Configuring SAP® ERP Sales and Distribution

Kapil Sharma
Ashutosh Mutsaddi

WILEY

Wiley Publishing, Inc.

Acquisitions Editor: Agatha Kim
Development Editor: Laurene Sorensen
Technical Editor: Dheeraj Oswal
Production Editor: Liz Britten
Copy Editor: Kim Wimpsett
Editorial Manager: Pete Gaughan
Production Manager: Tim Tate
Vice President and Executive Group Publisher: Richard Swadley
Vice President and Publisher: Neil Edde
Book Designer: Franz Baumhackl
Compositor: Craig Johnson, Happenstance Type-O-Rama
Proofreader: Word One, New York
Indexer: Ted Laux
Project Coordinator, Cover: Lynsey Stanford
Cover Designer: Ryan Sneed

Library of Congress Cataloging-in-Publication Data

Sharma, Kapil, 1975-
 Configuring SAP ERP sales and distribution / Kapil Sharma, Ashutosh Mutsaddi. — 1st ed.
   p. cm.

 1. SAP R/3. 2. Sales management—Computer programs. 3. Marketing—Management—Computer programs. 4. Physical distribution of goods—Management—Computer programs. I. Mutsaddi, Ashutosh, 1974- II. Title.
 HF5438.35S53 2010
 658.800285'53—dc22

                    2009052156

10 9 8 7 6 5 4 3 2

Dear Reader,

Thank you for choosing *Configuring SAP ERP Sales and Distribution*. This book is part of a family of premium-quality Sybex books, all of which are written by outstanding authors who combine practical experience with a gift for teaching.

Sybex was founded in 1976. More than 30 years later, we're still committed to producing consistently exceptional books. With each of our titles, we're working hard to set a new standard for the industry. From the paper we print on, to the authors we work with, our goal is to bring you the best books available.

I hope you see all that reflected in these pages. I'd be very interested to hear your comments and get your feedback on how we're doing. Feel free to let me know what you think about this or any other Sybex book by sending me an email at nedde@wiley.com. If you think you've found a technical error in this book, please visit http://sybex.custhelp.com. Customer feedback is critical to our efforts at Sybex.

Best regards,

Neil Edde
Vice President and Publisher
Sybex, an Imprint of Wiley

I dedicate this book to my grandmother and parents, because what I am today is due to their teachings and blessings, and to my wife Shweta, for all her support and encouragement, without which I could have never completed this book.

—Kapil Sharma

I would like to dedicate this book to my family—my son Atharva who understood that Daddy could not spend time with him due to the book deadlines, my wife Dipashri for her love and support, and my parents for who I am today. Thank you all for being with me throughout this (ad)venture!

—Ashutosh Mutsaddi

ACKNOWLEDGMENTS

We are grateful to the divine Universe for providing the inspiration for this book!

We would like to acknowledge the help and support received from our colleagues and the management of Intelligroup Inc. during the writing of this book. The opportunity to work on challenging projects over the years has helped us hone our technical skills and enabled us to write this book.

We thank Agatha Kim, our acquisitions editor, for her tremendous help at every stage. Special thanks to Dheeraj Oswal, our technical editor, and to the entire editorial and production teams for their suggestions and input.

Kapil Sharma and Ashutosh Mutsaddi

ABOUT THE AUTHORS

Kapil Sharma has more than eight years of experience in SAP. During this time, he has played various roles ranging from solution architect to project manager, and he has managed various projects involving full lifecycle implementations, production support, rollouts, upgrades, enhancements, acquisition and mergers, and process improvements in various industries such as consumer goods, retail, education, telecom and services, and high tech. He is an expert in business process analysis, configuration, implementation, and change management.

Ashutosh Mutsaddi is a senior SAP solutions consultant and a certified project manager. He has 10 years of experience in the design and implementation of SAP solutions. During his career, he has been a consultant to several Fortune 100 companies in Europe, North America, and Asia. He has diverse experience spanning industries such as high tech, automotive, electrical, media, and retail. Proficient in process reengineering, business blueprinting, and system configuration and upgrade, he has worked on all major SAP versions, from 3.1I to ECC 6.0. Besides consulting, he also fills a variety of strategic and leadership roles. As a senior project manager, he manages large teams and delivers cutting-edge SAP solutions to customers worldwide.

CONTENTS AT A GLANCE

TABLE OF CONTENTS

INTRODUCTION

This book provides a deep, working understanding of the essential concepts and customization settings related to the SAP Sales and Distribution (SD) application. SD is one of the most popular modules of the SAP ERP software and indeed the most interesting one to implement.

Over the years, we have worked on a variety of projects ranging from global implementation, support, upgrades, acquisition and mergers, rollouts, and integration. We've had the opportunity to study the business requirements of different industries and the best practices in customizing SAP to meet different challenges. Our goal was to bring the knowledge that we acquired during those projects to you through this book.

Who Should Read This Book

As the title implies, this book is intended for people who want to learn how to configure the SAP Sales and Distribution application. Whether you are a beginner who wants to make career in SAP as a SAP SD consultant, a business analyst from the IT/IS extended team of your organization, a member of the project implementation team responsible for implementing SD, a production support team member responsible for supporting the Sales and Distribution module after implementation, an experienced consultant from another SAP module who wants to learn SAP SD, or an experienced SAP SD consultant who wants to learn what's new in ECC 6 or how to handle some other functionality, you will find valuable information in this book related to customizing SAP SD.

If you are new to SAP, the learning curve can be steep. In this book, we tried to reduce that learning curve by providing easy-to-follow step-by-step instructions and case studies from a fictitious company called Galaxy Musical Instruments Inc.

How This Book Is Organized

You can use this book in several ways. The most straightforward way is to start at the beginning and proceed chapter by chapter. We have logically ordered the chapters according to the processes in a standard sales cycle. Each topic covers the prerequisite configurations before discussing how to configure a new submodule. We start with the basic concepts and travel all the way through to some very advanced configuration topics and techniques by the end of the book. If you already have configuration experience, you can skip around from chapter to chapter and follow the step-by-step instructions for a topic of interest in its individual chapter.

How Is This Book Different?

This book is different from others on the market in the following ways:

► The book covers the functionality offered by SAP in the latest version: ECC 6.0.

► It provides an overview of enhancement packages, which are the SAP road maps for delivering innovations in the coming years.

► It illustrates all the concepts with a real-life case study that runs through all the chapters of the book. This provides a cohesive picture of how a real-life organization can leverage SD to meet its requirements.

► It contains important tips, useful notes, and helpful links to other resources, such as SAP Service Marketplace (OSS) notes, where applicable.

What's Inside

Here is a glance at what's in each chapter:

Chapter 1: Introduction to Sales and Distribution   Gives you a brief overview of the SAP SD application and familiarizes you with the bare-minimum basics that you need to know before you step up to the next chapters.

Chapter 2: Enterprise Structure   Brings you to the customization world and provides easy-to-follow step-by-step instructions to help you set up your own SAP

SD enterprise structure. To demonstrate the customization, we'll set up the enterprise structure using the business requirement example from our fictitious company, Galaxy Musical Instruments.

Chapter 3: Master Data in SD   Introduces you to master data setup. Master data plays a key role in the core operation of a business. It may include data about clients and customers, employees, suppliers, products, and so on. Chapter 3 will teach you about how to set up and customize the master data in SAP SD.

Chapter 4: Partner, Text, and Output Determination   Takes your learning to the next level. You'll learn about the role of partners, output, and text determination in the overall sales cycle, followed by how to customize the same to meet your business requirement.

Chapter 5: Pricing and Tax Determination   Introduces you to the pricing and tax determination world. Here you'll learn about various pricing elements and will configure them to determine the final price at which the sales transaction can take place.

Chapter 6: Availability Check, Transfer of Requirements, and Backorders   Covers the available-to-promise functionality in detail. Promising accurate and reliable dates for delivery to your customers is a key element of the order fulfillment process in today's competitive environment, and this chapter talks about all the things you need to know in order to customize your SAP SD application to provide this reliability.

Chapter 7: Sales   Covers the customization and sales cycle flow for a variety of sales documents types that are available in standard SAP. You will learn about contracts, standard orders, third-party orders, debit/credit notes, consignments, warranty and maintenance contracts, quantity contracts, and so on.

Chapter 8: Shipping and Transportation   Covers shipping- and transportation-related activities in detail. This chapter covers topics such as delivery documents, routing, picking, packing, transportation, transfer orders, and shipment documents.

Chapter 9: Billing   Covers customer invoicing-related topics such as billing process, milestone billing, periodic billing, invoice lists, rebates, debit/credit notes, and payment card setup in SAP SD.

Chapter 10: Account Assignment and Revenue Recognition   Covers GL account determination for account posting of the invoice document. We'll also cover revenue recognition functionality in this chapter.

Chapter 11: Credit Management   Covers credit management in SAP SD in detail.

Chapter 12: Material Determination, Listing, Exclusion, and Proposal   Talks about various material-related functionalities in detail. This includes topic such as material determination, automatic product proposal, customer–material info records, and so on.

Chapter 13: Serial Numbers and Batch Management   Covers the serial number and batch management topics in detail.

Chapter 14: Advanced Techniques   Talks about various technical topics such as user exits, BAPI, EDI, IDOCS, and ABAP queries. This chapter also covers switch framework and enhancement packs in detail.

The appendix at the end of the book contains valuable information about transaction codes, database tables, and recommended web resources for further learning.

All through this book, we will use a case study of a fictitious company called Galaxy Musical Instruments; it's a trading organization that deals in musical instruments as well as related media and accessories, with operations in the United States and Mexico. This end-to-end case study will ensure continuity and help you understand how an organization can put SD's functionalities to use.

Here is the organization structure for Galaxy Musical Instruments.

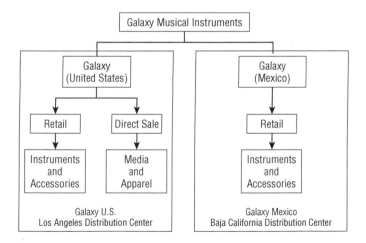

Introduction to Sales and Distribution

elcome to the world of SAP Sales and Distribution!

In this chapter, we will start with the basics about the SAP ERP system. We will discuss the various application areas and how they are structured. You will see that there are different menus offered to end users (who have to run transactions) and administrators (who configure or set up the system). We will introduce some basic transactions that you will need to know before you proceed with the rest of the book.

Sales and Distribution (SD) is one of the most important application areas in the SAP ERP system. In this chapter, we will explain how a general sales cycle is carried out in SAP. We will also give you an idea of how this book is structured.

Introduction to SAP

SAP is one of the most popular enterprise resource planning (ERP) solutions in the world. It offers an integrated system that supports major business functions such as sales, production, and financial accounting. Over the years, SAP has been enhanced, and new versions have been released. The older SAP R/3 has now developed into the SAP ERP system on which we have based this book.

The latest version of SAP ERP at this time is ERP Central Component, Release 6.0, often referred to as ECC 6.0. It consists of several application components closely integrated with one another. SD is one of these application components.

When any organization looks to implement SAP ERP, it first studies its business processes and decides on the ones that are to be mapped in SAP. Based on this, it can select the application components that are relevant. For example, a manufacturing organization may require a different set of applications than a service provider or a trading company.

The Sales and Distribution application caters to the business processes associated with customer order fulfillment. SD has several components offering diverse functionality. For example, there are components for pricing (which control how prices and costs are determined in a sales transaction), availability check (that control how product stocks are allocated to orders from various customers), and credit management (that check the credit worthiness of the customer before a transaction is permitted). Again, you have to select which processes are applicable to you.

In an integrated system, each application has to mesh with other related applications to ensure continuity and consistency. This is one of the strong points of the SD application.

Next we'll cover the first steps in accessing SAP. As we go through the application in this book, we will discuss each step in further detail.

First Steps in SAP

We'll now discuss some of the basic menus, screens, and transactions that you need to know when you log on to SAP. As we go along, we will also discuss the various features and applications that appear on each screen and how they relate to each other. This will help you understand the concepts better.

Easy Access Menu

After you log on to SAP, the first screen that greets you is the SAP Easy Access menu (Figure 1.1).

FIGURE 1.1   SAP Easy Access menu

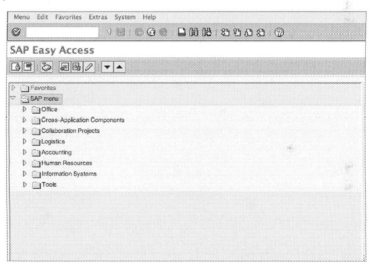

You can customize this menu based on your role in the organization. Specifically, you can arrange processes and transactions that you require for easy access and you can omit other transactions that you never use from the list.

Users can access transactions and run reports from this menu. However, they cannot carry out administrative functions from here. Those functions will be covered in the Customizing menu that we will discuss soon.

SAP ERP offers several business applications. As you can see, the major application areas in this menu are Accounting, Human Resources, and Logistics:

Accounting   If you drill down this menu, you will find diverse applications listed. Some of them are for financial accounting/controlling (FI/CO), financial supply chain management, and Project Systems (PS).

Human Resources   All the applications related to human resources management are grouped here. For example, you will find applications for personnel management, time management, payroll, and travel management.

Logistics   All the applications related to logistics functions are contained in this menu. Materials Management (MM), Production (PP), and Plant Maintenance (PM) are some of the applications listed here. The focus of this book—Sales and Distribution—is an application that falls under the Logistics menu. Logistics Execution (LE) is another application that is relevant here, because it covers the product delivery processes.

The Customizing Menu

You can configure and customize the SAP system to meet the specific requirements of your organization. The Sales and Distribution module has been developed with several business processes and various industries in mind. Some of these processes may not be relevant to your business. On the other hand, there could be some specific requirements that you will need to map in SAP through configuration.

During configuration, you can carry out various settings that control the process setup, such as the following:

► Activating or deactivating a certain process for your organization

► Configuring the look and feel of a transaction screen for a user

► Controlling which fields on the screen can be accessed, changed, or displayed

► Setting up a smooth flow of data from one document to another to ensure consistency and avoid the duplication of manual effort

You can access the Customizing menu in SAP using the following path: SAP Easy Access Menu ➤ Tools ➤ Customizing ➤ IMG ➤ Execute Project (transaction code SPRO).

NOTE A *transaction code* is a shortcut to a specific transaction in SAP. The menu path described would also lead you to the same destination. Whenever a transaction code is available, we will mention it alongside the path. You will also find a list of important transaction codes in the appendix.

This transaction code leads you to the Display IMG screen, as shown in Figure 1.2. You will find a menu with the various applications listed. It is called SAP Customizing Implementation Guide (or IMG for short). All the customization-related steps will be launched from this menu. If you click any application, you will find another menu that leads you to various submodules. Based on the exact path listed in the book, you can reach the specific transaction in the menu where the customization setting is to be carried out.

FIGURE 1.2 Customization menu

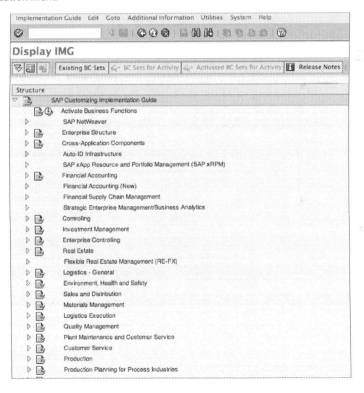

In this book, we also refer to the Display IMG screen as the Customizing menu or just IMG while explaining menu paths.

The focus of this book is the Sales and Distribution application. However, to complete the configuration steps, we will also touch upon some of the other topics, listed in IMG, under the nodes:

▶ Enterprise Structure

▶ Logistics – General

▶ Logistics Execution

In this book, we cover all the important settings that an SD expert should know. However, in an integrated system, a business process usually spans more than one application. You will need to work with experts in other areas (such as MM, FI/CO, WM, and so on) to complete the end-to-end process setup.

The Basic Sales Cycle

We'll now discuss the basic set of transactions that are most important in the SD area. The term *sales cycle* refers to the creation of a sales order document followed by delivery and a billing document. As we go along, we will tell you the transaction codes at each step. We will also point out how this book is structured to help you understand each area and functionality in the sales cycle.

Create a Sales Order

To create a sales order, follow the menu path SAP Menu ➢ Logistics ➢ Sales And Distribution ➢ Sales ➢ Order ➢ Create (VA01). Again, note that the transaction code mentioned in parentheses after the path will lead you to the same screen.

Figure 1.3 shows the sales order creation screen. Before you create a sales order, you must enter the organizational data such as sales organization, distribution channel, division, sales office, and sales group. This maps the organizational entities in your company.

To learn about how to set up the organizational structure in SAP, refer to Chapter 2, "Enterprise Structure." That chapter will explain how to configure SAP so the organizational entities are created and assigned to one another.

You must also specify the type of order document being created. After entering this information, you can proceed to the next screen, the Overview screen (Figure 1.4).

FIGURE 1.3 Creating a sales order

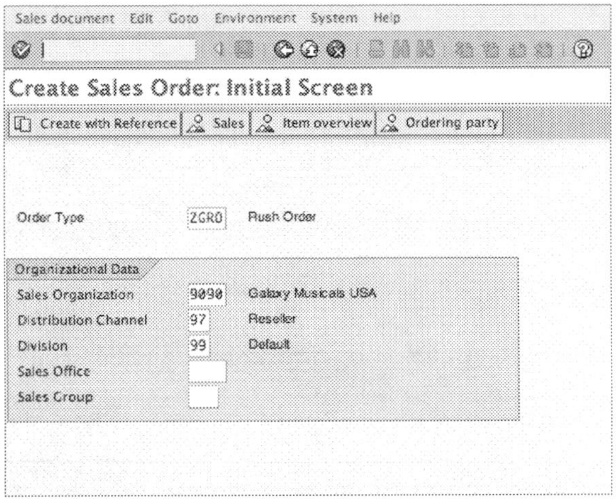

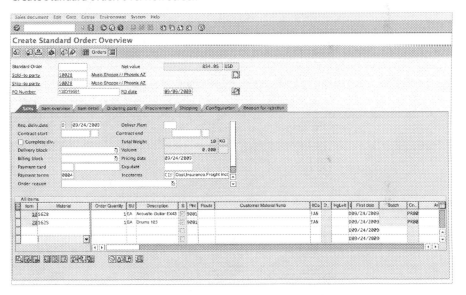

FIGURE 1.4 Create Standard Order: Overview screen

The sales document consists of header, item, and schedule line data. At the header level, you specify the details that are applicable to the entire document, such as the customer number (sold-to party) and the purchase order reference number. At the item level, you enter the products ordered. Details such as the material number, quantity, and item price, and so on, will be different on each line. The schedule line data pertains to delivery-related details such as delivery dates and delivery quantities.

You'll use master data at every step of the transaction. Data about your regular customers or the products and services offered are examples of master data. You have to maintain the repository of master data before using it in transactions. To learn more about master data setup, refer to Chapter 3, "Master Data in SD."

From the overview screen of a sales order, you can branch out to different screens to get into various aspects of the process such as pricing and availability dates. To navigate between screens, you can click the tabs that appear on the page. An alternative way is to use the Goto menu at the top of the screen. It lists all the detail tabs at the header and item levels.

For example, if you want to know all the partner functions associated with the sales transaction, you can select Goto ➤ Header ➤ Partner. As shown in Figure 1.5, this tab lists all the partners such as the sold-to party, ship-to party, bill-to party, and payer for this order. If you have different partners at each line item level, you can specify them on the Partners tab (which you can reach by selecting Goto ➤ Item ➤ Partner).

FIGURE 1.5   Sales order: Header Data, Partners tab

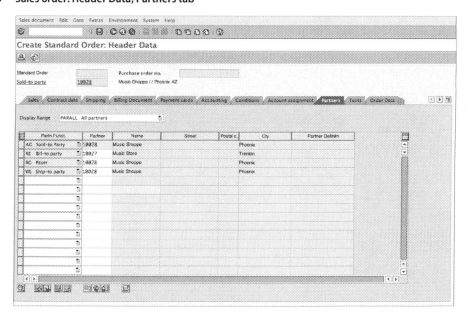

Another screen is the Texts tab, which appears at the header and item levels. The menu path is either Goto ≻ Header ≻ Text or Goto ≻ Item ≻ Text. Here you store all the text messages and instructions (as shown in Figure 1.6) that you want to flow with the order.

FIGURE 1.6   Sales order: Header Data, Texts tab

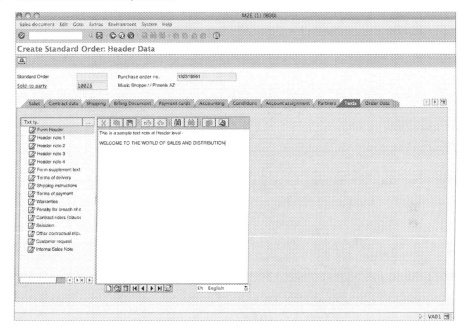

You can customize the setup for partners, texts, and outputs as per your requirements.

In partner determination, you can control which partner functions are of importance to you and make them mandatory. Text determination helps you set up how the texts are copied from one document to another. Output determination lets you customize the outputs from sales documents and transmit them to the business partners. For example, you can use it to send out a copy of an order confirmation document to the customer in print or by email or EDI.

Chapter 4, "Partner, Text, and Output Determination," will discuss how to maintain settings related to partners, outputs, and texts.

One of the most important parts of a sales transaction is the price that the customer has to pay. The price can be entered manually in the sales order. However, if your product prices are going to be stable for certain duration, you can maintain price records and set up automatic price determination to avoid manual entry.

To see how the exact price has been computed for a sales item, select Goto ➢ Item ➢ Conditions. As shown in Figure 1.7, the pricing schema gives you the details of the various pricing *conditions* in it. Pricing conditions are things such as base prices, discounts, freight conditions, or taxes. Certain pricing conditions can apply to the entire order (such as total freight charges). These are listed in the Header conditions tab.

To learn how to customize pricing, visit Chapter 5, "Pricing and Tax Determination."

FIGURE 1.7   Sales order: Item Data, Conditions tab

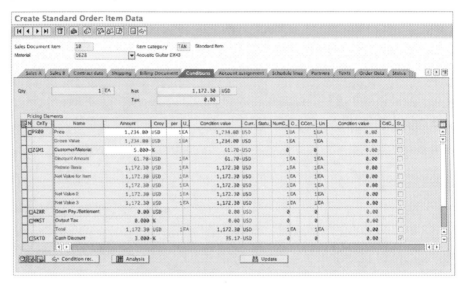

Availability check controls how product availability is checked and the date on which you can commit the delivery to the customer. As shown in Figure 1.8, as soon as you enter a material in the sales order, the system can be configured to carry out an availability check and display the earliest date on which this product can be delivered.

In a sales order, you can always check the schedule lines by selecting Goto ➢ Item ➢ Schedule Lines. As shown in Figure 1.9, you can check the dates on which the quantity can be confirmed.

Chapter 6, "Availability Check, Transfer of Requirements, and Backorders," will cover this topic in greater detail.

FIGURE 1.8   Availability Control

Standard Order: Availability Control

| Complete dlv. | Delivery proposal | Continue | ATP quantities | Scope of check | Other plants |

Item   10   Schd. Line   1
Material   1628
                Acoustic Guitar EX43
Plant   9001
Req.deliv.date 09/24/2009   Open Quantity   1 EA
End lead time   10/01/2009 ▾
☐ Fix qty/date   Max.Part.Deliveries   9

One-time del. on req. del. dte not possible
Dely/Conf.Date   09/24/2009 / 09/24/2009   Confirmed Quantity   0

Complete delivery
Dely/Conf.Date   09/28/2009 / 09/24/2009   ✓

Dely proposal
Dely/Conf.Date   09/28/2009 / 09/24/2009   Confirmed qty   1 ✓

FIGURE 1.9   Sales order: Schedule Lines tab

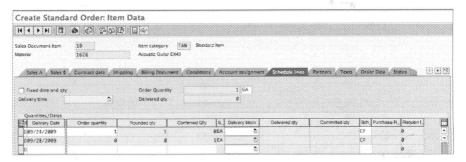

We have now covered some of the major screens in a sales order. Other sales documents may also need to be configured to meet different business processes. For example, you may have separate sales documents for returns or for presales such as inquiries and quotations.

Chapter 7, "Sales," will discuss the setup of sales documents for various business scenarios.

Creating a Delivery

To create a delivery, use the menu path SAP Menu ➢ Logistics ➢ Logistics Execution ➢ Outbound Process ➢ Goods Issue For Outbound Delivery ➢ Outbound Delivery ➢ Create ➢ Single Document ➢ With Reference to Sales Order (VL01N).

On this screen, you specify the shipping point (which is another organizational unit related to your plant), as shown in Figure 1.10.

FIGURE 1.10 Creating an outbound delivery

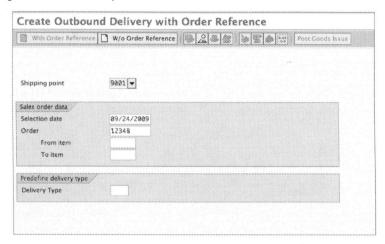

On the delivery overview screen, the relevant data has been copied over from the reference sales order. Product details and delivery quantity are the key fields here (refer to Figure 1.11).

From this step onward, the logistics processes of picking, packing, transportation planning and execution, and goods issue are carried out. The process extends all the way up to the goods leaving your premises and traveling to the customer's location.

The process is so vast that it has been placed under a separate application named Logistics Execution. In the customization menu, you have to refer to this node to maintain settings for deliveries.

To study the process in detail, refer to Chapter 8, "Shipping and Transportation."

FIGURE 1.11 Delivery Overview screen

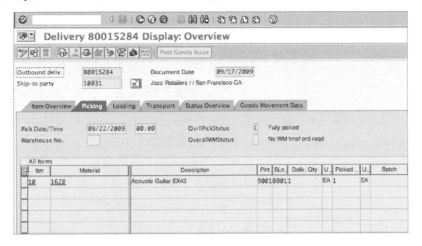

Creating a Billing Document

The last step in the sales cycle is to bill the customer for the goods delivered or the service rendered. To create a billing document, the path is as follows: SAP Menu ➢ Logistics ➢ Sales And Distribution ➢ Billing ➢ Billing Document ➢ Create (VF01).

A billing document is created with reference to either a sales order or a delivery. A correction document such as a credit or debit note can also be set up from this transaction. Enter the documents that are to be billed, and click Execute (Figure 1.12).

FIGURE 1.12 Creating a Billing Document

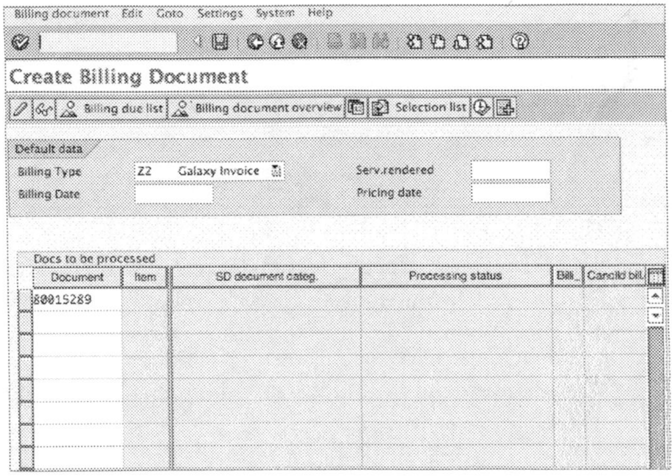

Again, you will observe that all the critical data is copied over from the reference document.

We mentioned the areas of pricing, outputs, and text in the context of sales documents. These also appear in the subsequent documents such as deliveries and billing documents. Chapter 9, "Billing," focuses exclusively on billing documents.

After a billing document is created, it is released to accounting. This updates all the relevant general ledger accounts with the transaction amounts. This is the interface between SAP's SD and FI/CO applications.

Some organizations require that billing the customer and updating the revenue books should occur at different times. The revenue recognition functionality helps you meet these requirements.

The settings for account assignment and revenue recognition are carried out within the SD module. Hence, it is important to know how they are controlled and determined. Chapter 10, "Account Assignment and Revenue Recognition," will help provide this perspective.

Credit management, material determination, serial numbers, and batch management are some of the other topics that are covered in Chapters 11 to 13.

The final chapter in this book is Chapter 14, "Advanced Techniques." It covers some of the more sophisticated tools and techniques offered by SAP.

This outline of a simple sales cycle should help you perceive the overall structure of the book. The actual processes can be very complex and diverse. In each chapter, we will cover the complex variations as well.

Getting Help

At this stage, we'll discuss the resources available to you if you are in the middle of a transaction and need to know more about any of the fields appearing on the screen.

From the transaction screen, you can get further details about a field by pressing the F1 key (the shortcut key for accessing Help) or by clicking the Help icon ⑦.

For example, in the sales order create transaction (VA01), if you need further information about the Net Worth field, you can access Help. As shown in Figure 1.13, the Help screen gives you more information about the field. In some cases, it also provides further links to learn more about some related important terms.

FIGURE 1.13 Using Help

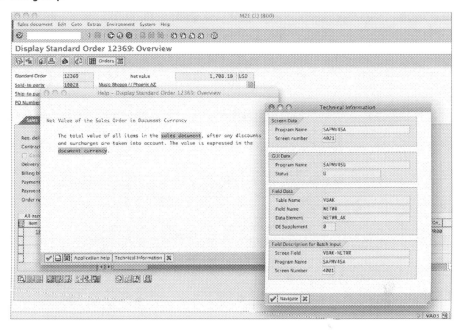

Clicking the Technical Information button at the bottom of the Help screen gives you more technical data about this field, such as the table name (VBAK) and field name (NETWR) where the data in this field is stored. We will discuss the technical topics such as database tables in the next section of this chapter.

SAP Help is also available on the Web at `http://help.sap.com`.

SAP also releases notes on its Online Service Marketplace website at `https://support.sap.com/support`. You will need login information from SAP to access this website. In this book, we have provided reference to such notes (also called *OSS notes*) where applicable.

Database Tables

During the discussion on sales cycle, you saw several transaction screens. Users access and enter data in the system using transaction codes. In the background, all this data is stored in database tables. As you learn more about configuration, it will be very helpful to understand and know how to access records from the database tables.

The first step is to know the important table names—at least the names of the tables commonly used in the SD application. Table 1.1 lists some of the most important tables. Once again, for convenience of understanding, we have tried to arrange them according to the transactions in the basic sales cycle. The appendix contains a list of all the important tables related to SD.

At this stage, do not try to remember the table names. It is more important to understand the concepts. As you progress further, however, you should make yourself familiar with these names.

TABLE 1.1   Database Tables in SD

Transaction	Table Name	Description
Sales orders	VBAK	Order header
	VBAP	Order item
	VBEP	Order schedule lines
Delivery	LIKP	Delivery header
	LIPS	Delivery item
Billing	VBRK	Billing header
	VBRP	Billing item
General process information	VBFA	Document flow
	VBUK	Header status
	VBUP	Item status

We'll now discuss how to access database records and explore the structure of a table.

Data Browser

The *data browser* allows you to search database tables and fetch stored records. To access the data browser, use the path SAP Menu ➤ Tools ➤ ABAP Workbench ➤ Overview ➤ Data Browser (SE16), and enter the name of the table that you want to study.

The next screen contains selection parameters that can help you search for appropriate database records. Figure 1.14 shows the selection screen for order header table VBAK. If you know the sales order number, you can enter it in the Sales Document field on the selection screen. If, on the other hand, you do not know the order number, you can carry out a search based on any of the parameters listed. For example, you may want to find all the sales orders created on a specific date.

FIGURE 1.14 Data Browser: Selection Screen

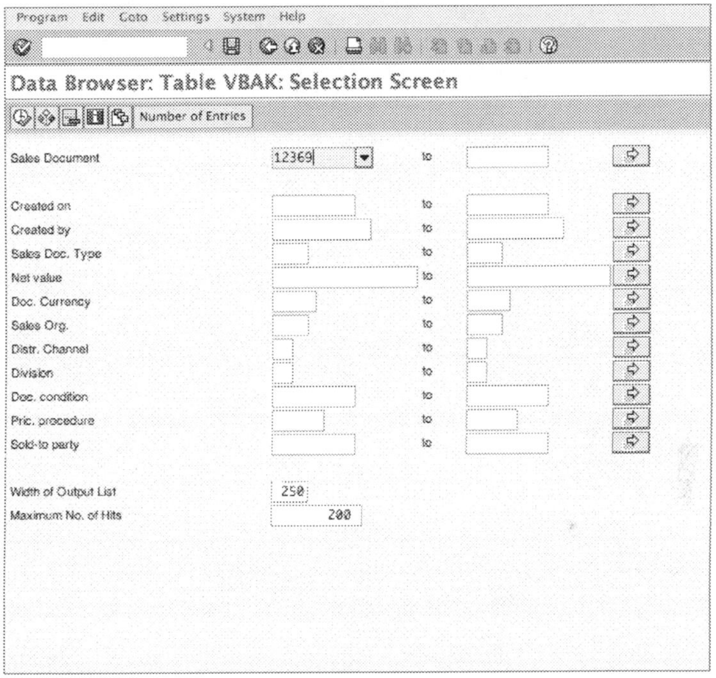

After entering the selection criteria, click the Execute button ⊕.

SAP will fetch the database record and display it on the screen. The details of the record (in our example, order details such as order type, sales organization, distribution channel, division, net value, and so on) will appear as shown in Figure 1.15.

Also note the Number Of Entries button on the selection screen. If you want to know how many records fit the selection criteria, click this button. It will give you the number of records found.

Another important field that controls the database search is Maximum Number Of Hits. If you enter a limiting value (say, 200) here, SAP will stop the search after finding the first 200 records. If the number of entries is high and you want to see all of them, make sure that your maximum number of hits is set to a higher number.

FIGURE 1.15 Data Browser: record display

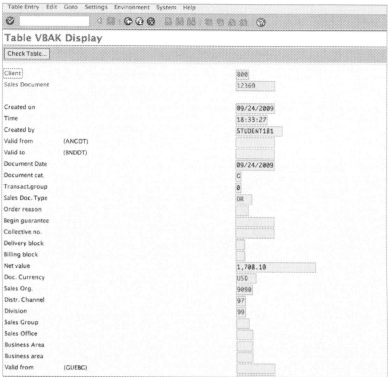

On the selection screen, you can change or add more selection parameters if the standard list does not meet your requirements. From the menu on the top of the screen, select Settings ➢ Fields For Selection. Then, from the list of fields, select the ones you need to be displayed as selection criteria.

You can use Settings ➢ User Parameters to control the display (Figure 1.16). This lets you choose to view the results in a standard list format or an ALV grid format. Also note the Keyword tab. Each field in the database table has a field label (a meaningful description) and a field name (a technical name). You can choose either mode of display.

To understand the difference between a field label and a field name, compare Figure 1.15 with Figure 1.17. They both show records from table VBAK for the sales order 12369. In Figure 1.15, you can see field labels such as Net Worth (the value is 1708.10). In Figure 1.17, you see the field name NETWR. This is the technical name for the net worth. The contents of the field are the same in both views.

FIGURE 1.16 User-Specific Settings for the Data Browser

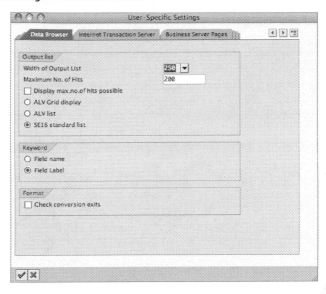

FIGURE 1.17 Data Browser: display showing field names

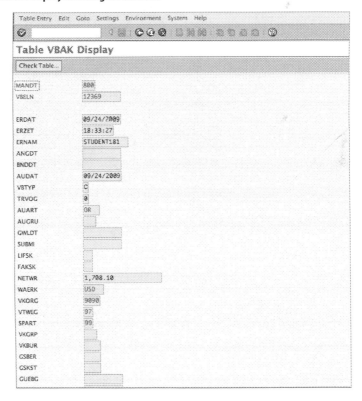

You will need to be familiar with field names to communicate effectively with your technical team. Furthermore, as we will discuss in Chapter 14, if you ever need to create a custom enhancement in SAP, you will need all the technical information, such as table and field names.

TIP   Note that there is new version of the standard data browser (SE16), called SE16N. It offers the same functionality of displaying database records, but it has some extra user-friendly features. As shown here, SE16N lets you see the field names *and* the technical names of the selection parameters. You can also choose the fields that you need in the output display.

ABAP Dictionary

While we are on the subject of tables and fields, we'll talk about another transaction code that you should know about. It is technical in nature, but it will help you understand the underlying structure of the tables we discussed earlier.

To access this transaction, the path is as follows: SAP Menu ➢ Tools ➢ ABAP Workbench ➢ Development ➢ ABAP Dictionary (SE11).

Figure 1.18 shows the Dictionary: Display Table view for VBAK. As shown, it includes the details such as field names, data elements, data type, length of field, and other technical attributes.

FIGURE 1.18 Dictionary: Display Table view

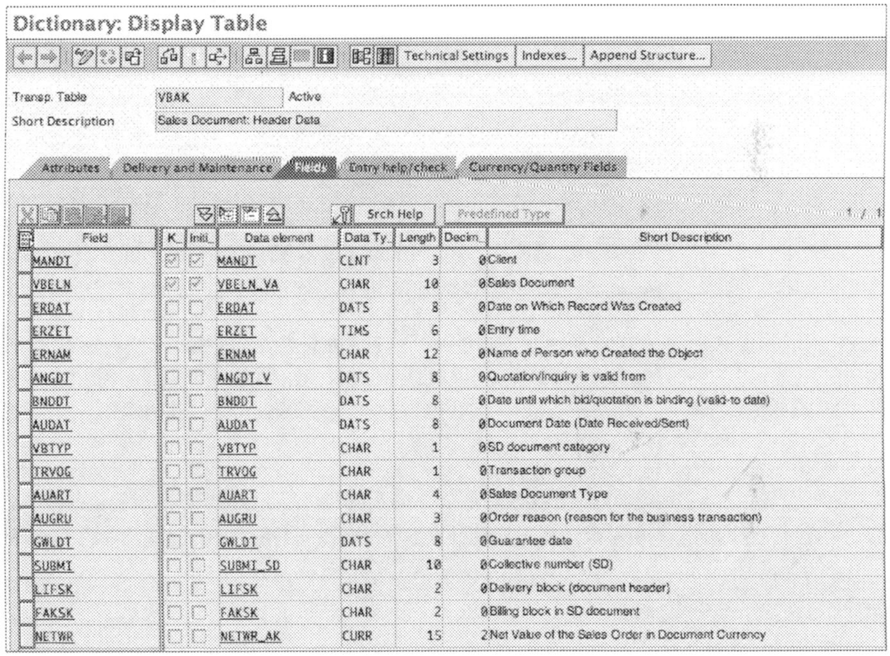

Field	K.	Initi.	Data element	Data Ty.	Length	Decim.	Short Description
MANDT	☑	☑	MANDT	CLNT	3	0	Client
VBELN	☑	☑	VBELN_VA	CHAR	10	0	Sales Document
ERDAT	☐	☐	ERDAT	DATS	8	0	Date on Which Record Was Created
ERZET	☐	☐	ERZET	TIMS	6	0	Entry time
ERNAM	☐	☐	ERNAM	CHAR	12	0	Name of Person who Created the Object
ANGDT	☐	☐	ANGDT_V	DATS	8	0	Quotation/Inquiry is valid from
BNDDT	☐	☐	BNDDT	DATS	8	0	Date until which bid/quotation is binding (valid-to date)
AUDAT	☐	☐	AUDAT	DATS	8	0	Document Date (Date Received/Sent)
VBTYP	☐	☐	VBTYP	CHAR	1	0	SD document category
TRVOG	☐	☐	TRVOG	CHAR	1	0	Transaction group
AUART	☐	☐	AUART	CHAR	4	0	Sales Document Type
AUGRU	☐	☐	AUGRU	CHAR	3	0	Order reason (reason for the business transaction)
GWLDT	☐	☐	GWLDT	DATS	8	0	Guarantee date
SUBMI	☐	☐	SUBMI_SD	CHAR	10	0	Collective number (SD)
LIFSK	☐	☐	LIFSK	CHAR	2	0	Delivery block (document header)
FAKSK	☐	☐	FAKSK	CHAR	2	0	Billing block in SD document
NETWR	☐	☐	NETWR_AK	CURR	15	2	Net Value of the Sales Order in Document Currency

Managing Customization Changes

Whenever you enter the Customizing menu and carry out any change in the system, the system tracks this change and records it. Every change has an impact on the way the system works. Hence, it is very important to understand the basic system landscape and the process of managing and transporting changes.

The System Landscape

The *system landscape* is the arrangement of the various servers. A generic system landscape consists of a production system (the one in which all the operations of the organization are carried out) plus other systems such as development and quality assurance systems. Although our focus is on the configuration of the SD application in this book, it is very important to understand the system landscape.

Figure 1.19 represents a typical SAP system landscape, consisting of a development system (DEV), quality assurance system (QAS), and production system (PRD). When any change is made during customization, it is essential to test it rigorously before it can be implemented in the production environment. To achieve this, you first make changes in the development system. At this stage, there is no impact on the production system at all. You can test the impact of the change locally and then choose to move it to the next level of testing in the quality assurance system.

This system usually has a large amount of test data. Often, it is a recent copy of the production environment so that the change can be tested in a real-life environment. It is also important to identify the system users who would be affected by this change and train them accordingly in this simulated environment.

Once the testing is complete, the change can move into production. Once this happens, the change is said to have "gone live."

Many organizations also have another system called a *sandbox*. It is an isolated system where you can carry out preliminary analysis and test new functionality and solution prototypes. Changes made in the sandbox never move to other systems in the landscape.

It is very important to record all the details of any change being made in SAP and transport it in steps through the system landscape. In the next section, we will cover the concept of transport request, which will help you understand how changes are recorded and tracked.

Transport Request

To capture the details of the change and manage its migration to production, SAP uses the concept of a *transport request*. When you make any changes to the Customizing menu, you will be required to create or choose a transport request number (Figure 1.20).

FIGURE 1.19 System landscape example

FIGURE 1.20 Transport request number

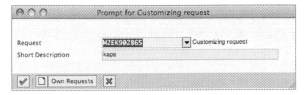

The data related to the change is stored in the transport request. This helps in controlling and tracking the change. The transport request can be moved from one system to another so that the same change is carried out in other systems. Changes made in the customizing domain are captured in a separate class of transport requests called *customizing requests*. Changes to ABAP programs are stored in *workbench requests*.

As shown in Figure 1.21, you can drill down a transport request number to see the customizing tasks that you have performed and the tables that have been affected by the change.

FIGURE 1.21 Transport request details

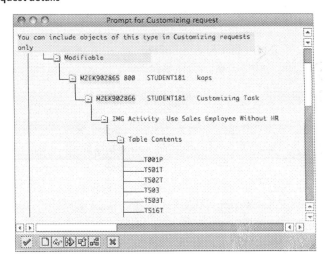

CASE STUDY OVERVIEW: GALAXY MUSICAL INSTRUMENTS

Throughout this book, we will use a case study of a fictitious company, called Galaxy Musical Instruments, which is a trading company that deals in musical instruments as well as related media and accessories.

Galaxy has operations in the United States and Mexico. Its main distribution center, located in California, caters to its wholesale and retail customers in the United States. Another plant in Baja California, Mexico, caters to all the customers there. In each chapter of this book, we will discuss how Galaxy uses SAP's SD application to map its business processes, and we will use graphics to depict how the settings were made.

We will consistently use the same product range, customers, and organizational units. This will help us present a cohesive picture and give you an idea of how an actual organization can use the SD application to map its business processes.

For instance, in Chapter 3, we will present Galaxy's master data requirements and how they were mapped in the system, including how the customer master data and hierarchical relationships were set up. Later, in Chapter 5, we will cover how the pricing procedure was set up for this customer. Later, in Chapter 8, we will cover how Galaxy set up routes to ship the products to the customer.

This end-to-end case study will ensure continuity and help you understand how to apply the functionalities in SD.

Once you have tested the change and are ready to move the changes to the quality assurance system, you have to release the transport request. Based on the process setup (which is not in our scope here), the change will be picked up for promotion to the next system. If you have transported the change to the quality assurance or production system and it is having an undesirable effect on the processes, you can reverse it at any time. This ensures that the production system remains safe from unwanted changes.

A useful transaction for checking and updating transport requests is SE10. The menu path is SAP Menu ➤ Tools ➤ Customizing ➤ IMG ➤ Transport Organizer (Extended View). As shown in Figure 1.22, you can enter the user ID and check all the transport requests created by that user. This transaction is also used to release the transport requests that are ready to be moved to other systems.

FIGURE 1.22 Transport Organizer screen

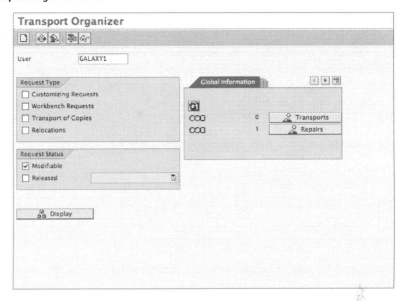

Summary

This chapter offered an overview of the SAP ERP system and the various applications contained in it. We covered the basic menu used to access transactions and the Customizing menu used to configure the system.

We also covered the basic sales cycle in SAP and other important transaction codes that will be needed throughout the SD application area.

We also touched upon the many functionalities in SD that will be covered in depth in the subsequent chapters of this book.

Thus, this chapter was a launching pad to start your journey in SAP SD. Good luck!

Enterprise Structure

Enterprise structure in SAP's SD application represents the organizational structure within the business entity that is selling and distributing goods and services. To help you map this organizational structure into the SAP ERP software, SAP offers a set of *building blocks*. In this chapter, we will discuss these building blocks and show how to arrange them to set up the SD enterprise structure.

Overview

The SD enterprise structure in SAP ERP represents the structure of the sales and distribution entity of an organization. To map this structure into the SAP ERP software, you use various building blocks provided by SAP. You use a *sales organization* to replicate the selling entity into the SAP system; *distribution channels* to represent various channels being used by the enterprise to distribute goods to market; *divisions* to represent various product divisions that exist in the organization; *sales areas* to define the relationship among selling entity, channels of distribution, and product divisions; *sales offices*, *sales groups*, and *sales districts* to represent the geographical locations; and *sales employee masters* (from SAP HR application) to denote sales employees and their positions in the hierarchical sales reporting structure. The organizational element for setting up a *plant* and the *plant* assignments to other organizational elements such as storage location, shipping/receiving point, and loading point, helps you set up the distribution structure. This structure defines where and how the goods will be stored and how they will be shipped to the customers. Both the sales organization and the plant are assigned to the company code so that the accounting entries resulting from the sale of goods and services, as well as those resulting from the material movements in the plant, are posted to accounting. Finally, the plant is assigned to the combination of the sales organization and the distribution channel, allowing the sales organization to use the assigned plant structure when distributing goods and services to the customers and completing the typical enterprise structure setup in SAP SD application.

Enterprise structure in SAP SD does not exist in isolation. It has dependencies with enterprise structures from other modules too. Dependencies with financial accounting and materials management enterprise structure is of vital importance because it impacts the use of materials in the SD application as well as the accounting posting of the sales transactions. Therefore, before you set up your SD structure, you should work with an SAP FICO consultant to make sure that the company code, chart of accounts, fiscal year, and other enterprise structure customizations related to the financial accounting application of SAP ERP are already set up. A *company code* represents your organization's legal entity, a *chart of accounts* represents the ledger accounts that you will use to post the sales transaction into accounting, and a *fiscal year* represents the financial reporting year for your company code. The bare minimum setup you need before you can start setting up the SD enterprise structure is the company code and fiscal year.

Setting up an enterprise structure is the foundation of your SAP implementation. It is therefore essential that you carefully analyze the structure of your client's organization before you map it into the SAP ERP software. You need to understand how your selling entity is structured and how it operates by considering whether it is centralized or decentralized; what products the sales entity deals in; how the sales are made (directly or via partners); what the various methods of distribution of goods to the customers are; how many plants/distribution centers there are and what geographical locations they belong to; the structure of the sales team; the geographical locations (how many regions, territories, sales offices, and branch offices there are); and what kind of internal reports, MIS reports, and external reports (if any) are generated. It is a good practice to analyze the enterprise's business requirements and draw a blueprint of the enterprise structure on paper before applying it to the SAP system.

TIP   A good structural design will accommodate the company's current needs and at the same time be flexible enough for the future. A good structural design will always yield better results in terms of operational control, reporting analysis, and smooth processing of the business transactions in the SAP ERP software.

Setting Up the Enterprise Structure

Setting up an enterprise structure entails two types of activity. You start with the definition activity and complete the setup with the assignment activity. Figure 2.1 represents the implementation guide (IMG) for SAP customizing, showing the definition and assignment activities menu path for setting up the enterprise structure in SAP ERP. Each of these activities is further divided into various application areas such as materials management (MM), logistics execution (LE), and financial accounting (FICO), to name a few. To set up an SD enterprise structure, we need to first define the SD structural elements in the definition activity for SD. We then need to assign these elements to each other to form an enterprise structure using the assignment activity. Let's start with the creation of a sales organization.

FIGURE 2.1   IMG menu path to maintain enterprise structure

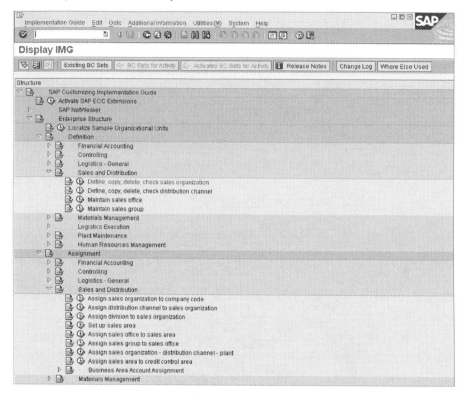

Setting Up the Sales Organization

The first step in setting up a sales structure in SAP is to set up a sales organization. A *sales organization* in SAP represents the selling entity of your client's organization. It is the highest level in the SD enterprise structure and the one to which all the other building blocks are assigned. A sales organization has its own master data. All sales-related transactions are executed within the framework of a sales organization. When you create a customer master or a material master, you must provide the sales organization for which you are creating this master data. You must even enter a sales organization while creating the sales order document in SAP. (Refer to Figure 1.3 from Chapter 1, "Introduction to Sales and Distribution," which shows sales organization 9090 on the order entry screen.) During processing of the sales cycle, the sales organization information gets copied over from order to delivery to billing and also helps you determine the company code while posting the sales transaction to accounting.

It is always advisable to keep the number of sales organizations to a minimum. You should only create multiple sales organizations when two or more selling entities operate on a totally different basis or when there is a legal requirement to have multiple sales organizations. For example, an organization running sales operations from multiple countries may end up having one sales organization for each country where it operates. Each of these sales organizations will then be assigned to the company codes that were set up for those countries.

Defining a Sales Organization

To create your own sales organization, use transaction code OVX5 or follow menu path IMG ➤ Enterprise Structure ➤ Definition ➤ Sales And Distribution. Click the Execute button ⊕ next to Define, Copy, Delete, Check Sales Organization. Following the Menu Path, you will be presented with the Choose Activity screen, as shown in Figure 2.2, providing you with the following two methods to define your own sales organization.

FIGURE 2.2   Choose Activity screen for defining a sales organization

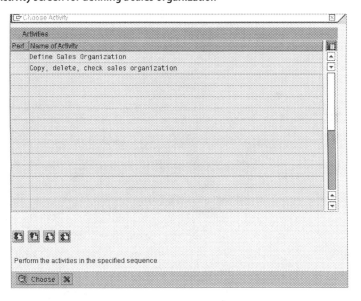

Define Sales Organization   Make this selection when you want to set up a new sales organization without copying it from any existing ones. You will have to manually enter all the required information to define your own sales organization.

Copy, Delete, Check Sales Organization   Select this when you want to set up your sales organization by copying it from an existing sales organization. With this copy option, you can copy the complete sales organization structure from the source sales organization to the target sales organization. This is really useful in scenarios where the source sales organization structure closely resembles the target sales organization structure. You can also use this option to check and delete an existing sales organization structure. We will cover this method in detail when we set up our Mexican sales organization (9091) for Galaxy Musical Instruments.

We'll define our first sales organization, "Galaxy Musical Instruments US (9090)," using Define Sales Organization option.

Select Define Sales Organization, and click the Choose button at the bottom of the screen in Figure 2.2. You now should see the sales organization configuration screen, as shown in Figure 2.3.

FIGURE 2.3   Overview screen for defining a sales organization

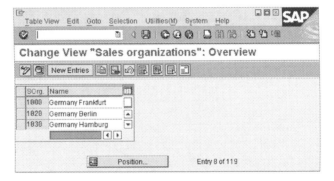

Here again, you are provided with the option to either create your own sales organization by using the New Entries button [New Entries] or by using the Copy button . Using the New Entries button provides you with a blank form where you fill in all the relevant details such as the name, address, and so on, for your sales organization. Using the Copy button will open a prefilled form with the name, address, and other information copied from the source sales organization. Depending upon your needs, you can completely or partially replace the information provided via the copy option and save your entry to create your sales organization. Let's use the Copy button in Figure 2.3 to create our first sales organization.

Now select the source, sales organization 1000, and click the Copy button . You will be presented with a screen like that shown in Figure 2.4 but with the values from sales organization 1000. Replace the data on the screen with what you want to maintain for your sales organization. We changed the values in Figure 2.4 to represent the Galaxy Musical Instruments USA sales organization (9090).

N O T E   Please note that the functionalities associated with the copy options in Figures 2.2 and 2.3 are very different. The copy option in Figure 2.2 will copy the complete sales organization structure along with all the assignments that were made to the source sales organization, whereas the one in Figure 2.3 will copy over only basic sales organization data such as the name, description, and address from the source to the target sales organization.

FIGURE 2.4   Defining the sales organization, Details screen

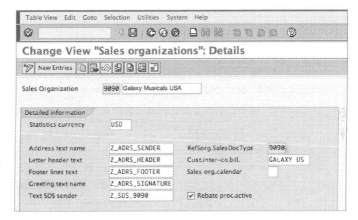

The following are the fields shown in Figure 2.4:

Sales Organization   Here you provide a four-character identifier and a description for your sales organization. This field is alphanumeric, which means that you can define the identifier key with only numbers, only alphabets or with a combination of numbers and alphabets.

Statistics Currency   Here you set the default statistical currency for your sales organization. When you generate sales statistics, the system uses this currency to report the statistics. Because it is a default, this currency can be overwritten during statistical reporting.

Content for form text modules   Address Text Name, Letter Header Text, Footer Lines Text, Greeting Text Name, and Text SDS Sender are five fields available in sales organization customization where you assign the text modules that carry information to be printed on the various outputs such as invoices, order confirmations and so on. (See the left column of Figure 2.4.) You first create and maintain the text module using transaction code SO10 and then assign the text modules to their respective positions in the sales organization customization screen as shown in Figure 2.4. Here text module Z_ADRS_SENDER stores the sales organization address, Z_ADRS_HEADER store the logo, Z_ADRS_FOOTER stores the footer lines and Z_ADRS_SIGNATURE stores the electronic signature for sales organization 9090. Always create your own text modules with a prefix Y or Z. This way your text modules will not be overwritten by SAP when you apply some software patches or perform a release upgrade on your SAP system.

RefSorg SalesDoc Type   This field sets up a reference between two sales organizations that share a common sales document type assignment. If you created your sales organization by copying from an existing sales organization, this field will automatically get populated with the source sales organization number from which you copied. Refer "Sales Document Type per Sales Area" section in Chapter, 7 "Sales," for more details on how to use this field.

Cust. Inter-co. Bill.   Here you enter the intercompany customer number for your sales organization. We will discuss intercompany billing process and customization in Chapter 9, "Billing."

Sales Org. Calendar   Here you enter the factory calendar for your sales organization. A factory calendar in SAP SD defines the working and nonworking days for your plant/factory/country setup and controls the shipping and billing activities. We'll discuss the customization of the factory calendar in the "Setting Up a Factory Calendar" section later in this chapter.

Rebate Proc. Active   Activating a rebate at the sales organization level is one of the prerequisites for rebate processing in SAP. Select this checkbox when you want to activate rebate processing for your sales organization. We'll discuss rebate processing in detail in Chapter 9.

Once you are done entering the values you want for your sales organization, click the check mark button ☑. This check mark button acts like the Enter key on your keyboard. Once clicked, SAP will automatically open the address data screen (Figure 2.5) for you to maintain the address details for your sales organization. Enter the address data, and save your entry by clicking the Save button 💾. Congratulations! You have successfully defined your first sales organization.

T I P   Notice the ▤ button on the screen now. This is the Address button. You can click this button to call up the address screen again for making any changes.

FIGURE 2.5   Address maintenance screen for a sales organization

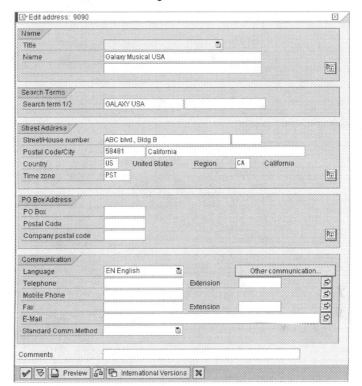

Defining a Sales Organization Using the Copy Method

In the previous section, we showed how to define a sales organization by using the Define Sales Organization option on the Choose Activity screen (shown earlier in Figure 2.2). In this section, we will cover the Copy, Delete, Check Sales Organization option to set up the sales organization. Remember that with this copy option, not just the address data but also the assignments that exist for the source sales organization are copied over to the target sales organization. This includes a distribution channel assignment to a sales organization, a division assignment to a sales organization, plants to sales organizations, and even sales document types to the sales organization. In other words, this copy option copies over the entire sales organization structure from the source sales organization to the target sales organization. Once you have defined the sales organization using this option, you will need to select the first option on the Choose Activity screen—Define Sales Organization—to make changes to the address and other details for your sales organization definition. You can also use the Copy, Delete, Check Sales Organization option to delete or check an existing sales organization structure.

Let's use this method to create our second sales organization, Galaxy Musical Instruments Mexico (9091). Follow the same steps as you did before to reach the screen shown earlier in Figure 2.2. Then choose the Copy, Delete, Check Sales Organization option. You should see a screen like the one in Figure 2.6.

FIGURE 2.6   Organizational Object Sales Organization, initial screen

The screen is blank, but there are a few buttons on the menu bar. Click the Copy button in the menu bar. You will now see a dialog box prompting you to provide the source and destination values for the sales organization (Figure 2.7). Enter the values and click the tick button on the dialog box to perform the copy.

Now, click the back arrow button on the screen to go back to the Choose Activity screen (shown earlier in Figure 2.2).

Now select the activity Define Sales Organization, which will open the screen shown earlier in Figure 2.3. Double-click the entry for sales organization 9091 to reach the Change Sales Organization screen (similar to what shown earlier in Figure 2.4), and make required changes to the fields, including Name, Description, Currency,

Address Data, and so on. *Voilá*, you have successfully created your second sales organization.

FIGURE 2.7   Organizational Object Sales Organization, copy options

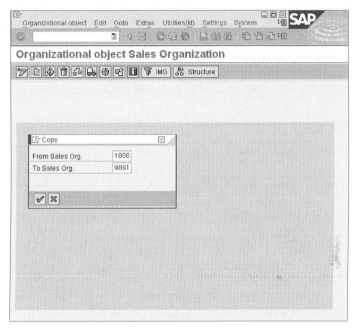

Assigning a Sales Organization to a Company Code

Once a sales organization has been defined, the next step in its setup is to assign the sales organization to a company code. Figure 2.8 shows the customization screen for assigning a sales organization to a company code. To reach this screen, you can use transaction code OVX3N or follow the menu path IMG ➢ Enterprise Structure ➢ Assignments ➢ Sales And Distribution ➢ Assign Sales Organization To Company Code. While posting the billing transaction into accounting, the SAP ERP system uses this assignment to determine the company code to which the accounting posting for sales needs to be booked.

NOTE   Always remember that a sales organization has a one-to-one relationship with a company code. You can assign more than one sales organization to a company code but cannot have a sales organization point to more than one company code.

FIGURE 2.8   Assignment Sales Organization – Company Code screen, default assignment

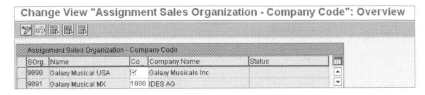

In Figure 2.8, notice that sales organization 9090 is not assigned to a company code, whereas 9091 is already assigned to company code 1000 by default. The reason for that is simple. We copied 9091 from 1000 using the Copy, Delete, Check Sales Organization option, whereas 9090 was created manually using the Define Sales Organization option. During the copy from 1000 to 9091, the system not only copied the address data but also applied all the assignments that were true for 1000 to 9091, thus bringing in the company code 1000 assignment to sales organization 9091. Figure 2.9 shows the Galaxy assignments, after we maintained the company code assignment for sales organization 9090 and corrected the company code assignment for sales organization 9091.

FIGURE 2.9   Assignment Sales Organization – Company Code screen, final assignment

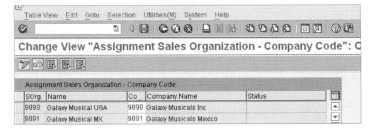

NOTE   Since the Copy, Delete, Check Sales Organization option copies over the entire structure, always use it when the source structure is very close in setup to what you want in the target structure. If the source and target are different and you use this copy option, you will be spending more time deleting the unwanted assignments that came with the copy. This is similar to what we'll be doing because we copied 9091 from 1000, which was not close to what we wanted to configure for Galaxy Musical Instruments Mexico. As we progress, we will find more assignments that originally belonged to 1000 but are copied to 9091 as well. We'll keep replacing them with what we need for 9091.

CASE STUDY—GALAXY MUSICAL INSTRUMENTS CONFIGURATION ANALYSIS: SALES ORGANIZATION

The sales operations for Galaxy Musical Instruments span the United States. The corporation also has a subsidiary in Mexico with its own sales entity to handle sales operations in Mexico. The U.S. and Mexican sales entities have different company codes. Galaxy decided to use numeric codes to represent the sales organizations and created two sales organizations: 9090 for Galaxy Musical Instruments USA and 9091 for Galaxy Musical Instruments Mexico. Each of these sales organizations is assigned to its respective USA (9090) or Mexican (9091) company code.

T I P   In SAP, there is no specific rule with respect to the naming convention for the organization structure components. You are free to use numeric, alphabetic, or alphanumeric values. Just try to keep it logical so that it is easy to identify the component by the value. For example, Galaxy Musical Instruments decided to use numeric values to define its sales organization. In Galaxy's naming convention, the first two characters represent the geographical region. Here 90 refers to the American region and covers all countries in the American region. The last two characters are a sequential number.

Configuring a Distribution Channel

A *distribution channel* represents the way you distribute your goods into the market. It may be wholesale, retail, or OEM, for example. In other words, a distribution channel is a grouping of various distribution methods that a company uses to distribute goods to its customers.

Configuring a distribution channel is a two-step activity. The first step is to create the distribution channel, and the second step is to assign the distribution channel to a sales organization. By assigning distribution channels to a sales organization, you set up a small structure that controls the methods of distribution that a sales organization can use to supply goods and services to its customers. Distribution channels are available across the sales organizations. This means you can assign the same distribution channel to multiple sales organizations.

Defining a Distribution Channel

You can define a distribution channel by using transaction code OVXI or by following menu path IMG ➣ Enterprise Structure ➣ Definition ➣ Sales And Distribution ➣ Define, Copy, Delete, Check Distribution Channel (shown earlier in Figure 2.1). Click ⊕ next to the Define, Copy, Delete, Check Distribution channel, and you will again see a Choose Activity screen providing you with the option to define your own distribution channel manually (Define Distribution Channel) or to copy it from an existing source distribution channel (Copy, Delete, Check Distribution Channel). Select the Define Distribution Channel option from the activity screen to get to the customization screen.

Once you are on the customization screen, click the New Entries button to open the New Entries screen, as shown in Figure 2.10.

FIGURE 2.10 New Entries screen for defining a distribution channel

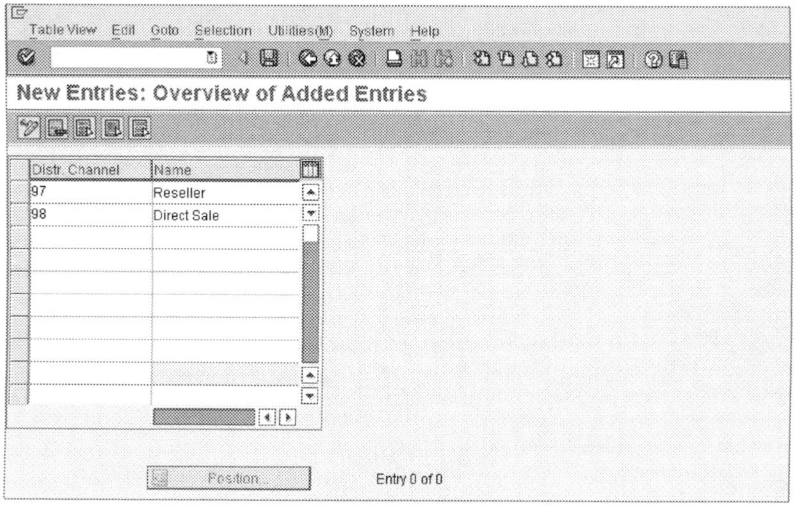

You'll see the following fields on the New Entries screen:

Distr. Channel   Here you enter a two-character identifier key for your distribution channel.

Name   Here you enter a meaningful description for your distribution channel. The description can be a maximum of 20 characters long.

Define your own distribution channel by entering the previous two entries. Figure 2.10 shows the two distribution channels that we have set up for Galaxy Musical Instruments.

MENU PATH CONVENTIONS

You will encounter the Choose Activity screen for almost all the components that you will configure under the enterprise structure. From now on, instead of writing about the Choose Activity screen every time and then asking you to choose an option, we will denote the step within the menu path. For example, we'll use IMG ➢ Enterprise Structure ➢ Definition ➢ Sales And Distribution ➢ Define, Copy, Delete, Check Distribution Channel ➢ Define Distribution Channel. The rest of the book will also follow this standard.

You also saw the use of copy option while setting up the sales organization. When used with other components, the functionality works the same way. When you use it for defining a sales organization, it allows you to copy, check, and delete the sales organization; when used with a distribution channel, it copies, checks, and deletes the distribution channel. Therefore, instead of going over this copy function every time, we will discuss customizing other components of the enterprise structure using the Define option.

Assigning a Distribution Channel to a Sales Organization

Now that we've defined the distribution channel, we can assign it to the sales organization.

You can assign a distribution channel to a sales organization via transaction code OVXKN or the menu path IMG ➢ Enterprise Structure ➢ Assignments ➢ Sales And Distribution ➢ Assign Distribution Channel To Sales Organization. Once you reach the assignment screen, click the New Entries button, and enter the assignments for your distribution channel and sales organization. Galaxy Musical Instruments distribution channel assignments are shown in Figure 2.11 and are discussed in the "Galaxy Musical Instruments Configuration Analysis: Distribution Channel" sidebar.

FIGURE 2.11 Assigning distribution channel to sales organization

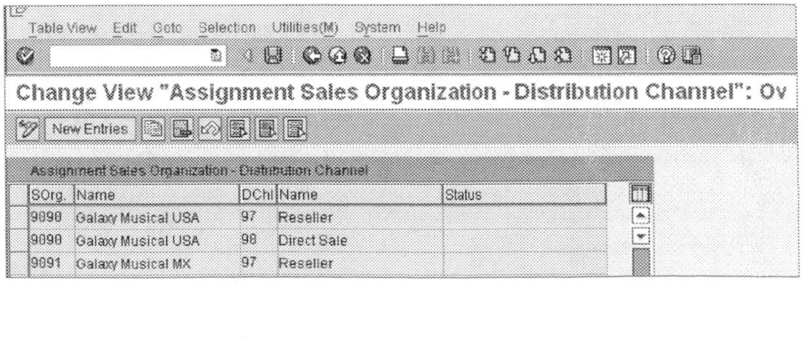

CASE STUDY—GALAXY MUSICAL INSTRUMENTS CONFIGURATION ANALYSIS: DISTRIBUTION CHANNEL

Galaxy Musical Instruments primarily distributes its goods through its retail partners in the United States and Mexico. In addition, U.S. customers can place orders with Galaxy using its website. To map this structure into SAP SD, we configured two distribution channels, namely, 97 for resellers and 98 for direct sales. These distribution channels were then assigned to respective sales organizations 9090 and 9091, allowing the United States to sell via both channels, while allowing Mexico to sell only through the reseller channel.

PREEXISTING CHANNEL ASSIGNMENTS

Just like in sales organization to company code assignment section, we noticed company code 1000 was pre-assigned to sales organization 9091; you will notice some distribution channels already assigned to sales organization 9091, which were copied over from 1000 to 9091. Let's keep deleting any unwanted assignments and keep only the ones that we need, just like we did for our Mexico enterprise structure setup. For this scenario, we only want sales organization 9091 (Mexico) to be assigned to distribution channel 97 (Reseller) and therefore we deleted all other pre-existing distribution channel assignments for Galaxy that came via copy from 1000.

Configuring a Division

A *division* in SAP refers to the product division that exists in your organization. It is a way to group similar products or product lines in SAP. When you create a material master record in SAP, you create it for a particular division. A division is also one of the rules used by SAP to determine the sales area, which we will discuss later in this chapter.

Configuring a division is also a two-step activity. The first step is to create the division, and the second step is to assign the division to a sales organization. By assigning a division to a sales organization, you set up a rule in SAP that controls which product divisions a sales organization can and cannot sell from. For example, if you assign the Media & Apparel product division only to the U.S. sales organization, then SAP SD will not allow you to sell the media and apparel products using the Mexican sales organization. Like distribution channels, divisions are also available across the sales organizations. This means that you can assign the same division to multiple sales organizations.

Let's now configure our division, starting with the definition step.

NOTE Division is a cross-application component within Logistics. It is also an integration point between the MM, PP, and SD applications. In SD we use divisions to create a sales area, but determining which product divisions are required to be set up is generally done by MM and PP consultants. You should make sure to work closely with your MM and PP counterparts before setting up a division in SAP SD.

Defining a Division

You can reach the required customization screen by using transaction code OVXB or by following menu path IMG ➤ Enterprise Structure ➤ Definition ➤ Logistics General ➤ Define, Copy, Check, Delete Division. Once you are at the customization screen, click New Entries to open the New Entries screen, as shown in Figure 2.12, which shows the division setup for Galaxy Musical Instruments.

FIGURE 2.12 New Entries screen for defining divisions

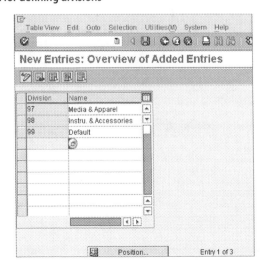

The fields on the displayed New Entries screen are Division and Name. Define your own division by filling in these two fields.

Division   Here you enter a two-digit numeric or alphanumeric identifier key for your product division.

Name   Here you enter a meaningful description for your product division. The description can be a maximum of 20 characters long.

Notice that in Figure 2.12 we created a default division: (99) for Galaxy Musical Instruments. The purpose of a default division is to allow cross-divisional sales. Without a default division, you can create a sales order only for Media & Apparel *or* for Instruments & Accessories. But what if a single customer order contains goods from both product divisions? You don't want to create separate orders in SAP just because your SAP software is configured to accept orders on an either/or basis. Default division 99 provides you with the ability to create a single order for goods from different divisions while maintaining the flexibility to report sales at individual divisions. This process is called *cross-divisional sales* in SAP ERP.

CASE STUDY—GALAXY MUSICAL INSTRUMENTS CONFIGURATION ANALYSIS: DIVISIONS

Galaxy Musical Instruments is a distributor of musical products in the United States and Mexico. It sells musical instruments, accessories, audio, video, books, and various apparel. To map this structure into SAP ERP, Galaxy's MM team came up with two product divisions: division 97, Instruments & Accessories, comprising all the musical instruments and related accessories, and division 98, Media & Apparel, comprising all video, audio, books, and wearable merchandise. In addition, we also created division 99 to allow cross-divisional sales within Galaxy Musical Instruments.

Assigning a Division to a Sales Organization

Now that we've defined the divisions, we can assign them to their respective sales organizations. You can assign a division to a sales organization via transaction code OVXAN or menu path IMG ➢ Enterprise Structure ➢ Assignments ➢ Sales And Distribution ➢ Assign Division To Sales Organization. Once you reach the assignment screen, click the New Entries button, and enter the assignments between sales organizations and divisions. Figure 2.13 shows an example of an assignment for Galaxy Musical Instruments.

FIGURE 2.13 The New Entries screen showing divisions assigned to sales organizations

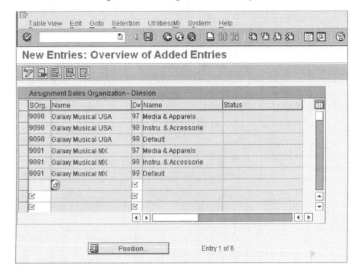

 TIP Before exiting the screen shown in Figure 2.13, make sure that you delete the unnecessary division assignments that were copied over from 1000.

So far, we have configured the sales organization, distribution channel, and division elements for Galaxy Musical Instruments. Now we will enter these values in a particular order to create a sales area.

Setting Up a Sales Area

A *sales area* is the bare minimum structure required to process a sales transaction in the SD module. It combines the sales organization, distribution channel, and division that we have created so far. You cannot create a sales document or enter a customer master record in SD without a sales area. So far, we have created two sales organizations (9090 and 9091), two distribution channels (97 and 98), and three divisions (97, 98, and 99). Now it's time to use our sales organization, distribution channels, and divisions to set up a sales area.

You can reach the required customization screen via transaction code OVXGN or menu path IMG ➤ Enterprise Structure ➤ Assignment ➤ Sales And Distribution ➤ Set Up Sales Area. Once you are at the customization screen, click the New Entries button to enter the required sales area entries. Figure 2.14 shows the sales areas setup for Galaxy Musical Instruments.

FIGURE 2.14 The New Entries screen for setting up the sales areas

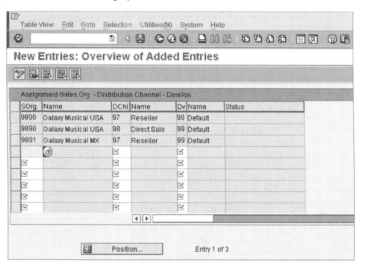

CASE STUDY—GALAXY MUSICAL INSTRUMENTS CONFIGURATION ANALYSIS: SALES AREA

With the data elements in hand (two sales organizations, two distribution channels, and three divisions), we could define up to 12 sales areas. Because Galaxy Musical Instruments sells in Mexico via a reseller channel and in the United States via both reseller and direct sale channels and also because the Galaxy's customer can place orders for cross-divisional products via a single order, we configured only three cross-divisional sales areas for Galaxy Musical Instruments, as shown in Figure 2.14.

Defining a Common Distribution Channel and Common Division

The next step in setting up the enterprise structure in SD is to define the common distribution channel and common division. In situations where your sales organization contains more than one distribution channel and more than one division, this customization setting is really helpful in reducing the master data maintenance efforts and avoiding master data duplication within a sales organization. Using a common distribution channel customization, you can define the master data for one distribution channel, and all other distribution channels that belong to that sales organization can use the same master data. You don't have to create the master data separately for all the distribution channels. Table 2.1 shows this customization assignment via the example of sales organization ABCD with distribution channels 01 and 02 sharing common master data. Row 1 in Table 2.1 shows that distribution channel 01 uses its own master data, and row 2 shows that distribution channel 02 uses the condition record and customer/material master data defined for distribution channel 01.

TABLE 2.1   Example of Common Distribution Channel Setup

Sales Organization	Distribution Channel	Reference Distribution Channel (Condition Master)	Reference Distribution Channel (Customer/ Material Master)
ABCD	01 – Wholesale	01 – Wholesale	01 – Wholesale
ABCD	02 – Retail	01 – Wholesale	01 – Wholesale

Common division customization works the same way for divisions that share common master data.

You can use transaction code VOR1 (Figure 2.15, top) or follow menu path IMG ➢ Sales And Distribution ➢ Master Data ➢ Define Common Distribution Channel to define a common distribution channel, and you can use transaction code VOR2 (Figure 2.15, bottom) or menu path IMG ➢ Sales And Distribution ➢ Master Data ➢ Define Common Division to define a common division setup.

FIGURE 2.15 Defining common distribution channels and common divisions

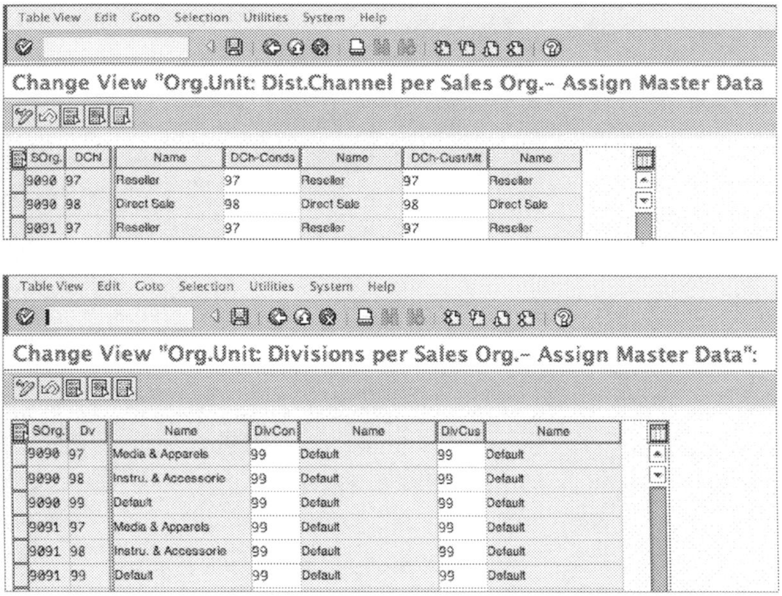

Always remember to define this setting irrespective of whether your business requirement setup needs a common distribution channel and common division. You won't be able to create master data using the sales area you just defined if this customization setting is missing. If you don't have a business requirement demanding a common distribution channel and common division setup, maintain the entry in VOR1 and VOR2 by keeping the source and target the same, as we did for Galaxy's setup (shown in Figure 2.15).

Setting Up a Sales Office

In SAP, you can maintain various sales-related geographical locations of your organization as *sales offices*. You can set up a sales office in SAP to represent a branch office or even a sales territory.

You can reach the required customization screen for defining a sales office by using transaction code OVX1 or by following menu path IMG ➤ Enterprise Structure ➤ Definition ➤ Sales And Distribution ➤ Maintain Sales Office. Once you are at the customization screen, click the New Entries button to open the New Entries screen, as shown in Figure 2.16.

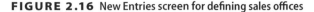

FIGURE 2.16 New Entries screen for defining sales offices

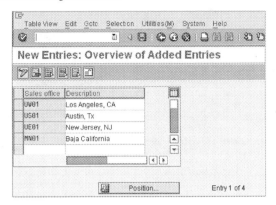

The fields on the New Entries screen are as follows:

Sales Office   Here you enter a four-character numeric or alphanumeric identifier key for your sales office.

Description   Here you enter a meaningful description for your sales office. The description can be a maximum of 20 characters long.

Address button   Here you enter the communication address for your sales office. To enter an address for a sales office, select the required sales office, and click the Address button ▤ on the sales office customization screen.

Define your own sales office by entering the previous three entries. Figure 2.16 shows various sales offices set up for Galaxy Musical Instruments.

Figure 2.17 shows the Edit Address screen that you will use to maintain the office address for the sales office.

Once you have defined a sales office, the next step is to assign the sales office to a sales area. You can reach the customization screen to assign a sales office to a sales area by using transaction code OVXMN or by following menu path IMG ➢ Enterprise Structure ➢ Assignment ➢ Sales And Distribution ➢ Assign Sales Office to Sales Area. Once you reach the assignment screen, click the New Entries button, and enter the assignments between your sales offices and sales area. Figure 2.18 shows an example of assignments for Galaxy Musical Instruments.

FIGURE 2.17 Edit Address screen for entering sales office data

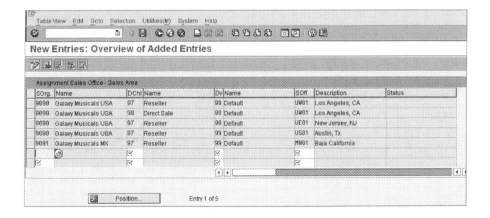

FIGURE 2.18 Assignment of sales office to sales area

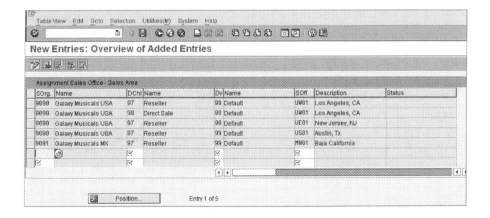

Setting Up a Sales Group

A *sales group* represents the grouping of your sales staff. This grouping is generally made on the basis of areas of responsibility. For example, you may have one group of sales staff that only solicits government contracts and another group that deals with everything else. You can set up a sales group in the SAP system either by using the transaction code OVX4 or by following the menu path IMG ➢ Enterprise Structure ➢ Definition ➢ Sales And Distribution ➢ Maintain Sales Group. Once you are at the customization screen, click the New Entries button to open the New Entries screen, as shown in Figure 2.19.

FIGURE 2.19 New Entries screen for sales group

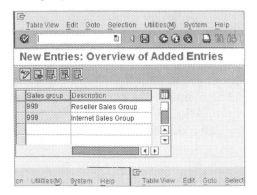

Directions for completing the fields on the New Entries screen are as follows:

Sales Group   Enter a three-character numeric or alphanumeric identifier key in this field for your sales group.

Description   Enter a meaningful description for your sales group. The description can be a maximum of 20 characters long.

Enter the required data into the screen shown in Figure 2.19 to define your own sales group. To illustrate this concept, Figure 2.19 shows the setup of various sales groups for Galaxy Musical Instruments.

Once you have defined a sales group, the next step is to assign the sales group to the sales offices from which it can operate. You can reach the required customization screen to assign a sales group to its respective sales office by using the transaction code OVXJN or by following the menu path IMG ➤ Enterprise Structure ➤ Assignment ➤ Sales And Distribution ➤ Assign Sales Group To Sales Office. Once you reach the assignment screen, click the New Entries button, and enter the assignments between your sales offices and sales group. Figure 2.20 shows a sample assignment for Galaxy Musical Instruments.

FIGURE 2.20 Assigning sales group to sales office

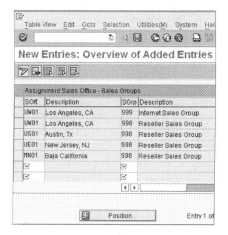

CASE STUDY—GALAXY MUSICAL INSTRUMENTS CONFIGURATION ANALYSIS: SALES GROUP

The sales group in Galaxy Musical Instruments is divided into two groups: an Internet sales group responsible for handling only sales from Galaxy's website and a reseller sale group for sales via reseller channels. To map this structure into SAP, we created two sales groups: 999 for Internet sales and 998 for resellers.

Configuring Plants

In SAP, a *plant* is an organizational entity central to the logistics operation. A plant can be a production facility, a material stock location, or even a repair facility. From the point of view of SAP SD, a plant can be defined as a material stock location from where you can source the delivery of goods to your customers.

You can reach the required customization screen to define a plant by using the transaction code OX10 or by following the menu path IMG ➢ Enterprise Structure ➢ Definition ➢ Logistics General ➢ Define, Copy, Delete, Check Plant ➢ Define Plant. Once you are at the customization screen, click the New Entries button to call up the New Entries screen, as shown in Figure 2.21.

FIGURE 2.21 New Entries screen used to define plant

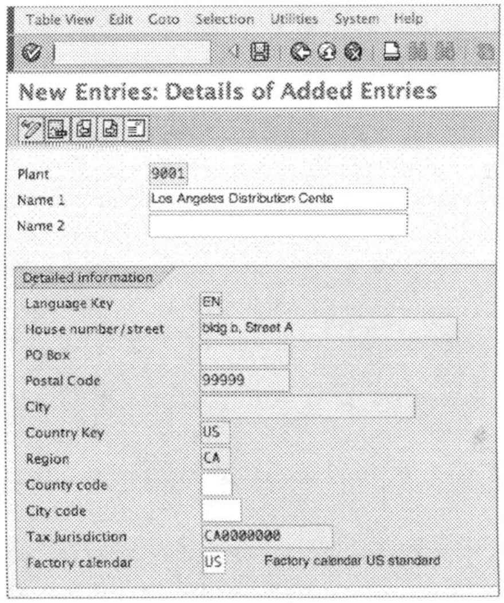

The fields on the New Entries screen are as follows:

Plant   Here you enter a four-character identifier key for your plant.

Name 1/Name 2   Here you provide an identifying name or description for your plant.

Detailed Information   The various fields under this grouping are used to capture the address details for the plant. This includes information such as the house number/street, region, country, city, postal code, and PO box. As you can see, all these fields are greyed out. You need to click the Address button to maintain this address data.

Tax Jurisdiction   This field is used to capture the tax jurisdiction code for the plant for the purpose of tax calculations. We will cover tax related settings in detail in Chapter 5, "Pricing and Tax Determination."

Factory Calendar   The value in this field represents the operational factory calendar for the plant. A factory calendar sets the working/nonworking days for a plant.

Enter the required data into the screen shown in Figure 2.21 to define your own plant. This figure shows the setup for plant 9001 in Los Angeles for Galaxy Musical Instruments.

Once you have defined a plant, the next step is to assign it to its respective company code. This is very important because all the material movements are carried out in the framework of a plant. Each material movement that results in a financial transaction requires posting to accounting. This setting provides the link between the plant and the company code for such a posting.

WARNING   A plant has a one-to-one relationship with a company code. You cannot assign the same plant to multiple company codes, although one company code can have multiple plants assigned.

You can reach the customization screen to assign a plant to its respective company code by using the transaction code OX18 or by following the menu path IMG ➢ Enterprise Structure ➢ Assignment ➢ Logistics General ➢ Assign Plant To Company Code. Once you reach the assignment screen, click the New Entries button, and enter the assignments between your plant and the company code. Figure 2.22 shows an example assignment for Galaxy Musical Instruments.

Assigning the Sales Organization and Distribution Channels to Plants

Once the plant is defined, the next step is to assign the combination of the sales organization and distribution channel to the list of allowed plants from where the sales organization can sell the goods. If you miss this setting, you will not be able to create an order in SAP. When you create an order in the SAP system, SAP looks into this customization setting to find out whether there is any plant assigned to the combination of sales organization and distribution channel used in the sales order. If no entry is found, SAP generates an error message stating that it could not find an entry for the plant.

FIGURE 2.22 Assigning a plant to a company code

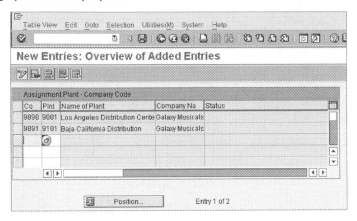

CASE STUDY—GALAXY MUSICAL INSTRUMENTS CONFIGURATION ANALYSIS: PLANT

Your sourcing and distribution strategy helps you decide the number of plants you need to set up in SAP. Galaxy manages all its distribution activities from its main plant and warehouse in Los Angeles. Galaxy has another plant in Mexico to handle local delivery within Mexico.

Galaxy Musical Instruments follows a strict naming convention to name the plants in SAP. The first two characters in the plant number represent the country where the plant is, and the last two sequential characters represent the number allocated to the plant. Therefore, the two plants for Galaxy Musical are named 9001 for Los Angeles (where 90 stands for the United States and 01 stands for the Los Angeles plant) and 9101 for Baja California (where 91 stands for Mexico and 01 stands for the Baja California plant). These plants were then assigned to their respective U.S. and Mexican company codes.

The transaction code here is OVX6N, and the menu path is IMG ➤ Enterprise Structure ➤ Assignment ➤ Sales And Distribution ➤ Assign Sales Organization and Distribution Channel To Plant. Once you reach the customization screen, click the New Entries button, and enter the assignments between the required sales organization, distribution channel, and plant. Figure 2.23 shows an example assignment for Galaxy Musical Instruments.

FIGURE 2.23 Assigning a sales organization and distribution channel to a plant

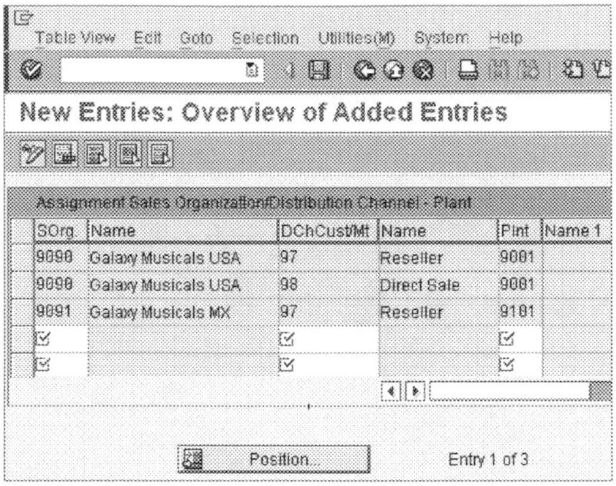

CASE STUDY—GALAXY MUSICAL INSTRUMENTS CONFIGURATION ANALYSIS: SETTING UP ALLOWABLE PLANTS

Galaxy Musical Instruments supplies goods to customers in Mexico locally from its 9101 plant in Baja California and to its U.S. customers via its 9001 plant in Los Angeles. For Galaxy to be able to sell from 9101 and 9001 using SAP, it needs to assign these plants to their respective sales organization and distribution channels. Figure 2.23 represents the setup for the allowable plants maintained in Galaxy Musical Instruments for the United States and Mexico.

Setting Up a Storage Location

A *storage location* in SAP represents the location in the plant where the goods are stored. The stock is maintained at this level. When the goods are received, the stock at the storage location goes up in the quantity received, and when the goods are sold, the stock at storage location is reduced according to the quantity delivered. You define the storage location using transaction code OX09 or using menu path IMG ➤ Enterprise Structure ➤ Definition ➤ Materials Management ➤ Maintain Storage Location. A storage location is always set up with respect to a plant, and therefore while customizing the storage location, the first screen you see is one like that shown in Figure 2.24. Here, enter the plant for which you want to set up the storage location, and click ✔ to reach the detailed customization screen shown in Figure 2.25.

FIGURE 2.24 Initial customization screen to define storage location

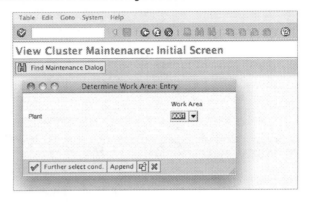

FIGURE 2.25 Defining a storage location, overview screen

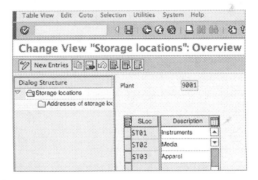

Click New Entries and define your storage location using an up to four-character unique identification key along with a meaningful description. Maintaining address data for your storage location is optional and is generally required only if your plant is very large and the storage location has its own address within the plant. To maintain address data for a storage location, select the required storage location and double-click the option for addresses of the storage location in the dialog structure on the left. You will see another screen like that in Figure 2.26. Click New Entries to open the New Entries screen, and use ⬚ to maintain the address data. Once you are done setting up your storage location, click 💾 to save your entry.

FIGURE 2.26 Defining a storage location, address maintenance screen

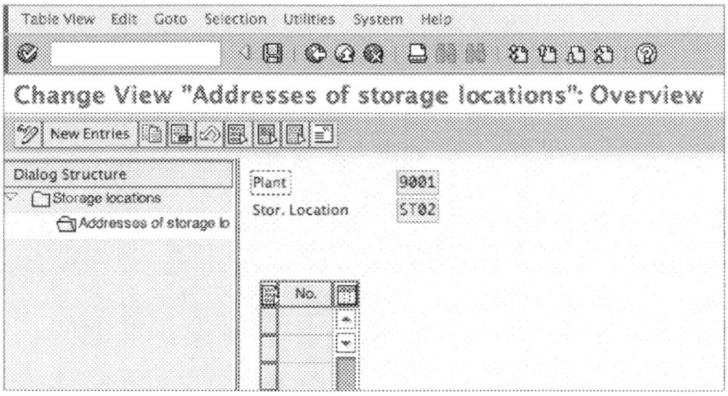

Setting Up a Shipping Point

A *shipping point* represents the organizational entity where the deliveries are processed. Each plant needs to have at least one shipping point from where the deliveries pertaining to that plant can be processed. You cannot create and process a delivery in SAP without a shipping point.

You define shipping points in SAP by using transaction code OVXD or by following menu path IMG ➢ Enterprise Structure ➢ Definition ➢ Logistics Execution ➢ Define, Copy, Delete, Check Shipping Point ➢ Define Shipping Point. Figure 2.27 shows the customization screen used to set up a shipping point in SAP. An explanation of the fields shown in Figure 2.27 follows.

Shipping Point   Here you provide a four-character identification and a description for your shipping point.

Location   The two fields in this section are Country and Departure Zone. These two fields represent the departure country and departure zone location for your shipping point. Country helps in determining taxes during pricing and determining country-specific standards, such as postal code length, for example. Departure Zone influences the delivery scheduling and also helps in route determination for deliveries being processed at the shipping point. To maintain the value in these two fields, you need to call up the address maintenance screen for the shipping point using the Address button 🖹 on the menu. Maintain the address data for the shipping point, and enter the country and departure region information on the address screen. When you close the address screen after the successful maintenance of the address data, the values for Country and Departure Zone will automatically populate the customization screen, as shown in Figure 2.27.

FIGURE 2.27 Customization screen for defining a shipping point

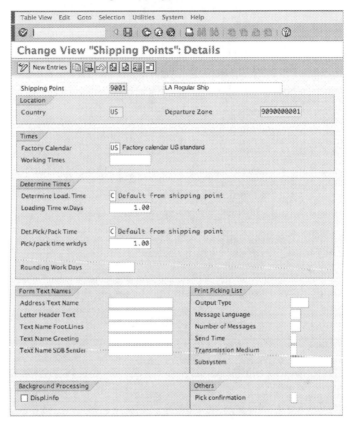

Times   Using the Factory Calendar and Working Times fields in this section of the screen, you can set up the working days and working hours for your shipping point.

Determine Times   The fields available in this section of the screen influence the delivery scheduling for the shipping point. The fields are explained here:

Determine Load. Time   This field helps determine the time taken for loading the goods. You can choose A for route-dependent and B for route-independent loading time determination. Choose C, and SAP will pick the loading time you defined for the Loading Time w.Days field. You can leave the value in this field blank if you do not want the loading time to be determined. (We cover route determination in detail in Chapter 8, "Shipping.")

Loading Time w.Days   Here you enter the loading time that you want to consider in delivery scheduling for your shipping point.

Determine Pick/Pack Time   This field helps determine the time taken for picking/packing the goods. You can choose A for route-dependent and B for route-independent pick/pack time determination. Choose C, and SAP will pick the time you defined in the Pick/Pack Time Wrkdys field. You can leave the value in this field blank if you do not want the loading time to be determined. (We cover route determination in detail in Chapter 8.)

Pick/Pack Time Wrkdys   Here you enter the picking/packing time that you want to consider in delivery scheduling for your shipping point.

Rounding Work Days   Here you enter the safety margin for the estimated time required for processing the delivery.

Form Text Names   Address Text Name, Letter Header Text, Text Name Foot. Lines, Text Name Greeting, and Text Name SDB Sender are the fields available in this section of the screen. This is where you can enter text that appears frequently on various shipping outputs. You maintain this text using transaction code SO10.

Print Picking List   The fields in this section control the output processing for picking lists. Here you define the output type, the output language (Message Language field), the number of times you want to generate output (Number Of Messages field), the timing for sending the output (Send Time field), and the medium in which you want to send the output such as print or fax (Transmission Medium field). We explain output processing in detail in Chapter 4, "Partner, Text, and Output Determination."

Background Processing   Selecting the Displ.info field check box will help you display information messages in addition to error messages in the delivery due list processing log.

Others   The Pick Confirmation field in this section controls the picking confirmation's applicability for a shipping point. Select A here if you want make confirmation compulsory for all the items processed via this shipping point. This is applicable only where you don't use MM–WM transfer orders to perform picking.

Once defined, the shipping points are assigned to plants. You can assign one shipping point to multiple plants, or one plant can have multiple shipping points. The transaction code is OVXC, and the menu path is IMG ➤ Enterprise Structure ➤

Assignment ➤ Logistics Execution ➤ Assign Shipping Point To Plant. Figure 2.28 shows the plant-shipping point assignment for Galaxy Musical Instruments.

FIGURE 2.28 Customization screen for shipping point assignment to plant

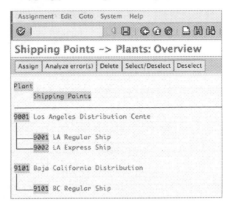

CASE STUDY—GALAXY MUSICAL INSTRUMENTS CONFIGURATION ANALYSIS: SHIPPING POINTS

Galaxy Musical Instruments created three shipping points: LA Regular Ship is 9001, LA Express Ship is 9002, and BC Regular Ship is 9101. Shipping points 9001 and 9002 were assigned to U.S. plant 9001, and shipping point 9101 was assigned to Mexico plant 9101. All regular shipments in the United States are processed at shipping point 9001, and all customer deliveries requiring express shipments are handled by shipping point 9002. For Mexico, all shipments are processed using shipping point 9101, which is called BC Regular Ship.

In SAP, you can divide a shipping point into multiple loading points. Setting up a loading point is optional. You can define a loading point by using transaction code OVX7 or by following menu path IMG ➤ Enterprise Structure ➤ Definition ➤ Logistics Execution ➤ Maintain Loading Point. Because a loading point is a subdivision of a shipping point, the first screen you will encounter will be a dialog box asking you to enter a shipping point. Here, enter the shipping point for which you want to set up the loading points, and click ✔ to reach the detailed customization screen in Figure 2.29. To define your own loading point, provide a two-character identifier and a meaningful description. Figure 2.29 shows the two loading points that we created for shipping point 9001.

FIGURE 2.29 Defining loading points

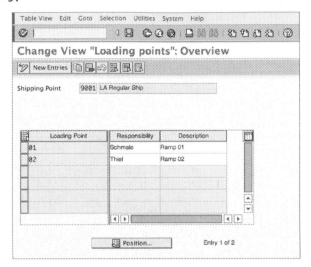

Setting Up a Transportation Planning Point

A *transportation planning point* is the organizational unit that manages transportation-related activities. The shipment documents are assigned to specific transportation planning points. You can define a transportation planning point using transaction code OVXT or following menu path IMG ➢ Enterprise Structure ➢ Definition ➢ Logistics Execution ➢ Maintain Transportation Planning Point.

To define your own transportation planning point, create a new entry as shown in Figure 2.30. Specify a four-character long alphanumeric name, as well as a description. Assign the entry to a company code. You can also maintain the address of this organizational entity.

FIGURE 2.30 Transportation planning point

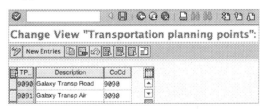

CUSTOMIZATION RULES

Before we define a factory calendar, there are a few technical points that we need to address while customizing:

► Always use *Y* or *Z* as prefix for the customization settings that you make in SAP. The enterprise structure that we configured earlier was an exception to this rule. The letters *Y* and *Z* are reserved in the SAP system for customer-specific customizations. When you make changes directly to SAP-provided customization objects without using a *Y* or *Z*, you run the risk of your changes getting overwritten by the next SAP system upgrade. All the customization settings that we will discuss in the remainder of this book will follow this rule.

► Customization changes in SAP are of two kinds: client dependent and client independent. A *client-dependent* setting is specific to the SAP instance you are customizing. A *client-independent* setting is independent of the current instance you are working. A client-independent setting affects all the instances of SAP that are installed on one system. Always take extra precautions when you configure a client-independent setting, because it will have a global impact across SAP clients.

Setting Up a Factory Calendar

In SAP, a *factory calendar* helps you define the number of working days for your organization. The transaction code is SCAL, and the menu path is IMG ≻ SAP NetWeaver ≻ General Settings ≻ Maintain Calendar. Figure 2.31 shows the initial screen for calendar maintenance. As you can see, you can use this customization screen to define factory calendars and holiday calendars in SAP. Calendars are part of the global settings in SAP and are used by many areas in the logistics and human resource applications of SAP. Setting up a calendar in SAP is a client-independent setting, and the changes to calendars are not automatically captured in a transport request. You have to manually capture these changes into a transport request for moving them between various instances of your SAP system—development, quality, and production, for example.

FIGURE 2.31 Main menu screen for defining SAP factory calendar

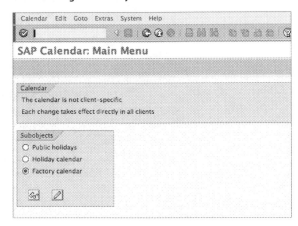

To define a factory calendar, select the factory calendar option on the customization screen shown in Figure 2.31, and click the pencil icon. Now you will see the overview screen for factory calendar customization, showing various factory calendars that exist in your SAP system (see Figure 2.32).

FIGURE 2.32 Overview screen for defining a factory calendar

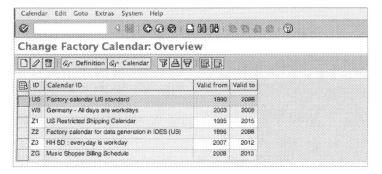

You can click the pencil icon on the menu to change an existing calendar, the recycle icon (to the right of pencil icon) to delete an existing calendar, and the create icon on the left of the pencil icon to create a new factory calendar. Let's click the create icon to create a new factory calendar called ZZ for Galaxy Musical Instruments USA. You will be presented with a calendar customization detail screen, as shown in Figure 2.33.

FIGURE 2.33 Customization screen for maintaining a factory calendar

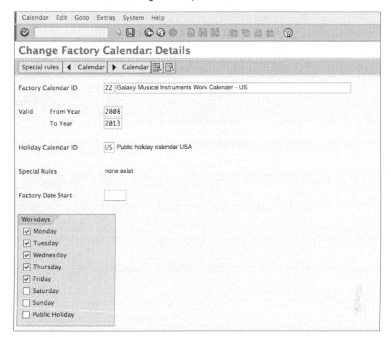

The screen is self-explanatory. Create the new factory calendar by providing a two-character identification key starting with a *Y* or *Z* prefix and by providing a meaningful description. Figure 2.33 tells you that the factory calendar ZZ is valid from year 2008 to 2013 with five working days per week (Monday to Friday) and a holiday calendar assigned as US.

For Galaxy, we created factory calendars ZZ for the United States and ZX for Mexico with both calendars having five working days per week.

Running a Consistency Check

Once you are done with all the customization related to enterprise structure setup, you should perform a consistency check in the SAP system to check whether the customization settings are correct in all respects. You can perform the consistency check using transaction code OVX8N or following menu path IMG ➤ Enterprise Structure ➤ Consistency Check ➤ Check Enterprise Structure For Sales And

Distribution. Figure 2.34 shows various checks that are performed by SAP when you run the consistency check for SD. For example, you can check whether the address is correctly entered in all the sales organizations, whether the distribution channel is correctly assigned to the sales organization, and whether the sales area is correctly set up.

FIGURE 2.34 Check Report for Customizing – Organization – SD screen for sales organization

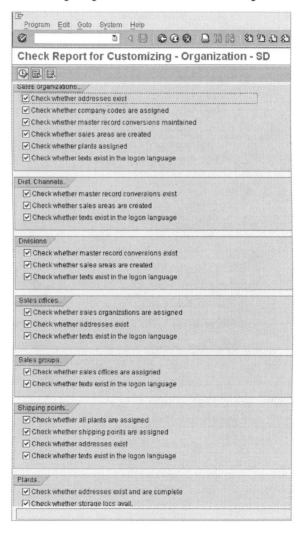

Always make sure to perform this consistency check once you are done with your customization settings for enterprise structure in SAP SD. If the consistency check report shows errors, go back to the respective customization screens and make corrections. You won't be able to use your structure if there are errors in customizing.

Summary

In this chapter, we showed you how to set up an enterprise structure in SAP SD. We explained the various elements of an enterprise structure, their use, and their arrangement in the structure. There is one more important component of the enterprise structure still to discuss. This is called *credit control*, and we will cover it in detail in Chapter 11, "Credit Management."

In Chapter 3, we will talk about master data in SAP SD.

Master Data in SD

aster data is any information that plays a key role in the core operation of a business. It may include data about clients and customers, employees, suppliers, products, and so on. Master data is typically shared by multiple users and groups. Hence, it is important to consult with the entire organization when you set it up. When you enter transaction data, the master data is copied over. This saves a lot of time and effort in data entry and ensures the consistency of information.

Master data comes in several types. The customer master and material master are the most important types and are the focus of our discussion in this chapter. In fact, all the subsequent chapters in this book will refer to topics in master data. Other master data types, such as the price master, output master, text master, customer–material information, and material determination, will be covered in the context of their respective chapters.

Customer Master

The *customer master* is a data record that contains all the information pertaining to a client, a customer, or any other business partner who plays a role in the business. As noted, a master data record is shared and updated across the organization. The customer master data is used and updated by the sales department (which maintains the customer groups, preferences, classification, and so on) and the finance/accounting department (which is more concerned with things such as bank details, credit classification, and account numbers). The common data—such as the customer's name and address—is used centrally. Based on this requirement, SAP structures customer master data into three parts:

▶ General data, which is common to the entire organization

▶ Sales data, which is specific to a sales area

▶ Company code data, which is specific to the company code

This breakdown enables you to segregate authorizations and structure the customer master data.

Common Terms in Customer Master Data

Before proceeding with how to set up the customer master, you need to understand what partner functions and account groups are.

Partner Functions

In each sales transaction, different groups or individuals can have different roles and responsibilities. For example, at the customer location, the party who places the order can be different from the receiving party. In addition, an invoice may need to go to a different address than that of the payer. Therefore, you have to map all these different roles in the system, which are called *partner functions*.

When you create customer master data, you also specify the roles that the customer will play. SAP then copies this information to all the sales documents for this customer. Thus, you can ensure that the delivery is shipped to the door of the ship-to party and that the correct payer is scheduled to make the payments.

The following partner functions are the most frequently used:

- ► Sold-to party (AG)
- ► Ship-to party (AU)
- ► Bill-to party (RE)
- ► Payer (RG)

We will discuss partner functions in more detail in Partner determination section of Chapter 4, "Partner, Text, and Output Determination."

Account Groups

Each partner function is assigned to an *account group*. Account groups are primarily used to control the screens and fields required to maintain data for each customer, based on the customer's roles. As you will see in the subsequent sections, you can control several important settings based on the account group.

Creating Customer Master Data

The menu path to access customer master data is SAP Menu ➤ Logistics ➤ Sales and Distribution ➤ Master Data ➤ Business Partner ➤ Customer.

Under Business Partner (see Figure 3.1), the nodes let you create or change other business partners such as sales partners and forwarding agents.

You can use three sets of transaction codes to create and update customer master records:

XD01   XD01 gives you the authorization to maintain all views of the customer master data. Hence, it's a master transaction code, which only a few individuals in the organization should have permission to use.

VD01   VD01 confines the user to maintaining the sales area data and general information, preventing access to the company code data.

FD01   FD01 is the converse of VD01. It permits the user to maintain the general information and company code data, preventing access to sales data.

In this chapter, you will work with XD01 only.

When you enter the transaction code, the screen shown in Figure 3.2 is displayed. Specify the sales area and company code for the data being set up.

To help expedite setting up the data, you can always copy data from an existing customer record. In the Reference tab of the screen shown in Figure 3.2, you can enter any existing customer number and specify the sales area. Data fields will be copied over from the reference customer. Then you can change them as required.

FIGURE 3.1   Menu for Business Partner

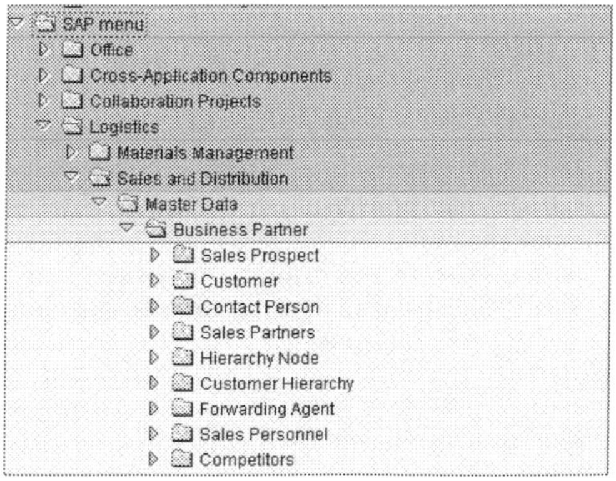

FIGURE 3.2 Customer Create: Initial Screen

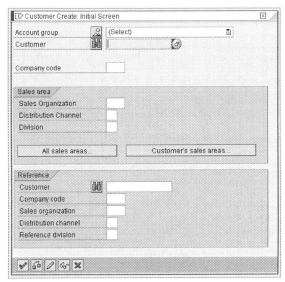

The customer master data is divided into three areas:

▶ The General Data section has common information such as the Address tab, which contains name and contact information details, control data (such as industry, transportation zone, and tax information), payment transaction (bank details and payment card details), marketing (Nielsen ID and other classification), and other tabs based on relevance to the business.

▶ The Sales Area Data section has tabs called Sales (containing information on sales groups, pricing classifications, and so on), Shipping (which controls items such as delivery priority, shipping conditions, and so on), Billing (for tax classifications, Incoterms, and so on), and Partner Functions.

▶ The Company Code Data section has tabs called Account Management (reconciliation account details) Payment Transactions, Correspondence, and Insurance. From the General Data and Sales Area Data sections, you can also branch out to Extras ➤ Additional Data to reach other fields.

Many of these data fields are copied over from the customer master to transaction documents (sales orders, delivery documents, and invoices) and control several functions.

One-Time Customers

Some customers require your service once in a lifetime. Therefore, it is not required to set up these types of customers. In such cases, you can set up a one-time customer master record. In this type of customer master, you do not capture any data specific to a single customer. This makes the customer master record reusable. Specifically, the same customer number has different names and address information in different sales documents, and whenever you use a one-time customer number in a sales order, the system prompts you to enter the actual name and address of the customer placing this specific order (Figure 3.3). Since this data is stored only in the current sales document, you can reuse the customer number. One of the common business processes where a one-time customer is used is in a regular cash sale. Because the customer pays immediately for the product or service, there is no need to track and maintain a record for future use.

FIGURE 3.3   Using a one-time customer in a sales order

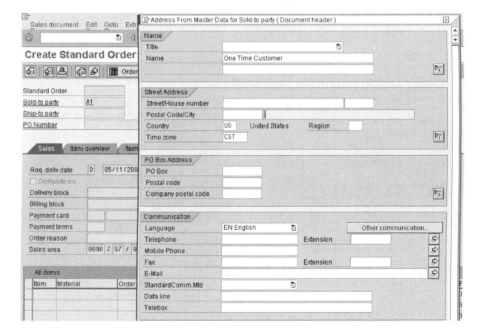

Maintaining Customer Master Records

The following transactions help you maintain existing customer master records in the system:

Change Customer Master (VD02, XD02, FD02)　These are the transactions to change or update customer master screens. As discussed earlier, each of these codes controls access to some or all of the data tabs.

Display Customer Master (VD03, XD03, FD03)　These transactions allow the user to display the master data without making any changes to it.

Block A Customer (VD05)　This transaction is used to block a customer from transacting business with your organization. As seen in Figure 3.4, you have options to block sales orders, delivery, and billing documents in some or all the sales areas.

FIGURE 3.4　Customer Block/Unblock: Details Sales Area screen

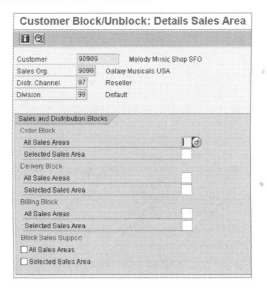

Flag For Deletion (VD06)　You can flag a customer master record for deletion using this transaction. Again, you have the option to delete the data specific to a sales area or across the organization. The system also gives you an option to retain the general data of the customer and delete business-relevant data such as Sales Area. This way, you can retain the basic customer record for future reference.

Change Account Group (XD07)   If you need to upgrade a customer to play a larger role or multiple roles, you can change its account group. In this transaction, specify the customer to be changed and the new account group. You get a checklist of any additional screens and fields that must be entered before you can promote the customer. You can then maintain the data and change the account group. In Figure 3.5, a payer is being promoted to a sold-to party.

You can use this transaction only to promote a customer from a lower-level to a higher-level account group. The converse is not possible. For example, you can promote a payer to a sold-to party, which would require additional fields to be maintained. However, you cannot change a sold-to party to a lower level such as a payer, since you cannot mask or undo fields that are already maintained.

FIGURE 3.5   Change Account Group screen

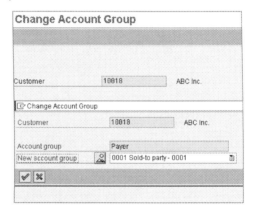

Customizing Customer Master Data

We've discussed how to create and maintain customer master data, so now we'll cover the various customization settings that you need to control.

Defining Account Groups

SAP comes with a set of standard account groups that should meet most business requirements. However, if you want to segregate different groups of customers with different number ranges or screen layouts, you can create additional account groups. For each account group, you can control the setup of various screens, fields, and attributes. If you need to set up a custom account group, use the following path: IMG ➢ Financial Accounting ➢ Account Receivable and Account Payable ➢

Customer Accounts ➤ Master Data ➤ Preparation For Creating Customer Master Data ➤ Define Account Groups With Screen Layouts.

CHANGE LOG IN THE CUSTOMER MASTER

Each customer master record is shared across the organization. Any changes made to it have to be tracked and recorded. Hence, the customer master has a *change log* that records each change made along with the date, the time, and the user who made it. To access the change log from the customer master record, use the path Environment ➤ Account Changes ➤ All Fields. This lists all the fields that have been changed along with the old and new values, a time stamp, and the user ID. Thus, you have total traceability for the changes. For example, you can see a change log for a customer address here. The change log clearly indicates the date, the time, and the user who changed the city of the customer from Trenton to Old Tappan.

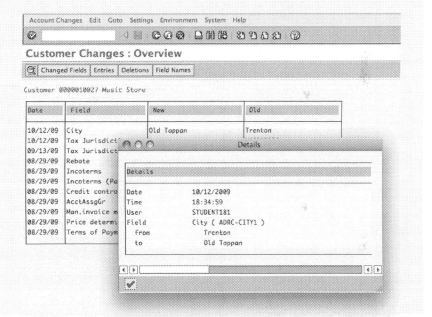

 TIP In most enterprises, account groups are maintained by the FI team. Thus, you should consult with your FI and MM teams before you make any changes.

In the customization menu, follow this path to get to the customer master setup menu (Figure 3.6): IMG ➢ Logistics – General ➢ Business Partner ➢ Customers ➢ Control.

FIGURE 3.6   Customer master customization menu

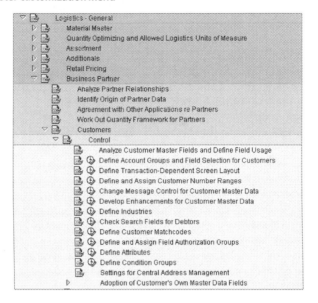

We'll now discuss some of the key settings you can access from the Control node.

Defining Account Groups and Field Selection for Customers (OVT0)

For each account group, you can customize the screens, mark fields as mandatory or optional, and even hide them. The purpose of this step is to keep only those fields that are relevant to your business.

To do this, start by specifying the account group that you want to customize, and then click the Details icon. In Figure 3.7, we have selected the account group 0001 (Sold-To Party).

The Details screen will show you the attributes of the account group, such as the number range and partner determination procedure. To customize the field selection, first choose from General Data, Company Code Data, or Sales Data. Double-click any of these to go to the Maintain Field Status Group: Overview screen (Figure 3.8).

FIGURE 3.7   Change View "Customer Account Groups": Details screen

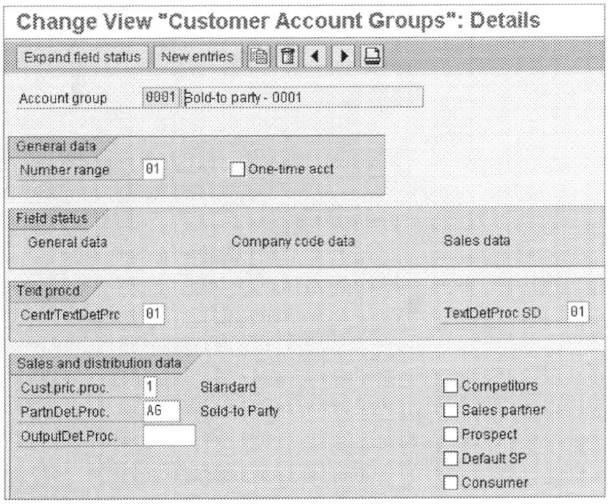

FIGURE 3.8   Maintain Field Status Group: Overview screen

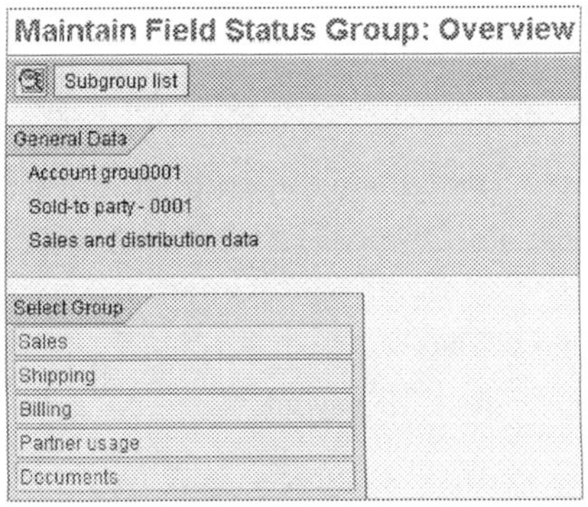

The fields are grouped together logically under tab names such as Address, Communications, and Marketing. Select the tab you want to configure, and click Choose (Figure 3.9).

The fields grouped under the chosen tab are now displayed. Radio buttons present four options for marking each field: Suppress (hidden), Req. Entry (required entry), Opt. Entry (optional entry), and Display (nonchangeable).

FIGURE 3.9   Maintain Field Status Group: Sales view

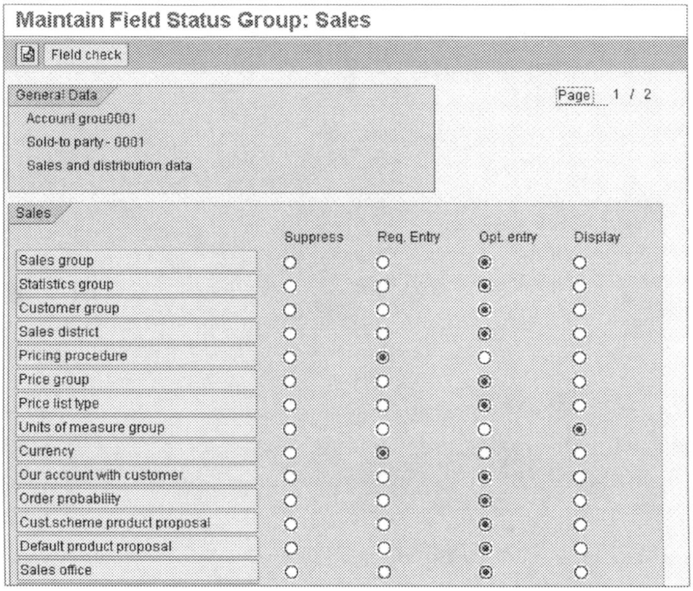

Defining a Transaction-Dependent Screen Layout (OB20)

In this option, you can control the fields and screens as discussed in the earlier section but based on each transaction code. This is not generally recommended and should be used selectively, only if you have typical requirements. For example if you need to mark a field as active in create mode (XD01) and as display only in change mode (XD02), you can use this option.

Defining and Assigning Number Ranges

Each account group is assigned a number range. Every new customer who you create will get a unique number from the specified number range. This helps in segregating and numbering similar partner functions serially. In the case of account group 0001, we have assigned number range 01 (Figure 3.10) and have defined the number range interval as between 10001 and 99999 (Figure 3.11).

FIGURE 3.10 Assigning a number range to the account group

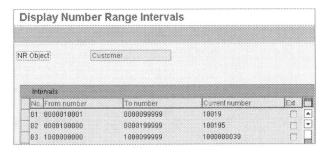

FIGURE 3.11 Defining a number range interval

Note the Ext. check box at the far right of Figure 3.11. This is where you can mark a number range as external. If you selected this box, the system would prompt you to choose a number for the customer being created. This is particularly useful if you have an external interface from which customer master data is being copied into SAP and you are required to keep the same number as was used in the parent system. In our case, we have opted for an internal number range.

After you have customized the screens and assigned a number range, you can proceed to configure the various key fields in the customer master data.

TIP Before you configure the fields in the customer master data, it is advisable to check the reporting requirements of your organization. Based on the reporting criteria, you can set up the grouping fields and hence derive reports easily.

Defining Industries

An *industry* is a group of customers with the same basic business activity. You can specify industries of your customers, such as trade, banking, service, manufacturing, healthcare, public service, media, and so on. The Industry appears in the general data of the customer master record (as seen in Figure 3.12) and can be an effective grouping term.

In the case of Galaxy Musical Instruments, we have specified MUSC (Musical) as one of the industries for customers. We can derive a report or control a pricing discount based on this grouping.

FIGURE 3.12 Specifying an industry in the customer master data

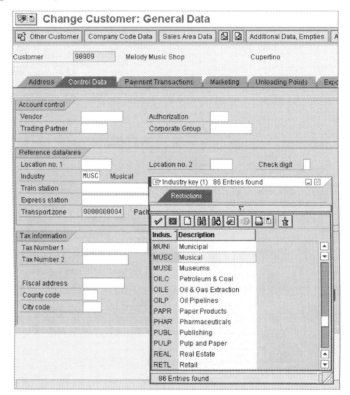

Defining Attributes

SAP provides 10 freely definable attribute fields. You can use these fields to capture various attributes or preferences of your customer. They are two-character fields. To add values applicable to your organization, click the attribute in the list, and enter new values.

CASE STUDY—GALAXY MUSICAL INSTRUMENTS: CUSTOM MASTER

In the case of Galaxy Musical Instruments, we will go with the standard SAP account groups, as shown in this table:

Account Group	Name
0001	Sold-To Party
0002	Ship-To Party
0003	Payer
0004	Bill-To
CPDA	One-Time Customer
0012	Hierarchy Nodes

The regular customers (such as retailers of the company's products) are mapped as sold-to parties (0001). The direct customers, who order over phone or online, are mapped as one-time customers (CPDA). We have set up a single account for them. We have also assigned internal number ranges. (Account group 0012 will be used in the "Customer Hierarchy" section of this chapter.)

We have then customized the data screens to mask the fields that are not relevant to us. For example, in the Sales view, we need only the fields Pricing Procedure and Currency to be mandatory. All other fields are marked as optional (as shown in Figure 3.9).

N O T E   The attribute fields come with predefined names like Attribute 1, Attribute 2, and so on. You can change the names to make them more meaningful to your organization. Contact an ABAP expert to make changes to the data dictionary.

Customizing Fields in the Sales Area Data

We have now covered the settings in the Logistics – General menu for customer master data. Next, the action moves to the Sales and Distribution node in IMG so you can configure fields in the Sales Area data. The path is IMG ➢ Sales And Distribution ➢ Master Data ➢ Business Partners ➢ Customers. The following are some of the key settings from the list of nodes appearing here (see Figure 3.13).

Marketing   An enterprise's sales and marketing team often classifies customers into various groups. External classifications such as the Nielsen ID for the customer can be defined here. These fields will appear in the Marketing view in the customer master.

Sales   In this section, you can define sales districts that cater to various geographical areas. You can also create different customer groups. This helps users track regional sales and derive reports.

Shipping   Among other functions, this tab lets you define delivery priorities. The value you input here will define the urgency of the order. Regular or important customers can be assigned a higher priority by default. This field gets copied into sales orders, where it can be changed manually, if needed. Delivery priority plays a critical role in getting stock committed to sales orders. You will study it in detail in Chapter 6, "Availability Check, Transfer of Requirements, and Backorders."

Billing Document   In this section, you can define Payment terms and Incoterms, as required. These are usually set up in consultation with the FI team.

Customer Hierarchy

You may need to map the client's organizational hierarchy in SAP. In the case of large customers, there could be various regional offices that order from you independently. Hence, each one of them could be a separate customer number in the system, yet there could be requirement to map them into a group. Often prices or rebates are determined at the level of the parent node of the hierarchy and apply to the entire family. This requirement is fulfilled by the customer hierarchy functionality.

The *customer hierarchy* is a grouping of customers in a flexible organizational structure. At each level you can specify the higher-level customer and thus build a multilevel structure. Any specific data (such as the price record, rebate agreements, and so on) is maintained at a higher-level node and then flows down to all the dependent nodes in the tree. A validity period is attached to the hierarchy so that if there is any change to the structure, it can be made effective from a specific date.

Partner determination (see Chapter 4) also plays a key role in reflecting the complete hierarchy in sales documents. Once a customer is entered in a sales document, SAP can trace all the higher-level nodes in its hierarchy up to the apex node.

Creating a Customer Hierarchy

Before you set up a hierarchy, always create an organizational chart where you plan the hierarchy and gather the following information:

- ▶ What are the customer numbers that need to be linked?
- ▶ What is the hierarchical relationship between these customers?
- ▶ Do I need to set up any additional nodes in the hierarchy? (Nodes may be required to set up intermediate grouping levels to complete the picture.)
- ▶ What are the account groups of all these customers?
- ▶ Which sales areas are these customers assigned to?
- ▶ Which sales document type would require this hierarchy?
- ▶ Which price and rebate conditions would depend on the hierarchy?

Prerequisite Steps

The following are the master data steps you will need to take before you can create a hierarchy:

Step 1: Create Customer Master Records   You should create customer master records for each of the customers you plan to link together in the hierarchy.

Step 2: Create Hierarchy Nodes   To complete the logical setup of a customer hierarchy, you sometimes need to define *hierarchy nodes*. These are not actual customers but logical grouping levels. A hierarchy node is set up as a customer with account group 0012. You can use VD01 or XD01 and specify the account group there. Alternatively, there is a special code, V-12, to set up hierarchy nodes. The path is SAP Menu ➢ Logistics ➢ Sales and Distribution ➢ Master Data ➢ Business Partners ➢ Hierarchy Node.

The procedure is the same as creating a customer master. In the sales billing view, there is a provision to activate relevance for price determination and rebates (Figure 3.14).

FIGURE 3.14 Creating a hierarchy node

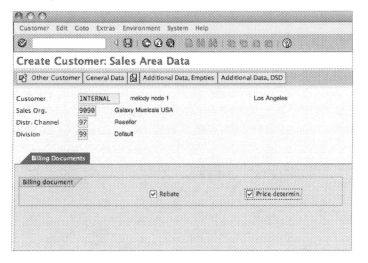

Creating the Customer Hierarchy

Once you have completed all the prerequisites, you can proceed to set up the customer hierarchy. Use this menu path: SAP Menu ➤ Logistics ➤ Sales And Distribution ➤ Master Data ➤ Business Partners ➤ Customer Hierarchy ➤ Edit (VDH1N).

You can also launch this transaction from within a customer master (VD02 or XD02) via Environment ➤ Customer Hierarchy.

Here are the steps:

Step 1: Specify Hierarchy Type On the Process Customer Hierarchy screen, you set up a hierarchy. The hierarchy type controls the purpose of the hierarchy (for example, pricing or reporting). It also controls which account groups are permitted and which sales areas can use the hierarchy. Also, enter a validity period and the customer details on this screen (Figure 3.15).

FIGURE 3.15 Process Customer Hierarchy screen

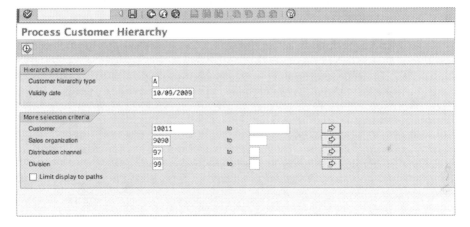

Step 2: Set Up Hierarchy Links Now set up the hierarchy, one link at a time. On the Assignment tab on the right of Figure 3.16, specify the two customers to be linked, and click Transfer. The updated hierarchy now appears on the left window. The Application Log tab, at the bottom right, signals whether the transfer was successful. If there is an error, you will find the details in the log.

FIGURE 3.16 Maintain Customer Hierarchy screen

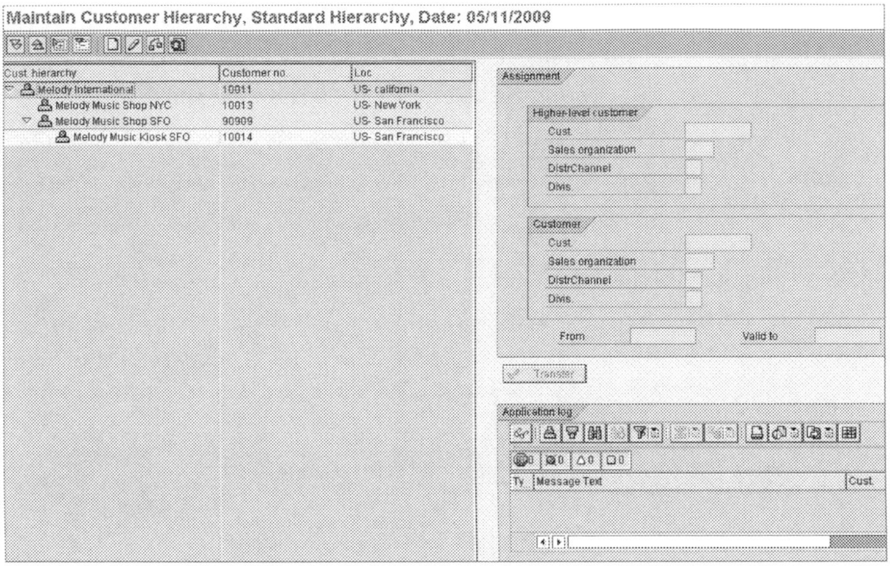

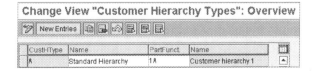

Customizing a Customer Hierarchy

To customize the settings in the customer hierarchy, use the following menu path in the customization menu: IMG ➤ Sales and Distribution ➤ Master Data ➤ Business Partners ➤ Customers ➤ Customer Hierarchy.

We'll discuss each step in this menu:

Step 1: Define Hierarchy Types (OVH1)   The Hierarchy type controls the purpose of the hierarchy. All the major settings for customer hierarchy are carried out at this level. In the setting shown in Figure 3.17, the SAP Standard Hierarchy type A is assigned to partner function 1A. This is the apex of the hierarchy.

FIGURE 3.17 Linking a hierarchy type to a partner function

Step 2: Set Partner Determination For Hierarchy Categories   Partner determination is important to copy the hierarchy data to sales documents. By customizing partner determination, the system will search for all the partners in the hierarchy of the customer in the order. They will appear as partners 1A, 1B, and so on, up to 1Z (26 levels). Use as many levels as required by your business.

Partner Determination can be set up for customer master, sales documents, delivery, shipment and billing documents. You can select one of these, from the menu. On the next screen, select the document type, and click Partner Functions In Procedure. As you can see in Figure 3.18, 1A to 1D (four levels) have been specified. They are marked as nonchangeable, and the source is specified as B (denoting a customer hierarchy).

FIGURE 3.18 Linking the hierarchy type to a partner function

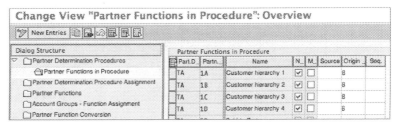

Step 3: Assign Account Groups (OVH2)   To control the assignment of customers in a hierarchy, you can set rules for account groups. For each account group, you specify which other groups are allowed to be at a higher level in the hierarchy. In Figure 3.19, for the hierarchy type A, the account group Sold-To Party (0001) can have another Sold-To Party group (0001), a Payer group (0003), or a Node group (0012) at a higher level. If you have defined any custom account groups, make sure this assignment is correct before you create your customer hierarchy.

FIGURE 3.19 Assigning account groups to a hierarchy type

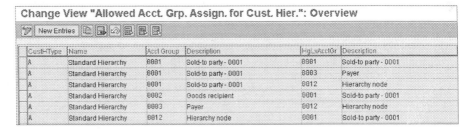

Step 4: Assign Sales Areas (OVH3)   Having set controls between account groups, you now check which sales areas are allowed at a higher level than others (Figure 3.20). If you need to link customers that belong to different sales areas, you can set up controls on which sales area is allowed to be at a higher level than the

other. If a user tries to link together customers that belong to sales areas that are not permitted together in this setting, the system will issue an error message stating that the sales area assignment is not permitted.

FIGURE 3.20 Assigning sales areas to a hierarchy type

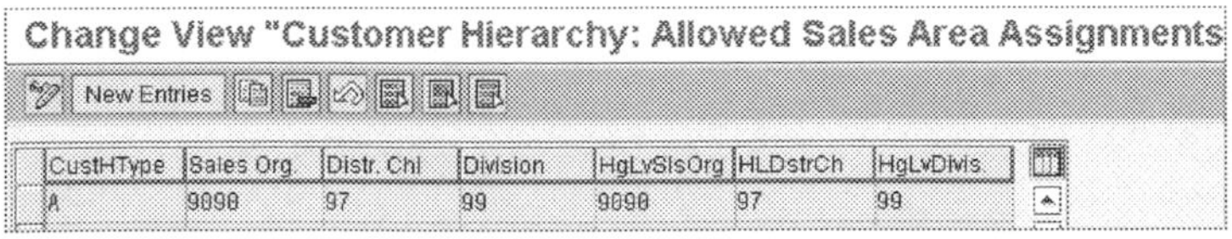

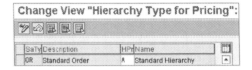

Step 5: Assign Hierarchy Type For Pricing By Sales Document Type (OVH4)
For each sales document type, you assign a hierarchy type using a screen similar to that in Figure 3.21. This is the critical link in transferring a customer hierarchy to a sales document and in determining pricing based on the hierarchy.

FIGURE 3.21 Assigning a hierarchy type to sales documents for pricing

CASE STUDY—GALAXY MUSICAL INSTRUMENTS: CUSTOMER HIERARCHY

One of our main customers is Melody International. Their regional offices and retail outlets have placed orders in the past, and each is registered in the database as a different customer. As part of a new agreement, we are offering a discount to all Melody group companies. We also have to track our sales across this strategic account. We use a customer hierarchy to structure the group companies.

The top of the hierarchy is a nodal company (10011). We will control the prices for the group at this level. The regional stores (90909 and 10013) form the second layer of the hierarchy. Any kiosks (10014) constitute the third layer. (Refer to Figure 3.16 for details.)

If a sales order is placed by the kiosk customer (such as 10014), the entire hierarchy will be traced up to the apex of the structure. The pricing agreement at the parent level will be determined and applied to the order.

Material Master

The *material master* contains all the information about the product or service being sold. This information is shared across the organization and maintained by different departments. Hence, it is structured in views according to the various functions such as Purchasing view, MRP view, Accounting view, and Sales view. SD-related data is structured in three views—Sales: Sales Org 1, Sales: Sales Org 2, and Sales: General/Plant. These three views will be the focus of the following discussion.

Common Terms in Material Master Data

In your organization, you manage different types of materials such as raw materials, semifinished goods, and finished goods. Materials with a similar set of attributes are grouped under the same material type. The *material type*, therefore, is the key to controlling screen sequence, data fields, and data. SAP has a set of predefined material types that meet most business requirements. Check whether the following terms match the materials and products you manage in your organization:

- *FERT*: Finished products
- *HALB*: Semifinished products
- *ROH*: Raw materials
- *DIEN*: Services
- *KMAT*: Configurable materials
- *HAWA*: Trading goods

From the sales and distribution angle, we will be most concerned with products and services sold to the customer. Hence, FERT, DIEN, and HAWA will be of greater interest to us than other material types.

Creating Material Master Data

You can create a material master record using transaction code MM01. The path is SAP Menu ➢ Logistics ➢ Sales and Distribution ➢ Master Data ➢ Products ➢ Material ➢ Other Material ➢ Create.

The screen shown in Figure 3.22 is where you specify the material type that you plan to set up. Use the Industry Sector field to specify the type of industry (Chemical, Pharmaceutical, Retail, and so on) to which the material belongs.

There is a provision to create a material by copying it with reference to an existing record. Use the Copy From field to specify the reference material and the organizational levels from which the data can be copied over.

The Select View(s) button allows you to choose which data screens you want to create. You can always create a material for a certain view first (such as Basic Data) and later extend it for other views. This is the typical scenario in most organizations, where different departments maintain their own piece of information and then hand it over to the next group. Based on your selection, you will then have to specify the organizational levels (plants, sales organizations, and so on) for which the data will be created.

The following are some views that you will come across in the material master. We will only discuss the major ones here.

FIGURE 3.22 Create Material screen: selecting views

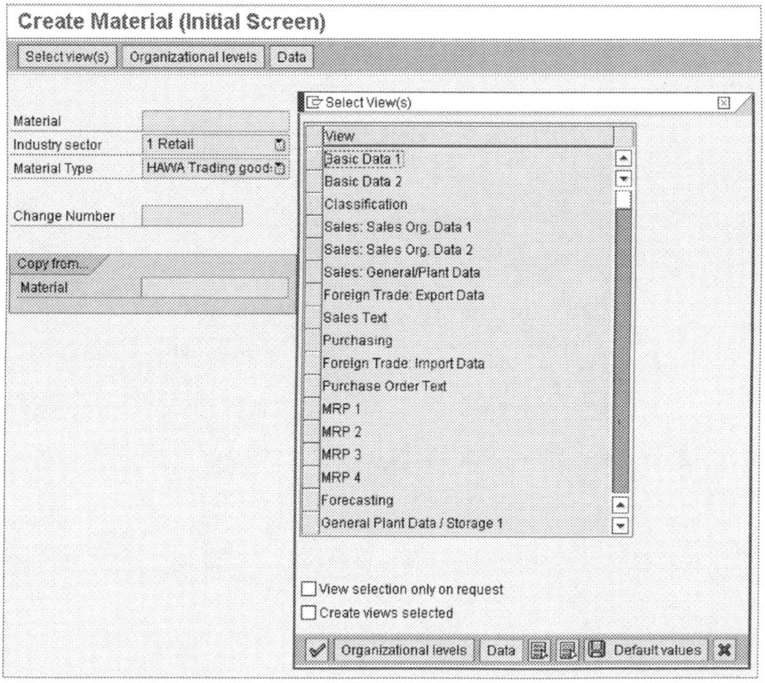

Basic Data

This view contains product data common to the entire organization. Hence, you do not have to specify any specific organizational level to create this view. The material description, units of measure, and attributes such as weight, volume, and status appear in this view.

TIP Fields in the Basic Data view should be maintained in conjunction with other departments in the organization.

There are three sales views in the material master: Sales Org. 1, Sales Org. 2, and General/Plant Data.

Sales: Sales Org 1 View

This data is specific to a sales organization and distribution channel. The following are some of the key fields:

Units Of Measure Here you specify one or more units of measure used for stocking, selling, delivering, or procuring the material. You can maintain three different units of measure for a material:

Base Unit Of Measure This represents the unit of measure in which the stocks of the material are maintained. This is the base unit of measure. All other units will be converted to the base.

Alternative Unit Of Measure If you have more than one unit of measure, you maintain the alternatives and their conversion to the base unit in the Additional Data section of the material master. For example, some music CDs are stored as individual pieces (EA) but could also be sold or procured in packs of 10 (PAC). In this example, EA is the base unit of measure; PAC is the alternative unit of measure. The conversion is 10 EA = 1 PAC.

Sales Unit Of Measure The unit of measure in which the material is sold is the sales unit. If you need to specify a different unit for sales, enter it here.

Quantity Stipulations You can specify any stipulations regarding material quantity in sales.

Minimum Order Quantity   This refers to the lowest quantity that a customer must order for this material. The marketing or pricing strategy of your organization may set a limit on the order quantity.

Minimum Delivery Quantity   This refers to the minimum quantity that must be delivered to the customer. This is often governed by transportation and logistical constraints.

Delivery Unit   This is the unit in which the material is delivered. If you specify the Delivery Unit setting as five pieces, then you can deliver in multiples of five only (5, 10, 15, and so on).

Sales Status   To signify the status of the material in the sales life cycle, you use the Sales Status setting. Certain products may be new and not yet released in the market. Others may have reached the end of their life cycle, become obsolete, or be discontinued. You can update the status in the material master in order to control or stop the sales of such items. In the material master, you can set the Sales Status setting specific to a distribution chain (using the field DChain - Spec. Status) or across the entire organization (using the field X-Distr. Chain Status). These fields are used in conjunction with the validity date to specify when the status will take effect.

Tax Data   This allows you to specify the tax classification for the material in each country. (We will cover the details and impact of this in Chapter 5, "Pricing and Tax Determination.")

Delivering Plant   This is where you specify the default plant chosen to deliver this material.

Sales: Sales Org 2 View

This view primarily contains various grouping terms:

General Item Category Group   This is a critical field that determines the item category. It controls the behavior and flow of the material across the sales documents.

Material Pricing Group   This field is used in pricing a product. It is used to group together materials that have the same price or pricing condition.

Material Group   There are five grouping terms provided to classify and group the material in various categories.

Product Attributes   You can capture the specific attributes of the product and control the sales transaction such that the order can be processed only if the attributes are acceptable to the customer.

Sales: General/Plant Data View

This view contains some general data and some fields that are plant specific.

Plant Specific Information   This includes fields such as availability checking group and loading group.

Availability Checking Group   The availability group controls how stocks are checked and committed to sales orders. Hence, it is a critical field. It plays a key role and will be covered in detail in Chapter 6, "Availability Check, Transfer of Requirements, and Backorders."

Loading Group   This field plays a role in logistics by determining the shipping point. It will be covered in detail in Chapter 8, "Shipping and Transportation."

General Information   Other general data fields include packaging material information, transportation groups, and weight.

Sales Text View

On the Sales Text tab, you can maintain a description or notes about the material in different languages. Through controls in text determination, the text is copied to sales documents.

Material Requirement Planning Views

Data in these views are specific to a plant and storage location. This data contains MRP-related information such as the MRP type, controller, and plant-specific material status. Information relevant to material requirements planning (MRP) is spread over four views in the material master. They are named MRP1 to MRP4. Settings here affect material availability check and inventory control.

Purchasing View

The data in this view is provided by the purchasing department. It includes information such as purchasing groups, handling and procurement of the material, tolerances, and order units.

Accounting and Costing View

This view contains data about valuation class, standard price, past price and costing data, and so on.

Other views

Other views that are beyond the scope of this chapter include the following:

▶ Warehouse Management

▶ Storage

▶ Work Scheduling

▶ Quality Management

Maintaining Material Master Records

As discussed earlier, you can create the material master using transaction MM01. The following transactions help you maintain existing material master records:

Change Material Master (MM02)   To make changes to any field in the material master, you proceed with this transaction code. You specify the material number and select the view(s) that are to be edited. You can then navigate to the required screen, make the changes, and save the record.

Display Material Master (MM03)   This transaction provides display rights to the user.

Flag For Deletion (MM16)   If any material master is to be discontinued, you can flag it for deletion using this transaction code.

Change Material Type (MMAM)   If the material type is to be changed at a later date, you can do so using this transaction code.

CHANGE LOG IN THE MATERIAL MASTER

Changes made to a material master are recorded in SAP. To check the changes done from within a material master record, select Environment ➢ Display Changes. You can get a log of old and new values along with a time stamp and user details.

Customizing Material Master Data

You can use several settings to configure the material master. However, the focus of this discussion is primarily on certain settings that are critical to SD.

Unit of Measure

You can customize all the required units of measure centrally from the General Settings menu. SAP lists all major ISO codes for measurement. If you need to add a custom unit of measure, follow this path: IMG ➢ SAP Netweaver ➢ General Settings ➢ Check Units Of Measurements (transaction CUNI). Here you can specify the following:

Dimensions   Specify the dimension for the unit of measure and the SI unit of measure.

ISO Code   This is a standard list of ISO codes. It is important in data exchange with other systems via EDI.

Unit Of Measure   Here you can set up a custom unit of measure, link it to an ISO code, and specify other details such as decimal places and rounding rules.

 Other settings for key fields appear in the menu when you follow the menu path Logistics – General ➢ Material Master ➢ Basic Settings ➢ Setting For Key Fields.

Defining a Material Group

In Figure 3.23, you'll find a list of existing material groups. To create a new group, click New Entry, and then enter a unique alphanumeric name and a brief description. For Galaxy Musical Instruments, we have grouped a wide range of products under material groups GM001 to GM005. As the business diversifies, we can add other material groups to this list. We can then design reports to get sales for each group.

FIGURE 3.23 Defining a material group

Matl Group	Material Group Desc.	Grp.	ID	Description 2 for the materia
GM001	String Instruments			
GM002	Percussion Instrumen			
GM003	Accessory/ Boutique			
GM004	Spare Parts			
GM005	Music Collection			

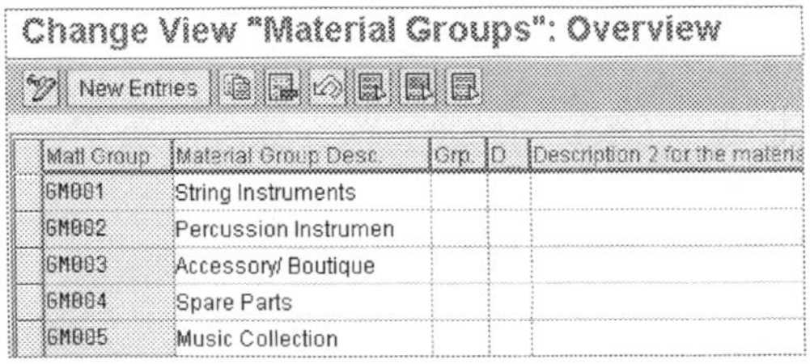

In the Setting For Key Fields node, there is a special submenu critical to sales and distribution. The path to it is Logistics – General Material Master ➤ Setting For Key Fields ➤ Data Relevant To Sales and Distribution. Two of the important settings here are Define Sales Statuses and Define Material Groups.

Defining the Sales Status

To set up a custom status, click New Entries (or Copy As to copy from a reference). Define a two-character status code with a description. In the same menu, you can specify whether the material is to be blocked in various sales documents, as well as the response of the system when this material is used.

When certain new products are launched, Galaxy Musical Instruments accepts bookings before the product release date. In this phase, the new products are flagged with a sales status of Not Yet Released.

As shown in Figure 3.24, we have defined a custom status of 91 (Not Yet Released). We have also specified that if we receive an inquiry, quotation, or sales order, the system will respond with a warning message. Any delivery will be blocked.

FIGURE 3.24 Defining the status of a material

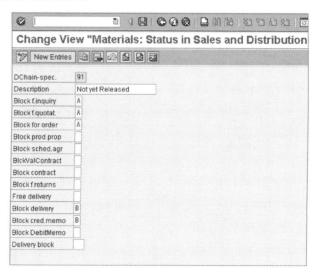

Defining the (Sales) Material Groups

SAP offers five grouping fields in this menu (Material Group1 to Material Group5). Select the material group for which you want to add custom values. Specify a three-character term and description. Effective use of these grouping terms facilitates data categorization and reporting. In the case of Galaxy Musical Instruments, Material Group1 has been used for the various musical instrument types such as guitars, drums, and keyboards (Figure 3.25).

FIGURE 3.25 Defining Material Group1

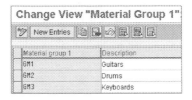

In Material Group2, you can specify further attributes. Guitars, for example, are grouped based on their properties (Figure 3.26).

FIGURE 3.26 Defining Material Group2

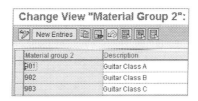

You can use some or all of the grouping terms provided, based on your requirements. The material group fields appear in the material master, Sales: Sales Org. 2 view.

NOTE   Mass Change: When you have a large number of master data records, it is difficult to make mass changes manually. In Chapter 14, "Advanced Techniques," we will study the MASS tool, which helps in mass maintenance of master data records.

Product Hierarchy

In the material master, you can enter the hierarchical classification of the product. This is very useful in pricing and statistical analysis. The hierarchy is broken down into different levels. Each level signifies a certain characteristic of the product.

Maintaining a Product Hierarchy

The Product Hierarchy field appears in the material master view Sales: Sales Org 2. To maintain the value, use transaction code MM01 (Create Mode) or MM02 (Change Mode).

Based on the structure of your product line, you can create your own product hierarchy. The standard SAP system offers a three-tiered product hierarchy. Level 1 and level 2 are five digits each. Level 3 is eight digits long (and is called the *5/5/8 schema*). Thus, the total length of hierarchy adds up to 18 digits.

Customizing a Product Hierarchy

To configure the product hierarchy, the path is as follows: IMG ➢ Logistics – General ➢ Material Master ➢ Settings For Key Fields ➢ Data Relevant For Sales and Distribution ➢ Define Product Hierarchies ➢ Maintenance: Product Hierarchy (V/76).

If the SAP standard schema (5/5/8) meets the requirements of your organization, you can maintain the hierarchy levels in this transaction. You can add new entries to set up the various levels in your product hierarchy. When you enter a hierarchy code, the level number is determined automatically by the system based on the number of characters you have entered. For example, if you enter a five-character entry, the system determines the level number as 1. Similarly, a 10-character entry would be level 2. Level 3 would have 18-character records.

Let us discuss this further with the example of Galaxy Musical Instruments, which has adopted the standard 5/5/8 schema shown in Figure 3.27 for its musical instrument inventory.

FIGURE 3.27 Standard 5/5/8 schema

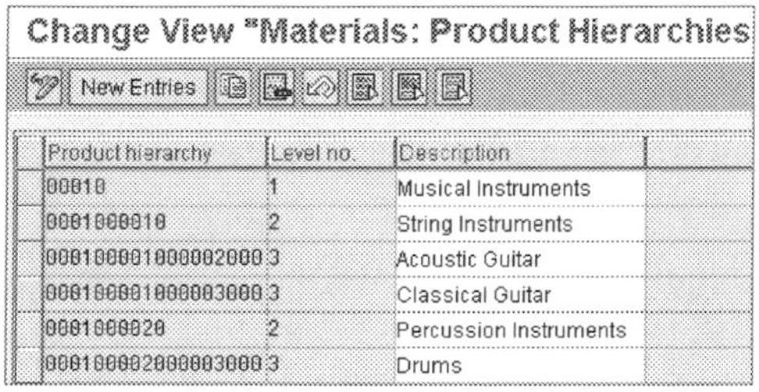
Change View "Materials: Product Hierarchies
New Entries

Product hierarchy	Level no.	Description
00010	1	Musical Instruments
0001000010	2	String Instruments
000100001000002000	3	Acoustic Guitar
000100001000003000	3	Classical Guitar
0001000020	2	Percussion Instruments
000100002000003000	3	Drums

CASE STUDY—GALAXY MUSICAL INSTRUMENTS: PRODUCT HIERARCHY

The following is the product hierarchy for Galaxy Musical Instruments:

> Level 1 (five digits long) shows the type of product, such as Musical Instruments.
>
> Level 2 (five digits long) classifies products into types of instruments, such as String Instruments, Percussion Instruments, and so on.
>
> Level 3 (eight digits long) tells us about the product, such as whether a guitar is electric or acoustic.

After setting up the structure, we maintain the exact product hierarchy in each of the material master records. Once the products are classified, we can then derive a report for the sales of all string instruments (0001000010). For pricing, we can run a special offer on all drums (000100002000003000) with a discount of 10%.

You can deviate from standard SAP and define your own hierarchy levels in the system by changing the data structure. This is a technical change and will require help from an ABAP resource. Product hierarchy structure (PRODHS) in SAP has to be changed to suit your own schema. You can define up to nine levels. Then you can create a template to represent the new structure. The detailed technical configuration is not in the scope of this book.

Summary

In this chapter, we introduced the concept of master data. We explained the processes of creating and maintaining master data records, focusing on how to customize and control the various fields and screens that appear in customer master data and material master data. Finally, we introduced you to the concepts of customer and product hierarchies.

In the next chapter, we'll cover more about partner, text, and output determination techniques.

Partner, Text, and Output Determination

Partner, text, and output determination are three of the important basic functions in the SAP SD application. You use partner determination to control the determination of parties involved in a sales transaction such as the sold-to party, ship-to party, forwarding agent, and so on; you use text determination to control text involved in a sales transaction such as terms of sales, special packaging or delivery instructions, and so on; and you use output determination to control the determination of any output forms involved in a sales transaction such as the invoice, packing list, and so on. In this chapter, we will discuss these three basic functions in detail, including how to customize them.

Partner Determination

The terms *partners* and *business partners* in the SAP SD application refer to the parties that are involved in a sales transaction. Each business partner has a specified role and can be identified based on the role or function they play in the processing of a sales cycle. Examples of business partners include a sold-to party ordering the goods, a forwarding agent delivering the goods, an employee responsible for processing the sales transaction, a customer contact person seeking regular updates about the delivery progress, a ship-to party location where the goods are to be shipped, a bill-to party who will receive the invoices, and a payer who will pay the bills. You set up these partners and their corresponding functions in SAP SD using a search technique called *partner determination*. The technique controls what partners are allowed, what roles they will play, and how they can be determined at the required stages (such as during sales document processing, delivery processing, transportation processing, and so on) in the processing of a sales cycle.

The customization of a partner determination procedure is a three-step process that we will discuss in more detail in the following sections:

1. Define partner functions.

2. Group partner functions into a partner determination procedure.

3. Assign the partner determination procedure to respective partner objects.

Define partner functions   In this step, you define a new partner function or modify an existing one to meet your specific business needs. A partner function in SAP is a two-character identification key that controls the partner's role and behavior. SP (sold-to party), SH (ship-to party), BP (bill-to party), PY (payer), and CP (contact person) are a few commonly used partner functions provided by standard SAP. Always remember that once defined, a partner function is valid across all the partner objects. This means that once you've created a partner function, you can use it in the partner determination procedure for a customer master, sales document header, sales document item, delivery document–related partner procedure, and so on, without having to re-create the partner function for each partner object.

Group partner functions into a partner determination procedure   In this step, you group the newly created or modified partner functions from step 1 into a two-character identifier key called the *partner determination procedure*. The customization settings in this step hold the determination logics for what, how, and when a partner function is determined.

Assign the partner determination procedure to respective partner objects In this step, you assign the partner determination procedures to the respective partner objects. This assignment completes the process of setting up the partner determination procedure. A customer partner determination procedure is assigned to a customer account group; a sales document header–related partner determination procedure is assigned to a sales document type; a sales document item–related partner determination procedure is assigned to an item category type; and so on. Table 4.1 represents this relationship.

TABLE 4.1   Partner Objects: Assignment Logic

Partner Determination Procedure	Assign To
Customer	Account group
Sales document header	Sales document type
Sales document Item	Item category type
Delivery header	Delivery document type
Shipment header	Shipment document type
Billing header	Billing document type
Billing item	Billing item category type
Contact	Contact type

Deciding the Scope of Customization

Before you set up a partner determination in SAP, it is always advisable to identify the scope of customization required. Specifically, you need to know how many partner functions are required and how to configure the determination logic. Answering the following questions may help to a great extent:

▶ How many partner functions are required per partner object? This means figuring out how many partner functions are required for the customer master, how many are required for the sales document header, how many are required for the sales document items, how many are required for the delivery document header, and so on.

▶ Can the existing partner functions be used as is or with some modification, or do you really need the new ones? For instance, if you can use the existing partner functions but need a new procedure, then your customization will only entail combining the partner functions into a new partner procedure and assigning the newly defined partner procedure to the respective partner object.

▶ Can existing partner functions can be reutilized by other partner objects? Reusing a partner function across objects helps reduce the unnecessary customization duplication in your SAP instance.

▶ Does the partner function require some sort of hierarchical setup? For instance, imagine a corporate head office signing a rate contract (the parent customer), after which various branch offices use the rates in the contract to place orders (the child customers). In such a case, you may need to set up determination logic involving a customer hierarchy. Please refer to Chapter 3, "Master Data in SD," for more details on customer hierarchy.

▶ What are the specific details of the partner determination logic? Answering this question will involve asking other questions:

   » Do you want to copy the partner function value from the customer master to the sales order and further down to delivery, and so on, in the sales cycle?

   » Do you want the partner function to be determined from an alternate master record, such as the ship-to party master, when it is missing from the sold-to party master record?

For this chapter's purposes, we will show the customization step by creating a new partner function and assigning it to a new partner determination procedure ZAG.

CASE STUDY—GALAXY MUSICAL INSTRUMENTS CONFIGURATION ANALYSIS: PARTNER DETERMINATION AND SCOPE FINALIZATION

The sales structure for Galaxy Musicals Instruments is divided into multiple sales regions, and each sales region is further divided into sales territories. Each sales territory is owned exclusively by a sales representative. Since sales commissions are a major part of a sales representative's remuneration, the SAP system must properly record the sales orders per sales representative. To achieve this, Galaxy decided to create a new partner function, Z9–Sales Representative, and assign the function's determination to a sold-to party master record. This way, Galaxy was able to assign a customer record exclusively to one sales representative.

Customizing Partner Determination

To call the customization screen for partner determination (Figure 4.1), use transaction code VOPAN or follow menu path IMG ➤ Sales And Distribution ➤ Basic Functions ➤ Partner Determination. As you can see, the customization screen has eight radio buttons. These radio buttons represent various stages in a sales cycle, called *partner objects*. You can define a partner determination for all the partner objects shown on this screen.

FIGURE 4.1   Partner determination, initial overview screen

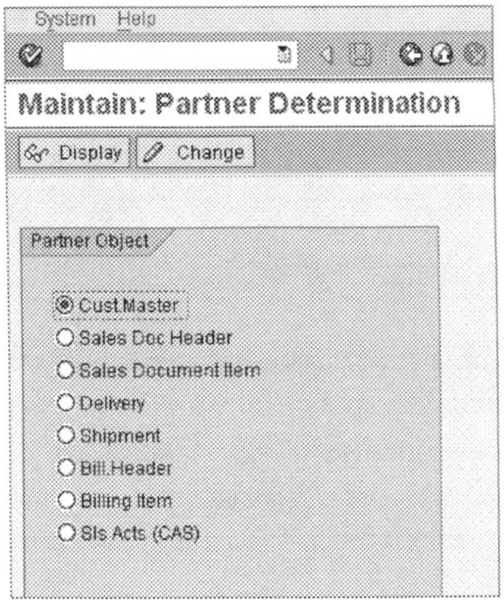

We'll first show how to set up the partner determination for the partner object Customer Master.

Setting Up Partner Determination for the Customer Master

The chronological order of activities is as follows:

1. Define a partner function.

2. Add the partner function to a partner determination procedure.

3. Assign the partner determination procedure.

Let's proceed with these activities one by one.

Define the Partner Function

To create your own partner function, select the Customer Master button on the VOPAN screen (shown earlier in Figure 4.1), and click the Change button to call up the partner determination customization screen. You will be presented with a customization screen divided into two parts, with a Dialog Structure pane on the left and the customization details of the partner functions on the right. Double-click the Partner Functions node in the Dialog Structure pane shown on the left to display the detailed list of available partner functions on the right, as shown in Figure 4.2.

As you can see in Figure 4.2, a large variety of partner functions are provided in SAP out of the box. You can either use these or create new ones if required. Before you define a new partner procedure, it's good practice to check whether you can use the existing partner functions to meet the needs of your business scenario.

Now click the New Entries button to call up the customization screen for defining new partner functions. To define a new partner function, provide a two-character identifying key, provide a meaningful description, and select the proper values for the rest of the fields (as described next). To bring more clarity, Figure 4.3 shows an example of partner function Z9 set up for Galaxy. Save your entry, and click the Back button to return to the screen shown in Figure 4.2. You will find your custom partner function successfully created in the list of partner functions on the right.

FIGURE 4.2 Partner determination customization screen for partner object, customer master

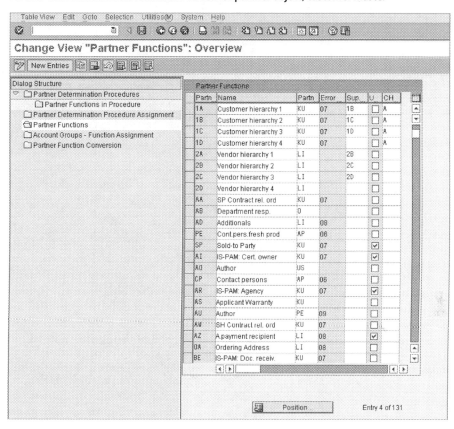

FIGURE 4.3 Partner function customization screen

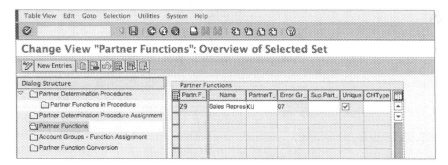

These are the fields on the partner function customization screen:

Partner Function   The first column on the screen, Partn.F., presents the partner function. Here you provide a two-character unique identifier (starting with a *Y* or a *Z*) for each partner function.

Name   In the column Name, maintain a meaningful description for this partner function. For Galaxy, we defined partner function Z9 as Sales Representative.

Partner Type   The column Partner T. presents the partner type. A partner type helps distinguish one partner function from another. It tells whether the partner function is for a customer (KU), a vendor (LI), a contact person (AP), and so on. SAP provides these partner types, and you cannot create your own partner type. You can use these partner types to define your own partner functions. For example, all four partner functions for a customer—in other words, SP, SH, PY, and BP—are of partner type KU, a forwarding agent (FA) is of partner type LI, and a customer contact person (CP) is of partner type AP. For Galaxy, we created partner function Z9 of type KU (customer).

Error Group   The column Error Gr is where you provide the two-character code for the partner incompletion procedure that you want to assign to your partner function. The incompletion procedure plays a vital role in controlling the further processing of the sales cycle when a required entry is missing. So if your partner function is missing in the sales document, whether the sales document can be delivered or not depends entirely upon the customization for the incompletion procedure that you assigned to your partner function in this Error Group field. In standard SAP, incompletion procedure 07 is available for partner type Customers, 08 is available for partner type Vendors, and 06 is available for partner type Contact Persons.

Superior Partner Function   The next column is Sup.Part. This is used to present a higher-level partner function for this partner function. The higher-level partner function is used in relation to customer hierarchies. For more information on customer hierarchies, please refer to Chapter 3.

Unique   Select the check box in the column Unique if you want your partner function to appear only once on the partners function screen of the customer master record. For Z9, we wanted only one sale representative per sold-to party account and therefore selected the Unique check box. This way, you will be able to assign only one sales representative on the Partner Function tab of the sold-to party account of the customer.

Customer Hierarchy Type   The column CHType specifies the type of customer hierarchy to be used for this partner function. If you are maintaining a hierarchy, enter the hierarchy type in this column.

TIP   Before you define a new partner procedure, it's good practice to check whether you can use the existing partner functions to meet the needs of your business scenario.

CASE STUDY—GALAXY: PARTNER FUNCTION

Galaxy created partner function Z9 with partner type KU. The partner is set up as unique in the customer master because one customer can have only one sales representative assigned to it. There is no customer hierarchy involved, and therefore the hierarchy fields are blank.

TIP   Always use a Y or Z prefix for your custom-defined partner functions so as to separate them from the standard partner functions provided by SAP. This way you can ensure that SAP doesn't overwrite your customization during the next patch or upgrade.

Add the Partner Function to a Partner Determination Procedure

Once you define a partner function, the next step is to add this partner function to its respective partner determination procedure. While you are still on the screen shown in Figure 4.3, double-click the Partner Determination Procedures node to reach the customization screen for partner determination procedures (Figure 4.4).

FIGURE 4.4   Partner determination procedure customization, overview screen

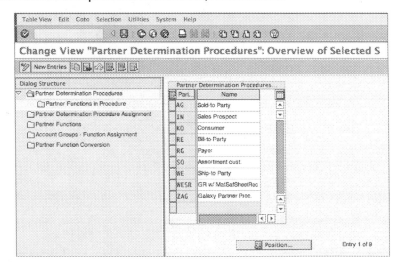

In SAP, the partner procedure AG is provided for the sold-to party, RE is provided for the bill-to party, RG is for the payer, and WE is for the ship-to party business partners. You can create your own Z partner procedure by clicking the New Entries button and providing a two-character identification key with a meaningful description for your custom partner procedure. For Galaxy, we created partner determination procedure ZAG as a copy of AG.

Now select the newly created partner procedure (in our case it is ZAG), as shown in Figure 4.4, and double-click the Partner Functions In Procedure node on the left screen to call up the next customization screen (Figure 4.5), which shows the partner functions allowed for partner procedure ZAG. Since ZAG was copied over from AG, you will find a long list of partner functions appearing in ZAG. Delete the unwanted ones, and keep only the ones you need as per your business requirement. For Galaxy, we required only four basic partner functions: SP, BP, PY, and SH. Now click the New Entries button to maintain the entry for the partner functions that you want to include in partner procedure ZAG (in our case it is Z9), and click the Save button to save your entry.

FIGURE 4.5   Partner functions on the procedure customization screen

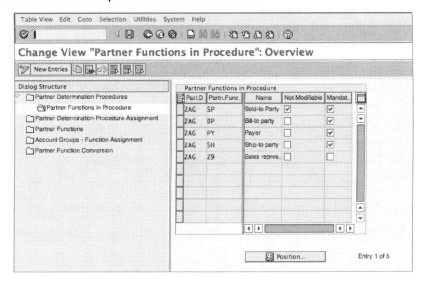

The following are the fields on the partner functions in procedure customization screen:

Partner Determination   The Part.D field denotes the partner determination procedure name. In this example, ZAG represents the partner procedure for partner object Customer Master, subobject Sold-To Party.

Partner Function   In the column Partn. Func., enter the two-character partner function that you want to include in the partner determination procedure. For Galaxy, we maintained the partner functions Z9, SP, BP, PY, and SH in this field.

Name   SAP automatically fills in the Name field with the description of the partner function once you enter the partner function.

Not Modifiable   If the check box Not Modifiable is selected, the partner function cannot be changed on the customer master maintenance screen.

Mandatory Function   Select the check box under the column Mandat. Funct. if you want to ensure that this partner function is mandatory for this partner procedure.

Notice that both the check boxes are selected for partner function SP, whereas only the Mandat. Funct. check box is selected for partner functions BP, PY, and SH. It is because of the settings of these two checkboxes in the partner determination customization for ZAG that when you are in the Sales Area Data ➤ Partner Function screen in a sold-to customer master record, you see all four partner functions—SP, SH, PY, and BP—appearing as mandatory, and that partner function SP is not modifiable.

CASE STUDY—GALAXY CONFIGURATION ANALYSIS: PARTNER DETERMINATION PROCEDURE

Partner function Z9 for Galaxy Musical Instruments was added to partner procedure ZAG. The Not Modifiable check box was not selected because Galaxy wanted the flexibility to modify the sales representative number assigned to the sold-to party master record in the event of a change in sales representative for a particular territory or for a particular customer in the sales territory. The Mandatory Function check box was not selected either, because Galaxy wanted the flexibility to maintain the sales representative name only when the customer account is active. For customers who are no longer dealing with Galaxy or new customers whose credit applications are still pending, Galaxy does not maintain sales representative information.

Assign the Partner Determination Procedure

Once the partner function is grouped under a partner determination procedure, the next step is to assign the determination procedure. For the customer master, partner function, and partner determination procedure, both are required to be assigned to a customer account group. (Yes, this is the same account group that you use for creating the customer master record in an XD01 or VD01 transaction.)

While you are still on the screen shown in Figure 4.5, double-click the Partner Determination Procedure Assignment node on the left to call up the assignment screen shown in Figure 4.6.

FIGURE 4.6   Customization screen for partner determination procedure assignment

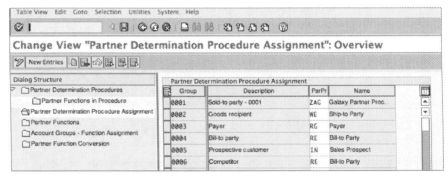

For Galaxy, we created partner determination procedure ZAG and will assign the same partner determination procedure to its respective account group, in other words, 0001. Since ZAG is assigned to 0001, you can only maintain those partner functions for a sold-to customer created under account group 0001 that are allowed under the partner procedure ZAG. Any partner function that is not available in the partner procedure will not even appear on the partner function screen for the sold-to party master record.

Now double-click the Account Groups – Function Assignment node to call up the customization screen for assigning the partner function to its respective account groups. Once you are on the customization screen and can see the entries showing the assignments between account groups and partner functions, click the New Entries button to call up the New Entries: Overview Of Added Entries screen. Now create the entry for your custom partner function, and click the Save button. Figure 4.7 shows the entry for partner function Z9 for Galaxy.

FIGURE 4.7   Customization screen for partner function assignment to account groups

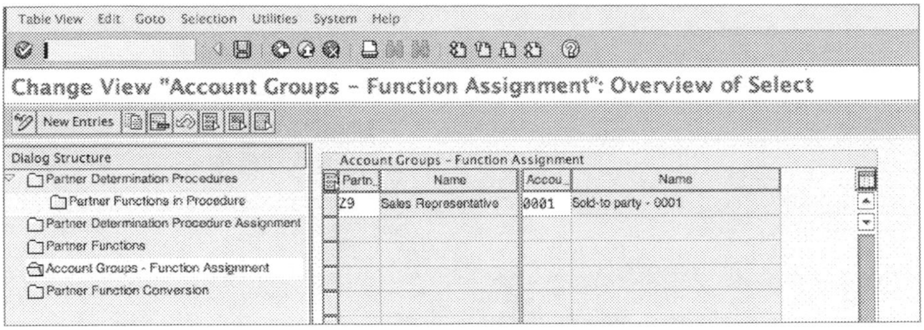

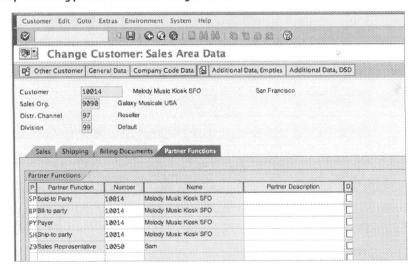

You have now configured your first customized partner function Z9.

To use this partner, you need to set up the master record for this newly created partner, i.e. a sales representative, and then assign this sales representative to all the customer accounts for which this sales representative is responsible. Since we created Z9 with partner type KU and assigned it to account group 0001, we use customer master maintenance transactions (XD*, VD*) to set up the master data account for the sales representative. For Galaxy, we created sales representative 10050 (Sam) and then assigned it to customer account 10014 with partner function Z9, as shown in Figure 4.8.

FIGURE 4.8   Example showing partner function Z9 assignment to customer master

Until now we have been discussing partner determination for customer master records. Partner determination is a bit different for sales headers and other partner objects such as sales item, delivery, shipment, and so on. The difference exists in the partner determination procedure setup. We'll now explore these differences by covering the partner determination customization settings for partner object Sales Document Header. For this chapter's purposes, we'll use standard SAP-provided partner procedure TA.

Setting Up Partner Determination for the Sales Document

To call up the customization screen for setting up the partner determination procedure for the Sales Document Header partner object, follow the same steps that you did for partner object Customer Master, but this time choose the Sales Document Header partner object. To get started, let's return to a couple of the screens we discussed earlier in the chapter. Call up the Maintain: Partner Determination screen (Figure 4.1), and select Sales Doc Header from the panel at left. You will be presented with a screen similar to Figure 4.2. On that screen, double-click the Partner Determination Procedures node to reach the customization screen for the partner determination procedure setup of the Sales Document – Header partner object. Select partner determination procedure TA, and double-click the Partner Functions In Procedure subnode to call up the customization screen (Figure 4.9).

This screen is similar to the Figure 4.5 with a few additional columns. The columns Part.Det.Proc. to Mandat. Func. have the same meaning as in Figure 4.5. The point to remember is that here the reference is to the sales document and not the customer master record.

The additional columns are as follows:

Source   The Source field acts as an alternative source for determining the sold-to party partner in the sales document. Standard SAP determines the partner functions from the sold-to party record of the customer. When you assign a partner function in this field, for example, SH for partner function Z9, and when you create a sales document, SAP will determine the sold-to party using the partner function Z9 assigned to the ship-to party record.

Origin (Table)   The Origin (Table) field defines the table from which the partner function should be determined during order processing. Here is an explanation of the available table origin values and when to select them:

FIGURE 4.9   Partner determination procedure customization, sales document header

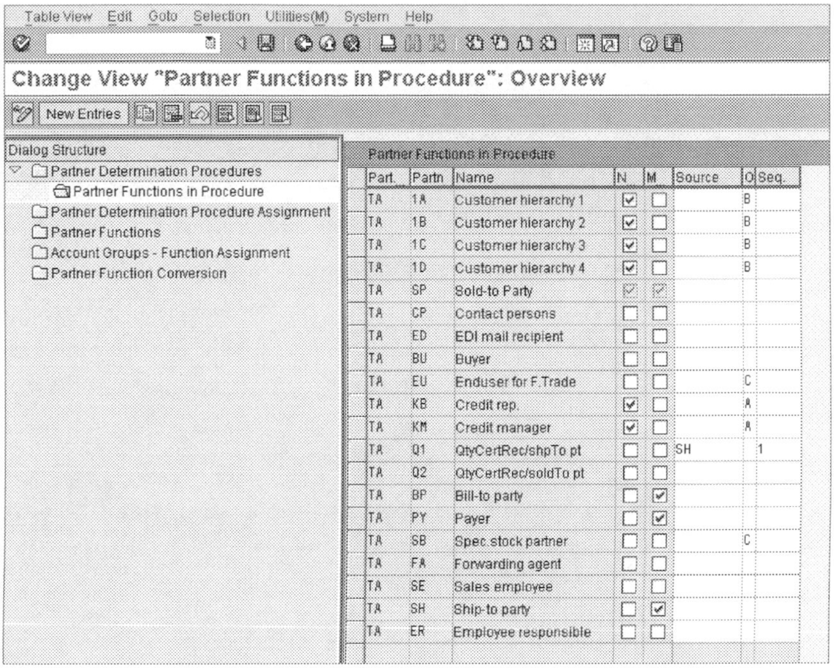

Table View	Edit	Goto	Selection	Utilities(M)	System	Help

Change View "Partner Functions in Procedure": Overview

New Entries

Dialog Structure
- ▽ ☐ Partner Determination Procedures
  - 🗐 Partner Functions in Procedure
  - ☐ Partner Determination Procedure Assignment
  - ☐ Partner Functions
  - ☐ Account Groups - Function Assignment
  - ☐ Partner Function Conversion

Partner Functions in Procedure

Part.	Partn	Name	N	M	Source	O	Seq.
TA	1A	Customer hierarchy 1	☑	☐		B	
TA	1B	Customer hierarchy 2	☑	☐		B	
TA	1C	Customer hierarchy 3	☑	☐		B	
TA	1D	Customer hierarchy 4	☑	☐		B	
TA	SP	Sold-to Party	☑	☑			
TA	CP	Contact persons	☐	☐			
TA	ED	EDI mail recipient	☐	☐			
TA	BU	Buyer	☐	☐			
TA	EU	Enduser for F.Trade	☐	☐		C	
TA	KB	Credit rep.	☑	☐		A	
TA	KM	Credit manager	☑	☐		A	
TA	Q1	QtyCertRec/shpTo pt	☐	☐	SH		1
TA	Q2	QtyCertRec/soldTo pt	☐	☐			
TA	BP	Bill-to party	☐	☑			
TA	PY	Payer	☐	☑			
TA	SB	Spec.stock partner	☐	☐		C	
TA	FA	Forwarding agent	☐	☐			
TA	SE	Sales employee	☐	☐			
TA	SH	Ship-to party	☐	☑			
TA	ER	Employee responsible	☐	☐			

[Blank]   Leave the Origin field blank when your partner functions are of partner type KU or you want to determine the partner from the partner functions maintained in the sold-to party customer master (table KNVP). If the system cannot determine all functions, it enters the number of the sold-to party (SP) for the remaining partner functions of the partner type customer (KU).

A   Use A for your credit management partner functions (for example, KB and KM), because those functions should be taken directly from the credit representative table (T024P). The credit representative or credit manager is an internal employee of your organization and therefore should not be created as a customer master record. Instead, this has to flow from the HR personnel records. These settings are made in credit management where you link partner functions such as KB and KM to the HR personnel number.

B   Use B if your partner functions should be taken from a customer hierarchy.

C   Use C when you want the partner function to determine exclusively from the partner screen entries in the customer master. So if you set up C for partner function ER (employee responsible) and the same is not maintained on the partner screen for the SP customer master record, it will not be determined in the concerned sales document. If you have defined an alternative source partner function such as SH along with C, then SAP will look at the Partner tab of the customer master record of the ship-to party for determining the partner number for the ER function and return that value in the sales document.

D   Use D when the personnel number of the system user should be used as the function, such as for sales executives.

E   Use E when the partner function should be replaced with a contact person from the contact person screen for the corresponding partner (table KNVK).

F   Use F when you want to determine the contact partners not only from the contact person screen but also from the partner screen of the partner with the current source partner function. In such a case, if the partner function is not available at the contact person screen, it will be determined from the partner screen.

X, Y, and Z   These refer to user-defined origins. You can define your own origins for partner determination by adding a code to the function exit EXIT_SAPLV09A_003.

Sequence   The column Seq. is used to define the priority in which the partner will be determined during document processing.

Table 4.2 shows an example of these features.

TABLE 4.2   Example Setup Showing Use of Partner Determination Procedure Fields

Partn.Funct.	Mandatory	Source Part. Funct	Not Changeable	Table of Origin	Sequence
SH	X				
CP	X	SH	X	E	1

Here, since Source is blank for SH, SH will be determined first from the sold-to party master records, and then CP is determined from the customer master record of partner function SH. Since the table of origin is E (table KNVK), the contact person will be picked from the contact person screen of the ship-to party record.

A sequence field value is required only if you are using an alternate source partner function for partner determination. When you use an alternative source for partner function determination, SAP needs to know the priority in which the records need to be determined. If you have specified a source partner function, then enter a figure in this field that is higher than the figure for the source partner function. So, value 1 in the sequence field in our example tells SAP to determine the partner for the AP function only after the ship-to party partner record is found. Once the SH partner is found, SAP will go into the contact person screen of that SH partner master data and determine the partner number for partner function AP. That's the kind of hierarchy you can maintain for the determination process if you use an alternative source partner function for partner determination.

As the final step in the customization of the partner determination procedure for partner object Sales Document Header, you assign the partner determination procedure to the respective sales document types, as shown in Figure 4.10.

FIGURE 4.10   Partner determination procedure assignment, sales document header

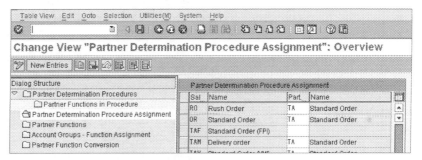

With this we've completed our discussion on partner determination setup. Our next topic of discussion is text determination in SAP SD.

Text Determination

Parties to a sales transaction often exchange various instructions and information during the course of the sales process. This information could be in the form of shipping instructions, packing instructions, delivery terms, explanatory notes, remarks maintained by the partner's agent, and so on. In SAP SD, you maintain all this information as *text*.

Text forms an important part of the SAP SD cycle processing. You maintain text in SAP to store and carry the important instructions throughout the sales cycle. You can maintain text in the customer master records and also in the sales documents at the header and item levels. For example, if the delivery text or shipping instructions are common for all the orders from the same customer, you maintain that in the customer master sales text, but if the instruction is specific to a sales transaction, you maintain that directly in the sales order. Further, you can copy text over to the subsequent process steps. This means that the delivery instructions maintained on a customer master Sales Area Data tab can be copied to the respective sales orders of that customer and can flow down the chain to the delivery and shipping documents. The information is available at the right time to the person processing the delivery in the warehouse, who can then read this additionally maintained information or instructions and proceed accordingly. You can even print the text associated with a sales transaction in document outputs such as invoices, order confirmations, or delivery notes.

TIP   It's always advisable to maintain repetitive text in the customer master record for a customer. This way you don't have to reenter the text in every sales order, and text automatically flows from the customer master to the sales document.

Maintaining Text in Customer Master Records

In a customer master record, you can maintain text at all three screen levels: General Data, Sales Area Data, and Company Code Data. To maintain text in a customer master record, call up the customer master maintenance screen in change mode (XD02). Once you are on the customer master maintenance screen, follow the menu path Extras ➢ Text to maintain the text for the respective screens.

▶ For maintaining central text, remain on the General Data screen, and then choose the menu path Extras ➢ Text.

▶ For maintaining contact person text, go to the Contact Person tab under the General Data screen. Select the contact person for whom you want to maintain the text by keeping the cursor on the respective contact person line, and then choose the menu path Extras ➢ Text.

▶ For maintaining sales text, go to the Sales Area Data screen, and then choose the menu path Extras ➢ Text. The text maintained at the sales area data level can be copied over for processing the sales transactions.

You can also maintain the text using transaction code XD01 (Create Customer Master). Figure 4.11 shows a text maintenance screen from the customer sales text.

Although this discussion covered maintaining text only in the customer master record, all the fields that we mentioned earlier in this section, such as marketing notes and shipping instructions, are likewise configurable in SAP. In other words, you can define them in customizing. Let's move forward and see how to define these text fields using SAP text determination customizing.

FIGURE 4.11   Customer master sales text maintenance screen

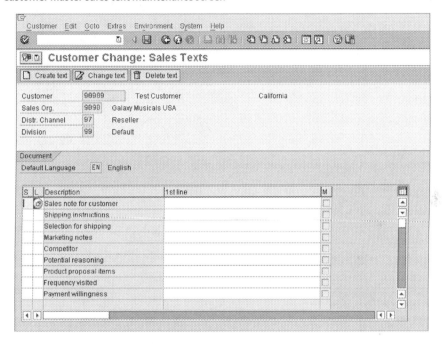

Setting Up Text Determination in SD

You set up the text determination procedure in customizing via transaction code VOTXN or menu path IMG ➢ Sales And Distribution ➢ Basic Functions ➢ Text Control. Figure 4.12 shows the customization screen for text determination.

As you can see in Figure 4.12, the customization screen has many selection options. These selection options represent various stages in a sales cycle for which you can define a text determination. Each stage is called a *text object*. You can broadly categorize these text objects into two categories:

Related to master data   This category covers the Customer, Info Req, and Pricing Conds options on the customization screen shown in Figure 4.12. Using these text objects, you can define the text determination related to the master data, such as the customer master, customer–material info master, and pricing master.

Related to sales documents   This category covers the remaining five text objects from the customization screen shown in Figure 4.12: Sales Document, Delivery, Billing Doc, SalesAct, and Shipment. Using these text objects, you can define the text determination for these types of sales documents.

FIGURE 4.12   Customizing screen for text determination setup

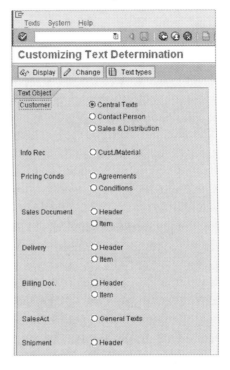

Customizing text determination involves three activities: setting up a text type, setting up the determination procedure, and assigning the determination procedure to the respective text object. For example, when you set up the text determination procedure for a customer master, you need to assign it to a customer account group; when you set up a text determination for a sales document, you need to assign it to sales document type; and so on. We will cover these three activities in detail shortly, but before we move forward, let's first decide on the scope of customization.

Deciding the Scope of Customization

Before you set up a text determination in SAP, it is always advisable to identify the scope of customization required as per the business requirements. Answering the following questions may provide you with some guidance:

▶ How many text types are required per text object? This means figuring out how many text types are required for the customer master, how many are required for the sales document header, how many are required for the sales document items, how many are required for the delivery document header, and so on.

▶ Can you use the existing sample text types available in SAP, or do you need to create new text types?

▶ If new ones are required, should the text be maintained manually in the transaction, or should it be determined automatically by SAP based on the source for text determination defined in the customizing?

▶ Can the text be referenced or duplicated?

The answer to these questions helps you in identifying the number of text types that are required for the sales processing and also the scope of customization. For instance, if you can use the existing text types, then your customization only revolves around combining the text types into a text procedure and assigning the text procedure to the respective text object.

For this chapter's purposes, we will show how to create a new text type, assign it to a new text procedure, and discuss all three customization activities in detail. Note that the setup of text determination is a bit different between the customer master and sales documents. Therefore, we'll cover the text determination setup for both the customer master and the sales document header. We'll start with setting up the text determination for a customer master.

CASE STUDY—GALAXY CONFIGURATION ANALYSIS: TEXT DETERMINATION AND SCOPE FINALIZATION

Galaxy Musical Instruments decided to go with a new text type called Internal Sales Note to capture various information/instructions that sales representatives want to capture while generating a new customer account or while making changes to an existing customer account. This new text type should be available in all four partners accounts: sold-to party, ship-to party, bill to party, and payer. Further, Galaxy wanted any Internal Sales Note to be automatically copied to the sales documents so as to provide this specific information about the customer to the departments processing the order. The sole purpose of the text is for internal use only and need not be printed on any customer communications such as order confirmations, invoices, and delivery printouts.

Setting Up Text Determination for the Customer Master

The activities here comprise three steps:

1. Defining the text type

2. Setting up a text procedure

3. Assigning the procedure to the customer account group

We'll cover these activities one by one.

Define Text Types

Creating a text type is the first step in configuring the text determination. To define a text type, select a text object from the customization screen shown in Figure 4.12, and then click the Text Types button. On the customization screen that appears next (shown in Figure 4.13), click the New Entries button, and create your text type by giving it a four-character identification key along with a meaningful description that explains and differentiates your text from other text. Figure 4.13 shows the customization screen for the Sales & Distribution text object for Galaxy.

FIGURE 4.13   Maintaining text types for the customer master, sales text

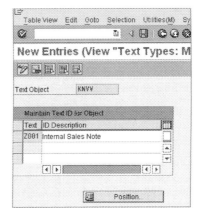

Now click the Save button to save your entry, and click the Back button to come back to the main screen (shown earlier in Figure 4.12). Congratulations, you have successfully defined the text type!

Set Up a Text Procedure

A text procedure is a grouping of different text types. You group all the required text types for a text object into a text procedure. To reach the customization screen for the text procedure setup, select the option for Sales & Distribution, and click the Change button on the Customizing Text Determination screen (shown earlier in Figure 4.12). You will be presented with a text procedure customization screen, as shown in Figure 4.14. You can define the text procedure using the New Entries button or using the Copy button. For Galaxy, we will define a new text determination procedure called Z1 and assign the text type Z001 – Internal Sales Note to this newly defined text procedure. We will also assign a few already existing text types that we want to include on the text maintenance screen for Galaxy's customer master–sales text.

FIGURE 4.14   Define text procedure for customer master–sales text overview screen

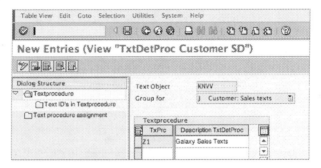

Now click the New Entries button, and provide a two-character identifier for your text procedure along with a meaningful description. For Galaxy, we created Z1. Now select your text procedure entry, and double-click the Text ID's In Textprocedure node on the left. You will be presented with the screen shown in Figure 4.15, which shows the customization setup for Galaxy. Now click the New Entries button, and create the entry by providing a sequence number and a text ID (which is the same as the text type, in other words, Z001). The text description will populate automatically. Click the Save button to save your entry.

FIGURE 4.15   Defining the text procedure for the customer master–sales text detail screen

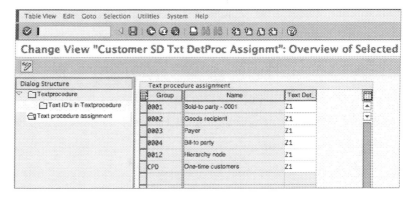

Assign the Text Procedure to Account Groups

The last step in the customization of a text determination procedure is to assign the text procedure to its respective text object. For the customer master, the respective text object is the customer account group. If you double-click the Text Procedure Assignment node on the left of Figure 4.15, it will open the customization screen for text procedure assignment. Enter your procedure number in the Text Det. column corresponding to the account group to which you want to assign your text procedure just like we assigned Z1, as shown in Figure 4.16.

FIGURE 4.16   Assigning the text procedure to an account group

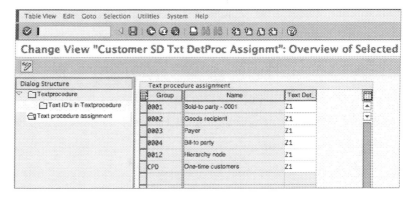

Click the Back button to return to the Customizing Text Determination screen. To verify whether the newly defined text type Internal Sales Note is appearing in the customer master, go to the SD screen for the customer master using transaction code XD02 and use menu path Extras ➤ Text to open the text maintenance screen.

You will find that your newly defined text now appears on the customer master text maintenance screen (which is the screen you saw in Figure 4.11) but with the text that you just assigned to procedure Z1.

For all other text objects that you saw in the master data category, the customization is similar. The only exceptions are Customer/Material Info Records and Contact Person text objects where the only configuration you need is to create the text type. Table 4.3 shows the customization for all these text objects.

TABLE 4.3   Text Determination Setup for Other Text Objects in Master Data Category

Text Object	Required Customization Steps	Procedure Assignment To
Agreement	All	Agreement type
Conditions	All	Condition type
Central Text	All	Customer account group
Customer/ Material Info Records	Define text type only	-
Contact Person	Define text type only	-

Setting Up Text Determination for the Sales Document

Now that we have successfully defined the text determination procedure for the customer master, let's move to the next step for Galaxy. That step is text customization and setup of the determination procedure for the sales document header with text Internal Sales Note automatically populated from the customer master to the sales document header. The setup for a sales document is a bit different than for a customer master. It includes an additional element for setup, called an *access sequence*. The steps are as follows:

1. Defining a text type

2. Setting up an access sequence

3. Setting up a text procedure

4. Assigning the procedure to the correct document type

We'll cover these activities one by one.

Define Text Types

The process for defining the text type is the same as for the customer master. On the Customizing Text Determination screen (shown earlier in Figure 4.12), select the Sales Document – Header radio button, and click the Text Types button. On the customization screen that appears next (Figure 4.17), click the New Entries button to call up the customization screen to create the entry for your new text type. Since you want this text to be copied over from the customer master to the sales document, keep the text ID the same as defined before, in other words, Z001 – Internal Sales Note. Click the Back button to return to the main screen (Figure 4.12). Figure 4.17 shows the customization setup performed for the sales document header text for Galaxy.

FIGURE 4.17   Defining text types for a sales document header

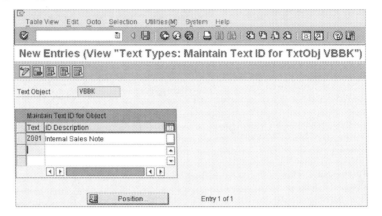

N O T E   **To copy the text between the customer master and the sales document, you need to keep the text ID the same between the two, or the copying won't happen.**

Define an Access Sequence

The next step in customization is to set up an access sequence. An *access sequence* in text determination setup refers to the search strategy you define in customization. SAP uses it to determine the required text value. It consists of various sources from where the text value can be obtained. For example, you can define that the internal sales note needs to be sourced from the text maintained on the customer master's Sales Area Data tab.

To reach the customization screen for access sequence setup, select the Sales Document – Header radio button, and click Change button on the VOTXN customization screen (shown earlier in Figure 4.12). On the next screen that appears

(Figure 4.18), double-click the Access Sequences option shown in the left part of the screen. Now click the New Entries button, and provide a two-digit numeric key for your access sequence followed by a meaningful description, similar to what we did in Figure 4.18 for Galaxy (99 – Internal Sales Note). Save your entry.

FIGURE 4.18 Defining access sequence, overview screen

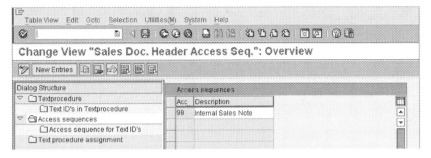

Now select your newly created access sequence, and double-click the access sequence for the Text ID's option shown in the left pane. You will be presented with a screen like the one in Figure 4.19.

FIGURE 4.19 Defining access sequence, detail screen

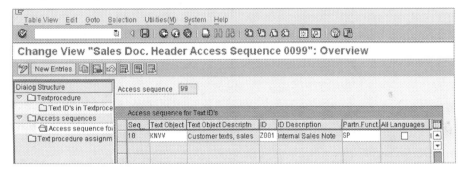

Before proceeding, let's discuss the important fields on the customization screen that are a must for defining an access sequence:

Sequence No.   Here you define the sequence in which you want SAP to search for the text from the source. For example, you may want the text to be sourced first from the sold-to party partner and then from the ship-to party partner.

Text Object   This refers to the actual source. In Figure 4.19, the text object KNVV tells you that the source for the text is the text maintained in the Sales Area Data table of the customer master.

Text ID   This is the text ID for the source. This is the same text ID that we defined in Figure 4.17.

Partner Function   This represents the partner function whose value needs to be copied.

Click the New Entries button to maintain entries for Sequence No., Text Object, Text ID, and Partner Function, as shown in Figure 4.19. Now, if you analyze the complete entry from Figure 4.19, you will see that we have defined the source value as the value maintained in text ID Z001 for a sold-to party record that is maintained in the KNVV table.

Save your entry.

Congratulations, you have successfully created the access sequence for use with your text determination procedure!

TIP   Before you create any new access sequence, always make sure to check whether the existing access sequence serves the purpose. Create a new access sequence only if the existing access sequence doesn't meet your needs.

Set Up a Text Procedure

The next step in customization is to set up a text procedure. We are already on the customization screen for text procedure setup. The customization screen shown in Figure 4.19 is used for defining an access sequence, defining a text procedure, and assigning the text procedure. Now double-click the Text Procedure option on the left to call up the text procedure creation screen. You can create your own Z text procedure by clicking the New Entries button and providing a two-character identification key with a meaningful description for your custom partner procedure. For Galaxy, we created text determination procedure Z1 as a copy of 01.

Now select the newly created text procedure (in our case it is Z1), and double-click the node Text ID's In Textprocedure on the left screen to call up the next customization screen (Figure 4.20). This screen shows the text types allowed in text procedure Z1. Since Z1 was copied over from 01, you will find a long list of text types appearing in Z1. Delete the unwanted ones, and keep only the ones you need as per your business requirements. Now click the New Entries button to maintain the entry for the text type that you want to include in the text procedure Z1 (in our case it is Z001), and click the Save button to save your entry.

FIGURE 4.20   Defining a text procedure for a sales document

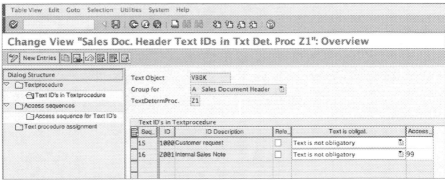

If you compare Figures 4.15 and 4.20, you will notice that Figure 4.20 has some additional elements that are not present in Figure 4.15. This is because text in documents has a greater role to play. Depending upon the scenario, you need to define whether the text will be copied or will be referenced only. You need to define whether the text will be copied from the master record to the sales document, will be copied from the preceding sales document, or will need a sequence of various sources to decide the determination. Before we proceed, we'll discuss these additional fields in detail:

Reference/Duplication Indicator For Copying Text   When this box in the column Refer/Duplicate is selected, the text value is referenced, and when it is left blank, the text value is duplicated from the source to the subsequent target object. For example, say you customized the text determination to copy text from the customer master to the sales document. If this check box is selected when you are customizing for your text type in the text procedure, any change in the original value maintained in the customer master will be reflected in all the existing sales documents for that customer. If the field is not selected, the text will be duplicated each time it gets copied from the master to the documents, and any change in the original is not going to change the text value in the existing documents.

Text Is Obligatory   This column controls whether it is mandatory to maintain the text value in the document. It's a kind of incompletion control for the text in a document. When you select the text as obligatory and do not maintain the value in the text in the document, the text field appears as part of the incompletion log. Leave this field blank if you do not want the text to be mandatory.

Access Sequence   In the column Access Seq., input the access sequence number that you want to apply to your text types.

Assign the Determination Procedure to Document Types

Now you are at the last step in customizing the text determination type for a sales document. In this step, you need to assign the text determination procedure to the sales document types. Figure 4.21 shows the assignment for Galaxy.

FIGURE 4.21   Assigning the determination procedure to sales document types

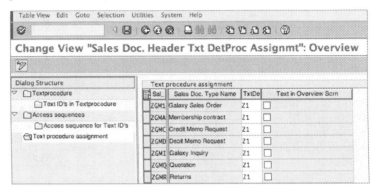

Table 4.4 represents various text objects for which you can define the text determination procedures and the corresponding document types/item types to which the procedures should be assigned in each case.

TABLE 4.4   Assignments for Other Text Objects in Sales Document Category

Text Object	Text Determination Procedure is Assigned to
Sales Document Item	Item categories
Delivery Header	Delivery document type
Delivery Item	Delivery item category
Billing Document Header	Billing document type
Billing Document Item	Billing item category
Sales Activity	Sales activity type

Output Determination

A sales transaction involves various stages such as presales, order, delivery, pick/pack, shipment, and billing. Each stage involves the generation of various documents specific to that stage. Sometimes these documents are required because of legal or commercial reasons, and sometimes they act as a milestone marking the completion of the stage. For example, an order acknowledgment that confirms the seller's acceptance of the order marks the completion of the order stage; an invoice sent by the seller to the buyer is a confirmation of the completion of the sales transaction; and so on. Processing and generating these documents in a sales transaction often involves a lot of conditional permutations too. They can have different formats and may be communicated using various communication media such as printed copies or using electronic media such as Electronic Data Interchange (EDI) email, fax, and so on. A customer may be satisfied with receiving fax copies of order acknowledgments but may want invoices sent via email, for instance. In SAP SD, all these documents (order acknowledgment, delivery note, pick/pack list, shipping order, invoice, etc.) are called *outputs*, and their processing is controlled using the output determination technique provided by SAP.

In SAP SD, you can define an output determination for the following stages of a sales cycle:

- Sales activities
- Sales documents such as quotation confirmations, order confirmations, and scheduling agreements
- Shipping and transportation–related documents such as delivery notes, packing lists, and handling units
- Billing-related documents such as invoices, credit notes, debit notes, and invoice lists

The process of setting up the output determination for the various stages mentioned here is fairly standard. Therefore, we will practice the customization using one sample only, namely, output determination for a sales document. Let's start the journey with scope definition for the customization.

TIP   Refer to Appendix A for the list of customization-related menu paths and transaction codes for defining output determination for various stages of a sales cycle, such as sales activities, sales documents, shipping and transportation, and billing.

Deciding the Scope of Customization

Before we move forward, let's identify the scope of customization required. Answering the following questions may provide you some guidance:

▶ How many output types are required per output object? This means how many output types are required for sales documents, delivery documents, billing documents, and so on. Sometimes a change in the format of the output also impacts the number of output types. For example, for Galaxy, if the formats for order confirmation for the United States and Mexico are entirely different, we may have to create two output types.

▶ Can you use the existing sample output types (RD00, BA00, RD04, and so on) available in SAP, or do you need to create new output? If you can use the existing output types, then your customization revolves around making cosmetic changes such as changing the output script/smart form.

▶ If new output types are required, should they be entered manually in the transaction, or should they be accessed automatically by SAP using the output condition records? The answer to this question decides whether you need to have an access sequence. In the former case, it does not need an access sequence, whereas in the latter case, it does.

▶ What communication media is the output to be configured for? In other words, is it a print output, an email output, a fax output, and so on?

▶ Is the processing for output type manual via the application's own processing transactions provided by SAP (such as VF31 for processing billing outputs), or is it required to be processed using scheduled background jobs running at a particular interval?

For better understanding of these concepts, let's go through the customization scope for Galaxy.

CASE STUDY—GALAXY CONFIGURATION ANALYSIS: CUSTOMIZATION SCOPE FOR OUTPUT DETERMINATION

In Galaxy Musical Instruments, the output processing for a sales document is generally controlled by the combination of the sales organization and distribution channels in which the order is created. In the case of the Direct Sale distribution channel where a customer orders directly from the Galaxy website, the website is capable enough to generate the order confirmations and mail them to customers. Still, as an exception for a few corporate customers, Galaxy requires SAP to generate the outputs. Order type also plays a vital role in the output determination because not all order types need an order confirmation generated. For example, order types for debit/credit note requests, quotations, inquiries, contracts, and so on, do not need an order confirmation.

Galaxy analyzed the existing output determinations available in SAP but could not find one that exactly fits its requirement. The nearest one Galaxy could find was SAP standard BA00, so the company decided to create a new one as ZBA9 by copying it from BA00 and making the necessary modifications to fit the company's needs. The access sequence for ZBA9 is also ZBA9, and it contains two condition tables: the first one with key combination Order Type/Customer and the second one with key combination Sales Organization/Distribution Channel/Order Type. The new determination procedure is Z0001 and is assigned to the relevant sales document types.

Setting Up Output Determination for Sales Documents

Output determination is a search technique based on the famous condition technique of SAP. Customization of an output determination, therefore, involves the following five steps:

1. Create the output condition tables.

2. Define the access sequences and arrange condition tables into the access sequence.

3. Maintain the output type and assign the access sequence to the output type.

4. Group output types into an output determination procedure.

5. Assign the output determination procedure to its respective output object.

Creating the Output Condition Tables

This is the first step in the customization of an output determination process. Here you define the key combinations/condition tables that are required for storing your output condition records. To create a condition table for the sales document output determination process, follow the menu path IMG ➢ Sales And Distribution ➢ Basic Functions ➢ Output Control ➢ Output Determination ➢ Output Determination Using The Condition Technique ➢ Maintain Output Determination For Sales Documents ➢ Maintain Condition Tables. You will be first presented with a Choose Activity dialog box, as shown in Figure 4.22.

FIGURE 4.22   Choose Activity dialog box

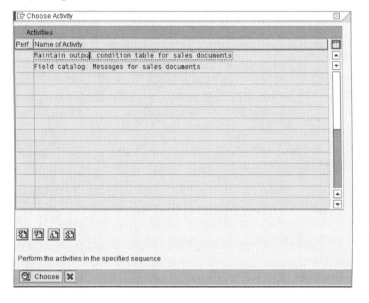

Choose the activity Maintain Output Condition Table For Sales Documents from the dialog box, and click the ![Choose] button to call up the customization overview screen. You will be presented with the customization screen for changing the condition tables. Now use menu path Condition ➢ Create to call up the Create Condition Table screen (Figure 4.23). Alternatively, you can use transaction code V/56 to directly reach this customization screen.

In SAP, condition table numbers greater than 500 are reserved for the customer name space. You can create your condition table by copying from some existing condition table or by creating it from scratch. To copy it from an existing table, provide the source table number in the Copy From Condition Table field while creating your condition table. To create your own condition table from start, select a number greater than 500 for your condition table, and press Enter to call up the detail customization screen (Figure 4.24). You can also leave this table number field empty, and SAP will automatically assign a number to your condition table upon its successful generation.

FIGURE 4.23   Create Condition Table (overview screen)

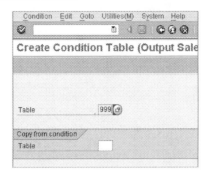

FIGURE 4.24   Create Condition Table (detail screen)

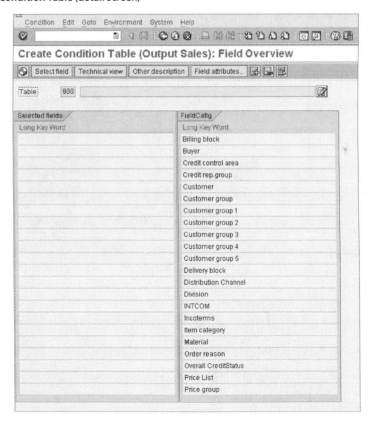

As you can see in Figure 4.24, the screen is divided into two columns: Selected Fields and Field Catalog. The Field Catalog column contains all the fields that you can choose from for creating your own condition table. The selected fields column shows all the fields that you selected for your condition table.

For Galaxy, we are creating two condition tables: condition table 999 and condition table 998. The example you see in Figure 4.24 is for condition table 999.

Now double-click the desired fields in the Field Catalog column on the right. The fields will be copied to the Selected Fields column on the left. You can also move fields from right to left by putting your cursor on the field on the right and clicking the Select Field button on the menu. Follow either of these directions until you get all the required fields to define your condition tables on the left. Figure 4.25 shows the customization settings for condition table 999 created for Galaxy. You will notice that SAP automatically proposed the condition table description using the sequence in which you selected the fields from the right. If needed, you can edit this description by using the ✎ button.

FIGURE 4.25   Creating a condition table (Galaxy example)

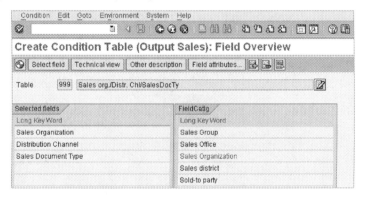

You can also insert a blank row before and after a field in the left window using the ⊞ button. For example, suppose while configuring table 999 in Figure 4.25 you selected Distribution Channel first and then wanted to make space to insert Sales Organization just before Distribution Channel. No worries, because you can do so using the ⊞ button on the menu. Similarly, use the ⊟ button to remove/deselect a field from the left window. Now, generate your condition table using the 🖲 button on the menu.

At this point, you should see a Create Object Directory Entry dialog box asking for package information to store the object directory entry for your condition table.

Provide a proper development class if you want to transport the condition table to the next SAP client in the landscape or use F7 to save locally. Next, you will be presented with another dialog box, called Prompt For Workbench Request. The purpose of this dialog box is to capture your customization setup into a transport request so that you can move your changes to other SAP clients on the landscape. Now either capture your customization table entry into the development/workbench transport request that appears in this dialog box or create a new one using the ▢ button for your customization.

With condition table generation, SAP also generates a log file that automatically pops up on the screen with the completion of the condition table generation process. Always make sure to check the log entries to find out any errors that arose while generating your condition table. Once the generation process completes without errors, your condition table becomes active and is ready for use with step 2 of the output determination process, that is, grouping condition tables into an access sequence.

CASE STUDY—GALAXY CONFIGURATION ANALYSIS: MAINTAIN CONDITION TABLES

Galaxy Musical Instruments named condition table 998 Order Type/Customer and named condition table 999 Sales Organization/Distribution Channel/Order Type.

Defining Access Sequences and Arranging Condition Tables into the Access Sequence

SAP uses access sequences as the search criteria to find the valid condition record during an output determination run. In this step, you define this access sequence and arrange the condition tables created in step 1 in the sequence in which you want SAP to access condition records. One rule of thumb is to arrange the tables in the most specific to most generic order.

To define an access sequence for the sales document output determination process, call the access sequence customization screen (Figure 4.26) using transaction code V/48 or following menu path IMG ➢ Sales And Distribution ➢ Basic Functions ➢ Output Control ➢ Output Determination ➢ Output Determination Using The Condition Technique ➢ Maintain Output Determination For Sales Documents ➢ Maintain Access Sequences.

FIGURE 4.26   Access sequence customization screen

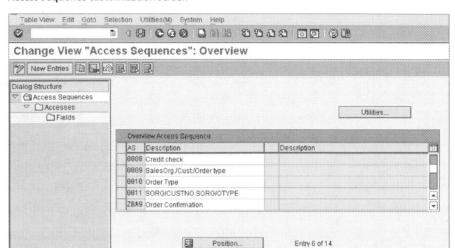

To define your own access sequence (which is what we did here for Galaxy), click the New Entry button, provide a four-character identification key starting with *Y* or *Z*, and provide a meaningful text description. In Figure 4.26, the last access sequence, ZBA9 – Order Confirmation, represents the access sequence we created for Galaxy.

Once you have defined your access sequence, select your entry, and double-click the Accesses node in the left window to call up the next customization screen. On this customization screen, click the New Entries button, and enter your condition tables in the sequence in which you would like SAP to perform the search. Once done, save your entry using the Save button. Figure 4.27 shows the customization performed for Galaxy access sequence ZBA9.

The following fields appear on the customization screen:

No.   The column No. indicates the number of the access within the access sequence.

Tab.   In the column Tab., enter the output condition table number.

Using these two fields, you set up the logical order in which you want SAP to read the records stored in condition tables.

In the current sequence shown in Figure 4.27, SAP will first read records from table 998; if nothing is found here, it will move to read records from the next table, 999.

Description   SAP automatically populates the field Description with the description of the condition table created in the previous step.

Requirement   A *requirement* is a piece of ABAP code that tells SAP when to read the records from a condition table in an access sequence and when not. If a requirement fails, the condition table is not accessed. For example, requirement 2 in Figure 4.27 tells SAP to process output type ZBA9 only if the sales document is complete and does not have a credit block or a delivery block. You can create requirements with the help of an ABAP person using transaction code VOFM. Again, like tables, the 900 series is available as the customer name space for naming your customized requirements. The requirement thus created is assigned in the column Requirement against the particular access.

Exclusive   Selecting the Exclusive check box tells SAP to stop searching further for a condition record once a valid condition record is found in the current access step. This also helps in improving the system performance because it avoids accessing further records if a valid record is found. In Figure 4.27, if Exclusive is not selected for any table, SAP will always perform the search until access step number 20, even though it found a valid record within step 10 and will always return the value from step 20 as a valid record value. If Exclusive is selected, as shown in Figure 4.27, SAP will move to the next step only if a valid record is not found in the previous step. So, if the valid record is found for the Sales Doc Type/Customer table, SAP will take that as valid record and stop performing the search.

FIGURE 4.27   Assigning condition tables to an access sequence

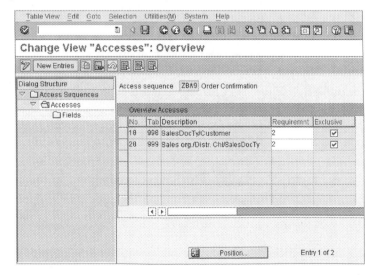

Now select line 10, and double-click the Fields node in the left window to call up the customization screen for fields assignment (Figure 4.28). Here you assign the fields of the condition table to the fields of the output communication structure so that the value flows from the source fields (condition tables) to the target fields (output communication structure) during various stages of sales cycle processing.

FIGURE 4.28   Populating fields for condition tables into the access sequence

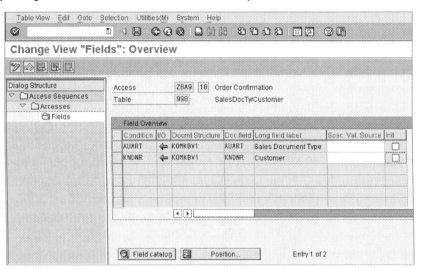

 TIP   When you double-click the Fields node, you may receive a warning message stating "The Field assignment has not yet been made." Just press Enter, and SAP will automatically assign the source and target fields to each other and take you to the next screen, as shown in Figure 4.28. When SAP is not able to find a suitable proposal for the source field, you need to provide one. In that case, click the Field Catalog button at the bottom of the screen to select the source field. You can also change SAP-proposed assignments for source fields using the Field Catalog button.

Now repeat the previous steps to perform field assignment for all other lines that you entered into the Accesses node for your access sequence. For Galaxy, we need to repeat the field assignment step, for line item 20. When you are done, save your entry using the Save button.

Once your entry is saved, double-click the Access Sequence node on the left to reach the customization screen shown in Figure 4.26. Now click the Utilities button to call up the Generate Access Sequences screen shown in Figure 4.29. Provide the value for your access sequence (ZBA9 for Galaxy), and press F8 or click the Execute button to activate your access sequence.

FIGURE 4.29   Activating your access sequence

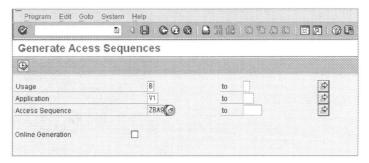

 NOTE   Remember that a condition table and an access sequence are client-independent configurations. Once set up, they will be available across all the clients on one SAP instance.

 NOTE   Always make sure to generate/activate after you create or make any changes to a condition table or an access sequence.

CASE STUDY—GALAXY CONFIGURATION ANALYSIS: SET UP ACCESS SEQUENCE

Galaxy Musical Instruments named its access sequence ZBA9 and arranged the two condition tables 998 and 999 in sequence so that 998 is accessed first. 999 is then accessed if there is no record found in 998. Further, Galaxy maintained a requirement type 2 to these condition tables to allow processing only when the sales document is complete.

Maintaining the Output Type and Assigning the Access Sequence to an Output Type

Here you set up an output type and assign the access sequence created in step 2 to it. An output type is a controlling element of the output determination process. An output type controls what output media (mail, print, fax) to use for sending output, which print script and print program to use, whether the output is to print manually or through a batch job, and so on. Further, you can set up an output type to be assigned manually to a sales document or to be determined automatically. If you want it to be determined automatically, you need to assign an access sequence.

Figure 4.30 shows the customization overview screen for defining an output type. You can call this customization screen using transaction code V/30 or via menu path IMG ➢ Sales And Distribution ➢ Basic Functions ➢ Output Control ➢ Output Determination ➢ Output Determination Using The Condition Technique ➢ Maintain Output Determination For Sales Documents ➢ Maintain Output Types. As in the previous examples, you can either use the New Entries button to create the new output type from scratch or use the Copy button to create the output type via the copy with reference function to an already existing output type. For Galaxy, we created the output type ZBA9 using the copy method and source output type BA00. For this chapter's purpose, we will cover the customization settings for an output type using our newly created output type ZBA9.

FIGURE 4.30   Output types overview screen

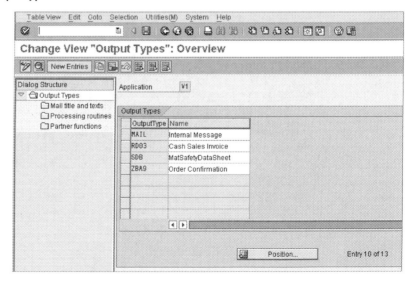

Double-click the output type ZBA9 shown on the right window in Figure 4.30 to call up the general data customization screen for output type ZBA9, as shown in Figure 4.31.

FIGURE 4.31   Defining the output type, general data

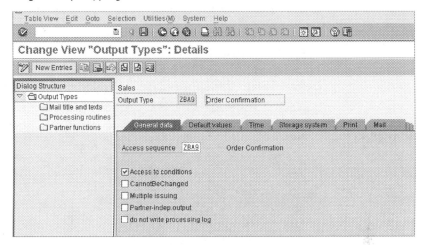

The screen is divided into two parts, which is a format that should be familiar by now. The left window (Dialog Structure) shows expandable customization options for the output type. The right window contains the customization screen divided into various tabs. These are the four major customization tabs:

General Data tab   This tab controls the general behavior of an output type. Here are the various customization fields shown in Figure 4.31, starting at the top left:

Output Type   This field represents the output type and its description. Here output type is ZBA9, and its description is Order Confirmation.

Access Sequence   This field represents the access sequence that is assigned to the output type for automatic output determination. Here the assigned access is ZBA9 that we created in step 2.

Access to conditions   This check box controls whether an output type should perform access to condition records. When selected, it means Yes; when it's unselected, it means No.

Cannot Be Changed   This check box controls whether SAP should allow the manual change of an output type in the documents, once it is successfully determined.

Multiple Issuing   This check box controls whether SAP should allow for repeat processing/multiple outputs for the same output type or whether the output type should be used only once in the document.

Partner-Indep. Output   This check box controls whether the output should depend upon the partner or should be partner independent.

Do Not Write Processing Log   This check box controls whether to write the processing log for the output type.

Default Values tab   The Default Values tab, as shown in Figure 4.32, is used for setting up the default values for the output processing–related customization.

FIGURE 4.32   Defining the output type, default values

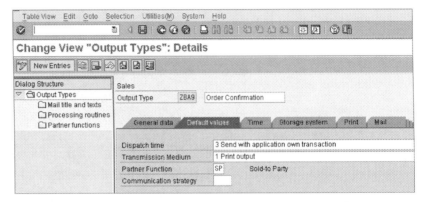

Here are the explanations for the fields in Figure 4.32:

▶ **Dispatch Time**   This specifies when and how to dispatch the output type. The available options are as follows:

  ≫ 1: When you select 1, your output type is dispatched with a scheduled job (RSNAST00 program scheduled with a SM37 job).

  ≫ 2: Option 2 acts like option 1 but with an earliest processing date and requested processing time. When you select 2, the program RSNAST00 processes the output message only when the processing date is reached.

  ≫ 3: Select 3 to manually use the application's own transaction (in other words, VF31 for billing, VL71 for delivery, and VT70 for shipping).

  ≫ 4: Select 4 for automatic dispatch once the document is saved.

Transmission Medium   This specifies what medium to use for dispatch, such as print, email, or fax.

Partner Function   This specifies which partner function to use for dispatch, such as BP for billing-related outputs, SP for sales-related outputs, SH for delivery-related outputs.

Communication Strategy   Here you specify the communication strategy that defines the sequence of communication methods that can be used while sending output messages externally.

Time   With the Time customization tab (Figure 4.33), you can restrict the output type from using a particular dispatch value, such as no processing by a job or no processing by an application's own transaction. For example, the selection for Timing 1 (Periodic Job) Not Allowed tells SAP that output type ZBA9 cannot be processed using a periodic batch job.

FIGURE 4.33   Defining the output type, time

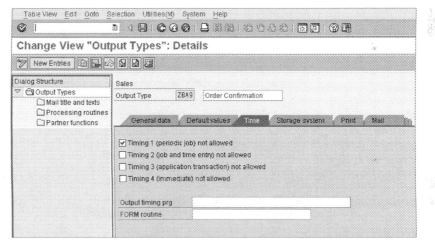

Storage System   The next tab, Storage System, helps you take control of whether the output type is to be used for printing only, for archiving only, or for both printing and archiving.

Once you have defined the general settings for an output type using all the various tabs that we've discussed, the next step is to customize the mail title and text, processing routines, and assignment of the output type to partner functions. These options are shown on the left side of the output maintenance screen (Figure 4.34).

FIGURE 4.34   Defining the output type, mail title, and text

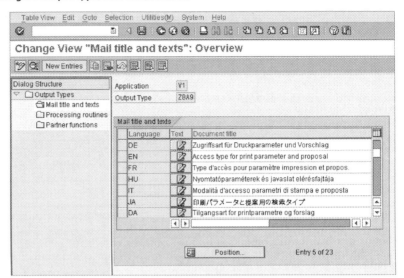

Mail Title And Text   Double-click the Mail Title And Text node, and SAP will provide you with the screen shown in Figure 4.34. Here you can maintain the title text for your output type in various languages. When you send the output via email, SAP uses this title text to generate the subject line for the email in the correct language. So, if you have maintained the output in the condition record or in the transaction document with the language as EN, the English title will be picked up, and when it is FR, the title text maintained in French will be picked up to generate the subject line.

Processing Routines   Now double-click the Processing Routines node, and you will be presented with a screen that looks like Figure 4.35. Here you define the processing programs and corresponding forms or form routines for your output type. Suppose you want to print the order confirmation document. You assign the print program and corresponding print form (order confirmation document template) to the print medium output on this screen. So in our example, a print program will pull the data from the order document and provide it to the order confirmation template, which is then processed as per the processing settings we maintained on the detail customization screen for the output type (Figures 4.31 to 4.33). Similarly, you can also define the processing parameters for another output medium, such as an EDI program with a form routine for EDI output.

FIGURE 4.35 Defining the output type, processing routines

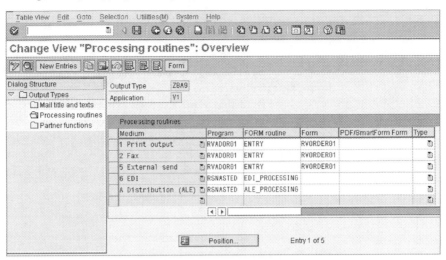

Partner Functions Next, you can define the partners relevant for output processing as shown in Figure 4.36. The output for a billing document is assigned to the bill-to party, the output for shipping documents is assigned to the ship-to party, and the output for sales documents are assigned to the sold-to party partner function in customizing.

FIGURE 4.36 Defining the output type, partner functions

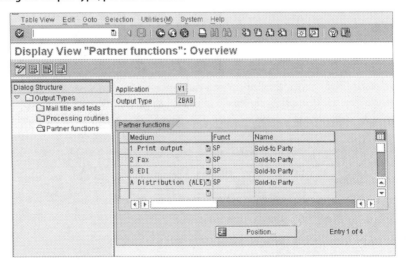

CASE STUDY—GALAXY CONFIGURATION ANALYSIS: DEFINE OUTPUT TYPE

With output type BA00 being the closest match, Galaxy Musical Instruments used the copy with reference method to create the output type ZBA9 with BA00 as the source output type. Access sequence ZBA9 was assigned to output type ZBA9 with the Access To Condition check box selected to allow automatic determination using the output determination technique. Default values from the Dispatch and Time tabs set the manual triggering for output type ZBA9 to printer, avoiding using any batch job for triggering the output to a printer. Print form RVORDER01 along with print program RVADOR01 constitute the actual print program and order confirmation template assignment to the output type ZBA9.

Grouping Output Types into an Output Determination Procedure

Once the output type is defined, the next step is to group the output type into an output determination procedure. An output determination procedure contains all the relevant output types arranged in a procedural sequence in which SAP will access them during output processing for a business transaction. Figure 4.37 shows the customization overview screen for the output determination procedure. You can call this customization screen using transaction code V/32 or menu path IMG ➢ Sales And Distribution ➢ Basic Functions ➢ Output Control ➢ Output Determination ➢ Output Determination Using The Condition Technique ➢ Maintain Output Determination For Sales Documents ➢ Maintain Output Determination Procedure. As usual, use the New Entries button to create the new output procedure from scratch or the Copy button to create the output procedure with reference to an existing one. With determination procedure V10000 being the closest match, Galaxy Musical Instruments used the copy with reference method to created the output type Z10000, with V10000 as the source procedure.

Now double-click the output procedure Z10000 shown in the right window in Figure 4.37 to call up the detailed customization screen, as shown in Figure 4.38. As in our other examples, you can use the New Entries or Copy button to maintain your entry.

FIGURE 4.37 Maintaining the output determination, procedures overview screen

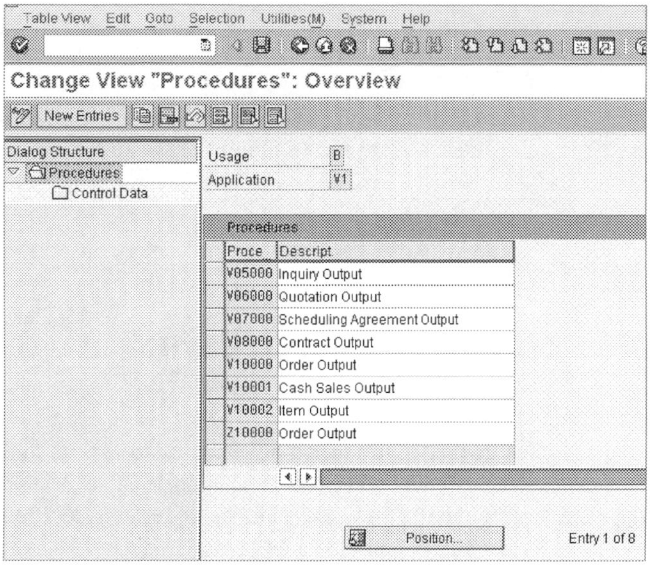

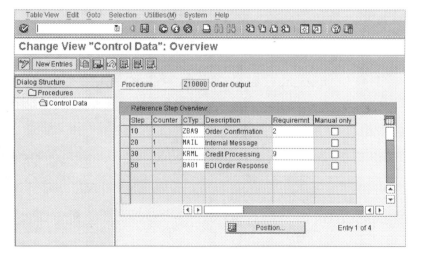

FIGURE 4.38 Maintaining the output determination, detail screen

The following are the various fields on this customization screen:

Step Use the field Step to set up the sequence in which the output types need to be arranged in the determination procedure.

Counter Use the field Counter to set up the subsequence in which the output types need to be arranged in the determination procedure.

Condition Type   Here you enter the output type that you created earlier.

Description   This field shows the description of the output type.

Requirement   The field Requirement allows you to specify the specific requirements that you want SAP to look into before accessing the output type. If the requirement fails, SAP will not access the output type.

Manual only   This check box, when selected, forces an output type to be processed manually only.

CASE STUDY—GALAXY CONFIGURATION ANALYSIS: MAINTAIN OUTPUT DETERMINATION PROCEDURE

Sending order acknowledgments to customers for incomplete/blocked/unconfirmed orders can be troublesome and has potential to create confusion. To avoid this, Galaxy wanted to stop the determination of output type ZBA9 in a sales order if the order is incomplete or blocked. To achieve this, Galaxy assigned a requirement type 2 to output ZBA9 in the output procedure Z10000.

Assigning the Output Determination Procedure to Its Respective Output Object

Finally, assign the output determination to its respective business object that needs output control such as the sales document, delivery, and billing, as the case may be. For Galaxy's example, we configured ZBA9 to generate an output message for order confirmation. Because order confirmation happens for a sales document, we will assign the output determination procedure Z10000 to the sales document header level, in other words, to the sales document type. You can call up the customization screen using transaction code V/43 or menu path IMG ➢ Sales And Distribution ➢ Basic Functions ➢ Output Control ➢ Output Determination ➢ Output Determination Using The Condition Technique ➢ Maintain Output Determination For Sales Documents ➢ Assign Output Determination Procedure. Figure 4.39 shows the customization screen for assigning the output determination procedure to a sales document type.

FIGURE 4.39   Assigning the output determination to a sales document type

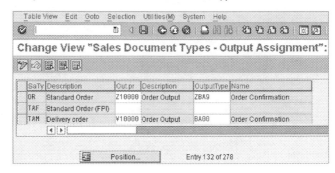

Unlike Galaxy's example where we configured the output for the sales document header level, if your output type is relevant for the sales document item level, you need to assign the output determination procedure to the sales document item category. You can call up the customization screen (Figure 4.40) using transaction code V/69. It shows a blank assignment because we have not configured any output procedure for use with sales documents at the item level.

FIGURE 4.40   Assigning the output determination to an item category

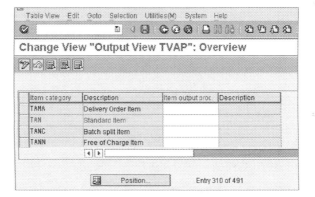

Summary

In this chapter, we covered how to set up the partner determination, text determination, and output determination in the SAP SD module. In the next chapter, we will cover customization and setup for pricing determination and tax determination.

Pricing and Tax Determination

O ne of the most critical areas in Sales and Distribution is pricing, in other words, determining the price at which a sales transaction takes place. In order to arrive at the final price, there can be several elements such as a base price, discounts, and taxes, linked together in a pricing schema. In this chapter, we will study the set up of a pricing procedure.

In addition, most sales are subjected to tax, as per the law of the land. The tax structure varies from region to region. Setting up and calculating tax is therefore important from both a legal and a sales perspective. Hence, in this chapter, we will focus on basic concepts of tax determination.

Pricing

A *pricing procedure* is a schema to arrive at the final price of a product or a service. For example, if a price of a product is determined as (base price – discounts + freight + tax), you would arrange these conditions in a sequence and specify the rules for arriving at a total. Each of these pricing elements in a pricing procedure is called a *condition type*. The conditions can either be at header level (applicable to the entire document) or at an item level. You can either enter the values for each condition type manually or determine them automatically using a condition technique. We discussed and showed how to apply this condition technique in Chapter 4, "Partner, Text, and Output Determination." To reiterate, when using this technique, you can assign an *access sequence* to each condition type. Following the sequence, the system looks up pricing records maintained in *condition tables* in a specific order. The *condition record* is then picked up from the tables and used in the pricing schema. Figure 5.1 gives you an overview of a pricing procedure and its constituents. You can refer to this figure as you go through this chapter.

To configure pricing, follow these major steps:

Step 1: Define the condition tables   First, you define the condition tables, with combinations of key fields. You then set up the pricing condition records for these key combinations.

Step 2: Define the access sequences   SAP uses access sequences as the search criteria to find the valid condition record during the pricing determination run. In this step, you define this access sequence and arrange the condition tables defined in step 1 in the sequence in which you want SAP to access the condition records. As in any condition technique, the rule of thumb is to arrange the tables in order from most specific to most generic.

Step 3: Set up the condition types   Here you set up condition types and assign the access sequence created in step 2 to them. Each condition type represents an element in the schema. You set up prices, discounts, freight conditions, tax, and costs as individual condition types.

Step 4: Define the pricing procedure   The pricing procedure is the schema to arrive at the final price. You link together the individual condition types defined in step 3 and maintain the relation between them. You can also attach complex formulae that may be required to compute any value.

Step 5: Assign the pricing procedure   You then determine the pricing procedure for each sales transaction. You can control which procedure is to be used for a specific customer and sales document type. In this step, you specify these rules for determining the pricing procedure.

FIGURE 5.1   Elements of a pricing procedure

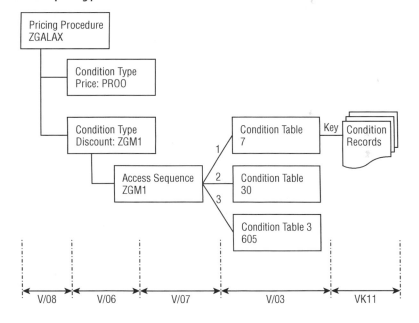

Deciding the Scope of Customization

As with any major customization activity, you should identify the scope of the customization based on your business blueprint. The following questions will help you understand the scope of work:

▶ How does your pricing schema look? It is often very useful to write down the complete schema in a spreadsheet. This gives you a picture of the various pricing elements and the formulae needed to arrive at a final price.

▶ Does the pricing schema vary by sales area? Do you have different document types that require a separate pricing schema?

▶ What are the pricing elements you require? Can you group them together under Prices, Discounts, Freight, Tax, and so on?

▶ What is the key to determining the value for each condition? Is the price of a material customer-specific? Or is it constant for all the customers in your sales area? Do you require multiple accesses to get the appropriate price? List all criteria for the price determination.

▶ What are the financial accounts to be updated? Where should you post the price, discount, and so on? What are the criteria for account determination?

▶ Are there any reporting requirements that need you to capture pricing subtotals as you go along computing the final price? You can capture gross price, net price, total discount, and so on, as intermediate subtotals and use the values in reports or in documents for customers.

Based on this list of answers, you should check the SAP standard pricing procedures in the system. Check whether those procedures meet your requirements or whether any customization is required.

For a better understanding of these concepts, let's go through the customization scope for Galaxy Musical Instruments.

CASE STUDY—GALAXY MUSICAL INSTRUMENTS CONFIGURATION ANALYSIS: PRICING PROCEDURE: SCOPE FINALIZATION

We analyzed Galaxy Musical Instruments' pricing requirements and documented the schema in a spreadsheet. Here we'll discuss some of the company's pricing-related requirements. As we go through the chapter, we will also discuss how we mapped these requirements in the system.

► *Base price*: The price records are simple and specific to each product. However, a special price applies to some of the customers. Hence, there should be a provision to maintain records for a key of (customer number + material number) and also a generic record irrespective of the customer (the material-specific price).

► *Discounts*: Galaxy offers several promotional discounts. Some of these discounts are specifically designed to attract certain new customers, and some are product discounts offered to a certain customer or a group of customers. We'll use the Customer Group field to determine discounts. Another requirement is to offer discounts based on customer hierarchy.

► *Shipping and handling charges*: There should be a provision for freight charges based on the total weight of the entire shipment.

► Besides this, we also assessed Galaxy's reporting requirements. We determined that the gross price, net price, freight, and costs have to be captured from the pricing schema for subsequent reporting and analyses.

Configure Pricing

We will follow the step-by-step procedure discussed earlier to build a pricing procedure, and we'll elaborate on each step of the procedure in the following sections.

Step 1: Define the Condition Tables

The first step is to define condition tables. To set up a condition table, you need to refer to a field catalog. From this list, you can pick up the fields that you require in your condition table.

Conditions: Allowed Fields

Use the menu path IMG ➢ Sales And Distribution ➢ Basic Functions ➢ Pricing ➢ Pricing Control ➢ Define Condition Tables ➢ Conditions: Allowed Fields (OV24).

Using this transaction, you can check the fields available in the standard field catalog (Figure 5.2). If this list does not meet your requirements, you can access a larger list of fields in the catalog by using the drop-down list (function key F4). Figure 5.3 shows the larger list.

FIGURE 5.2 Field catalog

Change View "Field Catalog (Pricing Sales/Distribution)": Overview

New Entries

Field Catalog (Pricing Sales/Distribution)

Field	Description
ADDNR	Additional
AKTNR	Promotion
ALAND	Country
ANZSN	No. serial numbers
AUART	Order Type
AUART_SD	Sales Document Type
AUBEL	Sales Document
AUGRU	Order reason

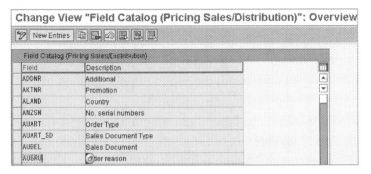

FIGURE 5.3 Field catalog, expanded

Change View "Field Catalog (Pricing Sales/Distribution)": Overview

Table Name Field Name	Short Description Short Description
KOMG	Maintenance
MANDT	Client
VKORG	Sales Organization
VTWEG	Distribution Channel
SPART	Division
KUNNR	Customer number
KDGRP	Customer group
PLTYP	Price list type
KONDA	Price group (customer)
KONDM	Material pricing group
WAERK	SD Document Currency
MATNR	Material Number
BWTAR	Valuation Type
CHARG	Batch Number
PRODH	Product hierarchy
MEINS	Base Unit of Measure
BONUS	Volume rebate group
EBONU	Settlement Group 1 (Purchasing)
PROVG	Commission group
ALAND	Departure country (country from which the goods are sent)
WKREG	Region in which plant is located
WKCOU	County in which plant is located
WKCTY	City in which plant is located
LLAND	Country of Destination
REGIO	Region (State, Province, County)
COUNC	County Code

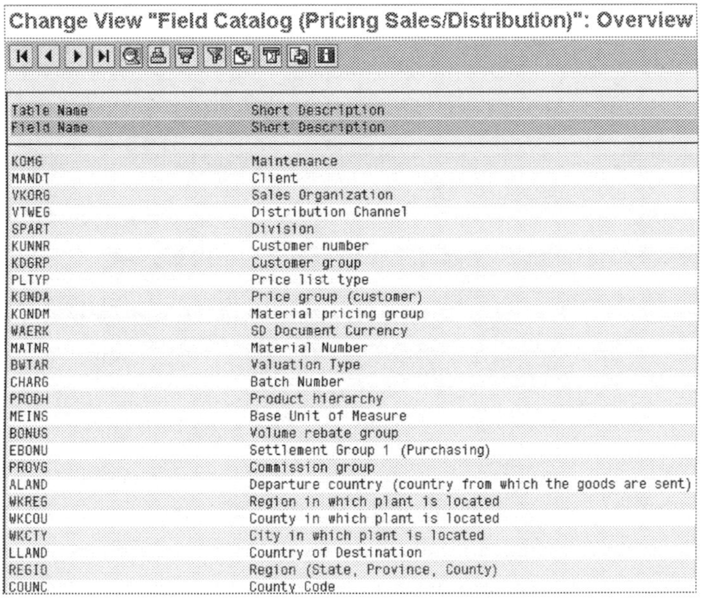

For Galaxy Musical Instruments, we need a table for a combination of Sales Organization and Customer Group. We first check in the field catalog and verify that these fields are available.

ADDING NEW FIELDS TO THE PRICING CATALOG

In some cases, you may find that the field you plan to use is not part of the field catalog provided by SAP. In those cases, you need to append the new fields to the catalog and populate the values of the new fields before they can be used. You will need the help of an ABAP expert to help you through the following steps:

1. *Add the new fields*: SAP uses the KOMG structure for all technical purposes. Append the new header field to the KOMK structure via "include KOMKAZ" and add the new item field to the KOMP structure via "include KOMPAZ." Once you add the fields in KOMK and KOMP via includes, they automatically add up to the KOMG structure.

2. *Populate the fields*: Use USEREXIT_PRICING_PREPARE_TKOMK (for the header fields) and USEREXIT_PRICING_PREPARE_TKOMP (for the item fields) from "include MV45AFZZ" to provide values to new fields during sales order processing. Similarly, use USEREXIT_PRICING_PREPARE_TKOMK (for the header fields) and USEREXIT_PRICING_PREPARE_TKOMP (for the item fields) from "include RV60AFZZ" to provide values to new fields during billing document processing.

3. *Add the fields to catalog*: Now you can add the fields to the catalog using OV24, as explained earlier.

Create Condition Table

Follow the menu path IMG ➤ Sales And Distribution ➤ Basic Functions ➤ Pricing ➤ Pricing Control ➤ Define Condition Tables ➤ Create Condition Tables (V/03).

This option allows you to set up a condition table. The steps are similar to the condition table set up and discussed in the "Output Determination" section of Chapter 4, "Partner, Text and Output Determination." You select the fields and generate a new table.

As shown in Figure 5.4, the selected fields appear in the list on the left. These fields will form the key to the new table. You can also choose to add a validity period and a release status to control the pricing records contained in the table. This option was not available in the condition technique discussed in "Output Determination."

FIGURE 5.4   Defining a condition table

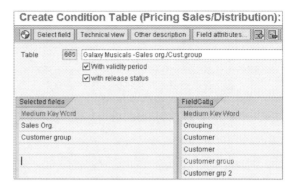

If you select the With Validity Period option, the pricing records get a Valid From date and a Valid To date. When you maintain the price, you can specify the exact duration for which the record should be active. Once the expiry date is reached, the record becomes obsolete. This feature enables you to maintain an archive record of all the previous prices over a period of time. You can also set up new pricing records in advance and release them using the Valid From date.

If you select the With Release Status option, you can control the pricing record further by adding a status field. Using this feature, you can flag a record as active or not yet released, depending on your requirements.

You will see how to use these fields (using transaction VK11) later in the chapter in the "Maintaining Price Records" section.

After you have selected the required fields, save and generate the new condition table. Figure 5.5 shows the generation log screen.

FIGURE 5.5   Saving and generating a new condition table

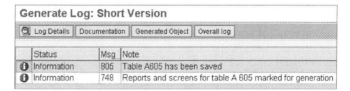

CASE STUDY—GALAXY MUSICAL INSTRUMENTS CONFIGURATION ANALYSIS: MAINTAIN THE CONDITION TABLES

Galaxy Musical Instruments required a custom condition table with a key-combination of Sales Organization and Customer Group. We created table 605, as shown in Figure 5.4. This table will help Galaxy maintain records specific to customer groups in the U.S. and Mexico sales organizations.

We also checked the list of existing tables in SAP to pick up the ones that would be relevant to Galaxy's other pricing requirements. Table 7 would let Galaxy maintain records for (Sales Organization + Distribution Channel + Division + Customer). Another one, table 30, is based on (Sales Organization + Distribution Channel + Customer + Material Pricing Group). We made a note of these table numbers so that we can link them together in an access sequence.

Step 2: Define the Access Sequences

To define an access sequence for pricing determination, the menu is as follows: IMG ≻ Sales And Distribution ≻ Basic Functions ≻ Pricing ≻ Pricing Control ≻ Define Access Sequence. From the Select Activity menu, choose Maintain Access Sequence. The transaction code is V/07.

From the Change View: Access Sequences: Overview screen, you can create a new access sequence by clicking the New Entry button and adding the condition tables in the required sequence (Figure 5.6). Please refer to the discussion on the exact steps in Chapter 4.

FIGURE 5.6 Defining an access sequence

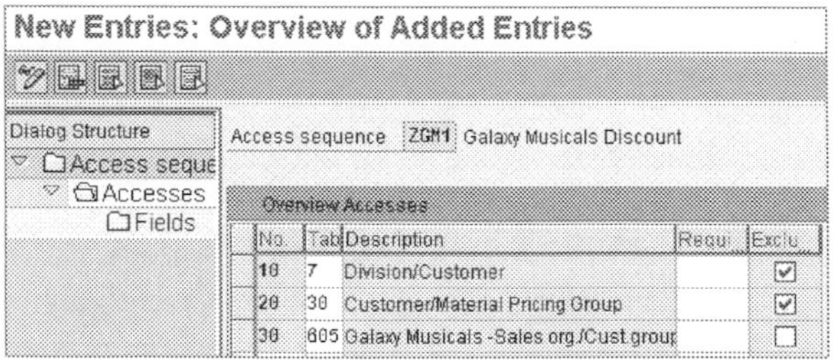

CASE STUDY—GALAXY MUSICAL INSTRUMENTS CONFIGURATION ANALYSIS: SET UP THE ACCESS SEQUENCE

After writing down Galaxy's table numbers, we set up a new access sequence: ZGM1. It consists of three tables, linked in a sequence, as shown in Figure 5.6. Our first access will use the standard table 7. This will be a customer-specific access. If the system cannot find a suitable record here, it will check table 30. Here it checks records for a material pricing group and a customer. If this draws a blank as well, it will proceed to the third access, which uses custom table 605, as we defined earlier. The Exclusive indicator is turned on to ensure that a unique record is determined.

In Figure 5.6, you can see the Exclusive indicator at the access steps. If the system finds a record at any step, it stops any further searching. If there are more records at subsequent levels, they will be ignored, and an exclusive record will be used to calculate the price.

We'll use an example to explain this concept further. If the access sequence ZGM1 finds a record at the first step (table 7), it stops any further searching and applies this rate. However, it is possible that a certain customer could have two or more conditions applicable to it. For example, a customer could have a special discount specific to it (using table 7) and another discount for the Customer group of which it is a part (table 605). If you turn off the Exclusive indicator, the system will continue the search and pick up both the records. It is advisable to have the Exclusive indicator on for better system performance and to avoid reading multiple records.

The Requirement field allows you to add a custom routine for the access step. You can add a prerequisite condition that has to be fulfilled before a specific access is carried out. An example is the standard access sequence MWST, used in the determination of tax conditions (Figure 5.7). The access sequence looks up tables for domestic and international tax rates. In this example, MWST has requirement routine 8 at the first step. This code checks whether the destination is an international address. If this prerequisite requirement is fulfilled, the system carries out the search for a tax record. Otherwise, this step is skipped, and the next access (for domestic taxes) is carried out. Requirement routine 7 checks for domestic destination. This way, you can improve the efficiency of the access sequence by checking prerequisites.

FIGURE 5.7 Access sequence using requirement routine

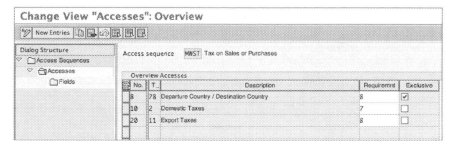

We will discuss how to set up a pricing requirement routine later in this chapter.

Step 3: Set Up the Condition Types

Pricing conditions are the basic pricing elements used in the pricing schema. Therefore, we'll start by showing how to set up a condition type to meet your requirements.

Define Condition Types

To define condition types, follow the path IMG ≻ Sales And Distribution ≻ Basic Functions ≻ Pricing ≻ Pricing Control ≻ Define Condition Types ≻ Maintain Condition Types (V/06).

On the overview screen, you can find a list of condition types that already are in the system. To define a new condition type, you can use the New Entries option or copy one from a reference condition type. You can specify a four-character alphanumeric name for the condition type. The following are the critical settings on the Details screen, as shown in Figure 5.8.

FIGURE 5.8 Defining a condition type: Control Data 1

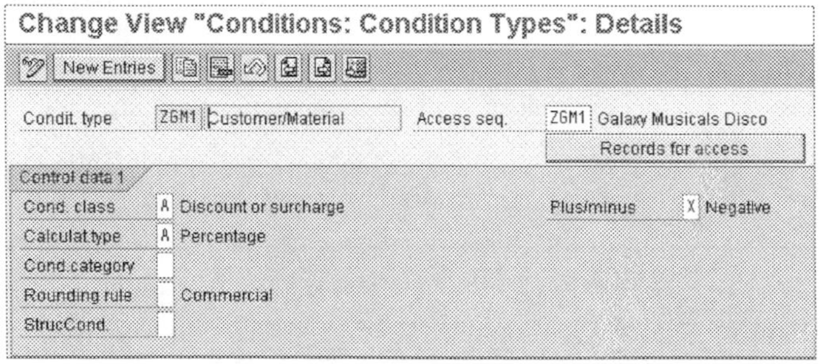

Access Sequence   If the condition type is to be linked to an access sequence, you can specify it in this field.

Records For Access   This link displays all the pricing records that have been maintained in the various tables listed in the access sequence.

Control Data 1 Tab: These fields are on the Control Data 1 tab:

Condition Class   This is the categorization of the condition that is being set up. It could be a price, a discount, a tax, and so on. It is also used to decide which condition types should be redetermined when copying from one document to another.

Calculation Type   This guides the system in calculating the value of a condition. For example, you can specify whether the value of a condition should be considered as a fixed value or a percentage based on quantity, volume, or other attributes.

Condition Category   This further classifies the condition into categories such as freight-related charges, taxes, and so on. This field also plays a key role in controlling which price conditions are copied from one sales document to another and which conditions need to be redetermined. The "Update Pricing" section in this chapter will explain this concept in detail.

Rounding Rule   This controls how SAP should apply the rounding rules to the condition calculations. Choose A for rounding up or B for rounding down, and keep this field as blank for commercial rounding.

Plus/Minus   This controls whether the resultant condition value will have a negative or positive impact on the value. Choose A to have positive impact, or choose X to have a negative impact; leave the field blank if you want the condition to leave both options open. For instance, a discount condition type would have a negative sign, whereas a surcharge condition type would have a positive sign.

Structure Condition   The field (Struc.Cond) controls the condition cumulation and duplication in case of structured materials such as a bill of materials and configurable materials. Choose A if you want to duplicate the condition to all the lower-level items in the structure, or choose B if you want the condition to contain the cumulative value from all the lower-level items. We will discuss this later in the chapter when we talk about cumulating conditions.

Below the Control Data 1 tab is the Group Condition tab. The following settings appear in Figure 5.9.

FIGURE 5.9 Defining a condition type: group conditions, master data

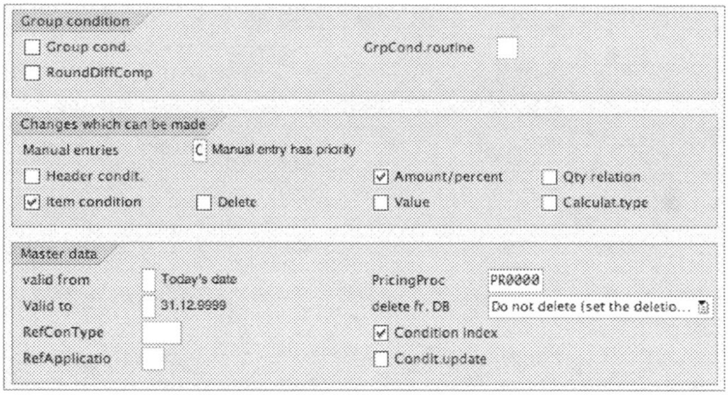

Group Condition: This field should be selected only if you want the system to calculate a condition value on the basis of more than one item in the order, grouped together by a certain criteria (such as a material group). You will study the application of this field later in the chapter, when we talk about condition types that use group condition functionality.

Changes Which Can Be Made: This section governs whether manual changes to the condition value should be permitted.

Manual Entries This setting decides which entry gets precedence. If, for example, the system determines a value of $100 for a price condition and you want to override it manually and make it $120, you can control it by specifying which value should take precedence. You can also prevent manual intervention altogether. The other fields in this section control other aspects of permitting changes.

Master Data: This section allows you to control default values such as validity dates when creating pricing master data (condition records).

Valid From, Valid To If a user does not specify any validity period, you can default these settings to Valid From Today and Valid To December 31, 9999.

Pricing Procedure This field (PricingProc in Figure 5.9) is used to specify a pricing procedure for determining condition supplements. We will discuss it later in the chapter.

Reference Condition Type The field RefCondType is useful when you have a reference condition that is similar to the one you are setting up. If a pricing record has been set up for the reference condition, the same will be copied over. This avoids multiple records to be maintained.

Reference Application   Here you can specify a reference condition type from an application other than sales.

Delete From Database   If a user wants to delete a condition record, you may want to warn him before deleting it from database. It is always a safe practice not to delete the records but to flag them as deleted. Thus, you still have traceability. You can specify this in the Delete Fr. DB field.

Next on-screen are the Scales and Control Data 2 tabs, as shown in Figure 5.10.

FIGURE 5.10 Defining a condition type: scales and control data 2

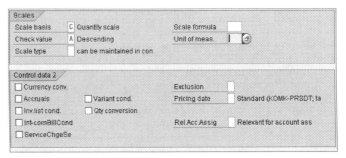

Scales: Sometimes you have scales in pricing, also known as *price slabs*. For example, from 1 to 49 pieces, the price is $50 apiece. From 50 to 99 pieces, it is $45 apiece. You manage this type of requirement using scales. We will show how to use this functionality later in this chapter. For now, we'll review some key settings on the Scales tab:

Scale Basis   This setting controls how the system interprets the scales. It can be a quantity-based scale (as in the previous example), or it can be based on weight, volume, distance, and so on.

Check Value   Here you can specify whether the scales have been entered in an ascending or a descending order.

Scale Type   You can specify a Scale Type such as a from-scale or a to-scale. This field is left blank to indicate that you can specify it in the condition record itself.

Scale Formula   If you have a complex formula to arrive at the scale base value, you can attach the formula routine here.

Control Data 2:   These fields are on the Control Data 2 tab:

Currency Conv   If the currency of a condition record (say EUR) varies from the document currency (say USD), the system applies the exchange rate (EUR to USD) to bring it to the document currency. The condition value is multiplied by the quantity to arrive at an amount. In this computation, you can control whether the currency conversion is to be done before or after the multiplication.

Accruals   This flag marks the value determined for this condition as statistical and posts it to financial accounting as accruals.

Pricing Date   This controls which date is used to check the condition record's validity at the time of pricing. By leaving this field blank, the system uses the standard pricing date. For tax conditions, it is the date on which the service was rendered.

Text Determination   This controls the text procedure and text ID that is to be associated with this condition type. Please refer to Chapter 4 for details.

Define Upper/Lower Limits for Conditions

The path here is IMG ➢ Sales And Distribution ➢ Basic Functions ➢ Pricing ➢ Pricing Control ➢ Define Condition Types ➢ Maintain Lower/Higher Limits For Condition Values (OVB2).

With this setting, you can specify limits on the value of a pricing condition (Figure 5.11). As you have seen earlier in the settings for condition types, you can allow manual changes to be made to the value of the condition. By limiting the value range, you can control the manual changes and help avoid human errors. At the time of the creation of condition records or in the sales order, the user will get an error message if she enters a value beyond the limits for the condition (Figure 5.12).

FIGURE 5.11 Defining limits for conditions

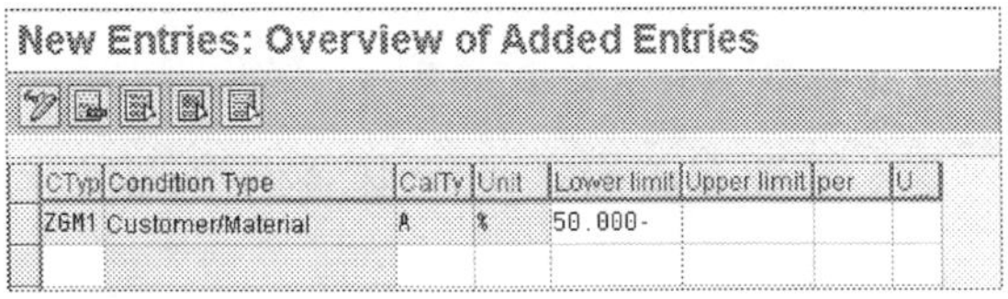

CTyp	Condition Type	CalTy	Unit	Lower limit	Upper limit	per	U
ZGM1	Customer/Material	A	%	50.000-			

FIGURE 5.12 Error message when limit is exceeded

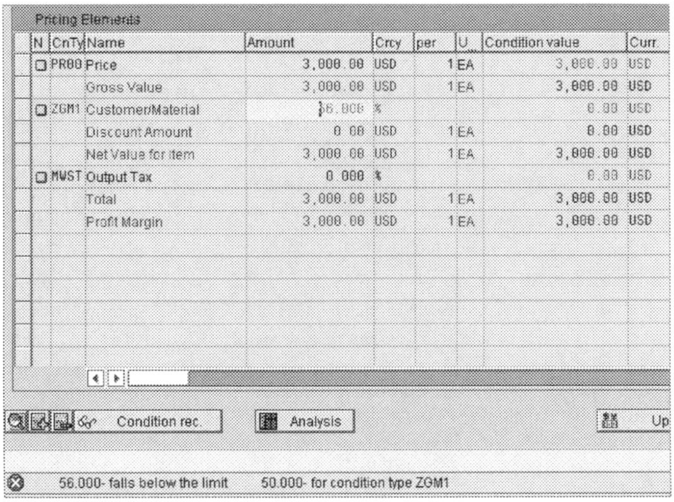

N	CnTy	Name	Amount		Crcy	per	U	Condition value		Curr.
		Pricing Elements								
☐	PR00	Price	3,000.00		USD		1 EA	3,000.00		USD
		Gross Value	3,000.00		USD		1 EA	3,000.00		USD
☐	ZGM1	Customer/Material	56.000		%			0.00		USD
		Discount Amount	0.00		USD		1 EA	0.00		USD
		Net Value for item	3,000.00		USD		1 EA	3,000.00		USD
☐	MWST	Output Tax	0.000		%			0.00		USD
		Total	3,000.00		USD		1 EA	3,000.00		USD
		Profit Margin	3,000.00		USD		1 EA	3,000.00		USD

Condition rec.   Analysis   Up

56.000- falls below the limit   50.000- for condition type ZGM1

Check Settings for Condition Types

Follow this path: IMG ➤ Sales And Distribution ➤ Basic Functions ➤ Pricing ➤ Pricing Control ➤ Define Condition Types ➤ Check Settings For Condition Types (VCHECKT685A).

It is advisable to run this report for any new condition types that you may have defined. It does not check all aspects of customization, but it does some critical checks on the use of scale types for group conditions, and so on.

Step 4: Define the Pricing Procedure

The pricing procedure is a sequential arrangement of a group of condition types. When you define a pricing procedure, you arrange various condition types in the sequence in which SAP should access them. Then you make settings that control the following:

- ▶ The way the values are calculated in the schema
- ▶ When the condition type should be accessed for reading the underlying price value

▶ Whether a condition type should be mandatory, statistical, or manually maintained during sales order processing

▶ Whether a pricing condition type is relevant for posting to accounting as revenue or as accruals

CASE STUDY—GALAXY MUSICAL INSTRUMENTS CONFIGURATION ANALYSIS: DEFINE CONDITION TYPE

Several condition types are required in the pricing procedure for Galaxy Musical Instruments. Besides using some standard conditions that met Galaxy's requirements, we had to set up a new condition type, ZGM1, for discounts. We did this by copying ZGM1 with a reference to the standard discount condition type K007. After checking all the settings and defining custom access sequence ZGM1, we attached access sequence ZGM1 to our new condition type, ZGM1. (Using the same name for the condition type and the access sequence makes it easier for the user to relate the two.)

We allowed manual changes to the value of the discount. This means that a user can override the value while creating a sales order. To guard against mistakes, we set a limit on the value of ZGM1 at 50 percent. If any user goes beyond the limit, he will get an error message. Finally, we ran a check on the consistency of our settings by using the check report.

Based on Galaxy's business requirements, we have now identified all the pricing elements that will be needed to build a pricing procedure. We have defined custom condition types wherever needed. Now we can proceed to the next step of joining the pieces together to make a pricing procedure.

To set up a pricing procedure, follow the path IMG ➤ Sales And Distribution ➤ Basic Functions ➤ Pricing ➤ Pricing Control ➤ Define And Assign Pricing Procedures ➤ Maintain Pricing Procedures (V/08).

Standard SAP provides a variety of pricing procedures. RVAA01 is a versatile standard procedure. SAP also provides some country-specific pricing procedures such as RVAAUS (Standard – USA w/out Jurisdiction Code) and RVAJUS (Standard – US w. Jurisdiction).

You can create your new pricing procedure by copying it from the existing pricing procedure that is the closest match to your requirements. You can also define a pricing procedure from scratch. We'll now show the pricing procedure customizing elements in detail, moving from left to right on the screen (shown in Figure 5.13).

FIGURE 5.13 Setting up a pricing procedure, part 1

Reference Step Overview

Step	Co..	CTyp	Description	Fr.	To	Ma..	R..	Stat..	(	SuTot	Reqt	CalTy..	BasTy..	AccK.	Accruals
11	0	PR00	Price			☐	☐	☐			2			ERL	
100	0		Gross Value			☐	☐	☐	X	1					
110	2	ZGM1	Customer/Material			☑	☐	☐	X		2			ERS	
111	0	HI01	Hierarchy			☐	☐	☐	X		2			ERS	
300	0		Discount Amount	101	299	☐	☐	☐							
800	0		Net Value for Item			☐	☐	☐	X	2		2			
801	0	NRAB	Free goods			☐	☐	☐	X		59		29	ERS	
810	3	HD00	Freight			☑	☐	☐		4				ERF	
815	0	KF00	Freight			☐	☐	☐		4				ERF	
900	0		Net Value 2			☐	☐	☐		3					
910	0	UTXJ	Tax Jurisdict.Code	900		☐	☐	☐			84				
911	0	JR1	Tax Jur Code Level 1	900		☑	☐	☐							
912	0	JR2	Tax Jur Code Level 2	900		☑	☐	☐							
913	0	JR3	Tax Jur Code Level 3	900		☑	☐	☐							
914	0	JR4	Tax Jur Code Level 4	900		☑	☐	☐							
915	0	DIFF	Rounding Off			☐	☑	☐			13	16	4		

Since the steps in the pricing procedure cannot fit in a single screen, you have to scroll down to see the other steps, shown in Figure 5.14.

FIGURE 5.14 Setting up a pricing procedure, part 2

Control

Reference Step Overview

Step	Co..	CTyp	Description	Fr.	To	Ma..	R..	Stat..	(	SuTot	Reqt	CalTy..	BasTy..	AccK.	Accruals
801	0	NRAB	Free goods			☐	☐	☐	X		59		29	ERS	
810	3	HD00	Freight			☑	☐	☐		4				ERF	
815	0	KF00	Freight			☐	☐	☐		4				ERF	
900	0		Net Value 2			☐	☐	☐		3					
910	0	UTXJ	Tax Jurisdict.Code	900		☐	☐	☐			84				
911	0	JR1	Tax Jur Code Level 1	900		☑	☐	☐							
912	0	JR2	Tax Jur Code Level 2	900		☑	☐	☐							
913	0	JR3	Tax Jur Code Level 3	900		☑	☐	☐							
914	0	JR4	Tax Jur Code Level 4	900		☑	☐	☐							
915	0	DIFF	Rounding Off			☐	☑	☐			13	16	4		
920	0		Total			☐	☐	☐		A		4			
940	0	VPRS	Cost			☐	☐	☑		B	4				
950	0		Profit Margin			☐	☐	☐				11			

Step   This represents the sequence in which the condition types will be accessed within the pricing procedure. Here you can assign first condition type at step 10, the second at step 20, and so on. It is advisable to use a spacing of 10 between steps in case you have to change the pricing procedure at a later date and then insert steps in between 10 and 20.

Counter   This represents a substep.

Condition Type   You must enter the condition type at each step. The system will read and compute each condition type in the sequence specified by the step number.

Description   If you have entered a condition type, then the description of the condition type automatically appears here. If you are defining a step for the subtotal, you can enter a meaningful description here (such as Gross Value).

From, To   These represent the basis of calculation for a step. For example, if the operation in step 30 is to be performed on the value appearing in line 20, then you specify From as 20. The From and To fields are also used in defining subtotals. Thus, if you want to compute the subtotal of all discounts, or all the tax conditions together, you can define a new step and enter the description of the subtotal in the Description column. For example, if you insert a subtotal at step 300 called Net Price and then specify that it will be the net of all values *from* step 101 *to* 299, the system will compute the subtotal, and it will appear at step 300 in the pricing procedure in the sales document.

Manual   When this box is selected, the condition value for the condition type is either provided manually by the user or is provided by a process external to SD such as costing.

Required   Selecting this box makes the condition mandatory. If SAP is not able to find a valid record for a condition type with the Req. check box selected, it issues an error message to the user that pricing is incomplete.

Statistical   Selecting this box makes the condition statistical. It will be calculated just like any normal condition, but the value will not impact or roll up to the total.

Print   This controls the printing of a condition line on printed outputs such as order confirmations and invoices. You can choose X to have condition lines printed at the item level, choose S to have condition lines printed at the total level, or choose to leave this field blank to skip the condition lines value being available for printing.

Subtotal   We have already discussed using subtotals in a pricing procedure. The Subtotal field is used to indicate the fields where the subtotal value is to be parked. Use this to store the condition amounts, condition rates, and subtotals values into Subtotal fields for use in further user-defined calculations or for use in reports. You can store the value into the fields KZWI1 to KZWI6 of structure KOMP or to internal auxiliary variables XWORKD to XWORKM. By default, SAP adds up the condition amounts, which are transferred to the same Subtotal field.

Requirement   This is a provision that attaches a routine before the value of a condition type is computed. It is like a prerequisite that has to be satisfied before you can proceed. If the requirement fails, the condition is not accessed. For example, requirement 2 in steps 11 through 110 tells SAP to access corresponding condition types only when the related sales line item in the sales document is relevant for pricing. If the sales-order line happens to be a free item, such as item category TANN, then SAP will not access PR00 for such line items.

Alternative Calculation Type   Use this field (shown in Figure 5.14 as CalType) when you want to apply your own calculation formula as an alternative to the standard condition technique. You can create a customer-specific formula as an alternate calculation type and assign it to the condition type in the pricing procedure.

Alternative Formula For Calculation Of Base Value   Use this field (shown in Figure 5.14 as BasType) when you want to change the calculation base value at the step. For example, for a condition type to compute a cash discount, the discount is to be applied on the net value (the amount less any taxes). A routine 2 is readily available to indicate this base value. Similarly, you can define your own custom routine, if required.

Accounting Key   Use this field (shown as AccK in Figure 5.14) for posting the condition type value to a revenue account in FI.

Accruals   Use the Accruals key (shown as Accru) to post the condition type value to an accrual or provision account in FI.

As you read the case study on maintaining the pricing procedure ("Galaxy Musical Instruments Configuration Analysis: Maintain Pricing Procedure"), please refer to Figures 5.13 and 5.14, and follow some of the key steps that we have defined.

CASE STUDY—GALAXY MUSICAL INSTRUMENTS CONFIGURATION ANALYSIS: MAINTAIN THE PRICING PROCEDURE

Based on the requirements discussed earlier, we've set up a new pricing procedure called ZGALAX for Galaxy Musical Instruments.

> Base price:

Step 11 has the condition PR00. We've added requirement 2 to make sure that only items relevant for pricing are picked up.

Step 100 is a subtotal field for Gross Price. This is the price before discounts are offered. We've designated this value to subtotal 1 (using the SubTo field). We can later pick up this value and use it in our reports, as required.

> Discounts:

At step 110 is our custom condition type ZGM1, defined earlier. We have already assigned a custom access sequence to it.

Step 111 uses condition type HI01. This enables us to offer a discount to our large customers linked by the customer hierarchy.

Step 300 captures the total discount. It is a summation of all the values from steps 101 to 299.

Step 800 is another subtotal to capture the net price. We use the standard alternative calculation type routine 2. We have also specified subtotal 2 field to populate this value.

> Freight:

Step 810 is the freight condition HD00. It is a header condition, based on the total weight of the order.

Step 815 is another freight condition, KF00, based on gross weight and at the item level.

> Tax:

Steps 910 to 914 are the tax conditions UTXJ and JR1 to JR4. We will discuss tax conditions later in the chapter.

Step 920 is a total value. We have specified this value in the subtotal A field.

Besides the pricing conditions, we also use some other conditions to capture cost (VPRS) and arrive at the profit margin for the sale.

Also note the entries in the different account keys we have specified for the price, discount, freight, and tax. We will then link them to different GL accounts in the account determination. (See Chapter 10, "Account Assignment and Revenue Recognition.")

Figure 5.15 gives you an idea of what this pricing procedure looks like in action. Imagine you are selling an acoustic guitar. The system computes the price for the product as $3,000. The customer qualifies for two discounts because of different promotional schemes running in parallel. Hence, it takes off $435 from the total. The system then adds freight, based on the total weight, to arrive at a total price of $2,665 for the customer.

FIGURE 5.15 Pricing in a sales order

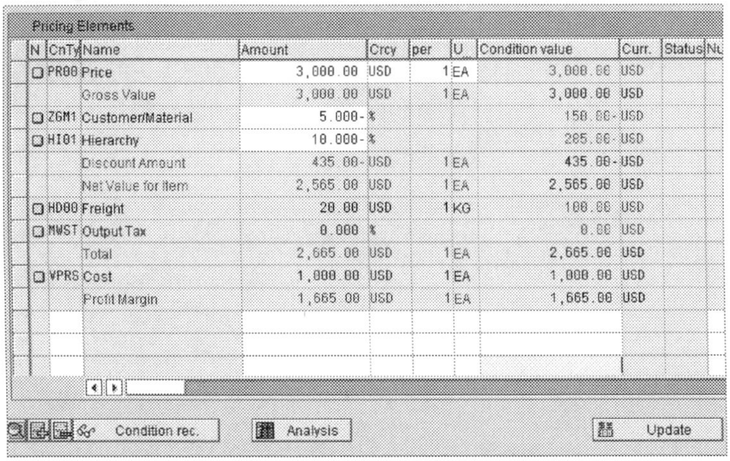

N	CnTy	Name	Amount	Crcy	per	U	Condition value	Curr.	Status	Nu
☐	PR00	Price	3,000.00	USD	1	EA	3,000.00	USD		
		Gross Value	3,000.00	USD	1	EA	3,000.00	USD		
☐	ZGM1	Customer/Material	5.000-	%			150.00-	USD		
☐	HI01	Hierarchy	10.000-	%			285.00-	USD		
		Discount Amount	435.00-	USD	1	EA	435.00-	USD		
		Net Value for Item	2,565.00	USD	1	EA	2,565.00	USD		
☐	HD00	Freight	20.00	USD	1	KG	100.00	USD		
☐	MWST	Output Tax	0.000	%			0.00	USD		
		Total	2,665.00	USD	1	EA	2,665.00	USD		
☐	VPRS	Cost	1,000.00	USD	1	EA	1,000.00	USD		
		Profit Margin	1,665.00	USD	1	EA	1,665.00	USD		

In a sales document, you can always study the pricing analysis log, which tells you how the system computed the total price. You can then drill down to study which condition types were accessed and what values were determined. Figure 5.16 shows you such a log for the acoustic guitar transaction just mentioned. You can drill down to each condition type and verify how the value was determined.

For example, if you click on condition type ZGM1, you will see further details as shown in Figure 5.17. The log tells you that discount ZGM1 was determined on the basis of access 30. The earlier accesses did not find any records. If you want to find the details of access 30, simply click it, and the details of the exact access appear on the right (Figure 5.18). The log reveals that the Sales Org (9090) + Customer Group (G1) was the key used and the value was 5 percent.

Finally, we captured the subtotals for this sales transaction to the database tables as subtotal fields and costs, as shown in Figure 5.19.

FIGURE 5.16 Pricing analysis

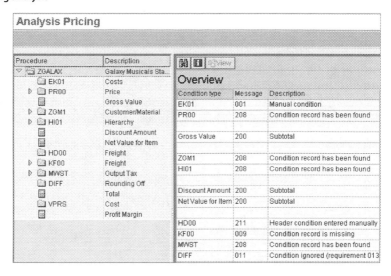

FIGURE 5.17 Pricing log at condition level

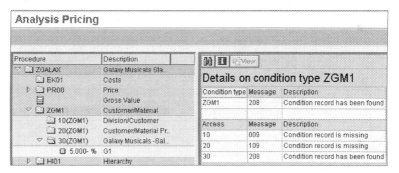

FIGURE 5.18 Pricing log at access sequence level

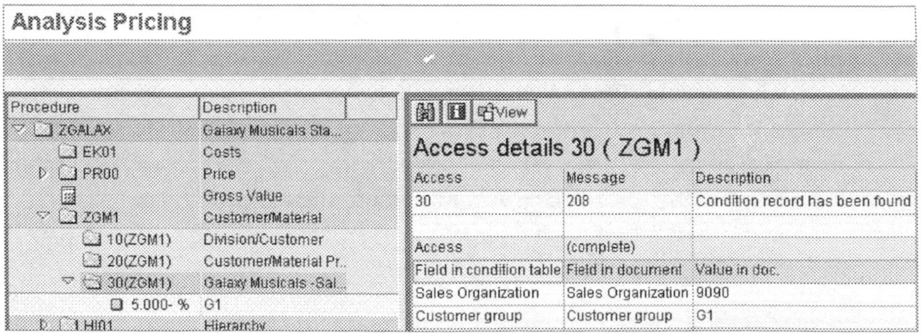

FIGURE 5.19 Condition subtotals in a database table

Data Browser: Table VBAP Select Entries

Cl.	Sales Doc.	Item	Material	Material ente
800	0000012192	10	000000000000001599	0000000000

Details

Group description	Cell Content
Pricing	X
Valuation Type	
Separate valuation	
Batch management	
Batch management	
Minimum delivery qty	0.000
Update group (stats)	
Cost	1,000.00
Subtotal 1	3,000.00
Subtotal 2	2,565.00
Subtotal 3	0.00
Subtotal 4	100.00
Subtotal 5	0.00
Subtotal 6	0.00

TIP   The standard system provides up to six fields to capture subtotal values. If you need more fields, refer to SAP Service Marketplace OSS note 155012 on the process of setting it up. OSS note 1022966 gives further information and clarification on the use of subtotal fields.

This completes the setup of a pricing procedure. At this stage, you may want to go back to Figure 5.1 to review the concepts discussed so far.

The pricing procedure is now ready for assignment!

Step 5: Assign the Pricing Procedure

The last step in the pricing setup is to define the determination rule to govern which pricing procedure will be used. The system determines the pricing procedure based on sales area, sales document type, and customer master record. You use the fields Customer Pricing Procedure and Document Pricing Procedure to control the determination.

Define the Document Pricing Procedure

Document Pricing Procedure (DoPP) is a one-character field that can be alphabetical or numeric. It serves as the link between a document and pricing. The menu path is as follows: IMG ➤ Sales And Distribution ➤ Basic Functions ➤ Pricing ➤

Pricing Control ➤ Define And Assign Pricing Procedures ➤ Define Document Pricing Procedure (OVKI).

You can use the standard options (Figure 5.20) or create a custom entry.

FIGURE 5.20 Defining a DoPP

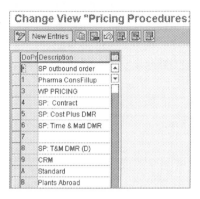

Assign the Document Pricing Procedure to Various Documents

Once defined, the DoPP has to be assigned to sales document types and billing document types. This allows you to have different pricing procedures assigned to different sales documents. For example, an inquiry or quotation may have a different pricing procedure than a regular sales order for the same customer.

The menu path is as follows: IMG ➤ Sales And Distribution ➤ Basic Functions ➤ Pricing ➤ Pricing Control ➤ Define And Assign Pricing Procedures ➤ Assign Document Pricing Procedure To Sales Document Types (OVKJ).

Figure 5.21 shows the assignment screen.

FIGURE 5.21 Assigning a DoPP

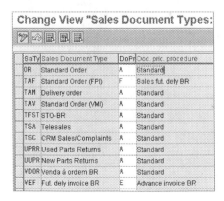

To assign a pricing procedure to billing documents, use the path IMG ➤ Sales And Distribution ➤ Basic Functions ➤ Pricing ➤ Pricing Control ➤ Define And Assign Pricing Procedures ➤ Assign Document Pricing Procedure To Billing Document Types (OVTP).

Define the Customer Pricing Procedure

The Customer Pricing Procedure (CuPP) field specifies which pricing procedure should be determined for a customer. It's a one-character field with a description that can be numeric or alphabetical. You can define a CuPP using transaction code OVKP or by following the menu path IMG ➤ Sales And Distribution ➤ Basic Functions ➤ Pricing ➤ Pricing Control ➤ Define And Assign Pricing Procedures ➤ Define Customer Pricing Procedure.

Figure 5.22 shows the customer pricing procedure screen. Once you've defined the customer pricing procedure, you assign this CuPP value to the respective customer master records. This field appears in the Sales view of the customer master. (Refer to the discussion on the customer master in Chapter 3, "Master Data in SD.")

FIGURE 5.22 Defining the CuPP

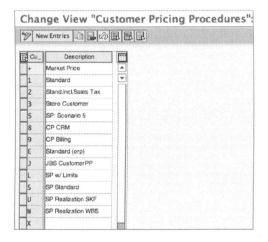

NOTE Always remember that the customer pricing procedure is picked up from the master data of the sold-to party.

Define the Pricing Procedure Determination

The last step is to link all the pieces together and define the determination. The transaction code is OVKK, and the menu path is IMG ➢ Sales And Distribution ➢ Basic Functions ➢ Pricing ➢ Pricing Control ➢ Define And Assign Pricing Procedures ➢ Define Pricing Procedure Determination.

As shown in Figure 5.23, you can set up a pricing procedure to be a combination of Sales Area + Customer Pricing Procedure + Document Pricing Procedure.

FIGURE 5.23 Pricing procedure determination

SOrg.	DChl	Dv	DoP	Cu	PriPr.	Pricing procedure	CTyp	Condition type
9090	97	99	A		1	ZGALAX Galaxy Musicals Standa	PR00	Price
9091	97	99	A		1	ZGALA2 Galaxy Musicals Test	PR00	Price

CASE STUDY—GALAXY MUSICAL INSTRUMENTS CONFIGURATION ANALYSIS: PRICING PROCEDURE DETERMINATION

Galaxy Musical Instruments needs to set up determination rules for its custom pricing procedures. We will be using different pricing procedures for the U.S. and Mexico sales areas.

We have used the document pricing procedure A (Standard), and we have assigned it to our sales document type OR.

We have used the customer pricing procedure 1 (Standard). We've updated this in the customer master records of our customers.

Next, we have set up the pricing procedure determination (as shown in Figure 5.23) so that the U.S. sales area gets ZGALAX, while the Mexico sales area uses ZGALA2.

Maintaining Price Records

After configuring the pricing procedure, you have to maintain the master data for the pricing condition records. The system will read the actual values of the pricing conditions from these master data records.

Follow this path: SAP Menu ➢ Logistics ➢ Sales And Distribution ➢ Master Data ➢ Conditions ➢ Select Using Condition Type ➢ Create (VK11).

When you specify the condition type, you will get a list of condition tables to choose from. This list depends on the access sequence that you have used for the condition type. Choose the table and proceed.

Each condition record contains its condition value and validity period. In addition to this, you can maintain other additional information in the record (Figure 5.24).

FIGURE 5.24 Maintaining price records

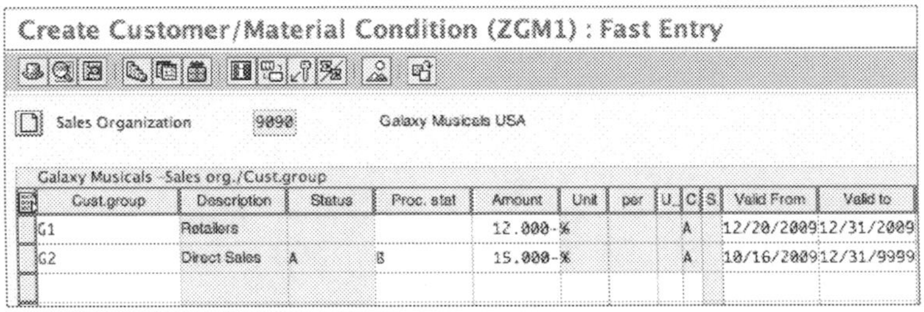
Create Customer/Material Condition (ZGM1) : Fast Entry
Sales Organization
9090
Galaxy Musicals USA
Galaxy Musicals -Sales org./Cust.group
Cust.group
Description
Status
Proc. stat
Amount
Unit
per
U
C
S
Valid From
Valid to
G1
Retailers
12.000-
%
A
12/20/2009
12/31/2009
G2
Direct Sales
A
B
15.000-
%
A
10/16/2009
12/31/9999

CASE STUDY—GALAXY MUSICAL INSTRUMENTS CONFIGURATION ANALYSIS: MAINTAIN PRICING RECORDS

After setting up the pricing procedure, we set up Galaxy Musical Instruments' condition records. Take the example of condition type ZGM1, as shown in Figure 5.24. We have specified the key (Sales Organization, Customer Group) and maintained the corresponding discount value. Note the use of validity periods in this example. For customer group G1, the special discount rates would apply for a holiday week in December. We can also set up the records in advance in the system so they take effect as per the validity period. In the record for customer group G2, the processing status (Proc. Stat field) has been set to B to block the condition. This enables you to get required approvals before the special discount is released to the customers.

In the pricing scenarios we explain later in the chapter, we will discuss some of the other information that can be updated using this transaction code.

> **TIP**   If you need to delete a condition record, it is always advisable to keep it in the database but set up a deletion indicator that marks the condition as inactive. Thus, you always have a log of the pricing record. Settings in V/06 control whether the record is to be deleted or flagged.
>
> Also note that you can check the change log for any condition record from the transaction to change the condition record (VK12) or display the condition record (VK13) using the menu path Environment ➢ Changes.

Other Key Settings in Pricing

In this section, we will discuss some of the other settings that influence how a pricing procedure works. We will cover some of the master data fields that are useful in the determination of pricing records. We'll also discuss the functionality of condition exclusion and how to set up pricing routines.

Maintain Price-Relevant Master Data Fields

Based on the requirements of your organization, you can use certain fields in the customer master and material master to determine the correct prices.

Define Price List Categories for Customers

Use the menu path IMG ➢ Sales And Distribution ➢ Basic Functions ➢ Pricing ➢ Maintain Price-Relevant Master Data Fields ➢ Define Price List Categories For Customers. You can set up a list of categories for the customers and then control the price determined in each price list category. To do this, create a two-character code and a brief description (Figure 5.25). In the customer master, this field appears in the Sales view. Choose the appropriate price list category from the drop-down menu. You can freely use this field to point to certain pricing condition records by using it as a key field in a condition table.

FIGURE 5.25 Defining a price list category

Define a Pricing Group for Customers

Follow this menu path: IMG ➤ Sales And Distribution ➤ Basic Functions ➤ Pricing ➤ Maintain Price-Relevant Master Data Fields ➤ Define Pricing Groups For Customers.

If you have to offer a special price to customers who meet certain grouping criteria, consider using a pricing group. It is another two-character field that can be used to determine prices.

Define Material Groups

Follow this menu path: IMG ➤ Sales And Distribution ➤ Basic Functions ➤ Pricing ➤ Maintain Price-Relevant Master Data Fields ➤ Define Material Groups.

Here you can define a two-character alphanumeric code and a brief description. You can use this grouping term in the material master and then determine the pricing condition on its basis.

This field appears in the material master in the Sales: Sales Org 2 view.

Condition Exclusion

In certain transactions, the system may determine records for more than one condition type in the pricing procedure. You saw this in Figure 5.15, where two discount condition types (HI01 and ZGM1) were applicable to the customer. As a result, the customer enjoyed a bigger discount. If you do not want this to happen, you can set up conditions or a group of conditions to be mutually exclusive. You can set up rules so that the system chooses one of them and ignores the other. This is called *condition exclusion*.

The following are the steps to set up a condition exclusion.

Define a Condition Exclusion Group

Follow this menu path: IMG ➤ Sales And Distribution ➤ Basic Functions ➤ Pricing ➤ Condition Exclusion ➤ Condition Exclusion For A Group Of Conditions ➤ Define Condition Exclusion Groups.

Condition exclusion groups house the condition types that are to be used in condition exclusion. To set up a group, click New Entries. Enter a four-character alphanumeric name and a meaningful description (Figure 5.26).

FIGURE 5.26 Defining a condition exclusion group

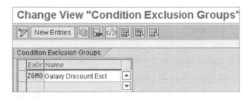

Assign a Condition Type to an Exclusion Group

In the next step, you assign condition types that are to be compared to the condition exclusion groups.

Follow this path: IMG ➢ Sales And Distribution ➢ Basic Functions ➢ Pricing ➢ Condition Exclusion ➢ Condition Exclusion For A Group Of Conditions ➢ Assign Condition Types To Exclusion Groups.

Click New Entries. In each row, enter the condition exclusion group and the condition that you want to include in that group. If more than one condition type is to be included in the same exclusion group, set up separate records for each (Figure 5.27). When you have finished, you will have exclusion groups each containing condition types to be compared.

FIGURE 5.27 Assigning a condition type to an exclusion group

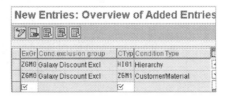

Maintain a Condition Exclusion for the Pricing Procedures

Before you can use a condition exclusion, you have to mark it relevant to your pricing procedure. Thus, if the same condition type (for example PR00) is used in several pricing procedures, you can still use it in a condition exclusion in a certain procedure without disturbing the others.

Use this menu path: IMG ➢ Sales And Distribution ➢ Basic Functions ➢ Pricing ➢ Condition Exclusion ➢ Condition Exclusion For A Group Of Conditions ➢ Maintain Condition Exclusion For Pricing Procedures.

From the list of pricing procedures, select the one to be activated, and click the Exclusion option in the left window. You can now set up the condition exclusion procedure in the right window (Figure 5.28).

FIGURE 5.28 Maintaining a condition exclusion for a pricing procedure

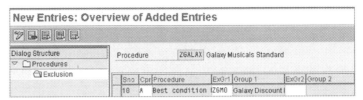

At each step, you can specify the condition exclusion groups to be compared and the rule for comparison. In the Condition Exclusion Procedure (CPr) field, choose from the list of rules offered in Figure 5.29. The options are as follows.

FIGURE 5.29 Rules for a condition exclusion

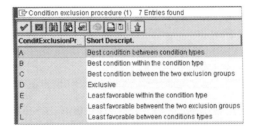

Choose favorable condition between condition types (options A and L)

Within a group, select the most favorable condition type *within* the group. Choose option A if you need the best value or option L for the least value. (If a group has two condition types, PR00 and ZPR0 and if PR00 has value $100, and ZPR0 has $200, you have to choose the most favorable. If the rule is A, ZPR0 will be retained. If you opt for L, PR00 will be retained.)

Choose favorable condition within the condition type (options B and E)

Select the most favorable (specify either the best with option B or the least with option E) condition record for a condition type, when more than one record has been determined. (If PR00 has two records found, choose the better of the two.) The access sequence should have its Exclusion indicator turned off so that it keeps on reading all records.

Choose favorable condition between two exclusion groups (options C and F)
Compare and select the more favorable value between two condition exclusion *groups*.
(Add group A and group B, compare the totals, and choose the more favorable.)
Choose option C if you want the best value or option F for the least value.

Exclusive (D)   If any one condition type from a group A has been selected, ignore
all the condition types from group B.

CASE STUDY—GALAXY MUSICAL INSTRUMENTS CONFIGURATION ANALYSIS: CONDITION EXCLUSION

There are two discount conditions in the pricing procedure ZGALAX. As per a new
policy, Galaxy decided to discontinue multiple discounts to a customer. Hence, we set
up a condition exclusion between the two discount condition types (HI01 and ZGM1).

We started by setting up condition exclusion group ZGM0. Next, we assigned both HI01
and ZGM1 to the group ZGM0. Finally, we selected our pricing procedure, ZGALAX, and
set up rule A (best condition between condition types). We specified the exclusion
group ZGM0 here.

As a result, the system visits the exclusion group, checks the contents of the two condition types in that group, compares the values, determines the best discount, and
applies it to the pricing procedure, while ignoring the other.

Now, if you carry out the same transaction of selling an acoustic guitar, you will see
a different price (Figure 5.30) because HI01, with a 10% discount, has been chosen
over ZGM1, which offered 5%. Both condition types are still displayed in the pricing procedure, but only one is applied.

FIGURE 5.30 Sales order with condition exclusion

N	CnTy	Name	Amount	Crcy	per	U	Condition value	Curr.	Status
☐	PR00	Price	3,000.00	USD	1	EA	3,000.00	USD	
		Gross Value	3,000.00	USD	1	EA	3,000.00	USD	
△	ZGM1	Customer/Material	5.000-	%			150.00-	USD	
☐	HI01	Hierarchy	10.000-	%			300.00-	USD	
		Discount Amount	300.00-	USD	1	EA	300.00-	USD	
		Net Value for Item	2,700.00	USD	1	EA	2,700.00	USD	
☐	HD00	Freight	20.00	USD	1	KG	100.00	USD	
☐	MWST	Output Tax	0.000	%			0.00	USD	
		Total	2,800.00	USD	1	EA	2,800.00	USD	
☐	VPRS	Cost	1,000.00	USD	1	EA	1,000.00	USD	
		Profit Margin	1,800.00	USD	1	EA	1,800.00	USD	

Pricing Requirements and Formulae

During the discussion of setting up a pricing procedure, we came across certain types of routines (or program codes) that are attached to the procedure at various stages. You will also come across other routines used in other areas of Sales and Distribution.

You can check and configure these routines centrally using the menu path IMG ➢ Sales And Distribution ➢ System Modifications ➢ Routines ➢ Define Formulas For Pricing (VOFM).

The top-level menu will have the following:

Requirements   We have covered the use of requirements in pricing. Similarly, there are requirement routines in other areas such as output determination, material determination, and so on. The setting basically checks whether certain prerequisites are met before a function can be performed.

Formula   This setting is used in pricing to define how to do a calculation as per a custom formula. The alternative condition base value and alternative condition base type are also types of formulae.

Copying Requirements   This routine checks certain prerequisites before copying data.

In subsequent chapters—specifically, Chapter 7, "Sales," as well as Chapter 8, "Shipping and Transportation," and Chapter 9, "Billing"—we will cover how data is transferred between orders and deliveries and billing documents.

Data Transfer   During copying, the actual data transferred between documents can be controlled by data transfer routines.

Each menu has further classification, based on usage in various functionalities such as pricing, output, account determination, and so on. For example, if you choose Requirements ➢ Pricing, you will see a list of routine numbers used in pricing, along with brief description (Figure 5.31). Select a routine you want to study. The Source Text button on the top will take you to the code in the routine. The Documentation option will give you some detailed documentation on the content and applicability of the routine.

FIGURE 5.31 Maintain: Requirements Pricing screen

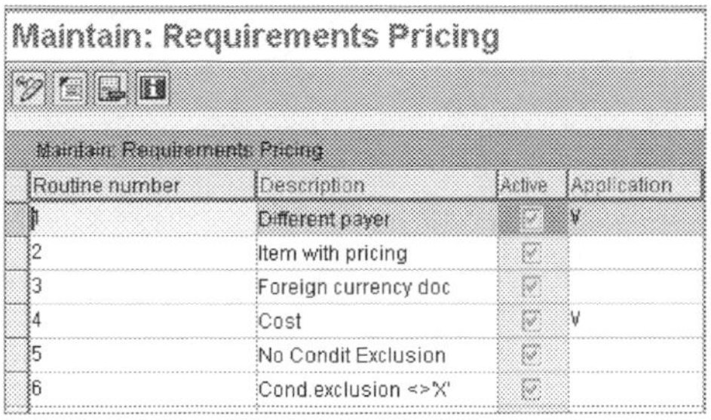

Maintain: Requirements Pricing

Maintain: Requirements Pricing			
Routine number	Description	Active	Application
1	Different payer	☑	V
2	Item with pricing	☑	
3	Foreign currency doc	☑	
4	Cost	☑	V
5	No Condit Exclusion	☑	
6	Cond.exclusion <>'X'	☑	

To define a custom routine, you can copy data from a standard routine and make the requisite changes. The number range for custom routines is from 601 to 999. It is a recommended best practice to document the number of the reference routine from which you cloned your custom routine.

TIP   It is always desirable to have an ABAP expert on hand to help you with any code change! You can also refer to SAP Service Marketplace OSS note 156230, which offers guidelines for writing custom pricing routines. OSS note 381348 answers some frequently asked questions and points to other related notes.

Pricing Scenarios and Notes

So far, you have seen how to configure a simple pricing procedure. You have also seen the various fields and settings that you can control. In real-world situations, pricing scenarios can be varied and complex. We'll discuss some of these scenarios and business requirements here. We will also cover how you can implement the various concepts and settings that you have studied so far to meet these pricing scenarios.

Use of Header Conditions and Group Conditions

You can enter pricing conditions at the header level (applicable to all the line items in the order) or at the item level (specific to one item).

Conditions that are applied at the header level are automatically distributed to the items. In case of a header condition with a fixed amount (calculation type B), there can be two kinds of requirements: applied to all line items equally or divided proportionately:

▶ If the header condition should be applied to all line items, use condition type RB00. This condition type has been specified as a header condition, allowing manual entries.

▶ If the header condition should be divided proportionately over the line items, use the concept of group conditions. Refer to condition type HB00. It has been flagged as a group condition (Figure 5.32). This automatically divides the amount proportionately over line items, based on the net value of each line.

FIGURE 5.32 Group condition

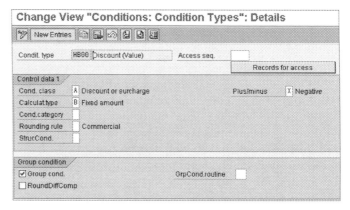

Let's look at a sample order that has three items with same unit price:

▶ *Item 10*: 20 pieces

▶ *Item 20*: 10 pieces

▶ *Item 30*: 20 pieces

Applying header condition RB00 = $100, $100 will be added to each of the three line items. Therefore, $300 will be added to the total.

Applying header condition HB00 = $100, the amount is divided proportionately as $40, $20, and $40, respectively, so that only $100 will be added to the total.

Rounding differences can occur during the distribution of absolute amounts. The system automatically evens these out by proposing the remainder to the largest item so that the value in the header is identical to the total of the values in the items.

Use of Cumulating Conditions

Some products have a complex structure in the sales order, with subitems arranged in multilevels. The pricing requirement may require computing the net value of an item and all the subitems belonging to it.

In such cases, consider the condition type KUMU. It can aggregate the net values of all subitems and add them up at the parent item level. In the definition of the cumulating condition (V/06), the StrucCond field (as shown earlier in Figure 5.8) comes into play.

Use of Condition Supplements

In some scenarios, you may want to apply a certain set of supplementary conditions (for example, discounts), whenever a certain condition (for example, a price) has been determined. In such cases, you can use condition supplements.

Suppose you want to apply discounts RB00 and RA00 every time you use the pricing condition PR00. First, when you define the condition type PR00 (in V/06), you specify the condition supplement pricing procedure PR0000 on the Master Data tab (Figure 5.9).

This pricing procedure lists the supplementary condition types (RA00, RB00) that you want to apply along with PR00.

To maintain the condition records for PR00 and the condition supplement, use VK11 (Figure 5.33). From the overview screen, select Goto ➤ Condition Supplement to set up the condition records.

When PR00 is determined in a pricing procedure, the system will also check the supplementary pricing procedure and pick up the discounts defined there. As shown in Figure 5.34, the order has picked up all the conditions we had maintained along with PR00. The pricing analysis too explains the fact that these conditions (such as RB00) are in fact condition supplements (Figure 5.35).

FIGURE 5.33 Setting up condition supplement condition records

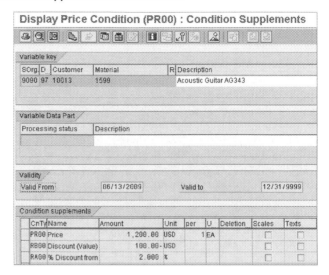

FIGURE 5.34 Sales order using condition supplement

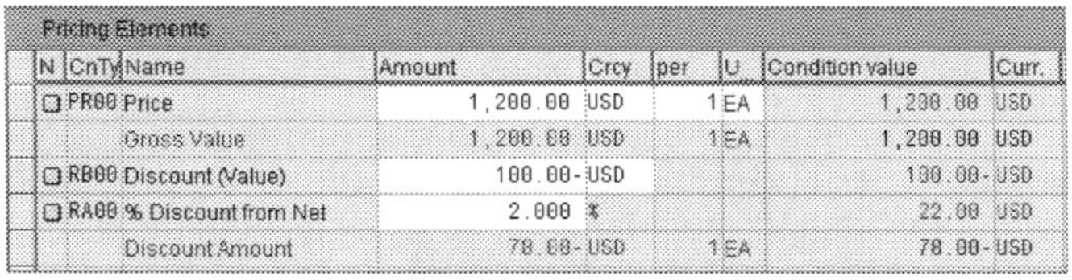

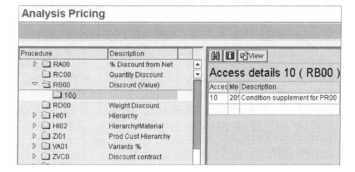

FIGURE 5.35 Pricing analysis log for condition supplement

Use of a Cost Condition

One of the common pricing requirements is to have the cost of the product added to the pricing procedure. This enables you to compute the profit margin on the sale.

The system provides condition type VPRS for this. It is defined by condition category G (Cost). This condition picks up the value from the valuation segment in the material master. You can control this further by opting to use condition category S (to pick up the standard cost) or T (to pick up the moving average cost).

The cost is captured in a subtotal B in the standard pricing procedure. It is passed to the database table VBAP as the cost (WAVWR). Further, you can use formula 11 to compute the profit margin by subtracting the cost (subtotal B) from the net value (subtotal 2). Refer to Figure 5.14, step 950, where you are computing the profit margin using formula 11.

In a sales order costing scenario, you can transfer the cost to the pricing procedure by using condition type EK01. If you want it at a statistical level, choose EK02. These conditions are in condition category C (Costing).

Free Goods

It's a common business requirement to offer free goods as an incentive to customers. There can be two scenarios:

Inclusive The customer pays for only a part of the goods he has ordered. For example, the customer buys 10 music CDs for the price of 8. (In other words, if a customer buys 10, he gets 2 of them free, included in the order quantity).

Exclusive The customer orders a certain quantity and gets additional items free. For example, the customer buys 10 music CDs and gets 2 extra for free. (In other words, if a customer buys 10, she gets 2 more, hence receiving a total of 12 CDs.)

You can map either case in SAP using the free goods functionality. Both scenarios rely on the same condition technique, following the five-step approach used for pricing procedures. However, the transaction codes and menu paths are different, as shown in Table 5.1.

TABLE 5.1   Configuring Free Goods

Menu Path	Transaction Code	Action
IMG ➤ Sales And Distribution ➤ Basic Functions ➤ Free Goods ➤ Condition Technique For Free Goods ➤ Maintain Condition Tables	V/N2	Create a condition table by selecting fields from the field catalog. Save and generate the table. (Similar to V/03 of pricing.)
IMG ➤ Sales And Distribution ➤ Basic Functions ➤ Free Goods ➤ Condition Technique For Free Goods ➤ Maintain Access Sequence	V/N1	Create an access sequence by adding condition tables in the required order. Save and generate the access sequence. (Similar to V/07.)
IMG ➤ Sales And Distribution ➤ Basic Functions ➤ Free Goods ➤ Condition Technique For Free Goods ➤ Maintain Condition Types	V/N4	Define a condition type. Assign an access sequence to it. (Similar to V/06.)
IMG ➤ Sales And Distribution ➤ Basic Functions ➤ Free Goods ➤ Condition Technique For Free Goods ➤ Maintain Pricing Procedure	V/N5	Define a pricing procedure. Add condition types in the desired sequence. (Similar to V/08.)
IMG ➤ Sales And Distribution ➤ Basic Functions ➤ Free Goods ➤ Condition Technique For Free Goods ➤ Assign Pricing Procedure	V/N6	Assign a pricing procedure for a combination of sales area, document pricing procedure, and customer pricing procedure. (Similar to OVKK.)

The transaction to create free goods condition records is VBN1. Here, you can specify whether an incentive is inclusive or exclusive. As shown in Figure 5.36, you can choose from three options. In the case of inclusive goods, you can choose option 1 (an inclusive rebate with item generation) if you want a separate line item to be generated for the free goods. The other alternative is option 3 (an inclusive rebate without item generation). Option 2 is for exclusive free goods.

FIGURE 5.36 Free goods options

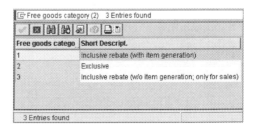

Here are the standard settings you can use:

- ► Condition tables:
    - ≫ *010*: Customer/Material
    - ≫ *017*: Campaign ID/Material
- ► Access sequences:
    - ≫ *NA00*: Free Goods (SD)
- ► Condition types:
    - ≫ *NA00*: Free Goods
- ► Pricing procedure:
    - ≫ *NA0001*: Free Goods (SD)

Use of Condition Updates

Some organizations offer special prices or discounts limited to the first few orders or up to a limited quantity, weight, volume, or certain budget. Any order that comes in after this limit is reached should not qualify for the pricing condition.

To map this requirement, make sure that the condition type you are using has Condition Update marked on in the settings in V/06. In such cases, the system keeps track of all orders or billing documents that have availed of this special price. Once the limit is reached, the condition is no longer applied to subsequent documents.

When you maintain the record using VK11, you can specify the limits (Figure 5.37). Galaxy Musical Instruments has set such a limit using the special pricing condition ZGMP. In this case, the first two orders for a particular customer will get the benefit of the special price.

At any point you can check the cumulative value of orders/weight/volume sold until date. On the VK11 overview screen, select Extras ➤ Cumulative Values.

FIGURE 5.37 Setting limits for pricing conditions

Display (Price): Additional Sales Data ZGMP

Variable key

SOrg	D	Customer	Material	R	Description
9090	97	10020	1625		Musical Drums 123

Validity

Valid From	06/13/2009	Valid to	12/31/9999

Assignments

Promotion	
Sales deal	

Assignments for retail promotion

Promotion	

Limits for pricing

Max condition value	0.00	USD
Max.number.of.orders	2	
Max.cond.base value	0	EA

Use of Pricing Scales

It is a common scenario to have a tiered pricing structure. To map these require-ments, you can set up scales in pricing conditions. Earlier in this chapter, in our discussion of V/06, we described the fields related to scales.

Galaxy Musical Instruments has set up pricing based on scales for one of its prod-ucts. For an order quantity up to four pieces, the price is $899. When five to nine pieces are ordered, the price is $850, and so on.

To maintain scales in pricing records, use VK11. On the overview screen, use the path Goto ➢ Scales. Then you can set up the pricing scales as required. Refer to Figure 5.38 for details.

FIGURE 5.38 Pricing scales

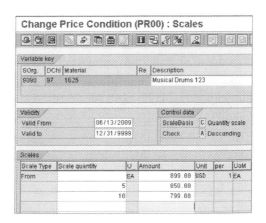

Change Price Condition (PR00) : Scales

Variable key

SOrg	DChl	Material	Re	Description
9090	97	1625		Musical Drums 123

Validity

Valid From	06/13/2009
Valid to	12/31/9999

Control data

ScaleBasis	C	Quantity scale
Check	A	Descending

Scales

Scale Type	Scale quantity	U	Amount	Unit	per	UoM
From		EA	899.00	USD	1	EA
	5		850.00			
	10		799.00			

Update Pricing

During a sales process, you create delivery and billing documents with reference to sales documents. You can also create new sales documents with reference to old orders. Sometimes the billing document is created days or months after the order was originally placed. During this time, the prices may have changed. Some organizations retain the old prices unchanged, whereas others need to carry out fresh pricing to pick up the latest prices. Others may choose to retain some price condition types and redetermine others, such as tax conditions. The functionality of Update Pricing caters to different business needs.

In Chapters 7 and 9, we will use this functionality in copy controls.

The users can also update pricing during sales order processing via VA01 or VA02. They can carry out fresh pricing using the Update Prices option in the Conditions tab. Sales orders can also be mass-updated for pricing via VA05.

The following are the some of the update rules you can choose from, as shown in Figure 5.39.

FIGURE 5.39 Pricing Update options

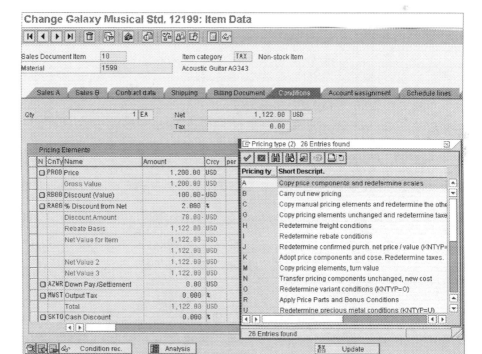

A: Copy Pricing Components And Redetermine Scales   The system does not determine any new condition types; it redetermines the scale prices for changed delivery quantities.

B: Carry Out New Pricing   The system carries out a completely new pricing (manually entered pricing elements are not copied from the reference document). It redetermines the taxes.

C: Copy Manual Pricing Elements And Redetermine The Others   The system carries out a new pricing, copies the manually entered pricing elements, and redetermines the taxes.

D: Copy Pricing Elements Unchanged   The system copies the pricing elements unchanged with automatically determined or manually entered surcharges and discounts from the reference document.

G: Copy Pricing Elements Unchanged And Redetermine Taxes   The system redetermines the following condition types: taxes (condition class D), rebates (condition class C), intercompany billing conditions (condition category I), invoice list conditions (condition category R), condition types with condition category L, cost conditions (condition category G), and cash discount conditions (condition category E).

H: Redetermine Freight Conditions   The system redetermines the following condition types: freight conditions (condition categories B and F) and condition types with condition category L.

As you can see, the condition categories can play a key role in controlling which conditions are copied over or redetermined.

TIP   Refer to SAP Service Marketplace OSS note 24832 on how the different condition types are processed and redetermined by SAP when pricing is updated.

Tax Determination

Any sales transaction has to take into account the taxes applicable. The key factors that determine taxes are the location of the delivery plant, the country and region of the customer, and the material and customer tax classifications. There is a lot of variation in tax laws and schema across the world. Therefore, it is important to document the exact requirements during business blueprinting, while working with your finance team.

Tax determination, like pricing, follows the condition technique. A tax condition appears in the pricing procedure as a condition type along with an account key, just like any other condition. This account key further maintains the link between SD and FI for tax posting to a tax GL account. Once customizing is done, you assign the tax classifications to customer and material master records. You set up the tax rates in the condition tables.

When a user creates a sales document, SAP reads the following:

- ▶ Customer tax eligibility from the customer master
- ▶ Material tax relevance from the material master
- ▶ Departure country and location from the plant used in the sales document at the item level
- ▶ Destination country and location from the ship-to party record

SAP then determines the applicable tax percentage and tax code from the master records and applies this percentage to the sales document.

During billing creation, SAP reads the pricing information from the sales document and service rendered date (Post Goods Issue date) from the delivery document and redetermines the applicable tax, based on settings. During the accounting posting of this billing document, the tax code and the account key determine the GL account to which the tax posting can be made.

Setting Up the Tax Determination

Following are the steps in the configuration of tax in SAP:

Step 1: Define Tax Determination Rules

The menu path is as follows: IMG ➤ Sales And Distribution ➤ Basic Functions ➤ Taxes ➤ Define Tax Determination Rules (transaction OVK1).

In this setting, you assign a tax category by country. Maintain the settings only for those countries that are relevant to your business scenario. This category is the pricing condition type that will be used for taxes in your pricing procedure. Only those condition types classified as tax (in the condition class) can be used here. Some countries can have more than one tax category assigned. In this case, you can use the sequence field.

Check whether the country appears in the list. To do this, click New Entries, and enter the country code and tax category, along with the access sequence number (Figure 5.40).

FIGURE 5.40 Assigning the tax category to a country

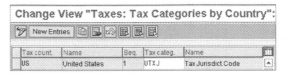

Step 2: Define Regional Codes

Some countries have regional taxes. Hence, it is necessary to define all the counties or cities in a country. Use this path: IMG ➢ Sales And Distribution ➢ Basic Functions ➢ Taxes ➢ Define Regional Codes ➢ Define County Codes. Specify the Country and Region entries, and then divide them into county codes as applicable (Figure 5.41).

FIGURE 5.41 Defining regions

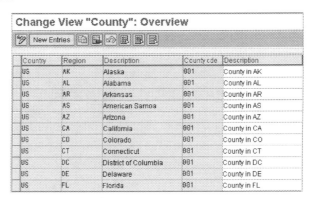

If you need to set up taxes at a city level, you can specify Country and Region and then divide them into city codes as applicable. To do this, the path is IMG ➢ Sales

And Distribution ➤ Basic Functions ➤ Taxes ➤ Define Regional Codes ➤ Define City Codes.

Step 3: Assign Delivering Plants for Tax Determination

Since the delivering plant determines the source address, it is important to set up the address details.

Follow the path IMG ➤ Sales And Distribution ➤ Basic Functions ➤ Taxes ➤ Assign Delivering Plants For Tax Determination (OX10).

Double-click the chosen plant. Specify the complete address, including the country, region, county code, city code, and jurisdiction code, as required. We covered this when we defined plants in Chapter 2, "Enterprise Structure."

Step 4: Master Data Classification

You next have to set up customers and materials so that the system determines the appropriate tax in a transaction. You can group your customers and materials into groups and control the tax by each group. Follow the path IMG ➤ Sales And Distribution ➤ Basic Functions ➤ Taxes ➤ Define Tax Relevancy Of Master Records ➤ Customer Taxes (OVK3).

For material taxes, follow IMG ➤ Sales And Distribution ➤ Basic Functions ➤ Taxes ➤ Define Tax Relevancy Of Master Records ➤ Material Taxes (OVK4).

In either case, specify the tax condition type (tax category), and define the tax classification codes (Figures 5.42 and 5.43). For example, materials in your product range could have no tax, half tax, or full tax. In this case, you would set up three material tax-classification codes and maintain them in the material master.

FIGURE 5.42 Defining the customer tax classification codes

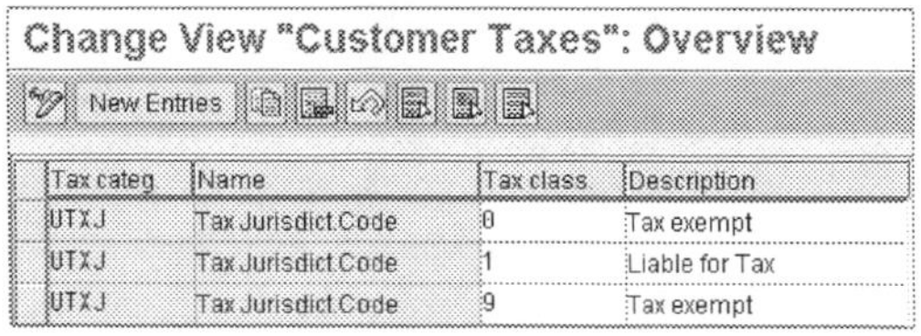

Tax categ	Name	Tax class	Description
UTXJ	Tax Jurisdict Code	0	Tax exempt
UTXJ	Tax Jurisdict Code	1	Liable for Tax
UTXJ	Tax Jurisdict Code	9	Tax exempt

FIGURE 5.43 Defining the material tax classification codes

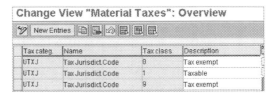

When you maintain the customer master data, you enter the tax classification on the Billing Document tab in the Sales Area Data section. As shown in Figure 5.44, for customer 10028, we have entered tax classification 1 (taxable). Note that the tax category (UTXJ) that appears on this screen is controlled by the tax determination rule maintained for the country (U.S.).

In the material master (using MM01 or MM02), you enter the tax classification on the Sales: Sales Org 1 tab. As shown in Figure 5.45, we have classified the material 1628 as taxable.

FIGURE 5.44 Maintaining the customer tax classification in the customer master

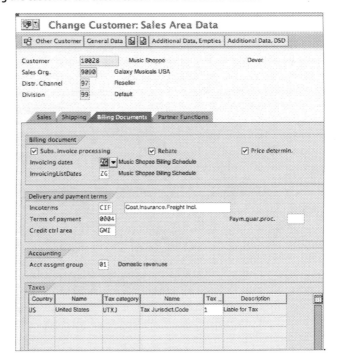

FIGURE 5.45 Maintaining the material tax classification in the material master

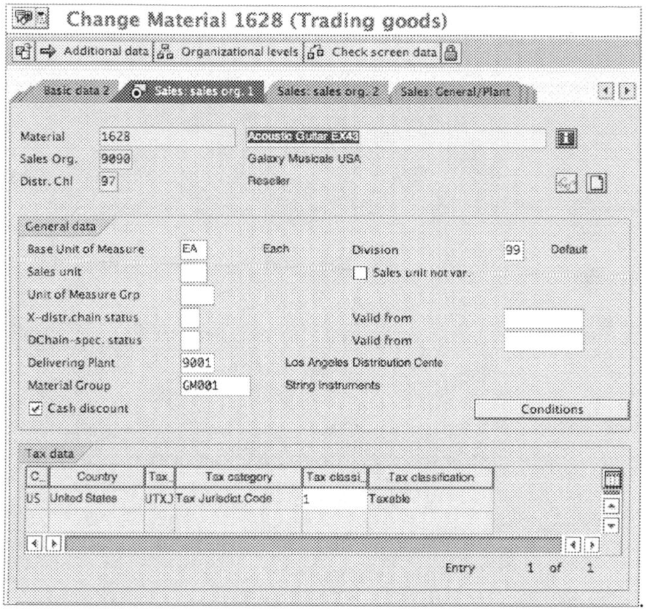

Step 5: Maintain Sales Tax Identification Number Determination

In this step, you can specify a rule to determine the VAT registration number in a sales order or billing document. The path is IMG ➤ Sales And Distribution ➤ Basic Functions ➤ Taxes ➤ Maintain Sales Tax Identification Number Determination.

Leaving the Tax Number field blank leads you to a default priority rule. You can specify other rules, such as A (determined from the sold-to party) or B (determined from the payer).

Step 6: Maintain Tax Codes

This is a setting in the FI domain. Always set up tax codes in consultation with your FI team.

Tax codes represent a tax category. You can define tax rate calculation rules for each tax code using this path: IMG ➤ Financial Accounting ➤ Financial Accounting Global Settings ➤ Tax On Sales/Purchases ➤ Calculation ➤ Define Tax Codes For Sales And Purchases (FTXP).

For a combination of country, tax code, and jurisdiction code, you can specify the tax percentage rate for each tax type.

Figure 5.46 shows that we are maintaining tax rates for the tax code S1 for the United States. In this example, we're showing the jurisdiction code for Colorado. We've set the sales tax at 3%.

Step 7: Maintain Tax Condition Records

You use the transaction VK11 to set up tax records, just like any other pricing record. Besides the tax rate, you also specify the tax code in the condition record.

Figure 5.47 shows the example with condition type UTXJ. You can set up a condition record for a combination of country, customer tax classification, and material tax classification. In this case, for country US, customer tax classification 1 (taxable customer), material tax classification 1 (taxable material), we have maintained the tax code as S1. The system then uses this tax code to determine the exact tax rates.

Note that we have not maintained any tax rate in the Amount field. The reason is that the exact tax rates will be picked up from tax code S1, based on the rates set up in the previous step (FTXP).

FIGURE 5.46 Maintaining tax codes

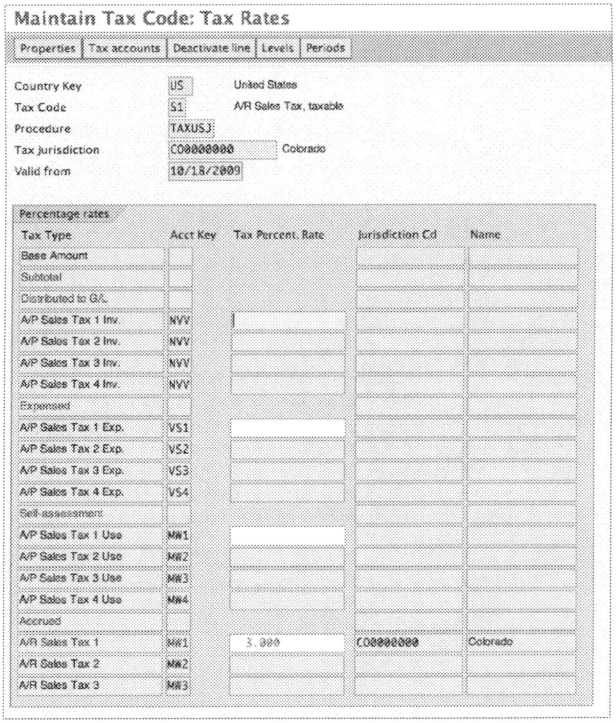

FIGURE 5.47 Maintaining the tax condition record

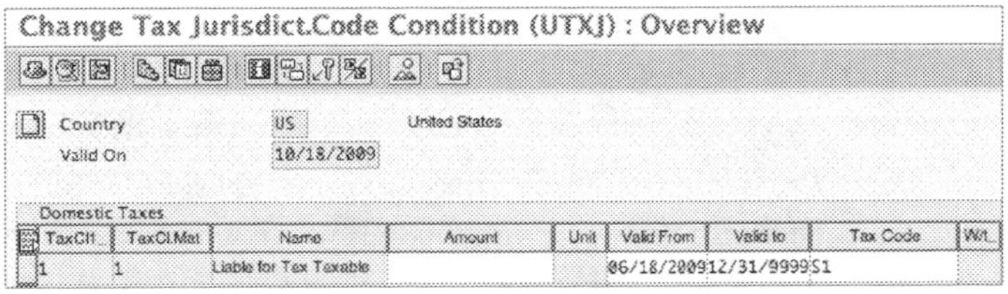

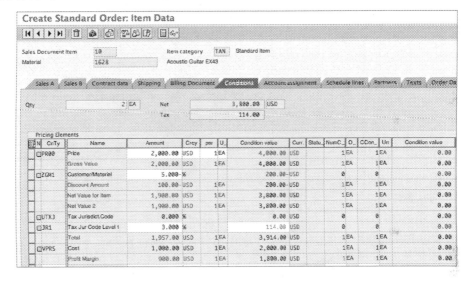

During pricing, the system picks up the tax rate and calculates the tax amount. Figure 5.48 displays the tax amount below the Net value. The value is also stored in the VBAP table in the field MWSBP.

FIGURE 5.48 Tax amount on the conditions screen in the sales order

The tax determination case study ("Galaxy Musical Instruments Configuration Analysis: Tax Determination") puts Figures 5.46 through 5.48 in a practical context.

CASE STUDY—GALAXY MUSICAL INSTRUMENTS CONFIGURATION ANALYSIS: TAX DETERMINATION

Galaxy Musical Instruments requires a tax determination based on jurisdiction codes for the United States. Therefore, in the pricing procedure, we added the conditions UTXJ, JR1, JR2, JR3, and JR4 for the various levels of tax jurisdiction. We also ensured that the tax determination rule for the United States points to UTXJ.

We have maintained the jurisdiction codes along with addresses in the customer master records. We have also maintained them in our plant address.

We have maintained tax classification in the customer and material master records.

Consider the sale of product 1628 (a guitar) to customer 10028, who is based in Denver, Colorado. The customer and material tax classification are both set up as 1 (taxable), indicating that the transaction is liable for tax calculation. The condition record for UTXJ (Figure 5.47) points to the tax code S1.

In consultation with the FI team, we've set up the tax code S1, showing a tax rate of 3% (Figure 5.46).

In the sales order, the system applies the tax and computes the amount, which is $114 (Figure 5.48).

Summary

Pricing and taxes are two of the most important areas in the SD application. In this chapter, we covered the steps to set up pricing, including how to use the condition technique to set up and determine pricing procedures. Then we discussed how to apply the concepts presented to some pricing-related requirements. We also discussed the basic concepts of tax determination and setup in this chapter.

In the next chapter, we will study availability check, transfer of requirements, and backorders.

Availability Check, Transfer of Requirements, and Backorders

P romising accurate and reliable dates for delivery to your customers is a key element of the order fulfillment process in today's competitive environment. In the SAP ERP software, the availability check functionality provides this accuracy and reliability. In this chapter, we will discuss the availability check functionality in detail including its relationship to transfer of requirements, backorder processing and order rescheduling. During these discussions, we will also walk you through the required customization settings for these functions and, as always, provide Galaxy Musical Instruments case studies to further clarify the topics.

Meaning and Relationship

The *schedule line* in a sales order contains information about the quantities of a material ordered by the customer and the corresponding delivery date requested by the customer for delivering the material. In the SAP ERP world, the delivery date quoted by the customer is called the *customer-requested delivery date*. When taken together with the delivery quantity requested by customer for such a date, the term used is *material requirement*. Material requirement–related information is vital to the MRP department's ability to make production/procurement-related decisions. In the SAP system, this information is transferred to MRP using the *transfer of requirements* (TOR). You can transfer requirements either individually or collectively. An *individual requirement* transfers the material demand for each schedule line to MRP, whereas a *collective requirement* transfers summarized data on a daily or weekly basis to MRP. Accordingly, you can trace back an individual requirement to the order from which it originated, while the same is not possible in a collective requirement.

An *availability check* (AC), on the other hand, is the functionality that helps you confirm the schedule line in an order and thus facilitate the customer's order confirmation/promise process. When carried out in the context of a sales order, the AC process checks the stock availability for the material in the delivering plant/ warehouse. If sufficient quantities are available to meet the customer-requested delivery date, the AC then confirms the customer-requested delivery date on the schedule line. In situations where the requested delivery date cannot be met because of a shortage of stock, the AC is also capable of proposing a future date when the delivery quantities can be confirmed for an order. While calculating, the availability check also considers various lead times such as procurement/production lead time, plant/warehouse processing time (including aspects such as pick/pack, load/unload, transportation planning time, and goods issue/receipt time), and shipment transit time. This helps you make accurate and reliable calculations about the delivery dates that you can promise to the customer. This also provides a visibility into manufacturing/procurement capacity, warehouse processing capacity, and transportation capacity.

The TOR functionality is a prerequisite for carrying out the availability check. You can configure TOR to work without an availability check but not the other way around. This is really beneficial in scenarios where you don't want the availability check to happen for the material but want the requirement to be transferred to MRP for production/procurement decision making. There is no hard-and-fast rule for what materials should be included for both the availability check and the transfer of requirements, what should be included only for the transfer of requirements, or what materials should be excluded from both the transfer of requirements and the availability check. The decision depends upon the business requirements and the way MRP strategies are used to handle such requirements. Therefore, it is always best that you work closely with your PP and MM counterparts when configuring the transfer of requirements and the availability check in the SAP ERP software. A few common examples of where the availability check is generally switched off are KANBAN-relevant materials, bulk materials, slow-moving inventory materials, and so on, where you control the procurement/production-related decisions using other planning strategies and methods available in the MM/PP application of the SAP ERP software.

Types of Availability Check

There are three types of availability checks:

- ► Check against available-to-promise quantities
- ► Check against product allocation
- ► Check against planning

Check Based on Available-to-Promise Quantities

Here the check is performed against available-to-promise (ATP) quantities. This check considers the currently available stock and also the stock that will be available in the near future for availability check calculations. In equation form, this can be depicted as follows:

Check against ATP = Available stock + Future receipts – Future issues

where

> ▸ *Available stock* refers to the stock available in hand at the delivering plant/warehouse.

> ▸ *Future receipts* represent all the inward movement of goods that can add stock in the delivering plant/warehouse. Purchase order, production order and stock transfer order are a few examples of documents that trigger inward movement of stock.

> ▸ *Future issues* are all the outward movement of goods that can lead to the consumption of stock from the delivering plant/warehouse. Sales orders, deliveries, stock transfer orders, and assembly orders are a few examples of documents that trigger outward movement of stock. Production order, assembly order, and stock transfer order play dual roles, because they are responsible for the addition as well as consumption of stock.

This type of check is performed dynamically for each transaction. In SAP SD, you can perform this check with or without *replenishment lead time* (RLT), which is the time to refill/replenish the inventory of the delivering plant.

Check Based on Product Allocation

Unlike the check based on ATP, in which allocation happens on a first-come, first-served basis, here you set up a maximum limit for the material quantity a customer can place order for. This check helps with the allocation of products to certain customers/regions so as to control the overall distribution. This is really helpful in scenarios such as new product launches, high-demand/hot sale products with limited supply, and products with higher lead times for production for which you want to restrict the stock quantity per customer so as to control the distribution of such products to the customer.

Check Based on Planning

Here the check is performed against independent requirements that are generated from demand-planning applications such as SAP APO-DP. These requirements are generally created for anonymous markets and are not customer-specific.

How the Availability Check Process Works

The availability check process confirms the delivery date on the schedule line in an order. To confirm this date, the system uses the *material availability date* (MAD) as the basis. This is the date on which the requested quantities for the material should be available to meet the customer-requested delivery date. The system determines the material availability date by calculating backward from the customer-requested delivery date and subtracting the delivering plant/warehouse processing time (pick/pack time, lead time for transportation planning, loading time) and transit time. This process is called *backward scheduling*.

The system then checks whether sufficient quantities of the requested material are available for this material availability date so as to make the delivery as per the customer-requested delivery date. If the requested quantities are not available as of the material availability date, the system performs another search in the future, taking into consideration the planned receipts and issues (if allowed in customization). It then redetermines the material availability date as the date in the future on which the sufficient quantities of the requested material will be available. Once the system determines the material availability date on which the requested quantities of material are available or will be available, it starts calculating forward and adding the time for pick/pack, transportation planning, loading, and transit to the material availability date and proposes or confirms the final date thus calculated as the confirmed schedule line date on the order. This process is called *forward scheduling*.

In equation form, this backward/forward scheduling can be represented as follows:

Schedule line confirmation = Material availability date + Pick/pack time + Lead time for transportation planning + Loading time + Transit time

Complete Delivery and Availability Check

Figure 6.1 depicts the concept we just discussed. As you can see, the customer placed an order on the 9th with a requested delivery date of the 14th. The available stock in the warehouse was 50 units with a planned receipt for another 50 units by the 10th. The warehouse processing time for the pick, pack, load, and goods issue activities takes a total of one day, and two days are needed for shipping time. The system first starts calculating backward from the 14th and determines the material availability date as the 11th. Because sufficient stocks will be available on this date (50 available on the 9th and 50 expected to be received into unrestricted stock by the 10th), the system performs forward scheduling from the material availability date, adding the warehouse processing time of one day and the shipping time of two days, and thereby confirms the schedule line for the 14th for 100 units.

FIGURE 6.1   Availability check in a complete delivery scenario

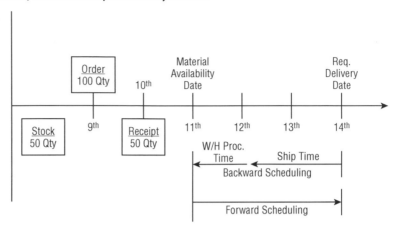

Figure 6.2 shows another variation of the same example, wherein the material availability date is already past because the customer ordered on the 9th with a requested delivery date of the 11th. The system performs backward scheduling and determines the material availability date as the 8th, which has already passed, and therefore it considers the current date, the 9th, as the material availability date. Sufficient quantities are not available on this date, and therefore the system redetermines the material availability date as the 10th, to which the system then adds three days of warehouse processing and shipping time and proposes the 13th as the confirmation date for the schedule line.

FIGURE 6.2   Availability check in a complete delivery scenario with material availability date already past

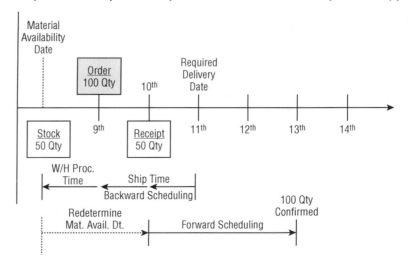

Partial Delivery and Availability Check

The scenario that you just saw was an example of the scenario wherein the customer will accept delivery for the goods in full only. What if the customer agrees to partial delivery? Figure 6.3 answers this very question by showing the influence of a partial delivery scenario on the availability check results. You can maintain the indicator to allow partial deliveries and the allowed number of partial deliveries directly in the sales document's "Shipping tab" or in the "Shipping tab" of the customer master sales data view. When you create a sales order, the partial delivery indicator defaults from the customer master data to the sales document. You can change this value in the sales document (if required).

FIGURE 6.3   Availability check in a partial delivery scenario

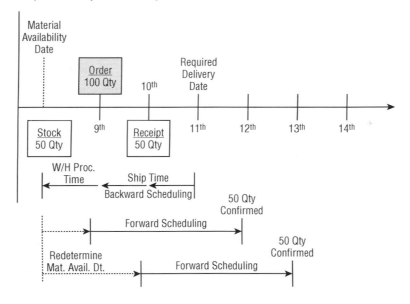

Now, if all other factors remain unchanged and if the customer agrees to partial delivery, the results will be as shown in Figure 6.3. As you can see from the figure, since the customer agrees to a partial delivery of goods, the system confirmed two schedule lines for two different dates. Against the requested delivery date of the 11th, 50 units were available on the 9th, and the receipt of the balance (50) is planned for the 10th. Adding three days for the pick, pack, post goods issue (PGI), and shipment time to these two availability dates, the system proposes the confirmation date as the 12th and the 13th.

One-Time Delivery and Availability Check

Another variation is also possible, wherein the customer agrees to take a one-time delivery of goods. In that scenario, the system confirms the quantities of the materials that are available for the customer-requested delivery date and cancels the balance of the order. Figure 6.4 shows this scenario.

FIGURE 6.4   Availability check in a one-time delivery scenario

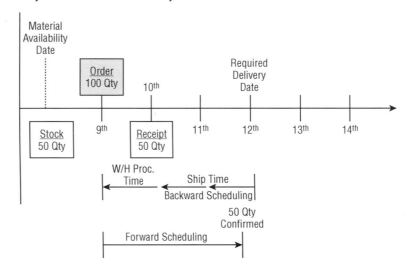

Availability Check with Replenishment Lead Time

In the SAP SD application, you can perform an availability check with or without replenishment lead time. As mentioned earlier, the RLT is the lead time to refill/replenish the inventory in the delivering plant/warehouse. In the case of in-house production, the RLT takes into consideration the production time. For external procurement, the RLT takes into consideration the goods receipt (GR) time.

Let's reconsider our example from Figure 6.1 with an RLT of two days, as represented by Figure 6.5. As you can see, one more order is received on the 9th for 120 quantities, and delivery is requested by the 14th. The system starts calculating backward and determines the MAD as the 11th. On this date, the system takes a look at the current situation and sees that the stock is not available (the stock in hand of 50 units and the 50 expected to be received are already consumed by 100 units in the order). Since there is no stock and an RLT is built into the availability check, the system starts calculating the time to replenish the stock from the current date and determines that the stock will be available by the 11th, which is the MAD. Therefore, the system will confirm the date of the 14th for the order.

FIGURE 6.5   Availability check with replenishment lead time

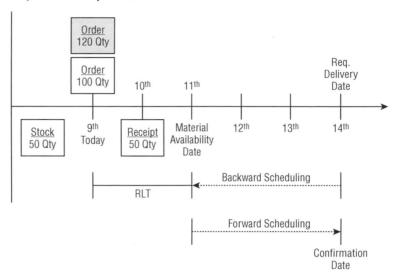

On the contrary, in Figure 6.6, the RLT is not considered. An order is received on the 9th for 60 units with a requested delivery date of the 14th. Another stock receipt is expected on the 12th. The system starts calculating backward and calculates the 11th as MAD. On this date, the stock quantity is not available, but a quantity of 50 will be available by the 12th, so the MAD for these 50 units is taken as the 12th, giving the 15th as the confirmation date. The balance (10 units) cannot be confirmed, because without a lead time, the system cannot say when the quantities will be available in stock, and thus the balance quantity falls into backorder status.

FIGURE 6.6   Availability check without replenishment lead time

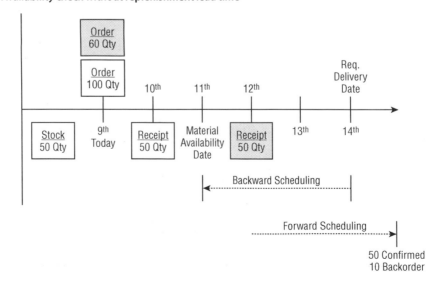

A common example of when you don't need RLT is consignment stock processing. In that case, you perform an availability check against the special stock, and thus there is no need for RLT. We will discuss more about consignment processing and its relationship to special stock in Chapter 7, "Sales."

Customizing the Availability Check and Transfer of Requirements

Both the availability check and transfer of requirements are controlled via a common set of customizing elements. These elements are arranged in six simple customization steps, as shown in Figure 6.7. Steps 1 to 5 are common to both the availability check and the transfer of requirements. Step 6 is required only for the availability check. In the following sections, we'll walk you through each of these customization steps in detail.

FIGURE 6.7   Customization steps for availability check and transfer of requirements

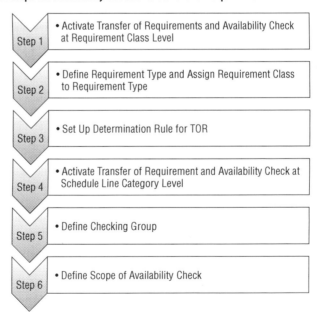

Step 1
• Activate Transfer of Requirements and Availability Check at Requirement Class Level

Step 2
• Define Requirement Type and Assign Requirement Class to Requirement Type

Step 3
• Set Up Determination Rule for TOR

Step 4
• Activate Transfer of Requirement and Availability Check at Schedule Line Category Level

Step 5
• Define Checking Group

Step 6
• Define Scope of Availability Check

Step 1: Activate Transfer of Requirements and Availability Check at Requirement Class Level

You start the customization activity for the availability check and transfer of requirements functions by activating these functions at the requirement class level. A requirement class controls MRP and other requirement-relevant functions such as requirement consumption strategy, requirement planning strategy, and so on. Once activated at this level, the transfer of requirements and availability check functions become globally activated for that requirement class in the SAP ERP software. You can further fine-tune to allow/disallow these two functions for a sales document type by activating/deactivating the two functions at the schedule line category level.

To activate/deactivate the availability check and transfer of requirements at the requirement class level, use transaction code OVZG, or follow the menu path IMG ➢ Sales And Distribution ➢ Basic Functions ➢ Availability Check And Transfer of Requirements ➢ Transfer Of Requirements ➢ Define Requirement Classes. Figure 6.8 represents the customization overview and detail screens for requirement class 041. Requirement class 041 is delivered in the SAP ERP software as a preconfigured requirement class for use with the SD application. The two fields that interest us in Figure 6.8 are check boxes for the availability check and transfer of requirements. Select these two check boxes if you want to activate the availability check and transfer of requirements for your requirement class. In requirement class 041, these two check boxes are preselected by SAP.

The customization screen also allows you to create your own requirement class. To do so, choose up to a four-character identifier key with a Z prefix and a meaningful description. Make selections into the relevant field as per your business requirements, and save your entry. Since the requirement class is a core of the PP/MM area with downstream impact on MRP calculations, it is advisable to work with a PP/MM consultant whenever you make any changes to a requirement class or create a new requirement class. In this book, we're only discussing the customization fields in the requirement class that are relevant for the availability check and transfer of requirements.

FIGURE 6.8   Overview and detail customization screens for setting up the requirement class

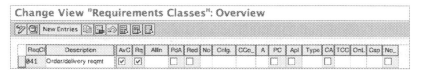

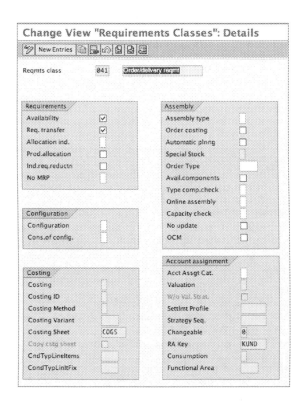

Step 2: Define Requirement Type and Assign a Requirement Class to a Requirement Type

A requirement type is a four-character key that uniquely identifies a requirement and helps differentiate requirements from one another. The transaction code is OVZH, and the menu path is IMG ➢ Sales And Distribution ➢ Basic Functions ➢ Availability Check And Transfer Of Requirements ➢ Transfer Of Requirements ➢

Define Requirement Types. Figure 6.9 shows the customization settings for requirement type 041 and its assignment to requirement class 041.

FIGURE 6.9   Defining a requirement type

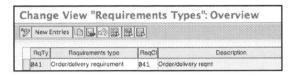

To define your own requirement type, click the New Entries button on the menu bar, and provide up to a four-character identification key with a meaningful description. Maintain the requirement class in the field next to the requirement type (as shown in Figure 6.9), and save your entry. Always remember that a requirement *type* can have only one requirement class assigned to it, whereas a requirement *class* can be assigned to multiple requirement types.

CASE STUDY—GALAXY MUSICAL INSTRUMENTS CONFIGURATION ANALYSIS: REQUIREMENT CLASS ACTIVATION AND REQUIREMENT TYPE SETUP

Galaxy Musical Instruments did not need to go for a new setup; instead, Galaxy decided to go with the standard SAP setup of requirement class 041 and requirement type 041 for carrying out the availability check and TOR.

Step 3: Set Up Determination Rule for TOR

In this customization step, you set up the rules for determining the requirement type based on the item category and MRP type combination and also the rules to determine the requirement type based on the item category only. The transaction code for this step is OVZI, and the menu path is IMG ➤ Sales And Distribution ➤ Basic Functions ➤ Availability Check And Transfer Of Requirements ➤ Transfer Of Requirements ➤ Determination Of Requirement Type Using Transaction. Figure 6.10 shows the customization screen for the rules setup.

FIGURE 6.10 Defining rules for the requirement type determination using transactions

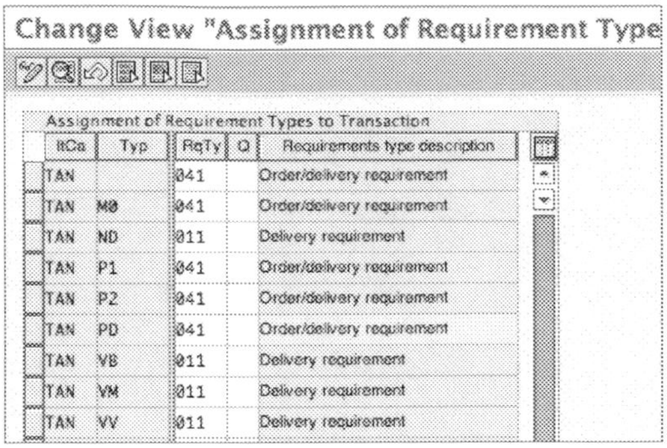

Change View "Assignment of Requirement Type

Assignment of Requirement Types to Transaction

ItCa	Typ	RqTy	Q	Requirements type description
TAN		041		Order/delivery requirement
TAN	M0	041		Order/delivery requirement
TAN	ND	011		Delivery requirement
TAN	P1	041		Order/delivery requirement
TAN	P2	041		Order/delivery requirement
TAN	PD	041		Order/delivery requirement
TAN	VB	011		Delivery requirement
TAN	VM	011		Delivery requirement
TAN	VV	011		Delivery requirement

This screen is a subset of the VOV4 customization screen. Transaction VOV4 is used to define the determination rule for the schedule line category using a combination of an item category and an MRP type as a determination key. If you want to maintain the requirement type determination rule in OVZI for a new item category or an item category and MRP type combination, you need to maintain it as a valid combination key in VOV4, before you can start using it in OVZI.

To maintain your entry in OVZI, select the key combination for the item category and MRP type or just the item category to which you want to assign the requirement type. Now enter your requirement type identification key in the Requirement Type field corresponding to your selected key combination. For reference purposes, Figure 6.10 shows the customization setup for the determination of requirement type 041.

CASE STUDY—GALAXY MUSICAL INSTRUMENTS CONFIGURATION ANALYSIS: REQUIREMENT TYPE DETERMINATION

In the Galaxy Musical Instruments setup, all the item categories that required an availability check and transfer of requirements, such as standard item (TAN) and free of charge item (TANN), were assigned to requirement type 041, whereas item categories for return orders (REN) and consignment returns (KRN) were excluded and were not set up for the requirement type determination.

REQUIREMENT TYPE DETERMINATION IN STANDARD SAP

Requirement type determination in standard SAP is performed using a six-level hierarchical sequence:

1. First, SAP tries to determine the requirement type using the strategy group from the material master record.

2. If the strategy group is not maintained, SAP determines the requirement type using the MRP group from the material master record.

3. If this is not maintained either, the SAP system determines the requirement type using the material type from the material master record.

4. If this also fails, the SAP system determines the requirement type using a combination of the item category and MRP type.

5. If this rule is not maintained, the SAP system at last tries to determine the requirement type using the item category itself.

6. If no requirement type is found at this level, the system treats the transaction as not relevant for the transfer of requirements or availability check.

If you do not want to use the hierarchical sequence provided by SAP and instead want the system to determine the requirement type based on, say, the item category and MRP type, you can select an alternative search strategy. This alternative search strategy has to be entered in column Q against the particular Item category and MRP type combination.

For assigning a search strategy in field Q, apart from the default option 0, SAP provides two more search strategy options: 1 and 2. Option 1 helps in determining the requirement type based on a combination of the item category and the MRP type. Option 2 is similar to 1 except that it also considers the allowed requirement types for this combination.

Step 4: Activate Transfer of Requirement and Availability Check at Schedule Line Category Level

This customization step allows further fine-tuning of the availability check and transfer of requirements settings. After activating the availability check or transfer of requirements at the requirement class level, if you don't want these functions to take place for a sales document type, you can deactivate these functions at the schedule line level. Always remember that activating the availability check and transfer of requirements at the requirement class level is a must before you can fine-tune them at the schedule line level.

Figure 6.11 represents the customization screen for schedule line level activation. The transaction code is OVZ8, and the menu path is IMG ➤ Sales And Distribution ➤ Basic Functions ➤ Availability Check And Transfer Of Requirements ➤ Transfer Of Requirements ➤ Define Procedure For Each Schedule Line Category.

FIGURE 6.11 Customization screen for schedule line category level activation of TOR and availability check

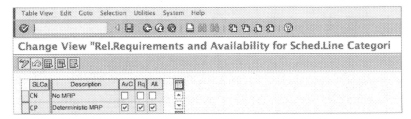

You can also activate the availability check and transfer of requirements using the schedule line category maintenance transaction VOV6.

CASE STUDY—GALAXY MUSICAL INSTRUMENTS CONFIGURATION ANALYSIS: ACTIVATION AT THE SCHEDULE LINE LEVEL

Galaxy Musical Instruments decided not to go for a new setup and instead to go with the standard SAP setup of the schedule line categories CP and CN for use with sales documents. Schedule line category CP is available in standard SAP for use with scenarios that use MRP, and CN is available for scenarios not requiring MRP. CP has both the requirement transfer and availability check fields selected, but CN contains no selection for these fields. As a result, sales documents using CP are eligible for transferring demand and carrying out the availability check, while the documents using CN aren't.

Step 5: Define Checking Group

A checking group is an important controlling element for the transfer of requirements and availability check processes. Whether the system should generate an individual or collective requirement, whether an availability check should happen with or without accumulation, and whether there should be no availability check at all are all controlled by the checking group function. You can define a checking group using transaction code OVZ2 or following the menu path IMG ➢ Sales And Distribution ➢ Basic Functions ➢ Availability Check And Transfer of Requirements ➢ Availability Check ➢ Availability Check With ATP Logic ➢ Define Checking Groups. Figure 6.12 shows the customization screen for defining a checking group. The entries in columns Av and Description show the checking group being configured and its description.

FIGURE 6.12 Defining a checking group

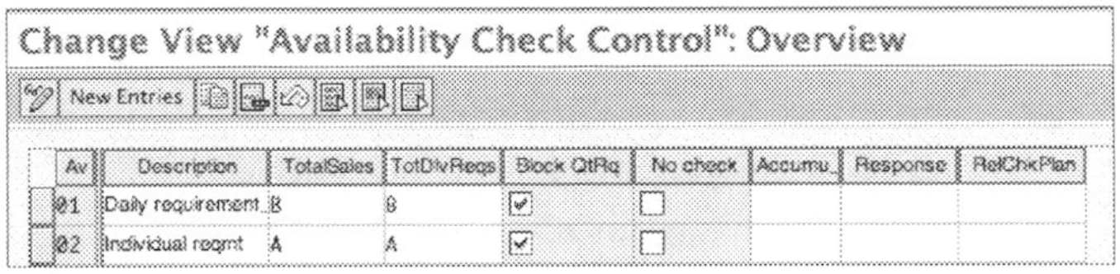

Let's quickly go through the other fields available on this customization screen:

Total Sales Requirements The field shown as TotalSales in Figure 6.12 controls the type of requirement that the SAP system generates and passes to MRP during sales order processing. Available values are A, B, C, and D. Choose A if you want to generate individual requirements per sales document, B if you want summarized requirements per day, C if you want weekly summarized requirements with a requirement date as Monday of the current week, and D if you want the weekly summarized requirements with a requirement date as Monday of the following week.

Total Delivery Requirements The field shown as TotDlvReqs in Figure 6.12 controls the type of requirement that the SAP system generates and passes to MRP during delivery processing. As with the previous field, the available values are A, B, C, and D. Choose A if you want to generate individual requirements per delivery document, B if you want summarized requirements per day, C if you want weekly summarized requirements with a requirement date as Monday of the current week, and D if you want the weekly summarized requirements with a requirement date as Monday of the following week.

Block QtRq This indicator is really helpful in preventing the problems that arise when more than one user carries out an availability check on the same material at the same time. When set, this indicator blocks the confirmed quantities and in turn avoids duplicate assignment of the same stock to multiple orders. This way, you can carry out the availability check for the same material/plant simultaneously without causing any duplicate or wrong assignments of stock. Always remember that although this indicator ensures accuracy, it also slows down performance, because each time the check is carried out, the SAP ERP system has to perform an extra step to block the confirmed quantities.

No Check   Not all the materials require an availability check. For instance, when materials are controlled via the KANBAN process, KANBAN makes sure that enough material is always available. Similarly, there might be certain low value or very low inventory turnover items that you might want to exclude from the availability check. The No Check indicator box serves the purpose in those scenarios. When you select it for a checking group and assign that checking group in the material master, that material is excluded from all further availability check processing. The standard SAP system offers checking group KP to handle such operations.

Accumulation   The field shown as Accumul. in Figure 6.12 helps you cumulate the confirmed quantities. Without accumulation, there is a chance that SAP will confirm more quantities to orders than are available to promise. Figure 6.13 shows the example scenario where order 1 got 100 units confirmed based on the available-to-promise situation at that point in time (available stock in hand [50 units] + planned receipt [50 units]). Later, the planned receipt was delayed from the 10th to the 12th. Since this delay of the planned receipt date does not retrigger the availability check for sales orders by itself, order 1 still shows confirmed for 100 units, whereas in reality, it has only 50 units available. Order 2 (50 units) was received on the 11th and also got confirmed against the planned receipt 1.

With the cumulation of quantities, you can avoid these inconsistencies. These are the available choices for this field:

0: No accumulation   Choose this when you don't want to use accumulation. If you don't use accumulation of quantities, you can still avoid the inconsistencies (shown in Figure 6.13) by running the reschedule and backorder processing transactions provided by SAP. These transactions are explained later in this chapter.

1: Accumulation of confirmed quantity when created and changed   Choose this when you want to use accumulation of confirmed quantities during sales order creation and while making any changes to the already confirmed quantities in a sales order. This means that for new orders to be confirmed, the sum of the receipts has to be more than the sum of the confirmed quantities.

2: Required quantity when created, no accumulation when changed   Choose this when you want to use accumulation of the confirmed quantities during the sales order creation only. No accumulation will happen when you change the sales order.

3: Required quantity when created, confirm quantity when changed   This is the recommended setting, because this allows you to accumulate the open requirement quantities during sales order creation and the confirmed quantities during sales order change. This means that for new orders to get confirmed, the sum of the receipts has to be more than the sum of the requirement quantities.

FIGURE 6.13 Example showing inconsistencies in ATP calculations when accumulation is not used

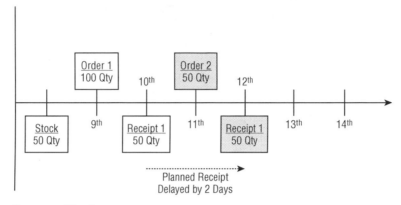

Sequence of Events

- Based on available stock (50 units) and planned Receipt 1 (50 units), Order 1 got confirmed for 100 units for requested delivery date of the 13th.
- Planned Receipt 1 got delayed by 2 days.
- Order 2 came in on the 11th for a requested delivery on the 14th and got confirmed for 50 units from planned Receipt 1.

Net Result at the End

Confirmed Quantities > Available-to-Promise (Available Stock + Planned Receipts)

Response   This setting works only if you have value 1, 2, or 3 maintained in the Accumulation field for your checking group. When you are processing an availability check using accumulation and there is a material shortage, this indicator helps control whether to issue an output (a dialog box with shortage information) to the user indicating the shortage. Available values are 0 and 1. Select 0, or leave the field blank, if you want no system response on a shortfall. Select 1 if you want a system response on a shortfall.

RelChkPlan   This indicator is relevant only if you are setting up the availability check against planning (in other words, planned independent requirements, which is out of the scope of this book).

To create your own checking group, click the New Entries button on the menu bar and provide up to a two-character identification key with a meaningful description.

Make the necessary selection for the customization fields shown in Figure 6.12 to match your business requirement, and save your entry by clicking the Save button. For Galaxy, we created a new checking group called Z9 with an individual requirement and confirmed quantity blocking, as shown in Figure 6.14.

FIGURE 6.14 Checking group customization screen showing checking groups defined for Galaxy Musical Instruments

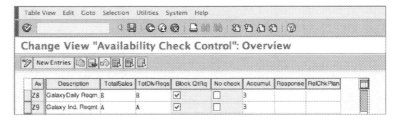

CASE STUDY—GALAXY MUSICAL INSTRUMENTS CONFIGURATION ANALYSIS: CHECKING GROUP

Galaxy wanted to transfer daily requirements for a few materials, individual requirement for a few others, and no requirement transfer for some materials. Therefore, we configured checking group Z9 for an individual requirement transfer with accumulation and Z8 for a daily requirement transfer with accumulation and then used SAP's existing checking group KP for no availability check.

Step 6: Define Scope of Availability Check

Once you have defined the checking group, the next step is to define the scope of the availability check. A combination of checking group and checking rule controls the scope of an availability check. SAP's SD application predefines checking rules. You use checking rule A for sales orders and B for deliveries. Figure 6.15 shows the customization screen for defining the scope of an availability check. You can reach the customization screen using transaction OVZ9 or by following menu path IMG ➢ Sales And Distribution ➢ Basic Functions ➢ Availability Check And Transfer Of Requirements ➢ Availability Check ➢ Availability Check With ATP Logic ➢ Carry Out Control For Availability Check.

FIGURE 6.15 Defining the scope of an availability check

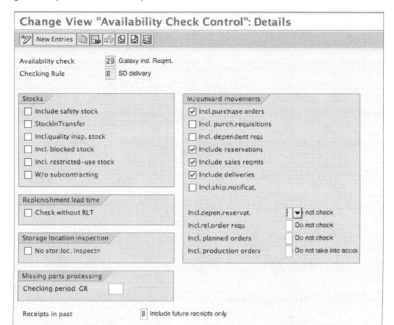

Let's take a look at the relevant fields available on this customization screen:

Stocks By default, the availability check in SD is carried out by considering the unrestricted stock available at the delivering plant/warehouse. This section of the customization screen allows you to include other stock, namely, safety stock, stock in transit, quality inspection stock, blocked stock, restricted use batch stock, and subcontractor stock, in the availability check calculations. By selecting the relevant check boxes on this tab, you can include these special stock situations in the availability check.

Replenishment Lead Time This tab allows you to include or exclude RLT in your availability check calculations. Select Check Without RLT if you want to exclude RLT; leave it deselected if you want to include RLT. The consignment process in the SD application is one example of a scenario that does not require RLT.

In/Outward Movements By making a selection in this part of the screen, you can include or exclude the material receipts and issues from various document types in your availability check calculations. As you can see from the customization screen shown in Figure 6.15, you can include the purchase order, purchase requisitions, reservations, deliveries, sales requirements, and so on. When checked, both inward and outward movement of the selected entry will be included in the availability check logic.

Storage Location Inspection   The No Storage Location Inspection field, when selected, switches off the availability check at the storage location.

Missing Parts Processing   When a goods receipt posting is made in the Inventory Management application of SAP, the value you enter in the Checking Period: GR field helps determine the number of days that the system should look into the future to check for missing parts.

The value you enter here helps in initiating the workflow in the SAP system to trigger an email to the MRP controller, if the goods receipt is carried out in Inventory Management for the missing part. Maintain the value in this field for the combination of the checking group and the checking rule you are setting up only when you want to carry out the missing parts processing in Inventory Management.

Receipt In Past   This field controls whether the sales order can consume the stock from receipts only in the future or from both the past and the future. Leave the field blank for including receipts from the past and future, choose A to do the same as leaving it blank but with a message, choose B to consume only future receipts, and choose C to perform the same as B but with a message.

To create your own scope, define the scope for a combination of the checking group and the applicable checking rule (A or B). Use the New Entries button to maintain the entry. Make the desired selections as per your business requirements, and save your entry.

Further Fine-Tuning in Customizing

In addition to the six steps of customization we just discussed, the SAP system also provides you with customization options to further fine-tune the availability check and transfer of requirements functionalities. Let's look at these customization options.

Defining the Checking Group Default Value

The checking group is assigned to the material master record in the Sales: General/ Plant view. When you create a material master record, you can either enter the checking group manually or have the system use a default value based on the customization settings done here in transaction code OVZ3. The menu path is IMG ➢ Sales And Distribution ➢ Basic Functions ➢ Availability Check And Transfer Of Requirements ➢ Availability Check ➢ Availability Check With ATP Logic ➢ Define Checking Group Default Value.

To define your checking group defaulting rule, click the New Entries button, and enter the material type and plant combination for which you want to default the checking group into the Material Type and Plant fields on the screen. Enter the checking group in the Availability Check field corresponding to your material type and plant field, and click the 🖫 button to save your entry. To help you visualize the setup, Figure 6.16 shows the customization setup for Galaxy Musical Instruments, where we have assigned checking group Z9 to material type HAWA and plant 9001.

FIGURE 6.16 Defining the checking group default value

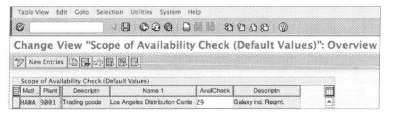

Defining the Default Availability Check Rule per Sales Area

This customization is really important because this controls the end result for the availability check run. The customization choices you make here will decide whether the system will perform an availability check as if the delivery is a one-time, complete delivery or whether it's a partial delivery; whether the SAP system shows a dialog box to the user when there is a shortage of stock; and how the system will behave while running the availability check in background mode. The determination rule here is set up by sales area. The transaction code is OVZJ, and the menu path is IMG ➢ Sales And Distribution ➢ Basic Functions ➢ Availability Check And Transfer of Requirements ➢ Availability Check ➢ Availability Check With ATP Logic ➢ Define Default Settings. Figure 6.17 shows the customization screen for this setup.

FIGURE 6.17 Defining default settings for the availability check by sales area

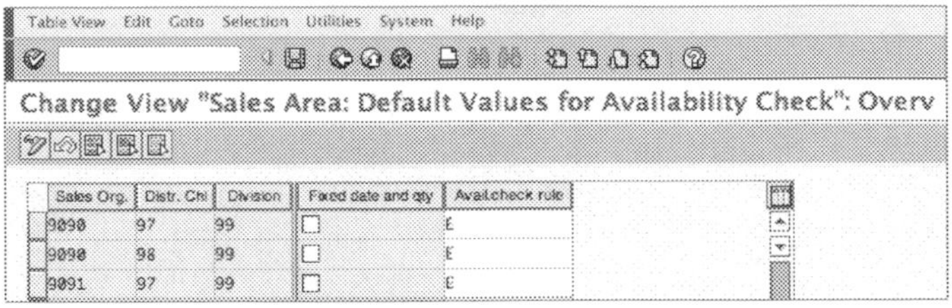

As you can see, the screen consists of five columns. The first three columns on the screen, taken together, represent the determination key, that is, the sales area for which you want the availability check defaults to be maintained. Here is what the other two fields do:

Fixed Date And Qty   Select this check box if you have a business requirement to default this field for a sales area. This field fixes the delivery date and quantity in a customer order and indicates the customer's confirmation of the delivery date proposed by the availability check run. In a scenario where the customer accepts delivery in full only and the availability check can only confirm a delivery date later than the customer requested date, marking this check box in the sales order schedule line or on the availability check overview screen confirms the customer's response to the delivery proposal suggested by the availability check run. If the customer agrees to accept delivery on a later date, you select the check box, and the requirements are transferred to MRP with the fixed delivery date and fixed quantity. The current available stock is not consumed by the order, and it becomes the job of the MRP department to meet the delivery deadlines as per the Fixed Date And Qty value transferred to MRP from the sales order.

Always remember that selecting this check box in a sales order also excludes the sales order from all subsequent order backlog processing and rescheduling job runs. This means that even if the goods do become available prior to the fixed date, you cannot allocate them to the order and therefore cannot ship prior to the fixed delivery date maintained in the order. To allocate them to this order, you need to deselect the Fixed Date And Qty field in the order document before you carry out the availability check processing. Therefore, to include orders in backlog processing and rescheduling, do not mark this field in scenarios where the customer accepts partial deliveries and wants deliveries to be made as early as possible.

Avail. Check Rule   In the case of a stock shortage, the SAP system generally brings up the availability check overview screen, asking the user to make a selection out of the delivery proposals that resulted from the availability check run. Using this field, you can control this system behavior by sales area and can force the SAP system to go with the proposal set up here in customizing instead of taking user inputs. You can select A for the system to automatically choose a one-time delivery proposal, B for full delivery, and C for the system to propose partial delivery proposals. Options D and E act just like A and C, respectively, when processing happens in background mode, but they provide a dialog box for user inputs when processing happens in foreground mode. Leaving this field blank brings up the dialog box in foreground mode and treats the proposal as a full delivery only in background mode. Select 1 if you want a delivery proposal from the product selection.

To maintain your rules, select the required sales area for which you want to maintain the availability check default rules, and make necessary selections in the Fixed Date And Qty and Avail. Check Rule fields based on your business requirements. Save your entry when finished with the setup process.

Defining the Material Block for Other Users

Unlike the soft block indicator (the Block Qt.Rq. check box) available in OVZ2 that only blocks a confirmed quantity and allows users to carry out an availability check simultaneously for the same material/plant, the material block functionality available in OVZ1 puts an exclusive ("hard") block on the material/plant, thereby restricting other users from simultaneously carrying out an availability check on the material/plant combination. The block is defined for a combination of the checking group and transaction (sales order or delivery) in customizing. The block is set when the availability check is carried out for the transaction document in create/change mode and is released when the document blocking the material/plant is saved. If both blocks (OVZ1 and OVZ2) are active in customizing, the block set at OVZ2 takes precedence.

The menu path is IMG ≻ Sales And Distribution ≻ Basic Functions ≻ Availability Check And Transfer Of Requirements ≻ Availability Check ≻ Availability Check With ATP Logic ≻ Define Material Block For Other Users. To set up a material hard block, select the required combination of the checking group and transaction, and select the corresponding Block check box. Leave the field deselected if you don't want to set up a material block. Save your entry when finished with the setup process. As a reference, Figure 6.18 shows the material block customization screen for Galaxy Musical Instruments.

FIGURE 6.18 Defining the material block for other users

AvailCheck	Description	Initiator	Block
Z9	Galaxy Ind. Reqmt.	A	☐
Z9	Galaxy Ind. Reqmt.	B	☑

Change View "Availability Check: Checking Criteria"

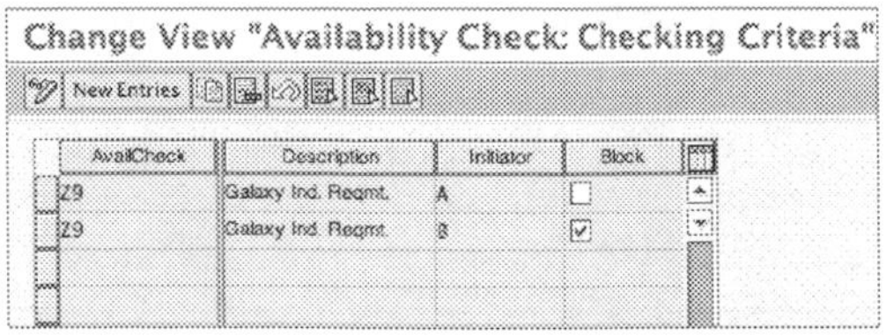

Creating a Block Quantity Confirmation in Delivery Block

A delivery block puts a stop on further processing for a sales order. Here, you can set up a delivery block to allow or disallow the quantity confirmation for a sales document. In addition, you can also set up a planned deferral of the quantity confirmation. This is really useful in situations where you don't want the availability check to confirm the quantity of the order if the order is under a delivery block, such as in the case of orders failing credit checks. This allows the stock to be available for other orders that are not under a delivery block. The transaction code is OVZ7, and the menu path IMG ➢ Sales And Distribution ➢ Basic Functions ➢ Availability Check And Transfer of Requirements ➢ Transfer Of Requirements ➢ Block Quantity Confirmation In Delivery Blocks. Figure 6.19 shows the customization screen for this activity.

FIGURE 6.19 Blocking quantity confirmation in delivery blocks

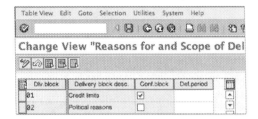

Let's look at the fields on the customization screen:

Dlv.Block and Delivery Block Desc.   These fields represent the delivery block identifier and corresponding description. These fields are autofilled for this customization screen with the number of delivery blocks configured in your SAP ERP system.

Conf.Block   This field controls quantity confirmation. Mark this check box if you want to block the quantity confirmation for a delivery block, and leave it unmarked if you don't want the quantity confirmation to be blocked.

Def.Period   This field allows you to put a planned deferral of quantity confirmation in a sales order. This is really useful for situations where you know the lead time required to complete all the necessary formalities in advance and you would like to defer the quantity confirmation until the end of the lead time. For example, let's say today is the 9th and you get an order from a new customer today for requested delivery by the 12th. The material is available in sufficient quantities on the 6th and the processing time is three days, which means that the system can confirm the delivery by the 12th. Your organization needs four days of lead time to set up the terms account for the customer (which involves getting a credit history and setting up the credit limits, payment terms, and so on). If you set up the delivery block called New Customer for a quantity confirmation with four days deferral, the SAP system will consider these four days of lead time while confirming quantities in the sales order and will propose the 13th (the 9th + four days) as the confirmation date. Note that the system starts calculating the lead time for deferral from the current date.

To fine-tune your delivery blocks for quantity confirmations, choose the required delivery block, and make selections in the Confirmation block and/or Deferral fields. Save your entry when finished with the setup process.

Refer to Chapter 7 for more details on customizing and using delivery blocks in sales and delivery processing.

Maintaining a User-Defined Requirement for Availability Check and Transfer of Requirements

For further fine-tuning of your availability check processing, SAP also lets you define your own requirements. You can add a technical piece of code to further allow/disallow quantity confirmation based on your business requirements. You have seen the use of requirements in Chapter 5, "Pricing and Tax Determination." Here also the requirements serve a similar purpose with respect to TOR and availability check calculations. SAP will execute your code only if the requirement is met.

You can use transaction VOFM followed by menu Requirements ➢ Subsequent Functions ➢ Reqs.Availability, or you can use the menu path IMG ➢ Sales And Distribution ➢ Basic Functions ➢ Availability Check And Transfer Of Requirements ➢ Transfer Of Requirements ➢ Maintain Requirement For Transfer Of Requirements. The standard SAP system provides requirement type 101 as an example of a user-defined requirement that contains a technical code to set a confirmed quantity on a sales order at zero if the document is under a credit block status.

WARNING When defining your own requirement, use ABAP help, and rigorously follow the naming convention for the customer namespace. Not following the SAP customer namespace rules puts your SAP ERP instance's code at risk of being overwritten by SAP code during SAP ERP software upgrades.

Determining the Procedure for Each Delivery Item Category

Once activated at the requirement class level, the availability check is valid for all delivery documents. But just like sales orders, not all delivery documents need an availability check. Return deliveries are a perfect example of when you don't need an availability check to be carried out. This customization screen gives you detailed controls to handle such situations. Using customization settings available on this screen, you can switch off the availability check for a delivery document via the delivery item category control. The transaction is OVZK, and the menu path is IMG ≻ Sales And Distribution ≻ Basic Functions ≻ Availability Check And Transfer Of Requirements ≻ Availability Check ≻ Availability Check With ATP Logic ≻ Determine Procedure For Each Delivery Item Category. Figure 6.20 shows the customization screen for this setup.

FIGURE 6.20 Determining the procedure for each delivery item category

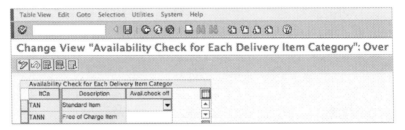

Here is an explanation of the three fields on this screen:

Item Category   The ItCa field represents the item category for which you want to fine-tune the availability check operations.

Description   The Description field shows the name of this item category. Both of these fields are autofilled by the system based on item categories configured in the system.

Avail. Check Off   The field Avail. Check Off is the one you need to select if you want to switch off the availability check for an item category. If this field is left blank, it means the availability check is on. An X here means the availability check is off.

To switch off the availability check for your item categories, select the relevant item category, and choose X in the corresponding Avail. Check Off field. Leave the value in this field blank for the item categories on which you want to carry out an availability check. Save your entry when done with the setup.

Checking the Rule for Updating Backorders

Here you assign the checking rule for SD transactions (A for sales order and B for delivery) to a plant. This is required before you can process backorders. The transaction code is OMIH, and the menu path is IMG ➢ Sales And Distribution ➢ Basic Functions ➢ Availability Check And Transfer Of Requirements ➢ Availability Check ➢ Availability Check With ATP Logic ➢ Checking Rule For Updating Backorders. Figure 6.21 represents this customization setup for Galaxy Musical Instruments.

FIGURE 6.21 Checking the rule for updating backorders

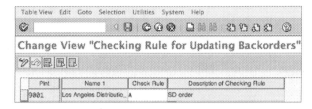

Working with the Availability Check

Now that we have covered the configuration setup, we'll show how these configuration elements work together to perform the availability check and transfer of requirements. Figure 6.22 summarizes how the complete availability check/transfer of requirements functionality works in SAP.

As you can see, when you create a sales order, the item category from the sales order, together with the MRP type from the material master record, determines the requirement type. The requirement type determines the requirement class, which in turn tells whether the transfer of requirements and availability check are activated in customizing. The next check is performed at the order schedule line level to determine whether the sales order is relevant to carrying out the availability check and passing on the material requirement to MRP. When found relevant, the availability check is carried out by SAP, taking into consideration the scope of check determined using the checking group from the material master record and the checking rule from the sales transaction as the determination key. If the check is successful, quantities are confirmed on the schedule line. If unsuccessful, the shortages are transferred to MRP to plan for the procurement/production of goods.

FIGURE 6.22 Availability check and transfer of requirements process

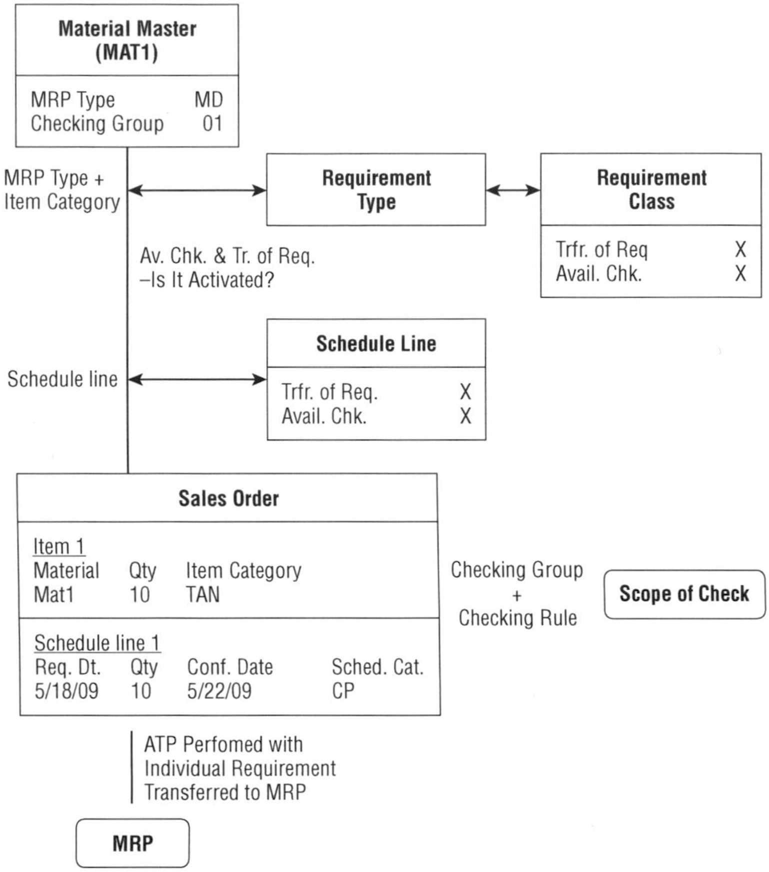

Availability Check in Sales Order

In a sales order, the availability check is carried out for the delivering plant. Figure 6.23 shows the availability check overview screen that is automatically displayed by SAP if a shortage of stock is encountered during an availability check run in a sales order. You can also call this screen from a sales order's create/change mode by clicking the ▓ button on the sales order screen.

FIGURE 6.23 Availability check overview screen

Take a close look at the screen. You will see that the screen contains the information from the sales order for which the availability check was carried out (such as plant, requested quantity and date, material number, and so on), and the bottom segment of screen represents the various proposals generated by the system as a result of the availability check.

As you can see, the customer ordered 192 units of material 1628 for a requested delivery date of 8/26/2009. After carrying out the availability check, the system found that only 84 units are available for delivery as of 8/26/2009. The system gave three proposals:

▶ *Proposal 1*: If customer wants only a one-time delivery, only 84 units can be delivered by the customer requested delivery date of 8/26/2009.

▶ *Proposal 2*: If customer wants only a complete delivery, all 192 units can be confirmed for delivery by 8/28/2009 (that is, the end of replenishment lead time).

▶ *Proposal 3*: If customer agrees to a partial delivery, 84 units can be delivered by 8/26/2009, and the balance (108) can be confirmed by the end of the replenishment lead time, in other words, 8/28/2009.

To choose a proposal, you can either click the ☑ button next to the proposal you want or click the respective buttons for the proposal that you want to choose from the menu buttons. Click Complete dlv. to select complete delivery, One-time delivery to select a one-time delivery, and Delivery proposal to select a delivery proposal with partial quantities.

You can perform an availability check on a plant other than 9001 by clicking the Other plants button on the menu. The ATP quantities button will provide you with information about the ATP quantities. Click the Scope of check button if you want to see what is included/excluded by the system while carrying out the availability check. You can also call this overview screen from outside a sales order using transaction code CO09. Figures 6.24 and 6.25 represent the selection and output screens for CO09: Availability Overview.

Table 6.1 describes the commonly used transactions for checking the stock availability in the SAP system.

FIGURE 6.24 Selection screen for availability check report (CO09)

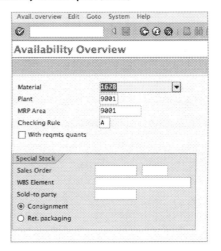

FIGURE 6.25 Output screen for availability check report

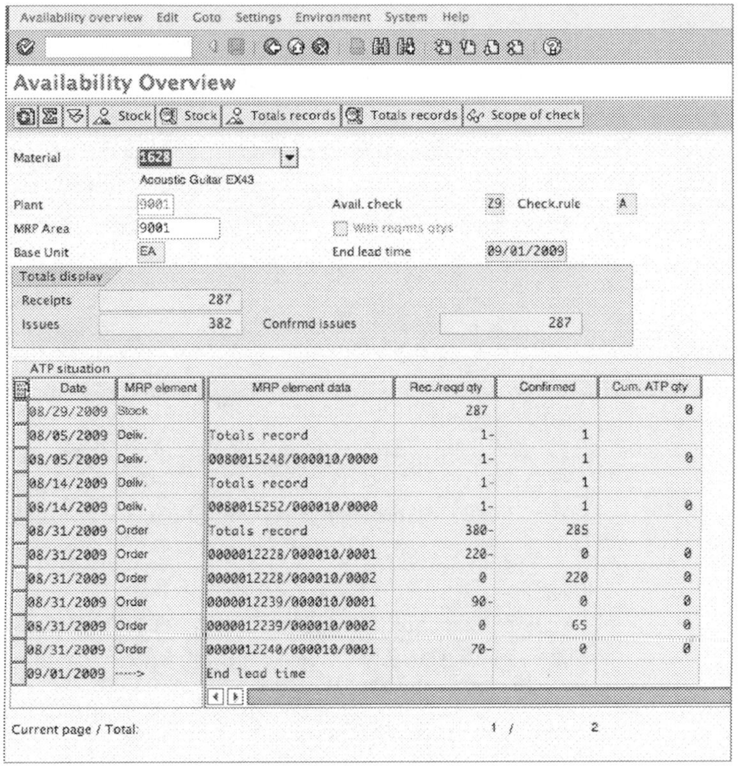

TABLE 6.1   Transactions to Check Stock Availability

Transaction Code	SAP Easy Access Menu Path	Title and Description
MB53	Logistics ➢ Materials Management ➢ Inventory Management ➢ Environment ➢ Stock ➢ Plant Stock Availability	Display Stock Availability: Provides a detailed report on the stock availability in a plant.
CO09	Logistics ➢ Materials Management ➢ Inventory Management ➢ Environment ➢ Stock ➢ Availability Overview	Availability Overview: Provides the availability overview for a material/plant combination.
MD04	Logistics ➢ Materials Management ➢ Inventory Management ➢ Environment ➢ Stock ➢ Stock/ Requirement List	Display Stock/Requirements Situation: Displays the current stock and requirements situation for a plant and material combination. This report provides a more detailed picture of the stock availability than does CO09.

Availability Check in Shipping

An availability check at delivery is required because of the dynamic nature of the availability check process and the elements that comprise the check. You should know by now that an availability check is performed based on the current stock in hand plus a planned inward and planned outward movement of goods. A planned future movement is always subject to change because changes in underlying factors can also affect the stock situation in the delivering plant. For example, a stock situation that existed during the sales order confirmation may not exist anymore during delivery. There are countless factors that can contribute to such situations— a planned future receipt coming later than expected or coming way before, lost output in production, release of confirmed stock from stock reservations to unrestricted stock, consignment stock picked up from customer location, a sudden or increased consumption of the finished goods by assembly orders because of an increase in demand for a kit or combo sale, cancellation of an already confirmed order, confirmed orders put on credit hold...these are several real-world examples of factors that consume or release stock and can change the stock situation in the delivering plant or warehouse between the order confirmation and delivery time. Stock transfers are the biggest contributor to such situations because they have the ability to steal stock from plant A and provide it to plant B, jeopardizing all the delivery schedules for plant A. Even a change in production capacity or warehouse capacity to process orders can bring a change in the availability check results. An availability check at delivery is, therefore, a must.

When you create a delivery, an availability check is initiated for the picking date along the same lines as sales orders. If the stock is not available at all, the system enters a delivery quantity of zero. You can process a delivery with a zero quantity only if it is permitted in delivery customization. If the quantity available is less than the order quantity requested and customer agrees to a partial delivery, then the available quantity is taken as the delivery quantity in the delivery document, and a corresponding reduction is made in the order quantity.

Backorder Processing

A *backorder* is an order stage that represents the orders for which an availability check is not able to find the sufficient quantities or no stock at all to confirm the customer-requested delivery date. When the stock situation changes in the delivering plant/warehouse, you can run the transaction for backorder processing to process these unconfirmed orders for confirmation. While processing backorders, you can assign the newly available stock (ATP quantities) to unconfirmed orders.

You can also adjust the stock by releasing it from an existing confirmed order and assigning it to another unconfirmed order manually. In the SAP system, you can run transaction V.15 to generate the list of backorders that exist in the system followed by transaction CO06 to process them manually. Alternatively, you can use transaction V_RA, which provides you with both the list and the screen used to process backorders. To explain backorder processing, we will use transaction V_RA.

Backorder Processing Using a Selection List

Figure 6.26 represents the selection screen for processing backorders using a selection list. Based on the choices you make on this selection screen, the SAP system will generate the list of backorders for processing, as shown in Figure 6.27.

FIGURE 6.26 Selection screen for backorder using selection list

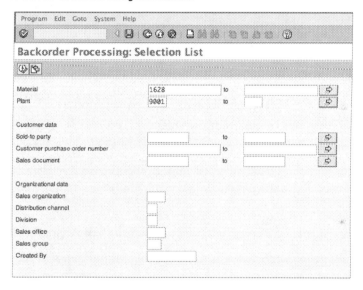

FIGURE 6.27 Output screen listing backorders

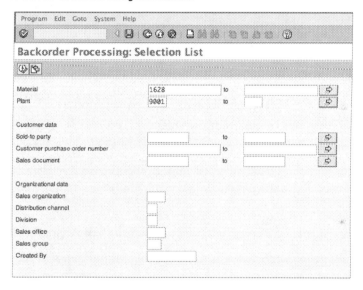

To process backorders, select the required documents, and click the Backorders button on the menu. Or use Edit ➤ Backorders to call up the backorder processing overview screen, as shown in Figure 6.28. If the stock is available, it will be shown in the Cumul. ATP Qty field. To adjust the stock confirmation for an order, double-click the required MRP element, and enter the new committed quantity in the Committed field in the Sales Requirements section at the bottom of the screen.

FIGURE 6.28 Screen for processing backorders

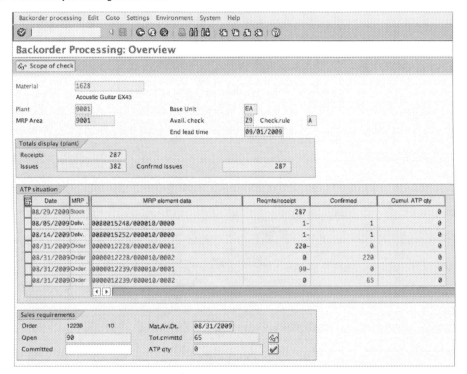

Rescheduling a Sales Document

The standard availability check allocates stock based on a first-come, first-served basis. In other words, the orders entered first in the system will be confirmed first. In practice, this is not always what you want. Sometimes you want the goods to be assigned to an order that came in last. A common example of such situations is consumption of available stock by a low-priority order that pushes a high-priority order into backorder status because the low-priority order was entered first into the SAP system. Rescheduling is handy in such situations, allowing you to release the quantity blocked by the low-priority confirmed order and reassign the same to the high-priority order so as to meet the delivery schedule for the high-priority customer. You can perform rescheduling using transaction code V_V2 or using the SAP Easy Access menu path Logistics ➢ Sales And Distribution ➢ Sales ➢ Backorders ➢ Rescheduling ➢ Execute. Figure 6.29 shows the selection screen for rescheduling a run.

FIGURE 6.29 Selection screen for the rescheduling report

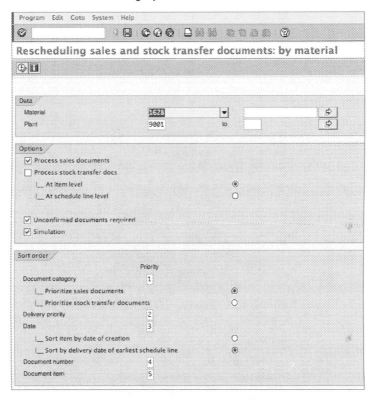

The screen is divided into three sections:

Data   This section of the screen allows you to enter the material and plant for which you want to run the rescheduling.

Options   This section of the screen allows you to further fine-tune your selection for the rescheduling run.

   Process Sales Documents   Select Process Sales Documents to include all the open sales documents (for the material and plant combination specified in the data section) in the rescheduling run.

Process Stock Transfer Docs   Select Process Stock Transfer Docs to include stock transfer orders, stock transfer scheduling agreements, and purchase order requests in the rescheduling run. You can include these stock transfer documents as an item-level selection or schedule line–level selection. Always remember that schedule line selection takes more processing time than item-level selection.

Unconfirmed Documents Required   Select the Unconfirmed Documents Required check box to include the backorders into the rescheduling run.

Simulation   Select the Simulation check box to run the rescheduling in test run mode without making any changes to the selected orders. You can also run transaction code V_R2 to run the rescheduling evaluation separately. The menu path for this is Logistics ➢ Sales And Distribution ➢ Sales ➢ Backorders ➢ Rescheduling ➢ Evaluate.

Sort Order   This section of the screen allows you to set the prioritization for the rescheduling run and also to set the sorting order for the rescheduling output. A maximum of five priority levels are allowed. The system will read the documents and process the rescheduling run based on these priorities.

Figure 6.30 and Figure 6.31 show an example of how priority can affect the end result of a rescheduling run. In Figure 6.30, customer 10014 is a low-priority customer who got all the stock allocated as order 12228, which was entered prior to order 12339 (a high-priority customer order) and 12240 (a next-day shipment order) [see *prev.confirmed qty* field in Figure 6.30]. Later, a stock of 70 units came as inward movement, raising the ATP stock availability in delivery plant 9001 for material 1628 to 70 units. When the rescheduling run is executed with the selection criteria shown in Figure 6.29, the SAP system will select all the undelivered confirmed and unconfirmed orders for plant 9001 and material 1628 and start allocating them on the basis of delivery priority (priority 1 is to select an order, and priority 2 is to allocate inventory based on the delivery priority). Thus, order 12240 (being the next-day shipment order) gets fully confirmed for 70 units from the available ATP stock. On the other hand, 25 units were released from low-priority order 12228 and got reassigned to high-priority order 12239, thus completely confirming order 12239 too [see *new confirmed qty* field in Figure 6.30].

If you reshuffle priority 2 and priority 3 on the selection screen (Figure 6.29) the whole calculation for rescheduling changes, as shown in Figure 6.31. Because Earliest Delivery Date became priority 2 and Delivery Priority became priority 3, order 12228 still gets to keep its old confirmation for 220 quantities, and the available ATP stock of 70 got assigned to the next-day shipment order 12240. The high-priority order 12239 remains without confirmation.

FIGURE 6.30 Log screen for rescheduling test run

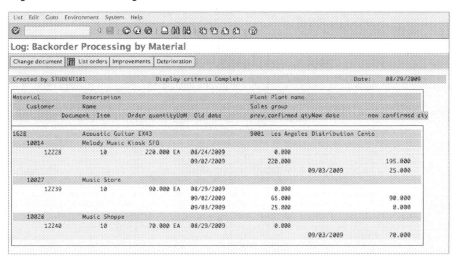

FIGURE 6.31 Log screen for rescheduling test run after reshuffling of priorities

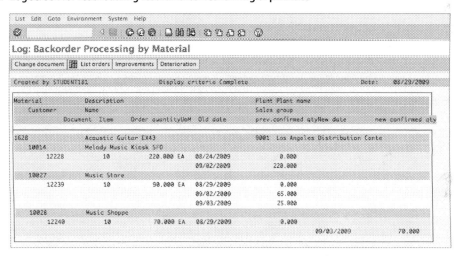

It is always advised to run rescheduling in background mode, because it is a performance-hungry transaction. Also, make sure that when you run the rescheduling transaction, there is minimal order-related activity in the system. Keeping an order open in change mode while rescheduling is running can lead to an order document being skipped from the run and in rare cases can lead to wrong allocation or duplicate allocation of stock.

Summary

In this chapter, we explained the customization steps for setting up the availability check and discussed the importance of an availability check in the overall processing of a sales transaction. During this discussion, we also covered two related functionalities—transfer of requirements and backorder processing—in detail. In next chapter, we will discuss sales document types and related customization.

Sales

The sales application in SAP SD deals with the business process involved with selling goods and services to the customer. A sales document is a vital component of the sales application that records and processes information related to a sales transaction and also marks the beginning of a sales cycle in the SAP system.

In Chapter 1, "Introduction to Sales and Distribution," you saw a brief overview of the sales cycle and experienced the look and feel of a sales document. In this chapter, we will discuss in detail sales documents, including their use in the SAP system, how they are structured, and how to configure and control them from a sales transaction perspective. We will also briefly touch upon the various sales document types that are available in the standard SAP system, including inquiries, quotations, orders, debit/credit notes, and contracts, to name a few.

Sales Documents

In SAP, the sales cycle begins with the creation of a sales document. The *sales document* stores and processes the sales-related data and controls the overall processing of the sales transaction. When you receive an order from the customer, the information contained in that physical customer order—such as ordered goods or services, ordered quantity, shipping location, delivery date, and so on—is all stored in a sales document. This sales document then forms the basis for carrying out subsequent SD process steps such as delivery, billing, and accounting postings.

In SAP, *sales document* is a generic term. You can use a sales document to store and initiate processing for inquiries, quotations, sales orders, contracts, credit/debit notes, invoice corrections, free-of-charge delivery, and other similar sales processes that a user in the sales function deals with on a day-to-day basis. Each of these processes is identified and controlled using a specific sales document type in SAP; for instance, document type AF is for inquiries, AQ is for quotations, and OR is for standard orders.

Each sales document in SAP is assigned a unique document number that can be set internally by the SAP system or externally by the user or interface program that is electronically creating the sales order in the SAP system. You can set up incompletion checks in a sales document to ensure the user enters the data entry completely and to also stop the processing of subsequent steps if the document is found to be incomplete. Status management in the SAP system documents the current status of the object and also controls what subsequent process step may be carried out next. While processing a sales document, SAP also carries out various basic functions such as pricing, taxation, partner determination, availability check, output determination, and so on, which we've already discussed in previous chapters.

You can create, change, delete, and reject these sales documents in SAP. You can also create a sales document electronically using the ALE, IDOC, EDI, and BAPI technologies provided by SAP. We discuss these technologies in Chapter 14, "Advanced Techniques."

TIP   Deletion and rejection are allowed only for those documents that are not yet processed for delivery and other subsequent processes.

Structure of a Sales Document

The structure of a sales document has three parts: a *header structure* that holds the information applicable to the whole document, an *item structure* that holds the information specific to an item, and a *schedule line* that stores the delivery schedule for the item. Data at the header level is valid for all the items. A sales document can have one header and one or multiple line items, and each line item further can have one or multiple schedule lines, as shown in Figure 7.1.

FIGURE 7.1   Structural breakdown of a sales document

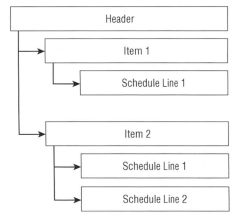

TIP   The header data for a sales document is stored in table VBAK, the item data is stored in table VBAP, and the schedule line data is stored in table VBEP. Business data—such as the terms of payment, for example—is stored in table VBKD, and partner data for the document header and item is stored in table VBPA.

Origin of Data in a Sales Document

Apart from the data that you entered manually or that came via an interface program, data in a sales document originates from a variety of other sources:

From master data to sales document   When you create a sales document, a majority of information required by the sales order is automatically derived by SAP from the master records of the customer and material number you provided on the sales document detail screen. Information derivation from the sold-to party master data includes pricing, shipping conditions, Inco terms, and so on. Information specific to the shipping location and taxation is pulled out from the ship-to party master, and information specific to the payment terms and credit checks is pulled from the payer master record. When the sold-to party performs all four partner functions for a sales document, all the partner-related data is pulled from the sold-to party master record. Information from the material master includes the delivery plant, weights, delivery priority information, and so on. Some miscellaneous information is also derived from various other master records such as the pricing master, customer–material info masters, output masters, and so on, based on the combination of customer and material numbers.

From document header to document item   Data for document items originates from the document header. Once copied from the header to the items in a document, this data can be manually changed in the sales document. In such a case, the manually entered data takes precedence over the automatically derived data. For example, say you have an initial customer order received with a requested delivery date of 03/09/09 for all three items; with the standard SAP system behavior, the date 03/09/09 is copied from the sales document header to all the items. But then say customer later sends a request to deliver item 20 by 04/09/09, keeping the schedule for item 10 and 30 intact. To incorporate this request, you manually change the requested delivery date at the item level for item 20 to 04/09/09. This manual change now takes precedence over the requested delivery date initially copied from the header data. So, the header data and items 10 and 30 show the requested delivery date as 03/09/09, and item 20 has a requested delivery date of 04/09/09.

From source document to target document   In SAP, data originated in the source document is copied to the target document. For example, when you create a sales order with reference to a quotation, SAP copies the data from the quotation document to the sales order. In this case, SAP will not do any derivation of data from the master records, and data copied from the quotation will be final. So, any changes made to the master data after creating the quotation will not be copied on to the sales order because the data for the sales order is copied from the quotation document that still contains the old information.

From customization settings to sales document   SAP copies the defaults defined in the customization settings to the sales documents. Values such as the default billing type and the default delivery type are copied to the sales document so that SAP can use these defaults to perform the subsequent steps without any user intervention. This makes the process more automated.

Customizing Sales Documents

A sales document is controlled via its customization settings. The customization of a sales document involves the following steps:

1. Defining sales document types

2. Defining item categories

3. Setting up an item category determination

4. Defining schedule line categories

5. Setting up a schedule line category determination

6. Setting up copy controls

In the following sections, we'll cover each of these steps in detail.

Defining Sales Document Types

The first step in sales document customization is to define the sales document types that meet your business requirements. A sales document type in the SAP system helps you differentiate one kind of sales document from another. Whether a sales document is an inquiry, a quotation, a sales order, or any other kind of sales document, you can identify each one exclusively based on its document type. In the customization of a sales document type, you can define various settings that not only control the overall behavior of the sales document but also impact the subsequent process steps, such as delivery and billing.

To customize a sales document type, you can use the transaction code VOV8 or follow the menu path IMG ➢ Sales And Distribution ➢ Sales ➢ Sales Documents ➢ Sales Document Header ➢ Define Sales Document Types. For discussion purposes, we will be breaking the customization screen into multiple screenshots and will discuss in detail all the important fields on the customization screen. During this discussion, we will be using document type OR – Standard Order for analyzing the various settings on the customization screen. Let's start with the General Control and Number Systems sections of the customization screen, as shown in Figure 7.2.

FIGURE 7.2   General Control and Number Systems sections of the customization screen for maintaining sales document types

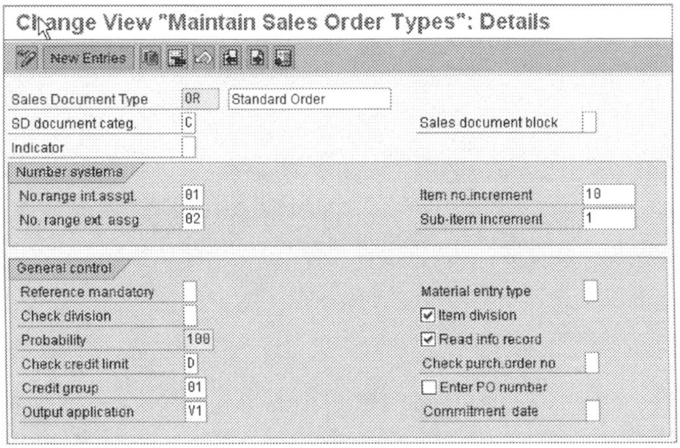

General Controls and Number Systems

In these sections of the screen, you define all the generic control settings required for your sales document type:

Sales Document Type   This field represents the identifier and description for your sales document type. You can define your own sales document type by providing an identifier key that is a maximum of four characters, along with a meaningful description. In Figure 7.2, OR stands for the document type, and Standard Order is the description for the document type OR.

Sales Document Category   The field SD Document Categ. classifies sales documents into various categories and enables the SAP system to provide status information about delivery and billing processing for the sales document. When you create your sales document via the copy with reference option, this category field enables the SAP system to provide the status information about the reference documents. You can use document category A for inquiries, B for quotations, C for orders, D for item proposals, E and F for scheduling agreements, G for contracts, H for returns, K for credit memo requests, and L for debit memo requests.

Sales Document Block   When you select this field for a sales document type, the sales document type is blocked for further use and is no longer visible in the list of available document types for processing with sales document create transactions, such as VA01, for example. This is useful in situations where your document type has become obsolete and you don't want the user to use it for transactional document creation by mistake. Always remember that once blocked in customizing, you cannot use that document type for creating new transactional documents, but the existing transactional documents can still be processed.

You can also use this field to mark a document type as relevant for automatic processing only. When you do so, the document type is no longer available for manual processing via maintenance transactions provided by SAP (VA01, for example). Rebate processing is one example where you do use this setting. Refer to Chapter 9, "Billing," for more details on rebate processing.

You can make one of the following selections for this field:

>> Leave the field blank if you do not want to block your sales document type.

>> Select X when you want to block the document type.

>> Select A to make the document available for automatic processing only.

Internal and external number range assignment   In SAP, you control the document numbering for your sales document using a two-character number range key. When customizing this key, you specify the starting number and the ending number for the number range that then controls the document numbering for your sales document.

In Figure 7.2, value 01 in field No.Range Int.Assgt. represents the internal number range that the SAP system will use to assign the document numbering to your sales document. Similarly, the value 02 in the field No. Range Ext.Assg. will control the document numbering for your sales document when the number is assigned externally by the user or the interface program that is creating the sales order. You can define a number range for your document type by using transaction code VN01 or by following the menu path IMG ➤ Sales And Distribution ➤ Sales ➤ Sales Documents ➤ Sales Document Header ➤ Define Number Range For Sales Documents.

Item No. Increment   Here you define the increments for an item number for your sales document. So if you set up an item increment as 10, then the first line in the sales document will have item 10, the second line will have item 20, and so on. Keeping a gap in item numbers is always good practice because it gives you some flexibility to insert a new line between two existing line items in a sales document.

Sub-item Increment   The subitem concept exists for structured materials such as a bill of materials (BOM). A BOM allows you to process materials in a specified structure. For example, a computer can be sold as one piece or as multiple parts separately. When you sell it as one piece, you define a BOM to set up the main piece of the item as a computer, with a mouse, keyboard, CPU, monitor screen, and so on, as subitems of that main piece. When you create a sales order, you enter the BOM for the computer as a material in the sales order. This BOM automatically explodes into multiple lines of individual materials to be delivered. What item numbers these subitems get depends upon what setting you made when customizing for the subitems increment. As per the increment value shown in Figure 7.2 for subitems, each subitem will have an increment of 1.

Reference Mandatory   Make a selection in this field if you want to create a document for your document type only by copying it from an existing document. For example, if your requirement says that a sales order can be created only with reference to a quotation document, you can choose B here for quotation to put this restriction on your sales order document type.

You can set up the SAP system to create a new sales document with reference to the following:

- A: An inquiry
- B: A quotation
- C: A sales order
- E: A scheduling agreement
- G: A contract
- M: A billing document

Remember that a selection in this field will only make it compulsory for the document to refer to an existing document. For the actual flow of data between the two documents, you also need to define the copy control between the documents.

Material Entry Type   This field defines the expected input value for the material field during the sales order entry. When you select B in this field, SAP expects you to enter a material number and product catalog combination as a valid input for creating the sales order. Select A, and the SAP expectation changes to the material order number and product catalog combination. Keep the value in this field as blank if you are not working with product catalogs.

Item Division   The Item Division check box is like an on/off switch that controls whether the division for an item in the sales order should originate from the material master or from the document header. When selected, it allows the item division to be copied from the material master data. If left unchecked, the item division is copied from the sales document header.

Check Division   The Check Division field checks whether the division at the document header is different from the document items. The following options are available:

- Leave the field blank: Different divisions between the header and the items are allowed without any message to the user.

- Select 1: Divisions can be different, but a warning message is issued.

- Select 2: Divisions cannot be different, and an error message is issued.

TIP   When to allow the fields to be different between the header and items depends upon what scenario you want to configure. For example, if you want to allow cross-divisional sales, which allow you to create a sales order with materials from different divisions, then keep the Check Division field blank and the Item Division check box selected for the document type you are configuring so that the division of the header can be different from the item, and at the same time the division at the item level can be copied from the material master.

Probability   You use order probability to measure the success rate of a presales process. For example, you use the probability percentage to measure the possibility of a quotation converting into an order. In SAP, the probability is allowed for the inquiry and quotation document categories only. The expected order value is calculated as the net value of the line item multiplied by the probability rate for that line item divided by the total net value for all the line items in the quotation. So, for a quotation containing two items, one for $100 with a 40 percent probability and the other for $100 with a 60 percent probability, the total order value equals $200, but the expected order value equals $100. In other words:

$$(100 \times 40\% + 100 \times 60\%) \div 200$$

Read Info Record   This check box controls the copying over of the customer-specific material description from the customer–material info record to the subsequent sales document. When selected in customizing for a document type, the customer–material info record gets copied to documents for that document type.

We'll cover customer–material info records in detail in Chapter 12, "Material Determination, Listing, Exclusions and Proposals."

Check Credit Limit   This field helps you activate/deactivate credit checks for your document type. The available options are as follows:

> » Blank: Select this if you do not want to run a credit check on your sales document type.

> » A: This runs a simple credit check with a warning message displayed when a credit check for the document fails.

> » B: This runs a simple credit check with an error message displayed when a credit check for the document fails.

> » C: This runs a simple credit check and blocks the delivery for the sales document if the credit check for the document fails.

> » D: This runs a rule-based automatic credit check. The value D in this field in Figure 7.2 represents that OR is using automatic credit checks.

We will cover credit checks and related settings in more detail in Chapter 11, "Credit Management."

Credit Group   In the standard SAP system, you can carry out the credit check at the sales order level and the delivery level and also while performing the goods issue step for your delivery. A credit group in the SAP system represents these levels. There are three credit groups available in standard SAP:

> » 01 for sales orders

> » 02 for deliveries

> » 03 for goods issue

If you want to carry out credit checks, you need to assign your document type to its relevant category. For sales orders, the credit group is always 01. Refer to Chapter 11 for more details on credit checks and related customization settings.

Check Purchase Order Number   The purpose of this field is to check for duplicate purchase order (PO) numbers during sales order entry. When you select A in this field, SAP gives a warning message during sales order creation if another sales document for same customer with the same PO number exists already. Leave this field blank if you do not want SAP to check for duplicate PO numbers.

Enter Purchase Order Number   When you select this box in customizing for your document type, SAP enters the sales document number in the PO number field, provided that this field is blank when the document is saved. This is useful for scenarios such as return material authorization (RMA) wherein you would like to save your sales document number of the RMA document type in the PO field as a reference to be provided to the customer. The customer will use this number as a reference number for all their communications related to that specific RMA transaction.

Output Application   An output application is a two-character identifier that controls the overall processing of output at the application level. If you want to carry out output determination for your sales document, then apart from the customization settings that you defined in Chapter 4, "Partner, Text, and Output Determination," you also need to assign your document type to its relevant output application. For sales documents, the output application is V1.

Commitment Date   Commitment dates are relevant for when your customer contracts have certain obligatory delivery dates to be met. This situation can exist most commonly in customer make-to-order production where there might be bottlenecks and you want SAP to give a commitment date in addition to a confirmed date and quantity. Select an entry in this field when you want SAP to calculate a commitment date for your sales document type.

Transaction Flow

Figure 7.3 represents the Transaction Flow section of the sales document type customization screen. Here you can customize the look and feel of the order entry screen, define the screen sequencing, and define the various transactional flow–related settings for your sales document. We'll now give you a detailed look at the various fields on this screen.

FIGURE 7.3   Transaction flow section of customization screen for maintaining sales document types

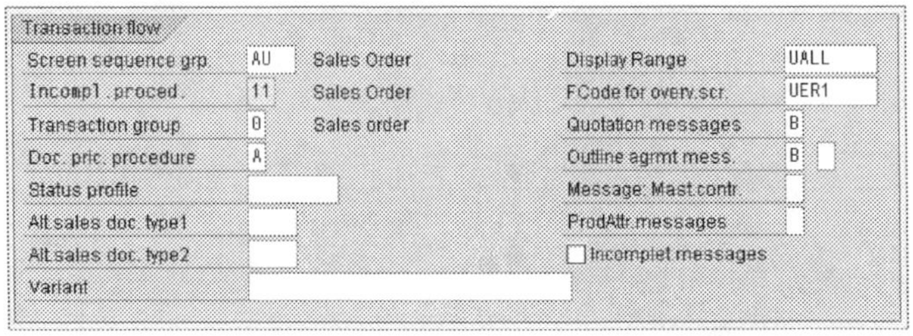

Transaction flow					
Screen sequence grp	AU	Sales Order	Display Range	UALL	
Incompl. proced.	11	Sales Order	FCode for overv.scr.	UER1	
Transaction group	0	Sales order	Quotation messages	B	
Doc. pric. procedure	A		Outline agrmt mess.	B	
Status profile			Message: Mast.contr.		
Alt.sales doc. type1			ProdAttr.messages		
Alt.sales doc. type2			☐ Incomplet messages		
Variant					

Screen Sequence Group   A data entry screen that you use for a contract document might not be relevant for a sales order, and vice versa. Therefore, based on the individual needs of the sales document categories, SAP has grouped the screens into various screen sequence groups. By choosing a screen sequence group for your document type in the field Screen Sequence Grp., you tell SAP what screens and fields should appear and in what sequence they should show up when you create the documents using your document type. In standard SAP, screen sequence group AG is available for inquiries and quotations, AU for sales orders, GA for credit and debit memo, KM for contracts, and RE for returns.

Display Range   The value you select in this field controls which details for a structured item, such as a BOM, will be shown during the sales document display. If you choose UALL, both the main and subitems are displayed, and if you choose UHAU, only the main item is shown.

Incompletion Procedure   As we mentioned earlier in this chapter, an incompletion procedure helps you check the sales document for incomplete data and stops the further processing steps such as delivery, billing, and so on, for the sales document, until the data in the sales document is complete. In Figure 7.3, value 11 in field Incompl.Proced. represents the two-character identifier for the incompletion procedure that is assigned to order type OR. Incompletion procedure customization and its assignment are explained in detail later in this chapter.

FCode For Overview Screen   The selection made in the field FCode For Overv. Scr. tells SAP which overview screen to display first when you are processing a sales document. You have a choice to select either general overview (UER1), item overview (UER2), and ordering party overview (UBST).

Transaction Group   There are six different transaction codes to process the six different varieties of sales documents in SAP, as shown in Table 7.1.

TABLE 7.1   Relationship Between Transaction Codes and Transaction Groups

Transaction Code	Transaction Group	Document Type
VA01, VA02, VA03	0	Sales orders
VA11, VA12, VA13	1	Inquiries
VA21, VA22, VA23	2	Quotations
VA31, VA32, VA33	3	Scheduling agreements
VA41, VA42, VA43	4	Contracts
VA51, VA52, VA53	5	Item proposals

Which transaction code to use for processing your document type will depend on what transaction group you choose while configuring your document type. So if you are configuring a sales document, make sure that you select 0 as the transaction group for your document type to process with transaction code VA01-VA03. Apart from this, the transaction group also controls updating the reporting indices in tables TINPA (Business Partner Index) and TVIND (Material & Validity Index).

Quotation Messages/Outline Agrmt Mess./Message: Mast.Contr./ProdAttr. Messages The purpose of these fields is to provide a message to the user during order creation if any open quotation, outline agreement, master contract, or product attributes exists. The available choices in these fields are self-explanatory.

Document Pricing Procedure In the field Doc. Pric. Procedure, you choose which document pricing procedure key to assign to your document type. The key you assign here will be one of the factors determining the pricing procedure for your sales document. At this point, if you feel the need for a quick revision/recall on the pricing procedure and its determination-related concepts, please refer to Chapter 5, "Pricing and Tax Determination."

Status Profile In this field, you assign the default status profile for your document type. Using the status profile, you can define your own status management for a sales document or individual line items of a sales document. Suppose you want to set up a small workflow for your sales document wherein your sales document should be under the Initial status just after creation, should be under the In Process status when it is with the approval authority for approvals, should be under the Reassign status when it is reassigned back, and finally should show the status as Released when some authorized person releases it for further processing.

In a status profile, you define the status steps (in other words, the four statuses we mentioned earlier). For each status step, you define which business function you want to allow when the document is under the said status. Thus, each status step then controls what business function is allowed and what is not. So that only an authorized person can perform the status change, each status line within a status profile is linked to an authorization code. Only the users who have this authorization code assigned to their user roles can change the status of the document. You can assign this status profile to the sales document type or an item category type to make it work for a sales document or a line item, respectively. For defining and assigning your own status profiles, follow the menu path IMG ➢ Sales And

Distribution ➤ Sales ➤ Sales Documents ➤ Define And Assign Status Profile. Define your own status profile by providing an eight-digit alphanumeric value and maintaining the various statuses.

Alternate Sales Document Types   By making a selection in the field Alt.Sales Doc. Type1, you allow the user to switch between the document types during the sales order entry. This is really helpful in a telesales scenario where the telesales representative does not know whether the prospect customer will end up placing an order or an inquiry. With a choice to switch between the document types without leaving the document creation screen, the telesales representative can keep on entering the information as they talk with the customer and can choose the document type while saving the document. You can set up two alternate sales document types when customizing for your sales document type using the fields Alt.Sales Doc. Type1 and Alt.Sales Doc. Type2. Choose the sales document type in this field that you would like to use as an alternative sales document during sales order processing.

Incompletion Messages   Unlike the incompletion procedure that allows you to save the incomplete sales document but disqualifies it for further processing steps such as delivery and billing, the Incomplet.Messages check box, when selected, prevents you from even saving the incomplete sales orders. You should select this only if you want SAP to stop an incomplete sales document from getting saved that was created using your sales document type.

Variant   Transaction variants consist of a sequence of screen variants and are assigned to the transaction codes. Using these variants, you can change the normal behavior of various screens called in a transaction during document processing. You can change the "ready for input" status of the fields, hide and change the table control column attributes, hide menu functions, and hide the entire screens. You define the transaction variants using transaction code SHD0. If you would like to use a transaction variant for processing your document, then provide that transaction variant here in this field, or leave this field blank so SAP will use the standard variant.

Shipping and Billing Information

In this section of customizing a sales document type, you assign default values for delivery-related and billing-related fields. SAP then uses these defaults (as shown in Figure 7.4) while performing the subsequent steps of shipping and billing for your sales document.

FIGURE 7.4   Shipping and billing section of the customization screen for maintaining the sales document types

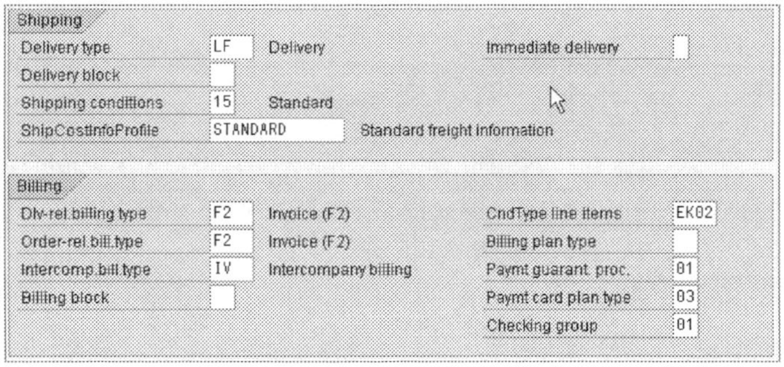

Delivery Type   Delivery Type here represents the delivery document type that you would like SAP to use while creating a delivery for your document. Choose a default delivery type only when your document is relevant for delivery. Leave this field blank if your sales document is not relevant for delivery such as with an inquiry, quotation, debit, or credit note request or any service-related billings. For document type OR, SAP uses delivery document LF.

Delivery Block   When you make a selection in this field, SAP prevents your sales document from getting delivered until an authorized person checks the documents and releases them from the delivery block. For example, in case of free-of-charge deliveries, you might want to make someone responsible to validate and justify the reasons for free-of-charge delivery before the actual delivery happens. Delivery block customization is discussed in detail later in this chapter.

Shipping Conditions   Make a selection in this field if you would like to copy the default shipping condition from the document type customization to your sales document. SAP copies shipping conditions from the customer master to the sales documents, but when you define a default in the sales document type, that default takes precedence over the customer master shipping condition.

Immediate Delivery   When you make a selection in this field, SAP creates the delivery for your document immediately on saving the document. In the standard SAP system, this setting is generally used for cash sales and rush orders. You can select from the following available options:

> Select A for immediate deliveries.

> Select X for immediate deliveries only for confirmed quantity line items.

> Leave the field blank if you do not want to create immediate deliveries.

Dlv-Rel.Billing Type   The SAP system will use the billing document type you enter in this field as a default billing document type when creating billings for your sales document type for delivery-relevant billing scenarios. A delivery-relevant billing refers to those scenarios where the sales cycle involves creating a delivery document before creating a billing document.

Order-Rel.Bill.Type   Here you enter the default order-relevant billing document type that you want to use to bill your sales document. An order-relevant billing refers to a billing document created directly from a sales order without involving a delivery step in between. This refers to service billing orders and debit/credit note processes.

Intercomp.Bill.Type   Here you enter the default intercompany billing document type that you want to use to bill your sales document in an intercompany scenario. An intercompany billing document records the sales transaction happening between the two companies of the same group.

Billing Block   The purpose of this field is to block your sales document from getting billed. Make a selection in this field only when you want to prevent your sales document from getting billed until an authorized person checks the documents and releases them from the billing block, such as credit notes. Please note that the billing block you assign here will work at the header level and will be applicable throughout the sales document.

Billing Plan Type   A billing plan controls the billing timelines and schedule of billing for periodic and milestone-based billing. In SAP, you can have a billing plan at the header level as well as at the item level. Make a selection in this field only when your sales document is either relevant for periodic billing or is a milestone billing and you want to keep the billing plan at the header level for your sales document type. For more details on billing plans, refer to Chapter 9.

Payment Guarantee Procedure   A payment guarantee procedure controls the risk management settings for your sales document type. A letter of credit, bank guarantee, and export credit insurance are a few examples of risk management documents that are commonly used in foreign trade. Maintain the value in this field if your document type is relevant for risk management control.

Payment Card Plan Type and Checking Group   Make a selection in these fields only when your sales document is relevant for payment cards processing. Payment cards are discussed in detail in Chapter 9. For standard orders of document type OR, SAP uses value 03 (Payment Cards) for the Payment Card Plan Type field and uses 01 (Standard) for the Checking Group field.

Requested Delivery Date/Pricing Date/Purchase Order Date

Figure 7.5 shows the set of fields from the sales document type customization screen where you maintain proposals for determining the requested delivery date, the pricing date, and the purchase order date for your sales document type. A requested delivery date is the date by which the customer expects to receive the delivery of the goods. It can be a date provided by the customer or proposed by the SAP system. A pricing date, on the other hand, helps in finding out the valid price for a sales document line item. We'll now cover how these fields impact the determination of various dates in a sales document.

FIGURE 7.5   Requested Delivery Date/Pricing Date/Purchase Order Date section of the customization screen for maintaining sales document types

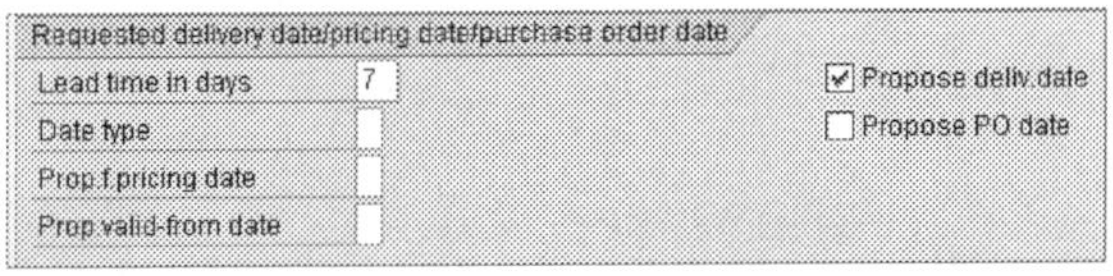

Date Type/Propose Delivery Date/Lead Time In Days   These three fields control the value and display format for the requested delivery date field on the sales document:

- ▶ Date Type controls the display format of the requested delivery date. You can make selections from the list of available values and can set up the display of the requested delivery date to be a day format (day, month, year), a week format (week, year), and a month format (month, year).

- ▶ The Propose Deliv.Date check box, when selected, proposes the current system date as the requested delivery date for your sales document.

- ▶ Lead Time In Days postpones the requested delivery date by the number of days you enter in this field.

Proposal For Pricing Date   The field Prop.F.Pricing Date helps in determining the pricing date for the sales document. From the list of available options, you can select A to have the pricing date equal the requested delivery date from the document header, you can select B to have the pricing date be valid from the date of the document header, you can select C to have the pricing date equal the contract start date from the document header or item, and you can leave the field blank to have the pricing date equal the current system date.

Propose PO Date   Use this check box when you want to propose the current system date as the purchase order date for a sales document.

Proposal For Valid From Date   The field Prop.Valid-From Date helps in determining the date value for the valid from date in the sales document. The fields on the sales document have no proposal when the value is left blank in customizing, they will be valid from today's date when A is selected for the value in customizing, and will be valid from the date that equals the beginning of next month when the value B is selected in customizing.

The customization screen for the sales document type also contains a section for setting up contracts. We intentionally skipped that section of the customization here and will be covering that later in this chapter while discussing contracts.

Defining Item Categories

The next step in customizing a sales document is to define an *item category*. An item category controls the behavior of an item by controlling the various elements relevant for item processing, such as item price, delivery, ATP, transaction flow update, and so on. The customization settings that you define at the item category level determine how the item will behave within a sales document and how it will impact all the next steps in the sales document cycle.

By using customization settings for delivery relevancy, billing relevancy, and pricing relevancy in the item category setup, you can bring various flavors to an item to fit your business needs. For example, to set up an item category that should cater to free-of-charge deliveries, you can make a standard item relevant for delivery and billing but not relevant for pricing.

Standard SAP comes with a long list of predefined item categories that work for various business scenarios. You have item category AFN for document type AF (inquiry), item category AGN for document type AG (quotation), and so on. You can make use of these item categories if they match your business requirements or can create your own by copying from these standard item categories.

To define a sales item category, use transaction code VOV7 or follow menu path IMG ➤ Sales And Distribution ➤ Sales ➤ Sales Documents ➤ Sales Document Items ➤ Define Item Categories. Let's take a detailed look at the various fields shown in Figure 7.6 and their impact on line items in a sales document. For this chapter's purposes, we will be covering the settings for standard item category TAN.

FIGURE 7.6   Business Data section of the customization screen for maintaining item categories

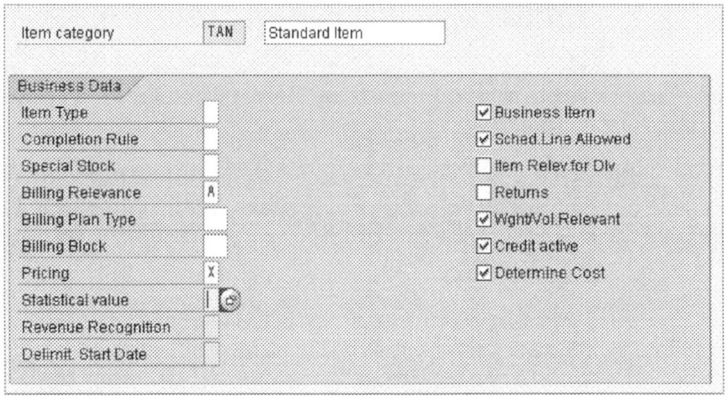

Business Data

Here you define business data for the item category. The following are the fields shown on this part of the screen:

Item Type   In SAP, items are classified as text items, value items, or standard items:

> **Text items**   Text items are generally used for sending print materials such as flyers, catalogs, and so on, to the customer. These items are generally not billable to the customer and therefore are not relevant for pricing. Text items can be added directly to the sales order without requiring you to create a material master record first. In standard SAP, item category TATX is available for use with text items.

> **Value items**   SAP provides value items for scenarios where you bill your customer for a fixed lump-sum amount for the goods or services rendered. The value is fixed and does not change with changes in quantity, volume, weight, or time units associated with the material.

> **Standard items**   For all other scenarios, you use standard items in SAP. The pricing for a standard item takes into consideration the change in quantity, weight, volume, and time units associated with the material.

By selecting a value in the field Item Type, you classify your item category as one of the three items. Choose A to define your item as the value item, choose B for defining it as a text item, or keep this field blank to define your item category as a standard item.

Completion Rule   The Completion Rule field controls the completion status for an item in inquiries, quotations, and contract documents. It tells that at what point in time your item will be considered completely processed. For example, choose A in this field for your quotation item category, and SAP will set the status of your quotation document as complete on its first reference by an order. Once the status is complete, you cannot refer to that quotation again for another order. The available options for this field in customizing are self-explanatory.

Special Stock   Make a selection in this field when you want your item category to use the inventory of some special stock location. For example, in the case of consignment processing, the scenario demands billing the customer only for the stock quantity physically consumed by the customer from the consignment stock location. This stock at the consignment location is tracked in SAP using the special stock indicator W (Customer Consignment). Standard item categories KEN (Consignment Issue) and KRN (Consignment Returns) have the value W in this field. This helps SAP to use the stock from the customer consignment location for all the inventory-related postings during consignment issue and consignment returns processing. Customer consignment processing is explained in detail later in this chapter.

Billing Relevance   Whether your item category is relevant for billing is controlled by the Billing Relevance field. Available choices for this field are self-explanatory. A few important ones are as follows:

> » B for configuring the item category relevant for order-related billing

> » A for delivery-related billing

> » D for pro-forma billing

> » I for billing plan–relevant billing

Leave the value blank in this field to configure your item category as not relevant for billing.

Billing Plan Type   In this field, you enter a default billing plan type key for your item category that in turn will control the billing plan for your sales item. If your item category is relevant for periodic or milestone-based billing (billing relevancy = I), you need to assign the two-character billing plan identifier here. Item category WVN for use with warranties and maintenance contracts and item categories MVN for use with rental contracts use this setting. Contract documents are explained later in this chapter. For more details on billing plans, refer to Chapter 9.

Billing Block   Using this field, you can default a billing block for your item category. When you create the sales document using the item category with a billing block set in customizing, the item in the sales document will get blocked for billing and can be billed only when an authorized person validates the sales item and removes the billing block. If your business requirement demands that the item should be blocked for billing by default, you should use this field.

Pricing   Here you set the pricing indicator for your item category. A pricing indicator tells whether the item category is relevant for pricing and whether SAP should automatically carry out pricing for the item in the sales document that uses this item category. You can choose among the following indicators:

- » X makes your item category relevant for standard SAP item pricing.
- » A sets your item category relevant for pricing for empties.
- » B applies free goods pricing to your item category.

Keep the value in this field blank to make your item category not relevant for pricing.

Statistical Value   In SAP, item values are totaled up to calculate the document value at the header level. When you set a statistical value indicator for your item category, the item value does not roll up to the header for calculating the document totals. Unless you want your item values to act statistical, keep the value in this field blank so SAP can consider the item values while calculating the document totals. If you choose X, SAP performs no cumulation, and the value cannot be used statistically. If you choose Y, SAP likewise performs no cumulation, but the value can be used statistically.

Revenue Recognition and Delimit/Start Date   These two fields control the revenue recognition and accrual processing for your item category. Keep the data in these two fields blank if your item category is not relevant for revenue recognition processing. For more details on revenue recognition including the explanation for these two fields, refer to Chapter 10, "Account Assignment and Revenue Recognition."

Business Item   This check box, when selected for an item category, allows the business data in the header and item for a sales document to be different. Select it when you want to allow different data between the header and the item for your sales document, and deselect it if you want the data to be same between the header and item.

Schedule Line   When this check box is selected, it allows the item to have schedule lines. The Schedule Line tab in the sales document item level appears only when you select this check box when customizing for your item category. You need the schedule line only for those items that are relevant for delivery. Items that are not relevant for deliveries, such as credit note items, debit note items, and service items, do not need a schedule line. Text items as an exception can exist both with and without a schedule line.

Item Relevant For Delivery   Text and value items do not contain schedule lines and therefore cannot be delivered as such. When the check box Item Relev.For Dlv is selected, it allows the text and value items to be relevant for delivery. By making them relevant for delivery, it does not deliver text items from stock but allows them to copy to the delivery document for informational purposes. Do not select this check box unless you are configuring an item category for text or value items that you want to make relevant for delivery.

Returns   This check box tells whether the item in the sales order is a return item. Select this if you are setting up the item category for return goods or a similar process.

Weight/Volume Relevant   This check box specifies whether SAP should calculate the weight and volume for the item.

Credit Active   This check box tells whether the item is relevant for credit checks. Select this if you want to perform credit checks on your items.

Determine Cost   Selecting this check box tells SAP to use the cost condition type VPRS in pricing to calculate the cost of the item. For more information on VPRS, refer Chapter 5.

General Controls

The next set of fields when customizing an item category are a few check boxes, as shown in Figure 7.7. These check boxes act as yes/no indicators and exercise some general controls over a sales document item with respect to batch determination and order quantity.

FIGURE 7.7   General Control section of the customization screen for maintaining item categories

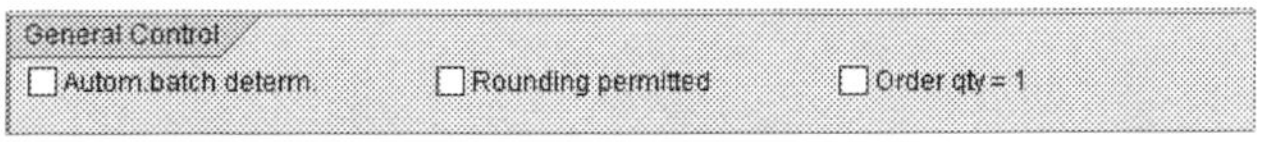

Automatic Batch Determination   This check box controls the batch determination for an item. When selected for an item category, it tells SAP to use automatic batch determination to find out the matching batch for a material entered into a sales order line item. Use this only when your materials are batch relevant. You will learn about batch management in detail in Chapter 13, "Serial Numbers and Batch Management."

Rounding Permitted check box   This controls whether a required order quantity can be rounded to match the deliverable units. When selected, it activates the rounding feature for an item category, and vice versa. In addition, you also need to define a rounding profile and assign it to either a customer-material record or a material master record. A rounding profile consists of the threshold values and round-up/round-down percentage.

Order Qty = 1   Select this check box if you want the order quantity for each sales item to be limited to one per line item in the sales document.

Transaction Flow

The fields shown in Figure 7.8 control the transactional flow for an item in a sales document.

FIGURE 7.8   Transaction Flow section of the customization screen for maintaining item categories

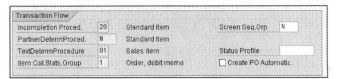

Screen Sequence Group   A screen sequence group controls the fields that appear on various screens related to an item and the sequence in which these screens appear during the processing of a sales item. This field should always contain an N to represent the standard item screens, unless you have defined your own item screen sequence group and you want to use that instead of the standard.

Status Profile   Select a value here only if you want to attach a default status profile to your item category. Using this status profile, you will be able to control the user-defined statuses for a line item in a sales document. For details about the status profile, please refer to the status profile explanations in the sales document type customization process, as explained earlier in this chapter.

Create PO Automatically   This check box was available only for ALE in previous versions, but now it is also available for third-party PO creation. When selected, it creates a purchase requisition for a third-party schedule line and a purchase order in the background when you save the order. Select this check box only if your item category type is relevant for third-party order processing.

Incompletion Procedure/Partner Determination Procedure/Text Determination Procedure/Item Category Statistics Group   If you take a look at Figure 7.8, you will see that the fields on the left in this group are not available for data entry here. This is because these fields are assigned to the item categories on their respective customization screens. For example, you assign the item incompletion procedure to an item category while configuring the incompletion procedure for a sales item. We'll briefly summarize them here:

Incompletion procedure   An item incompletion procedure will ensure that when you save the document, the required data for an item is duly filled in, and its incompletion status is complete.

Partner determination procedure   An item-level partner determination procedure will ensure that the required partner data is present at the sales item level.

Text determination procedure   An item text determination procedure will control what text fields should be determined for an item and how.

Item category statistics group   An item category statistics group will control the update of item data in the logistics information system (LIS).

Bill of Material

Figure 7.9 shows the next set of fields in the customization of an item category. These fields control the variant configuration and bill of materials processing for an item category.

FIGURE 7.9   BOM/configuration section of the customization screen for maintaining item categories

Structure Scope   Entry in this field determines how a BOM is going to be processed in a sales document. You can choose from the following options:

> » Select A to explode the single-level BOM.

> » Select B to explode the multilevel BOM.

> » Keep the value in this field blank for no BOM explosion.

Create Delivery Group   Use this field when your item category is BOM relevant and you want to combine all the deliverable subitems of a BOM in one delivery group so as to deliver on the same date. When you select this check box, SAP groups the subitems into a delivery group with same dates. When you choose A in this field, SAP creates a delivery group with correlated schedule lines.

Manual Alternative   This check box, when selected, allows the user to manually pick an alternative BOM for an item during the BOM explosion in a sales document, provided that multiple BOM exist for that item in SD.

Figure 7.10 shows the fields relevant for value contracts, repair management, and resource-related billings. You make a selection in these fields only when your item category type is relevant for any of these three processes. Contracts are explained later in this chapter, and repair/resource-related billing is out of scope of this book.

FIGURE 7.10   Maintaining item categories: value contract, repair service management, and resource-related billing

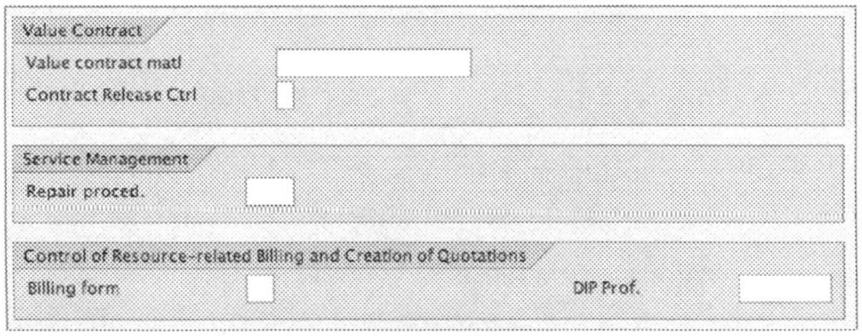

Setting Up an Item Category Determination

Before we set up the item category determination rule, we'll discuss a few elements we are going to use in the determination process.

Item Category Group

An item category group is a grouping of various material types. An item category group is assigned to a material master through material types and is linked to SD via an item category determination rule. The item category group, together with item usage, a higher-level item category, and a sales document type, helps in the determination of the item category during sales order processing. A long list of item category groups comes with standard SAP, and they should be sufficient for any business need. Still, if you ever need to create a new item category group, you would do so by providing a four-digit or less alphanumeric key starting with the letter Z and by providing a description. To define a new item category group, follow the menu path IMG ➢ Sales And Distribution ➢ Sales ➢ Sales Documents ➢ Sales Document Item ➢ Define Item Category Groups. You can also define a default item category group for a material type by following the menu path IMG ➢ Sales And Distribution ➢ Sales ➢ Sales Documents ➢ Sales Document Item ➢ Define Default Values For Material Types.

Item Category Usage

This controls the usage of an item. For example, during automatic product selection, you use the Item category usage PHSP (product selection main item) and PSEL (product selection subitems) to differentiate the main item and subitems. To define an item category usage, follow the menu path IMG ➢ Sales And Distribution ➢ Sales ➢ Sales Documents ➢ Sales Document Item ➢ Define Item Category Usage.

Setting Up an Item Category Determination Rule

Unlike a sales document type where you manually enter the sales document type on the initial screen, an item category is determined automatically by SAP during sales order processing. This is made possible by assigning the item category to a determination key in customizing. You can assign an item category to the determination key by using transaction code VOV4 or following menu path IMG ➢ Sales And Distribution ➢ Sales ➢ Sales Documents ➢ Sales Document Item ➢ Assign Item Categories. Figure 7.11 shows the customization screen for assigning an item category. The first four fields on the screen, Sales Doc Type (SA), Item Category Group (ItCGr), Item Usage (Usg.), and Higher-Level Item Category (HLevItCa), form a determination key. You can assign one default item category and up to 11 manual item categories to a determination key. During determination, the default item category automatically copies to the required item line in the sales document, but you can always override it with any of these 11 manual ones you assigned to the same determination rule in customizing.

FIGURE 7.11 Assigning item categories to sales documents

SaTy	ItCGr	Usg	HLevItCa	DfltC	MItCa	MItCa	MItCa
OR	NORM			TAN	TAP	TAQ	TANN

How SAP Determines an Item Category

The process followed by SAP for determining an item category is explained in the following steps and is also graphically represented by Figure 7.12:

FIGURE 7.12 Determination of an item category in SAP

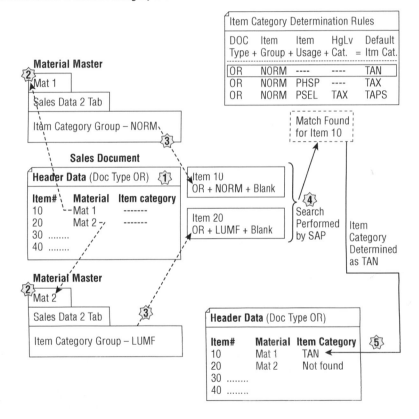

1. SAP reads the document type from the sales document.

2. SAP reads the item category group from the material master of the sales item material. At this point, it also checks whether the item is a main item or subitem to find out whether a higher-level item category (linked to the main item) will have any role to play in item category determination. SAP also checks if there is any Item usage that needs to be considered for item category determination.

3. SAP creates a determination key from the data received.

4. SAP searches for this key in arrangement for determination rules.

5. SAP returns the item category for the sales item to the sales document.

Defining Schedule Line Categories

The next step in customizing a sales document is to define a schedule line category. A schedule line consists of confirmed delivery quantities and corresponding confirmed delivery dates when these quantities can be delivered. A schedule line category controls this delivery scheduling process and impacts logistics by controlling various relevancy indicators and other values related to delivery, purchase requisition generation, availability check, goods movement, transfer of requirement, product allocation, and MRP applicability for an item. The behavior of a schedule line, whether to create delivery, by default blocked for delivery, whether to allow MRP, and so on, depends upon the configuration options you set when customizing the schedule line category.

You define a schedule line category by using transaction code VOV6 or by following the menu path IMG ➤ Sales And Distribution ➤ Sales ➤ Sales Documents ➤ Schedule Lines ➤ Define Schedule Line Categories. Once you are at the customization screen, enter a two-digit alphanumeric key with a description to define your own schedule line category. Always remember to follow the rule of naming your objects with the prefix Z. Standard SAP provides a variety of schedule line categories, but still you may come across situations where you need to customize a schedule line category of your own. Let's now take a look at various customization settings of a schedule line category, as shown in Figure 7.13.

FIGURE 7.13 Defining schedule line categories

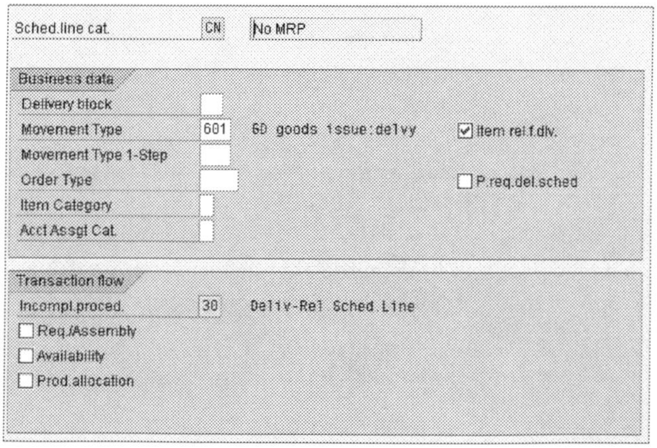

Schedule Line Category Key and Type   At the top of the screen shown in Figure 7.13, CN represents the schedule line category key, and No MRP represents the description for the schedule line category type.

N O T E   In standard SAP, the first character in a schedule line category always represents the sales process where the schedule line category will be used, such as A – Inquiry, B – Quotations, C – Sales Orders, and so on. The second character represents the impact of the schedule line on the logistics process, such as N – No MRP, P – MRP applicable, T – No Inventory Management, and so on. So, schedule line category CN, as shown in Figure 7.13, is for sales orders with no MRP checks.

Delivery Block   The delivery block key that you enter in this field gets copied over as a default delivery block on the schedule line in the sales document. Select the delivery block, which you would like to default to your schedule lines.

Movement Type   A movement type in SAP controls the "to and from" movement of goods and thus controls the inventory update. For instance, movement type 601 (Figure 7.13) is used for goods issue from the inventory, and therefore it reduces the inventory to the tune of delivered quantities. The SD module uses goods movement from 601 to 699. Select the relevant movement type for your schedule line category in this field.

Item Relevant For Delivery Indicator   When selected, the check box item Rel.F.Dlv. allows the items attached to a schedule line to be relevant for delivery. Leave this field deselected for those schedule line categories where you do not want the items to be delivered such as inquiry- and quotation-related schedule line categories.

Movement Type 1-Step   This field allows you to enter the movement type for one-step movement of goods.

Processes such as STO can have both single-step and two-step movement of goods possible. Example of a two-step process would be transferring goods from plant A to plant B, where step 1 is goods issue (GI) of goods from plant A and step 2 would be performing goods receipt (GR) in plant B when the goods are physically received in plant B. A one-step process would be transferring goods from plant A to plant B where step 2 is deemed performed when you perform GI from Plant A. In this case, you will not wait for goods to be received physically in plant B in order to perform the GR step. Rather GR at plant B will be automatically performed by SAP the moment you perform GI step at plant A. One-step process is generally used when the plants are physically located very close to each other and therefore cross plant movements need not involve two separate steps.

Order Type/Item Category/Account Assignment Category   With ATP checks and TOR, you can check the availability of the goods in stock and can transfer the shortage requirement to PP or the Purchasing module for production planning or procurement. These three fields together allow the automatic creation of a purchase requisition for the requirements transferred from a sales order.

Purchase Requisition Delivery Schedule   The check box P.Req.Del.Sched indicates whether the sales line item is relevant for delivery rescheduling. Keep this deselected for third-party orders processing because it is possible to have a direct shipment of goods from your vendor to your customer, and you do not require SAP to reschedule the delivery timelines in such a case. Use this when the goods come to your warehouse first and then move to a customer's purchase order on receipt of the requirements from the sales order so that SAP can add those times into the delivery scheduling.

Incompletion Procedure   The field Incompl.Proced. is for display only in the customization screen for schedule line categories. You enter a default value for an incompletion procedure for a schedule line in the customization of incompletion procedures.

Req./Assembly   This check box acts as an on/off switch for transferring requirements. When selected, requirements from a sales order can be transferred to the PP or the Purchasing module by creating the relevant purchase order or purchase requisition. It also acts as a prerequisite for an availability check to happen. If you do not select the requirement field and select only the availability field, the check will not function.

Availability/Prod. Allocation   When selected, this check box activates the availability check/product allocation for a sales order. For more details on availability checks, please refer to Chapter 6, "Availability Check, Transfer of Requirements, and Backorders."

Setting Up a Schedule Line Category Determination

Just like an item category, schedule line categories are also determined automatically by SAP. This is made possible by assigning the schedule line categories to a combination of item categories and MRP type. The MRP type is stored in the MRP view of the material master record and is responsible for the requirement planning for the material. You can assign a schedule line category via transaction code VOV5 or via menu path IMG ➤ Sales And Distribution ➤ Sales ➤ Sales Documents ➤ Schedule Lines ➤ Assign Schedule Line Categories.

Figure 7.14 shows the customization screen for assigning a schedule line category. As you can see on this screen, the default schedule line category CN is assigned to item category TAN (Standard Item And MRP Type ND – No Planning). You can also assign three additional manual schedule line categories (field MSLCa) for your determination rule. When you create a sales order with a material line having item category TAN and if that material master has the MRP type ND, SAP automatically determines the schedule line category as CN. You can then overwrite it with any of these three manual schedule line categories values that you set up in customizing for schedule line category determination.

FIGURE 7.14 Assigning schedule line categories

ItCa	Typ	SchLC	MSLCa	MSLCa	MSLCa	
TAN	ND	CN				

Setting Up Copy Controls

A copy control transfers the data from one document to another and thus saves on data entry time, automates the sales process, and reduces the chances of manual mistakes. It also updates the document flow and ensures easy traceability between the documents. For example, if you know the sales order number, you can trace the delivery document, billing document, and accounting posting for that sales document using the document flow generated via the copy control setups. If you know the accounting document number, you can still trace the whole flow back up to the sales document number from where the whole transaction started.

In a sales application, you can define copy control for the following:

► Copy from sales document to sales document (transaction code VTAA)

► Copy from billing document to sales document (transaction code VTAF)

You need to define a copy control from a sales document to another sales document when you want to copy one sales document's data into another sales document such as when performing a copy from an inquiry to a quotation or from a quotation to an order. On the other hand, copying from a billing document to a sales document is usually set up in debit and credit notes scenarios where you want to create the debit or credit note request by copying data from a billing document.

Because a sales document is structured into header data, item data, and schedule line data, you need to maintain the copy control setup at all three levels. To maintain the copy control setup for a sales document, use transaction codes VTAA and VTAF, or follow the menu path IMG ➤ Sales And Distribution ➤ Sales ➤ Maintain Copy Control For Sales Documents. For this discussion, we'll cover how to customize a copy control at all these levels, with the help of a sales document–to–sales document copy setup and by using copy controls for standard orders as an example.

Setting Up Copy Control: Header Data

A copy control customization screen consists of an overview screen and a detail screen. On the copy control overview screen, you define the source object from where you want to copy and you define the target object to which you want to copy. Figure 7.15 is an example of a copy control overview screen. Here, IN and QT represent the source document type, and OR represents the target document type. You can define a new copy source and target relationship by clicking the new entries button on the menu. The dialog structure menu shown in Figure 7.15 contains an icon for each of the levels for which you need to define a copy control setup. Double-clicking the icon will take you to the overview screen of the specified level. Currently the icon is on the header level, and we are maintaining the copy control at the sales header level.

FIGURE 7.15 Header Overview screen for sales document–to–sales document copy

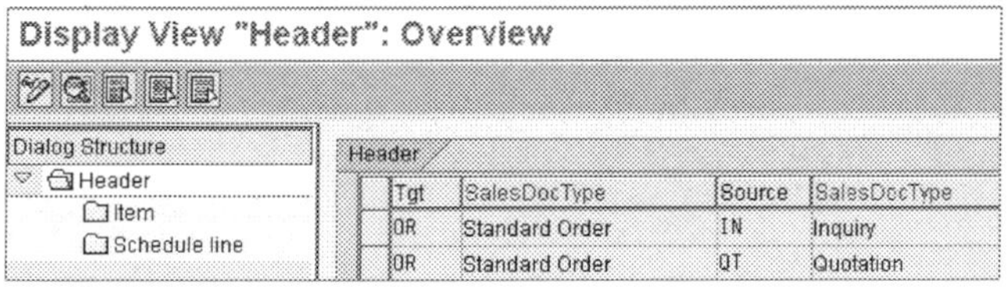

A copy control setup primarily consists of three main elements: a data transfer routine, a requirement, and a few check boxes. A data transfer routine controls whatever data needs to be copied over, a requirement controls when (and when not) to copy data, and a check box field acts as an on/off switch to activate or deactivate a particular functionality during copy. Let's take a look at all these elements with reference to Figure 7.16.

FIGURE 7.16 Header Details screen for sales document–to–sales document copy

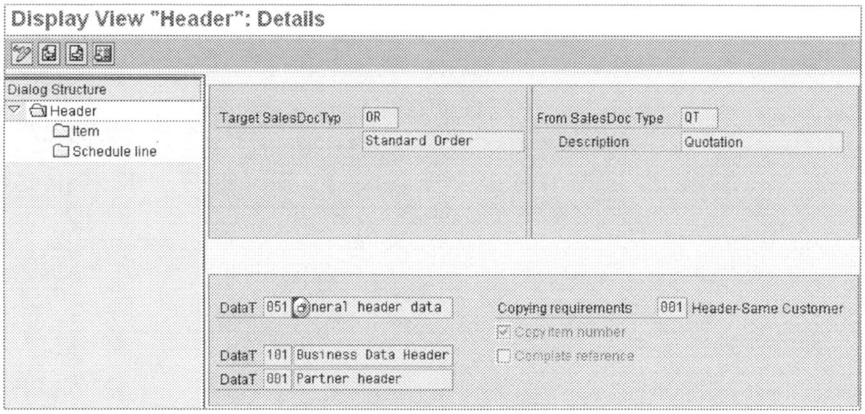

Data Transfer Routine (DataT field)   A data transfer routine contains the ABAP code for the field-to-field transfer of data from the source object to the target object. Routines 051, 101, and 001 in Figure 7.16 specify that when the QT document is copied into an OR document, the general header data, the business data at the header level, and the partner data at the header level all will be copied from the source to the target document, in other words, from QT to OR.

Copying Requirements   The Copying Requirements field controls when the data should be copied over and when it shouldn't be. Here, copy requirement 101 tells SAP that the copy should happen only when the header partners of both the documents (in other words, QT and OR) matches each other. With this setting, if you go ahead and try to create an order for customer A from the quotation document of customer B, SAP will show an error on the document copy screen telling you that the sales document cannot be copied because the header data between the two documents are not same.

Copy Item Number check box   The Copy Item Number check box controls whether item numbers should be copied from the source to the target. This setting makes sure that the item number for the item in the source and target documents is the same. Since this is selected in Figure 7.16, the item numbers will be copied over from QT to OR.

Complete Reference   The Complete Reference check box, when selected, tells SAP to update the status of the source document as complete on the first reference of the source document by the target document. Once the source document status becomes complete, you will not be able to copy that source document again to any other target document.

Setting Up Copy Control: Item Data

Once the copy control is defined between the header for a source and target document type, you need to define the copy control between the relevant item categories for these two documents. Figure 7.17 shows the overview screen for item category copying. To reach this screen, click the Item icon shown on the left of Figure 7.16. Item category AGN on the screen is the source item category.

FIGURE 7.17 Item Overview screen for sales document–to–sales document copy

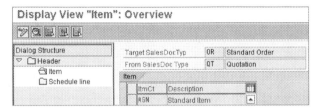

For the purposes of this chapter, we will analyze the standard item category AGN. To reach the detail screen shown in Figure 7.18, double-click the item category line AGN.

FIGURE 7.18 Item Details screen for sales document–to–sales document copy

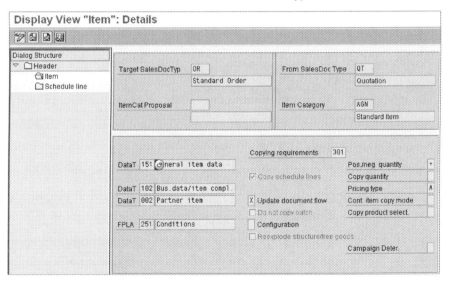

We'll now discuss the customization fields shown in Figure 7.18 in detail, starting at the left of the lower pane:

Item-level data transfer routines   Starting from the top, you can see the item-level data transfer routines 151, 102, and 002, which respectively ensure the copying of general data, business data, and partner data that's relevant for the item.

FPLA   FPLA contains the copy requirement for the data transfer of billing plans. If the check as per the copy requirements for FPLA is successful, the billing plan fields are copied from the source to the target item.

Copying Requirement   Copying requirement 301 ensures that the rejected lines are not copied from the source item to the target item.

Copy Schedule Line   The Copy Schedule Line check box, when selected, ensures that the schedule lines from the source item are copied to the target item.

Update Document Flow   The Update Document Flow check box controls the updating of document flow during the copying.

Do Not Copy Batch   The Do Not Copy Batch check box controls whether the batch can be copied from the source item to the target item.

Configuration   The Configuration check box controls the copying behavior of configurable items. When you copy a configurable item from the source to the target document, the target document uses the configuration of the source document, and the BOM is not re-exploded. Now, if you change the source document, the target document also gets that change passed over. By using the available options in this field, you can change this behavior.

Re-explode Structure/Free Goods   This option is used for BOM-based materials. When selected, this check box ensures that the main items are copied as such and the BOM is re-exploded in the target document with a new date and new quantities contained in the target document.

Positive/Negative Quantity   This controls whether, during copying of an item, the quantity or the value of the item will have a positive impact, a negative impact, or no effect at all. For example, a contract to a return will have a negative effect, a quotation to an order will have a positive effect, an order to an order copy will have no effect, and so on.

Copy Quantity   This controls what quantity should be copied from the source to the target document. You can choose between copying from the target quantity and copying from the order quantity, and you can even leave the field blank. If you do not choose any value in the field, SAP tries to determine the most appropriate quantity. For example, if you leave this field blank for a copy between QT and OR, then the open quotation quantity is determined and copied as the order quantity.

Pricing Type   This controls how the pricing should behave during the copy between the source and the target. With the available options from the field, you can set the pricing to completely determined, partially determined and partially copied, or completely copied from the source to the document without any changes.

Cont. Item Copy Mode   This sets the limits for the copy of the value contract items. You can select B to allow the copy of the value contract items and restrict the others from copying, or you can select A to restrict the value contract item from copying but allow other items to copy. You can also leave the field blank if you do not want to apply any restrictions.

Copy Product Selection   This is relevant for product selections. By selecting a value here, you can set up whether the product selections should be copied over from the source to the target documents. For copying from an order to an order, do not copy the product selections from the source. Rather, you should leave the field blank so that the product selection is carried out again for the target document.

Campaign Determination   The Campaign Determination field is related to the campaign determination in SD.

The next screen (Figure 7.19) represents the copy control at the schedule line level. This screen is pretty simple; the only requirements are to decide when to copy or when not to copy the schedule line and to set a data transfer routine to control what data to be copied.

FIGURE 7.19 Schedule Line copy screen for sales document–to–sales document copy

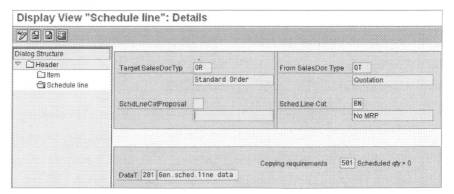

DEFINING YOUR OWN ROUTINES AND REQUIREMENTS

The routines and requirements you saw in the detail screens of the copy control setup at various levels are the ones provided by standard SAP. Using transaction code VOFM, you can define your own routines and requirements for the cases where existing routines and requirements are not sufficient to handle your business needs. Please refer to OSS note 327220 – "VOFM functions and its objects" for more details on VOFM functionality.

Copy Control in Other Document Types in SAP SD

SAP provides the copy controls for deliveries and billing documents as well as for sales documents. Table 7.2 shows the various copy controls that you can set up in delivery and billing along with their transaction codes and menu paths.

TABLE 7.2   Transaction Codes and Menu Paths for Setting Up Copy Controls in Delivery and Billing Documents

Description	Transaction Code	Menu Path
Copy Control for Delivery Documents		
Sales document to delivery document	VTLA	IMG ➤ Logistics Execution ➤ Shipping ➤ Copying Control ➤ Specify Copy Controls For Deliveries
Copy Control for Billing Documents		
Billing document to billing document	VTFF	IMG ➤ Sales And Distribution ➤ Billing ➤ Billing Documents ➤ Maintain Copying Control For Billing Documents
Sales document to billing document	VTFA	
Delivery document to billing document	VTFL	

Delivery and billing documents are structured into a header and an item data only. Therefore, maintaining a copy control for these documents involves only two levels: a header copy and an item copy. Otherwise, the process is the same as you saw earlier for sales-to-sales copy. There will also be routines, requirements, check boxes, and fields for extra information to be copied over from source to target document during copying.

TIP Throughout the sales process, you need to define various copy controls in order to complete a cycle. For example, if your cycle is for a quantity contract, then your first copy control is between the quantity contract and release order, followed by between the release order and delivery, followed by between the delivery and billing and between the billing and debit/credit request if you need the data from billing to be copied directly into the debit/credit requests. Copying from inquiries to quotations, from quotations to orders, from orders to delivery documents, and from delivery documents to invoice billing documents are a few examples of using copy control in SD. To identify which application to choose for setting up these controls, follow this rule of thumb: identify the target document. If the target document happens to be a sales document, you need to define the copy controls in the sales application. If the target document happens to be a delivery document, you need to define the copy controls in shipping, and if the target document happens to be a billing document, you need to define the copy controls in billing.

Common Sales Document Customizations

In addition to the settings that have we already defined in this chapter, there are various miscellaneous customization settings that you can define for sales documents. We'll cover these other settings one by one.

Allowable Sales Doc by Sales Area

By default, the sales document types you create are available to be used across all sales areas. But if you ever want to use them only with a particular sales area, you then need to assign them to that sales area by following the menu path IMG ➢ Sales And Distribution ➢ Sales ➢ Sales Documents ➢ Sales Document Header ➢ Assign Sales Area To Sales Document Types. Next you will be presented with the activity dialog screens with the following four activities.

- ▶ Combine sales organizations
- ▶ Combine distribution channels
- ▶ Combine divisions
- ▶ Assign sales order types permitted for sales areas

These four activities need to be configured in the sequence they are explained next. Remember that all four steps are mandatory if you want to set up the sales document by sales area.

Combine sales organizations   Here you assign your sales organization to a reference sales organization for the purpose of sharing the document types between the two. You can also reach this customization screen directly using transaction code OVAO. Figure 7.20 shows the customization screen for OVAO. Here, sales organizations 9090 and 9091 are set up to share the document types that are defined for sales organization 9090.

FIGURE 7.20   Defining a reference sales organization for assigning document types

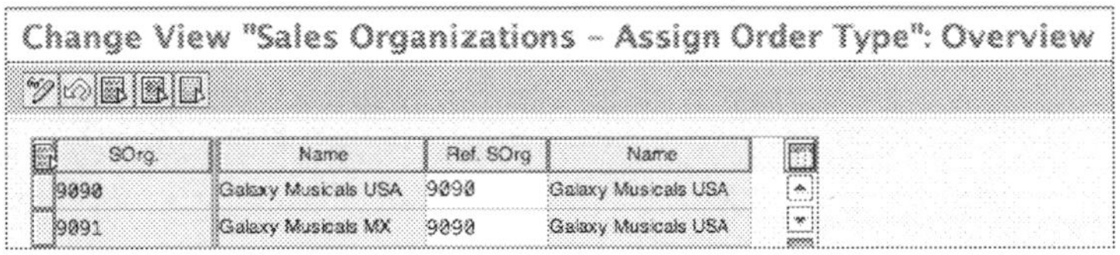

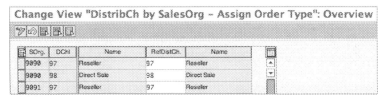

Combine distribution channels   Here you assign your sales organization and distribution channel combination to a reference distribution channel for the purpose of sharing the document types. You can also reach this customization screen directly using transaction code OVAM. Figure 7.21 shows the customization setting for OVAM setup. Here, the sales organization and distribution channel combination for 9090-97 and 9091-97 will share the document types, whereas 9090-98 is set up to have its own document types.

FIGURE 7.21   Defining reference distribution channel by sales organization for assigning document types

Combine divisions   Here you assign your sales organization and division combination to a reference division for the purpose of sharing the document types. You can also reach this customization screen directly using transaction code OVAN. Figure 7.22 shows the customization setting for OVAN setup. Here, as you can see, all the sales organization and division combinations for Galaxy US and Mexico are set up to share the document types that are defined for division 99.

FIGURE 7.22 Defining reference divisions by sales organization for assigning document types

Change View "Divisions by SalesOrg - Assign Order Type": Overview

SOrg.	Div	Name	RefDivDoc	Name
9090	97	Media & Apparels	99	Default
9090	98	Instru. & Accessorie	99	Default
9090	99	Default	99	Default
9091	97	Media & Apparels	99	Default
9091	98	Instru. & Accessorie	99	Default
9091	99	Default	99	Default

Assign sales order types permitted for sales areas At the end, you assign the sales document types to the reference sales area. You can also reach this customization screen directly using transaction code OVAZ. Figure 7.23 represents this customization setting for Galaxy Musical Instruments. As you can see from the customization setup shown on this screen, we assigned the document types to sales areas 9090-97-99 and 9090-98-99. The document types that were assigned to 9090-97-99 will be shared between 9090-97-99 (the U.S. reseller sale) and 9091-97-99 (the Mexico reseller sale), whereas the document types defined for 9090-98-99 (U.S. direct sales) will be exclusively used by sales area 9090-98-99 only.

FIGURE 7.23 Assigning sales document types to sales area

Change View "Sales Documents: Allowed Order Types per Sales Org.": Ove

Ref.S	Name	RefD	Name	Div	Name	SaTy	Description
9090	Galaxy Musicals USA	97	Reseller	99	Default	ZGM1	Galaxy Sales Order
9090	Galaxy Musicals USA	97	Reseller	99	Default	ZGMC	Credit Memo Request
9090	Galaxy Musicals USA	97	Reseller	99	Default	ZGMD	Debit Memo Request
9090	Galaxy Musicals USA	97	Reseller	99	Default	ZGMI	Galaxy Inquiry
9090	Galaxy Musicals USA	97	Reseller	99	Default	ZGMQ	Quotation
9090	Galaxy Musicals USA	97	Reseller	99	Default	ZGMR	Returns
9090	Galaxy Musicals USA	97	Reseller	99	Default	ZGPV	Item Proposal
9090	Galaxy Musicals USA	97	Reseller	99	Default	ZGQC	Galaxy Qty Contract
9090	Galaxy Musicals USA	97	Reseller	99	Default	ZGRK	Invoice correct. req
9090	Galaxy Musicals USA	98	Direct Sale	99	Default	ZGM1	Galaxy Sales Order
9090	Galaxy Musicals USA	98	Direct Sale	99	Default	ZGMA	Membership contract
9090	Galaxy Musicals USA	98	Direct Sale	99	Default	ZGMC	Credit Memo Request
9090	Galaxy Musicals USA	98	Direct Sale	99	Default	ZGMD	Debit Memo Request
9090	Galaxy Musicals USA	98	Direct Sale	99	Default	ZGMI	Galaxy Inquiry
9090	Galaxy Musicals USA	98	Direct Sale	99	Default	ZGMQ	Quotation
9090	Galaxy Musicals USA	98	Direct Sale	99	Default	ZGMR	Returns
9090	Galaxy Musicals USA	98	Direct Sale	99	Default	ZGPV	Item Proposal
9090	Galaxy Musicals USA	98	Direct Sale	99	Default	ZGRK	Invoice correct. req
9090	Galaxy Musicals USA	98	Direct Sale	99	Default	ZGRO	Rush Order

Converting the Language for Each Sales Document Type

In SAP, you can set up the language-specific identifier key for your document type. The menu path is IMG ➢ Sales And Distribution ➢ Sales ➢ Sales Documents ➢ Sales Document Header ➢ Convert Language For Each Sales Document Type. Figure 7.24 shows the customization screen with an example showing the sales document type key conversion into Chinese.

FIGURE 7.24 Converting the language for each sales document type

Change View "SD: Language-dependent Con

New Entries

Language	SDTy	Description	Lang.key
ZF	GENE		授權
ZF	HITK		找到
ZF	HITS		模擬
ZF	HITW		找到
ZF	INIT		起始
ZF	INSE		建立
ZF	INSG		建立

Defining Purchase Order Types

Your customer can send orders to you using various transmission services, such as phone, EDI, fax, mail, email, and so on. In SAP, you can define a four-character identifier key for each of these transmission methods that your customer has used to send the orders into your organization and thereby can take statistical reports on this basis. This is one of the factors an organization uses to determine whether its investment in electronic ordering techniques is showing any results. The menu path is IMG ➢ Sales And Distribution ➢ Sales ➢ Sales Documents ➢ Sales Document Header ➢ Define Purchase Order Types. Figure 7.25 shows the customization screen for defining the purchase order type.

FIGURE 7.25 Defining PO types

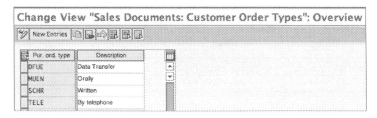

Change View "Sales Documents: Customer Order Types": Overview

New Entries

Pur. ord. type	Description
DFUE	Data Transfer
MUEN	Orally
SCHR	Written
TELE	By telephone

Maintaining Order Reasons

The reasons that led the customer to place an order or returns for your product can be maintained in SAP as order reasons. A sales call, television advertisement, trade fair activities, excellent price, existing customer recommendation, and so on, are a few examples of order reasons. Be it an inquiry, quotation, sales order, contract, return, or any other sales document, you can use an order reason for all of them. An order reason helps you analyze your marketing and presales activities' effectiveness and efficiency. It also help you judge your product performance in the market and capture quality failures and problems that led to customers returning your goods, so that you can improve in the future.

The transaction code is OVAU, and the menu path is IMG ➤ Sales And Distribution ➤ Sales ➤ Sales Documents ➤ Sales Document Header ➤ Define Order Reasons. For defining your own order reason, provide a three-character identifier for your order reason along with a meaningful description.

It is always best to define a naming convention before you create an order reason in SAP. Galaxy decided to use an alphabetic prefix for order reasons that will help them to easily identify the order reasons. Galaxy named all the order reasons that are applicable for returns processing with the prefix *R* and all the order reasons that are applicable for sales orders with the prefix *S*. Figure 7.26 shows the order reasons that were customized for Galaxy Musical Instruments.

FIGURE 7.26 Defining order reasons

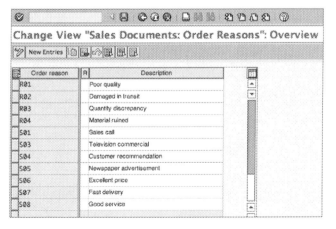

Customizing Order Blocks

Order blocks are available in SAP to block a customer master record from being able to create a new sales document. For example, assume your customer is a defaulter, and you do not want any new order for this customer to be entered into your SAP system. You can simply assign an order block into the customer master record that blocks the customer from placing any order in SAP.

When customizing an order block, you first create the reason for which you would like to block your customer from placing further orders. You then assign this order blocking reason to the respective document types. Once set up, this order block reason can then be assigned to the respective customer master records that you want to block.

The menu path for setting up an order blocking reason is IMG ≻ Sales And Distribution ≻ Sales ≻ Sales Documents ≻ Define And Assign Reasons For Blocking. You will be presented with activity dialog boxes where you can define blocking reasons and allocate them to sales order types.

Defining blocking reasons   This activity allows you to define an order block. Figure 7.27 shows the customization screen for defining the order blocks. You can also reach this customization screen directly using transaction code OVAS. To define your own order block, provide a two-character identifier for your block reason along with a meaningful description.

FIGURE 7.27 Defining order block reasons

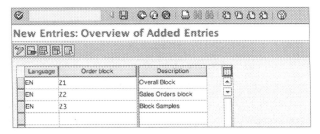

Allocating blocking reasons to sales document types   This activity allows you to assign the order blocks to their respective sales document types. Figure 7.28 shows the customization screen for assigning order blocks to document types. You can also directly reach this customization screen using transaction code OVAL. The assignment shown in Figure 7.28 represents the assignment for Galaxy Musical Instruments.

FIGURE 7.28 Assigning blocking reasons to sales document types

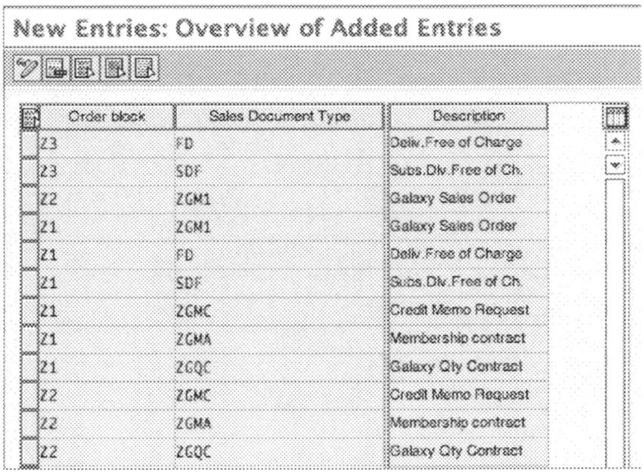

	Order block	Sales Document Type	Description	
	Z3	FD	Deliv.Free of Charge	
	Z3	SDF	Subs.Dlv.Free of Ch.	
	Z2	ZGM1	Galaxy Sales Order	
	Z1	ZGM1	Galaxy Sales Order	
	Z1	FD	Deliv.Free of Charge	
	Z1	SDF	Subs.Dlv.Free of Ch.	
	Z1	ZGMC	Credit Memo Request	
	Z1	ZGMA	Membership contract	
	Z1	ZGQC	Galaxy Qty Contract	
	Z2	ZGMC	Credit Memo Request	
	Z2	ZGMA	Membership contract	
	Z2	ZGQC	Galaxy Qty Contract	

New Entries: Overview of Added Entries

Reasons for Item Rejections

In SAP, you can reject individual line items of a sales document or a complete sales document (done by rejecting all the lines in it). You reject individual line items by entering a rejection reason for your line item on the Reasons For Rejection tab on the sales document overview screen. This way, you can provide different rejection reasons for different lines. Alternatively, using the fast-entry option in sales document change mode (the menu path is Edit ➤ Fast Change Of ➤ Reasons For Rejection), you can reject multiple lines at once, provided that they all belong to same rejection reason. What kind of subsequent functions (billing, printing, and so on) a rejected line can perform is controlled via customizing the rejection reason.

Defining Reasons for Rejections

To set up the rejection reasons, follow the menu path IMG ➤ Sales And Distribution ➤ Sales ➤ Sales Documents ➤ Sales Document Item ➤ Define Reasons For Rejection, or use the transaction code OVAG.

Figure 7.29 shows the customization screen for item rejection reasons.

FIGURE 7.29 Defining reasons for rejection for a sales item

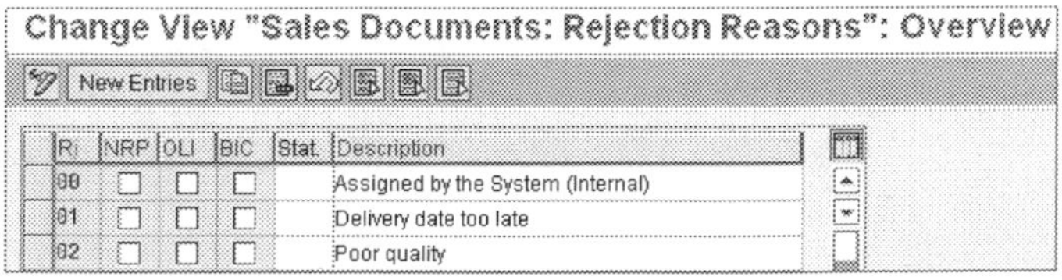

Change View "Sales Documents: Rejection Reasons": Overview

R	NRP	OLI	BIC	Stat.	Description
00	☐	☐	☐		Assigned by the System (Internal)
01	☐	☐	☐		Delivery date too late
02	☐	☐	☐		Poor quality

Here is an introduction to the fields in Figure 7.29:

Rj   This field represents the two-character identifier for a rejection reason. The key can be numeric or alphanumeric.

Description   This field represents the logical description of the rejection reason.

NRP check box   This field controls the printing of the rejected line. This checkbox, when selected for a rejection reason (and if that rejection reason is selected for a sales line in document), makes that sales line item not relevant for printing. This way you will restrict the rejected line to print on the order confirmation and other print outputs.

OLI check box   This field controls the rejection for a resource-related billing document. When selected, this check box allows you to create a new sales document or new sales item line in an existing sales document for a rejected line, provided the rejected sales document or the line item was triggered via the resource-related billing process.

BIC check box   This field controls the copy of the rejected line for billing purposes. This check box, when selected for a rejection reason (and if that rejection reason is selected for a sales line in document), makes that sales line item not relevant for billing.

Statistical   By selecting a value from the list of available values for this field, you tell SAP whether the rejected line item value should be added to the header totals of the sales document or whether it should be used only as a statistic. The available selection values are self-explanatory.

Incompletion Procedure

As we progress in the sales cycle, data gets copied between the sales order, delivery, and billing documents, and it is required that the proper control is maintained so that any important information does not gets missed during the sales cycle processing. An incompletion procedure helps in identifying such missing data elements and gives you more control by stopping the sales cycle from proceeding if some of the key fields are missing in the sales cycle. You can set up an incompletion procedure to ensure the completeness of the following:

- ► Sales document at the header, item, and schedule line levels
- ► Delivery document at the header and item levels
- ► Sales activity
- ► Partner data (sales document, delivery document, and sales activity)

The configuration process starts with defining a status group that is assigned to individual fields in the incompletion procedure, and then this incompletion procedure is assigned to the sales document at the header, item, or scheduled line for which you customized the incompletion procedure. Figure 7.30 diagrams the customization involved in setting up an incompletion procedure.

FIGURE 7.30 Incompletion procedure

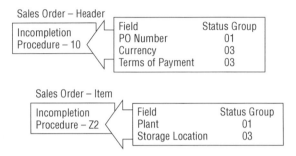

Once set up in customizing, the incompletion log can be called automatically while saving the document or via the menu from the sales document screen. When the incompletion log is called, SAP checks whether the fields maintained in the incompletion procedure are filled up. It then creates a log for all the fields that are part of the incompletion procedure being assigned to that sales document and decides on the action to be taken. Action can be either to allow the incomplete document to be saved but blocked for further processing or to disallow the incomplete document from saving. The decisions related to further processing of the documents are controlled by the combination of statuses being chosen in the status group.

TIP   An incompletion check should not be confused with field validations because it checks only whether the field is maintained and cannot validate the correctness of the values being maintained in that field.

Incompletion configuration is a three-step activity:

1. Defining the status group

2. Defining the incompletion procedure

3. Assigning the incompletion procedure

We'll now cover this configuration in detail.

Defining a Status Group

For this step, you choose the various available statuses such as general status, delivery status, billing status, pricing status, and so on, and put them into a status group (with a two-digit alphanumeric number), which controls what impact a particular field assigned to a particular status group will have on the document if it is part of an incompletion log. You can define a status group using transaction code OVA0 or following menu path IMG ➤ Sales And Distribution ➤ Basic Functions ➤ Incompletion Log ➤ Define Status Groups. Figure 7.31 represents the customization screen for defining a status group. What impact each of these status fields, shown in the customization screen in Figure 7.31, has on your status group, and in turn on incompletion procedure, is explained in Table 7.3.

FIGURE 7.31 Incompletion Control: Status Group

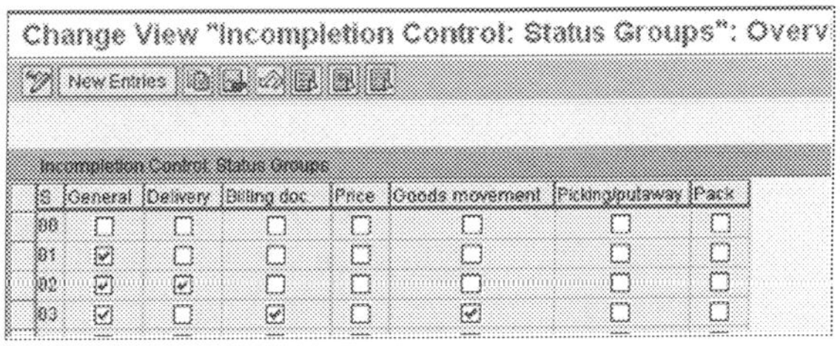

TABLE 7.3 Status Fields and Their Impacts

Status Field	Impact
General	Document or item is generally incomplete but can be processed further
Delivery	Delivery not possible for document or item
Billing	Billing not possible for document or item
Price	Order confirmation or billing not possible for the document
Goods movement	Goods movement not possible
Picking/put-away	Picking/put-away not possible for the document or item
Pack	Packing not possible

When working with status groups, first try using the default status groups provided by SAP such as 01, 02, and so on. If these status groups cannot serve the purpose, then create a new one by copying from any of these available status groups and using a Z prefix. Choose the necessary statuses required for your scenario in the new user-defined status group.

Defining an Incompletion Procedure

An *incompletion procedure* is a grouping of individual fields that are to be checked for completion during document processing in a sales cycle. You can define your incompletion procedure using transaction code OVA2 or following the menu path IMG ➢ Sales And Distribution ➢ Basic Functions ➢ Incompletion Log ➢ Define Incompletion Procedure. Figure 7.32 shows the incompletion procedure definition screen listing seven incompletion procedure groups provided by standard SAP.

FIGURE 7.32 Incompletion procedure, groups

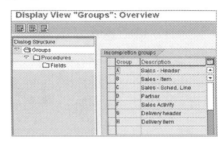

For our configuration study, we'll show the example of using the sales document header Incompletion – Group A.

Choose Sales – Header, and click the Procedures icon in the left window. The next screen will list all the available incompletion procedures for the Sales – Header group (Figure 7.33).

FIGURE 7.33 Incompletion procedure: Groups ➢ Procedures

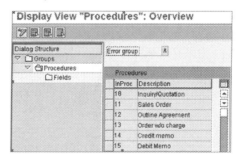

Choose incompletion procedure 10 (Inquiry/Quotation), and double-click the Fields icon on the left. The new screen (Figure 7.34) will show all the fields that are part of incompletion procedure 10.

FIGURE 7.34 Incompletion procedure: Groups ➤ Procedures ➤ Fields

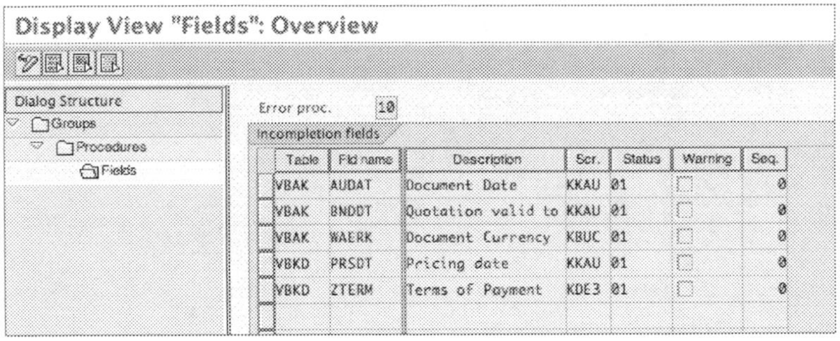

Table Here you enter the name of the table whose field needs to be checked for completion. In Figure 7.34, sales document header tables VBAK and VBKD are being used for setting up the sales header incompletion procedure 10.

Fld Name Here you enter the name of the field from the table that needs to be checked for completion. In Figure 7.34, incompletion procedure 10 is configured for checking incompletion for the fields document date, quotation validity to, and document currency from table VBAK and the fields pricing date and terms of payment of table VBKD.

Description This is the description of the field.

Scr. This field stores the function code that displays the screen on which you can correct the error. When your document is incomplete, the system creates an incompletion log. When you select the incomplete item from the incompletion log for maintaining the missing value, the system uses the function code mentioned in this field to display the relevant screen where you can maintain the missing data.

Status This is the status group assigned to the individual field that will control the field behavior during sales order processing.

Warning This controls whether to show any warning to the user when the user does not make an entry in the required field.

Seq. This is the sequence in which the SAP system should check for the incomplete fields in the sales document.

If a need arise to change the incompletion procedures provided by standard SAP such as 10, 11, 12, and so on, as shown earlier, you can make a copy of the one that is a good match to your requirement and then save it with prefix Z. Now remove the fields that you don't want to check for incompletion from this newly created Z procedure and add the fields that you want this Z procedure to check during incompletion with the required table, screen name, status group, warning, and sequence.

TABLES THAT CAN BE USED FOR THE MAINTENANCE OF INCOMPLETION PROCEDURE

You can use the following tables in the maintenance of incompletion procedures:

- ▶ VBKD for business data
- ▶ VEDA for contract data
- ▶ VBAK for a sales document's header data
- ▶ VBAP for a sales document's items data
- ▶ VBEP for a sales document's schedule line data
- ▶ LIKP for a delivery's header data
- ▶ LIPS for a delivery's item data
- ▶ LIPSD for the dynamic part of a delivery item
- ▶ LIPSVB for a delivery's reference structure for XLIPS/YLIPS
- ▶ V50UC for a delivery's dynamically generated item and header data
- ▶ FM111 for funds management account assignment data
- ▶ VBKA for sales activities
- ▶ VBPA for partner data

Assigning the Incompletion Procedure

The last step in configuring an incompletion procedure is to assign the incompletion procedure to the appropriate activity. The transaction code is VUA2, and the menu path is IMG ➤ Sales And Distribution ➤ Basic Functions ➤ Incompletion Log ➤ Assign Incompletion Procedures. For the seven incompletion groups provided in the incompletion procedure, SAP provides seven different activity groups while assigning them. For example, the Sales Header Incompletion group corresponds to sales document types, the Sales Item Incompletion group corresponds to item categories, and so on.

So, in the Sales-Header incompletion group procedure configuration, the next step is to assign it to a sales document type. Go to T-code VUA2, and double-click Assign Procedures To The Sales Document Types, as shown in the Figure 7.35.

FIGURE 7.35 Assigning incompletion procedures

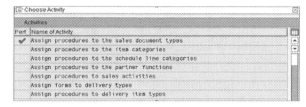

On the next screen, shown in Figure 7.36, assign the incompletion procedure to the required sales document type. Please note the field IC-Dialog in Figure 7.36. This field controls whether you can save an incomplete sales document.

FIGURE 7.36 Assigning procedures to the sales document types

SaTy	Description	Proc.	Description	IC-dialog
01	Cust.Independent Req			☐
AA	Promotion Order	11	Sales Order	☐
AE	Qtn from Serv. Order	19		☐
AEBO	Standard order	11	Sales Order	☐
AEBQ	Offer	18	Inquiry/Quotation	☐
IN	Inquiry			☐
QT	Quotation	18	Inquiry/Quotation	☐

To define an incompletion procedure for a sales document, you need to define the incompletion procedure for the sales document header, item, and schedule line and assign it to the respective sales document type, item category, and schedule line category.

Similarly, for activating an incompletion log in a delivery document, you need to define the incompletion procedure for both the delivery header and the item and assign it to the respective delivery document type and delivery item category.

The incompletion group for a partner needs to be defined to have the control on the partner data in the sales document flow (table VBPA). A partner incompletion procedure defined and assigned to a partner acts globally for the sales activity, sales document, and delivery document.

Calling the Incompletion Log

Once set up in customizing, the incompletion log can be called automatically while saving the document or via the menu Edit ➤ Incompletion Log from the sales document, sales activity, or delivery document screen. Once called, the incompletion log generates a log screen and will show the list of fields that are missing values. The list comprises fields from the header, item, and schedule lines. Whether the document can or cannot be saved or processed further will depend upon the customizing settings you made in the incompletion procedure configuration. To maintain these fields, just select the check box next to the field and then click the Complete button on the top. This action will take you to the individual screen for each of the fields; keep pressing the F5 key on the keyboard to toggle between the screens that are to be maintained. Once all the fields are maintained, you can save the document to be processed further. Table 7.4 shows the reports available in standard SAP that you can use to generate the list of incomplete sales documents.

TABLE 7.4   Incompletion-Related Standard Reports Available in SAP

Transaction Code	Report Description
V.00	Incomplete SD documents
V_UC	Incomplete delivery documents

Delivery Blocks

Delivery block functionality in SAP allows you to block the sales order and delivery documents from further processing. You can apply the delivery blocks to the sales document either at the header level (Shipping tab) or at the schedule line level (Schedule Line tab). Further, you can assign the delivery block manually in the sales document, or the system can automatically propose it. For automatic proposal at the header level, the delivery block needs to be entered in the sales document type customization (VOV8). For autoproposal at the schedule line level, the delivery block needs to be entered in the schedule line customization (VOV6). Always remember that for the delivery block to be effective at the sales document header level, the delivery block assignment to the respective delivery type is a must. A delivery block at the schedule line can work even without this setting. You can also enter a default delivery block in the customer master data, and SAP will copy over the same delivery block to all the sales documents of the customer, thereby blocking the sales documents from getting delivered.

The menu path for setting up an order blocking reason is IMG ➤ Logistics Execution ➤ Shipping ➤ Deliveries ➤ Define Reasons For Blocking In Shipping. You will be presented with an activity dialog window where you can select the activity to define the delivery blocking reasons and the Delivery Blocks activity to allocate the delivery blocks to the delivery document types.

Defining Delivery Blocking Reasons/Criteria

The Deliveries: Blocking Reasons/Criteria activity allows you to define the delivery blocking reasons and criteria. Figure 7.37 shows the customization screen for defining the delivery blocking reasons. You can also reach this customization screen directly using transaction code OVLS. To define your own delivery block, provide a two-character identifier for your blocking reason along with a meaningful description, and select the relevant check boxes for the delivery blocking criteria.

FIGURE 7.37 Defining delivery blocking reasons

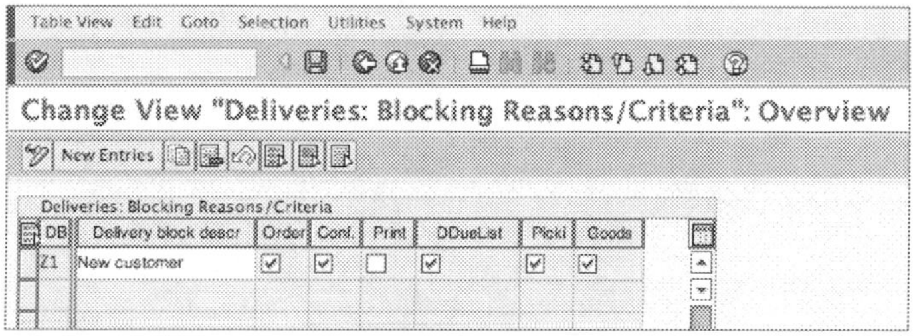

Order   You can use this check box to block the sales orders from getting delivered.

Conf.   You can use this check box to block the order quantities from getting confirmed.

Print   You can use this check box to block the output generation for sales documents that are blocked for delivery.

DDueList   This check box helps you exclude the sales document blocked for delivery from the delivery due list.

Picki   This check box stops the deliveries from getting picked that are under the delivery block.

Goods   This check box stops the deliveries from getting PGIed that are under the delivery block.

Assigning Delivery Blocks to Delivery Document Types

The Delivery Blocks activity allows you to assign the delivery blocks to their respective delivery document types. Figure 7.38 shows the customization screen for assigning delivery blocks to delivery document types representing the assignment for Galaxy Musical Instruments.

FIGURE 7.38 Assigning blocking reasons to delivery document types

This activity is required only if you want to use the delivery blocks for blocking the sales order from getting delivered. For scenarios where you want the delivery block to be applied at the sales order schedule line level or directly in the delivery document, this setting is optional.

Types of Sales Documents

We briefly touched on the sales cycle in Chapter 1 and discussed the customization for standard orders (document type OR) during our discussions on sales document customization.

Apart from the document type OR, standard SAP comes with the following pre-configured sales document types that you can use as-is or can use as a referencing template to create your own customized document types:

▶ Presales documents such as inquiries and quotations

▶ Order documents such as cash sales, rush orders, standard orders, and consignment orders

▶ Outline agreements such as contracts and scheduling agreements

▶ Complaint-processing documents such as debit/credit notes, invoice correction requests, sales returns, and free-of-charge and subsequent free-of-charge deliveries

We'll take a quick look at each of these sales document types in the following sections.

Inquiries and Quotations

An *inquiry* is a request that a buyer places on the seller to get the required information about the seller's products. It is an indication of the buyer's interest toward the seller's products. A customer inquiry may contain questions about the cost of a product, its availability on a particular date, use of a product, and so on. You reply to the customer's inquiry by sending a quotation. A quotation usually contains information about the product price, any applicable terms and conditions, and the answers to any other question from the buyer's inquiry.

Standard SAP provides document type IN for inquiries and QT for quotations, with the item categories AFN and AGN controlling the item data for inquiries and quotations, respectively. You can create an inquiry and quotation document for both goods and services. You can also use structured materials, such as bill of materials, in inquiries and quotations. While creating any of the two documents (IN or QT), you can give the choice to your customer by providing one or more alternatives for a particular product. To maintain an alternative for an item in an inquiry or a quotation document, enter the alternative item just below the main item with the reference number of the main item in the alternate item field on the alternate item line. Figure 7.39 shows this, where item 20 is the alternative for item 10.

FIGURE 7.39 Inquiry and quotation process in SAP

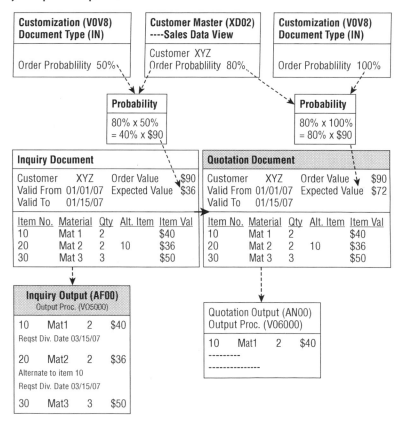

If the customer quotation converts into a confirmed order and the customer has agreed on the alternative item, you can copy the alternative item into the sales order with reference to the quotation. To do so, you have to use the selection list function from the dialog box that appears when you copy a document with reference to another document. You can also maintain a validity period for your inquiry or quotations and thus can monitor the processing time of your inquiry and quotation process in SAP against the benchmarks that exist in your organization.

A quotation is copied from an inquiry or can be created stand-alone. Copy controls exist in standard SAP for IN-QT, IN-IN, and QT-OR for allowing the copy between an inquiry to a quotation, from an inquiry to an inquiry, and from a quotation to an order.

Sales Returns

A *sales return* or *goods return* is a process where the buyer sends back the goods to the seller and the seller credits the customer for the value of the goods by creating a returns billing document. The process involves creating a sales return document type followed by a returns delivery and a returns invoice/credit note.

You can create returns in SAP with or without reference to a billing document. If you want to create them with a reference to a billing document, make sure that you have copy control set up between the billing and sales documents to allow this copy for your sales document.

In standard SAP, sales document type RE with the default delivery document type LR and a default billing document type RE represents the sales return cycle. The SD document category is H, and the screen sequence group is RE. The document is under the default billing block that ensures the validation of the return document by an authorized person before giving credit to the customer. Since it is an inward movement of goods, the return documents are not relevant for credit checks.

The item category REN for returns processing is a standard return item relevant for delivery, billing, and pricing, and it allows schedule lines.

Debit and Credit Notes

Mistakes do happen in the processing of a sales transaction. This creates a need for an adjustment or correction process. *Debit notes* and *credit notes* are these adjustment documents in SAP. You create a debit note in SAP to debit the customer for any underbilled amount and a credit note to credit the customer for any overbilled amount, without involving any goods movement.

Underbilling and overbilling are not the only criteria for creating debit and credit notes. There may be various other reasons too. For example, you may have an agreement with your customer to get reimbursed for any expense you incurred on behalf of your customer with relation to the sales transaction, such as freight charges, insurance, and so on. In such cases, a debit note is also used for charging these actual expenses to the customer.

You can create a debit or credit note with a reference to a sales document, a contract, or a billing document, and you can even create one without a reference to any document. The structure of a debit and credit note document consists of a header and item. Since no delivery is involved, the schedule line category is not required. Because there is no delivery step involved in a debit or credit document and they straightaway hit accounting, organizations generally keep these documents under a default billing block. An authorized person then reviews these documents and releases the billing block. If you are not satisfied with this two-level validation process and need something like a release strategy, you can define one by using status profiles. For example, you can set up the user-defined statuses as initial, blocked, rejected, and released, and you can then provide the authorizations for these different individuals. Once the documents are approved or released from the billing block, they can be processed using billing process and posted to accounting.

In standard SAP, the document type CR with the document category K and billing type G2 exists for a credit note, and document type DR with document category L and billing type L2 exists for a debit note. The screen sequence group is GA, which controls the display of the screens in VA01, VA02, and VA03 transactions, which you use for the maintenance of credit/debit note request documents.

Item categories available in standard SAP are G2N, GFN and L2N, and LFN, where G2N and L2N are for normal sales order–related credit/debit documents, and GFN and LFN are for billing plan–related credit/debit sales documents. All these item categories are set up for order-relevant billing.

Invoice Corrections

Invoice corrections (document type RK) represent the process of adjusting or correcting the customer's invoice. Unlike debit and credit sales documents where you create two separate documents (one for debit and one for credit), the document type RK allows you to create a single correction document for your invoice. The structure of the document consists of a header and item data. The item data always consists of two items. The first item is always a debit item, and the second is the credit item. The net invoice correction amount is a sum total of both the lines leading to an upward or downward revision of the original invoice amount.

A combination of the document category (value K) and the indicator field (value D) categorizes document type RK as an invoice correction document. The reference mandatory field in customizing for document type RK contains value M. This forces the document type to be created only with reference to an invoice document. The document type RK is not relevant for delivery and creates an order-relevant billing, G2. A default billing block exists in customizing for document type RK, which ensures proper validation by an authorized person before the RK document can be billed. The item categories G2N and L2N are available in standard SAP for use with the document type RK.

Free-of-Charge Delivery and Subsequent Free-of-Charge Delivery

Certain sales scenarios demand free-of-charge delivery of goods, such as samples. In standard SAP, you can send free-of-charge deliveries to your customer using sales document type FD (free-of-charge deliveries) and document type SDF (subsequent free-of-charge deliveries). You use transaction code VA01 for entering these documents into the SAP system.

Free-of-Charge Delivery (FD)

You use sales document type FD with default delivery type LF to send samples of your products to your customer. The sales cycle for FD only involves the order and delivery step and is not relevant for billing. In customizing, the document type FD is set up with document category I, which categorizes the sales document type FD as a free-of-charge order. For a free-of-charge delivery, the order reason is compulsory and is part of the incompletion procedure 13 assigned to the document type FD.

The item category is KLN and is set up as a standard item with schedule lines allowed so that you can perform an availability check and maintain schedule lines for free-of-charge deliveries. The item category is not relevant for pricing or credit checks and is also not relevant for billing. Since no billing is involved, the copy control setting exists only for copying a sales document to a delivery (copying FD to LF).

Subsequent Free-of-Charge Delivery (SDF)

SAP provides a free-of-charge delivery sales document (SDF), on the other hand, to handle situations where goods were billed to a customer but found damaged on arrival when received by customer. In some cases, it is not worth having these goods returned, and a subsequent delivery needs to be carried out. For example, as a result of a customer complaint, you now want to send a subsequent delivery to your customer free of charge. An SDF document is always created with reference to the original sales document and, similar to document type FD, involves only the order and delivery step. You don't bill the customer a second time, and therefore the document is not relevant for billing.

From a customization standpoint, sales document type SDF is like a mirror image of document type FD with the major exception that referencing the original sales document is mandatory for an SDF sales order, and it need not access customer–material information records because all the values are supposed to flow from the reference sales order to the SDF document. The SAP system is capable of keeping track of how many quantities you copied from the reference document into the SDF document for delivering free to the customer.

The document type SDF also uses item category KLN and therefore, similar to FD, is relevant for delivery but not for billing and pricing. The copy control setting exists only for copying a sales document to delivery (copying SDF to LF).

Cash Sales

Cash sales is a special order type available in SAP to handle those business scenarios where the customer places the order, pays for the goods, and receives the delivery at the same time. An example of this business process would be an over-the-counter sale.

Process

You create cash sales using transaction code VA01. Once you save the sales document type, SAP automatically creates the delivery. You cannot save an incomplete cash sales document unless you maintain all the required entries. The customer may receive the delivery of the goods at the counter, they may pick up the goods from the warehouse, or you can even deliver the goods at the customer's specified location. The delivery document can be configured to meet all these business needs. In a standard setup, though, it works as if the delivery is required at the counter.

Unlike the standard SAP process of taking the invoice printout from the billing document, the invoice printout for cash sales is generated from the sales document itself. The customer makes the payment against this document, and therefore the sales order number is also stored as a payment reference in the accounting entry for cash sales.

The billing for cash sales is an order-related billing; in other words, you create the billing with reference to a cash sales order and not with reference to the delivery document. Copy control for cash sales exists only between the order to delivery and the order to billing in standard SAP. While creating the billing document for cash sales, SAP also checks that the quantity ordered in the cash sales order should exactly match with the PGI quantity of the delivery. If the quantities do not match, you cannot create the billing document.

Since the invoice printout is generated from the sales document, the billing document is relevant only for posting the accounting entry. The accounting entry is passed into the revenue, and the offset goes to a cash account. If there are any cancellations, credit notes, returns, and so on, against cash sales, then that follows the standard SAP process.

Apart from the salient features mentioned earlier, the cash sales order cycle uses basic functions just like any other standard order. This includes an availability check, credit check, pricing, partner determination, and so on. Normally, for over-the-counter cash sales purposes, businesses use a one-time customer (account group CPD/CPDA). This helps them avoid the hassle of creating customer masters for cash customers.

Customization Settings in Cash Sales

In standard SAP, the sales document type CS with the default delivery document type BV and a default billing document type BV represents the cash cycle. You select the option for immediate delivery in the sales document type customization to achieve immediate delivery for document type CS. This triggers the delivery only the first time the document is saved, and therefore any changes in the quantity or any additions of new lines in the cash sales document will not create a subsequent delivery. So that the sales order for cash sales cannot be processed unless complete in all respects, the check box for an incompletion check is selected in the customization setting when assigning the document header incompletion procedure to the billing document type.

Item categories BVN and BVNN exist in standard SAP for cash sales. BVN is for a standard item, and BVNN is for a free-of-charge item. They both are relevant for order-related billings. This is what allows the document type CS to be created only with reference to an order and not a delivery. If you try creating the billing for CS using a delivery number, SAP gives you an error message telling you that you cannot generate a BV billing document from the BV delivery document.

To take the invoice printout from the sales document, output type RD03 is available in the standard output determination procedure for cash sales, which is V10001. To allow the retriggering of the invoice printout again if there is a change in the net value of the sales order, a requirement 14 is also assigned to the output type RD03 in the procedure V10001.

Copy control exists between the order to delivery (CS to BV) and the order to billing (CS to BV) to allow the delivery and billing documents to be created from the sales order CS. For the item-level copy control between order and billing, a copy routine 002 is assigned in standard SAP that ensures that the cash invoice is not created unless the quantity in the sales order CS matches with the PGI quantity of the delivery document CS.

Once the billing is created, the accounting posting happens by crediting the revenue, and offset entry is passed to the cash account. In general, SAP picks up the customer account from the billing document for offset entry, but in the case of cash sales, since the entry has to flow to the cash account, the account key EVV is assigned to the billing type BV when assigning the revenue account determination procedure customization. An entry for this account key, EVV, is then maintained in VKOA tables, and that triggers the accounting offset entry for the cash account for BV billing documents. Since the payment is collected against the invoice generated from the CS sales document, a reference of the same is required in the accounting entry being passed. This is achieved by selecting the value B in the assignment and the reference number field at the header-level copy control between order and billing.

Rush Orders

A *rush order* is a special order type provided by SAP to handle situations where you would like to create an immediate delivery from the sales order, for example, in same-day delivery scenarios. The moment an order is saved, a delivery document is created, and the warehouse can start processing the order. The billing for rush orders is created with reference to the delivery document, and the billing output is also generated from the invoice document.

From a customization standpoint, a rush order is like a mirror image of a standard order (order type OR); the only major exception is that the delivery document for a rush order is created immediately. You create a rush order using transaction code VA01. In standard SAP, the sales document type RO with default delivery document type LF and a default billing document type F2 represents the rush order cycle. You can still use all the item categories that you generally use with a standard order like TAN, TANN, and so on.

Consignment Processing

A *consignment* is a type of sales process where the goods are not sold to the customer in the first place. You manage the stock levels at a customer-consigned location. The customer consumes the goods on a needed basis from the location, and you bill the customer only for the goods consumed. The goods at the customer's location are your property, and the transfer of ownership happens once they are consumed by and billed to the customer.

In SAP, the customer consignment location is represented by special stock locations within the plant, and the stock in these locations is tracked separately with a special stock indicator W (Customer Consignment Stock). The complete consignment cycle in SAP involves four document types. These document types are explained in the following sections.

Consignment Fill-Up

Consignment fill-up is the process under which you fill up the stock at the customer's location. You create a consignment fill-up order using transaction code VA01. In standard SAP, the document type KB with item category KBN is available for consignment fill-up. The item category is relevant for delivery but not relevant for billing. When you do the PGI for a delivery for a consignment fill-up order, the consigned stock is moved from unrestricted stock to a special stock location. The ownership for the stock is still with you, and therefore there is no billing to the customer at this stage of the consignment sales cycle. Since the goods are moved within the plant from the regular storage location to a customer consigned location, there is no material valuation entry posted to accounting either.

Consignment Issue

Consignment issue is the process under which you bill the customer for the consumed stock from the consigned location. You create a consignment issue order using transaction code VA01. In standard SAP, document type KE with item category KEN is available for consignment issue. The item category is relevant for delivery and billing, and the special stock indicator in item category customization is set up to consume from special stock inventory W. The availability check is also performed against the consignment stock. When you do the PGI for a delivery for a consignment issue order, the consigned stock is depleted to the tune of the quantity delivered via the consignment issue order, and an accounting entry for material consumption is passed (cost of goods consumed). A billing document is generated with reference to the delivery document and posts the sales revenue into the accounting books.

Consignment Pickup

Consignment pickup is the process where you pick up the excess, slow-consuming, or unutilized stock from the consigned location and bring it back into your unrestricted inventory. You create a consignment pickup order using transaction code VA01. In standard SAP, document type KA with item category KAN is available for consignment pickup. The item category is relevant for delivery but not for billing. The special stock indicator in item category customization is set up to pick up from special stock inventory W. When you do the post goods receipt (PGR) for a delivery for a consignment pickup order, the consigned stock is depleted to the tune of the quantity picked up via the consignment pickup order, but no material-related accounting entry is passed because the stock is just moving from the consignment location within the plant to the regular storage location. No billing is created either.

Consignment Returns

Consignment returns is the process where you take returns for the goods that were originally billed to the customer via document type KE (Consignment Issue). You create a consignment returns order using transaction code VA01. In standard SAP, document type KR with item category KRN is available for consignment pickup. The item category is relevant for delivery and for billing. The special stock indicator in item category customization is set up as blank because the incoming stock is actually a customer return and not a pickup of your own inventory from a consignment location. When you do the PGR for a delivery for a consignment returns order, an accounting entry for a cost of goods sold (COGS) reversal is passed. A credit note is generated with reference to the delivery document, and it posts the sales returns entry into the accounting books.

Third-Party Order Processing

Third-party order processing is a type of sales process wherein your vendor directly supplies the goods to your customer, and you bill your customer for these goods on receipt of delivery proof from the vendor. The distribution of goods directly by your vendor to your customer provides you with benefits such as no inventory management, warehouse management, or transportation hassle; no storage cost; no special training or staff to handle the vendor's product in your warehouse; and so on. Third-party processing provides your business, to an extent, with a low-cost approach toward achieving the same objectives as it would achieve by maintaining inventory in your own warehouse and distributing the goods yourself.

Process

As you can see in Figure 7.40, the process starts when you create a sales order with a line item relevant for third-party processing (a line item with item category TAS). SAP creates a purchase requisition (P/R) for this line item, which then converts it into a purchase order following the regular procurement process. The purchase order is released and is sent to the vendor, and the vendor supplies the goods to the customer and sends you an invoice for the goods delivered. You post the invoice receipt (I/R) against the purchase order via transaction code MIRO. This I/R then updates the VPRS cost and sales order billing status for the line item (I/R done— billing due), and the billing document is created for the delivered quantities as per the normal billing process.

Customization Settings

To support the third-party processing, standard SAP comes with item category TAS and schedule line category CS. Schedule line category CS contains the defaults for the purchase requisition type, item category, and account assignment and thus is responsible for triggering the P/R for the order line items. You can have one or more line items in the purchase requisition, depending upon how many schedule lines exist in your third-party line item in the sales order. So, a one-line item with two schedule lines means two individual line items in the purchase requisition.

Item category TAS comes with billing relevancy F, which means that the billing for the order item will be possible only when the I/R for the purchase order is posted. The indicator F also controls the billing status for the sales order, because the billing status remains not due for billing until you post the invoice receipt. This way, you bill multiple invoices to the customer based on the I/R quantities. Each I/R updates the invoicing status only for the quantity received by the I/R. If you don't want to wait for the I/R posting for billing your customer, you can set up the billing relevancy for your third-party item category as B (relevant for order-related billing on the basis of the order quantity). In this case, the customer will be billed for the entire order quantity irrespective of the I/R processing.

FIGURE 7.40 Third-party process flow

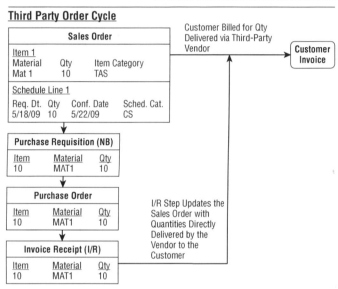

You can configure SAP to do manual as well as automatic third-party order processing. If you normally fulfill the customer order from your own stocks and require case-to-case procurement only for a particular product via third-party processing, you can follow the manual process. In manual processing, you change the item category on the overview screen of the sales order to TAS, which then triggers the purchase requisition process. If you have a particular product that is always procured via a third party, you can set up an automatic process also. In an automatic process, you assign the item category group BANS on the Sales Data2 tab of the material master. In standard SAP, under item category determination rules, BANS is linked to item category TAS, and therefore when you create an order with a material having BANS, SAP automatically determines the item category as TAS.

When you create a third-party order, SAP takes into account the lead times for automatic delivery scheduling for the third-party line item in the sales order. This means that the time required by the vendor to deliver the goods and also the time taken by your purchasing department for processing the purchase order together impact the schedule line confirmation date for the corresponding third-party line item in the order.

When you create a purchase order using the purchase request corresponding to the third-party order line, SAP automatically updates the purchase order number in the document flow of the sales order. Any changes in the delivery dates or quantity thereafter in the purchase order automatically updates the confirmed quantity and confirmation date in the corresponding schedule line on the third-party sales order, but the reverse way is not allowed. Any changes in the quantity or date in the sales order does not change the purchase order quantity or delivery dates. It is therefore always suggested to make changes in the purchase order and not in the sales order. You can also use report SDMFSTRP to find any quantity differences that exist between the sales order and the purchase order.

If you want to copy any text from the sales order to the purchase order, enter that into the text field PO text at the sales order item level because this gets copied over to the purchase order item text field during the third-party processing.

Sales Contracts

A sales contract is a legal agreement that not only has all the essential elements of a sales order but also has a validity period. By signing a sales contract, the seller agrees to supply the goods and services to the customer, and the customer agrees to receive and pay for the goods and services as per the terms and conditions of the contract. The breach of a contract has its own consequences and can lead to penalties and other related fees. Because of its legally binding nature, a sales contract provides an exact picture of the current period of revenues and the future period of revenues and thus also serves as a revenue assurance tool to the companies.

A *sales contract* in SAP is nothing but another sales document type you define via transaction code VOV8, but with a few more functionalities that are made possible by the use of the set of fields available specifically for contracts.

You create a contract document in SAP using transaction code VA41 or menu path Logistics ➤ Sales And Distribution ➤ Sales Contract ➤ Create. You can create a contract for goods as well as services. Unlike a sales order, a contract document does not contain a schedule line or requested delivery date. You maintain the validity of the contract using the Valid From and Valid To fields available at the header level on the contract entry screen. You can maintain the contract validity at the header level, and this validity is then applicable to the complete document. To capture the contractual data into a contract sales document, SAP provides a contract tab in the sales document customization transaction VOV8. To activate this contract tab for your document type, you need to make a selection when customizing the contract document type, as shown in Figure 7.41. You can have a header pricing procedure and an item pricing procedure for a contract. A contract in SAP can lead directly to a billing document (such as service contracts) or can be copied to an order followed by a delivery and then a billing document (quantity contracts).

FIGURE 7.41 Contracts section from the VOV8 customization screen

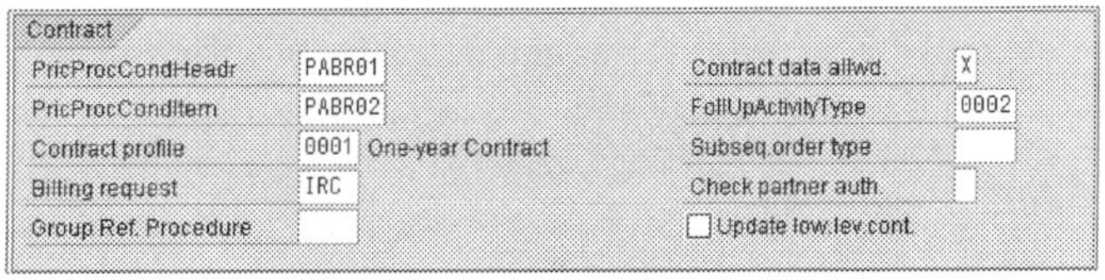

Let's take a look at these customizing fields in VOV8:

Pricing Procedure Condition Header/Pricing Procedure Condition Item
Unlike a sales document, where you generally set up a pricing master record before creating the transactional sales document, the pricing for a contract can be set up while creating the contract document itself. This is really beneficial in situations where you sign up a fixed lump-sum value contract with your customer, leaving very limited space for setting up masters because each contract has a different price, and it does not follow any price list/rate card. Sometimes a service sale that includes a variant configuration also comes under this category. The header pricing procedure PABR01 with condition type PKAR and item pricing procedure PABR02 with condition type PPAR and PPAG are provided in the standard SAP system for such purposes. When you create the contract, the pricing is saved with a reference of the contract number.

Contract Profile Here you assign the default contract profile for your contract document that in turn controls the contract start and end dates rule, default validity period for the contract, cancellation procedure to be used when the contract is cancelled, subsequent action required in case the contract is expired or about to expire, and action date rule that calculates the date when that subsequent action is supposed to take place. You set up these date rules and the contract profile when customizing the contract data using menu path IMG ➤ Sales And Distribution ➤ Sales ➤ Sales Documents ➤ Contracts ➤ Contract Data.

Billing Request   Here you assign the billing request type that you would like to use to initiate the billing processing for your contract document.

Group Reference Procedure   This field is relevant for the master contracts document setup. Here you assign a reference procedure that defines the rules according to which data from a master contract is copied over to lower-level contracts.

Contract Data Allowed   Here you define whether your sales document type should allow the contract data screens to show up when you are entering a sales transaction using your sales document type. You can choose X to allow the contract data for the sales document, you can use Y to force the item contract data to flow from the header contract data, and you can leave the value in this field blank to suppress the contract data screens for your sales document type.

Follow Up Activity Type   When a contract document is about to expire, you can use the follow-up action work list to trigger the subsequent follow-up activity. For example, you may define the follow-up activity as creating a quotation or mail to the account manager, or initiating a telesales call to customer, and so on. In SAP, follow-up activities can be identified based on the follow-up activity types. Here you enter the follow-up activity type that you want SAP to propose when you run the follow-up work lists.

Subsequent Order Type   When you run the subsequent processing for an expired contract, SAP uses this field to automatically propose the default document type for subsequent processing such as a quotation for a new contract.

Check Partner Authorizations   This field is used with quantity contracts with release orders. In real world, there may be situations where a customer may designate only a few branch offices to make a release against the sales contract, and therefore SAP provides you with the field check partner authorizations in the sales document type customization. If you select A in this field, SAP allows any partner in the quantity contract with partner type AG (sold-to party) or AA (party authorized to release) to release the contract. Selecting B in this field allows any partner to release the contract who holds a lower position in the customer hierarchy than the sold-to party of the contract. Leaving this field blank makes it wide open for any partners to release the contract.

Update Lower Level Contracts   This check box is provided in SAP for master contracts. If you want to update the flow when a master contract is copied to a lower-level contract, select this check box in the customization of the master contract.

Common Customizations in Sales Contracts

We'll now explain the various customization settings that are common for all the contract document types.

Define Validity Period Category

The validity period category is a two-character key that SAP uses to propose the validity periods in a contract. The key is assigned to a contract profile from where it defaults to the contract document. You can use the validity period category as one of the key terms in pricing determination for contracts and also in statistical evaluations on contracts.

You can define a validity period category key by using transaction code VOVO or by following the menu path IMG ➤ Sales And Distribution ➤ Sales Documents ➤ Contracts ➤ Contract Data ➤ Define Validity Period Categories. Figure 7.42 represents the customization screen for defining the validity period category.

FIGURE 7.42 Defining the validity period category

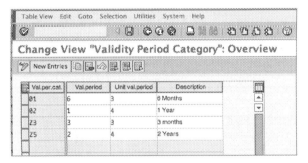

To define your own validity period category, provide a two-character identification key starting with a Y or Z. Specify a validity period value and the unit for the validity period in the Val.Period and Unit Val.Period fields, and provide a meaningful description for your validity category. Available choices for Unit Val.Period are 1 (day), 2 (week), 3 (month), and 4 (year). For the Z5 validity period category in Figure 7.42, we maintained 2 as the validity period, chose 4 as the unit for the validity period, and provided a description, thus creating a two-year validity period represented by category Z5.

Rules for Determining Dates

Here you define the rules for determining the start and end dates for your contracts. The transaction code is VOVP, and the menu path is IMG ➢ Sales And Distribution ➢ Sales Documents ➢ Contracts ➢ Contract Data ➢ Define Rule For Determining Dates. Figure 7.43 and Figure 7.44 show the two-date determination rules that were defined for Galaxy Musical Instruments. Rule Z2 is for determining the end date for the contract as today's date + two years, and rule Z1 determines the date when a follow-up action on the contract should be due, in other words, two months prior to the contract's end date. Both the rules use factory calendar ZZ – factory calendar US (the one we defined in Chapter 2, "Enterprise Structure") to determine the number of working days.

FIGURE 7.43 Defining rules for determining dates (rule Z1)

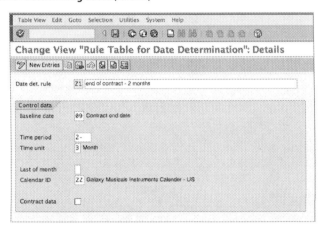

FIGURE 7.44 Defining rules for determining dates (rule Z2)

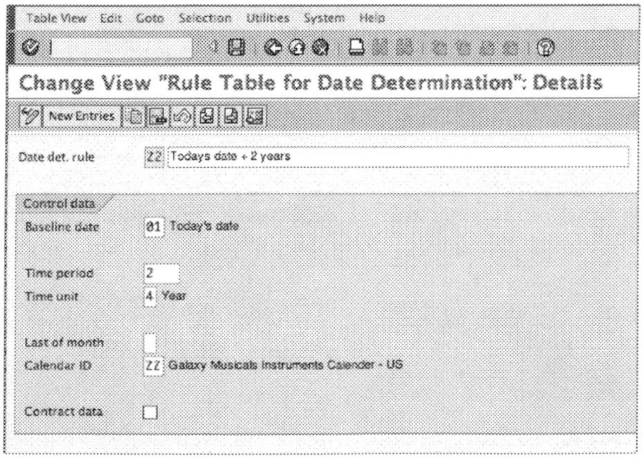

Controlling Contract Cancellations

Here you define the cancellation rules for your contracts. The setup activity involves setting up cancellation reasons, setting up cancellation procedures, setting up cancellation rules, and assigning cancellation rules to cancellation procedures.

Defining cancellation reasons   Here you define various cancellation reasons that exist in your organization for terminating a contract. Once defined in customizing, you can use these cancellation reasons in contract documents to cancel a particular line item or to cancel a complete contract document. The transaction code is VOVQ, and the menu path is IMG ➢ Sales And Distribution ➢ Sales ➢ Sales Documents ➢ Contracts ➢ Contract Data ➢ Control Cancellation ➢ Define Cancellation Reasons. Figure 7.45 shows various cancellation reasons we created for Galaxy Musical Instruments.

FIGURE 7.45 Defining cancellation reasons

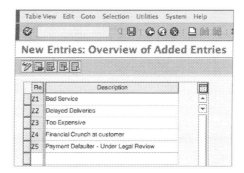

Defining cancellation procedure   A cancellation procedure is a four-character key that controls the cancellation process for a sales document. The transaction code is VOVM, and the menu path is IMG ➢ Sales And Distribution ➢ Sales ➢ Sales Documents ➢ Contracts ➢ Contract Data ➢ Control Cancellation ➢ Define Cancellation Procedures. Figure 7.46 shows the cancellation procedure that we created for Galaxy.

FIGURE 7.46 Defining cancellation procedures

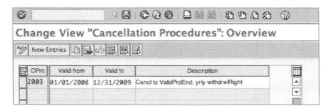

Defining cancellation rules Here you set up the contract's cancellation-specific rules. The transaction code is VOVL, and the menu path is IMG ➢ Sales And Distribution ➢ Sales ➢ Sales Documents ➢ Contracts ➢ Contract Data ➢ Control Cancellation ➢ Define Cancellation Rules. Figure 7.47 shows the cancellation rule we created for Galaxy.

FIGURE 7.47 Defining cancellation rules

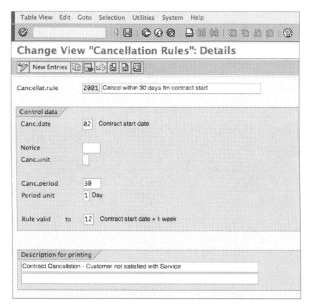

Assigning cancellation rules to cancellation procedures Finally, you assign the cancellation rules to cancellation procedures. The transaction code is VOVN, and the menu path is IMG ➢ Sales And Distribution ➢ Sales ➢ Sales Documents ➢ Contracts ➢ Contract Data ➢ Control Cancellation ➢ Assign Cancellation Rules And Cancellation Procedures. Figure 7.48 shows the cancellation procedure assignment for Galaxy.

FIGURE 7.48 Assigning cancellation rules to procedures

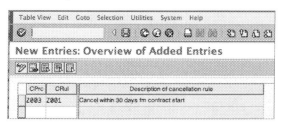

Contract Profile

A contract profile controls the contract start and end dates rule, default validity period for the contract, cancellation procedure to be used when the contract is cancelled, subsequent action required in case the contract is expired or about to expire, and action date rule that calculates the date when that subsequent action is supposed to take place. You set up these date rules and contract profiles when customizing the contract data using menu path IMG ➢ Sales And Distribution ➢ Sales ➢ Sales Documents ➢ Contracts ➢ Contract Data ➢ Define Contract Profiles. Figure 7.49 shows the contract profile defined for Galaxy Musical Instruments.

FIGURE 7.49 Defining a contract profile

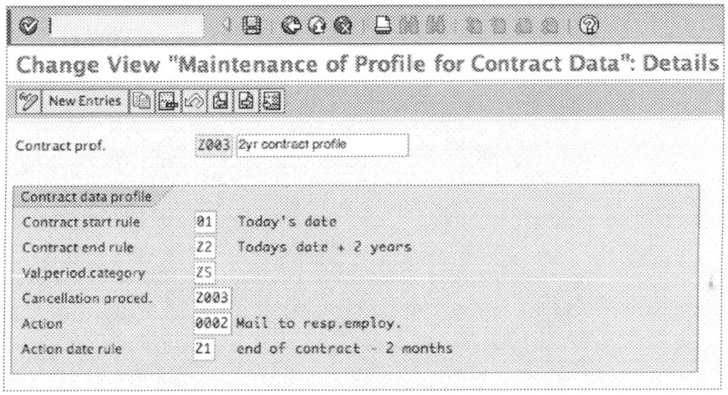

Quantity Contracts

A *quantity contract* is a type of contract where your customer agrees to purchase a certain quantity of your product within a certain period of time but the information related to delivery scheduling, such as when, where, and how many quantities will be required, might not be available at the time of the contract. This delivery scheduling information is provided later by the customer as individual purchase orders referring to the sales contract. An example of the quantity contract is when, to get bulk-purchase benefits (discounts, for example), your customer's head office signs a sales contract with you for a certain quantity of your product, at a particular rate, and with a year validity, but you receive the delivery schedule information from the individual branch offices in the form of release orders against the contract, as and when they require the product in the next one-year period.

In SAP, you handle the quantity contracts via document type CQ. Figure 7.50 shows the processing of a quantity contract in SAP. The process starts with the creation of a quantity contract using the document type CQ by providing all the necessary information into the contract such as the customer, contracted quantity, validity period, contracted rate, and so on. The contracted quantity of product is maintained in the target quantity field in the quantity contract. When you receive the individual customer purchase order, you create a release order with reference to the quantity contract using order type OR. SAP then maintains the released quantity in the order quantity field in the quantity contract, thus providing you with a control over contracted vs. released quantity. This also helps you in booking and backlogs reporting for quantity contracts. The release order also updates the document flow and is later processed like a normal sales order falling into delivery and billing.

FIGURE 7.50 Quantity contract processing

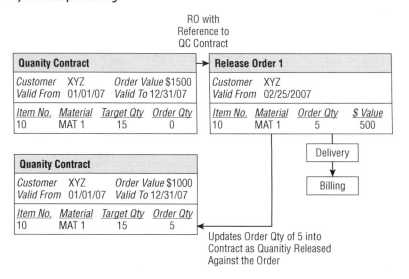

Service and Maintenance Contracts

A *service contract* in SAP is used to record and process service-related transactions between the service provider and service recipient. These transactions can be periodic in nature or once-off services. Here are some examples:

► Periodic flat-rate services such as billing for monthly gym/club membership fees, monthly flat-rate contracted cell phone charges, monthly Internet/cable TV/telephone service usage charges, tuition fees, and any other such services that are billed periodically at a flat rate.

- ▶ Milestone-based billings on the completion of an event.

- ▶ One-time services such as installing and commissioning equipment at the customer site, performing a repair on a product, giving product-related service call/phone support, and providing professional services such as consulting, medical, legal, and so on.

You create a service contract in SAP using contract maintenance transaction code VA41. The document type for a service contract available in standard SAP is SC. Like any other contract, you can use validity periods and cancellation procedures in service contracts to handle the contract validity and cancellation processing. Service contracts do not involve a delivery document or schedule line category setup. These contracts are billed directly from the contract just like any other order-related billing documents. You can use the SC contracts with or without billing plans. Standard SAP provides the item category WVN, which is preconfigured for use with services that require a billing plan. You can have service contracts created with a milestone billing plan or with a periodic billing plan (refer to Chapter 9 for more details on billing plans).

Depending upon your business requirement, you may configure a service contract to bill services in advance or in arrears, on periodic time buckets, as one-time once-off charges, or on an event/milestone completion basis. A service contract also provides you with the flexibility of separating the revenue from the billing. You can bill the customer in advance or arrears and can recognize revenue separately in accounting in periodic buckets. We discuss revenue recognition in detail in Chapter 10.

When used with the customer service module in SAP, a service contract can be linked to technical objects (equipment, serial numbers, and functional location) and helps in storing the warranty information for a serialized unit. This information can then be used for validating warranty- and service-level coverage in the event you receive a service request for the product from the customer. Standard SAP provides material type DIEN for service items.

CASE STUDY—GALAXY MUSICAL INSTRUMENTS: EXTENDED WARRANTY SERVICE CONTRACT

Galaxy Musical Instruments offers an extended one-year warranty on musical instruments. The company bills the customer up front for the warranty. For selling this extended warranty, we configured a warranty service contract ZAMC for galaxy by taking a copy of standard SAP contract type SC. ZAMC is not relevant for delivery and is configured to use billing document type F2 for billing the customer. The item category ZWVA is created as a copy of WVN with time based revenue recognition selected.

Since the extended warranty contract was offered at the time of purchase of equipment and cannot be purchased stand-alone at a later date, today's date rule is used to determine the warranty start date on the contract. The galaxy's service contract profile Z004 (1 year validity) is assigned to the ZAMC contract, which gives the contract a validity of 1 year from the date of purchase (today's date). Z004 contract profile uses following rules:

- ► Contract start rule = 01 (Today's date)

- ► Contract end rule = Z3 (Today's date + 1 yr)

- ► Validity period category = 02 (1 yr)

- ► Cancellation Procedure = Z003

- ► Action rule = 0002 (mail to responsible employee)

- ► Action date rule = Z1 (end of contract – 2 months)

Summary

In this chapter, we walked you through the various details of a sales document. We covered the use of sales documents in the SD cycle, its structure, and its customization. We also discussed various sales-related business processes and the sales document types that are available in standard SAP to support these processes. In next chapter, we'll discuss shipping and transportation processing.

Shipping and Transportation

This chapter covers the Distribution part of SD Module. The processes and configuration discussed in this section are grouped in SAP under a separate application called Logistics Execution. In this chapter, you will study the order fulfillment process steps, including creating a delivery document, picking, packing, shipment, goods issue, and transportation of the goods to the customer. The same steps are also applicable to handling customer returns, which result in an inbound delivery and goods receipt.

In most cases, a delivery is created with reference to a sales order. A lot of business data must be copied from order to delivery. We will cover the copy control in this chapter. We will also be referring to certain topics covered in Chapter 7, "Sales." Other settings that are applicable to deliveries are covered in Chapter 4, "Partner, Text, and Output Determination," and Chapter 5, "Pricing and Tax Determination."

The Shipping Process

Shipping is part of the order fulfillment process. It starts with the creation of a delivery document. This document can be created with or without reference to a preceding sales document.

The typical process consists of delivery document creation (commonly called *delivery creation*), followed by picking, packing, shipment, and goods issue:

Delivery creation   In a sales order, when the material availability date or transportation scheduling date is reached, the order becomes due for delivery, and it is time for various planning and execution activities to start. The delivery document is the medium of conveying the information to the Logistics Execution team. In most organizations, this team is located at a different location (a plant, shipping point, or warehouse) from the sales team.

Picking   Picking is an optional step. It involves the physical pickup of goods from their storage place and setting them aside for shipping. Hence, some of the items in the delivery document (such as services) may not be relevant for picking. The picking process can be done automatically during delivery creation or can be a scheduled activity that takes place in batches at regular intervals.

Packing   Packing is the step of assembling all the picked items and packing them. It can be a multistep process, such as packing musical instruments into a special box, then packing six such boxes into a crate, and finally loading ten crates into a truck. All of these groupings are called *handling units*. Each one can be located and managed by a unique identification number.

Shipment   Shipment is the step of transportation planning and execution. In this step, one or more deliveries are grouped into a shipment document. The transportation for the various legs is then planned, and as each leg is executed, the shipment document status is updated until the goods reach the customer.

Goods issue   Goods issue is the last step. When you post a goods issue, the delivery has physically been shipped. The material and accounting documents get created in the background, and the user cannot change or influence any data at this stage.

With this overview out of the way, we'll now cover how the process is carried out in SAP. Then we will proceed with the configuration of this process.

Delivery Creation

A delivery document can be created in several ways. Based on your requirements, you can create an individual delivery manually or use a batch program that runs a delivery-due list and creates deliveries.

Before a delivery is created for a sales order, the system carries out the following checks:

- ▶ Is the sales order data complete?
- ▶ Are the items in the order relevant to delivery creation?
- ▶ Is there a credit block or a delivery block?
- ▶ Are the schedule lines for one or more items in the order due for delivery?
- ▶ Has the customer asked for complete delivery?

The Delivery Creation Process

In SAP, a delivery can be created as an individual document or in batch mode by running periodic jobs.

Creating Individual Delivery from the Logistics Execution Menu

To access this menu, the menu path is as follows: SAP Menu ➤ Logistics ➤ Logistics Execution ➤ Outbound Process ➤ Goods Issue For Outbound Process ➤ Outbound Delivery ➤ Create ➤ Single Document ➤ Create With Reference To A Sales Order (VL01N).

Take a look at Figure 8.1. The shipping point is the most important organizational unit in delivery creation. Specify the shipping point from where the delivery would originate. Also enter the sales order number and (if needed) the range of items for which this delivery is to be created.

FIGURE 8.1   Creating a delivery using VL01N

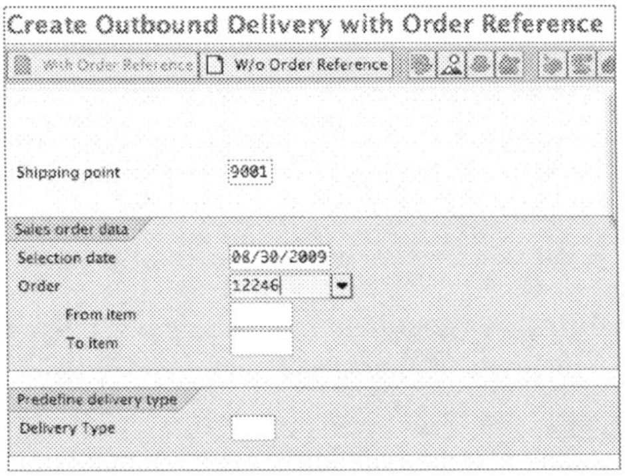

You can also create a delivery without any sales order reference. Follow the same menu path as shown earlier, and choose Create Delivery Without Order Reference (VL01NO). In this case, because there is no reference sales order, you also have to specify the sales area.

Creating Individual Delivery from Within the Sales Order Screen (VA01 or VA02)

From the sales order screen, you can use the menu Sales Document ➤ Deliver to create a delivery.

You can use this option only if you are authorized to create sales orders and deliveries.

Collectively Processing Documents Due for Delivery

When the volume of sales transaction is very high, it is convenient to create deliveries in batches by executing a delivery-due list. To access the transaction codes, the path is as follows: SAP Menu ➤ Logistics ➤ Logistics Execution ➤ Outbound

Process ➢ Goods Issue For Outbound Process ➢ Outbound Delivery ➢ Create ➢ Collective Processing Of Documents Due For Delivery.

As you can see, there are several transaction codes in the list in Figure 8.2, offering various selections to choose from. The program called up in each case is the same; the variations are controlled from the User Role tab. Thus, the transaction codes offer different selection criteria to call up and execute a list of documents due for delivery. Figure 8.3 shows one such transaction—VL10A—from the list.

FIGURE 8.2   Collective delivery processing menu

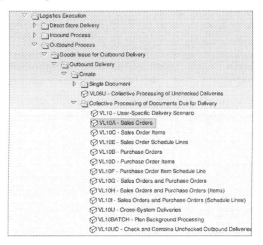

FIGURE 8.3   Collective processing with VL10A

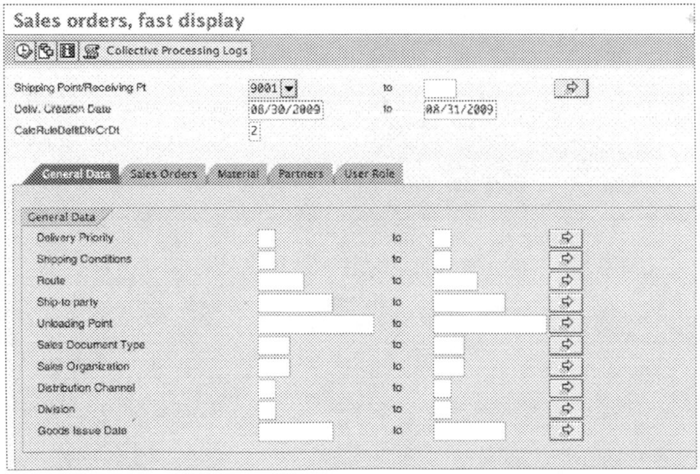

Using these variants, you can also set up a batch job to run at certain intervals and create deliveries in the background.

Customizing Delivery Documents

We'll now cover the important settings required to configure a delivery document and control the data flow in it.

Setting Up the Delivery Type

The first step in the configuration is to set up a delivery document. The path to configure delivery types is IMG ➢ Logistics Execution ➢ Shipping ➢ Deliveries ➢ Define Delivery Type (0VLK).

You can create a new delivery type or copy from an existing entry. You can refer to the SAP standard delivery type LF.

Figure 8.4 shows the configuration screen for delivery types. We'll discuss some of the critical settings in this screen. Please note that we are not discussing every option on this screen here—just the most important ones.

Document Category   The Document Category field at the top of the screen is used by the system to classify various documents (such as sales documents, deliveries, billing documents, and so on). For a standard delivery, this category is J.

Number Systems tab   This is where the delivery documents can be assigned an internal or external number range

> **NR Int. Assgt**   Assign the internal number range in this field.. In the case of an internal number, the system assigns the next available number to each new delivery that is saved.

> **No. Range Ext**   Specify an external number range in this field. For external number ranges, the user can specify a number from within the number range specified. As in the case of number ranges for sales documents, you can define the number range intervals for delivery in a separate transaction.

> **ItemNoIncrement**   This field is used to specify the interval between successive items in the delivery.

Order Reference tab   The following are the important fields on this tab:

> **Order Required field**   The Order Required field is used to specify the document type to be referenced in the creation of this delivery. In the case of standard

SAP delivery LF, you would specify X (Sales Order Required). However, other deliveries, such as NLCC (a cross-company replenishment delivery), are created with reference to a purchase order. Hence, the value is B (Purchase Order Required). Some deliveries are created without reference to any preceding document. An example is document type LO. In this case, the field is blank (meaning no preceding document is required).

Default Ord. Ty.   Specify the default order type here. If a delivery is to be created without reference, you need to specify a "pseudo" order type, which is a reference order type that is required from an internal control point of view. For example, in the case of delivery type LO, the default order type is DL. This order type is configured like any other sales document.

ItemRequirement   This is a provision to attach a requirement routine for delivery items without reference to a sales document.

FIGURE 8.4   Setting up a delivery type

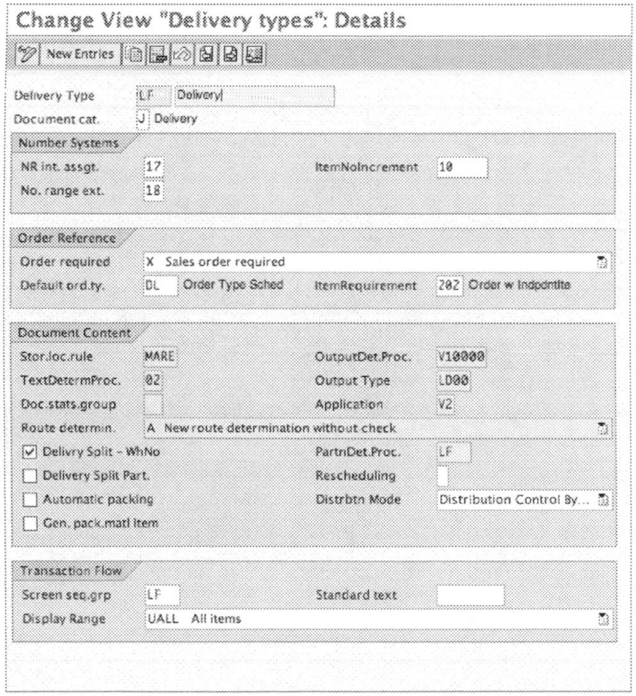

Most of the fields on the Document Content tab cannot be changed from this transaction. They appear here in display mode only.

Defining Delivery Item Categories

The Item Category field controls how the system processes the delivery item. It is conceptually similar to the Item Category field in a sales document.

To set up item categories, the path is IMG ➢ Logistics Execution ➢ Shipping ➢ Deliveries ➢ Define Item Categories For Deliveries (0VLP).

If you have to define a new item category, it is advisable to copy it from an existing standard one. This ensures that all the critical fields are copied over, and then you only have to change those fields that you want to change from original.

We'll now discuss some of the major fields in the delivery item categories screen, as shown in Figure 8.5.

FIGURE 8.5   Setting up a delivery item category

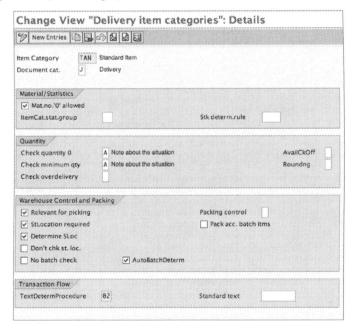

Quantity tab   There are certain controls based on quantity in the delivery. Through the settings on the Quantity tab, the system can check for zero quantity and respond with an error or a notice. Similarly, you can control the checks for a minimum delivery quantity and over-delivery situation.

Warehouse Control And Packing tab   On the Warehouse Control And Packing tab, you can decide whether picking and packing are relevant for this item category. In the case of packing relevance, you can also specify whether it is mandatory or optional. We will discuss the processes of picking and packing later in this chapter. You can also control the role of storage location in the delivery. You can make it a mandatory field in the document. You can also request automatic determination of storage location. (We will return to this a little later in this chapter.)

Determining Item Category

In Chapter 7, we discussed item category determination in sales documents. In deliveries, the item category is determined along similar lines. The following are the determining factors:

- ▶ Delivery type
- ▶ Item category group
- ▶ Item usage
- ▶ Higher-level item category

In the case of items copied from a sales document into a delivery, the item category determined in the order is copied over. Items created without reference or added new in the delivery would follow the rules of item category determination.

The Item Category Group setting comes from the material master record. Item category usage, however, can be defined using the path IMG ➤ Logistics Execution ➤ Shipping ➤ Deliveries ➤ Define Item Category Usage. Specify a four-character usage. You can then use this as a key in item category determination.

To set up item category determination, the path is IMG ➤ Logistics Execution ➤ Shipping ➤ Deliveries ➤ Define Item Categories Determination In Deliveries (transaction 0184).

As shown in Figure 8.6, for each combination, you can specify a default item category and other permitted item categories that the user is allowed to change in the delivery document.

FIGURE 8.6   Item category determination

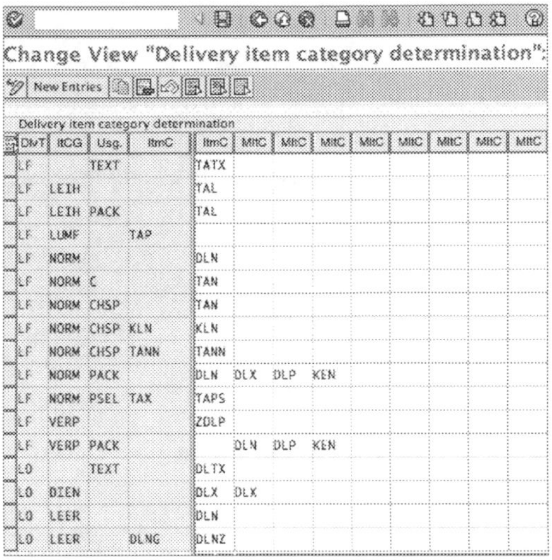

DMT	ItCG	Usg.	ItmC	ItmC	MltC	MltC	MltC	MltC	MltC	MltC	MltC	MltC
LF		TEXT		TATX								
LF	LEIH			TAL								
LF	LEIH	PACK		TAL								
LF	LUMF		TAP									
LF	NORM			DLN								
LF	NORM	C		TAN								
LF	NORM	CHSP		TAN								
LF	NORM	CHSP	KLN	KLN								
LF	NORM	CHSP	TANN	TANN								
LF	NORM	PACK		DLN	DLX	DLP	KEN					
LF	NORM	PSEL	TAX	TAPS								
LF	VERP			ZDLP								
LF	VERP	PACK			DLN	DLP	KEN					
LO		TEXT		DLTX								
LO	DIEN			DLX	DLX							
LO	LEER			DLN								
LO	LEER		DLNG	DLNZ								

Setting Up Copy Controls for Deliveries

In the case of deliveries that are created with reference to a sales document, you have to control the flow of data into the delivery. This step ensures continuity of data, copies essential information, and avoids manual data inputs in delivery creation. The copy controls between sales and delivery documents can be controlled at the Header and Item levels using copy routines. The copy controls can be set up as follows: IMG ➤ Logistics Execution ➤ Shipping ➤ Copying Controls ➤ Specify Copy Controls For Deliveries (VTLA).

Select the source and target documents.

At the Header level screen, there are three tabs, as shown in Figure 8.7.

Conditions tab   Here is a summary of the main options on the Conditions tab:

Order Requirements routine   On the Conditions tab, there is an Order Requirements field. The copy routine assigned here checks whether certain prerequisites are fulfilled before a delivery can be created from a sales document.

Combination Requirement routine   The Combination Requirement routine checks for certain conditions to be met before multiple sales documents can be combined into a single delivery.

Data Transfer tab   Here is a summary of the main option on the Data Transfer tab:

Header Data routine   The Header Data routine controls the data that is copied from order to delivery. Technically speaking, if you want certain data to be copied from the VBAK (order header) table, for example, and the destination is the LIKP (delivery header) table, you can set up a routine and attach it here.

Control Data tab   If you select the check box Copy Item Number on the Control Data tab, the items would retain the same item number as in the sales document. It would make sense to keep this check box selected if you are dealing with large orders that may result in multiple deliveries and post-delivery analysis is required.

At the item level, you have to specify the Item category and select the Details view, as shown in Figure 8.8.

FIGURE 8.7   Order to delivery, copy controls at Header level

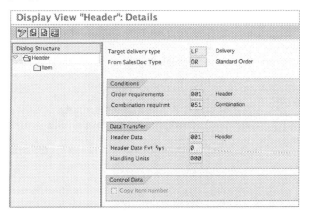

FIGURE 8.8   Order to delivery, copy controls at Item level

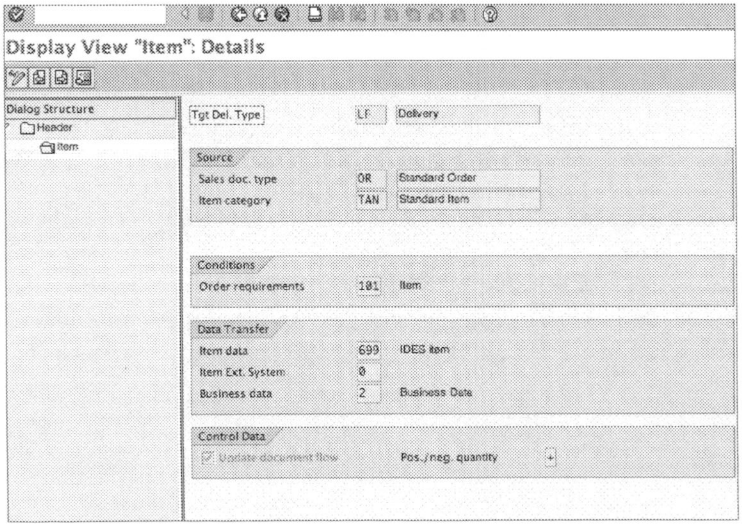

Conditions tab   The Conditions tab has an Order Requirement routine that performs item-level checks before the order is copied into the delivery.

Data Transfer tab   Here is a summary of the main options on the Data Transfer tab:

Item Data routine   The Item Data routine on the Data Transfer tab controls the data that will be copied at the Item category level. Technically, the data in the LIPS (delivery item) table is controlled here.

Business Data routine   The Business Data routine controls the copying of business data. If you need any data stored in the VBKD table to be copied over into your delivery, this is the routine you can use.

Control Data tab   The Update Document Flow setting on this tab controls whether the source and destination documents will be shown as linked in the document flow.

Determining the Shipping Point

The shipping point is the organizational unit for a delivery. In Chapter 2, "Enterprise Structure," we discussed the relevance of shipping points.

A shipping point is determined based on the following criteria:

▶ Plant

▶ Shipping conditions

▶ Loading groups

We'll now discuss each of these determining factors and how they influence shipping point determination:

Plant   The delivering plant is determined in the sales order line item. To determine a plant, the system looks up the customer-material information records. If the plant is not specified there, it then checks the customer master for a preferred plant. If no such preference is maintained for a customer, it is determined from the delivering plant field in the material master.

Shipping conditions   The shipping condition defines the strategy for the delivery. For example, there can be different shipping conditions for regular delivery and express delivery. This field is specified in the customer master record on the Shipping tab. You can also assign a shipping condition to a sales document type. In the sales order, a user can manually override shipping conditions.

To define a shipping condition, follow the path IMG ≻ Logistics Execution ≻ Shipping ≻ Basic Shipping Functions ≻ Shipping Point And Goods Determination Point Determination ≻ Define Shipping Conditions. As shown in Figure 8.9, you can either use an existing set of conditions or define a new one here.

FIGURE 8.9   Defining shipping conditions

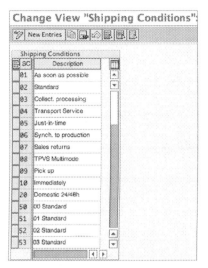

You can assign a shipping condition to a sales document type and overrule the value coming from the customer master. The menu path is as follows: IMG ≻ Logistics Execution ≻ Shipping ≻ Basic Shipping Functions ≻ Shipping Point And Goods Determination Point Determination ≻ Define Shipping Conditions By Sales Document Types.

Select the document type from the list. Assign a shipping condition to the document type. Now, whenever this order is created, the shipping condition will be picked up from this setting rather than referring to the customer master.

As shown in Figure 8.10, we have assigned shipping condition 07, which is Sales Returns, to the sales document type RE. In this case, the returns can be diverted to a different receiving point.

FIGURE 8.10 Assigning shipping conditions to a sales document type

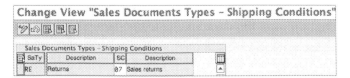

Loading group   A loading group is a grouping of materials with same loading requirement. For examples, materials that require the same equipment (cranes, forklifts) can be placed together in a common loading group. The loading group is copied from the material master record. To define a loading group, follow the path IMG ➤ Logistics Execution ➤ Shipping ➤ Basic Shipping Functions ➤ Shipping Point And Goods Determination Point Determination ➤ Define Loading Group.

As shown in Figure 8.11, you can create loading groups that are four characters long. This field is then used in the material master, specifically, in the Sales: General/Plant data view. For example, we have used the manual loading group 0003 (Manual Loading) for the material master 1628, as shown in Figure 8.12.

Once you have configured the factors that influence shipping point determination, you have to set up the determination rules.

Follows the menu path IMG ➤ Logistics Execution ➤ Shipping ➤ Basic Shipping Functions ➤ Shipping Point And Goods Determination Point Determination ➤ Assign Shipping Points.

Click New Entries, and specify a combination of plant, shipping condition, and loading group. Assign a default shipping point. You can also specify other shipping points that the user will be allowed to change manually (Figure 8.13). See the case study "Galaxy Musical Instruments: Shipping Point Setup" for an example of how this works.

Shipping point determination can also be carried out based on storage location, in addition to the factors mentioned earlier. The settings are similar to those you have already seen. The menu path is IMG ➤ Logistics Execution ➤ Shipping ➤ Basic Shipping Functions ➤ Shipping Point And Goods Determination Point Determination ➤ Set Up Storage Location–Dependent Shipping Point Determination.

FIGURE 8.11 Define loading groups

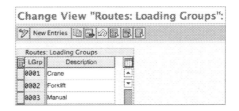

FIGURE 8.12 Key fields in material master, Sales: General/Plant view

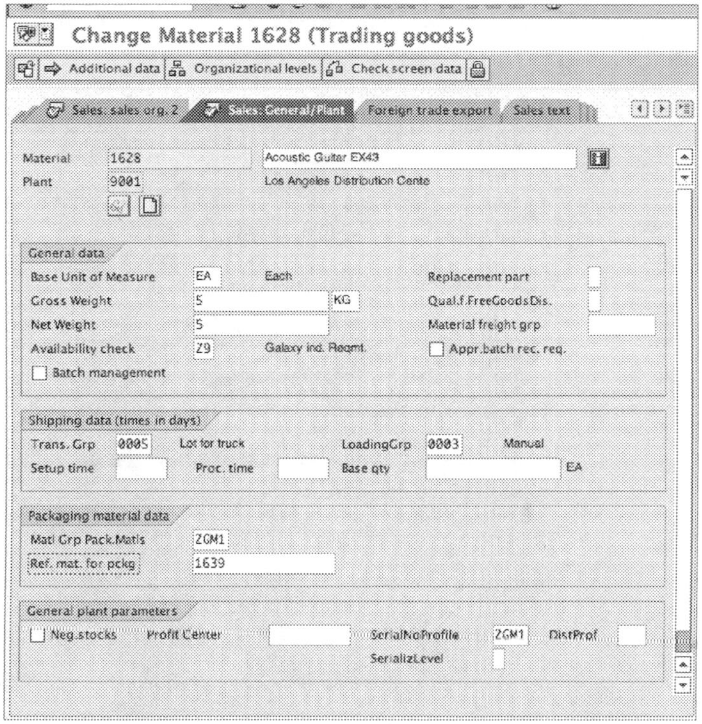

FIGURE 8.13 Shipping point determination

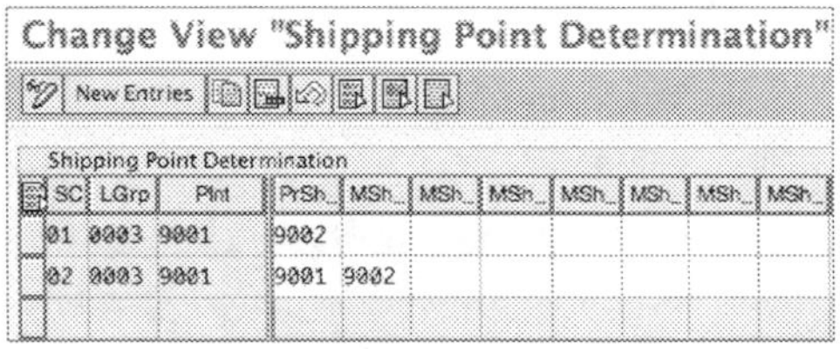

Defining Delivery Blocks

It is sometimes necessary to block an order from being delivered. You can either block an entire order or certain schedule lines from delivery. We discussed the definition and assignment of delivery blocks in Chapter 7.

Note that besides defining the block reasons, it is important to assign it to a delivery type.

The menu path is as follows: IMG ➤ Logistics Execution ➤ Shipping ➤ Deliveries ➤ Define Reasons For Blocking In Shipping ➤ Delivery Blocks.

CASE STUDY—GALAXY MUSICAL INSTRUMENTS: SHIPPING POINT SETUP

There are two shipping points defined for the Los Angeles Distribution Center (Plant 9001) of Galaxy Musical Instruments:

- ▶ 9001: Regular shipping point
- ▶ 9002: Express shipping point

This enables Galaxy to segregate and prioritize urgent shipments. The delivery-due list for the express shipping point is run every hour.

The shipping conditions are used to show the urgency of the order. The following shipping conditions are used:

- ▶ As soon as possible
- ▶ Regular

Loading group 0003 is used in the material master for all the products.

The shipping point determination is as follows:

> Plant + Shipping Condition + Loading Group = Shipping Point
>
> 9001 + 01 + 0003 = 9002
>
> 9001 + 02 + 0003 = 9001

Thus, the shipping condition for expedited shipping (01) points to the express shipping point (9002).

Also note that in the case of the regular shipping condition (02), the user is allowed to manually change the shipping point to 9002. Galaxy uses the Manual Shipping Point field for this purpose.

Picking

Picking is the process of physically collecting the items to be shipped. It can be done in the plant or in a warehouse location. If the Warehouse Management (WM) module of SAP has been implemented, then the picking process is carried out there, through a document called *transfer order*.

The Picking Process

You can access the picking screen in delivery create/change transactions. When picking has been completed in the warehouse, you can update the quantity in the picking tab of the delivery document.

The transaction VL06P generates a list of all deliveries that are due for picking. This list helps in planning the workload for the day. Used in conjunction with WM, you create transfer orders en masse with this transaction.

Customization for Picking

The following sections describe some important settings you will need to know in order to configure the picking process in SAP.

Determining Relevance for Picking

You can activate picking using the transaction OVLP. The path is IMG ➤ Logistics Execution ➤ Shipping ➤ Picking ➤ Define Relevant Item Categories.

Refer to Figure 8.14. On this screen, select the item categories that are relevant to picking, and activate the picking flag.

FIGURE 8.14 Item categories relevant to picking

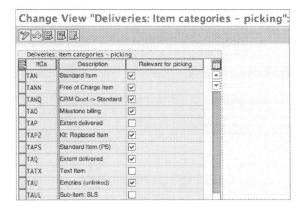

Specifying Rules for Picking Location

When you mark an item as relevant to picking, you have to specify the location from where it is to be picked up. In SAP, this is the storage location. To make these settings, you need to work in consultation with your WM or MM/IM team to get the list of storage locations where the finished product will be stored.

Storage locations can be determined automatically in the delivery. Two options, or *rules*, are predefined in SAP (the MM module) for this purpose:

- ▶ MALA rule: The storage location is determined based on plant, shipping point, and storage condition.

- ▶ RETA rule: The storage location is determined based on plant, shipping point, and situation.

The details of these rules are not in the scope of SD. For purposes of this discussion, we will use the MALA rule. To select the rule, the path in customization is as follows: IMG ➤ Logistics Execution ➤ Shipping ➤ Picking ➤ Determine Picking Location ➤ Define Rules For Picking Location Determination.

In this setting, you can assign the rule for every delivery type.

Setting Up Automatic Picking Location Determination

The factors that determine the picking location (storage location) are the plant, shipping point, and storage condition. By now you should be familiar with the terms *plant* and *shipping point*. These have already been determined in the delivery. We'll now cover the third factor, storage condition.

This field is maintained in the material master and is used to signify the conditions in which the item is to be stored. (For example, refrigeration is a special storage condition.)

To define the possible storage conditions in customization, the menu path is IMG ➤ Logistics Execution ➤ Shipping ➤ Picking ➤ Determine Picking Location ➤ Define Storage Conditions.

As shown in Figure 8.15, you can define a two-digit code for the new storage condition and add a description. In the case of Galaxy, there are two special storage conditions: 90 and 91. This field appears in the material master in the Plant Data/Stor. 1 view (see Figure 8.16).

Next, we will cover how to set up the actual determination of storage locations.

Use the menu path IMG ➤ Logistics Execution ➤ Shipping ➤ Picking ➤ Determine Picking Location ➤ Assign Picking Location. Then, specify the storage location for each combination of plant, shipping point, and storage condition.

FIGURE 8.15 Defining a storage condition

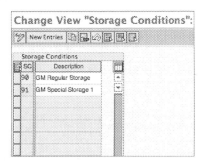

FIGURE 8.16 Assigning a storage condition in the material master

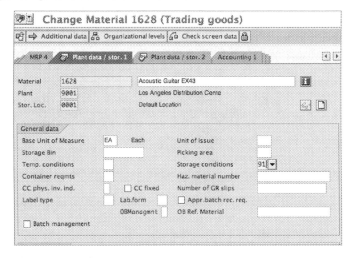

In Figure 8.17, we specified a storage location for plant 9001, shipping points 9001 and 9002, and each storage condition.

Also note that we included a general record (in the first row) without specifying any storage condition. This means that for materials for which we haven't specified any special storage condition, the default storage location 0001 will be picked up based on plant and shipping point alone.

FIGURE 8.17 Storage location determination

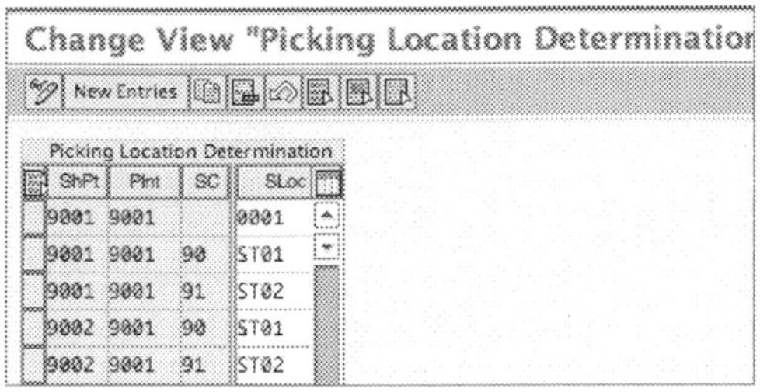

Picking with Transfer Orders in Warehouse Management

If warehouse management has been implemented for a storage location, the picking process will be carried out in the Warehouse Management application of SAP.

If this is the case, there is an additional transaction: creating a transfer order (LT03). The picking process is then carried out in WM. Based on the requirements in the transfer order, the stock is physically picked up from the storage bins in the warehouse. Once the process is completed, the transfer order is confirmed using transaction LT12.

The remaining steps in the logistics execution process are then carried out in the delivery document.

Wave Picking

In large warehouses or plants, picking runs are planned in advance. The deliveries that are due for picking at around the same time are grouped together. This process, called *wave picking*, enables the picking team to go around the warehouse and gather products for all deliveries at one time.

Now refer to Figure 8.18. Transaction VL06P allows you to run a periodic job to pick up all the deliveries that are due for picking during a specified time interval. As you can see from the results, if WM is enabled, a transfer order for all the deliveries can then be created in batches, or *waves*.

FIGURE 8.18 Picking due list

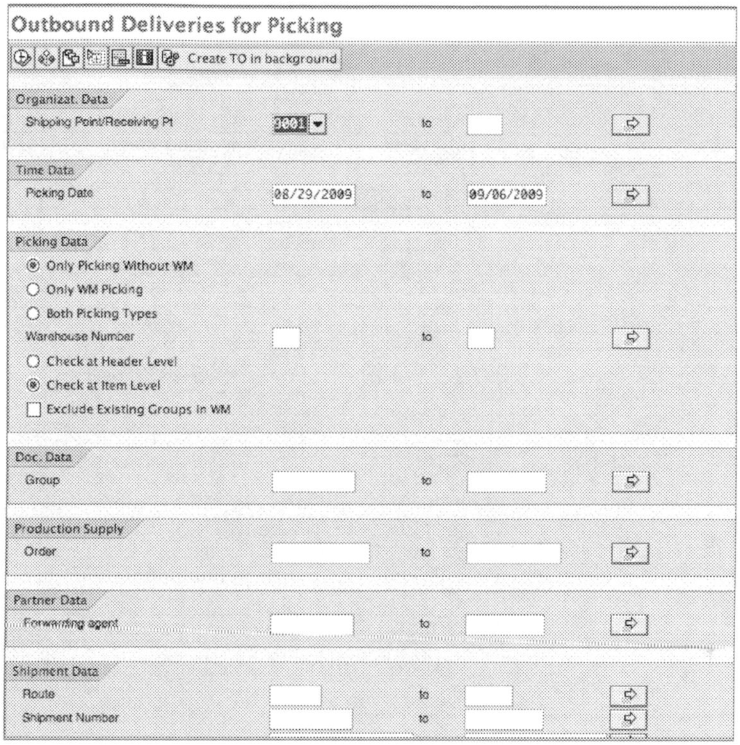

Packing

After picking the items, the next step is to pack them for shipment. The packing functionality in SAP covers the aspects of planning and execution of this process.

Packaging materials such as boxes and crates are also set up in SAP, using unique material master records. These materials are distinguished by a different material type: VERP. During the course of packing, you have to select the appropriate packaging material for the items being shipped. Certain customers may also send you special packaging instructions to follow for all shipments sent to a specific ship-to location. You can control these factors through customization steps. We'll now discuss these steps in detail.

The Packing Process

Packing can be done for each delivery or by using a special transaction designed for packing stations.

Packing in Individual Delivery Documents

In the delivery document, you can reach the packing screen (Figure 8.19) by selecting the Edit ➤ Pack option in VL02N.

The items that are due for packing appear in the lower window, whereas the new handling units (HUs) will appear in the upper window as the packing progresses.

FIGURE 8.19 Packing overview screen

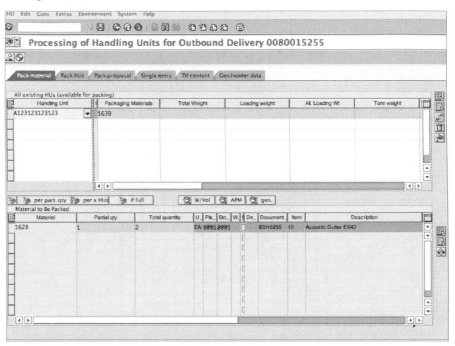

On the Pack Material tab, you can enter packaging material(s) and continue creating handling units until all items have been packed.

On the Pack HUs tab, the handling units can be packed into higher units. For example, you can pack several boxes into a crate, or several crates into a truck, using this feature.

As shown in Figure 8.20, the New HU Per X HUs button allows you to pack two boxes (packaging material 1639) into a crate (packaging material 1671).

At any point, you can see which packing materials can be used to pack the item. For this, use the menu path Extras ➤ Allowed Packaging Material. When you follow this path, a dialog box like that in Figure 8.21 will appear, giving you the options that are available for packing your products. This narrows down the search easily and prevents mistakes.

FIGURE 8.20 Packing handling units

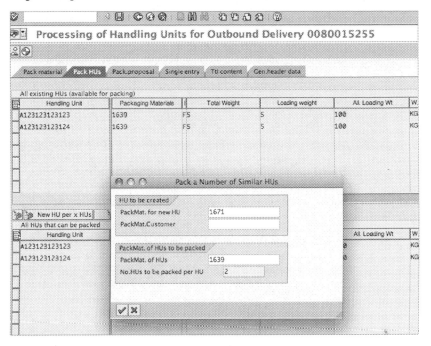

FIGURE 8.21 Using allowed packaging material to limit options

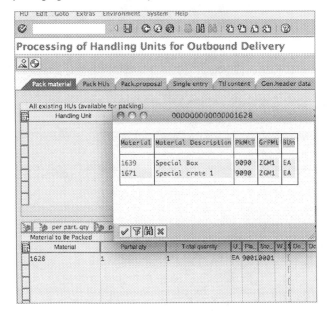

Packing Stations

We have just described the process of packing from within a delivery document.

However, it is also possible to configure and use a separate transaction code for packing that is specially meant for *packing stations*, which are special locations in the plant or warehouse where packing is being carried out.

To access the packing station transaction, follow the path SAP Menu ➢ Logistics Execution ➢ Outbound Process ➢ Goods Issue For Outbound Delivery ➢ Pack ➢ Packing Station (transaction HUPAST). Specify the packing station, and hit Enter. As shown in Figure 8.22, a complete packing cockpit screen appears, where you can pack materials into HUs and further pack the HUs into higher handling units.

You can also create or change handling units in a delivery or create a new HU without any reference. This is useful if any excess picked material is to be returned to the warehouse. You can also print labels and update or modify weights of HUs that are already created.

FIGURE 8.22 Packing station

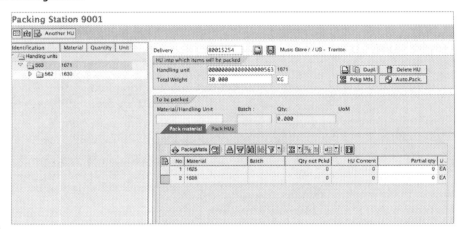

We'll now cover the customization settings for packing.

Customizing for Packing

You'll start the customization by identifying the items that are due for the packing process. Then you will configure the packaging materials and the packing station.

Setting Relevance for Packing

To start, you have to identify whether packing is relevant for the material being delivered. Like picking relevance, this is controlled at the item category level. Follow this menu path: IMG ➤ Logistics Execution ➤ Shipping ➤ Packing ➤ Packing Control By Item Category.

Select the item category that you plan to use. On the packing control screen, you can choose from three options. As you can see in Figure 8.23, packing can be made mandatory, optional, or disallowed totally. Choose the appropriate option for your requirements. If you are not certain, it is advisable to leave this field blank, in which case it will automatically default to optional packing.

If you chose mandatory packing, the system will not allow goods issue until this step has been completed.

FIGURE 8.23 Packing relevance at the item category level

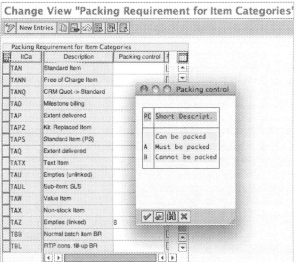

Determining Allowed Packaging Material

There can be a wide variety of packaging material. In the packing stage, it is important to have rules to determine the right type of packaging materials that are allowed for a particular delivery item.

Before you set up these rules, you'll have to configure two grouping terms: packaging material types and material groups for packaging materials.

Packaging material types   *Packaging material type* is a grouping term for similar packaging materials. This term can be used to identify a family of packaging materials that would then be allowed or disallowed. To configure this, use the menu path IMG ➤ Logistics Execution ➤ Shipping ➤ Packing ➤ Define Packaging Material Types. To create a new entry, specify a four-character alphanumeric code and description, as shown in Figure 8.24.

FIGURE 8.24 Defining the packaging material type

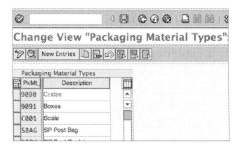

In the case of Galaxy Musical Instruments, there are several packaging materials. Galaxy has set up two groups:

➤ 9090: Crates

➤ 9091: Boxes

When you set up material master records for packaging materials, this field will appear in the Sales: General/Plant data. You will maintain this field for all packaging materials.

Material groups for packaging materials   This term groups together materials that require similar packing. For example, all string instruments require special boxes for secure packing. You can define a grouping term and assign it in the material master record for all the string instruments. To configure this, you can use the menu path IMG ➤ Logistics Execution ➤ Shipping ➤ Packing ➤ Define Material Groups For Packaging Materials.

In the case of Galaxy Musical Instruments, we have set up group ZGM1 for all the string instruments (Figure 8.25).

FIGURE 8.25 Defining material groups for the packaging material

This field appears in the material master in the Sales: General/Plant data. Refer to Figure 8.12; like Acoustic Guitar (Material 1628), you will find this field in the Packaging Material section. The group ZGM1 has been attached here.

Setting rules for allowable packaging materials   The next step is to set up rules to control the list of packaging materials users will be allowed to choose from. To set up the rules, use the menu path IMG ➢ Logistics Execution ➢ Shipping ➢ Packing ➢ Define Allowed Packaging Materials. As shown in Figure 8.26, we have specified that material group ZGM1 can be packed using packaging material 9091 (Boxes) and 9090 (Crates). This rule helps you in selecting the correct packaging material.

FIGURE 8.26 Rules for allowable packaging material

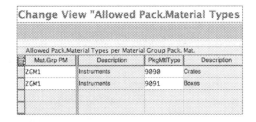

Configure Packing Stations

Packing station transactions can be customized for your organization. To configure a packing station, the menu path is IMG ➢ Logistics Execution ➢ Shipping ➢ Packing ➢ Set Profile For Packing Station.

Define a new packing station. You can customize the settings as shown in Figure 8.27. The default plant, storage location, and packaging material can be set up in this screen so that default data is proposed when a user logs on to this station. Also note that on the Scale tab there is a provision to link to external systems (such as a scanner or a weighing scale) that are commonly used at packing stations.

FIGURE 8.27 Configuring a packing station

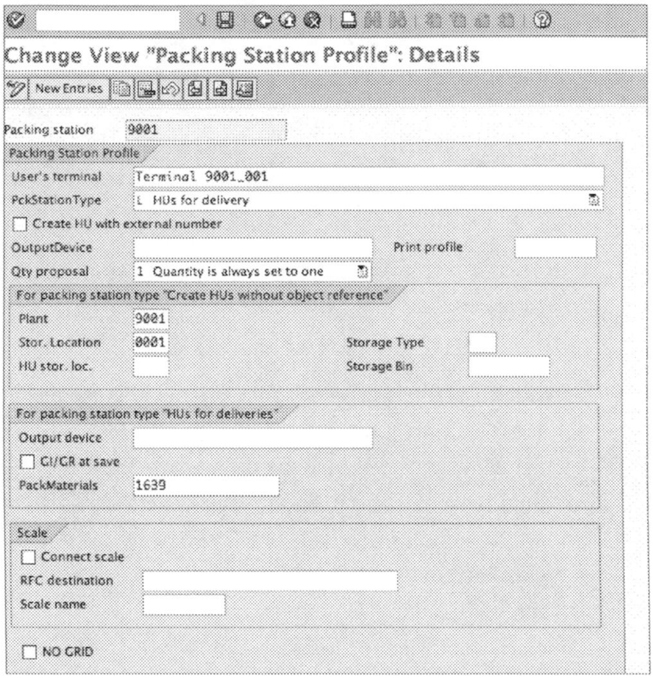

Transportation

The shipment document is the basis of transportation planning and execution. This document contains all the shipping-related information for the end customer and the other business partners, such as forwarding agents and vendors.

Depending on the complexity of your distribution model, the shipments can be the following types:

Individual shipment   One or more deliveries are combined in one shipment document. It starts from the same starting point (such as a shipping point) and ends at a common destination. For example, all deliveries originating from the same shipping point A and going to the same destination, transportation zone C, by truck can be clubbed together into the same shipment.

Collective shipment   One or more deliveries, originating from different starting points (such as different plants) and shipped to different destinations, may be clubbed together in a common shipment. An example is *milk-run shipments* in which a single truck travels from plant A to plant B and then continues to the final customer destination C. Some of the deliveries are to be carried from A and dropped at B. Other deliveries may originate in B and be added to the truck. Then the total deliveries are taken to the customer location C.

Transportation chains   The scenario gets complex when more than one mode of transport is used for shipment. You may need to plan each leg separately with different sets of documents and instructions to each driver. Within the organization, there can be different teams doing transportation planning, such as for air cargo, ocean, and surface. In such cases, you can create multiple shipment documents. For example, deliveries originating from plant A and plant B are carried in different trucks to an international airport cargo hub C. These are called *preliminary legs* of the journey. From there, they are combined in a second shipment and carried by air on the major leg of the journey. On arrival at airport D, they are then picked up by different trucks and shipped to end locations E and F, respectively. These are called *subsequent legs*.

The shipment process requires mapping of major routes in the system. The duration of travel by each route would play a role in planning the date of arrival at the customer location. We'll now discuss the configuration of routes in SAP before proceeding with the setup for the shipment process.

Maintaining Routes

Most organizations use predefined routes in conveying material from source to destination. You can set up and maintain a central repository of your primary routes in SAP. This master record contains all details about the route such as the duration, the means of transport, and the service provider. SAP's automatic route determination functionality populates the appropriate route in the sales document. We'll discuss the process of defining and determining routes.

Before you configure route setup, you should ask the following questions:

▶ Does the organization use predefined routes?

▶ What are the modes of transport being used? Road? Air?

▶ Do you want to plan shipments by taking transit time into account? If so, do you know the transit duration of each route?

▶ How should you group the destination regions into transportation zones? What should be the right level of aggregation? For example, transportation zones could be regions (northeastern United States), states (New York state), cities (New York), ZIP codes, and so on. Increasing the level of detail may improve accuracy, but the number of routes would increase as well.

▶ Does the choice of transportation route depend on weight of the shipment? What are these weight groups (1 to 99 pounds, greater than 99 pounds, and so on)?

▶ Do any specific vendors (freight forwarders or logistics service providers) cater to a specific route? If so, can they be mapped to the route?

▶ Are there any major transportation connection points to be mapped with the routes? These could be airports, transportation hubs, customs office, harbors, and so on. What is the length of stay at each point?

Based on the answers to these questions, you can then configure the routes at the right level of detail.

Configuration of Routes

The configuration of routes consists of two major steps:

1. Route definition: Setting up routes and defining attributes such as distance, time, and so on

2. Route determination: Setting up rules for automatic determination of routes in sales documents

We'll now discuss the configuration steps that you should carry out before you can define and assign routes.

Defining Modes of Transport

To configure the modes of transport, use the following path: IMG ➢ Logistics Execution ➢ Shipping ➢ Basic Shipping Functions ➢ Routes ➢ Define Routes ➢ Define Modes Of Transport. On this screen, (which will look like Figure 8.28), you can specify the mode of transport in the column ShTy using a two-digit alphanumeric code. If needed, you can assign a mode-of-transport type in the column SType. This field is relevant only in the case of movement of dangerous goods.

FIGURE 8.28 Defining modes of transport

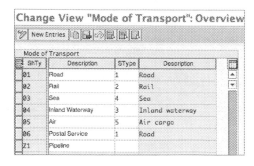

Defining Shipping Types

After defining the modes of transport, you define the shipping types (such as trucks, trucks with trailers, and so on) and assign them to modes (such as Road).

Follow the menu path IMG ➤ Logistics Execution ➤ Shipping ➤ Basic Shipping Functions ➤ Routes ➤ Define Routes ➤ Define Shipping Types. On this screen (Figure 8.29), define the shipping type in the column PT using a two-digit alphanumeric code. Assign it to the mode of transport (MdTr) defined earlier.

Another field, STPG (shipping type procedure group), shown in the figure is used during shipment cost calculation.

FIGURE 8.29 Defining shipping types

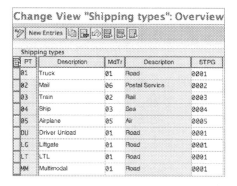

Setting Up Transportation Connection Points

In this step, you can set up all major transportation connection points. As you will see later, you will use them as transit points during the setup of routes. The menu path in customization is IMG ➤ Logistics Execution ➤ Shipping ➤ Basic Shipping Functions ➤ Routes ➤ Define Routes ➤ Define Transportation Connection Points.

Define a new entry, identified by a unique name and description (as shown in Figure 8.30). You can specify the type of location, such as an airport, train station, and customs office, as well as other relevant attributes and details such as transit time at the location.

FIGURE 8.30 Defining the transportation connection point

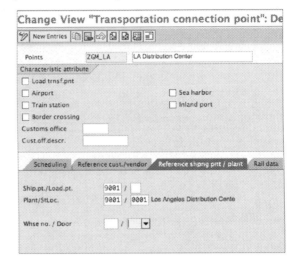

Defining Transportation Zones

Define the transportation zones to specify all the regions that you plan to cover with your routes. Routes will flow from a departure zone to a destination zone. The menu path in customization is IMG ➤ Logistics Execution ➤ Shipping ➤ Basic Shipping Functions ➤ Routes ➤ Route Determination ➤ Define Transportation Zones.

Here you can select a country and define transportation zones with a meaningful description, as shown in Figure 8.31.

The zones you set up here will be used in the master data. The location of each customer and vendor will be identified using the Transportation Zone field on the Address tab in the customer (or vendor) master record.

FIGURE 8.31 Defining transportation zones

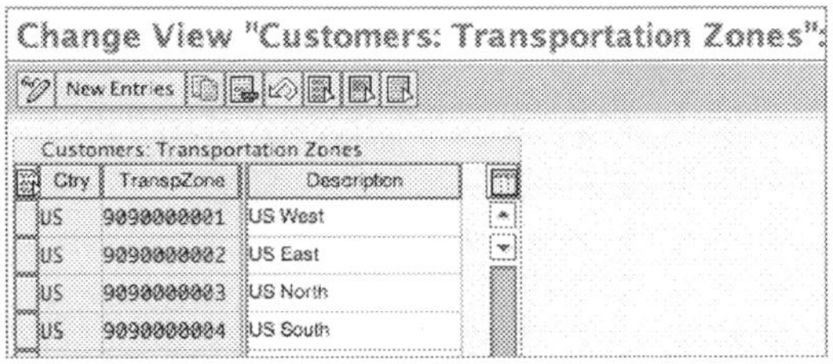

You can also specify the zones for each of your shipping points by following the menu path IMG ➢ Logistics Execution ➢ Shipping ➢ Basic Shipping Functions ➢ Routes ➢ Route Determination ➢ Maintain Country And Transportation Zone For Shipping Point.

On the screen shown in Figure 8.32, select the shipping point, and specify the country and transportation zone.

As an alternative, when you define a shipping point as discussed in Chapter 2, you can specify the transportation zone on the address screen.

FIGURE 8.32 Specifying the transportation zone for each shipping point

Creating Transportation Groups

A *transportation group* combines all materials that share the same transportation requirements. For example, you can group all liquids into a transportation group that requires special tankers for transport. To create transportation groups, use the menu path IMG ➢ Logistics Execution ➢ Shipping ➢ Basic Shipping Functions ➢ Routes ➢ Route Determination ➢ Define Transportation Groups.

Figure 8.33 shows the screen for defining transportation groups.

FIGURE 8.33 Defining transportation groups

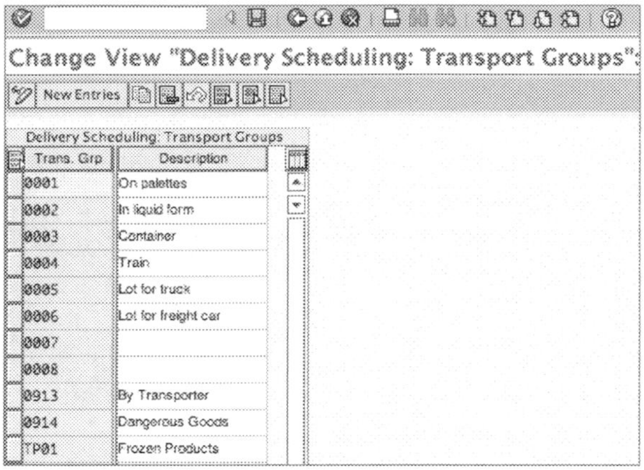

Setting Up Weight Groups

If the exact weight of the delivery plays a role in route determination in your organization, you can set up weight groups in SAP by following the menu path IMG ➤ Logistics Execution ➤ Shipping ➤ Basic Shipping Functions ➤ Routes ➤ Route Determination ➤ Define Weight Groups.

On the default screen, Maintain Weight Group, create a new weight group with a meaningful description. From the navigation menu on the left, you can go to Maintain Details For Weight Group. On this screen, you can specify the maximum weight that is allowed in each weight group.

At the time of delivery creation, the system will take into account the weight and then determine an appropriate route. This is an optional setting. If you choose not to use it, route determination will take place in the sales order and be copied into the deliveries.

Configuring Shipping Conditions

We discussed shipping conditions earlier in this chapter. They also play a role in route determination.

Defining and Assigning Routes

Now that you have explored how to configure these key factors, we will show you how to define and assign routes.

Defining Routes

The path to set up routes is as follows: IMG ➤ Logistics Execution ➤ Shipping ➤ Basic Shipping Functions ➤ Routes ➤ Define Routes ➤ Define Routes And Stages (transaction 0VTC).

This will bring you to an overview screen that lists all the routes that have been defined in the system. To define a new route, click New Entries, or copy from an existing route. A screen similar to Figure 8.34 appears. On this screen, identify the new route with a unique number. Other fields in this screen are discussed here:

Identification tab   Use these fields to add a meaningful description of the route.

Processing tab   If the route is managed by a specific vendor, you can specify it in the Service Agent field. You can also fill in the Shipping Type field here.

Scheduling tab   These are the important fields on the Scheduling tab:

TransitTime   Transit Time is the total time taken for the goods to reach the customer following the route. It is specified in calendar days. The time entered here is taken into account for planning purposes and for determining the date on which the product will reach the customer.

Trav.Dur.   Travel Duration, expressed in hours, is a subset of the total transit time. It is the time taken for the actual travel along the route.

TransLdTm.   Transportation Lead Time is the time needed for planning and arranging transportation. SAP uses it to arrive at the transportation planning date. It is specified in calendar days and in hours.

When you have defined the attributes of the route, click the Route Stages tab in the left menu in Figure 8.34. You will see a screen that looks like Figure 8.35. On this screen, specify the departure and destination points from the list of transportation connection points defined earlier. Also specify the duration and shipping type details for each stage.

TIP   A route can have either a single stage (from point A to point B) or multiple stages, each of which is likely to involve a different means of transport. You can specify all these details in the route stages.

FIGURE 8.34 Defining routes

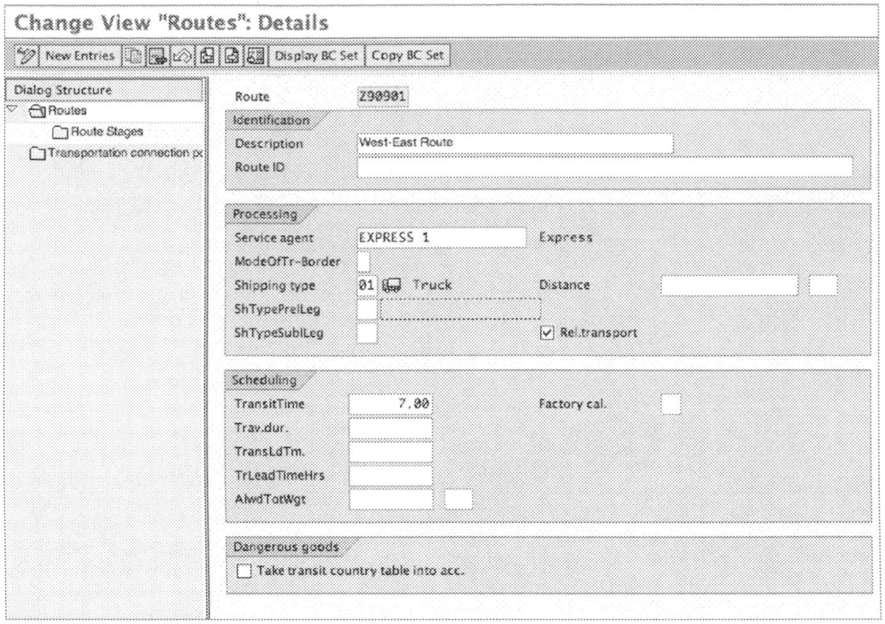

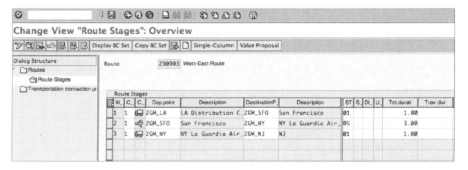

FIGURE 8.35 Defining route stages

Determining Routes

Automatic route determination is based on the following factors:

▶ Country/departure zone (picked up from the address of shipping point)

▶ Country/destination zone of the recipient (from the ship-to party address)

▶ Shipping condition

▶ Transportation group (from the material master)

In the case of deliveries, you can also add weight groups to the list of controlling factors, if that is applicable to your organization.

The menu path for route determination is as follows: IMG ≻ Logistics Execution ≻ Shipping ≻ Basic Shipping Functions ≻ Routes ≻ Route Determination ≻ Maintain Route Determination.

To set up a new record, enter the country and transportation zone of the source and destination locations. You can also specify generic routes between countries, leaving the Transportation Zone field blank.

Click Route Determination Without Weight Group (Order), as shown in Figure 8.36, and then click the New Entries button. This enables you to specify a route for every combination of shipping condition and transportation group.

FIGURE 8.36 Setting up route determination

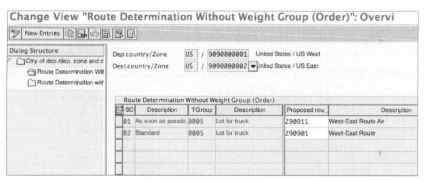

You can also choose Route Determination With Weight Group (Deliveries) if it is applicable. During delivery creation, the routes will be redetermined based on the weight of the delivery.

TIP   The shipping condition comes from the customer master record of the sold-to party, and the destination address (transportation zone) comes from the customer master record of the ship-to party.

CASE STUDY—GALAXY MUSICAL INSTRUMENTS: CONFIGURATION OF ROUTES

We'll now discuss how Galaxy Musical Instruments set up some of its major routes.

All the major transportation connection points were set up. The Los Angeles distribution center as well as other major hubs, airports, and load transfer points have been set up (as shown in Figure 8.30).

The regions were divided into transportation zones (such as 9090000001 for the Western United States). Galaxy assigned this transportation zone to the shipping points of the Los Angeles–based plant. This specified the country and transportation zone of the source location.

Similarly, the addresses of major customers were updated with corresponding transportation zones. This completed the setup of destination locations.

There are two major shipping conditions: regular shipment and express shipment.

As shown in Figure 8.36, Galaxy assigned express (air) routes such as Z90911, corresponding to the express shipping condition.

The regular shipping condition was mapped to ground routes such as Z90901.

The Shipment Process

You can create individual shipment documents or use a collective processing option.

Follow the path SAP Menu ➤ Logistics ➤ Logistics Execution ➤ Transportation ➤ Transportation Planning ➤ Create ➤ Single Document (VT01).

On the selection screen, specify the transportation planning point and shipment type. The next screen is the overview of the new shipment document. As shown in Figure 8.37, various activities in shipment planning and execution are recorded and updated in the shipment document. One or more deliveries can be added to the shipment. The leg determination functionality (on the Stages tab) will help you plan the stages of the shipment. The document status is updated on completion of every step of the process. You can also assign activity profiles so that certain activities (such as posting goods issue) happen once a certain status has been reached.

FIGURE 8.37 Shipment overview

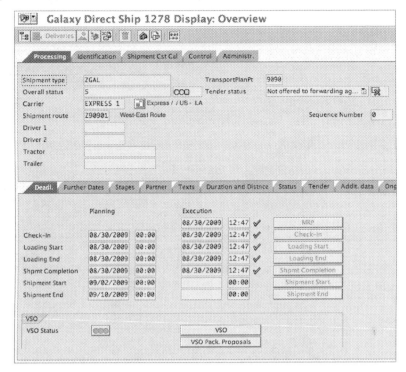

To access collective processing, use the path SAP Menu ➤ Logistics ➤ Logistics Execution ➤ Transportation ➤ Transportation Planning ➤ Create ➤ Collective Processing (VT04).

This transaction allows collective processing for creating shipment documents. On the selection screen (Figure 8.38), you can specify a variant for selection of delivery documents that are due for shipment. Specify a meaningful name for your variant, and click the Maintn option to create it. This will take you to a screen similar to Figure 8.39. You can choose from several selection criteria to select the deliveries. For example, in the case of Galaxy, we have specified that the shipping point in the delivery should be 9001. Technically, the system uses the report SAPLV56L to select deliveries.

FIGURE 8.38 Creating shipments in collective processing

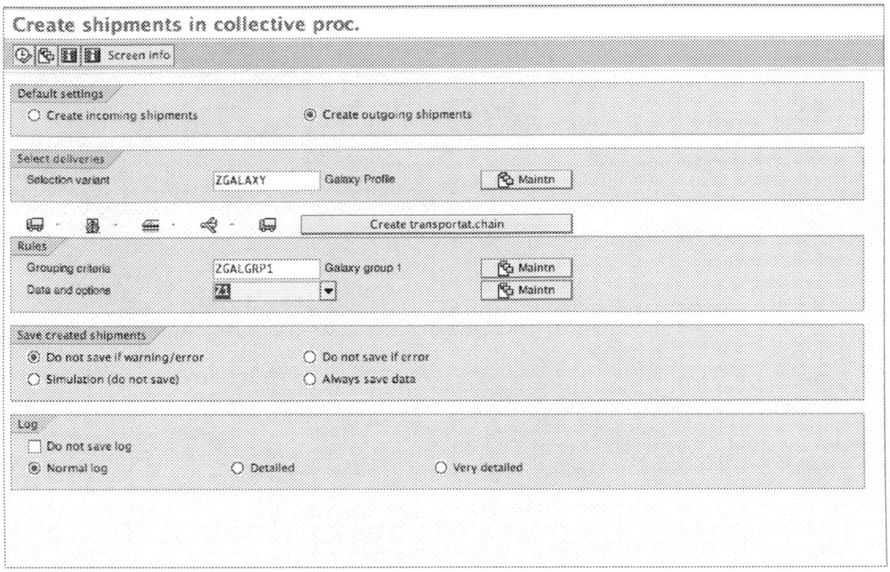

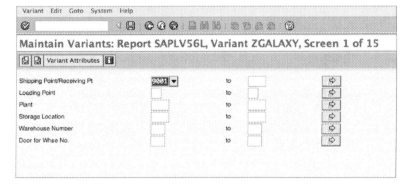

FIGURE 8.39 Maintaining variants for delivery selection

You can use the grouping criteria to specify rules for combining deliveries together in a shipment. You can also specify the weight and capacity limitations per shipment. Use the Maintn option to define a selection variant, as shown in Figure 8.40. If you select Routes as a criterion for combination, you can specify the routes that can be grouped together in the same shipment.

FIGURE 8.40 Maintaining variants for grouping criteria

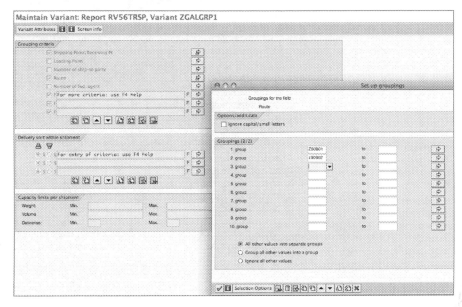

Configuration of Shipments

The following are the steps in the configuration of shipments.

Maintain Transportation Relevance

Before we move on to configuring shipment documents, we have to select the relevance to our business processes. To carry out this activity, the menu path is IMG ➢ Logistics Execution ➢ Transportation ➢ Shipments ➢ Maintain Transportation Relevance.

There are three activities listed here. Follow the sequence, and select the relevance of the following:

► Delivery type

► Delivery item type

► Route

Figure 8.41 shows the screen for marking delivery types relevant to transportation.

FIGURE 8.41 Setting up relevance for transportation

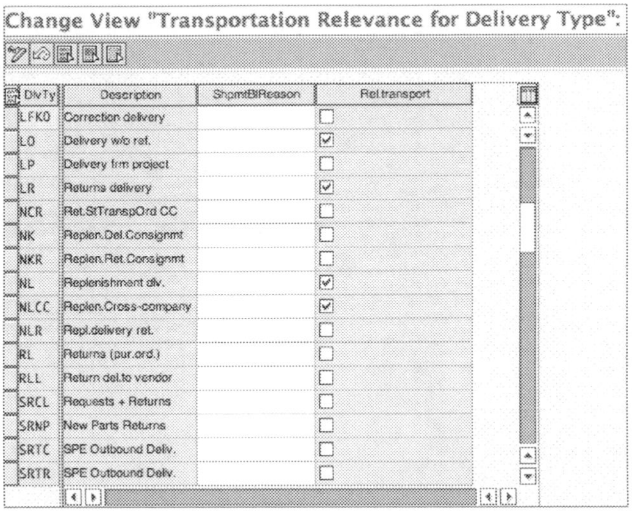

Change View "Transportation Relevance for Delivery Type":

DlvTy	Description	ShpmtBlReason	Rel.transport
LFKO	Correction delivery		☐
LO	Delivery w/o ref.		☑
LP	Delivery frm project		☐
LR	Returns delivery		☑
NCR	Ret.StTranspOrd CC		☐
NK	Replen.Del.Consignmt		☐
NKR	Replen.Ret.Consignmt		☐
NL	Replenishment dlv.		☑
NLCC	Replen.Cross-company		☑
NLR	Repl.delivery ret.		☐
RL	Returns (pur.ord.)		☐
RLL	Return del.to vendor		☐
SRCL	Requests + Returns		☐
SRNP	New Parts Returns		☐
SRTC	SPE Outbound Delv.		☐
SRTR	SPE Outbound Delv.		☐

Set Up Transportation Planning Points

After you decide on transportation relevance, you need to configure the organizational elements that look after transportation. The shipment documents are created for a transportation planning point.

We discussed the steps to set up a transportation planning point in Chapter 2.

Define Shipment Type

To configure the shipment type document, the menu path is IMG ➢ Logistics Execution ➢ Transportation ➢ Shipments ➢ Define Shipment Types.

Define a four-character alphanumeric code and description for the shipment type.

Figure 8.42 shows some of the critical fields to be configured.

Number Systems tab On this tab, you can specify an internal and external number range for the shipment documents that will be created. This is identical to any other number range settings that we covered earlier.

Document Content Perhaps this is the most important tab that defines the shipment type in detail. The following are some of the important settings on this tab:

> **Shipment Completion Type** The field ShpmtComplType specifies the type of shipment being created. You can specify whether it is an inbound or outbound shipment and whether it is filled or empty.

Shipping Type The field Shipping Type signifies whether the shipment will be by road or air or other means of transport. (We covered this when talking about route definition.)

Process Control The field Process Control defines the way the shipment will be planned. The options here are as follows:

> Individual Shipment With Single Mode Of Transport

> Individual Shipment With Multi Mode Of Transport

> Collective Shipment With Single Mode Of Transport

> Collective Shipment With Multi Mode Of Transport

FIGURE 8.42 Defining the shipment type

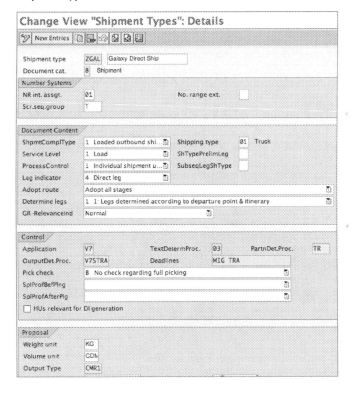

Leg Indicator In the field Leg indicator, you can specify whether a leg is a direct leg of a shipment or whether it is a primary leg, mail leg, or subsequent leg of a transportation chain. If you select Direct Leg or Return Leg, the entire process will be carried out in a single shipment document. However, if you select Primary Leg,

Main Leg, or Subsequent Leg, it will be a transportation chain with multiple shipments interlinked to complete the shipment. You can also specify the transportation type of the preliminary and subsequent legs through the fields ShTypePrelimLeg and SubseqLegShType.

Determine Legs   Using the field Determine Legs, you can select a rule; based on this, the system then tries to structure the legs of the shipment. For example, if you choose type 1 (1: Legs Determined According To Departure Point & Itinerary) for a collective shipment, leg determination will be carried out on the basis of the sequence of departures and destinations. In other words, assume there are two deliveries in a shipment. Both originate from the same shipping point, 9001, in Los Angeles. The first delivery is being sent to a customer in New York. The other is being shipped to New Jersey, which is near New York. The first leg of the journey is from Los Angeles to New York (carrying both the deliveries). After the first delivery is offloaded at the customer's location, the subsequent leg is from New York to New Jersey (with the second delivery only). In the shipment document, if you click Leg Determination, the system will check the points of origin and destination of each delivery and automatically propose the stages of the journey. You can override or modify the proposal manually. Note that leg determination is not an optimization algorithm. Rather, it is a simple tool to help create legs on the basis of rules that you specify.

Define and Assign Activity Profile

You can use activity profiles to define which actions are to be performed once a shipment reaches a particular status. For example, once the shipment reaches "completion" status, the system should perform the goods issue activity for each of the constituent delivery documents.

There is a provision to attach different activity profiles for each status of the shipment.

To maintain and assign an activity profile, the path is IMG ➢ Logistics Execution ➢ Transportation ➢ Shipments ➢ Define And Assign Activity Profiles.

Select your shipment type. The columns in Figure 8.43 denote the various statuses of a shipment document, such as check-in, completion, and so on. For each status, you can specify an activity profile. Select from the list of available profiles. To set up a new activity profile, enter a profile name, and click the Maintain button.

FIGURE 8.43 Assigning activity profiles to shipment types

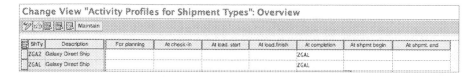

As shown in Figure 8.43, on the Activity Profiles For Shipment Types screen, we chose shipment type ZGAL. Against the status At Completion, we want to set up a custom activity profile named ZGAL. We enter the name and click Maintain.

On the next screen (Figure 8.44), we have selected the post goods issue and billing options.

FIGURE 8.44 Defining activity profiles

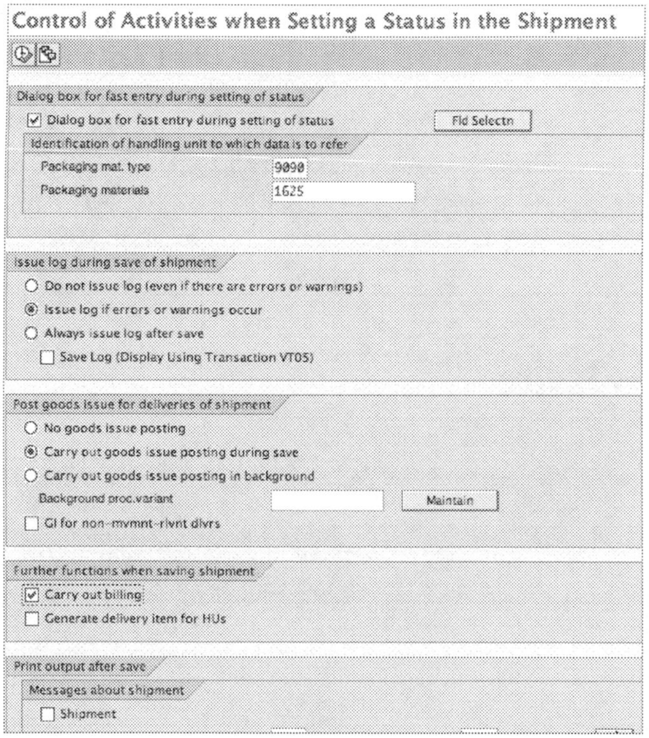

Technically, the program RV56ABST is being called in this transaction. You can set the options on the selection screen of this program and save the variant for further use.

CASE STUDY—GALAXY MUSICAL INSTRUMENTS: CONFIGURATION OF SHIPMENTS

Galaxy Musical Instruments has marked all the delivery types and routes as relevant for shipment. The organizational setup at Galaxy is such that it has two different groups to manage air transportation and road/rail transportation, respectively. Hence, we have set up two transportation planning points:

► 9090: Galaxy Transportation Road

► 9091: Galaxy Transportation Air

Both entities are assigned to company code 9090.

The shipment type defined is ZGAL. It is an example of individual shipment. Deliveries that are being shipped to the same destination are grouped together in a single shipment. For example, all deliveries for customers in New York City are loaded in the same truck, from LA to NY.

Galaxy's requirement is that, once shipment is completed, the goods issue and billing should occur in the background, without further manual intervention. We have achieved this through configuring activity profile ZGAL, as shown in Figure 8.44.

Once we create shipments of type ZGAL, we will find that once it reaches the completion, the goods issue and billing will be carried out in the background.

Goods Issue

Goods issue is the last step in the shipment process. Once the goods leave your shipping point, you confirm it by posting a goods issue. In the background of this transaction, several important updates are occurring in the system:

► The physical stocks are updated. The inventory in the shipping plant/warehouse is reduced by the quantity that was shipped.

► The requirements in the stock requirement list are updated. The delivery quantity is no longer "open," and the requirement is now marked as completed.

► Accounting documents are posted in the background, reducing the value of inventory and increasing the cost of goods sold.

If the delivery contains service items or items that have no physical inventory, the transactional equivalent of goods issue is the *confirmation of service*. There is no inventory update in this case.

In SAP, the Post Goods Issue button appears in delivery processing transactions (such as VL01N or VL02N). The entire process is carried out by a single click of this button. If you are using Returns Delivery (document type LR), you will find the Post Goods Receipt button instead. It allows you to receive returned goods.

For collective posting of goods issue for a batch of deliveries, you can use the transaction VL06G.

If the goods issue is to be reversed, you can do this using transaction VL09.

TIP   When we defined schedule line categories (using transaction VOV6) in Chapter 7, we specified a movement type for updating inventory. When a goods issue is done, the system posts the movement type based on this setting.

System Modifications in Deliveries

There are several routines, user exits, and business add-ins available in shipping if you need to modify the system setup.

You have already seen (when we talked about copy controls) that VOFM routines are required to control the flow of data from sales documents into deliveries. You can reach this menu from Logistics Execution, using the path IMG ➢ Logistics Execution ➢ Shipping ➢ Copy Controls ➢ Define Copying Requirements.

Similarly, you can define a custom routine with specific requirements for the picking process. You can attach it at the following location: IMG ➢ Logistics Execution ➢ Shipping ➢ Picking ➢ Define Picking Requirements (OVB6).

For packing, you can attach the Requirements routine using the menu path IMG ➢ Logistics Execution ➢ Shipping ➢ Packing ➢ Define Requirements For Packing (VPBD).

For the list of Business Add-Ins (BAdIs) and user exits, refer to the menu path IMG ➢ Logistics Execution ➢ Shipping ➢ System Modifications.

Another resource on this topic is SAP Service Marketplace note 198137, which explains the enhancements and user exits available to customize the delivery-due list. For example, you can follow the guidelines in this note to set up custom rules to control the delivery dates (From date and To date) that appear as the default in the VL10 set of transactions.

Summary

In this chapter, we covered the process of shipping, starting with delivery creation and moving on to picking, packing, shipment and transportation, and finally goods issue. This vast process is part of the Logistics Execution module in SAP.

After goods issue, the delivery becomes due for billing. We will cover the billing process in the next chapter.

Billing

B illing is the one of the most important process in a sales cycle. In this step, customers are invoiced for the services rendered or goods supplied. If there are any corrections in the billed amount or if the customer has returned the goods for any reason, the difference is settled by issuing credit or a debit memo or a credit for returns. All these documents are termed *billing documents* in SAP.

During the process of billing, you can choose to carry out a final repricing for some or all the pricing conditions before the invoice is created. The billing documents are then released to accounting. The determination of the accounts, the accounting document type, and other information is initiated during the billing process.

In this chapter, we will cover the billing process, explain some of the important scenarios, and show you the configuration settings.

Billing Process

A sales document becomes due for billing once a product has been delivered or a service has been rendered. Actions such as posting goods issue (or a confirmation of service) in a delivery can make the document due for billing. Order-related billing is another scenario.

As covered in Chapter 7, "Sales," when you define item categories, you choose the options for billing relevance such as order-related billing, delivery-related billing, and so on. These settings govern the items that show up in the billings-due list.

Another factor that determines items due for billing is the Billing Date field in the sales document. The item cannot be billed until the billing date is reached.

Billing Document Creation

In SAP, a billing document can be created as an individual document or in batch mode by running periodic jobs. The following sections cover the ways to create a billing document.

Creating an Individual Billing Document

To access this transaction, the menu path is as follows: SAP Menu ➢ Logistics ➢ Sales And Distribution ➢ Billing ➢ Billing Document ➢ Create (VF01).

This will lead you to a screen similar to Figure 9.1. Enter one or more documents due for billing. These can be sales documents (in the case of order-related billing and credit/debit memos) or delivery documents. The billing type can be entered manually or determined automatically, based on the customization settings. The Execute function creates a billing document.

FIGURE 9.1   Creating a billing document using VF01

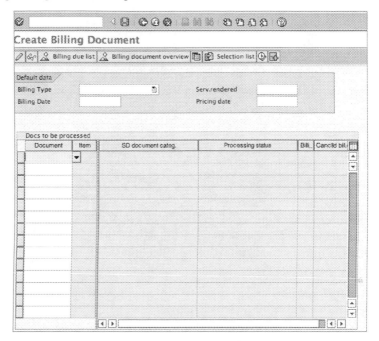

Creating Individual Billing Document from the Sales Order Screen (VA01 or VA02)

From the sales order screen, you can use the menu Sales Document ➢ Billing to create a billing document in the case of order-related billing.

This option is available if the user is authorized for sales order and billing document creation.

Collective Processing of Documents Due for Billing

When the volume of sales transaction is high, it is not always feasible to create individual billing documents. Collective processing of billing documents enables you to create documents in batches. The path is SAP Menu ➢ Logistics ➢ Sales And Distribution ➢ Billing ➢ Billing Document ➢ Process Billing Due List (VF04).

The selection screen allows you to control the parameters for which the list can be executed. As shown in Figure 9.2, you can use criteria such as billing data (with options like billing type and billing dates), organizational data (such as sales organization), and/or customer-specific data (such as the sold-to party number). You can further limit the documents to be selected by choosing scenarios such as order-related billing, delivery-related billing, and so on.

FIGURE 9.2 Billings-due list

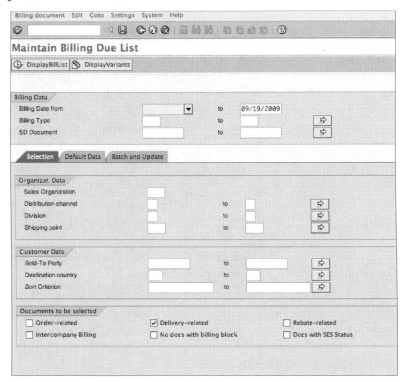

Some Important Billing Types

In SAP, several types of billing documents exist to fulfill different business processes. The billing type determines the kind of billing document that is created in the process. We'll now discuss some of the major document types and the business scenarios where they are used; after that, we'll discuss the customization settings.

Customer Invoice

You can invoice the customer for services rendered or items delivered by using regular invoices. Depending on the reference document, billing type F1 is defined for order-related billing; F2 is defined for delivery-related billing.

As discussed in Chapter 7, when you define a sales document (VOV8), you specify the billing type to be used in the case of order-related and delivery-related billing scenarios.

Credit and Debit Memos

You can make any corrections to the invoices amount or give any refunds to the customer using credit memos (G2) and debit memos (L2). These documents are usually created with reference to a credit (or debit) memo request. In that case, it is an order-related billing. However, credit and debit memos can be created with reference to invoices as well.

You can also issue a credit to a customer in the event of a return. In this case, you can use a special billing type, RE. This is usually created with reference to a return order and/or returned delivery.

Pro-forma Invoice

A pro-forma invoice is used as documentation to accompany shipments. It has details about the shipment contents and value. A pro-forma invoice has no impact on financial accounting. You can print out any number of pro-forma invoices at any stage of the sales cycle.

You can create a pro-forma invoice with reference to a sales order (billing type F5) or a delivery (billing type F8).

Intercompany Invoice

In an intercompany sales scenario, the delivering plant in a sales order belongs to a different company code than the sales organization. In this case, the plant delivers the shipment to the customer and bills the ordering company code for the goods or services provided. This internal document is called *intercompany invoice*. The billing type in this case is IV.

We will discuss this process later in this chapter.

Invoice List

Some customers prefer to receive a periodic statement that lists the details of all the billing documents created in a certain period. This document is called an *invoice list*. You can combine one or more billing documents in an invoice list. In the case of a large group of companies, there can be several sold-to parties but a common payer. In such cases, it is common to issue a periodic invoice list to the payer, who will make the payment on behalf of the entire group. The group payer internally collects the amount from each sold-to party within the group. In some cases, the payer is given a discount (called a *factoring discount*) for these services.

To create an invoice list, proceed through the SAP Easy Access menu via the menu path Logistics ➤ Sales And Distribution ➤ Billing ➤ Invoice List ➤ Create (VF21).

The transaction is similar to VF01 but used exclusively for an invoice list. You can combine one or more invoices and debit notes in a common invoice list. SAP offers the billing type LR. Credit memos are combined into a separate invoice list, called LG.

The billing documents to be included in an invoice list should already have been posted to accounting.

Invoice Cancellation Documents

If any invoice that has been posted to accounting has to be deleted, you can create another billing document called a *cancellation document* to offset the effect. The cancellation document is also posted to the accounting and offsets entries there.

At this time, the reference document (order or billing) once again becomes due for billing. S1, S2, LRS, and LGS are examples of cancellation billing types.

To create a cancellation document, follow the menu path SAP Menu ➤ Logistics ➤ Sales And Distribution ➤ Billing ➤ Billing Document ➤ Cancel (VF11). Enter the billing document to be cancelled, and execute the transaction. The transaction is similar to VF01.

Table 9.1 summarizes the important billing types used in SAP.

TABLE 9.1   Billing Types

Billing Type	Description
F1	Order-related billing
F2	Delivery-related billing
L2	Debit memo
G2	Credit memo
RE	Credit for returns
F5	Pro-forma for order
F8	Pro-forma for delivery

TABLE 9.1   Billing Types *(continued)*

Billing Type	Description
IV	Intercompany billing
LR	Invoice list
LG	Invoice list for credit memos
S1	Cancellation document

Customizing Billing Documents

We'll now cover the important settings required to configure a billing document and control the data flow in it.

Setting Up a Billing Type

The first step in the configuration is to set up a billing document. The path in IMG to configure delivery types is IMG ≻ Sales And Distribution ≻ Billing ≻ Billing Documents ≻ Define Billing Types (VOFA).

You can select from the existing list of billing documents or define a custom document here. It is helpful to copy with reference to an existing document type. Choose a two-character alphanumeric code and a meaningful description. Refer to Figure 9.3.

FIGURE 9.3   Define billing types, general controls

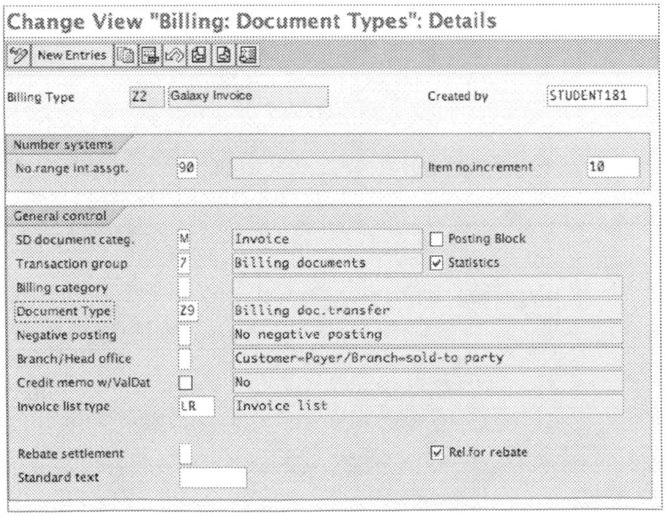

Change View "Billing: Document Types": Details

Billing Type	Z2	Galaxy Invoice	Created by STUDENT181

Number systems
No.range int.assgt.   90   Item no.increment   10

General control
SD document categ.   M   Invoice   ☐ Posting Block
Transaction group   7   Billing documents   ☑ Statistics
Billing category
Document Type   Z9   Billing doc.transfer
Negative posting   No negative posting
Branch/Head office   Customer=Payer/Branch=sold-to party
Credit memo w/ValDat ☐   No
Invoice list type   LR   Invoice list

Rebate settlement   ☑ Rel.for rebate
Standard text

Some of the important fields in this screen are as follows:

Number Range: Internal Number Assignment   You can specify a number range for the billing document in the field No.Range Int.Assgt. on the Number Systems tab. SAP allows only internal number range assignments for billing document types.

SD Document Category   The code in the field SD Document Categ. signifies the type of billing document you're configuring. In this book's earlier chapters, we showed you how to maintain the document category for sales and delivery documents. For billing documents, some of the major document categories are as follows:

>> M: Invoice

>> O: Credit memo

>> P: Debit memo

>> 3: Invoice list

>> U: Pro-forma invoice

Posting Block   If you select this check box, the billing document is blocked from posting to accounting. The document has to be released manually.

Transaction Group   This field is used for document control in SAP. For billing documents, the transaction group is 7. For pro-forma invoices, it is 8.

Document Type   You can specify an accounting document type that will be linked to this billing type.

Negative Posting   This field is used to control whether negative values are permitted in the document.

Branch/Head Office   This field allows you to control which partner function is forwarded to accounting, if the payer and sold-to party are different in the sales order. The default setting passes the payer to financial accounting.

Invoice List Type   If this billing type is going to be used in invoice lists, you can specify the type of invoice list document that can be created.

Rebate Settlement   If this billing type is going to be used for settlement of rebates, you have to specify the type of settlement in this field. For example, billing type B1 is a rebate credit memo used in final rebate settlements (option A). The other options here are rebate correction document (B), partial settlement (C), and manual accruals (D). Leave this field blank if the billing type is not used for rebate settlements.

Relevant For Rebate   If you flag the Rel. For Rebate check box, the billing document is considered relevant for rebates. The value of the billing document will be added to the total sales for the customer and will contribute to the rebate calculated for the customer. For example, regular invoices (such as F1 and F2) are relevant for rebates, whereas pro-forma documents (such as F5 and F8) are not.

We will discuss the rebates functionality later in the chapter.

Let's look at the other important fields shown in Figure 9.4.

FIGURE 9.4   Defining billing types, other settings

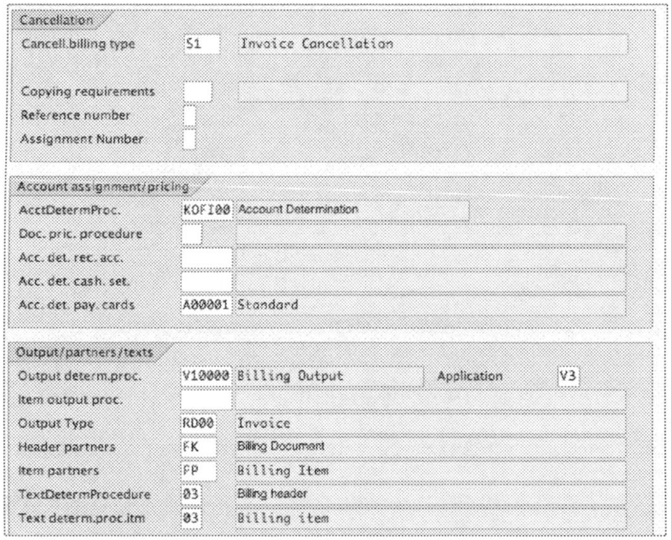

Cancellation   The settings on this tab control the process of cancellation of invoices. In the Cancell. Billing Type field, specify the document type to be used for cancellation of this document.

Reference and Assignment numbers   When a billing document is posted to accounting, you can forward document numbers as reference for the financial accounting team. In the Reference Number field, you can choose whether, for example, the sales order number or the delivery number is to be passed to accounting for reference. You can choose another reference document in the Assignment Number field.

The other settings on the Account Assignment/Pricing tab (see Figure 9.4) will be covered in Chapter 10, "Account Assignment and Revenue Recognition." We covered the settings on the Output/Partners/Texts tab in Chapter 4, "Partner, Text, and Output Determination."

> **NOTE** When a billing document is released, it creates an accounting document. It is a common requirement that the billing and accounting document numbers be the same for easy cross-reference.
>
> To achieve this, there are some settings in the FI application area . You need to set up identical number range intervals for the billing type and the corresponding accounting document type. Make sure that for the accounting document type, the number range is specified as External. This ensures that the billing document and the accounting document number have the same number.
>
> For example, as seen in Figure 9.3, we have linked the billing type Z2 with the accounting document type Z9. To synchronize the numbers, we have assigned the same number range interval (0900000000 to 0999999999) for both and ensured that we have flagged External number range for Z9.

Copy Controls in Billing

A billing document can be created with reference to a sales document, a delivery document, or another billing document. You can set up copy controls between the documents based on what is relevant for you. You can set up the copy controls as follows: IMG ➢ Sales And Distribution ➢ Billing ➢ Billing Documents ➢ Maintain Copy Controls For Billing Documents.

Then choose the reference document (sales order, delivery or billing) to copy from.

On the next screen, select the source and target document types. The copy control settings are at the header and item levels.

Figure 9.5 shows the copy control settings at the document header level when copying data from a delivery (LF) to a billing document (Z2). We'll discuss some of the key fields on this screen.

Copying Requirements   At the header level, there is a provision to attach a requirements routine that checks that some prerequisites are met before a billing document is created.

Reference Number and Assignment Number   These are additional reference fields used to forward information from SD to FI when the accounting document is created. For example, you can choose the delivery number be passed to accounting as a reference number. You can decide which document types are set in the

Assignment Number and Reference Number fields in consultation with your FI team.

Copy Item Number   The Copy Item Number check box indicates whether the system copies the item numbers from the source document into the target document. If this box is not selected, the system does not copy the item numbers from the source document, and the item numbers in the target document are regenerated to avoid gaps in the numbering.

FIGURE 9.5   Copy controls at the header level

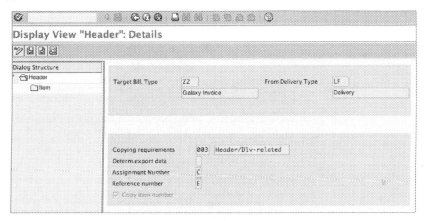

At the item level, the controls are at the item category level, as shown in Figure 9.6. It shows the copy control settings at the item category (TAN) level from a delivery (LF) to a billing document (Z2). The following are the key fields in this screen.

FIGURE 9.6   Copy controls at the item level

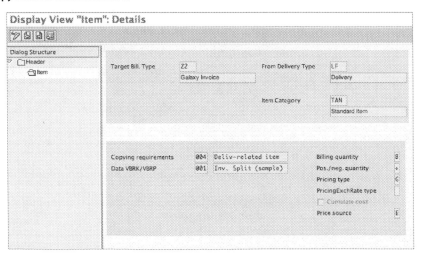

Copying Requirements   You can attach an item-level copy control routine, which checks for certain prerequisite conditions before a document can be copied into a billing document.

Data VBRK/VBRP routine   In this field, you can specify a routine that can carry out additional checks before data is copied into the billing tables. This routine governs the combination and splitting criteria in the creation of billing documents. Thus, based on the routine here, it is possible that multiple deliveries/orders can be billed together in one invoice. On the other hand, a single delivery may result in a split invoice if certain combination criteria are not met. You can use this routine to specify the fields that should be checked as criteria for splitting data into multiple billing documents.

Billing Quantity   This controls the quantities due for billing that are carried into the billing document. For example, for invoicing a customer, you can choose option B (the delivery quantity less the invoiced quantity). This ensures that the customer is billed for the right quantity. For pro-forma invoices, there is no such restriction. You can create pro-forma invoices for the complete quantity. Hence, you can select D.

Positive/Negative Quantity   The setting in the field Pos./Neg. Quantity controls whether the quantity in the billing document will have a positive, negative, or neutral impact on the open quantity in the source document.

Pricing Type   At the time of copying, you may require repricing or redetermination of some of the pricing conditions. You can specify the rule in this field. We already discussed this in Chapter 5, "Pricing and Tax Determination."

Pricing Exchange Rate Type   The field PricingExchRate Type controls the source of exchange rate, in case the document currency is different. For example, you can pick up the rate valid on the pricing date or the date of billing.

Cumulate Cost   This check box enables you to control whether the costs of subitems are to be copied to the parent item. It is useful in the case of products with a main item and several subitems. If the subitems are not relevant to billing, you still need to capture their cost and add it up to the cost of the parent item. The parent alone will appear in the billing document.

Price Source   This field controls the reference documents (such as sales order or delivery) from which pricing conditions are copied to the billing document.

Invoice List

An *invoice list* is a collection of one or more billing documents. The configuration of the billing type used for an invoice list is same as any standard billing type. The copy controls are set up between billing documents. The following are some of the configuration and master data steps before you can create an invoice list:

1. Define a billing document for the invoice list (using VOFA). You can use LR and LG as the reference document.

2. Using transaction VTFF, maintain Copy Controls: Billing Document To Billing Document. Set up copy control settings between your billing document type (such as F1 and F2) and the invoice list document type (LR and LG). The standard invoice list in SAP is LR for billing documents and debit memos and LG for credit memos. These will be the target documents in the copy control.

3. Assign the invoice list type to each billing type. The menu path is IMG ➢ Sales And Distribution ➢ Billing ➢ Billing Documents ➢ Invoice Lists ➢ Assign Invoice List Type To Each Billing Type (OVV7).

As shown in Figure 9.7, assign the invoice list type to each billing type.

FIGURE 9.7   Assigning an invoice list type to a billing document type

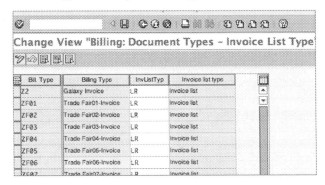

4. Besides these steps in the configuration, there is also an important field in the customer master that controls the invoice list. In Figure 9.8, note the InvoicingListDates field appearing on the Billing Documents tab in the Sales Data section of customer master. Attach a customer calendar showing the invoice list schedule. Based on the dates selected as workdays in this calendar, the invoice list will be run for the payer.

FIGURE 9.8   Invoice list date calendar in the customer master

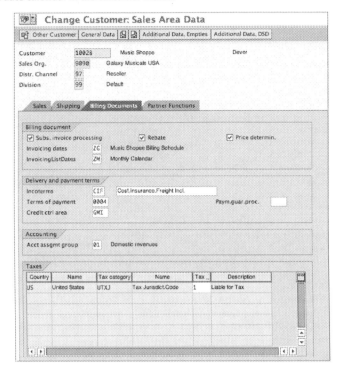

You can maintain output and pricing for invoice lists. The output condition types normally used for the invoice list are LR00 and RD01. Maintain records for these condition types, or create custom condition types using them as reference.

In some business scenarios, a factoring discount is offered to the payer of the invoice list. If your business scenario requires a factoring discount, use condition type RL00 as a reference. There is also the factoring discount tax condition type MW15, if required. These condition types must be added to the pricing procedure. The condition type RL00 has condition category R, which defines this condition type as used for invoice lists. SAP delivers the condition type RL00 with an exclusion indicator A.

Figure 9.9 shows a pricing procedure with condition RL00. As shown in the figure, when you use this condition type, it should always be flagged as statistical, with requirement routine 23 (which invokes this condition only in billing documents) and with base type routine 2 (to apply the discount to base value). A pop-up message from SAP prompts you to make these settings when you add RL00. Condition records should be maintained for RL00 using transaction VK11.

FIGURE 9.9   Adding RL00 to a pricing procedure

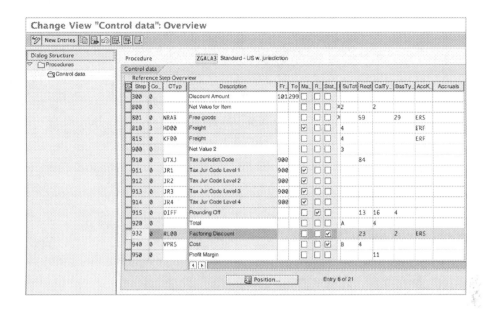

Figure 9.10 shows an invoice list with a factoring discount. On the overview screen, you can see that the net value is reduced by the factoring discount to arrive at the final amount.

FIGURE 9.10 Invoice list with factoring discount

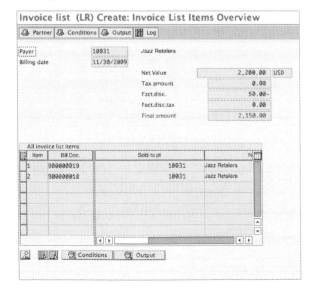

Billing Blocks

Billing blocks are sometimes required to stop or hold a document from being billed to the customer. For example, you may want to scrutinize all documents for a particular customer. You can achieve this by setting up an automatic billing block at the customer level.

There are two steps in configuration of billing blocks: defining the blocks and assigning them to billing documents.

Defining Billing Blocks

The first step is to define a billing block. The path in customization is as follows: IMG ➢ Sales And Distribution ➢ Billing ➢ Billing Documents ➢ Define Blocking Reasons For Billing ➢ Billing: Blocking Reasons.

Create a new billing block, and add a meaningful description (see Figure 9.11, where we have added a billing block G1 to the list of standard blocks).

FIGURE 9.11 Defining billing blocks

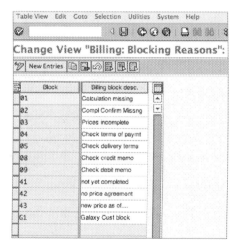

Assigning Billing Blocks to Billing Type

The purpose of this step is to specify the billing document types that should not be allowed if a sales document has a billing block in it.

Follow this menu path: IMG ➢ Sales And Distribution ➢ Billing ➢ Billing Documents ➢ Define Blocking Reasons For Billing ➢ Assign Blocking Reasons To Billing Types.

In this setting, you assign the billing block to the billing type that has to be blocked. As shown in Figure 9.12, we have assigned the billing block G1 to billing types (such as Z2). Now when a user applies a block G1 in the sales order, you cannot create a billing document of type Z2 with reference to the order, unless the block is removed.

FIGURE 9.12 Assigning billing blocks to a billing type

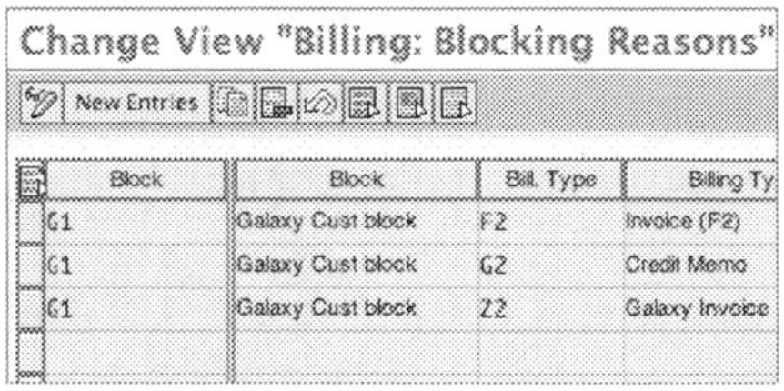

You can use the billing block in the following ways:

Customer level   In the customer master record, you can specify a billing block. From the transaction Change Customer Master (VD02), use the menu path Extras ➤ Blocking Data, and add a billing block for a particular sales area or for all sales areas. An alternative transaction for setting blocks is VD05 (discussed in Chapter 3, "Master Data in SD"). The billing blocks will be applicable for all relevant documents for this customer. In Figure 9.13, billing block G1 has been applied in the customer master record in the blocking data.

FIGURE 9.13 Billing block in customer master

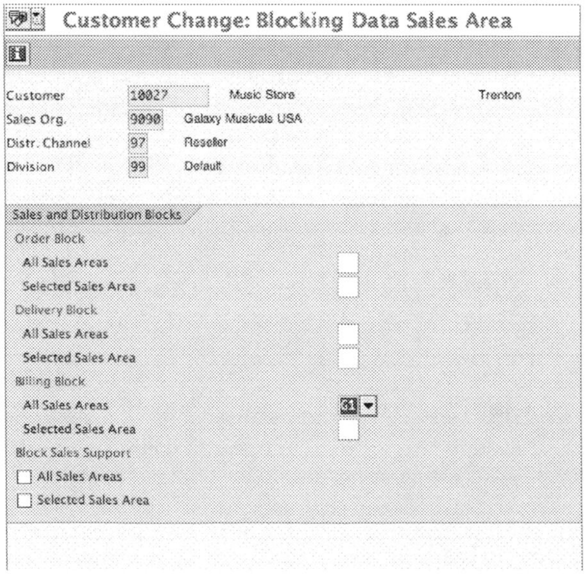

Item category level   You can define a custom billing block in the configuration of item categories (VOV7). We discussed this setting in Chapter 7. This selectively blocks items in a sales document from billing.

Document level   In the individual sales document, you can manually insert a billing block (using VA02) if the document is to be blocked individually.

The transaction V23 will give you a list of all sales documents blocked for billing.

Complaints Processing

Complaints management is one of the most critical business processes. As soon as you receive a complaint from a customer, you may have to initiate several actions such as create a return order, issue replacement items, and so on.

The complaints processing functionality enables a user to trigger actions based on a complaint received from a customer. You can set up an action profile and define what subsequent documents are to be initiated based on the reason for the complaint. To carry out this setting, follow this menu path: IMG ≻ Sales And Distribution ≻ Billing ≻ Billing Documents ≻ Define Reasons For Complaint.

Click New Entries to define a new reason for complaint. Enter a brief code for the reason in the Abb. field, as shown in Figure 9.14.

FIGURE 9.14 Customizing complaints reason

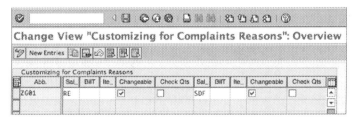

For each reason, you can specify the sales document type (Sal), the item category (Ite.), and/or the billing document (BillT) that has to be created automatically, when the complaint reason is entered.

If the Changeable field is selected, the user is allowed to make changes manually during transaction processing.

The Check Qts field checks whether the quantity referenced in the complaint exceeds the billed quantity, and it issues a message.

In the Reason For Complaint field at the end, add a meaningful description of the reason. (You'll have to scroll to the right to see this field.) This reason will be displayed in document processing.

To use the complaints workbench, use the following menu path: SAP Menu ➤ Logistics ➤ Sales And Distribution ➤ Billing ➤ Billing Document ➤ Complaints Processing (CMP_PROCESSING).

On this screen, enter or search for a reference document for which the complaint is to be entered.

The header data and item data are both displayed for the document. On the lower portion of the screen (as shown in Figure 9.15), you can identify the items and quantity for which you have to register a complaint. Specify the complaints reason for the selected item(s).

FIGURE 9.15 Complaints processing

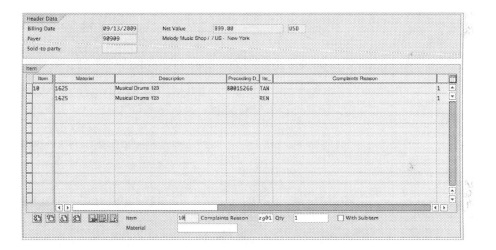

Upon saving, the system processes the document as per the configuration. The processing log is then displayed on the screen for your reference (as shown in Figure 9.16).

FIGURE 9.16 Complaints processing log

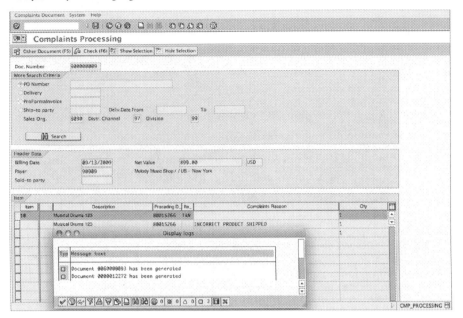

CASE STUDY—GALAXY MUSICAL INSTRUMENTS: COMPLAINTS PROCESSING SETUP

Customer satisfaction is of great importance to Galaxy. One of the important policies is efficient handling of complaints.

For a certain category of complaints, Galaxy wanted to initiate a return order (RE) and a subsequent delivery free of charge (document type SDF). We used the complaints processing functionality of SAP.

As shown in Figure 9.14, we have defined a reason for complaints as ZG01 (Incorrect Product Shipped). For such complaints, Galaxy immediately issues a replacement order with the correct product to the customer. Galaxy also wants to initiate a returns order to receive the incorrectly shipped item, back in the plant. Hence, we have specified the SDF (Subsequent Delivery, Free Of Charge) order type and the RE (Returns) order type to be created.

When a billing document number is entered as a reference for the complaint, along with the reason for complaints, the system processes the document, as per the action profile. As shown in Figure 9.16, the RE and SDF documents are created in the background.

Intercompany Billing

Intercompany billing is an important business scenario. We will now discuss the four key steps in configuration of intercompany billing. They are defining order types relevant to intercompany process, assigning organizational units to plants, defining internal customer numbers by sales organizations, and defining pricing conditions for intercompany billing.

Step 1: Define order types relevant for intercompany process   Use menu path IMG ➢ Sales And Distribution ➢ Billing ➢ Intercompany Billing ➢ Define Order Types For Intercompany Billing.

For this setting, select the order type, and assign an intercompany billing document type to it. The standard SAP document for intercompany billing is IV. With this setting, you can activate intercompany billing for the chosen sales document types. Refer Figure 9.17 for this setting.

FIGURE 9.17 Sales documents relevant for intercompany scenario

Change View "Sales Order Types for Inter-Company Billing"

SalesDocTy	Sales Document Type	Interco.	Intercomp.bill type
OR	Standard Order	IV	Intercompany billing
TAF	Standard Order (FPI)	IV	Intercompany billing
TAM	Delivery order	IV	Intercompany billing
TAV	Standard Order (VMI)	IV	Intercompany billing
TFST	STO-BR	ZIVU	IB Stock Transfer
TSA	Telesales	IV	Intercompany billing
TSC	CRM Sales/Complaints	IV	Intercompany billing
UPRR	Used Parts Returns	IG	Internal Credit Memo
UUPR	New Parts Returns	IG	Internal Credit Memo
VDOR	Venda à ordem BR	IV	Intercompany billing
VEF	Fut. dely invoice BR	IV	Intercompany billing
VEFR	Fut. dely shipmnt BR	IV	Intercompany billing
WA	Rel. to value contr.	IV	Intercompany billing

Step 2: Assign organizational units to plants   To identify that a sales transaction includes an intercompany transaction, you have to first clearly identify the sales area to which each plant belongs. This enables the system to check the delivering plant in the sales order and determine whether it belongs to the same or different sales area.

To carry out this setting, follow this path: IMG ➢ Sales And Distribution ➢ Billing ➢ Intercompany Billing ➢ Assign Organizational Units By Plant.

Refer to Figure 9.18. In our case, we have assigned the U.S. plant and the Mexico plant to their respective sales areas.

FIGURE 9.18 Assigning sales area to plant

Step 3: Define internal customer numbers by sales organizations   Having defined the sales areas for each plant, you can now set up the sales organizations as customers for each other. To enable the system to create an intercompany invoice, you require a customer number to be billed. This customer number will then be used in the creation of an intercompany invoice.

The menu path is as follows: IMG ≻ Sales And Distribution ≻ Billing ≻ Intercompany Billing ≻ Define Internal Customer Number By Sales Organization.

Before making this assignment, you have to create customer master records for each sales organization participating in intercompany sales. You can then assign these customer numbers to the sales organizations (see Figure 9.19). For this example, we have created a customer master using the account group 0120 (a branch with intercompany billing) that uses an external number range.

FIGURE 9.19 Assigning internal customer numbers to sales organizations

T I P   This is a rare instance in SAP where the master data is part of a customization setting! As shown in Figure 9.19, the intercompany customer GALAXY US is assigned to sales organization 9090. Before you transport this configuration to other systems (such as the quality assurance or production system), remember to create a customer master record with the same number (such as GALAXY US) in every system. Using an account group with an external number range allows you to control the customer number.

Step 4: Define pricing conditions for intercompany billing　This step is applicable only if the intercompany billing is to be carried out at a transfer price. To determine this price, standard SAP offers the pricing conditions PI01 (quantity based price) and PI02 (transfer price as a percentage). Based on your requirements, you can add these pricing conditions to the pricing procedure used in the intercompany scenario. Refer to the steps in pricing procedure set up in Chapter 5.

If these conditions are used, the commercial invoice (to the customer) will be at sales price, whereas the intercompany invoice will be at transfer price.

CASE STUDY—GALAXY MUSICAL INSTRUMENTS: INTERCOMPANY BILLING

Galaxy serves customers in the United States and Mexico. Sales organization 9001 is set up in the United States, and 9091 is set up for Mexico.

However, sometimes the product has to be shipped from the U.S.-based distribution center in Los Angeles (plant 9001) to the customer in Mexico. This plant belongs to the U.S. company code. The sales order has been created by Mexico sales organization, and the delivering plant is from the United States. This is a typical intercompany scenario. To set up intercompany scenario, we assign each plant to its sales area. Thus, plant 9001 is assigned to the U.S. sales area (9001, 97, 99).

We have defined internal customer records GALAXY US and GALAXY MX and assigned them to the sales organizations 9090 and 9091, respectively. This makes them "customers" of each other.

We have checked that the customer master records have been extended to the correct sales areas. A sales order is created for a customer in Mexico City. However, the product is not locally available and has to be delivered from the U.S. plant 9001. In such cases, after the customer receives delivery from the U.S.-based plant, there are two billing documents created:

► A regular invoice from the selling organization (9091) to its local customer. This document would have the selling price for the customer.

► An intercompany billing document from the United States (9001) to Mexico (9091) for the supplied products. This document could have an intercompany transfer price, instead of the selling price.

The system carries out checks based on the configuration and executes the intercompany billing process.

Billing Schedule

As mentioned, the Billing Date field in the sales order controls the date on which the item becomes due for billing. If you want to execute the billing transaction for a customer only on particular dates, you can control it by setting up a billing schedule.

A billing schedule is similar to a factory calendar and accessed using the same transaction. However, you can define a specific schedule (calendar) containing the dates (workdays) on which billing is permitted. Later, you assign the calendar to the customer master record.

To define a billing schedule, use the path SAP Menu ➤ Logistics ➤ Sales And Distribution ➤ Master Data ➤ Others ➤ Billing Schedule (SCAL).

Define a factory calendar, and assign a two-digit identification code and description (see Figure 9.20). The fields here are self-explanatory.

FIGURE 9.20 Defining a billing schedule

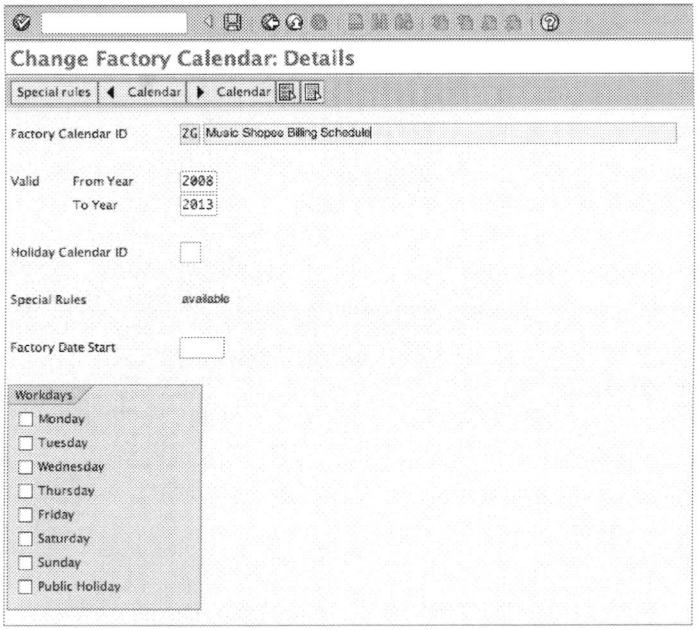

If you want to set up billing schedule on certain dates of the month, click the Special Rules option.

Create new rule and in the From Date and To Date fields add the specific date required. For example, in Figure 9.21, November 30 is the "from" date as well as the "to" date. Flag it as a Workday, and save it with a meaningful name. Similarly, set up rules for all the other days on which you want to schedule billing and save them in the calendar.

FIGURE 9.21 Defining special rules in the billing schedule

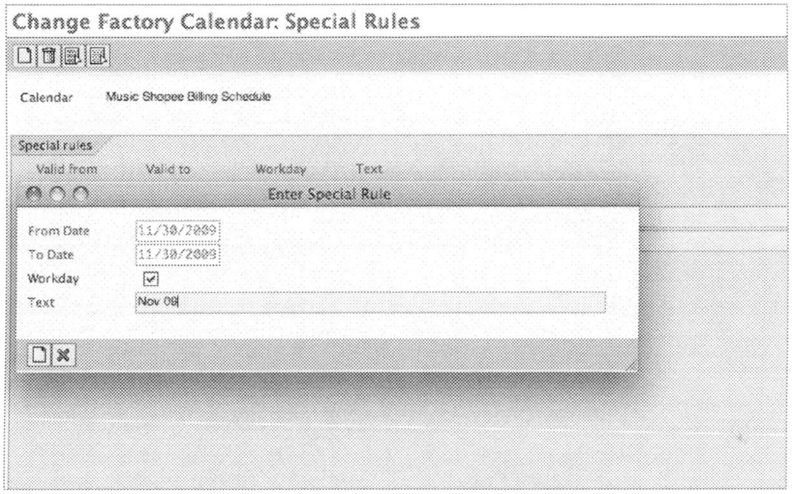

The billing schedule calendar is to be assigned in the customer master in the sales data on the Billing Documents tab. Refer to Figure 9.8 shown earlier. On the same screen, you can use the field Invoicing Dates to attach a custom billing calendar.

When a sales document is created, system checks the next workday from the calendar and copies it in the Billing Date field. Thus, the document becomes due for billing when the billing date is reached.

Billing Plans

Billing plans are useful when the customer is to be billed over a period of time or in installments. A billing plan is a schedule for billing the customer. It specifies how much is to be billed and when.

There are two types of billing plans. Each is based on a different business scenario.

Periodic Billing

In this scenario, the customer is to be billed a fixed amount regularly over a period of time. An example is a lease under which the same rent is charged at the beginning of every month.

Milestone Billing

The customer is charged a portion of the total price when certain milestones are achieved. For example, during execution of a project, a certain percentage of the total project value is billed on completion of each project phase.

When a sales document is created, the item category determines whether it is relevant for a billing plan. Based on the settings, the amount to be billed is determined along with the date.

We'll now discuss the major steps in customization for the two different types of billing plans. The first step is to set up the controls for the billing plan type. Use the menu path IMG ➤ Sales And Distribution ➤ Billing ➤ Billing Plan ➤ Define Billing Plan Types. From the activity node, choose Periodic or Milestone Billing Plan.

Defining Periodic Billing (transaction OVBI)

You can create a new billing plan type by specifying a two-character code and description.

The following are some of the fields relevant to periodic billing. Refer to Figure 9.22 for each field mentioned here.

Under Origin Of General Data, you'll find these settings:

Start Date and End Date   You can select rules to govern the start and end date of the plan. For example, the date could be today's date (rule 01), the contract start date (rule 02), or something else.

Horizon   This specifies the rule used to determine the last planned billing date. This rule generally specifies a baseline date and a duration. For example, rule 10 would specify today's date + 1 year (as would be the case for an annual lease contract).

FIGURE 9.22 Maintaining the billing plan type for a periodic billing

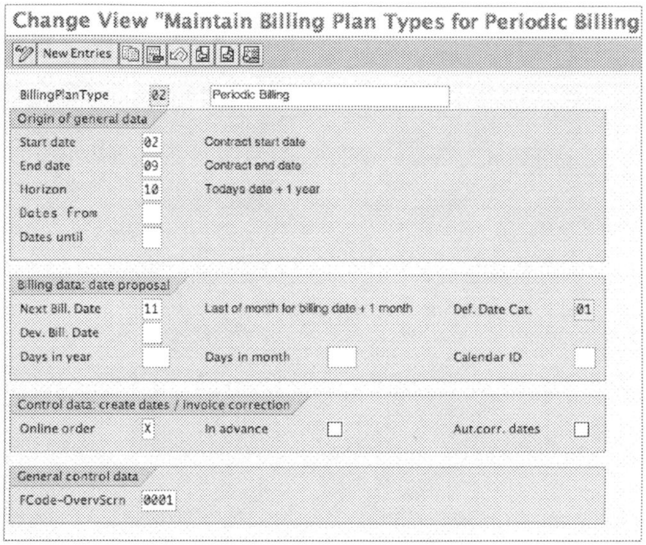

The next section, Billing Data: Date Proposal, deals with proposing the next date for billing:

Next Bill. Date   This rule controls how the next date is proposed by the system. For example, the next date could be determined by rule 50, which is monthly, so it would fall at the end of the month.

Dev. Bill. Date   This rule accommodates deviations and additional rules needed to determine the next billing date. For example, if you want to bill the customer three days before the end of the month, then you can specify a custom rule that subtracts three days from the end of month and determines the date. You can leave this field blank if it is not applicable.

Calendar ID   You can attach your custom calendar so the system can use it to determine the working schedule for the year.

The Control Data section provides these boxes:

Online Order   If you want the system to determine the billing plan dates automatically, at the time of document creation you can select this box.

In Advance   If you select this box, it means that the customer is to be billed in advance. If you leave it blank, the default rule is to bill in arrears. For example, if you want to charge monthly rent at the beginning of the month, you should select this box.

Defining Milestone Billing (Transaction Code OVBO)

Since the billing dates are determined by events and milestones, there are no rules to determine dates, as was the case in periodic billing. Hence, some of the fields that you saw in the periodic billing setup do not appear here (as shown in Figure 9.23).

FIGURE 9.23 Maintaining the billing plan type for milestone billing

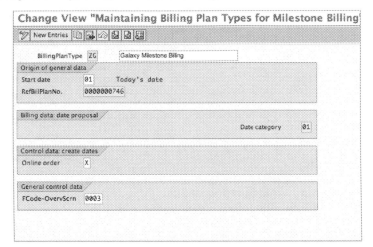

The important difference in milestone billing setup is the reference billing plan number (in the field RefBillPlanNo). It contains the detailed schedule of the milestone billing. In the next step, we will maintain the details in the reference billing plan, such as the exact dates and the amount (either as a percentage value or as an exact amount) to be billed.

Maintain Date Proposals for Billing Plan Type

This step is applicable only if you are setting up milestone billing plans.

Use menu path IMG ➢ Sales And Distribution ➢ Billing ➢Billing Plan ➢ Maintain Date Proposals For Billing Plan Types (OVBM).

This transaction leads you to a screen similar to the milestone billing definition screen (OVBO). The difference is the Maintain Date button next to the reference billing plan number, as shown in Figure 9.24.

FIGURE 9.24 Maintaining the date proposal for the billing plan type

Change View "Date Proposal Maintenance for Billing Plan Type"

BillingPlanType   ZG   Galaxy Milestone Billing

Origin of general data
Start date   01

RefBillPlanNo.   0000000746   Maintain date

Billing data: date proposal
                                              Date category   01

Control data: Create dates
Online order   X

General control data
FCode-OvervScrn   0003

Clicking the Maintain Date button leads you to the date proposal maintenance screen (Figure 9.25). You can specify the billing dates for each milestone. The BR (rule in billing plan) field controls the billing amount (in the field Bill. Value) as either a percentage or an exact amount. It also explains if it is a down payment, regular milestone charge, closing amount, and so on. Based on your requirement, select from the options provided for this field. For example, we have selected BR as 2 (milestone billing on value basis). Here we have specified the amounts in USD so that on October 1, 2009, the amount to be billed is $10,000, and so on.

FIGURE 9.25 Maintaining the date proposal

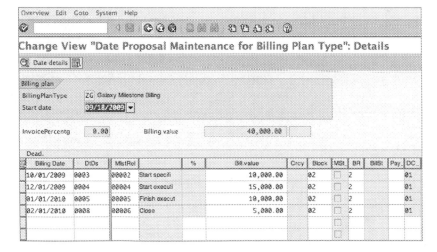

Billing Date	DtDs	MlstRel		%	Bill.value	Crcy	Block	MSt	BR	BillSt	Pay	DC
10/01/2009	0003	00002	Start specifi		10,000.00		02	☐	2			01
12/01/2009	0004	00004	Start executi		15,000.00		02	☐	2			01
01/01/2010	0005	00005	Finish execut		10,000.00		02	☐	2			01
02/01/2010	0008	00006	Close		5,000.00		02	☐	2			01
								☐				
								☐				

After entering all the dates, use the back arrow key to go to the main screen, where you can save your changes.

Date Categories

The Date Category field gives more information about the date appearing in the billing plans. For this setting, you define date categories for the billing plan. You can assign rules and add blocks to stop any billing before a milestone is reached. Use the menu path IMG ➢ Sales And Distribution ➢ Billing ➢ Billing Plan ➢ Define And Assign Date Categories ➢ Maintain Date Category For Billing Plan Type (OVBJ).

On this screen, you can specify the categories of dates that you plan to use in each billing plan type, as shown in Figure 9.26.

FIGURE 9.26 Maintaining date category for billing plan type

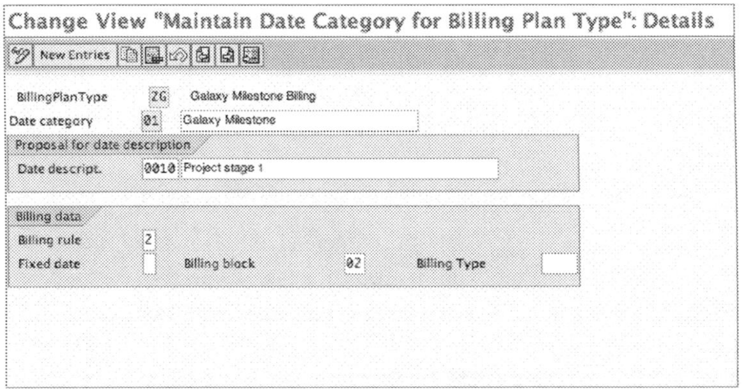

In the proposal for the date description, you can select the date description (such as the monthly rent in the periodic billing) or contract sign date, assembly completion, or other project milestone dates. In the Billing Data section, the Billing Rule field controls whether the billing will be on a percentage basis or a value basis. The Billing Block field specifies the block applied against billing date in the plan.

Since there can be several date categories assigned to a billing plan type, you assign a default date category in the next step. Follow the path IMG ➢ Sales And Distribution ➢ Billing ➢ Billing Plan ➢ Define And Assign Date Categories ➢ Allocate Date Category.

Assign a default date category for your billing plan type.

Maintain Rules for Date Determination

In the definition of billing types, we used several rules for defining start and end dates, horizon, and so on. If you need to set up custom date rules, you can use this setting: IMG > Sales And Distribution > Billing > Billing Plan > Define Rules For Determining Dates (OVBS).

Create a new entry or copy from an existing rule. As shown in Figure 9.27, in the field Baseline Date, you have to specify a rule for determining the baseline date. Use the Time Period and Time Unit fields to specify whether the time is to be added or subtracted from the baseline to arrive at the billing date. You can specify the unit of time in days, weeks, months, or years. In the Calendar ID field, you can also assign a calendar to this rule. For example, if the rule ZG is used, it will propose the start date as the current date, and the end date will be six months from now. The calendar ID ZG will be used to determine the working days and holidays during this six-month period.

FIGURE 9.27 Maintaining rules for date determination

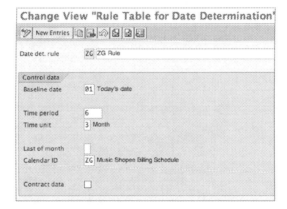

At this stage, you have completed the definition of the billing plan. The next step is to assign the billing plan to sales documents and item categories.

Assignment of Billing Plan Types

Two settings are involved in assignments. You assign the billing plan type at both the sales document level and the item category level.

Use the menu path IMG > Sales And Distribution > Billing > Billing Plan > Assign Billing Plan Types To Sales Document Types (OVBP).

For this setting, you can select the sales document types that are relevant for your billing plan type and make the assignment, as shown in Figure 9.28.

FIGURE 9.28 Assigning the billing plan type to a sales document type

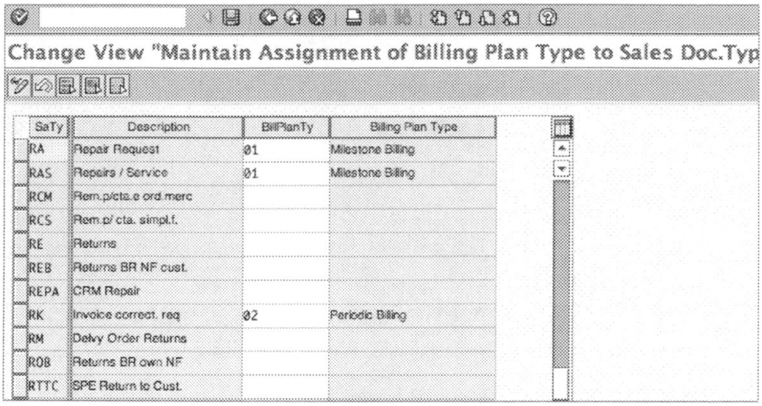

SaTy	Description	BillPlanTy	Billing Plan Type
RA	Repair Request	01	Milestone Billing
RAS	Repairs / Service	01	Milestone Billing
RCM	Rem.p/cts.e ord.merc		
RCS	Rem.p/ cta. simpl.f.		
RE	Returns		
REB	Returns BR NF cust.		
REPA	CRM Repair		
RK	Invoice correct. req	02	Periodic Billing
RM	Delvy Order Returns		
ROB	Returns BR own NF		
RTTC	SPE Return to Cust.		

Now follow the menu path IMG ≻ Sales And Distribution ≻ Billing ≻ Billing Plan ≻ Assign Billing Plan Types To Item Categories (OVBR).

Assign the billing plan type (in the BillPlanTy field) to the item categories, as shown in Figure 9.29. The billing relevance (the BilRl field, also discussed in Chapter 7 in transaction VOV7) can also be maintained here. In this case, you set it to I(Order–Relevant Billing– Billing Plan).

FIGURE 9.29 Assigning the billing plan type to an item category

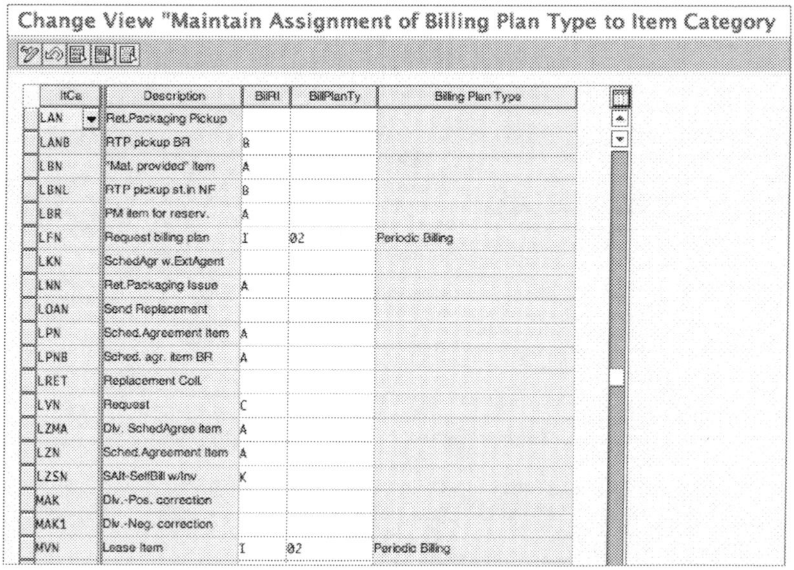

ItCa	Description	BilRl	BillPlanTy	Billing Plan Type
LAN	Ret.Packaging Pickup			
LANB	RTP pickup BR	B		
LBN	"Mat. provided" Item	A		
LBNL	RTP pickup st.in NF	B		
LBR	PM item for reserv.	A		
LFN	Request billing plan	I	02	Periodic Billing
LKN	SchedAgr w.ExtAgent			
LNN	Ret.Packaging Issue	A		
LOAN	Send Replacement			
LPN	Sched.Agreement Item	A		
LPNB	Sched. agr. item BR	A		
LRET	Replacement Coll.			
LVN	Request	C		
LZMA	Dlv. SchedAgree item	A		
LZN	Sched.Agreement Item	A		
LZSN	SAlt-SelfBill w/Inv	K		
MAK	Dlv.-Pos. correction			
MAK1	Dlv.-Neg. correction			
MVN	Lease Item	I	02	Periodic Billing

Rebates

A *rebate* is a sales promotion technique that a seller applies to improve sales volume. It is generally a time-bound, after-sale discount that is based on a volume of sales made to a particular customer and has either a prospective or retrospective effect. For example, a customer might be entitled to a 2 percent discount as a rebate for total purchases of more than $100,000 in the next six months. Another example can be a $1 discount on every piece eligible for the rebate, if a customer buys 5,000 pieces of a particular product over a period of four months, including one month in the past and three months in the future. Rebates can also be independent of sales volume. An example is performance rebates.

To provide rebates, the seller generally signs an agreement with the customer that includes all the necessary details such as the agreed sales targets, the time period in which these targets are to be completed, and the discount conditions such as percentage rate, dollars per piece, or lump sum. The seller then tracks the volume of sales made to the customer for the rebate-eligible products and periodically accounts for the rebate accruals as per the organization's accounting policies. When the targets are successfully achieved, the seller pays the rebate amount to the customer. This step is called *rebate settlement*.

In SAP, rebates are handled by the rebate processing component of the billing application. Here you can provide rebates based on both sales volume and performance. Performance rebates are manually accrued, whereas sales volume dependent rebates can either accrue manually or be set up for automatic accrual by SAP. The settlement can be made via check or credit memo to the customer. You can also process either partial or full settlements pursuant to a rebate agreement. The partial settlements can be manually processed or automated to run on a periodic basis.

The Rebate Process

In SAP, the rebate process consists of three main processing steps. You initiate the process by creating a rebate agreement followed by the automatic or manual posting of accruals, and you complete the process by running rebate settlements. A detailed explanation of these process steps follows.

Creating a Rebate Agreement

A rebate agreement stores the rebate-related data and controls the overall rebate processing. The pricing condition records for rebate processing are also stored within the rebate agreement. You can create a rebate agreement for a particular customer by using following menu path: SAP Menu ➤ Logistics ➤ Sales And Distribution ➤ Master Data ➤ Agreements ➤ Rebate Agreement ➤ Create (VBO1).

In the initial screen that appears, you provide the rebate agreement type and the organizational data for which you want to create a rebate agreement. Standard SAP provides five types of rebate agreements to choose from:

Agreement type 0001 (Group Rebate)   This agreement type allows condition records to be created for a combination of customer/material or a customer/ rebate group. The rebate group is a field on the material master Sales Org.2 view. Additional rebate groups may be created through customizing. The customer is the payer, and the rebate is specified in terms of a percentage. If the rebate agreement is not material-specific (as would be the case if you use a customer/rebate group as a criteria), you have to specify a rebate material that will be used in the payment documents, such as credit memos. Typically you have to set up a material master record for a dummy material and then use it in the settlement documents. The delivering plant in the material master record will default into the payment documents for use in determining business areas if needed.

Agreement type 0002 (Material Rebate)   This agreement type allows condition records for a customer/material and uses a quantity-dependent calculation. The customer is the payer.

Agreement type 0003 (Customer Rebate)   This agreement type allows condition records based solely on the customer and uses a percentage for the calculation. The customer is the payer. As with 0001, a rebate material must be specified.

Agreement type 0004 (Hierarchy Rebate)   This agreement type allows condition records for a customer hierarchy node/material or by hierarchy alone. The calculation is based on a percentage. The hierarchy nodes must be established in customer hierarchy maintenance before using this type of rebate agreement.

Agreement type 0005 (Independent of Sales Volume)   This agreement type allows a lump-sum payment to a customer. Because it is independent of sales volume, no accruals will be automatically generated. Typically a manual accrual is generated for the amount of the agreement, and payments are made over the life of the agreement until final settlement is carried out.

The next screen is the rebate agreement overview screen (Figure 9.30). Here you provide all the information related to a rebate agreement. A *rebate recipient* is a customer who is supposed to receive the rebate and whose sales are to be tracked for rebate processing. *Validity period* represents the validity of the rebate, and *verification level* represents the level at which you would review a report on sales volume for this rebate agreement.

FIGURE 9.30 Creating a rebate agreement, overview

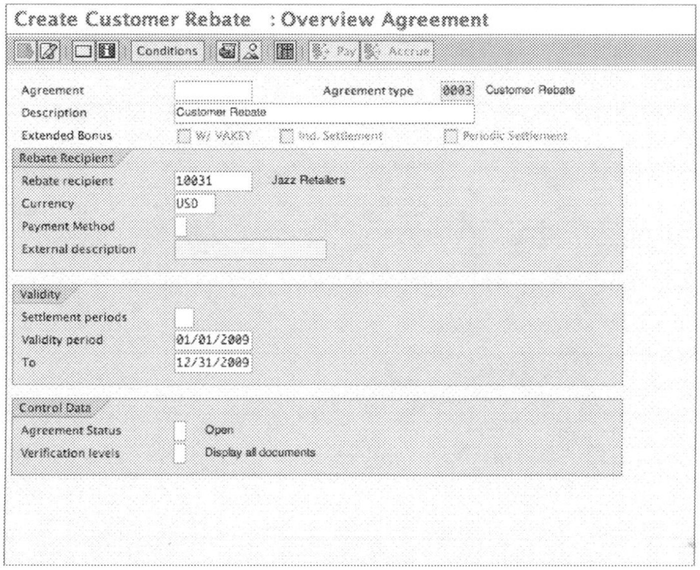

Click the Conditions button to reach the condition maintenance screen (Figure 9.31). This screen looks similar to the transaction VK11, used for pricing condition records discussed in Chapter 5. You can enter the rebate condition record on this screen. You can use the Goto menu at the top to navigate to other screens in the agreement. If the agreement type is not material-specific (as in the case of 0001 and 0003), you have to specify a dummy settlement material on the Material For Settlement screen shown in Figure 9.32.

FIGURE 9.31 Creating condition records in a rebate agreement

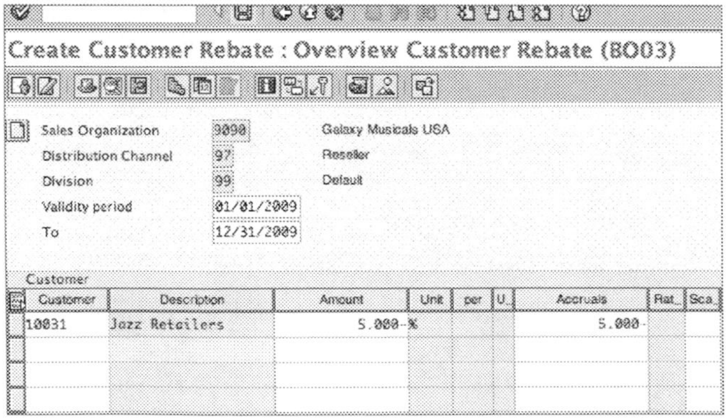

FIGURE 9.32 Maintaining the material for settlement in a rebate agreement

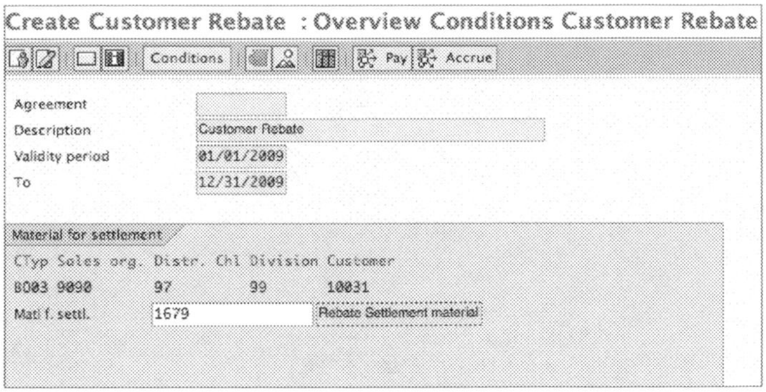

Posting Accruals

Manual accruals may be used in any of the agreement types where the configuration of the agreement type allows them. Most often, manual accruals are used in agreements that are independent of sales volume. The agreed-upon payment may be accrued up front and then be reduced with each payment.

To create a manual accrual, use the Change Material Rebate transaction VBO2. From the overview screen, select Extras ➢ Manual Accrual. On this screen, which looks like Figure 9.33, you can manually enter the amount to be accrued. When you save the agreement, a rebate credit memo request is created. You can then create a credit memo with reference to the credit memo request. The accrual amount is then posted to accounting.

From the manual accrual screen (Figure 9.33), you can follow the path Goto ➢ Payment Data, which will lead you to an overview screen displays cumulative accrual and payment information for this rebate agreement.

Once the billing documents relevant for rebates are processed, you can check the sales volumes from the VBO2 screen; just follow the menu Rebate Payment ➢ Sales Volume. The level at which the details will be shown to you depends upon what verification level you set up.

Carrying Out Settlements

At the end of the rebate agreements, you can carry out the final settlement before closing the agreement. You can also carry partial settlements manually at any time. These are limited to the cumulative accrued amount.

FIGURE 9.33 Manual accrual process

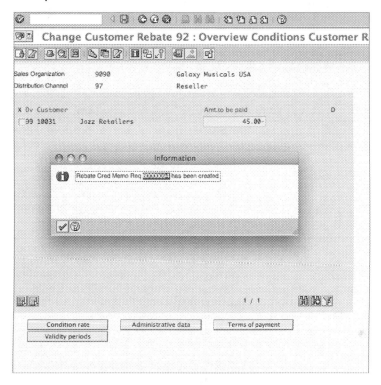

To carry out the final settlement from the Rebate Agreement screen (change mode VBO2), click Execute Settlement. This allows you to manually check and verify the amount for settlement before a credit memo request is created. If you do not want to verify or change the amount, choose the Create Final Settlement option, which automatically creates a credit memo request in the background.

Before an agreement can be settled, the system will prompt you to update the status of the agreement to B (released for settlement), based on the configuration. This makes sure that you do not accidentally settle and close an agreement.

You can carry out the final settlement in batch mode using the menu path SAP Menu ➢ Logistics ➢ Sales And Distribution ➢ Billing ➢ Rebate ➢ Rebate Settlement [VB(7].

Sometimes, when you set up a rebate agreement, the system displays a message that the sales volume is not current. This may happen after changes have been made to the rebate conditions. When this happens, you have to execute the report SDBONT06 (from the transaction SE38) to carry out the proper updates.

Rebate Configuration

We'll now discuss the major steps in rebate configuration.

Activating Rebates

Rebates are deactivated in standard SAP by default. You have to activate the functionality at three levels: the sales organizations, the billing types, and the customer level. You can activate the rebates at the first two levels—the sales organization and billing type—in customization. The menu path is as follows: IMG ➤ Sales And Distribution ➤ Billing ➤ Rebate Processing ➤ Activate Rebate Processing.

You have two actions to perform here. In the first step, you select the billing documents that are relevant for rebates. In the second step, you activate rebates for your sales organizations.

As shown in Figure 9.34, we have selected billing type Z2 for rebates. In Figure 9.35, we have ensured that sales organization 9090 is ready for rebate processing.

The third step is done through master data maintenance. You have to activate rebates for a customer in the customer master record.

On the Billing Documents tab of the customer master, there is a check box for activating rebates. (Figure 9.8 shows the Rebate check box) of the sales. Make sure this has been selected for your customers in the payer role.

FIGURE 9.34 Activating rebates for billing types

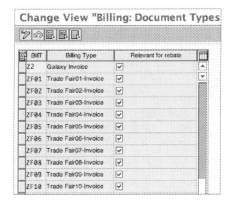

FIGURE 9.35 Activating rebates for sales organizations

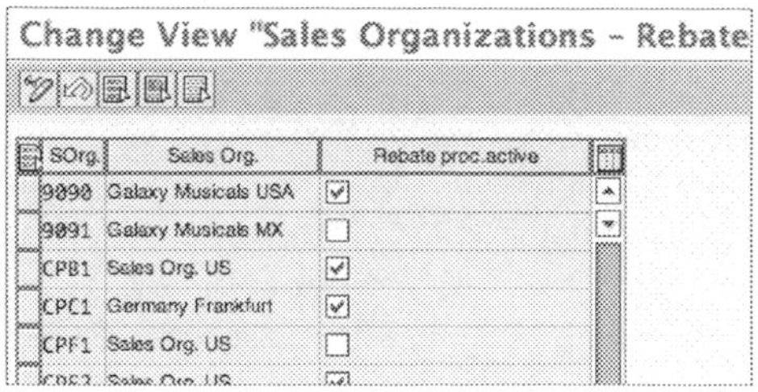

Defining Rebate Agreements

To set up a rebate agreement, the path is as follows: IMG ➤ Sales And Distribution ➤ Billing ➤ Rebate Processing ➤ Rebate Agreements ➤ Define Agreement Types ➤ Define Agreement Types [VB(2].

You can check the existing rebate agreement types or define a new one. The following are some of the important fields in the details screen, as shown in Figure 9.36.

FIGURE 9.36 Defining rebate agreement types

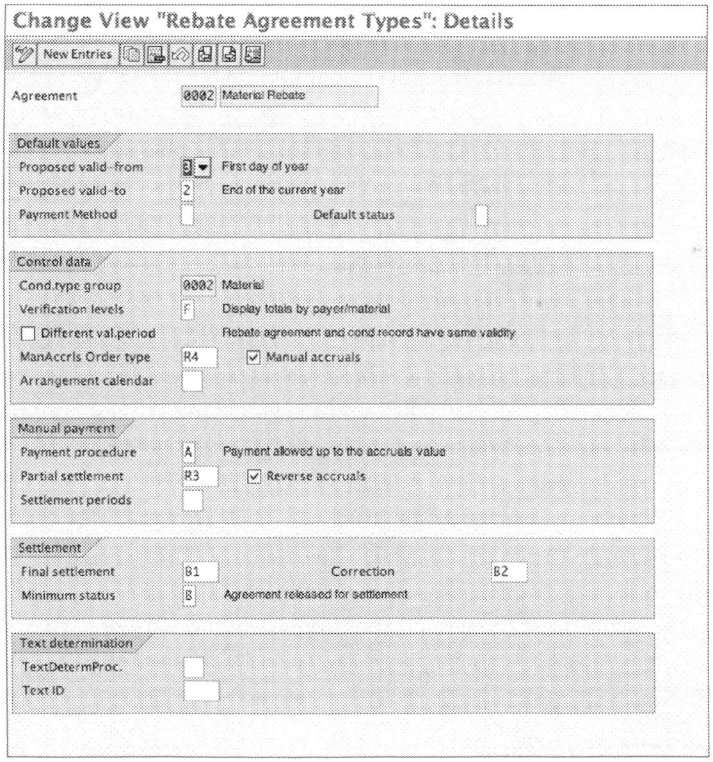

Proposal Valid-From   Here you set up a default proposal for the validity start date for your rebate agreement. You can choose the start date as today's date, the start of the week, the start of the month, or the start of the year, or you can even leave the field blank if you don't want SAP to propose any start date.

Proposal Valid-To   Here you set up a default proposal for the validity end date for your rebate agreement. Available proposal options include the end of the month, the end of the year, a fixed date of 12/31/9999, a proposal as per settlement calendar, today's date, and no proposal.

Payment Method   Here you set up a default proposal for the payment method that will be used by SAP for the settlement of your rebate agreement. For example, if you leave this field blank, SAP will use credit notes that you can apply against the customer's outstanding receivables as the method to settle the rebate agreements. If you choose C here, SAP will still create a credit note, but the credit note will post to accounting with a payment method indicator of C. This means that the credit note cannot be applied against the customer receivables and can be settled only via a check to the customer for the credit note amount.

Default Status   Here you set up a default status at the time of creation of the agreement. The default value here is blank, which means that the agreement is in open status.

Verification Levels   This field controls the level of detail you want to see in the report when you review the rebate-relevant invoices for a rebate agreement. For example, you can either choose to display each document separately or choose to display totals using grouping criteria such as sold-to party, payer, materials, and so on.

Different Validity Period   You select the Different Val.Period check box if you want to allow the rebate agreement and the underlying condition record to have different validity periods. An example of a business scenario where you may want to select this check box is seasonal rebates. You may agree to give an additional 0.5 percent rebate to your customer for purchases they make during Thanksgiving week. If this check box was already selected in customizing, you would be able to create another condition record in your rebate agreement for the Thanksgiving season with a validity of one week. SAP will be able to track and provide additional 0.5 percent rebates on the sale during that period.

You should leave this check box deselected if you want the agreement and condition records to always have the same validity.

Manual Accruals Order Type   In the ManAccrls Order Type field, you define the default order type for any manual accruals such as accruals for performance rebates or accruals for retroactive rebates. When you process the manual accrual for a rebate agreement, SAP uses this sales document type to create the credit memo request for manual rebate accrual.

Manual Accruals   This check box controls whether manual accruals should be allowed for a particular agreement type. In standard SAP, agreement types 0002 and 0005 are set up for manual accruals.

Arrangement Calendar   An arrangement calendar defines the end of the validity period for a rebate agreement and also helps in extending the rebate agreement to the next period. SAP provides report RV15C005 for extending rebate agreements to the next periods. You can access it using transaction code VB(D.

> **TIP**   You can only extend a rebate agreement to the next period if the agreement type had an arrangement calendar defined in customizing.

Payment Procedure   The value in this field controls the upper limit for making manual payments against a rebate agreement. Here, you can choose A to allow the manual payments up to the accruals value, B to allow the manual payments up to the value of pro-forma settlement, or C for no limits, or you can leave the field blank, in which case SAP will not allow the manual payments.

Partial Settlement   This field tells what order document type SAP should use when partial settlement needs to be made for a rebate agreement. When you execute the partial settlement process, SAP will use this document type to create a credit memo request for the partial settlement value.

Reverse Accruals   This check box controls whether you want SAP to reverse the accruals when a manual payment is made.

Settlement Periods   If you want to make periodic partial settlements, you can attach a calendar here with the required settlement dates. If you schedule a batch job for settlements (VB(7, discussed earlier in the chapter), the rebate agreement will come up for partial settlement on the dates in the calendar.

Final Settlement and Correction   In these fields you can specify the document types that will be used for final settlement or corrections, respectively.

Minimum Status   This field specifies the minimum status that is required before you can process a rebate agreement for settlement. For example, if you enter B here, the agreement needs to be in this status (or higher) before settlement can be carried out.

Configuring Rebate-Related Pricing Conditions

The rebate functionality requires some special pricing condition types. The basic concept and settings are similar to standard pricing using condition techniques (discussed in Chapter 5). You must add the rebate-related pricing conditions to your pricing procedure.

These conditions are called during pricing, only in billing documents.

To define these settings, the path in customization is IMG ➤ Sales And Distribution ➤ Billing ➤ Rebate Processing ➤ Condition Technique For Rebate Processing.

We'll now discuss the major points to be noted in rebates configuration. Note that the steps here are similar to the pricing configuration menu discussed in Chapter 5.

Setting up rebate condition types   SAP offers the standard condition types BO01 to BO06 for use with rebates. The setting that differentiates the rebate condition types from other pricing condition types is condition class. For rebate condition types, the condition class is C. Fewer fields are required to be filled up for such conditions. It is this value in condition class that makes sure that the condition type for a rebate cannot be processed via any of the pricing maintenance transactions such as VK11 and VK12. Table 9.2 summarizes the pricing conditions, access sequences, and condition tables used in rebates.

Setting the pricing procedure   In standard SAP, rebate condition types BO01 to BO06 are assigned to the pricing procedure, as shown in Figure 9.37

If you are setting up your own rebate conditions, make sure that you have attached requirement routine 24. This ensures that the conditions are called up in billing documents only. Also note that account keys ERB and ERU must be assigned to the conditions. We will discuss the account assignment aspects later in this chapter.

TABLE 9.2 Condition Types in Rebates

Condition type	Access sequence	Condition table(s)
BO01—Group Rebate (% based)	BO01—Material Rebate/Rebate Group	001—Customer/Material 002—Customer/Rebate Group
BO02—Material Rebate (Qty based)	BO02—Material Rebate	001—Customer/Material
BO03—Customer Rebate (% based)	BO03—Customer Rebate	003—Customer
BO04—Hierarchy Rebate (% based)	BO04—Rebate Hierarchy	004—Customer Hierarchy
BO05—Hierarchy Rebate/Material (% based)	BO05—Rebate Hierarchy/Material	005—Customer Hierarchy/Material
BO06—Sales Independent Rebate (fixed amount)	BO03—Customer Rebate	003—Customer

FIGURE 9.37 Pricing procedure with rebate conditions

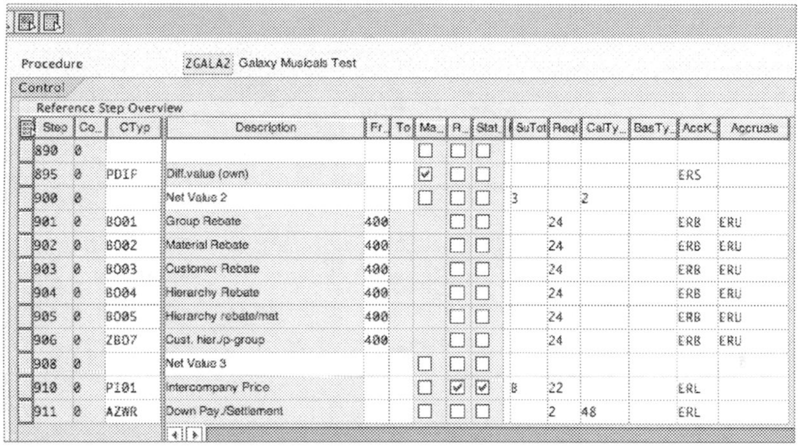

Procedure ZGALAZ Galaxy Musicals Test

Control

Reference Step Overview

Step	Co..	CTyp	Description	Fr..	To	Ma..	R..	Stat	SuTot	Reqt	CalTy..	BasTy..	AccK..	Accruals
890	0					☐	☐	☐						
895	0	PDIF	Diff.value (own)			☑	☐	☐					ERS	
900	0		Net Value 2			☐	☐	☐	3		2			
901	0	BO01	Group Rebate	400			☐	☐		24			ERB	ERU
902	0	BO02	Material Rebate	400			☐	☐		24			ERB	ERU
903	0	BO03	Customer Rebate	400			☐	☐		24			ERB	ERU
904	0	BO04	Hierarchy Rebate	400			☐	☐		24			ERB	ERU
905	0	BO05	Hierarchy rebate/mat	400			☐	☐		24			ERB	ERU
906	0	ZBO7	Cust. hier./p-group	400			☐	☐		24			ERB	ERU
908	0		Net Value 3			☐	☐	☐						
910	0	PI01	Intercompany Price			☐	☑	☑	B	22			ERL	
911	0	AZWR	Down Pay./Settlement			☐	☐	☐		2	48		ERL	

Defining condition type groups The next step in customization is to assign one or more rebate conditions to a condition type group. Then, you attach this group to the rebate agreement type. This way, you can create the rebate agreement and the associated rebate conditions using the same transaction.

To define the condition type groups, the path is IMG ➢ Sales And Distribution ➢ Billing ➢ Rebate Processing ➢ Rebate Agreements ➢ Condition Type Groups ➢ Define Condition Type Groups.

Here you can define a condition type group and assign it to a condition type group category, as shown in Figure 9.38.

FIGURE 9.38 Defining the condition type group

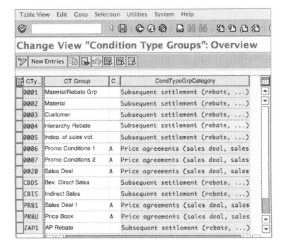

Assigning rebate conditions to the group   Follow the menu path IMG ➤ Sales And Distribution ➤ Billing ➤ Rebate Processing ➤ Rebate Agreements ➤ Condition Type Groups ➤ Assign Condition Types/Tables To Condition Type Groups.

The screen is shown in Figure 9.39. Here you assign the rebate condition types and the underlying condition tables to a condition type group. For example, consider the condition type group 0001. The condition type BO01 is assigned to this group. You can maintain condition records for BO01 either for the customer/material (in condition table 1) or for the customer/rebate group (in table 2). Hence, there are two records for condition type group 0001 in Figure 9.39.

FIGURE 9.39   Assigning condition types to condition type groups

Change View "Assignment of Condition Type/Table for Agreement'

CTyGr	Cond.type group	Cntr	Cn.	Condition type	N.	
0001	Material/Rebate Grp	1	BO01	Group Rebate	1	Customer/Material
0001	Material/Rebate Grp	2	BO01	Group Rebate	2	Customer/Rebate Group
0002	Material	1	BO02	Material Rebate	1	Customer/Material
0003	Customer	1	BO03	Customer Rebate	3	Customer
0004	Hierarchy Rebate	1	BO04	Hierarchy Rebate	4	Customer Hierarchy
0004	Hierarchy Rebate	2	BO05	Hierarchy rebate/mat	5	Customer Hierarchy/Material

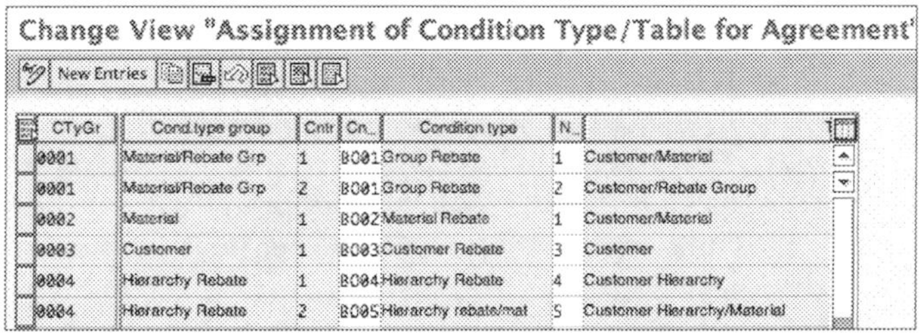

Attaching the group to rebate agreement types   To perform the last step in the assignment process, follow the menu path IMG ➢ Sales And Distribution ➢ Billing ➢ Rebate Processing ➢ Rebate Agreements ➢ Condition Type Groups ➢ Assign Condition Type Groups To Rebate Agreement Types (see Figure 9.40).

FIGURE 9.40 Assigning condition types group to rebate agreement types

Select the rebate agreement type that you plan to use, and assign a condition type group to it.

Thus, in our example, agreement type 0001 has condition type group 0001 linked to it. Further, the group is linked to condition type BO01 with two condition tables, 1 and 2, thus completing the assignment.

Configuring Account Assignment for Rebates

Account determination for rebates consists of two account keys: account key ERU for posting the accruals and account key ERB for posting the actual rebate expenses. We have attached these keys in the pricing procedure illustrated in Figure 9.37. The account key ERU points to two accounts: an accrual G/L account and a rebate expense provisional account. Account key ERB points to the actual rebate expense G/L account. Between accrual and settlement, having two separate GL accounts helps in tracking the rebate expenses separately. However, you can use the same G/L account. Please consult your FI/CO team before making these settings.

When SAP posts an accrual (either automatic or manual), the G/L account for posting the accruals into accounting is taken from the ERU account key, and the accounting entry is posted by debiting the rebate expense provisional account and crediting the rebate accrual account. When you run the rebate settlement, SAP takes the G/L account from ERU and reverses the previously posted accruals and the G/L account from ERB to post the entry into customer receivables and rebate expense account.

We will discuss account assignment in detail in Chapter 10. However, at this stage, we will cover how accounts are maintained for rebates processing by using the menu path IMG ➤ Sales And Distribution ➤ Billing ➤ Rebate Processing ➤ Account Determination For Rebates ➤ Assign G/L Accounts (VKOA).

In Figure 9.41, we have assigned G/L accounts for the posting keys ERB and ERU, as discussed earlier. Figure 9.42 depicts the impact of accrual and settlement transactions on the G/L account posting.

FIGURE 9.41 Account assignment for rebates

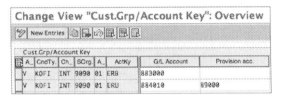

FIGURE 9.42 Accounting postings

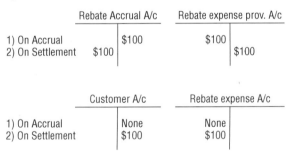

Payment Card Interface

One of the increasingly popular and convenient means to pay is using payment cards. You can specify the basic settings for entering payment card information in sales documents and set up an interface with an external clearinghouse to authorize and settle the card charges. The interface details vary depending on the external partner and are not in the scope of this book. However, in this section, we will discuss the setup and functioning of payment cards in SAP.

The payment card functionality allows you to store customer card information in the customer master records. You can enter the details in the Payment Transactions tab in General Data section, (which you can access using XD01 or XD02) from where the details get copied into sales documents. You can also enter payment card information manually during sales order processing. There is a separate tab in the order header for payment cards.

The Payment Card Process

You can create a sales order with a payment card in the usual way, using VA01. There is no change in the process, except that an additional screen for payment card data comes into play at the header level.

On this screen, you enter the payment card details, such as card type, number, expiration, cardholder's name, and so on. It is possible to enter more than one payment card to cover the sales order. The Limit To field is used to limit the amount that may be charged on a particular card.

At the time of saving the sales order, the system carries out an authorization check using the interface. Depending on the settings, the system gets authorization for an amount required to cover any immediate delivery (see Figure 9.43). The authorization is valid for a limited time. Hence, at the time of delivery creation, the system will check to ensure that the authorization is still valid, before it permits a delivery.

The Manual Authorization button (at the bottom of Figure 9.43) allows a user to manually trigger authorization during sales order processing.

When the order is fulfilled and a billing document is created, the payment card details are copied into the invoice. Once the billing document is posted to accounting, the payment card clearinghouse assumes the liability for the amount.

Going back to the Payment Cards tab in the sales order, you will notice another button: Settled In Billing Docs. After the invoice has been created against the sales order, you can use this button to show the corresponding billing document(s) in which this card was used and settled.

FIGURE 9.43 Payment Cards tab in sales orders

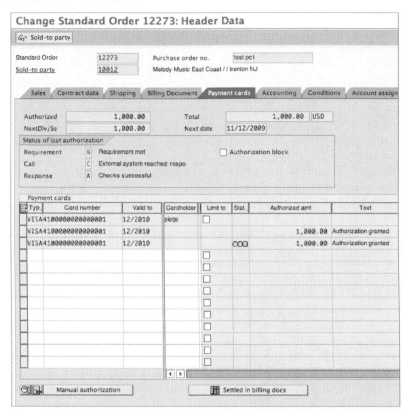

During the subsequent settlement run (again using the interface), the invoice amount is settled with the clearinghouse.

In cases where a return order is created with reference to a payment card order or invoice, the system will not automatically copy over the card details. Instead, you will get a message warning you that the original order was a payment card order. You then must manually key in the card details that are valid at that time. Remember that if you do not enter card details, a regular credit memo will be issued to the customer.

You can also schedule a background job to carry out authorizations in batch mode (use transaction code S_ALR_87014369). The underlying program RV21A010 checks all the open sales documents for which fresh authorization or reauthorization is required and processes them in a batch mode.

The transaction code VCC1 provides a useful worklist of all sales documents containing payment cards.

Payment Card Configuration

We'll now discuss some of the major settings for configuring payment cards in SAP. They can be grouped into two major steps:

- ▶ Payment card definition settings
- ▶ Authorization- and settlement-related settings

Defining the Payment Card Type

The first step is to define the types of payment cards that you plan to use. Use the menu path IMG ≻ Sales And Distribution ≻ Billing ≻ Payment Cards ≻ Maintain Card Types.

On this screen, you can maintain a four-character name and description for the payment card (see Figure 9.44). In the Check field, you can define a program to carry out preliminary checks on the card details entered. For example, you can run a check to verify if the leading digit is correct under the rules of the payment card company.

FIGURE 9.44 Defining a payment card type

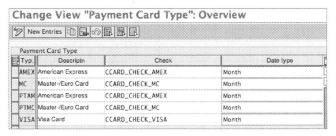

The date type controls the date format (for example MM/YYYY) of the validity dates on the payment card.

Standard SAP has Visa, MasterCard, American Express, and other major cards predefined.

Defining and Assigning Card Categories

The next step is to categorize the cards as credit cards, procurement cards, or any other user-defined category.

Follow the menu path IMG ≻ Sales And Distribution ≻ Billing ≻ Payment Cards ≻ Maintain Card Categories ≻ Define Card Categories.

On the screen shown in Figure 9.45, define the card type. You can also set a limit of one card per transaction for a card category.

FIGURE 9.45 Defining card categories

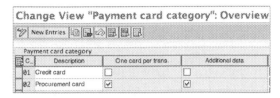

On the same menu, the Determine Card Categories setting allows you to assign the card category to each card type. For example, in Figure 9.46, SAP has identified American Express and Visa as credit cards by assigning them to card category 01.

FIGURE 9.46 Assigning card category to payment card types

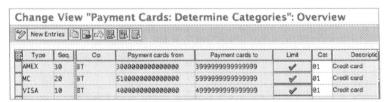

In this step, you also define the number range for the cards. When a payment card number is entered in a sales transaction, the system will identify the card category based on this setting and check whether the number entered is within the range specified here.

Linking Payment Cards to Sales Documents

Having defined the cards, you now will link them to the sales documents where these cards will be used. The menu path is IMG ➤ Sales And Distribution ➤ Billing ➤ Payment Cards ➤ Maintain Payment Card Plan Types.

A payment card plan controls how the sales document will be settled for payment. Standard SAP uses plan 03. You may never need to define any custom plans, in which case you can use the standard one for all scenarios.

It is important to assign your payment card plan type to all the sales document types where you plan to use this functionality, as shown in Figure 9.47.

FIGURE 9.47 Assigning payment card plan type to sales documents

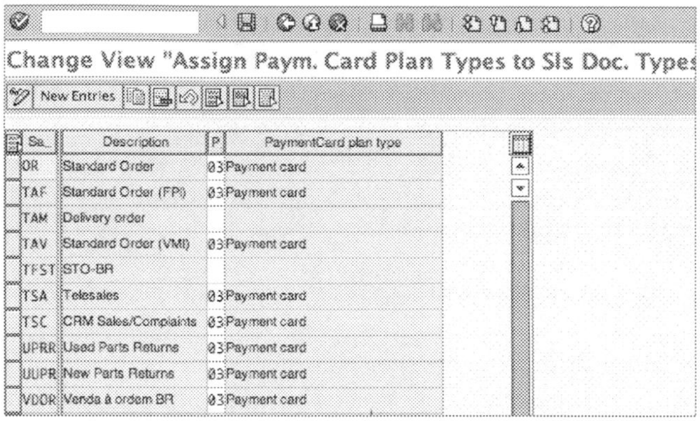

In the sales documents, this setting activates the Payment Cards tab in the header data. So, if you are unable to see the Payment Cards tab in a particular sales document type, you would have probably failed to perform this step.

Assigning a Payment Guarantee Procedure

Just like a pricing procedure, you have to set up and assign a payment guarantee procedure, which determines which form of payment guarantee is valid for a particular document and customer. In this section, we will cover how to define and assign payment guarantee procedures to sales documents using the condition technique. The menu path is IMG ➤ Sales And Distribution ➤ Billing ➤ Payment Cards ➤ Authorization And Settlement ➤ Risk Management For Payment Cards ➤ Maintain Payment Guarantee Procedures. We'll now discuss the steps in this menu.

Define a Payment Guarantee Schema

Standard SAP offers schema 000002 for payment cards. The payment guarantee form assigned to it is 02. Although you may never need to define a custom payment guarantee schema, you will still need to carry out the assignment settings.

As you did with the pricing procedure determination, you will use a document determination schema and a customer determination schema (optional) as keys to the determination of payment guarantee procedure. In the next steps, we will define customer and document determination schemas and then define rules for determination.

Define a Customer Determination Schema

You should make this setting only if you want to set up different payment guarantee procedures for different groups of customers. You can define a four-character customer determination schema using the customer payment guarantee procedure 0002 as a reference.

In the customer master record, you have to specify the customer determination schema in the Payment Guarantee Procedure field in the Billing Documents tab in the sales data section

You can choose to skip this step and the master data maintenance altogether.

Define a Document Determination Schema

You can use the standard option 01 or create a copy. The document payment guarantee procedure has to be assigned to the sales document types in the next step.

Assign the Document Schema to Order Types

In this step, select the sales document types that you plan to use, and assign a document payment guarantee procedure.

In Figure 9.48, you can see we have used the standard document payment guarantee procedure 01 and assigned it to sales document types.

FIGURE 9.48 Assigning document schema to sales documents

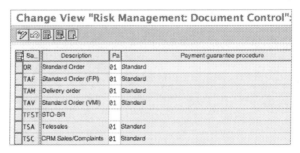

Define Payment Guarantee Schema Determination

In this step, you can specify the rules for the determination of the payment guarantee procedure. For a combination of customer determination schema and document determination schema, you will assign a payment guarantee procedure. You can also choose not to use the customer determination schema and leave this field blank. This way, the rule applies to all customers. As shown in Figure 9.49, the document payment guarantee procedure (Pa) 01 points to payment guarantee procedure 000002, irrespective of the customer procedure (CusP), which is left blank.

You can add other rules based on your requirements.

FIGURE 9.49 Payment guarantee schema determination

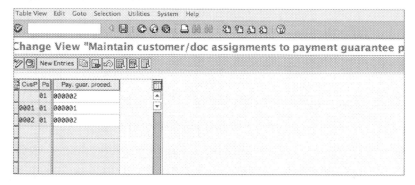

Maintaining Checking Groups

Checking groups control how SAP checks card data before authorization. You can define custom routine checks, authorization horizons, and validity at the checking group level. In this step, you will first define checking groups and then assign them to the appropriate sales document types.

Setting Up a Checking Group

The path is IMG ≻ Sales And Distribution ≻ Billing ≻ Payment Cards ≻ Authorization And Settlement ≻ Maintain Checking Groups. On the Define Checking Groups screen, you'll start by setting up a checking group. Refer to Figure 9.50. You can define a two-character checking group (in the CkGroup field) and add a description.

FIGURE 9.50 Defining a checking group

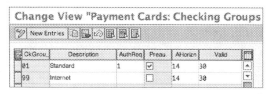

The AuthReq field allows you to add a custom routine to check whether certain prerequisites are met before authorization is carried out. For example, standard routine 1 checks whether the sales document is complete before authorization can be done.

When a sales order is created with payment card data, it is not authorized for the entire amount. The system takes into account the material availability date or billing date. In the case of partial delivery, only that portion of the total amount that is required to cover the immediate delivery is authorized. You can control how many days in advance the system should start authorization. This is known as an *authorization horizon*. You can specify the number of days in the AHorizn field.

If the entire sales order is beyond the horizon (that is, if there are no confirmed schedule lines within the horizon), then you can opt for a preauthorization by selecting the Preau. box. In this case, you get authorization for a nominal amount (usually a dollar), just to make sure that the card credentials are correct.

At this stage, it is also important to check the card expiry date. It should remain valid for a certain number of days after the sales order has been created. This is to make sure that at the time the order is delivered and billed, the card will still be valid. You can specify the number of days in the Valid field.

Assigning the Checking Group to a Sales Document Type

The next step is to assign the checking group to a sales document type. You can make this assignment using the menu path IMG ≻ Sales And Distribution ≻ Billing ≻ Payment Cards ≻ Authorization And Settlement ≻ Maintain Checking Groups ≻Assign Checking Groups.

Figure 9.51 illustrates this simple assignment step.

FIGURE 9.51 Assigning checking groups

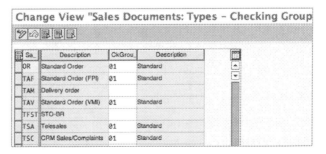

This completes our discussion of the assignment of checking groups to sales documents.

Maintaining Authorization Validity Period

For each payment card type, you can define a period in days for which the authorization will remain valid. Go to IMG ➤ Sales And Distribution ➤ Billing ➤ Payment Cards ➤Authorization And Settlement ➤ Specify Authorization Validity Periods.

Add the number of days for which the authorization is to remain valid. At the end of this period, the authorized amount will expire, and you will have to carry out a fresh authorization check for the sales order.

The batch job for authorization that we discussed earlier is very useful in reauthorization without manual intervention.

Maintaining Settings for a Clearinghouse

In this section, you set up the interface with the clearinghouse. You also have to assign reconciliation and clearance accounts for authorization and settlement transactions.

These steps involve setting up accounts in FI to post the various transactions to. Please make these settings in consultation with your finance team, taking their requirements into account.

Assigning Reconciliation Accounts

In this step, you need to assign a receivables account for each card type. You may choose to have separate accounts for, say, MasterCard and Visa. Use the following path to set this up: IMG ➤ Sales And Distribution ➤ Billing ➤ Payment Cards ➤ Authorization And Settlement ➤ Maintain Clearing House ➤ Account Determination ➤ Assign G/L Accounts (OV87).

As shown in Figure 9.52, we have assigned a receivables account for each card type.

FIGURE 9.52 Receivables account assignment

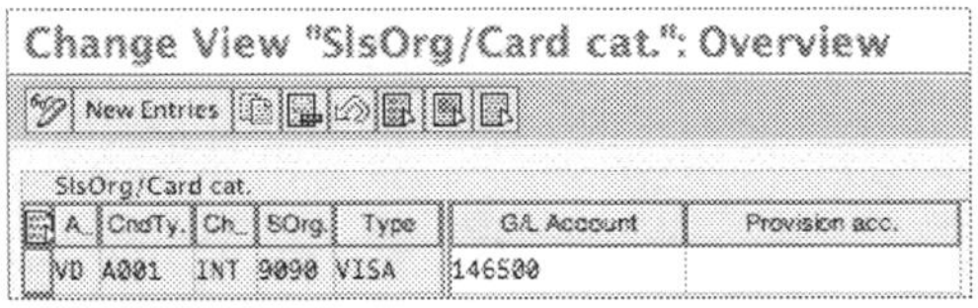

Change View "SlsOrg/Card cat.": Overview

New Entries

SlsOrg/Card cat.

A	CndTy.	Ch.	SOrg.	Type	G/L Account	Provision acc.
VD	A001	INT	9090	VISA	146500	

The clearinghouse assigns each enterprise a merchant ID to uniquely identify it in each payment card transaction. You can also define this merchant ID in SAP and assign it to each receivables account.

TIP We will discuss the other concepts in account determination using condition techniques in Chapter 10. At this stage, you can assume that you will have to assign G/L accounts to proceed with other settings

Setting Up Controls for Authorization and Settlement

In this step, you make two important settings. First, you link each receivables account to a clearing account. Second, you specify the routines used in the external interface to the clearinghouse.

To do this, use the menu path IMG ➤ Sales And Distribution ➤ Billing ➤ Payment Cards ➤ Authorization And Settlement ➤ Maintain Clearing House ➤ Set Authorization/Settlement Control Per Account. As shown in Figure 9.53, you can specify a clearing account corresponding to the receivables account in your chart of accounts.

FIGURE 9.53 Maintaining clearing account and external interface

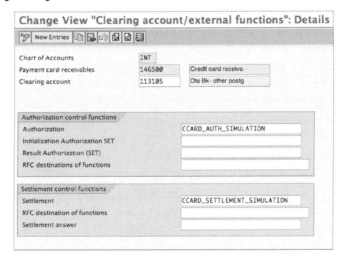

On the Details tab, specify the authorization and settlement control functions.

In the Authorization and Settlement fields (Figure 9.53), assign your custom function modules per your requirements. Standard SAP offers simulation codes for authorization (CCARD_AUTH_SIMULATION) and settlement (CCARD_SETTLEMENT_SIMULATION) so that you can test the concepts before establishing a real connection to the clearinghouse.

NOTE   Each payment card contains a three-digit credit verification value (CVV) code to increase the security of the card transactions. SAP Service Marketplace note 914147 contains some FAQs on the use of this functionality. It also points to other notes that explain how to activate CVV in your version of SAP.

For security reasons, payment card numbers must now be stored in an encrypted format. The display to users should be in a masked format with only the last few digits appearing on the screen.

To implement these security features, refer to SAP Service Marketplace note 1029819, which guides you through the steps and notes that you have to follow for encrypting and masking payment card data.

Summary

In this chapter, we covered the process of creating different billing documents and the steps in configuration. We also discussed rebate functionality and the payment card interface.

Billing is the last step in the sales cycle. Before a billing document is released to accounting, you have to configure account assignment. We will discuss this in the next chapter.

Account Assignment and Revenue Recognition

A fter a billing document is saved, it is released to accounting, where it updates the various general ledger accounts. In this chapter, we will study how to configure SAP to determine the accounts and post the billing document automatically. Further, based on the requirements of the finance team, various pricing elements such as discounts, taxes, and price can be posted to different accounts. In this chapter, we will cover how to control the determination of various accounts.

Some organizations require that billing the customers and updating the revenue books should happen at different points in time. The *revenue recognition* functionality separates billing from revenue and lets you control when to recognize revenue using a separate transaction. In this chapter, we will explain the fundamental scenarios for revenue recognition.

Account Assignment

Account determination is the procedure used to establish the correct G/L accounts for posting a billing document to accounting. Using this procedure, SAP carries out account determination for billing documents such as invoices, credit notes, debit notes, and so on. Revenue account determination provides the G/L account for revenue, discounts, surcharges, and taxes.

Account assignment uses the condition technique to determine general ledger accounts. The *account determination procedure* is a schema that consists of elements called *condition types*. An *access sequence* is assigned to each condition type. Following the sequence, the system searches for G/L accounts maintained in condition tables in a specific order. The *condition record* is the account number set up for a combination of determination criteria. The following sections describe the major steps you will use to configure account assignment.

Set Up Account Assignment

We will show the step-by-step procedure you can use to build an account determination procedure and assign the G/L accounts. Before we show you how to build the procedure, we'll discuss some master data elements that influence account determination.

Material Account Assignment Group

The *material account assignment group* is used to distinguish accounts based on different materials. For example, the requirement may be to separate the revenue from the sale of finished goods from the revenue of services. You can create account groups and assign them in each material master record. You can then use this field as a key to point to different accounts.

To maintain the values in this field, follow the path IMG ➤ Sales And Distribution ➤ Basic Functions ➤ Account Assignment/Costing ➤ Revenue Account Determination ➤ Check Master Data Relevant For Account Assignment ➤ Materials: Account Assignment Group. As shown in Figure 10.1, you can check the list of predefined account assignment groups or define a new entry by specifying a two-character alphanumeric identifier and description. In the material master, this field appears on the Sales Org 2 tab.

FIGURE 10.1 Material account assignment group

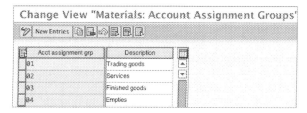

Customer Account Assignment Group

Use the *customer account assignment group* to distinguish accounts based on groups of customers. For example, one of the common requirements is to segregate revenues of domestic customers from those of foreign customers. You can create account groups and assign them in the customer master record. You can then use this field as a key to point to different accounts.

To maintain the values in this field, follow the path IMG ➤ Sales And Distribution ➤ Basic Functions ➤ Account Assignment/Costing ➤ Revenue Account Determination ➤ Check Master Data Relevant For Account Assignment ➤ Customers: Account Assignment Group (OVK8).

As before, you can check the list of predefined account assignment groups or define a new entry, as shown in Figure 10.2. In the customer master, this field appears on the Sales Data tab.

Now let's set up the account determination procedure following the condition technique. The following sections explain the step-by-step procedure.

FIGURE 10.2 Customer account assignment group

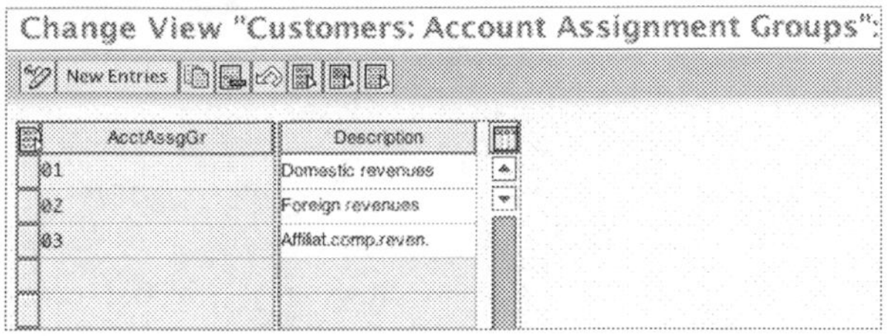

Step 1: Create Condition Tables

Condition tables specify the key combinations required for account determination. Before setting up new condition tables, check the standard tables provided by SAP.

If you have to set up a custom table, refer to the field catalog, and search for the fields you require to be part of your condition table.

The menu path is IMG ➤ Sales And Distribution ➤ Basic Functions ➤ Account Assignment/Costing ➤ Revenue Account Determination ➤ Define Dependencies Of Revenue Account Determination ➤ Field Catalog: Allowed Fields For The Tables.

You can check the fields available in the standard field catalog. If this list does not meet your requirements, you can use function key F4 to access the full list of fields in the catalog (refer to Figure 10.3). Note that, unlike with pricing, there is a very limited set of fields to choose from.

Once you have checked the availability of required fields, pick up these fields, and create a condition table. For this step, follow the path IMG ➤ Sales And Distribution ➤ Basic Functions ➤ Account Assignment/Costing ➤ Revenue Account Determination ➤ Define Dependencies Of Revenue Account Determination ➤ Account Determination: Create Tables (transaction code V/12).

As shown in Figure 10.4, table 001 has a key consisting of the sales organization, customer and material account assignment groups, and account key.

We covered the steps to create a condition table in Chapter 4, "Partner, Text, and Output Determination," when we discussed output determination. Please refer to that discussion for the exact steps.

FIGURE 10.3 Field catalog for account assignment

Change View "Field Catalog (Accnt Determination Sales/Distribution)

Table Name	Short Description
Field Name	Short Description
KOMCV	Maintenance
VKORG	Sales Organization
VTWEG	Distribution Channel
KTGRD	Account assignment group for this customer
WERKS	Plant
KTGRM	Account assignment group for this material
KSCHA	Condition type
KVSL1	Account key
SPART	Division
CCINS	Payment cards: Card type
LOCID	Payment cards: Point of receipt for the transaction
LIFNR	Account Number of Vendor or Creditor
MWSKZ	Sales Tax Code
BEMOT	Accounting Indicator
AUGRU	Order reason (reason for the business transaction)
KDUMMY	Dummy function in length 1
PDUMMY	Dummy function in length 1
PSTYV	Sales document item category
KOMKCV	Determination header
KTOPL	Chart of Accounts
VKORG	Sales Organization
VTWEG	Distribution Channel
KTGRD	Account assignment group for this customer

FIGURE 10.4 Defining a condition table

Display Condition Table (Accnt Determination Sales

Technical view | Other description | Field attributes...

Table   001   Cust.Grp/MaterialGrp/AcctKey

Selected fields	FieldCatlg
Long Key Word	Long Key Word
Sales Organization	Account key
AcctAssgGr	Acct assignment grp
Acct assignment grp	AcctAssgGr
Account key	Condition type
	Distribution Channel
	Division
	Order reason
	Plant
	Sales Organization

Step 2: Define an Access Sequence

To define an access sequence for the pricing determination, the path is as follows: IMG ➢ Sales And Distribution ➢ Basic Functions ➢ Account Assignment/

Costing ➢ Revenue Account Determination ➢ Define Access Sequence And Account Determination Types ➢ Maintain Access Sequence For Account Determination.

On the Change View: Access Sequences: Overview screen, create a new access sequence using the New Entries button. We covered the steps to create an access sequence in Chapter 4 when we covered output determination. Please refer to that discussion for the exact steps.

As shown in Figure 10.5, the access sequence KOFI has five accesses arranged in a specific sequence. The condition tables defined (or identified) in the previous step are used in the access sequence. There is a provision to attach a requirement routine to steps in the access sequence. In the case of KOFI, requirement routine 3 checks that the CO account assignment is not active. If this condition is fulfilled, it carries out the access; otherwise, it skips the step. This initial check helps improve the performance of the access sequence and prevents unnecessary steps.

FIGURE 10.5 Defining an access sequence

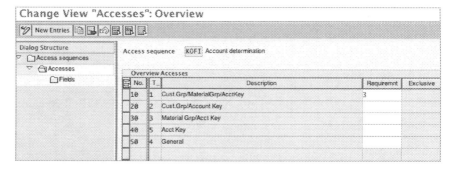

Step 3: Maintain Account Determination Types and Assign the Access Sequence

Account determination types are the condition types that you will use in the account determination procedure.

To set up condition types, follow the path IMG ➢ Sales And Distribution ➢ Basic Functions ➢ Account Assignment/Costing ➢ Revenue Account Determination ➢ Define Access Sequence And Account Determination Types ➢ Define Account Determination Types.

In this transaction, you can define a condition type. There are no other controlling parameters to be maintained here (unlike pricing condition types that required configuration using V/06, which we discussed in Chapter 5, "Pricing and Tax Determination"). You can assign the access sequence to the condition types here.

Standard SAP offers two account determination types: KOFI (standard account determination) and KOFK (account determination with costing). The access sequence KOFI (covered in step 2) is assigned to both conditions (Figure 10.6).

FIGURE 10.6 Defining account determination types and assigning the access sequence

CT	Name	AS	Description	Valid from	Valid to
KOFI	Account Determinat.	KOFI	Account determination		
KOFK	Acct Determ.with CO	KOFI	Account determination		

Change View "Conditions: Types": Overview
New Entries
Overview of Condition Types

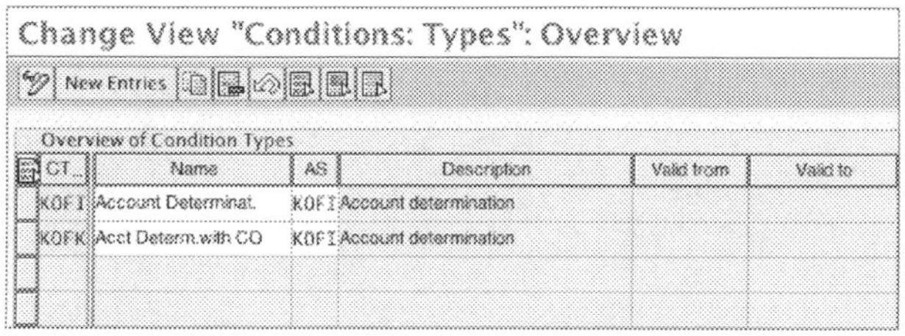

Step 4: Set Up the Account Determination Procedure

The account determination procedure contains the list of condition types defined in the previous step.

To set up an account determination procedure, follow the path IMG ➢ Sales And Distribution ➢ Basic Functions ➢ Account Assignment/Costing ➢ Revenue Account Determination ➢ Define And Assign Account Determination Procedure ➢ Define Account Determination Procedure.

The Account Determination procedure has condition types linked together in a schema. Standard SAP offers the procedure KOFI00, which consists of two condition types, KOFI and KOFK, as shown in Figure 10.7.

FIGURE 10.7 Account determination procedure KOFI00

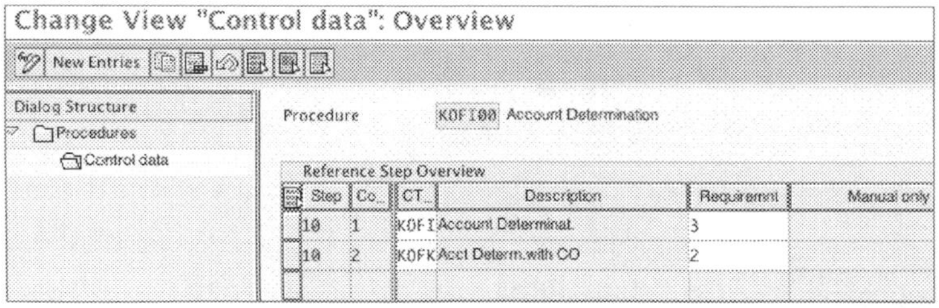

Change View "Control data": Overview
New Entries

Dialog Structure
▽ ☐ Procedures
   ☐ Control data

Procedure   KOFI00 Account Determination

Reference Step Overview

Step	Co.	CT	Description	Requirement	Manual only
10	1	KOFI	Account Determinat.	3	
10	2	KOFK	Acct Determ.with CO	2	

Step 5: Assign the Account Determination Procedure

In this step, you assign the account determination procedure to a billing document.

To assign the account determination procedure, follow the path IMG ➤ Sales And Distribution ➤ Basic Functions ➤ Account Assignment/Costing ➤ Revenue Account Determination ➤ Define And Assign Account Determination Procedure ➤ Assign Account Determination Procedure.

Select the billing document. Attach the appropriate account determination procedure to it, as shown in Figure 10.8. This setting ensures that when billing document F2 is created, the account determination will be done following the procedure KOFI00. Similarly, assign a procedure to all other billing documents (such as credit and debit memos) that you use. The CaAc column here enables you to specify a cash allocation key. With this, the system posts to a general ledger account for cash rather than to a receivables account.

FIGURE 10.8 Assigning an account determination procedure to the billing document

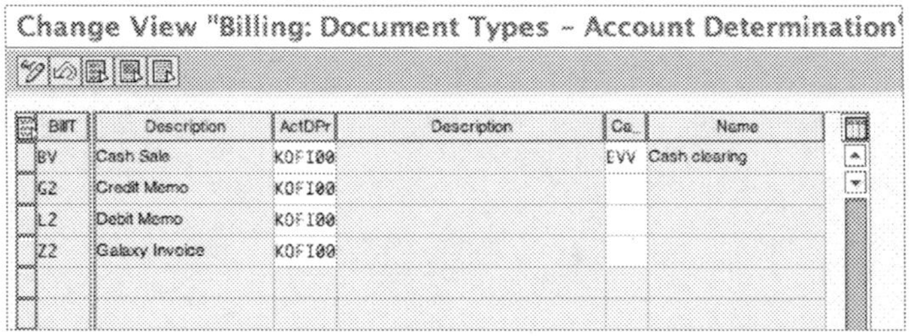

Change View "Billing: Document Types – Account Determination"

BllT	Description	ActDPr	Description	Ca.	Name
BV	Cash Sale	KOFI00		EVV	Cash clearing
G2	Credit Memo	KOFI00			
L2	Debit Memo	KOFI00			
Z2	Galaxy Invoice	KOFI00			

Step 6: Define and Assign an Account Key

Account keys are used to group together similar accounts in financial accounting. You can also use an account key to point to a specific account number in account determination. For example, the account key ERL is used to point to a revenue account. In the pricing procedure, you will assign this key to the pricing conditions related to the product price.

The path in SAP to define and assign account keys is as follows: IMG ➤ Sales And Distribution ➤ Basic Functions ➤ Account Assignment/Costing ➤ Revenue Account Determination ➤ Define And Assign Account Keys ➤ Define Account Keys.

Refer to Figure 10.9, where you will see the standard account keys offered by SAP, such as ERL (Revenue), ERF (Freight), and ERS (Discounts). You can add a new account key by specifying a three-character identifier.

FIGURE 10.9 Defining an account assignment key

Change View "Account Key"
New Entries
ActKy
Name
ERF Freight revenue
ERL Sales revenues
ERS Sales deductions
ERU Rebate accruals
ERZ Revenue increase(PL)
EVV Cash clearing

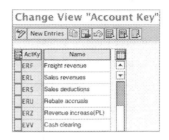

The next task is to assign the account key. Follow the menu path IMG ➢ Sales And Distribution ➢ Basic Functions ➢ Account Assignment/Costing ➢ Revenue Account Determination ➢ Define And Assign Account Keys ➢ Assign Account Keys.

Refer to the pricing procedure that you are using. The table lists all the pricing condition types used in the procedure, as shown in Figure 10.10. You can specify an account key for each condition type.

FIGURE 10.10 Assigning the account assignment key

Change View "Pricing Procedures: Revenue Account Determin
New Entries
Proc. Step Cntr CTyp Name ActKy Name Accrls Name
ZGALAX8 0 EK01 Costs ERL Sales revenues Sales revenues
11 0 PR00 Price ERL Sales revenues
110 0 ZGM1 Customer/Material ERS Sales deductions
111 0 HI01 Hierarchy ERS Sales deductions
801 0 NRAB Free goods ERS Sales deductions
810 3 HD00 Freight ERF Freight revenue
815 0 KF00 Freight ERF Freight revenue
900 0 UTXJ Tax Jurisdict.Code MWS Taxes on sls/purch.
901 0 JR1 Tax Jur Code Level 1 MWS Taxes on sls/purch.
902 0 JR2 Tax Jur Code Level 2 MWS Taxes on sls/purch.
903 0 JR3 Tax Jur Code Level 3 MWS Taxes on sls/purch.
915 0 MWST Output Tax MWS Taxes on sls/purch.
919 0 DIFF Rounding Off ERS Sales deductions
940 0 VPRS Cost

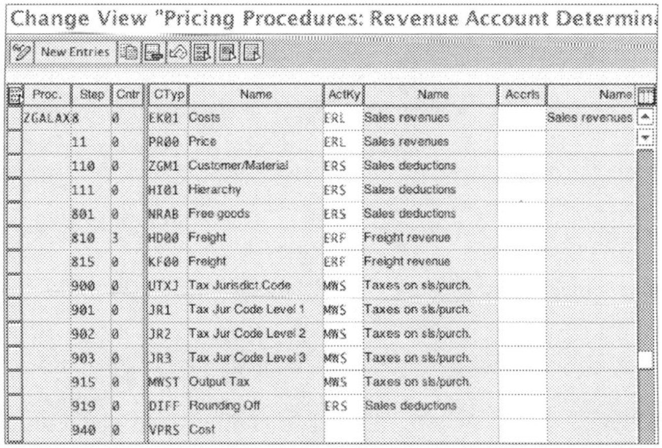

Another way to assign an account key is when you define a pricing procedure (using transaction V/08). Refer to Chapter 5 (specifically Figure 5.13), where the account key is specified in the AccK column.

Step 7: Assign G/L Accounts

In the final step, specify the actual account numbers for each combination key. Follow the path IMG ➢ Sales And Distribution ➢ Basic Functions ➢ Account Assignment/Costing ➢ Revenue Account Determination ➢ Assign G/L Accounts.

You now should see a screen like that shown in Figure 10.11. That displays all the condition tables with key combinations.

FIGURE 10.11   Assign G/L Accounts overview screen, with tables to choose from

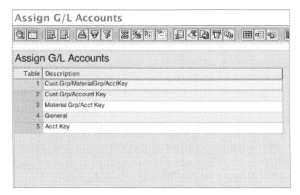

Select the table for which you want to maintain the account numbers and set up condition records. For example, select table 1 (customer group, material group, and account key), and go to the details screen (Figure 10.12) where you can set up condition records, specifying a G/L account for the key combination.

FIGURE 10.12   Assign G/L Accounts details screen to set up condition records

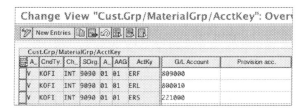

In Chapter 9, "Billing," during the discussion of the rebates and payment card interface, we used account assignment and specified G/L accounts but deferred the discussion of detailed configuration to this chapter. Note that you can also follow the previous steps 1–7 in rebates and in payment card setup to control the determination of accounts.

CASE STUDY—GALAXY MUSICAL INSTRUMENTS: ACCOUNT DETERMINATION SETUP

Galaxy Musical Instruments has set up pricing procedure ZGALAX (discussed in Chapter 5). Now, Galaxy is designing an account determination procedure that goes hand in hand with this pricing procedure. The requirement is that when a billing document is posted to accounting, the different pricing elements in the pricing procedure—such as discounts and freight—must be posted to separate G/L accounts.

The standard account determination procedure offered by SAP (KOFI00) meets Galaxy's requirement. It consists of two conditions, KOFI and KOFK. Galaxy will use KOFI for account determination. The access sequence attached to it is also named KOFI (shown earlier in Figure 10.5). It consists of five condition tables, from specific to generic.

The account assignment keys were previously assigned in the pricing procedure ZGALAX. The customer and material account assignment keys are also maintained in the respective master data records.

To specify account assignment for Galaxy Musical Instruments, take the example of table 1. As shown in Figure 10.12, it has a key composed of the following fields:

- ▶ Application (V for sales and distribution)
- ▶ Condition Type (KOFI)
- ▶ Chart of Accounts (INT is used by Galaxy Musical Instruments)
- ▶ Sales Organization (9090 is used by Galaxy Musical Instruments US)
- ▶ Customer Account Assignment Group
- ▶ Material Account Assignment Group
- ▶ Account Key

Galaxy Musical has specified G/L accounts for each combination of customer account assignment group, material account assignment group, and account key, such as ERL, ERF, and so on. Thus, the amounts in all the revenue conditions (such as condition PR00, with account key ERL) will be posted to G/L account 800010. Discount conditions that use account key ERS (like ZGM1 and HI01) would be directed to 221000, and so on.

Whenever a billing document is saved, you can use *account determination analysis* to understand which G/L accounts have been picked up and which key was used to fetch the records. To access the analysis, use the transaction VF02 or VF03, specify the billing document number and follow the menu path Environment ➢ Account Determination Analysis ➢ Revenue Accounts. Figure 10.13 shows an example from a typical billing document (Z2) for Galaxy Musical Instruments. The analysis confirms that the PR00 amount has been posted to account 800010. If there is an error in account determination, the analysis report is very helpful in finding which records are missing or could not be determined.

FIGURE 10.13 Account determination analysis

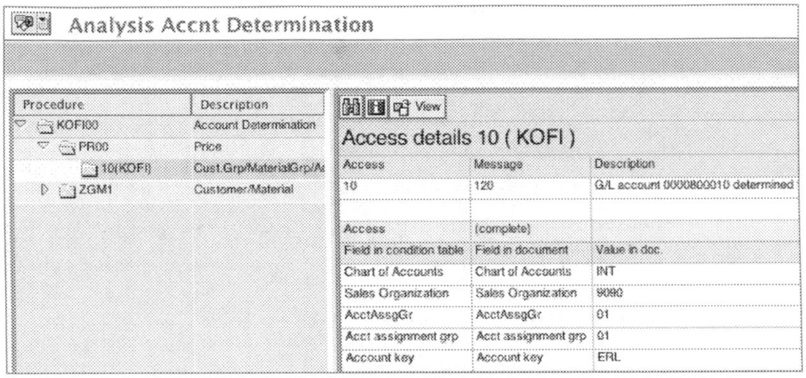

Revenue Recognition

SAP's revenue recognition functionality enables you to post the billing documents and recognize revenue at different points in time. In the regular process, SAP recognizes revenue as soon as the billing document is posted to accounting. The receivables account (customer account) and the revenue account are posted with this transaction. However, certain business scenarios require revenue to be recognized either before or after the invoice has been created. The revenue recognition function provides a separate transaction (VF44) to trigger the recognition of revenue. Here, two additional G/L accounts come into play: the deferred revenue and unbilled receivables accounts. If you bill the customer first and recognize revenue at a later point, the amount is classified as *deferred revenue* in the interim. On the other hand, if the business requires you to recognize revenue periodically but bill the customer later, then the amount is kept in the *unbilled receivables* account.

Suppose you have to bill the customer first and recognize revenue later. Here's what will happen:

1. *The billing document is posted*: The receivables account and the deferred revenue account are updated. Thus, you are billing the customer but not realizing the revenue yet.

2. *The revenue recognition is posted*: This offsets the deferred revenue account with the revenue account. The revenue recognition is thus completed.

Revenue Recognition Process

The revenue recognition process has several variations. To discuss the process flow, we'll present a simple example. Suppose a customer has purchased a one-year warranty from Galaxy for a specific musical instrument. The customer has to be billed up front, but the revenue has to be recognized on a monthly basis over the life of the contract. This is an example of time-based revenue recognition with up-front billing.

In this example, you'd set up a service contract in SAP specifying the start and end dates. (For details on contract creation, refer to Chapter 7, "Sales.") You would also create a billing document with reference to the contract using VF01.

When it comes to revenue recognition, the system uses the contract start and end dates to create equal "buckets" in which the revenue will be recognized. If the customer is billed for $1,200, the revenue recognized per period will be $100 each, for 12 months.

The transaction that triggers the revenue recognition is VF44. You can access it from SAP Menu ➢ Logistics ➢ Sales And Distribution ➢ Billing ➢ Revenue Recognition ➢ Edit Revenue List.

Figure 10.14 shows the selection screen of VF44. In this case, we have specified the contract document number and the posting period as the entire life of the contract.

The details are displayed, as seen in Figure 10.15. The Revenues data is displayed in the upper window, and the Control Lines data appears in the lower one. The Control Lines record contains information such as the total value of the contract. The Recog. Rev. field shows the total revenue recognized until date. Unrec. Rev. is the balance, which is an unrecognized component. In this case, the customer has been invoiced for $1,200. The revenue has been deferred; hence, the unrecognized revenue is $1,200.

FIGURE 10.14 Revenue recognition, post revenue selection screen

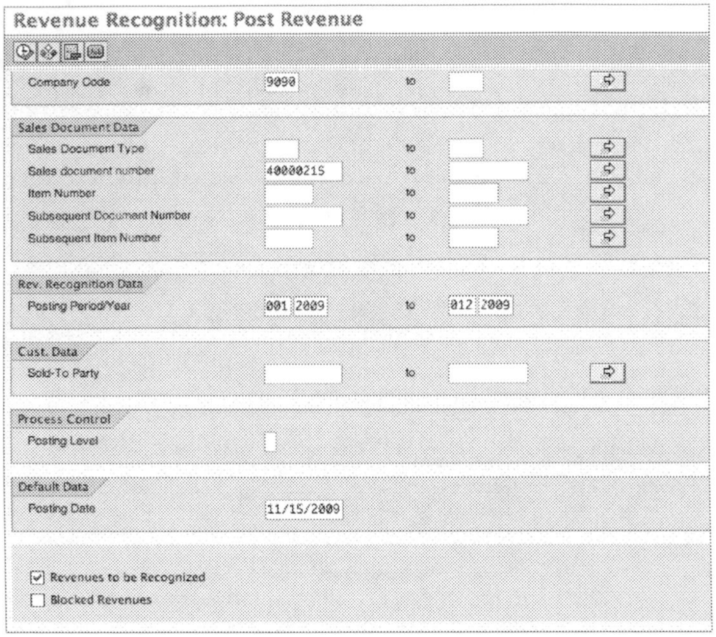

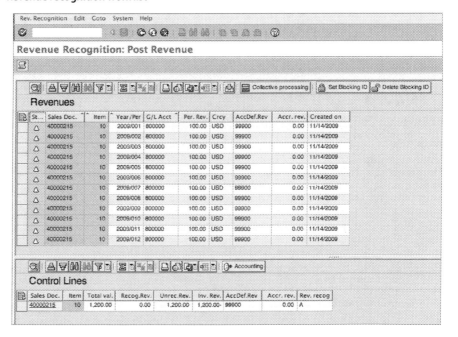

FIGURE 10.15 Revenue recognition work list

The Revenues list shows the revenue amounts that would be recognized in the selected posting period. Since in this example we are checking data for the entire life of the contract, we can see 12 revenue buckets spread over the posting periods. The Year/Per. field shows the posting period and year. In every period, revenue will be recognized in equal amounts ($100). The corresponding G/L accounts appear in the list.

In this example, suppose at the end of first period, the user selects the first line (for period 2009/001) and clicks Collective Processing. The accounting document is generated, and revenue is recognized to the extent of the amount specified.

Figure 10.16 shows the accounting entries that are made at every step of the process. The amount billed ($1,200) is placed in the deferred revenue account. Each month, a revenue recognition entry is made for $100. It updates the revenue account and offsets the deferred revenue account. This process continues every period until the total revenue has been recognized.

FIGURE 10.16 Accounting view, deferred revenue scenario

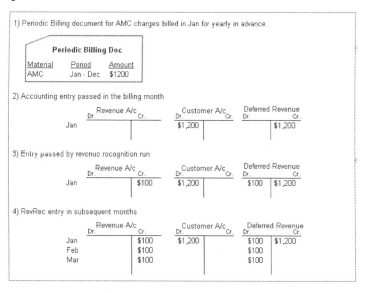

If there is a mistake in recognizing revenue, you can cancel the entry using transaction VF46. Follow the path SAP Menu ➢ Logistics ➢ Sales And Distribution ➢ Billing ➢ Revenue Recognition ➢ Maintain Cancellation List (transaction code VF46).

You can derive a revenue report using transaction VF45. It lists all the details related to a given sales document. You can check all the revenue documents and cancellation documents that have been posted over a period of time. It is possible to display the accounting documents that have been created. You can access this report using the path SAP Menu ➤ Logistics ➤ Sales And Distribution ➤ Billing ➤ Revenue Recognition ➤ Revenue Report (transaction code VF45).

This was a simple example of a revenue recognition process. There can be other variations as well. For example, you can use sales orders with billing plans instead of contracts. In this case, the billing plan dates control the revenue postings.

Another variation is when the revenue is to be recognized before the customer is billed. Consider the example of Galaxy's warranty. A variation could be that the customer is not billed up front but instead billed quarterly, as per a billing plan attached to the contract. The revenue will be recognized in each period. At the end of first period, a revenue of $100 is recognized, but it has not been billed yet. In this case, it updates the Unbilled A/R account. Figure 10.17 shows the accounting entries for this variation of the process.

FIGURE 10.17   Accounting view, unbilled A/R scenario

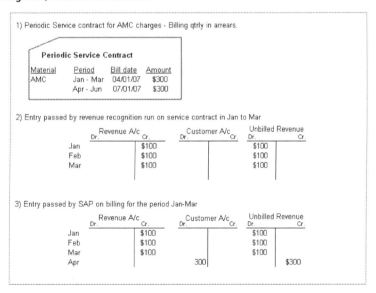

Now let's turn to service-based revenue recognition. In this case, the revenue recognition is triggered by a specific event, such as posting a goods issue. Suppose a customer has placed an order with Galaxy for some musical instruments. As per the delivery schedule, some instruments are to be delivered in the first quarter of the year, and others in the second. The customer will be sent a combined invoice at the end. Whenever a delivery is created and a goods issue is posted, you can trigger the recognition of revenue. This ensures that revenue is recognized in each financial quarter, although the customer is billed at a later point in time.

Set Up Revenue Recognition

Configuring revenue recognition requires close coordination with your finance team and SAP FI/CO expert. Since it is complex functionality, it is not open for configuration, and you have to contact SAP through an OSS message to get it activated. Refer to SAP Service Marketplace OSS note 779366 for the initial activation.

As discussed earlier, the FI/CO experts have to set up G/L accounts to be used for deferred revenue and unbilled receivables. SAP Service Marketplace OSS note 777996 provides detailed guidance on the setup of these accounts.

Once this initial setup is completed, you can proceed with the steps in the following section.

TIP   Before you proceed with configuring revenue recognition functionality, please read the SAP Service Marketplace OSS note 1256525. It contains a best-practice document and recommendations from SAP. It also covers the process variations and flow diagrams. Be advised that the content of the document is frequently updated, and new notes are often released. Please search for the latest note number in OSS Search before proceeding.

Set Up Revenue Recognition for Item Categories

Revenue recognition is controlled at the item category level.

To create the settings, follow the path IMG ➤ Sales And Distribution ➤ Basic Functions ➤ Account Assignment/Costing ➤ Revenue Recognition ➤ Set Revenue Recognition For Item Categories (OVEP).

Select the item category that you plan to activate, and go to the details screen. Figure 10.18 shows this screen with the Business Data tab in it.

FIGURE 10.18 Maintaining item categories for revenue recognition

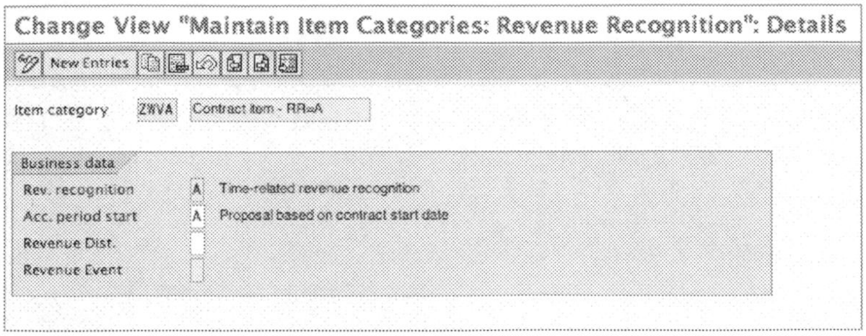

Let's look at the fields in this screen:

Revenue Recognition In this field, specify the type of process you plan to use. In this field, you can specify the revenue recognition category you are using, such as time-based or service-based revenue recognition. Here are the options to choose from:

Time-based revenue recognition (A) Choose this option if your business scenario calls for revenue recognition over a period of time, usually the length of a contract or the duration of a service. The process starts with a contract document (or sales document with a billing plan). In this process, revenue is recognized in equal parts, over the duration of this contract.

Service-based revenue recognition (B) In this scenario, you carry out revenue recognition based on an event, such as rendering a service. The process starts with a contract or a sales order. As soon as a goods issue is posted for the delivery or when there is a confirmation of service, you can run VF44 to recognize revenue. It creates an accounting document that posts to the unbilled revenue account and the revenue account. When the customer is invoiced, another accounting document offsets the unbilled account and impacts the receivables account. There can be other variations of this process, such as invoicing first and then recognizing the deferred revenue later. There can also be contracts with call-off orders. In this case, the call-off order will be delivered and billed.

Time-based and invoice-related revenue recognition (D) In this scenario, the recognition of revenue is done on the basis of an invoice, over a time period. The process is triggered when the invoice is created and posted to accounting. The process is similar to a variation of option A in which the customer is billed first and deferred revenue is recognized later. The major difference is that option A allows you to either bill first or bill later. Option D limits you to billing first.

Credit/debit memo revenue recognition with reference to predecessor (F)
Choose this option for credit and debit memos created with reference to documents that used revenue recognition functionality. The revenue recognition category in the preceding document should be either A or B. If the preceding document is A (time based), it is possible to recognize revenue in the credit/debit memo over the same duration of time as the original document. If it is B (service based), it is possible to recognize revenue on the basis of a specific event as in the original document.

Proposed start date for accrual period   This field controls the start of the accrual-posting period. There are two options, as shown in Figure 10.19. Choose the appropriate option depending on your business requirements and whether you plan to use contract documents in the process flow.

FIGURE 10.19 Proposed start date for accrual period

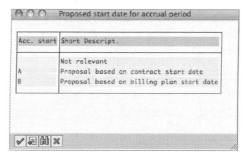

Proposal Based On Contract Start Date   The contract start date will be used as the accrual start as well.

Proposal Based On Billing Plan Start Date   Use this option when you want to refer to the billing plan rather than contract dates.

Revenue Distribution   This field is used to control the distribution of amounts over a certain period. It is used in conjunction with revenue recognition category A (time-based). There are various options to control how the total value and correctional value are divided over the periods, as shown in Figure 10.20. A correctional value can arise if, for example, there is a correction in the pricing of an order or contract, after revenue recognition has already been started. In this case, the correctional value has to be distributed over the remaining periods for which revenue has not been recognized as yet.

FIGURE 10.20 Revenue distribution type

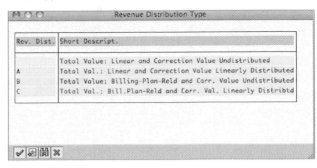

Using the options, you can specify whether the correctional value is to be divided equally over all posting periods or is to be booked entirely in the first open posting period. Please check on the exact requirements with your FI/CO expert before making these settings.

Revenue Event   This field is used only in the case of revenue recognition category B (service-based). You can leave this field blank if revenue is not event related. Choose from the events in the drop-down list. In the case of a third-party business scenario where a vendor directly delivers goods or services to your customer, you can specify that an event such as an incoming invoice (B) should trigger revenue recognition. The customer acceptance date (C) can be another such event. SAP has also provided a business add-in (BADI_SD_REV_REC_PODEV) to define custom events.

Maintain Account Determination

In this section, you will specify the G/L accounts to be used for deferred revenue and unbilled receivables, respectively. Follow the path IMG ➤ Sales And Distribution ➤ Basic Functions ➤ Account Assignment/Costing ➤ Revenue Recognition ➤ Maintain Account Determination ➤ Assign G/L Accounts For Revenue And Deferred Revenue (transaction code VKOA).

You can choose the appropriate table from the list, based on the key combination. In the G/L Account field, specify the revenue account. In the Provision Acc. field, specify the deferred revenue account (Figure 10.21).

The other setting you need to define is for the unbilled receivables account. Follow the menu path IMG ➤ Sales And Distribution ➤ Basic Functions ➤ Account Assignment/Costing ➤ Revenue Recognition ➤ Maintain Account Determination ➤ Assign Accounts For Unbilled Receivables (transaction code OVUR).

FIGURE 10.21 Assigning accounts for revenue and deferred revenue

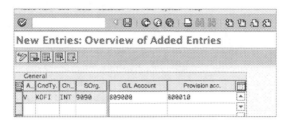

For the chart of accounts and reconciliation account, you can specify the unbilled receivables account here (see Figure 10.22).

FIGURE 10.22 Assigning accounts for unbilled receivables

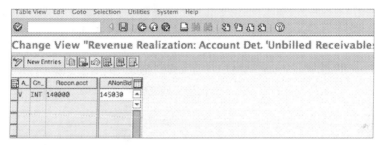

Item Category Settings

Besides the revenue recognition–related settings mentioned earlier, you may require other settings for an item category if you are going to use billing plans. In the definition of the item category, there are fields where you can specify billing relevance and billing plan type (Figure 10.23).

To define these settings, use the menu path IMG ➤ Sales And Distribution ➤ Sales ➤ Sales Document Item ➤ Define Item Categories (transaction code VOV7).

If you want to use a billing plan, set the Billing Relevance field to I. (Figure 10.24 shows the options to choose from.)

Then specify the type of billing plan from the list, as shown in Figure 10.25.

FIGURE 10.23 Item category settings for billing relevance and billing plan

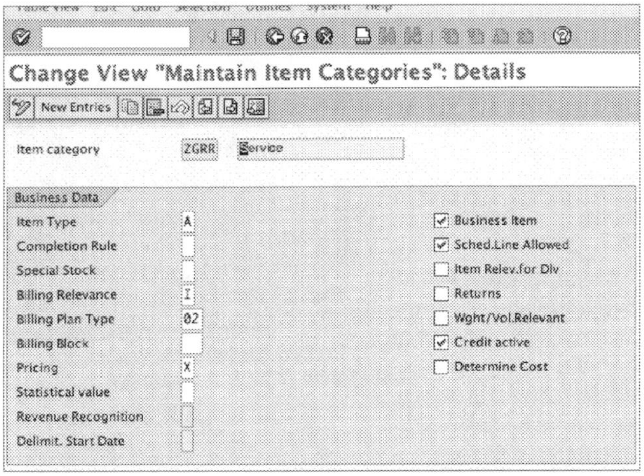
Change View "Maintain Item Categories": Details
New Entries
Item category ZGRR Service
Business Data
Item Type A
Completion Rule
Special Stock
Billing Relevance I
Billing Plan Type 02
Billing Block
Pricing X
Statistical value
Revenue Recognition
Delimit. Start Date
Business Item
Sched.Line Allowed
Item Relev.for Dlv
Returns
Wght/Vol.Relevant
Credit active
Determine Cost

FIGURE 10.24 Choosing billing relevance I for billing plan

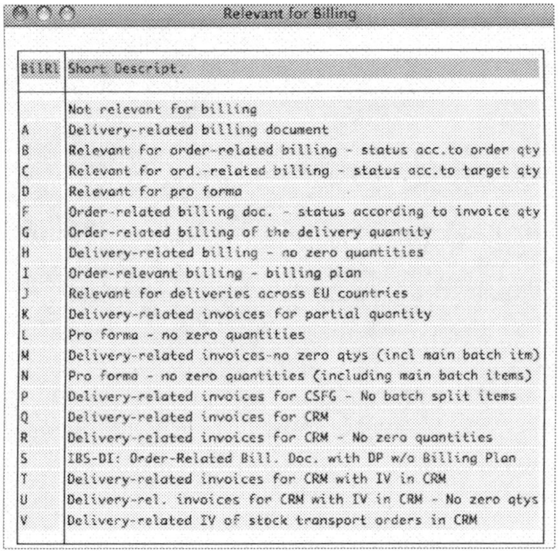
Relevant for Billing
BilRl Short Descript.
Not relevant for billing
A Delivery-related billing document
B Relevant for order-related billing - status acc.to order qty
C Relevant for ord.-related billing - status acc.to target qty
D Relevant for pro forma
F Order-related billing doc. - status according to invoice qty
G Order-related billing of the delivery quantity
H Delivery-related billing - no zero quantities
I Order-relevant billing - billing plan
J Relevant for deliveries across EU countries
K Delivery-related invoices for partial quantity
L Pro forma - no zero quantities
M Delivery-related invoices-no zero qtys (incl main batch itm)
N Pro forma - no zero quantities (including main batch items)
P Delivery-related invoices for CSFG - No batch split items
Q Delivery-related invoices for CRM
R Delivery-related invoices for CRM - No zero quantities
S IBS-DI: Order-Related Bill. Doc. with DP w/o Billing Plan
T Delivery-related invoices for CRM with IV in CRM
U Delivery-rel. invoices for CRM with IV in CRM - No zero qtys
V Delivery-related IV of stock transport orders in CRM

FIGURE 10.25 Options for billing plans

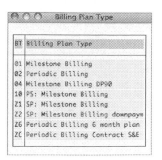

CASE STUDY—GALAXY MUSICAL INSTRUMENTS: REVENUE RECOGNITION SETUP

Galaxy Musical Instruments offers an extended one-year warranty on musical instruments. The company bills the customer up front for the warranty. The requirement is that the warranty charges are to be placed in a deferred revenue account. They have to be recognized in equal installments over the life of the warranty (12 months).

To map this scenario, Galaxy has chosen time-based revenue recognition (category A) in the settings for the selected item category. The Proposed Start Date field for the accrual period is set to A (proposal based on contract dates). It carries out revenue recognition in equal parts over the life of the contract, referring to the contract start and end dates.

Refer to the discussion in the "Revenue Recognition Process" section of this chapter for the steps in this business scenario.

Summary

In this chapter, we discussed a couple of topics that require close integration between SD and FI/CO. We discussed the account assignment process and the steps to set up and control account determination. We also examined the revenue recognition functionality, which allows you to bill the customer and recognize revenue at different points in time.

In Chapter 11, we will discuss the credit management functionality.

Credit Management

L ong-outstanding, uncollectable receivables are never good for the financial health of an organization. If a customer defaults on paying outstanding amounts by the end of the allowed payment term, the company needs to monitor that customer's allowed credit more closely in future transactions. The credit and risk management function in an organization is therefore responsible for creating policies and exercising continuous control in order to minimize credit risks. The Credit Management application in SAP allows you to map your organization's credit policies at various stages of the order to the cash cycle such that the policies act as the determining rules and help in controlling the credit decision-making process.

In this chapter, we will cover how the credit management functionality available in the SAP SD application supports the credit management function in an organization. We will discuss the concepts of credit management, look closely at customization, and show you the process/setup with the help of the settings we have created for our imaginary company, Galaxy Musical Instruments.

Introducing Credit Management in SAP

SAP Credit Management is an application that helps organizations monitor, evaluate, and control credit situations and credit allocations. It allows you to grant credit terms to your customers and also perform credit checks on the sales transactions. When you implement Credit Management in your SAP instance, you map your organization's credit policies into the Credit Management application. Customers are aligned with these credit policy rules on the basis of the information collected from various sources, such as the customer's past transactional history, the customer's credit reports available from credit agencies like Dun & Bradstreet (D&B), the customer's financial stability in the market, the geographical and political situations of the regions where the goods are sold, and so on. Each credit-related sales transaction is then monitored and evaluated with respect to these rules or policies, and the results of the evaluation help your organization decide whether to sell the goods on credit.

A credit check is a comparison of the customer's credit exposure with the customer's available credit limit setup in the credit master records. *Credit exposure* is a sum total of the open orders, open deliveries, open billings, open receivables, and open special liabilities. *Credit limit* is the maximum amount for which you allow your customer to purchase goods from you on credit. You store credit limits in the customer's credit master records.

Whenever you create a new document that is relevant for credit checks, SAP calculates the current credit exposure for the customer and compares it with the customer's available credit limit that is maintained in the customer's credit master. If the exposure is more than the credit limit, the credit check fails. Figure 11.1 shows an example of applying credit management in a sales cycle.

FIGURE 11.1 Example showing credit processing

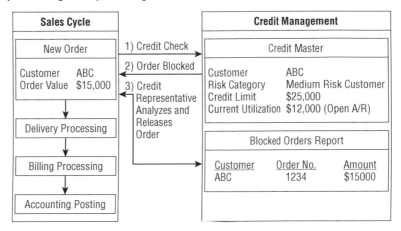

As you can see, a new sales order for customer ABC was created with an order value of $15,000. Since credit management is active and the document is relevant for a credit check, the SAP system inquires for the current credit utilization and maximum credit limit for the customer from the customer credit master. The total credit exposure for this customer (current utilization + current order value = 12,000 + 15,000 = 27,000) is greater than the credit limit ($25,000), and therefore SAP blocks the customer order. The credit representative then analyzes the document using the credit-blocked order reports and, after carefully evaluating the risk involved in releasing the order, approves and releases the order. The order is picked up by delivery processing and billed, and the SAP system posts the receivables to accounting.

In SAP, a credit limit check is carried out whenever a document is created or changed. You can perform credit checks at three points, namely, when a sales order is created or changed, when a delivery document is created or changed, and at the time of PGI. When the check is performed at the time of the order or delivery, the resultant document gives a warning, triggers an error message, or may even be blocked, based on the customization settings defined in IMG. When a check is performed at PGI, it behaves a bit differently. Since PGI is the last step in delivery processing, a credit check failure at the time of PGI cannot block the delivery document. Rather, it triggers an error message and stops the PGI from posting.

THE LINK BETWEEN A CREDIT CHECK AND THE PRICING PROCEDURE

A SAP credit check is linked to SD pricing via the Subtotal field. For SAP to be able to derive the credit value (VBAP-CMPRE) from the sales document, the net value (final price + tax) line in the pricing procedure must have selection A in the Subtotal field. Without this setting in the pricing procedure, the credit check will not work.

Setting Up Credit Masters

A customer credit master in SAP stores all the credit-related information for the customer. The credit master is set up for the combination of payer partner account and the respective credit control area. You can set up the credit master data by using the transaction FD32 or by following the SAP easy access menu path SAP Menu ➤ Accounting ➤ Financial Accounting ➤ Accounts Receivables ➤ Credit Management ➤ Master Data ➤ Change. Figure 11.2 shows the customer credit master data maintenance screen.

FIGURE 11.2 Customer credit master data

You maintain the customer credit limit in the Credit Limit field, and you maintain the risk category to which the customer belongs in the Risk Category field. The SAP system automatically calculates the sales value as a sum total of all the open orders, open deliveries, and open billing documents that are relevant for the credit check and that belong to the credit account. The open receivables value is taken from the customer A/R records, and the credit exposure is automatically calculated as the sum total of all the open values. The credit limit used is calculated by comparing the credit limit with the current credit exposure.

You can set the dates when the last internal credit review on the customer account was performed and when the next internal credit review for the customer account should be due. Using the Goto, Extras, and Environment menu paths in the menu bar at the top of the screen, as shown in Figure 11.2, you can pull up a variety of valuable information about the customer account, such as A/R summary, dunning summary, change log, and so on.

TIP   *Open orders* are the orders that are not yet processed for deliveries, *open deliveries* are deliveries that are created but not yet processed for PGI, and *billing* and *open billing* are the billing documents that are generated but not yet posted to accounting.

Processing the Credit-Blocked Documents

SAP provides a set of five transaction codes to process documents that are blocked because of a credit check. You can use these transactions to generate a work list of credit-blocked documents. From the work-list screen, you can then do the following:

▶ Release the blocked documents so that they can be processed further for delivery and billing steps.

▶ Reject a credit-blocked document. The document is rejected and cannot be processed further.

▶ Reassign the documents to your peers.

▶ Forward the documents to another credit manager or credit representative for evaluation.

Table 11.1 discusses the five transactions for processing the blocked documents.

TABLE 11.1   Transactions to Process Blocked Sales Documents

Transaction Code	Description	Use
VKM1	List of blocked documents	Lists all the credit-blocked documents.
VKM2	List of released documents	Lists all the documents that are manually released (status D).
VKM3	Sales documents	Allows work-list generation based on sales document numbers. The list contains all the documents irrespective of whether the status is blocked (B), released (D), or approved (A).
VKM4	List of all documents	Allows work-list generation including all the documents that are relevant for a credit check (i.e., deliveries and orders). The list contains all the documents irrespective of whether the status is blocked (B), released (D), or approved (A).
VKM5	Delivery documents only	Allows work-list generation for delivery documents only.

IMPORTANT NOTES AND PROGRAMS RELATED TO CREDIT RELEASE TRANSACTIONS

Note the following:

▶ So that a credit representative releases only the documents that they are eligible to release, SAP allows you to set authorization limits. Refer to SAP OSS note 1259643, which talks in detail about how to use authorizations.

▶ If you ever want to add new fields to the VKM* reports, you can use user exit DBKMVF02. Refer to SAP OSS note 779389, which talks about the details of how to add user-defined fields to VKM* reports.

▶ You can use programs RVKRED06 and RVKRED09 in the background job mode for automatic credit checks. This will reduce the load on credit representatives so they only have to deal with the scenarios that are exceptions and therefore need their approvals.

When you release a document manually using one of the VKM* transactions, the document's overall credit status is set to D. This denotes that the document was under a credit block and has been manually released. Other document statuses used in SAP in Credit Management are as follows:

- ► A denotes the documents for which the credit check was successful.

- ► B denotes the documents that are in blocked status due to an unsuccessful credit check.

- ► Blank denotes the documents for which the credit check is not applicable.

To decide whether to release a document from a credit block, a credit representative needs information from various sources such as the customer's past payment history, the customer's A/R ageing, the oldest open item in A/R, the customer's account summary, the dunning information on the customer, and so on. SAP provides this information to credit representatives via a set of reports available in the SAP FICO module (Table 11.2). For an SD consultant, it is good, but not essential, to know about these reports.

TABLE 11.2   Credit Information Reports

Transaction Code/Program Name	Description
F.31/RFDKLI40	Credit overview
F.33/RFDKLI30	Brief credit overview
S_ALR_87012218/RFDKLI41	Credit master sheet
FCV3	Early warning list
F.32/RFDKLI10	Missing data
F.28/RFDKLI20	SD, FI: re-creation of credit data after organizational changes
S_ALR_87012215	Changes to credit management
FDK43	Master data list
FD11	Account analysis
FD10N	Customer balances
FBL5N	Customer line items

Customizing Credit Management

The credit management functionality in SAP spans SD and FICO and so does its customization. There is no predefined sequence that needs to be followed; the process we explain in the following sections is based on what we prefer to choose while configuring Credit Management in SD.

The customization at a high level involves the following steps:

1. Defining a credit control area
2. Assigning the credit control area to a company code and sales area
3. Defining the permitted credit control area for a company code
4. Defining credit risk categories
5. Setting up credit groups
6. Assigning credit groups to sales documents and delivery documents
7. Determining active receivables per item category
8. Setting up credit checks

The following sections cover these customization steps in detail.

Defining a Credit Control Area

A *credit control area* is an organizational unit responsible for monitoring, evaluating, and controlling the credit management operations. Defining a credit control area is the first step in the customization of the credit management functionality in the SAP SD application. You can define the credit control area by using the transaction code OB45 or by following the menu path IMG ➢ Enterprise Structure ➢ Definition ➢ Financial Accounting ➢ Define Credit Control Area. On the customization overview screen that appears next, click the New Entries button to define your credit control area. Figure 11.3 shows the customization screen that appears.

The fields on this screen are as follows:

Credit Control Area   Here you provide the identifier key for your credit control area along with a meaningful description. The key can be up to four characters long. For Galaxy Musical Instruments, we defined the key as GMI.

FIGURE 11.3 Customization screen for setting up a credit control area

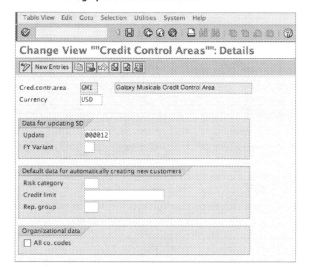

Currency   Here you maintain the currency for the credit control area. Credit limits are maintained in the credit control area currency. In scenarios where the currency of the assigned company code is different from the credit control area currency, the credit exposure of the customers under such company codes is converted into the credit control area currency for the purpose of credit checks and related decision making.

Update rules   In SAP, *credit exposure* is a sum of special liabilities, open receivables, open orders, open deliveries, and open billings. Update rules control when and how the data related to open orders, open deliveries, open billing, and open A/R is updated in the calculation of credit exposure. You can choose one of the following update groups that are available in standard SAP:

[Blank]   If the field is left blank, the SAP credit management application ignores the SD documents and considers only open receivables and open special G/L items for calculating credit exposure.

000012   This update rule is available for a sales order cycle that involves delivery. In the event that a new order is created, the open order value is added to the exposure. When the order is delivered, the open order value is subtracted from the exposure, and the open delivery value is added to the exposure. On billing the delivery, the open delivery value is subtracted from the exposure, and the open billing value is added to the exposure. When the billing posts to accounting, the open billing value is subtracted, and the open A/R value is added to the exposure. The exposure is finally reduced when the cash is applied against the open A/R.

000015   Use this rule if you want SAP to calculate the exposure without considering the open sales order value. In this rule, when the order is delivered, the open delivery value is added to the exposure. On billing generation, the open delivery value is subtracted from the exposure, and the open billing value is added to the exposure. When the billing posts to accounting, the open billing value is subtracted, and the open A/R value is added to the exposure. The exposure is finally reduced when the cash is applied against the open A/R.

000018   This is relevant for nondelivery-relevant orders only. When a new order is created, the open delivery value is added to the exposure. When the order is billed, the open delivery value is subtracted from the exposure, and the open billing is added to the exposure. When the billing posts to accounting, the open billing value is subtracted, and the open A/R value is added to the exposure. The exposure is finally reduced when the cash is applied against the open A/R.

FY Variant   In SAP, the fiscal or financial year of an organization is divided into a number of periods (a posting period and special periods). *Fiscal year variant* is the term used to represent and control these posting periods. When a document is posted into accounting, a fiscal year variant, along with a posting date, helps determine the posting period and fiscal year for posting the accounting entry into the correct period.

You should enter a fiscal year variant for your credit control area if the company codes that you will be assigning to your credit control area use different fiscal year variants. If they all use the same fiscal year variant, you can leave this field blank. The reason for this is that in SAP the credit values updated in the tables (S066) are recorded per posting period. In cases where the assigned company codes have different fiscal year variants, determining the correct posting period becomes difficult. The posting period in such scenarios can be determined only if you assign a default fiscal year variant to your credit control area.

Default Data For Automatically Creating New Customers   The fields in this section of the customization screen are for creating the default credit check–related settings for new customers who have not yet been granted any credit terms. Provide default values in these fields if you want to perform credit checks on orders from new customers who have not yet been granted credit terms. We will discuss the credit check setup for new customers later in this chapter.

All Co. Codes   Select this check box if you want to apply your credit control area to all the company codes that exist in your SAP instance.

CASE STUDY—GALAXY MUSICAL INSTRUMENTS CONFIGURATION ANALYSIS: CREDIT CONTROL AREA DEFINITION

Galaxy wanted centralized credit management and therefore decided to use centralized credit control area GMI with the USD currency. Galaxy wanted to perform credit checks by including open orders, open deliveries, and open billing values in the calculation of credit exposure and therefore chose update group 000012 to manage credit management for both the United States and Mexico. The Fiscal Year Variant setting is blank because both the company codes for Galaxy use the same fiscal year variant.

Assigning the Credit Control Area to a Company Code and Sales Area

Once defined, the credit control area needs to be assigned to the required sales areas and company codes. This way, you maintain a link between Credit Management, FI-A/R, and the SD application so you can monitor, evaluate, and control the credit transactions taking place in the assigned company codes and sales areas.

You assign a company code to a credit control area by using transaction code OBY6 or by following menu path IMG ➤ Enterprise Structure ➤ Assignment ➤ Financial Accounting ➤ Assign Company Code To Credit Control Area. Always remember that a credit control area can have multiple company codes, but a company code can be assigned to only one default credit control area. Figure 11.4 shows the customization screen for assigning company codes to a credit control area. The assignment is very simple. The company code data is already populated on the customization screen. You just need to maintain the corresponding credit control area in the CCAr field for all the required company codes.

FIGURE 11.4 Assigning a company code to a credit control area

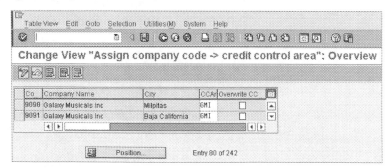

> **NOTE** Remember that this is the default assignment for a credit control area for the respective company codes. For example, company codes 9090 and 9091 will always have a default credit control area of GMI. If you want to have the flexibility to overwrite the default credit control area during document postings, you need to select the Overwrite CC check box for the particular company code for which you want this flexibility.

You can assign a sales area to a credit control area by using transaction code OVFL or by following menu path IMG ➢ Enterprise Structure ➢ Assignment ➢ Sales And Distribution ➢ Assign Sales Area To Credit Control Area. Figure 11.5 shows the configuration screen for assigning a sales area to a credit control area. As you can see, this assignment is also very simple. The sales area is automatically populated on the configuration screen. Use the Position button to position the cursor on the required sales area, and maintain the credit control area in the CCAr field for each required sales area.

CASE STUDY—GALAXY CONFIGURATION ANALYSIS: CREDIT CONTROL AREA ASSIGNMENT

Galaxy wanted to implement centralized credit management, and therefore both the company codes were assigned to the same credit control area, GMI (Figure 11.4). Since the credit management is to be used to perform credit checks on sales transactions, all the U.S. and Mexico sales areas were also assigned to the GMI credit control area (Figure 11.5).

The currency for the credit control area GMI is USD. Therefore, the credit limits for GMI can only be maintained in USD, and the credit checks will also be performed in USD, irrespective of the currency of the company codes. For performing credit checks on sales transactions belonging to 9091 (Galaxy Mexico), the SAP system will first internally convert the sales transaction value from Mexican currency into USD so as to calculate the credit exposure in USD and will then perform the credit check on the sales transaction.

FIGURE 11.5 Assigning a sales area to a credit control area

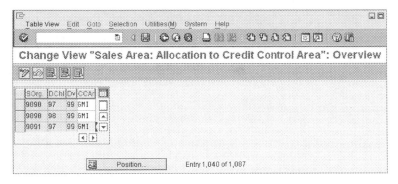

CENTRALIZED VS. DECENTRALIZED CREDIT MANAGEMENT

In SAP, credit management can be categorized as either centralized or decentralized.

Credit management is *centralized* when you assign all the relevant company codes to a single credit control area, as shown in following example:

Credit Control Area	Company Code
1000	1000
1000	1100
1000	1200

In this case, the credit limits assigned to the customer are valid across all the company codes assigned to the centralized credit control area. This chapter talks only about centralized credit management in SAP.

Credit management is *decentralized* when you have more than one credit control area to handle your credit operations. In decentralized credit management, you assign company codes to their individual credit control areas, as shown in the following example:

Credit control area	Company Code
1000	1000
1100	1100
1200	1200

Defining a Permitted Credit Control Area for a Company Code

In SAP, a credit control area can have multiple company codes, but a company code can have only one default credit control area. If you ever come across a situation where the business requirement demands use of an alternate credit control area instead of using the default credit control area assigned to the company code in OB38, you can configure an alternate credit control area using "permitted credit control areas for a company code" customizing. You can reach the customization screen by using transaction code OBZK or by following menu path IMG ➤ Financial Accounting ➤ Accounts Receivable And Account Payable ➤ Credit Management ➤ Credit Control Account ➤ Assign Permitted Credit Control Areas To Company Code.

As usual, use the New Entries button to maintain the customization entry, and maintain all the alternatives that you want to permit for a company code. For your alternate credit control area to work, the default credit control area assignment in OB38 must have the Overwrite CC check box selected. This selection tells SAP that the default credit control area can be overwritten.

Once both these settings are done, you can use your alternate credit control area in the transactions by manually replacing the default SAP-proposed credit control area with your permitted alternative credit control area. If you want to default this alternative credit control area for a specific customer, you can assign this on the Billing tab of the sales area data of the customer master as a default credit control area for that customer. You may also use user exit EXIT_SAPFV45K_001 to define your own determination rules, which will help overwrite the SAP-proposed default credit control area with your permitted alternative credit control area.

Defining Risk Categories

Risk categories help you group the customers based on their credit ratings. You can define separate controls for each risk category to monitor, evaluate, and control the credit situations and credit allocations.

You define a risk category by using transaction code OB01 or by following menu path IMG ➤ Financial Accounting ➤ Accounts Receivable And Account Payable ➤ Credit Management ➤ Credit Control Account ➤ Define Risk Categories. Figure 11.6 shows the customization screen for setting up the risk categories.

To define your own risk categories, you just need to click the New Entries button, maintain an up-to-three-character identifier for the risk category with a meaningful description, and then assign the identifier to the appropriate credit control area. Figure 11.6 shows the risk categories that we set up for Galaxy Musical Instruments.

FIGURE 11.6 Defining risk categories

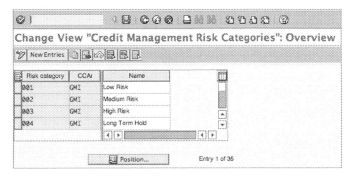

DETERMINING CREDIT CONTROL AREA

A credit control area controls the credit operations. You assign a credit control area in customization to the company code and sales area. The credit control area is also assigned to the customer credit master record. You could even set up your own determination rules for your credit control area, as we just discussed. When you create a sales document, SAP uses these assignments to determine the credit control area for the sales transaction. For a sales transaction, a credit control area can be determined in the following sequence:

▶ Via user exit (EXIT_SAPFV45K_001)

▶ Customer master/sales area data (the Credit Control Area field on the Billing tab)

▶ Sales area (customization)

▶ Company code of the sales organization (customization)

CASE STUDY—GALAXY CONFIGURATION ANALYSIS: RISK CATEGORIES

Every organization has its own way to rate its credit customers. For Galaxy, we grouped customers into four risk categories: Low Risk, Medium Risk, High Risk, and Long Term Hold. The Long Term Hold risk category was created to control credit allocations and credit checks for defaulters who have not paid off their long-outstanding receivables.

Defining Credit Groups

A *credit group* represents the business transaction where the credit check can be applied. Figure 11.7 represent the three credit groups that are provided in the standard SAP system to cover the three major business transactions in sales and distributions. You can reach this customization screen by using transaction code OVA6 or by following menu path IMG ≻ Sales And Distribution ≻ Basic Functions ≻ Credit Management/Risk Management ≻ Credit Management ≻ Define Credit Groups. As you can see, the available credit groups cover all three vital steps in sales order processing. It's not very common that you have to define a new credit group for your credit management settings, but if the need arises, you can define one by clicking the New Entries button on the customization screen and providing a two-character identifier and a meaningful description.

FIGURE 11.7 Defining credit groups

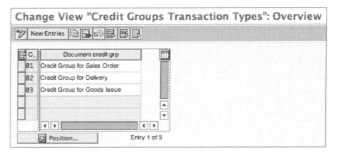

Assigning Credit Groups to Sales Documents and Delivery Documents

In this step, you assign all the sales order and delivery document types that you would like to include in credit checks to their respective credit groups. To perform the assignments, you can use menu path IMG ➢ Sales And Distribution ➢ Basic Functions ➢ Credit Management/Risk Management ➢ Credit Management ➢ Assign Sales Documents And Delivery Documents. After you follow the menu, you will see a Choose Activity dialog box providing two options: Credit Limit Check For Order Types and Credit Limit Check For Delivery Types.

Credit Limit Check For Order Types   Here you assign the sales document to the respective credit group. Figure 11.8 shows the customization screen for this assignment activity. You can also reach this screen using transaction code OVAK.

The assignment process is very simple. You just need to assign the sales document types to their respective credit groups. Galaxy is using credit group 01 to perform credit checks on sales order type ZGM1, as shown in Figure 11.8.

Another field visible here is the Check Credit field. This field controls whether the system runs credit checks during sales order processing and, if yes, whether it will be a simple credit check or an automatic credit check. We will discuss the selection value for this field later in the chapter, along with how to set up simple and automatic credit checks.

FIGURE 11.8 Defining credit groups

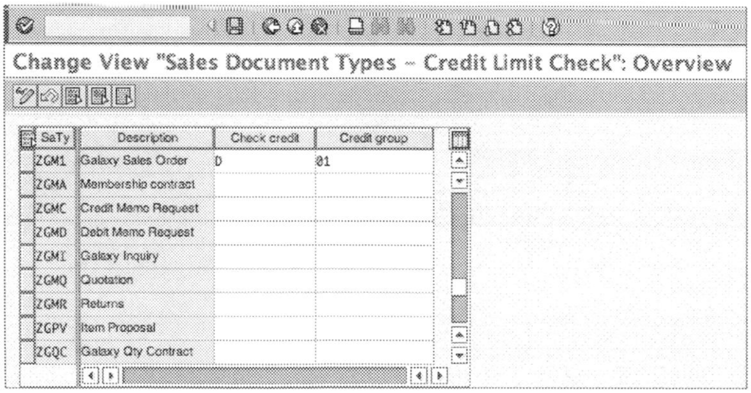

Change View "Sales Document Types – Credit Limit Check": Overview

SaTy	Description	Check credit	Credit group
ZGM1	Galaxy Sales Order	D	01
ZGMA	Membership contract		
ZGMC	Credit Memo Request		
ZGMD	Debit Memo Request		
ZGMI	Galaxy Inquiry		
ZGMQ	Quotation		
ZGMR	Returns		
ZGPV	Item Proposal		
ZGQC	Galaxy Qty Contract		

Credit Limit Check For Delivery Types   This activity allows you to set up the credit groups for delivery documents. Figure 11.9 shows the customization screen for this assignment activity. You can also reach this screen using transaction code OVAD.

Here again, you just need to assign the delivery document types to their respective credit groups. Galaxy is using credit group 02 for performing credit checks at the delivery document (create/change) level for delivery type LF and is using credit group 03 to perform credit checks at the post goods issue (PGI) level for delivery type LF.

FIGURE 11.9 Defining credit groups

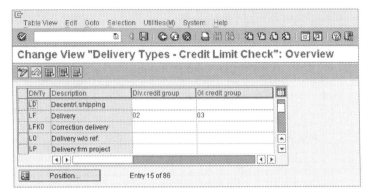

Determining Active Receivables per Item Category

In this step, you set up the item category relevancy for credit checks. This setting helps calculate the net order value that is relevant for the credit check. So, in the case of an order with four line items of $100 each, if three line items are set up as relevant to a credit check (based on their item categories credit check relevancy setup in OVA7), SAP considers only $300 as the net credit value for calculating the credit exposure for that sales order and excludes $100 for line 4, which is not relevant for the credit check.

To reach the customization screen, you can use transaction code OVA7 or follow menu path IMG ➢ Sales And Distribution ➢ Basic Functions ➢ Credit Management/Risk Management ➢ Credit Management/Risk Management Settings ➢ Determine Active Receivables Per Item Category. Figure 11.10 shows the customization screen for setting up item category relevancy for credit checks. To make the assignment, you need to select the check boxes for all the required item categories that you want to make eligible for credit checks.

FIGURE 11.10 Setting up item category relevancy for a credit check

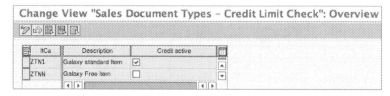

Always remember that credit checks in SAP are performed against a payer partner after accumulating all the necessary financial figures and all the open order, open delivery, and open billing documents. When you create an order document, all the credit relevant line items from the order are summed up to calculate the total sales order credit value. SAP then searches the credit existing exposure for the payer account from the sales order by looking into the credit master data record for the payer and add the credit value from the sales order to the existing credit exposure to calculate the total credit exposure value. This total exposure value is then compared against the total credit limit available to the payer and accordingly SAP blocks or approves the credit check on the sales order and updates the credit status at the document header level.

Setting Up Credit Checks

SAP provides two types of credit check, namely, a simple credit check and an automatic credit check:

Simple credit check   A simple credit check, as the name suggests, is very simple in nature. The functionality is limited and considers only open A/R items and open items from special G/L and sales orders for performing the credit checks. When you create/change a sales order that is relevant for a simple credit check, SAP calculates the payer/customer's credit exposure by adding the open A/R balance for the customer, open item balances from the special G/L, and the net sales order value. This credit exposure is then compared against the customer credit limit maintained in the customer's credit master. If the credit exposure is greater than the credit limit, the system sets the credit check status as "fail" and shows a warning, generates an error message, or performs a delivery block.

Automatic credit check   An automatic credit check is more robust than a simple credit check. Unlike a simple credit check, where you apply a standard rule across all the credit check–relevant documents, an automatic credit check allows you to pick and choose from a variety of credit check rules available in the standard SAP system to base your credit checks on. You can specify when and when not to perform a credit check, can include seasonal factors, and can even define and use your own credit check rules.

Setting Up a Simple Credit Check

You set up a simple credit check in customizing by using transaction code OVAK or by following menu path IMG ➢ Sales And Distribution ➢ Basic Functions ➢ Credit Management/Risk Management ➢ Simple Credit Limit Check. Figure 11.11 shows the configuration screen for maintaining simple credit checks.

FIGURE 11.11 Customization screen for configuring a simple credit check

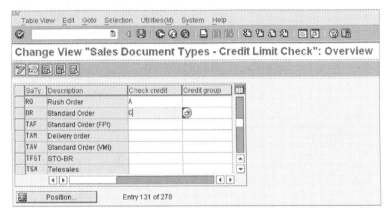

To set up a simple credit check, you need to maintain values in the Check Credit field corresponding to each and every sales document type for which you want the simple credit check to happen. The Check Credit field specifies whether the system runs credit checks for sales documents and, if it does, what types of credit check the system would run and what impact it would have on the corresponding sales order document. Table 11.3 lists the possible values that you can maintain for the Check Credit field and their impacts.

TABLE 11.3 Possible Values for Simple Credit Checks and Their Impacts on Sales Orders

Selection Value	Impact
Blank	No credit check occurs.
A	The system shows a warning message; the sales order can be delivered and allowed to perform further processing.
B	The system shows an error message; the sales order cannot be saved.
C	The system sets up a delivery block on the sales order; the order can be saved but cannot be delivered.

Setting Up an Automatic Credit Check

You set up the automatic credit check by using transaction code OVA8 or by following menu path IMG ➤ Sales And Distribution ➤ Basic Functions ➤ Credit Management/Risk Management ➤ Credit Management ➤ Define Automatic Credit Control. Figure 11.12 represents the overview screen for defining automatic credit checks. In SAP, each automatic credit check rule is defined for a unique combination of credit control area, risk category, and credit group. This provides you with the flexibility to assign different checks for different combinations, thus allowing new-customer sales order credit check rules to differ from a high-risk credit customer sales order. Take a look at Figure 11.12, and you will notice that we defined a couple of credit control rules for Galaxy, each identified on the basis of a unique combination of credit control area, risk category, and credit group field.

FIGURE 11.12   Defining automatic credit control, overview screen

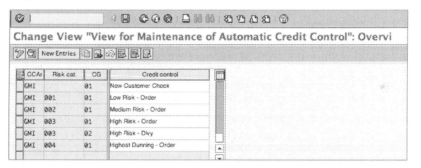

As always, you can use the New Entries button to define your own automatic credit checks or you can use the Copy button to create one by copying from an existing one.

TIP   If you are configuring an automatic credit check, in addition to OVA8 setup, make sure that the sales document types on which you would like to perform the automatic credit check are configured, as shown earlier in Figure 11.8.

Figure 11.13 shows the customization detail screen for automatic credit control setup. For the purposes of this chapter, we will break this customization screen into logical sections and will show examples (wherever required) to explain the use and impact of section/field in the credit check. The first section on the customization screen shows the key combination that controls the credit check, which we already discussed. The Currency and Update settings in Figure 11.13 are automatically proposed by the system from the credit control area customization (from OB45 setup) and cannot be changed.

FIGURE 11.13   Defining automatic credit control, detail screen

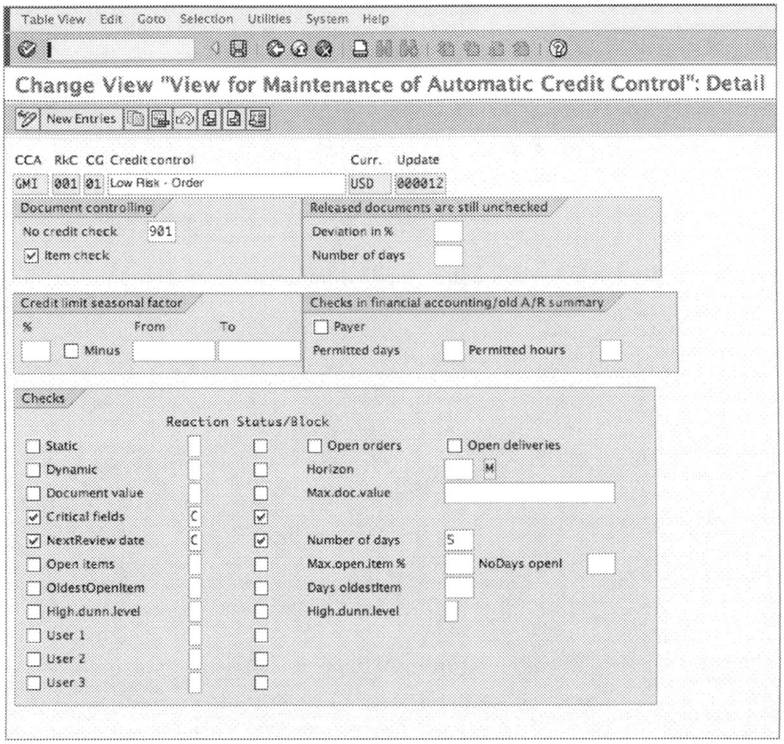

The other sections of the screen are as follows:

Document Controlling   Here you set the overall document-level controlling for your credit check rule. There are two fields:

No Credit Check   Here you can set up your own requirement to not trigger credit checks on certain documents or in a certain situation. A common use of this field is for manually released documents. In standard SAP, manually released documents are rechecked when there is a substantial change. If you would like to not check the manually released documents with a credit check again, you can create a requirement using ABAP help and can assign the requirement number in this field.

Item Check If you select this check box, SAP takes into consideration the item category relevancy for credit checks. The credit check happens for all the items in the document that are relevant for credit checks. When this check box is not selected, the credit check is performed at the document header level.

Released Documents Are Still Unchecked Here you set the rule that controls when to recheck the documents for credit checks if they were originally released manually.

If the dollar value for any manually released document is changed beyond the threshold percentage defined in the Deviation In % field, the document is rechecked for credit check calculations.

If a manually released document has passed the threshold limit specified in the Number Of Days field, the document will be again rechecked for credit check calculations after taking into account whether the new value exceeds the calculation as per the Deviation In % field.

Checks In Financial Accounting/Old A/R Summary This check against the A/R summary helps you ensure that the credit checks are always happening against the latest open A/R summary for a payer. Here you define the permitted number of days and permitted number of hours for an A/R summary to be used for credit check calculations.

> **N O T E** In SAP, you use transaction code FCV1 to generate an A/R summary. The A/R summary is beneficial for decentralized credit management where you have sales transactions happening in system X and you want to transfer the open A/R balances from system Y for performing credit checks on sales documents in system X. In the case of centralized credit management, an A/R summary is helpful in improving system performance because every time SAP checks open A/R balances for credit check calculations, it doesn't need to go to various FI tables and instead can easily pick up information from the A/R summary table (KNKKF1). In SAP, you can define the validity for the A/R summary and can put the A/R summary program in periodic batch job runs for regular updates to the KNKKF1 table.

Role Of Seasonal Factors In Credit Check In SAP, you can add seasonal factors to your credit check. For example, during holiday seasons, if you wanted to relax or restrict your customer's purchasing power by some percentage, you can do it using this customization check.

Reaction   By making an appropriate selection in this field, you can control how the system reacts in situations where the credit check for a document is unsuccessful. The available options are as follows:

> » Blank: No message is sent to the user.

> » A: A warning message is issued to the user informing them that the credit check was unsuccessful.

> » B: An error message is issued to the user with information about the unsuccessful credit check, and the document cannot be saved.

> » C: This is just like A, but it tells the user the exact amount by which the credit exposure is above the credit limit.

> » D: This is just like B, with the information provided to user about how much more the credit exposure is above the credit limit.

Status   Using the Status field, you can set the document status as blocked or unblocked. When selected, the document will be blocked if it fails the credit check; otherwise, it will not be blocked.

Static Credit Checks   As the name suggests, a static credit check is static in nature. There is no time factor in play when the credit check is calculated. SAP provides two check boxes, Open Orders and Open Deliveries, which control the credit checks. Based on whether you select only sales orders, only deliveries, or both sales orders and deliveries for a static check, SAP selects the documents.

Dynamic Credit Checks   A dynamic credit check allows you to use horizon periods for calculating credit checks. Which documents should be picked for a credit check by SAP depends upon what horizon periods you set when customizing in this check. You can define a horizon in days, weeks, and months. So if you set a dynamic credit check in customization with a two-month horizon, SAP will only pick up documents for the customer that fall in this two-month horizon period to calculate the credit exposure. If there are any sales documents from the customer that fall outside this horizon period, they are excluded from the credit check. Dynamic credit checks can be performed only on sales order documents.

Document Value Check   This field, in conjunction with the value in the field Max.Doc.Value, decides how the system behaves when the maximum allowable document value is exceeded. Figure 11.14 shows how the document value check impacts the credit check for a sales document.

FIGURE 11.14   Example showing the document value check

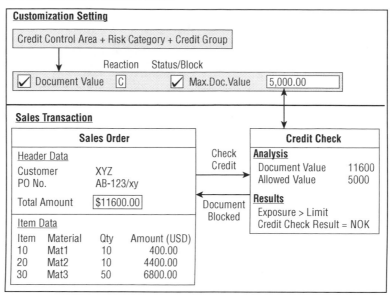

Critical Fields Check   Payment Terms, Fixed Value Date, and Additional Value Days are the three predefined critical fields in the standard SAP system. With this check, the SAP system compares and ensures that the values for these critical fields in the sales document are exactly similar to what is maintained in the corresponding customer master record for the customer. If the values are the same, the document passes the credit check; otherwise, the credit check is unsuccessful.

Next Review Date Check   The credit review is a periodic activity. Organizations do perform credit reviews on a regular basis and make sure that the credit terms in the customer master are appropriate with respect to the current credit analysis on the customer account. This check allows you to block the sales documents of a customer whose credit review information is old, such as if the next review date has already passed and the customer account is still pending credit review.

Open Items Check   Long-open A/R balances often turn into bad debts if the proper controls are not in place to stop an A/R from falling into the long-term A/R bucket. This check helps you block customer sales orders if the customer open A/R balance has reached a certain threshold. This check works on the combined result of two fields: the number of days outstanding and the percentage of total A/R. If both the conditions hold true, only then the credit check is successful. Figure 11.15 shows how an open item check impacts the credit check for a sales document.

FIGURE 11.15   Example showing open items check

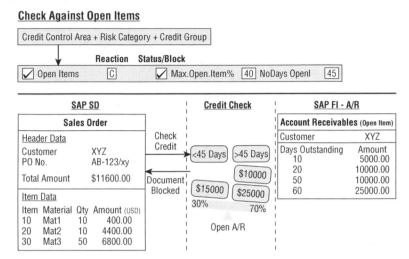

As you can see, customer ABC has a total A/R balance for $50,000. The overdue balance of more than 45 days is $35,000, which is 70 percent of the total A/R. As per the credit check rules, if the outstanding balance of more than 45 days is above 40 percent of the total A/R, the credit check will block the document, and thus the sales document gets a credit block.

Oldest Open Items Check   Just like the previous check, this check takes into consideration a customer's open A/R values. This check gives you control to block the customer's sales document in situations where customer is defaulting for a particular invoice payment that is about to cross the threshold limit set in customizing and that may turn into a bad debt. For example, suppose customer X is a medium-risk customer and in customizing for medium-risk credit-check rule, you entered that the oldest open items allowed for a medium-risk customer is 90 days with status checkbox checked. Now the day customer X has any A/R item outstanding more than 90 days, SAP will start blocking the orders for customer X.

Highest Dunning Level Check   In SAP, you send dunning letters to customers as a payment due reminder. *Dunning level* refers to the number of times you have sent a dunning letter to a customer for the same A/R. Level 1 may be configured as a friendly reminder sent one week before the payment is due, level 2 may be configured as a reminder one week after the payment was due, level 3 may be configured as a reminder one month after the payment was due, level 4 may be a reminder two months after the payment was due, and so on.

Using this check, you set a threshold for dunning letters when customizing. For example, you can set a credit check rule to block all the sales documents for the customer if they've been sent three letters of dunning and the payment for A/R is yet to be received.

Custom Defined Checks   In SAP, you can define up to three user-defined credit check rules. For defining your own credit check rules, SAP provides the user exits LVKMPFZ1, LVKMPFZ2, and LVKMPFZ3 that correspond respectively to the User 1, User 2, and User 3 check boxes on the OVA8 screen.

To give you an idea of how you can use these rules in real time, Table 11.4 shows the credit rules configured for Galaxy Musical Instruments.

CASE STUDY—NEW-CUSTOMER CREDIT CHECK FOR GALAXY MUSICAL INSTRUMENTS

To have better credit controls, Galaxy felt a need to put all the newly opened accounts into one default category called New Customer. As a process in Galaxy, a new customer account is opened by a sales representative, and the credit allocation and processing is performed by a credit representative working in the finance department. The lead time for setting up the credit master for the new customer is one day. Galaxy wanted to have the flexibility to allow the creation of a sales order without waiting for a credit master to be set up in SAP, but at the same time Galaxy wanted these orders to be in a default credit block, which could later be released by the credit managers once they have set up the credit master for each new customer. To do so, Galaxy set up the credit rule (GMI + blank + 01) for new customers in Automatic Credit Checks. To make sure that this rule was called up in SAP while processing transactions for a new customer, Galaxy activated the new customer settings available in OB45 by assigning a default credit limit of $1.

As a result, Galaxy was able to provide parallel processing to the sales and credit teams: the sales team got the flexibility of creating orders for new customers without waiting for the credit team to set up their credit masters, and at the same time the credit team was not worried about a credit risk due to new customers because all the orders for new customers are under a default credit block.

TABLE 11.4   Galaxy's Credit Rules

Credit Control Area	Risk Category	Credit Group	Credit Rule	Applies To	Checks Maintained	Credit Check Failed—System Response	Special Requirements
Blank	Blank	01	New customers: create and block	New customer not yet assigned to any risk category. Order documents to be blocked.	Dynamic, document value	Blocked with warning	None
ZGMI	001	01	Low risk	Low-risk customers: order documents should only be checked for any changes to the critical fields and next review dates.	Critical fields, next review date	Blocked with warning	901
ZGMI	002	02	Medium risk	Medium-risk customers: order documents should be checked for dynamic credit check, taking into consideration the credit limit assigned to the customer master.	Dynamic	Blocked with warning	901
ZGMI	003	01	High risk	High-risk customers: order documents should be checked with a dynamic credit check along with a check for any open A/R and oldest open A/R too.	Dynamic, open A/R, oldest open A/R	Blocked with warning	901
ZGMI	004	01	Highest dunning	A/R defaulters who have been sent three dunning letters. Order creation not allowed; will error out when saved.	Highest dunning check with level 3	Error message	None
ZGMI	003	02	High risk	High-risk customers: delivery documents should be checked for any open A/R and oldest open A/R too.	Open A/R, oldest open A/R	Blocked with warning	902

ZGMI is the centralized credit control area for Galaxy.
Risk category 01 is for low risk, 02 is for medium risk, 03 is for high risk, and 04 is for the highest dunning. New customers are taken care of by using a blank risk category.
Credit group 01 represents sales documents, and 02 represents delivery documents.
Requirement 901: Do not perform credit checks again for documents released manually from a credit block. Applicable only to orders.
Requirement 902: Do not perform credit checks again for documents released manually from a credit block. Applicable only to deliveries.

TROUBLESHOOTING CREDIT MANAGEMENT: HELPFUL OSS NOTES

► 18613, Checklist for Credit Management: This OSS note provides a general customizing checklist that you can use if you face any customization-related trouble with credit management.

► 377165, Update Open Credit Values for Credit Management: This note provides valuable insight about how open values are updated in SIS structures S066 and S067 in SAP.

Summary

In this chapter, we discussed credit management in detail, including concepts, processes, and customization, and also used the Galaxy Musical Instruments case study to provide examples for customization. We discussed how credit management works in SAP and how can you customize it to suit your business needs. In the next chapter, we will discuss various material-related functionalities that are available in SAP SD.

CHAPTER 12

Material Determination, Listing, Exclusion, and Proposal

T his chapter covers various material related functionalities that are available in standard SAP. These include material substitution, item proposals, automatic product selection, material listing and exclusion, and customer–material information records. Each of these functionalities has its own use and importance in the overall sales cycle. In this chapter, we'll cover these functionalities in detail, including how to use and customize them. We'll start with material determination.

Material Determination

Material determination (also called *material substitution*) is a technique provided by SAP to allow you to substitute one material for another during the processing of a sales cycle. The technique is really useful for providing solutions for a variety of day-to-day business requirements that demand material substitutions. Here are a few real-world examples:

- ▶ Replacing an obsolete/discontinued material with a new one so as to avoid entering an order that erroneously commits the enterprise to sell a discontinued material to the customer

- ▶ Automatically substituting the agreed-upon alternative material in an order when the original ordered material is out of stock

- ▶ Supplying specially packaged versions of the original material during holiday seasons such as Christmas or Thanksgiving

- ▶ Executing a sales promotion in which you want to enclose flyers or promotional materials along with the materials ordered by the customers

You can use material determination to automatically substitute one material for another or to propose a list of alternative materials for the user to select among. Further, the substitute material either can replace the original material on the main order line or can be added as a subitem to the original material in the order. With material determination, not only can you substitute the materials, but you can also check the stock availability for the original or substitute material and control whether the shortage is to be transferred to the MRP for the original or for the substitute materials.

Material determination and automatic product selection make a great combination. With this combination, you can replace the materials and can also check whether the customer has agreed to the replacement. You achieve this using the product attributes fields available in the customer and material master records. In the following sections, we'll cover material determination in detail, including automatic product selection. But before we move ahead, we'll talk about how to maintain material determination records.

Maintaining Material Determination Records

You maintain the material determination record by using transaction code VB11 or by following the SAP Easy Access menu path Logistics ➤ Sales And Distribution ➤ Master Data ➤ Products ➤ Material Determination ➤ Create. Figure 12.1 shows the material determination overview screen. To maintain the material determination record, choose the key combination for which you would like to maintain the material substitution. In our example, it is A001, which stands for the material substitution based on the material number.

FIGURE 12.1 Overview screen for maintaining a material determination record

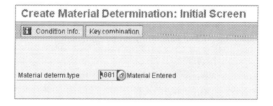

Now press the Enter key on the keyboard to go to the detailed maintenance screen (Figure 12.2). Here, you maintain the original material on the left in the MatEntered column and enter its substitute on the right in the Material column. Enter a reason for the substitution in the Reason column, and enter a validity date for your material substitution record. A substitution reason controls the overall substitution process, including whether the substitution will be automatic or manual and whether it will include an ATP check. We will cover in detail the reasons for substitution, along with the customization setup for material determination, later in this chapter. The material determination functionality also allows you to maintain more than one substitute in your material record. If you see the check box in the Alternative Materials column selected for your substitution entry, this means that more than one substitute material has been maintained for the entered material, as is the case here.

FIGURE 12.2 Fast Entry screen for maintaining a material determination record

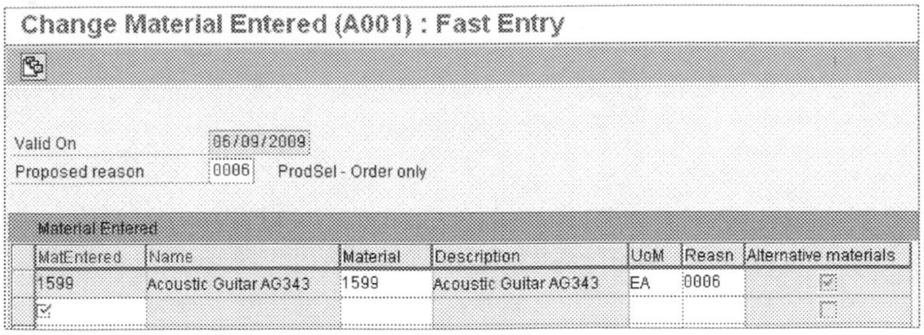

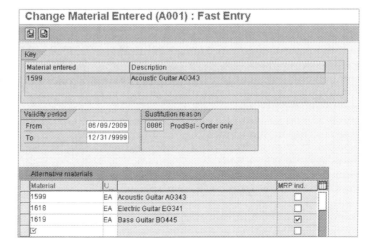

This is really helpful in situations such as material substitution for stock shortages, because you can maintain all the alternative materials in the required prioritized sequence in the VB11 record. The SAP system then replaces the original material on the order with the next available material alternative in stock.

To enable this functionality, double-click the required substitution entry line while you are on the screen shown in Figure 12.2. You will be provided with the screen shown in Figure 12.3. Here you can maintain all the alternative materials in the sequence in which you want them to be determined in the sales order. Since substitution reason 0006 is configured to perform an ATP check, when the stock is insufficient for material 1599, SAP will first allocate all the available stock from 1599 to the order and will then allocate the available stock from alternative materials 1618 and 1619, respectively.

FIGURE 12.3 Maintaining multiple alternatives

The checkbox shown in MRP Ind. column on this Fast Entry screen plays a vital role in controlling the transfer of material shortage to SAP's planning application. As you can see in the top portion of Figure 12.4, when the MRP Ind. box was selected for material 1619, the shortfall for three quantities after the successful substitution run was reported for material 1619, but when the MRP Ind. check was removed (Figure 12.4, bottom portion), the shortage of three quantities was instead reported for material 1599.

FIGURE 12.4 Example showing use of MRP indicator

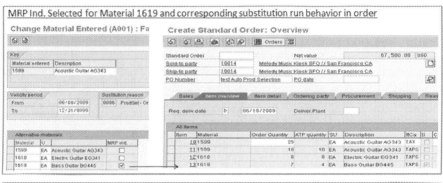

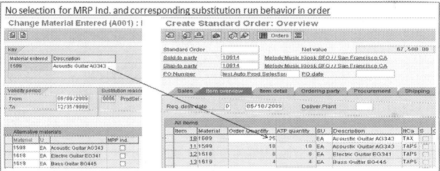

This setup can also be useful for clearance situations when you would like to sell off all the available inventory of a material you are planning to discontinue in the near future and start replacing it thereafter with a new material. By creating the setup shown in Figure 12.3, you tell SAP that if an order comes for material X, it should first deplete the available stock for material X and then start substituting alternative material X1. During this process, if any shortfall is encountered, transfer it to planning for the alternate material X1.

Now we have covered the benefits of material determination in SD and how to maintain the condition record for material substitution, let's move forward and take a look at the customization settings required to set up the material determination in the SAP system.

Deciding the Scope of Customization

Before you start customizing the material determination, it is necessary that you know the scope of substitution, and you also should be able to evaluate the complete end-to-end substitution process. Answering the following questions will help you determine the scope of customization:

What is the purpose of the Material Determination?   Do you need material determination to offer an additional subitem to the main item, such as discount coupons, promotional flyers and so on, or do you need material determination to perform material substitution for the main item in the sales document, such as a new material substituted for a discontinued material?

How is the substitute product going to be determined?   This question points to the determination rule. Will you need to substitute products according to the material entered into the order, the material group, or any other material attribute? This helps you decide the fields you need to include into your condition tables.

Is it possible to use an existing setup, or do you need to create a new one?   Standard SAP provides substitution condition type A001, item category TAPS, TAX along with schedule line category CX, and PP to handle the material determination in orders. Before you set up your new customization entry, always make sure to check whether this existing setup, as available out of the box in standard SAP, is appropriate for your business requirements. Refer to Chapter 7, "Sales," for more details on how to set up item categories and schedule line categories.

For what scenarios can a substitute be offered, how many and in what priority can substitutes be offered, and for which material is the shortage to be reported?   Recall the discussions related to Figure 12.3 and check if you need that kind of setup.

Is there any seasonal or time factor involved in substitution?   For example, material X might be substituted for by its specially packaged holiday version (material Y) during the Christmas season, whereas for the rest of the year, the substitute might be alternate material Z.

Do you need to configure the product attributes?   In cases where your customers are picky about the substitute material, you may want to configure the product attributes so as to consider customer consent before substituting the material on the order document.

What material number will you print on documents such as order confirmations, deliveries, invoices, and so on?   Will it be the number of the original product, the substituted product, or both?

How is the pricing performed during product substitution?   Will the prices be based on the original material or on the substituted material?

CASE STUDY: GALAXY MUSICAL INSTRUMENTS CONFIGURATION ANALYSIS: MATERIAL DETERMINATION, SCOPE FINALIZATION

Galaxy Musical Instruments required the ability to substitute a material for the purposes of promotions, responding to stock shortages, and as a standard replacement for discontinued or to be discontinued materials. This determination needed to occur automatically based on the material number entered into the customer order. Galaxy further required that the pricing for the original material would prevail even after the substitution, but both the substitute and original materials were to be shown on the output documents. After analyzing these requirements against the available out-of-box setup for the material determination, we concluded that material determination A001 serves Galaxy's purpose, and therefore we did not need to create a new setup. A001 maintenance, when used along with substitution reasons, allows substitution in the case of shortages, promotions, and so on, based on the material number entered into the order, without disturbing the original material pricing.

Customizing the Material Determination

Customization for a material determination is based on the condition technique. You start with setting up the determination using the condition technique followed by defining the substitution rules. You then also perform item categories and schedule line categories setup, provided if standard item categories TAPS and TAX along with schedule line category CX and PP are not sufficient to cater to your business requirement. Since we've discussed the condition technique in detail in earlier chapters of this book and applied it a number of times while configuring various basic functions such as pricing determination, partner determination, text determination, and output determination, we will just summarize the material determination customization and focus on substitution rules customization.

Follow the steps in the next sections to customize the material determination setup.

Step 1: Set Up a Condition Table for Material Determination

To create your own material determination key combination/condition table, follow menu path IMG ➢ Sales And Distribution ➢ Basic Functions ➢ Material Determination ➢ Maintain Prerequisites For Material Determination. The menu path will take you to a Choose Activity screen listing the steps for setting up material determination using the condition technique. Select the activity for Create Condition Tables from this screen to setup your own condition table. Alternatively, you can use transaction code OV16 to call the customization screen. You can use numbers greater than 500 in your condition table, or you can leave the condition table number field blank, in which case SAP automatically assigns the next available number from the customer namespace (501 and above) to your condition table. Select the required fields as per your business requirement from the field catalog, and generate and save the table.

Step 2: Set Up the Access Sequence

To create your own access sequence, use transaction code OV11, or choose the activity for *Maintain Access Sequences* from the Choose Activity screen.

1. Create your own access sequence by providing a four-character identification key along with a meaningful description.

2. Assign the condition tables you created earlier to your access sequence in the sequence of the most specific to the least specific or generic condition.

3. Maintain any requirements that you want to assign to your access sequence.

4. Generate your access sequence using the Utilities button available on the access sequence overview screen.

Figures 12.5 to 12.7 show this customization setup for access sequence A001 that is available in the standard SAP system for the material determination. Both access sequences A001 and A002 are available in standard SAP system for the material determination.

ADDING FIELDS TO THE FIELD CATALOG

If some fields that you want for your condition table do not exist in the field catalog, you can add them using the following steps:

1. Add the new fields to the KOMKDZ (header) and KOMPDZ (item) structures.

2. Add these new fields to the field catalog via transaction OV26 or using the activity for Maintain Field Catalog from the Choose Activity screen.

3. Use USEREXIT_MOVE_FIELD_TO_KOMKD (header fields) and USEREXIT_ MOVE_ FIELD_TO_KOMPD (item fields) from "include MV45AFZZ" to provide values to new fields during sales order processing. Remember that for step 1 and step 3, you will need an ABAP resource.

FIGURE 12.5 Defining access sequences

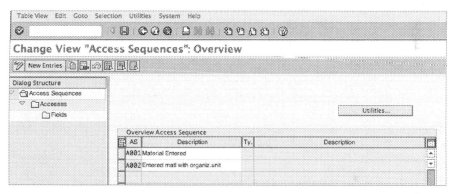

FIGURE 12.6 Assigning condition tables to access sequence

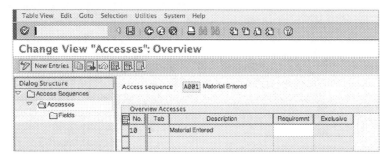

FIGURE 12.7 Assigning data source for condition table fields

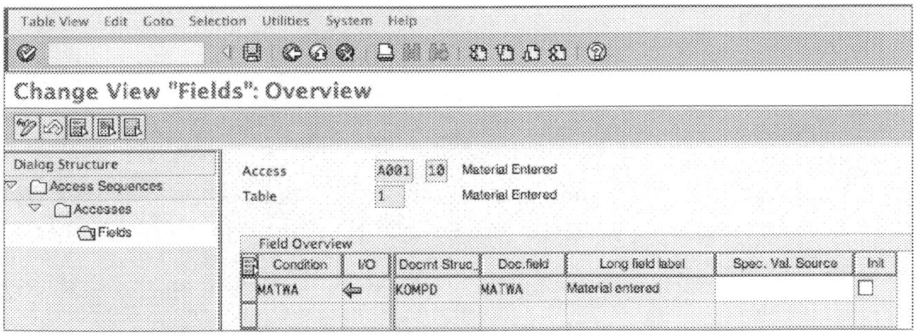

Step 3: Set Up Material Determination Types

Use transaction code OV12 to create your own material determination condition types or choose the activity for Define Condition Types from the Choose Activity screen. Here's how to create your own material determination type:

1. Provide a four-character identification key along with a meaningful description for your material determination condition type.

2. Assign the access sequence you created in the "Step 2: Set Up the Access Sequence" section to your condition type. You can even set up validity rules for your condition type that can control the condition record validity.

Figure 12.8 shows the customization setup for condition type A001 that is provided in the standard SAP system for the material determination.

FIGURE 12.8 Defining condition types

CTyp	Name	AS	Description	Valid from	Valid to
A001	Material Entered	A001	Material Entered		

Step 4: Maintain the Material Determination Procedure

To define your own determination procedure, use transaction code OV13 or choose the activity for Maintain Determination Procedures from the Choose Activity screen.

1. Provide a six-character identification key along with a meaningful description for your determination procedure.

2. Assign the condition type you created to your procedure.

Figure 12.9 shows this customization setup for procedure A000001 that is available in the standard SAP system for the material determination.

FIGURE 12.9 Defining a determination procedure

Step 5: Assign the Material Determination Procedure to Sales Document Types

Now assign the material determination procedure you have created to all the sales document types that will make use of material determination technique for material substitution.

This is shown in Figure 12.10. To reach this customization screen, you can use transaction code OV14 or follow menu path IMG ➤ Sales And Distribution ➤ Basic Functions ➤ Material Determination ➤ Assign Procedures To Sales Document Types.

FIGURE 12.10 Assigning a material determination procedure to sales document types

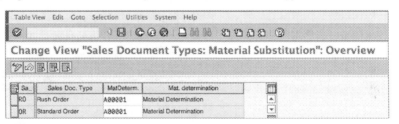

Step 6: Create the Substitution Reasons

Substitution rules control the material substitution process. You can define a substitution reason via transaction code OVRQ or menu path IMG ➤ Sales And Distribution ➤ Basic Functions ➤ Material Determination ➤ Define Substitution Reasons.

To create your own substitution reason, enter a four-character identification key along with a meaningful description, followed by making the required selections in the controlling fields, as shown in Figure 12.11.

FIGURE 12.11 Creating substitution reasons

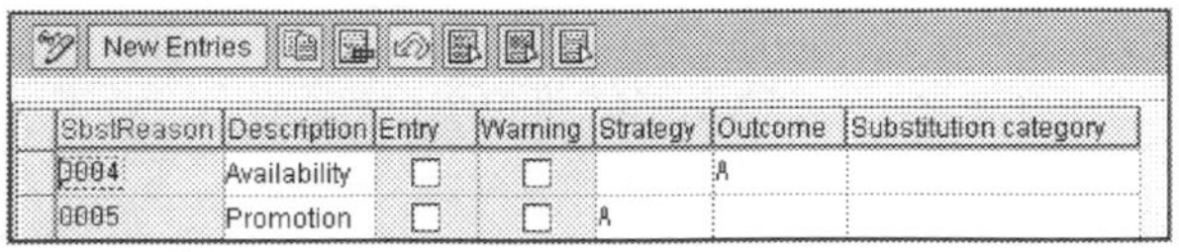

SbstReason	Description	Entry	Warning	Strategy	Outcome	Substitution category
0004	Availability	☐	☐		A	
0005	Promotion	☐	☐	A		

The following are the fields shown in this figure:

Substitution Reason The column SbstReason contains the four-character identification key for the substitution reason.

Description The column Description contains a meaningful description for this substitution reason, with the maximum field length being 20.

Entry check box This check box controls the printing of the material number on the output form during output processing. When selected, SAP prints original material and its description on the output such as invoices, order confirmations, and so on.

Warning check box This check box provides a warning to the user before substituting a material. This warning works only for manual substitutions, not for automatic ones.

Strategy This field defines the substitution strategy. If you leave the value in this field blank, substitution is automatic. When the value is A, substitute products are displayed to the user for making a selection. At this time, an ATP check is also performed by the SAP system. Selection value B is similar to A but with no ATP check.

Outcome This field controls whether the substitute material should replace the original material entry in the sales order or should be created as a subitem of the original entry. When the value in this field is blank, the items are replaced. When the value is A, the substitution products are displayed as subitems. Value B acts like A but applies only when creating items in sales orders. To help you understand the importance of the Strategy and Outcome fields, Table 12.1 shows the nine possible combinations for values in these fields that can be used to set up a substitution reason and also explains what impact these nine combinations will have on the order document and the situations where you can use them.

TABLE 12.1   Possible Substitution Combinations and Result

Strategy	Outcome	Substitution	Response	ATP	Shortage Reported to Planning	Possible Use for this Rule
Blank	Blank	Automatic Substitution	Main item Replaced	No	Yes	EAN replacement, obsolete replacement, special packaging
Blank	A	Automatic Substitution	Subitem generated	Yes	Yes	Substitution for stock shortage
Blank	B	Automatic Substitution	Subitem generated	Yes	Yes	Substitution for stock shortage (sales order only)
A	Blank	Manual Proposal List	Main item Replaced	Yes	Yes	Promotions with samples
A	A	Manual Proposal List	Subitem generated	Yes	Yes	Substitution for stock shortage
A	B	Manual Proposal List	Subitem generated	Yes	Yes	Substitution for stock shortage (sales order only)
B	Blank	Manual Proposal List	Main item Replaced	No	No	EAN replacement, obsolete replacement, special packaging
B	A	Manual Proposal List	Subitem generated	No	No	Promotional flyers or text materials requiring no ATP
B	B	Manual Proposal List	Subitem generated	No	No	Promotional flyers or text materials requiring no ATP (sales order only)

Substitution Category   This field is used only for service orders. When you select A in this field, the serviceable equipment on the service order gets replaced with the service product, thus allowing pricing to happen at the service product level and not at the serviceable equipment level.

Automatic Product Proposal

Automatic product selection is one step beyond the plain material determination technique in SAP ERP. Here you not only substitute material A with material B but also check whether the customer agrees with such substitution. The setup consists of three simple steps:

Step 1: Define the product attribute   The standard SAP system comes with 10 product attribute fields, namely, PRAT1 through 9 and PRATA. These fields correspond to product attributes 1 through 10. The first step is to give a meaningful label to these fields that can help you identify the nature of the product attribute. For example, you may rename product attribute 1 as "gift-wrapped," product attribute 2 as "discount coupons," product attribute 3 as "promotional material," and so on. Since renaming is a technical change, you will need an ABAP consultant to help you with the renaming.

Step 2: Assign the product attribute to the material   Next you assign the product attribute to the material. This assignment is set up in the Sales Org. Data 2 view of the material master record for the material. Here you select all the product attributes that apply to the material. For example, you may select product attribute 1, "gift-wrapped," to indicate that the material always comes as gift-wrapped and product attribute 3, "promotional material," to indicate that marketing promotional material also ships along with this material.

Step 3: Assign the product attribute to the customer   Finally, you assign the product attributes to the customer. This assignment is set up on the Sales tab of the Sales Data view of the customer master record. You click the product attribute button on the Sales tab to call up the product attributes screen and then select the attributes that the customer is not willing to accept. For example, if the customer is not willing to accept any material that is gift-wrapped and contains marketing material, select attribute 1, "gift-wrapped," and attribute 3, "promotional material." If the customer accepts the materials that are gift-wrapped with no promotional material, choose attribute 3 only.

Material Listing and Exclusion

Material listing/exclusion is functionality in SAP SD that controls what materials a customer can buy. When you maintain a material listing for a customer, the customer can only buy those goods contained in the material listing assigned to the customer. Conversely, material exclusions allow you to set up a list of materials that a customer cannot buy. Figure 12.12 shows two examples.

FIGURE 12.12 Examples for material listing/exclusion

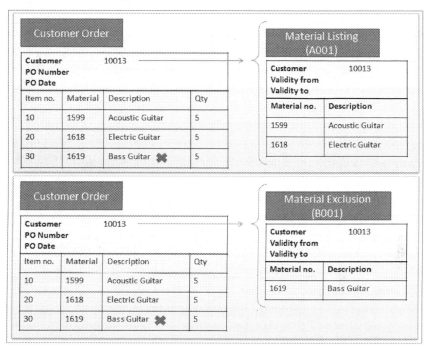

The first example shows how a material listing record maintained for a customer restricts a customer order to be processed only for listed materials, whereas the second example shows how material exclusion helps you exclude a particular material in customer order processing. The end results from both the approaches are same.

You can maintain a material listing at a sold-to level and also at a payer level. In the event the sold-to and payer are different and the material listing is maintained at both levels, the sold-to material listing takes precedence over the payer material listing. If the listing is only maintained at either the sold-to level or the payer level, SAP picks that level. If there is no listing maintained at either level, the customer is allowed to purchase any material without any restrictions.

If your business scenario demands a new configuration setup for material listing/exclusion, you can configure that by setting up the condition technique for material listing/exclusion.

CASE STUDY—GALAXY MUSICALS INSTRUMENTS CUSTOMIZATION SCOPE: MATERIAL LISTING/EXCLUSION

Galaxy Musical Instruments has a requirement to restrict the sale of a few musical instruments to customers who buy directly from its website. For retail customers buying via the retail channel, the restriction is enforced by individual retailers on their customers. To enforce this restriction in SAP ERP, Galaxy decided to use material exclusions for such customers. The initial design study was performed, and we decided to use standard condition type B001 as-is to maintain material exclusions.

Customizing the Material Listing/Exclusion

Material listing/exclusion also uses the condition technique. You start the customization with condition table setup, followed by the access sequence, condition types, and the determination procedure. In this section, without going into details of the condition technique setup, we will discuss the key customization elements related to material listing and exclusion setup. To get to the customization screen for material listing/exclusion, follow the menu path IMG ➢ Sales And Distribution ➢ Basic Functions ➢ Listing/Exclusion. You will be presented with a Choose Activity dialog box showing various customization activities for material listing/exclusion, as shown in Figure 12.13.

FIGURE 12.13 Initial configuration screen for material listing/exclusion

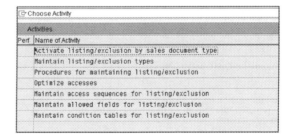

Step 1: Set Up the Condition Table

As always with the condition technique, the first step is to maintain a condition table. From the Choose Activity dialog box, choose Maintain Condition Tables For Listing/Exclusion. Alternatively, you can use transaction code OV05. As usual, you can either choose a three-digit number from the customer namespace along with a meaningful description to define your own condition table or use condition tables provided by standard SAP.

ADDING FIELDS TO THE FIELD CATALOG

If some fields that you want for your condition table do not exist in the field catalog, you can add them using the following steps:

1. Depending on whether you need a header or an item field, append the KOMKG (header) or KOMPG (item) communication structure and add the new field to the respective customer includes, KOMKGZ and KOMPGZ. When you add fields to KOMKGZ and KOMPGZ, the fields automatically get included in the main communication structure, KOMGG.

2. Add these new fields to the field catalog using the activity Maintain Allowed Fields For Listing/Exclusion in the Choose Activity dialog box.

3. Use USEREXIT_MOVE_FIELD_TO_KOMKG (header fields) and USEREXIT_ MOVE_ FIELD_TO_KOMPG (item fields) from "include MV45AFZA" to populate values for the new fields during sales order processing.

Step 2: Set Up the Access Sequence

Once done with the condition table creation/selection, the next step is to define the access sequence. In the Choose Activity dialog box shown in Figure 12.13, choose Maintain Access Sequences For Listing/Exclusion. Alternatively, you can use transaction code OV01. Figures 12.14 and 12.15 show the customization setup for access sequence A001 and B001 available in standard SAP for material listing/exclusion.

FIGURE 12.14 Overview screen for defining the access sequence

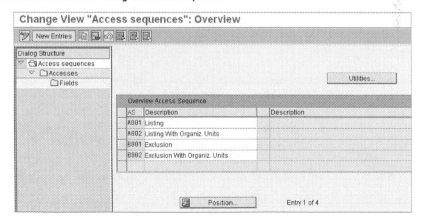

FIGURE 12.15 Assigning condition tables to the access sequence

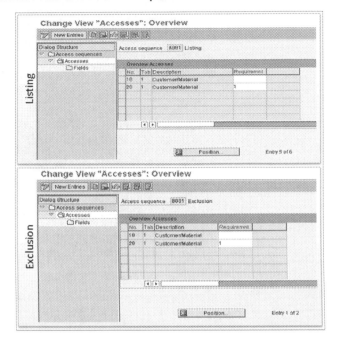

You can use this standard setup if it suffices for your business needs or else create your own access sequence using a four-character identification key along with a meaningful description. (Always use *Y* or *Z* for your own creations.) Set up the condition tables that you defined in previous steps from most specific to least specific, and assign requirements wherever you think necessary. Here, requirement 1 (Figure 12.15) is provided in standard SAP to handle the scenario where you have a different sold-to and payer and both have material listings. The first access (10) is for the scenario where the sold-to and payer are the same. Access 20 is for where the sold-to and payer are different. When you are finished, don't forget to click the Utilities button to generate the access sequence.

Step 3: Set Up the Condition Types

Once done with the access sequence maintenance, the next step is to set up the condition types. In the Choose Activity dialog box shown in Figure 12.13, choose Maintain Listing/Exclusion Types to maintain the condition types for listing and exclusion. Alternatively, you can use transaction code OV02. As usual, you can either use standard SAP condition types if they suffice for your business needs or define your own condition types for material listing and exclusion using a four-character identification key along with a meaningful description. (Here again, always use *Y* or *Z* for your own creations.) Once the condition types are defined, assign the access sequences created in the previous steps to their respective condition types.

Figure 12.16 shows the customization setup that is available in the standard SAP system for condition types A001 and B001. As you can see, listing condition type A001 is assigned to access sequence A001, and exclusion condition type B001 is assigned to access sequence B001. You can also provide a default validity to your listing/exclusion records by selecting from the available values for the Valid From and Valid To fields. For example, you can set up your conditions to be valid from the first day of the year to the end of current year, from the first day of the month to the end of the current month, or even from today's date until December 31, 9999.

FIGURE 12.16 Maintaining listing/exclusion types

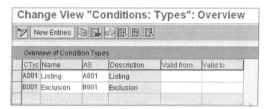

Step 4: Set Up the Determination Procedure

Once done with the listing/exclusion type setup, the next step is to set up the determination procedure. In the Choose Activity dialog box shown in Figure 12.13, choose Procedures For Maintaining Listing/Exclusion to maintain the determination procedure for listing and exclusion. Alternatively, you can use transaction code OV03. Figures 12.17 and 12.18 show the customization screens for the listing/exclusion determination procedure setup. In standard SAP, procedure A00001 is provided for listing, and B00001 is provided for exclusion.

FIGURE 12.17 Maintaining the listing/exclusion procedure

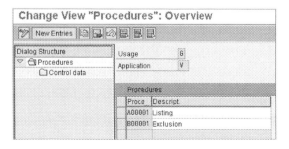

FIGURE 12.18 Assigning the listing/exclusion type to the procedure

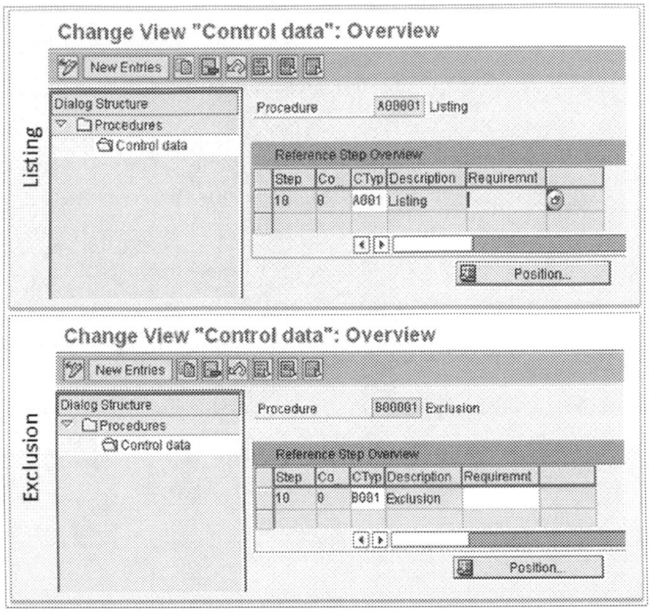

To create your own material listing/exclusion determination procedure, provide a six-character unique identification key starting with *Y* or *Z* along with a description. Assign the condition types you created in previous steps to your procedure, and save your entry.

Step 5: Assign the Procedure to a Sales Document Type

Now you are at the last step for listing/exclusion customization, which is assigning the listing/exclusion procedure to the sales document type. From the Choose Activity dialog box shown in Figure 12.13, choose Activate Listing/Exclusion By Sales Document Type to maintain the assignment. Alternatively, you can use transaction code OV04. Figure 12.19 shows the customization screen for assignment.

FIGURE 12.19 Activating the listing/exclusion by sales document type

SaTy	Sales Doc Type	Pro	Listing	Listing	Exclusion	Exclusion
OR	Standard Order		A00001	Listing	B00001	Exclusion

Unlike in access sequences for other determination procedures, we don't have an exclusion indicator in the access sequence for material listing/exclusion to handle situations where there are multiple condition records. Here, the Pro (procedure) field in Figure 12.19 controls the system reaction when there is more than one listing. We'll cover the impact of various available values in the Pro field with the help of an example.

Say you maintain two separate material listings: at the customer level and at the customer group level. The customization setup contains a material listing access sequence with two accesses: step 10 for the customer and step 20 for the customer group. When you enter an order for a material that is maintained in both the material listings, the access that will apply to your sales order will depend upon what customization you have maintained for the Pro field:

- If the Pro field contains value A, then SAP will use the last listing in the access sequence (here, 20 for the customer group).

- If the Pro field contains value B, then SAP will make sure that at least one listing must apply.

- If the Pro field contains value C, then SAP will apply all listings. (Here, both 10 for customer and 20 for customer group will be applied.)

- If the Pro field value is blank, then SAP will use the first listing in the access sequence (here, 10 for the customer).

Table 12.2 summarizes what we have discussed so far about material listing/exclusion customization.

TABLE 12.2   Material Listing and Exclusion Setup Available in Standard SAP

Determination Procedure	Condition Types/ Access Sequences	Condition Table
A00001: Material Listing	A001/A001	501: Customer Hierarchy/Article
		001: Customer/Material
B00001: Material Exclusion	B001/B001	001: Customer/Material

Handling the Material Listing/Exclusion in Deliveries

When a delivery is created with reference to an order, material listing/exclusion is carried out in the delivery with reference to the underlying sales document. If material listing/exclusion is active for the underlying sales document, you will be able to perform the listing/exclusion for newly added items to the delivery. However, you cannot perform the material listing/exclusion in the delivery document for the items copied over from the sales order to the delivery.

Stand-alone delivery documents (delivery type LO) are not created with reference to a sales order. Therefore, material listing/exclusion functionality in these documents is handled through the Default Order Type field in the delivery type customization (0VLK). In standard SAP, sales order type DL is assigned to delivery type LO. So, if material listing/exclusion is activated for sales document type DL, you will be able to use material listings/exclusions in stand-alone delivery documents too. Similarly, the assignment of a default billing type to an LO delivery type is also controlled by sales order type DL.

Maintaining the Material Listing Master Records

You can maintain material listing/exclusion condition records for a customer by using transaction code VB01 or by following menu path Logistics ➢ Sales And Distribution ➢ Master Data ➢ Products ➢ Listing/Exclusion ➢ Create. When you are at the overview screen, choose condition types A001 for material listing and B001 for material exclusion if you are using the standard SAP setup. If you are not using the standard SAP condition types, use the one you customized for use with material listing/exclusion. Now click the key combination button to call up the key combination record, as shown in Figure 12.20. Choose the key combination for which you want to maintain condition record, and click the ✔ button to call up the detail maintenance screen, as shown in Figure 12.21. To finish, maintain your condition records, and save your entry.

FIGURE 12.20 Creating a material listing, initial screen

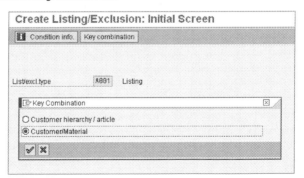

FIGURE 12.21 Creating a material listing, details screen

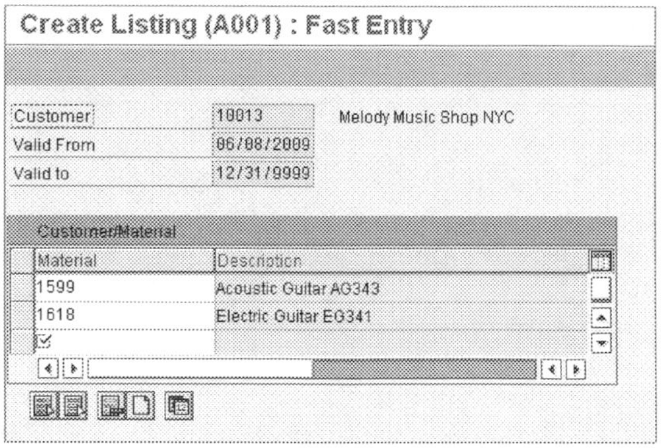

Once condition records for listing/exclusion are maintained for a customer, SAP uses the condition technique to search the suitable record and apply the restrictions as per that record to customer sales and delivery document processing.

Customer–Material Info Records

Parties to a sales transaction (the buyer and the seller) sometimes use different material numbers and descriptions for the same material. A seller may call the material XYZ, whereas the buyer calls it ABC in his books. In SAP, you bridge this gap using a *customer–material info record*. The purpose of a customer–material info record is to maintain the customer-specific number and description of the seller's material in the seller's books so as to avoid any confusion that may arise because of different naming conventions used by the buyer and seller for the same material. Once the record is maintained, you can make an order entry using any of the two material identifiers, that is, the seller's or the buyer's. You can even print the customer-specific material number on the various outputs such as order confirmations and invoices.

Creating the Customer–Material Info Record

You create a customer–material info record using transaction code VD51 or via menu Logistics ➢ Sales And Distribution ➢ Master Data ➢ Agreements ➢ Customer Material Information. Figure 12.22 shows the initial screen for setting up a customer–material info record.

FIGURE 12.22 Customer–material info record, initial screen

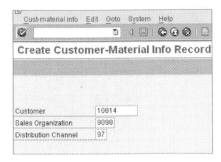

To maintain your record, provide the customer, sales organization, and distribution channel information on this screen, and click ✔. You will see an overview screen like that shown in Figure 12.23.

FIGURE 12.23 Customer–material info record, overview screen

On this screen, enter your material number in the field Material No., and enter the corresponding customer-specific material number in the field Cust. Material to maintain the cross-reference. On this screen you can also maintain the value for the rounding profile (RdPr) and for the unit of measure group (UMGr) to be used with the rounding profile. (A *rounding profile* allows you to round the order proposal quantity to deliverable units.)

NOTE You can maintain text for the customer–material info record by following the menu path Goto ➤ Text. Text for a customer–material info record is customizable. You can perform your own text determination setup for a customer–material info record using transaction code VOTXN. For more details on how to use VOTXN, please refer to the discussion of text determination in Chapter 4, "Partner, Text, and Output Determination."

Apart from facilitating a cross-reference between the two materials, a customer–material info record allows you to maintain default proposals for delivery tolerance and shipping-related data specific to the customer–material info record. As usual, these defaults can be overwritten manually in the sales order. Always remember that the defaults you maintain in customer–material info records (VD51) are applicable only to the particular customer and material combination, whereas the defaults maintained in the customer master record (XD01) are applicable to all the materials ordered by that customer. In scenarios where you have maintained both these defaults, the ones maintained in the customer–material info record takes precedence over any defaults maintained in the customer master record during the order entry.

For example, imagine that you maintain a default delivery plant 9002 in the customer master record and 9001 in the customer–material info for material X and customer Y. Now, when you create a sales order for material X, SAP will pick the default delivery plant as 9001 (using the customer–material info record). For any other material, SAP will pick the default plant as 9002 from the customer master record.

DETERMINATION OF THE DELIVERING PLANT IN THE SALES ORDER

The system searches for the delivering plant for a material in the sales order in the following sequence:

1. It picks the delivering plant from the customer–material info record.

2. If it finds no plant in the customer–material info record in step 1, the system looks for the delivering plant in the shipping view of the customer master and picks it.

3. Finally, if the system fails to find the delivering plant in either of the previous steps, it picks the delivering plant from the sales organization view of the material master.

To maintain the defaults, double-click the cross-referenced entry you maintained on the overview screen (in Figure 12.23, it is the row with material 1619) to reach the item screen shown in Figure 12.24.

FIGURE 12.24 Creating a customer–material info record, item screen (for setting defaults)

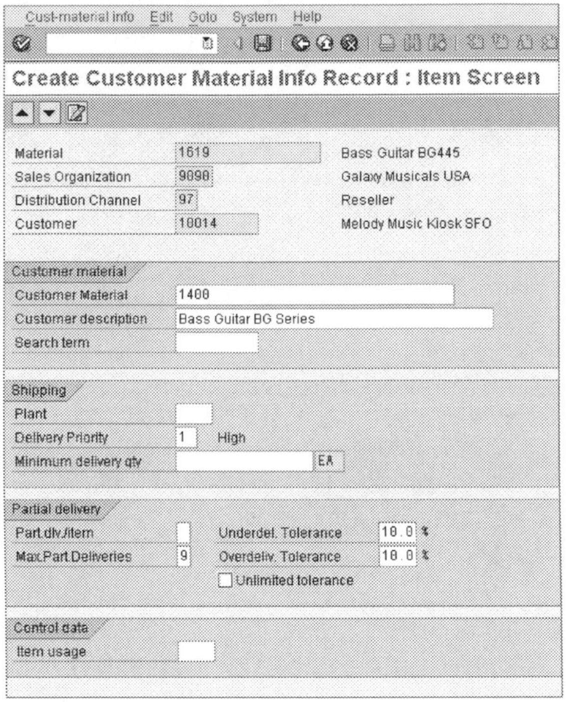

As you can see, this screen allows you to maintain a variety of additional data for your customer–material info record and make the data searchable. Here are the main properties of the four tabs on this screen:

Customer Material   This is where you can set up the customer description for the material. The Search Term field helps you in searching this material in various order-processing screens and work lists.

Shipping   This is where you can set a default shipping plant and delivery priority for this customer–material info record. You can also maintain defaults for a minimum delivery quantity that a customer should purchase for this material.

Partial Delivery   This is where you can set whether the customer allows partial deliveries for this material and if yes, then how many partial deliveries can be made. You can also set the range for the delivery tolerance agreed upon with the customer.

Control Data   There is only one item, Item Usage, on the Control Data tab. This is where you define the item usage for this material, which in turn will help in determining the item category for this material in sales and delivery documents. We discuss item categories in detail in Chapter 7.

Now, maintain the required data on this screen, and save your newly created customer–material information record.

Creating Orders Using the Customer Material Number

The order entry screen in the SAP system contains fields to accept and display customer and material-specific information, that is, a customer-specific material number and a customer-specific description. Once you have maintained the cross-reference between the identifier you used and the one that is used by the customer for the same material using the customer–material info record, you can perform the order entry for that customer using the customer material identifier.

To do order entry using a customer's identifier, call up the create order screen (Figure 12.25), and fill in the required information such as the customer, order quantity, and purchase order number. Now enter the customer material number identifier in the Customer Material Numb field. You will see that SAP will automatically populate the Material and Description fields with the values from the customer–material info record. In our example, when we entered 1400 in the customer material number field, SAP automatically populated the Material and Description fields with the values 1619 and Bass Guitar BG Series, respectively.

FIGURE 12.25 Customer–material info record in action

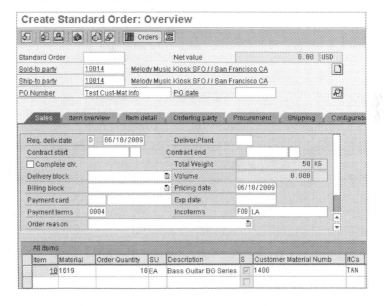

Dependencies Between Material Functionalities

The sequence of events for various material-related functionalities can be defined as follows:

1. Customer–material info records

2. Material determination

3. Material exclusion

4. Material listing

In standard SAP logic, the customer–material info record is applied first to the sales order. This is followed by the material determination. At the end, restrictions as per material listing/exclusion record are applied. Let's imagine a situation where you have maintained material determination for material 1619 to replace it with material 1599 and have also maintained a customer–material info record for 1619 as 1400. Now, when you create a sales order and enter material number 1400 in the order, the SAP system will first apply the customer–material info record to get to the seller's material number, that is, 1619. Next it will apply the material determination record on 1619, thus giving an end result of an order entry maintained for material 1599. If you also have maintained the material exclusion record that restricts the sale of material 1599 to this customer, this record kicks in next and sends a message telling the user that material 1599 is restricted for sale to the customer. The SAP system always applies material exclusion prior to the material listing.

Item Proposal

Item Proposal (Figure 12.26) is a tool that helps you to perform the order entry process more efficiently by allowing you to copy over the items into your order from a customer-specific or generic item proposal list. In this process, you first maintain as a proposal document a list of frequently ordered materials, along with the quantities in which the material is ordered or can be ordered by the customer. Next, when you need to create an order for such materials, you just call the item proposal screen from within the sales order creation screen and copy over the required materials with or without quantities to the customer order. This definitely saves a lot of the valuable time and effort that goes into searching for the material when you create the order.

FIGURE 12.26 Process example, item proposal

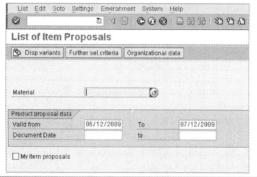

SAP provides a set of four transaction codes to maintain an item proposal in the ERP software. You can use transaction code VA51 to create, VA52 to change, and VA53 to display an item proposal. Transaction code VA55 allows you to generate the list of existing item proposal records with the selection based on material number, validity dates, or records created by you. You can further filter your report output by using the Organizational Data and Created By options available on the selection screen in the VA55 report. Figure 12.27 shows the selection screen and report outputs for the VA55 report.

FIGURE 12.27 List Of Item Proposals by material, selection screen, and report output

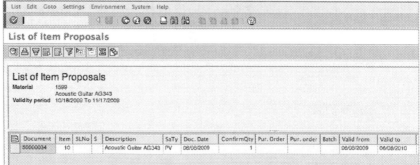

You can check the change history for an item proposal using menu path Environment ➤ Changes while you are in a change or display transaction (VA52 or VA53). Figure 12.28 shows the overview screen for the item proposal change log and the log of all the changes that were made in the item proposal document.

FIGURE 12.28 Item proposal change log, selection screen, and item proposal change log

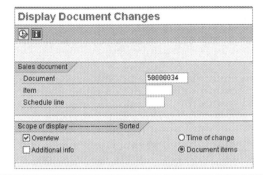

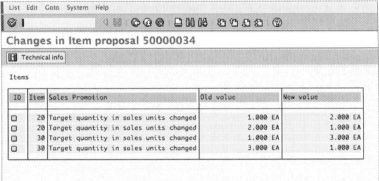

Creating an Item Proposal Record

You create an item proposal record by using transaction code VA51 or by following menu path Logistics ➤ Sales And Distribution ➤ Master Data ➤ Products ➤ Item Proposal ➤ Create. Figure 12.29 shows the initial overview screen for setting up an item proposal record.

Once you are at this screen, provide the values for the document type and sales area fields, and click ✔ to reach to the detail maintenance screen shown in Figure 12.30.

FIGURE 12.29 Customer item proposal, overview screen

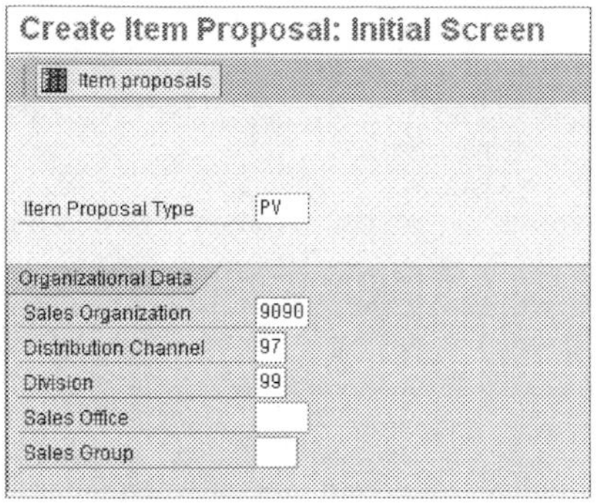

FIGURE 12.30 Customer–material info record, detail screen

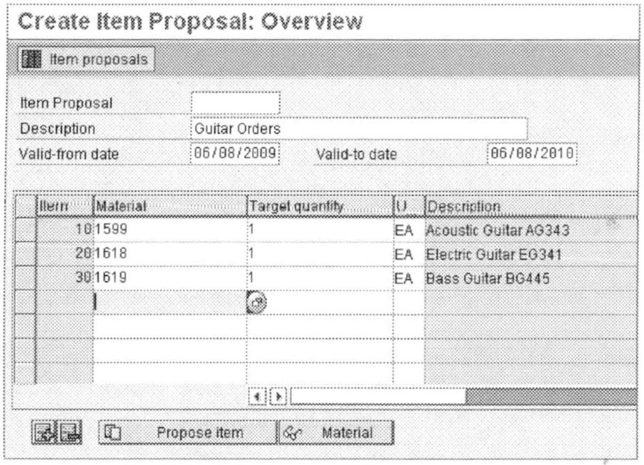

On this screen, provide a meaningful description and validity dates for your proposal record, and maintain all the materials along with the default quantity that you want to set up in a single proposal document. Unlike other sales documents, an item proposal maintenance screen does not contain a Copy With Reference button to allow item proposal creation by copying from an existing item proposal. But, you can still propose items from an existing item proposal using the Propose Item button  .

Now use the menu path Edit ➢ Incompletion Log to check the completeness of your item proposal record, and save your entry.

Seeing Item Proposals in Action

While you are at the order entry screen, you can propose items into a sales order by using the Propose Item button 🗋 Propose item , using the hotkey Ctrl+F11, or following the menu path Edit ➢ Additional Functions ➢ Propose Items. After you do one of these things, you will be presented with a Propose Items dialog box, as shown in Figure 12.31. If you know the item proposal number, you can enter it in the Sales Document field. Otherwise, you can search for your item proposal by triggering an F4 search on the Sales Document field. As you can see in Figure 12.31, this dialog box provides you with various options to copy the material. You can copy the material with or without quantity information and can choose materials to be copied using the Selection List button. When you make the desired selection, SAP copies over the materials to the customer order, as per the selection chosen.

FIGURE 12.31 Item proposal in a sales document

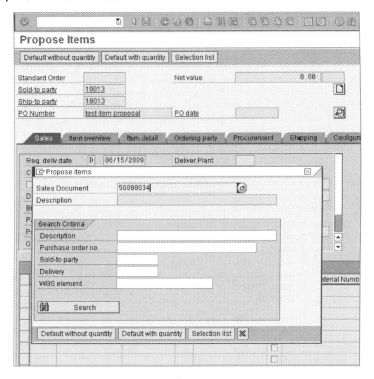

Seeing Customer-Specific Item Proposals in Action

Unlike other sales document types, you don't need a partner determination setup for an item proposal. You can set up the link between a partner and an item proposal by maintaining the item proposal record number in the customer master record. An item proposal assigned in this way is also known as a *customer-specific item proposal*. The assignment works as shown in Figure 12.32.

FIGURE 12.32 Item proposal maintenance in customer master

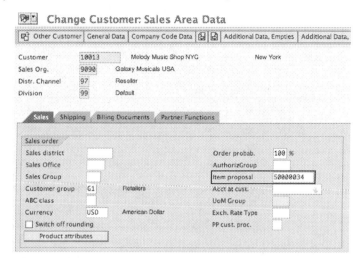

This is really useful in situations where your customer places recurring orders for particular products. You can simply create an item proposal and assign it to a customer master record, and SAP will automatically propose and copy over the materials from this assigned item proposal into the new customer orders, saving you the time and effort required when searching the material every time you create orders for such customer.

NOTE   Always remember that an item proposal is just a frequently used material listing that helps in the order entry process. No basic functions from SAP SD application are triggered or determined from within or for an item proposal document. When you create an order using Item Proposal, first the items are copied to the order document, and then all the other functions such as availability check, BOM explosions, material determinations, and material listing/exclusions are triggered in their logical sequence.

Customizing an Item Proposal

Unlike the other sales document customizations that we studied in Chapter 7, you don't need to configure the item category, schedule line category, or copy controls for an item proposal. Therefore, customizing an item proposal consists of only two steps:

Step 1: Customize the document type for item proposals   To do this, use transaction code VOV8 or follow menu path IMG ➤ Sales And Distribution ➤ Sales ➤ Sales Documents ➤ Sales Document Header ➤ Define Sales Document Types.

Step 2: Define number ranges to be used with item proposals   To do this, use transaction code VN01 or follow menu path IMG ➤ Sales And Distribution ➤ Sales ➤ Sales Documents ➤ Sales Document Header ➤ Define Number Ranges For Sales Documents.

Since we have already covered sales document customization at length in Chapter 7, we will skip that topic here. However, for your convenience, we are providing a configuration screenshot (Figure 12.33) demonstrating the setup for item proposal document type PV. PV is the item proposal document type available out of the box in the standard SAP system. If you want to create your own item proposal type while customizing, make sure to create it as a copy from PV and prefix it with a *Y* or *Z* to differentiate it from standard SAP document types. Once it's copied, make the necessary changes in your newly created document type as per your business requirements.

NOTE   When configuring item proposals, you only need to configure an incompletion procedure at the sales document header level. In the standard SAP ERP setup, incompletion procedure 16 is available for item proposals. It is always advisable to analyze the settings for existing setup provided by SAP in incompletion procedure 16 before you create your own customized version. For more details on how to perform customization on an incompletion procedure, please refer to the discussion of incompletion procedures in Chapter 7.

FIGURE 12.33 Item proposal customization screen

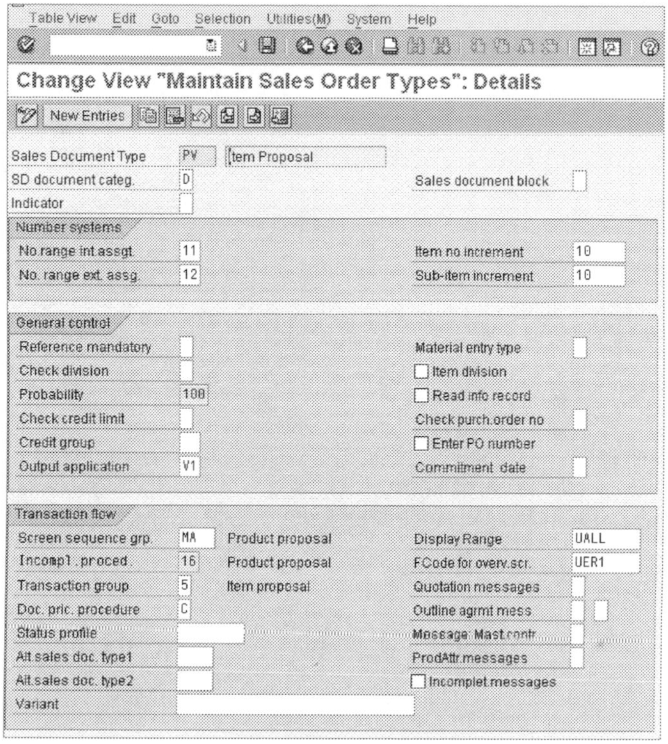

Summary

In this chapter, we covered the various material/product-related functionalities that are available in SAP SD. We also talked about their use and customization setup and discussed their relationship to each other and to sales and delivery document processing. In Chapter 13, "Serial Numbers and Batch Management," we will cover two other important material functionalities that can help you track individual units of materials.

Serial Numbers and Batch Management

T he serial number and batch management functions have their presence in almost all parts of the logistics chain in SAP. Although the former provides the ability to trace and track materials at an individual unit level, the latter provides the same at the batch level. In this chapter, we will cover the setup and use of the serial numbers and batch management functionality that is provided in the SAP ERP system.

Serial Numbers

A *serial number* is a unique number allocated to an individual piece of a product that helps organizations identify, record, and track that individual piece throughout its life cycle. Starting from when the item was produced, you can record and track many types of information for an individual serialized unit using serial number management, including the following:

- ▶ Whether it is under blocked or unrestricted inventory status

- ▶ Which plant it is available in

- ▶ Whether it is at your warehouse or at a customer's location

- ▶ When and to whom it was sold

- ▶ What its warranty coverage is

- ▶ Whether it came back for repairs and how many times it has undergone repairs

- ▶ Whether it came back into the warehouse as a return

- ▶ Whether it was it resold after being refurbished

- ▶ Whether the item was installed at a customer site or it was kept dismantled

In the SAP system, serial number management is part of logistics and is available across applications. You can use it in a production application to assign serial numbers during production and refurbished orders processing. In a quality management application, it allows serial number assignment during quality inspection processing. Using serial numbers in an inventory management application allows you to capture serial numbers during various inventory transactions resulting from goods receipts, goods issues, stock transfers, stock transport orders, and physical inventory processing, and thus it provides inventory control at an individual unit level. When used in a plant maintenance and customer service application, a serial number not only provides you with control over the products sold but also lets you identify, record, and track your own assets, including their maintenance records. In a sales and services application, you can assign serial numbers to the individual units that are delivered to the customers via a delivery document. You can also capture serial numbers in the return delivery document.

A serialized product provides better controls during after-sales support. Not only can you easily track and validate warranty coverage on a serialized unit, but a serialized unit also helps detect fraud in RMA processing and can help determine whether the unit reported in RMA is actually a counterfeit or stolen unit. When a serialized unit is registered, it creates a direct relationship between the consumer and the manufacturer/service provider, thus providing a platform to organizations for strengthening the relationship with their customers and improving brand presence. Product recalls are easier when the material is serialized and registered.

In the SAP system, the serial numbers can be generated internally by the system or can be provided externally by the user. The field length is a maximum of 18 characters. The field can store numeric as well as alphanumeric serial numbers.

Controlling Serial Number Management

In SAP ERP, the serialization of products is controlled by the serial number profile assigned to the product's material master record in the Sales: General/Plant Data view, as shown in Figure 13.1.

FIGURE 13.1 Assigning a serial number profile to the material master record

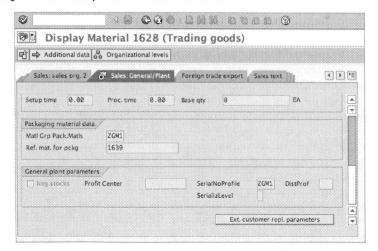

You can assign a serial number at various stages of a business process. You can assign serial numbers when the goods are produced/procured, when the goods are delivered to the customer, during the handling unit management (HUM), and so on. However, whether the serialization can happen in a particular business transaction like production, delivery, HUM, and so on, depends solely on the serial number profile settings. The serial profile, along with the serialization procedures assigned to it, controls the creation of serial master records and the assignment of serialized units while carrying out business transactions, such as delivery processing.

A serialization procedure controls whether the serial number can be assigned in a particular business transaction. You can switch on/off the use of the serial number in a particular business transaction using serialization procedures. For example, if you don't want to use a serial number in order, don't assign the SDAU procedure to the serial number profile.

Standard SAP comes equipped with 10 serialization procedures, as explained in detail in Table 13.1.

TABLE 13.1 Serialization Procedures

Serialization Procedure	Description and Use
HUSL	Allow serial numbers maintenance during handling unit management.
MMSL	Allow serial numbers maintenance during inventory management, i.e., goods receipt, goods issue, stock transfers, stock transport orders, and physical inventory.
PPAU	Allow serial numbers maintenance during production and refurbished orders processing.
PPRL	Allow serial numbers maintenance when production and refurbished orders are released.
QMSL	Allow serial numbers assignment during the quality inspection on the serialized material in the quality management application of the SAP ERP system.
SDAU	Allow serial numbers assignment in sales documents such as sales orders, inquiries, and quotations.
SDLS	Allow serial numbers assignment during delivery processing.
SDCC	Allow serial numbers assignment when performing a completeness check for deliveries.
SDRE	Allow serial numbers assignment during return delivery processing. Common uses are sales returns from the customer, returns for repairs, material recalls, replacements, and so on.
SDCR	Allow serial numbers assignment when performing a completeness check in return deliveries.

NOTE In the SAP system, you are not allowed to create your own serialization procedures.

Customizing Serial Number Management

Customizing serial number management in the SAP system involves setting up a serial profile and assigning the required serial number procedures to the serial profile. You then assign the serial profile to the material master record of the material that you want to manage using serial number management.

Deciding the Scope of Customization

Before we start discussing customization, we'll answer a few questions that can help you decide the basic scope of customization that you need:

▶ **What specific areas of business do you want to implement serial number management for?** Is it only for selling the serialized unit, or does it have a bigger scope? For example, if you want to be able to sell the serialized units, then you should also be maintaining the serialized stock; similarly, if you want to provide post-sales service for the serialized product, you should be able to take the serialized returns and validate them against the serialized sales too. The answer to this question will help you decide the serialization procedures that you need to assign to your serial profile in customizing.

▶ **What materials need serialization?** Do you want all finished goods and parts to be serialized or only specific ones? The answer to this question will help you decide how many serial profiles you need and what materials they should be assigned to.

▶ **How are the serial numbers to be assigned to a serialized unit?** If you use an external system to control the assignment of serial numbers to the units, you would most likely require external number range setup in the SAP system.

▶ **Do you need special user statuses to track the whereabouts of the serialized unit?** For example, after the unit is shipped to the customer (system status ECUS), is it installed, pending for installation, or dismantled? Here, installed, pending for installation, and dismantled are the user-defined statuses, and ECUS (unit at the customer's place) is a system-provided status.

▶ **What partners need to be captured?** For instance, do you want to capture only the sold-to party partner in the serial number master record, or do the business requirements also call for capturing the retail partner who sold the serialized unit to the end customer or the authorized service partner who will service the serialized unit for that region?

To illustrate these concepts, let's look at the customization scope analysis for Galaxy Musical Instruments.

CASE STUDY—GALAXY MUSICAL INSTRUMENTS: SCOPE ANALYSIS

Galaxy decided to manufacture its own brand of acoustic guitar. So that it can track the guitar throughout the logistics cycle, the company decided to implement serial numbers and batch management for this new product. So, Galaxy created the finished goods material master record for the new product (model EX43) with material number 1628, which is serialized and relevant for batch management.

A non-SAP system controls the serial number assignment for Galaxy during the production process, and therefore the serial numbers in SAP are maintained as external numbers. The scope of serial number management implementation for Galaxy involves the ability to allocate serial numbers to the units when the stock is received in the plant, the ability to capture serial number information on the sales and delivery document, and the ability to capture serial numbers when the goods are returned by the customer.

Maintaining a Serial Profile

The transaction code is OIS2, and the menu path is IMG ≻ Sales And Distribution ≻ Basic Functions ≻ Serial Numbers ≻ Determine Serial Number Profiles.

Figure 13.2 represents the customization screen showing serial number profile ZGM1 configured for Galaxy Musical Instruments. Profiles 0001 to 0003 on the screen are standard profiles that come out of box with the SAP system.

As always, define your own serial profile with the prefix Z, taking the copy from the existing profile that matches your business requirement closely. You can give an identification key (four characters or less) along with a description for your serial profile generation.

FIGURE 13.2 Serial number profile customization screen

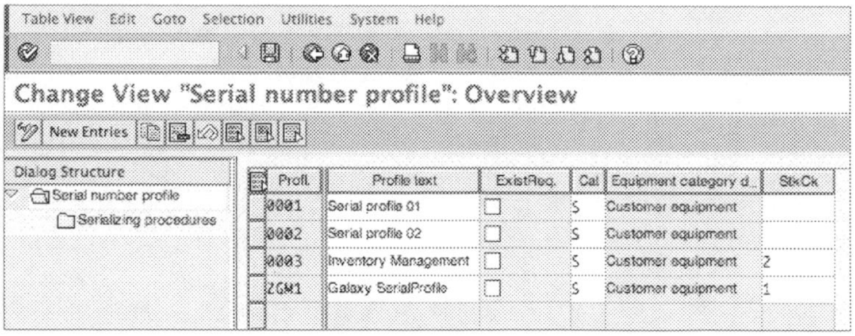

Let's take a look at the fields and check boxes on this screen:

Profl./Profile Text   The profile is displayed in the field Profl., and the description is displayed in the next field, Profile Text.

ExistReq.   The check box for ExistReq., when selected, ensures that the serial number master record for the individual unit should exist before it can be used in the delivery or in any other business transaction. With this setting, it won't be possible for the business transaction to automatically create the serial number master record. You will have to create serial number master record manually using maintenance transactions (IQ*) before you can use the serial number in delivery or any other transaction.

Category   The Category field controls the link between the serial number profile and the equipment category.

StkCk   This field controls whether the system should perform a stock check when the serial number is assigned and controls whether to throw a warning or error if a stock discrepancy is found. Choose 1 to perform a stock check with a warning for stock discrepancies, choose 2 to perform a stock check with an error for stock differences, and leave the field blank to not perform the stock check at all.

Assigning the Serialization Procedures

In this step, you assign various serialization procedures to your serial profile. Figure 13.3 shows various serialization procedures assigned to serial profile ZGM1.

FIGURE 13.3 Assigning serialization procedures to a serial number profile

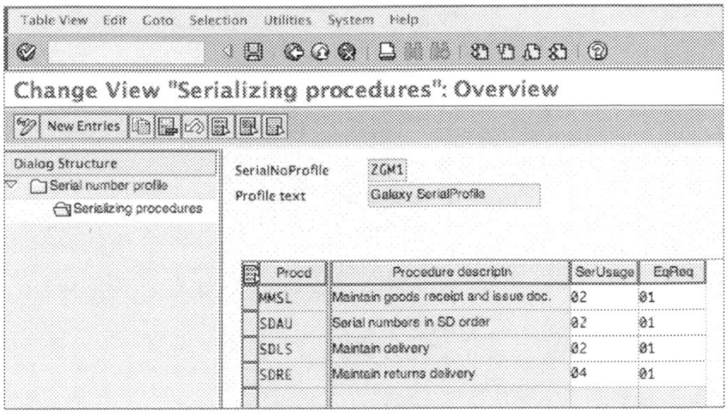

Select all the required serialization procedures that are applicable as per your business requirement. Depending upon whether you want a serial number to be optional, mandatory, or automatic, you can make the required selection in the SerUsage field. The EqReq field allows you to maintain a serial master record with or without equipment. When you choose 01 in this field, the creation of equipment master record for each serial number master record is optional, and when you choose 02, the equipment record creation is mandatory.

Maintaining Serial Numbers Master Record

In the SAP system, a unique combination of material number and serial number constitutes a *serial number master record*. You maintain a master record for each serialized unit in the SAP system. You can set up the serial number master record by using transaction code IQ01 or by following the SAP Easy Access Menu Path: Logistics ➤ Sales and Distribution ➤ Master Data ➤ Products ➤ Serial Numbers. You can also use transaction IQ02 for changing serial number master record, IQ03 for displaying serial number master record, IQ04 for creating serial numbers via list entry, IQ08 for making mass changes, and IQ09 for displaying work lists for serial numbers. Figure 13.4 represents the serial number master maintenance screen.

Here the material number and serial number together define the unique key for the serial number master record.

You can maintain stock-related information for the serialized unit under the Stock Information section. You can then use this information to track the serialized unit in the stock. The stock information can be autopopulated by the SAP system if the serial numbers are generated while loading the stock into the SAP system. In that case, you will find fields for the stock type, plant, storage location, and batch already filled in with the relevant data. You can also maintain the stock batch and master batch–level information for a serialized unit. In fact, you can even maintain the serialized unit warranty information and back-to-back warranty information of the vendor using the fields available on the Warranty tab.

FIGURE 13.4 Serial number master maintenance screen

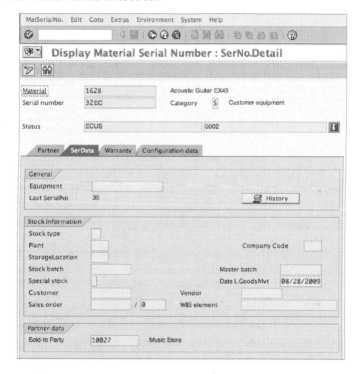

For each serial number master record, you can maintain the current status of the serial number. When you create the record for the first time, it is under either AVLB status or ESTO status. When the goods are sold, the status changes to ECUS, representing that the goods are at the customer's location now. At the same time, SAP captures the customer details and the details of any other required partners that you want to maintain for the serialized unit. These details are shown on the Partner Data tab and in the Sold-To Party field on the SerData tab, as shown in Figure 13.4.

You can also maintain further qualifier statuses called *user statuses*, if they are set up in customizing.

You can maintain and change the serial number status manually using the menu path Edit ➤ Special Serial No. Functions ➤ Manual Transaction. You can also change the serial number assignment to the material or change the material number assignment to the serial number by using the menu path Edit ➤ Special Serial No. Functions ➤ Change Serial No. and the menu path Edit ➤ Special Serial No. Functions ➤ Change Material No., respectively.

Using the Extras ➤ Serial Number History menu path, you can get the complete history for the serialized unit including when it was procured, when it was sold, when it was returned, when the inventory was transferred, when it was repaired, and so on, along with the document numbers, provided the serial number profile allows the serial numbers assignment in these business transactions and provided the serial number was captured while carrying out the business transaction.

NOTE Always remember that a serial number cannot be deleted from the system once created. You can only mark it for deletion and can later archive it.

Assigning Serial Numbers to Deliveries

Once the master record for the serialized unit is ready, you can select the serialized unit during delivery processing and other allowed business transactions. You can also create a new serial number master record at this time by clicking the Create Serial Number button to generate and assign a new serial number to the delivered unit, provided it is allowed in customizing. Figure 13.5 shows an example of the assignment of serial numbers during outbound delivery processing. To reach this serial number assignment screen, you have to select the line item in delivery that requires the serial number assignment and then follow the menu path Extras ➤ Serial Numbers. If you set up the Serial Usage field as obligatory while customizing the serial number profile, the SAP system will automatically bring up the serial number screen for maintenance because without it the document will be incomplete.

FIGURE 13.5 Assigning serial numbers during delivery processing

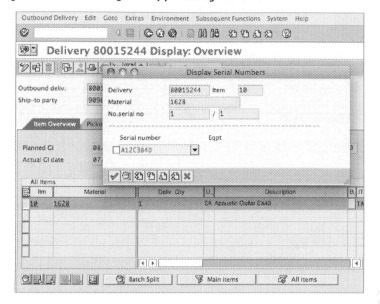

Batch Management

Batch management refers to managing, tracking, and processing products produced/procured in batches. A *batch* can be defined as a partial quantity or subset of a material quantity procured/produced that differs from other subsets of the same material based on certain distinguishing characteristics or properties. For instance, during a first process run, say 1,200 gallons of milk are processed and packed into 1-gallon milk bottles (sellable units) with an expected shelf life of 10 days. During the second process run, 1,500 gallons of milk are processed and packed into milk bottles with an expected shelf life of 12 days. Thus, the material stock record for milk has two distinctive batches (based on when it was produced and the shelf life/expiry date) with 1,200 and 1,500 stock quantities, respectively.

Batches are used by a lot of industries. For some industries, such as industries manufacturing food, pharmaceuticals, and medical devices, batch management is a legal requirement governed by the regulatory Good Manufacturing Practice (GMP) Act. For other industries, batch management is more of an internal business requirement to track products at the batch level.

Batch management functionality in the SAP system deals with managing and processing of batches across the logistics component. You can create batches when the goods are produced, assembled, or procured. Each batch is identifiable based on the unique batch number, which can be externally assigned by the user or can be internally assigned by system. Each batch number corresponds to a batch master record that contains all the specifications and attributes of a batch. You can use these attributes as a selection parameter to perform automatic batch determination during the processing of a sales cycle.

You can perform quality inspection on the batch stock and can put the batch under restricted or unrestricted use. During outbound delivery processing to the customer and transport orders in warehousing, you can run batch determination to select the relevant batches. You can also use the SAP batch management for defect tracking and product recall management. Using Batch Info Cockpit report, you can even perform quite an exhaustive analysis on the batches.

Understanding Batch Levels

In the SAP system, you can define batches at three levels: the client level, the material level, and the material/plant level:

Client level   Batch maintenance at the client level makes a batch unique throughout the client. This means that the batch number, once assigned to a material, cannot be reassigned to another material within the same client. Here, the batch master record is maintained for a combination of the material number and the batch number, and the batch class type used is 023.

Material level   Batch maintenance at the material level makes a batch unique for a material: you can assign the same batch number to more than one material within a client, with batch specifications varying from one material to another but with the same specifications across all plants for the same material. When batch maintenance is at this level, all material movement between plants for one material will involve only one batch. Here, the batch master record is maintained for a combination of the material number and the batch number, and the batch class type used is 023.

Material/plant level   Batch maintenance at the material/plant level makes the batch assignment very flexible and therefore is widely used. It is also the default setting for batch-level maintenance available in the standard SAP system. Here, the batch number is unique for a combination of a material and a plant. You have the flexibility to assign the batch number again and again for a different material with different specifications at each plant level. You can even transfer stocks from one plant to another plant between batches with the same number and different specifications. In such cases, the SAP system automatically assumes the specifications of the destination batch. Here the batch master record is maintained for a combination of material number, plant, and batch number, and the batch class type used is 022.

Figure 13.6 represents the three levels we just discussed.

FIGURE 13.6 Batch levels

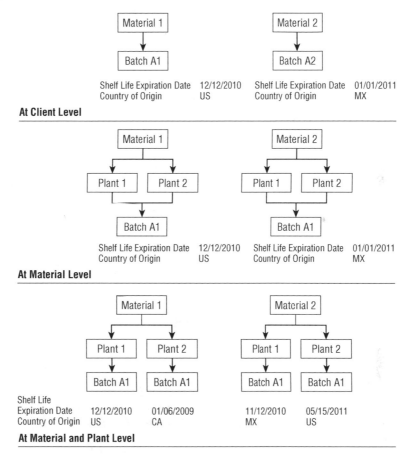

In SAP, if you started using batch management at a particular batch level and you need to switch to another batch level, you can easily switch as long as you are switching to a higher level in the batch-level hierarchy; in other words, you can switch from a material/plant level to a material level, from a material/plant level to a client level, and from a material level to a client level. Switching to a subordinate level is, however, allowed only between the client level to a material level; that is, you cannot switch from a material level to a material/plant level or from a client level to a material/plant level, but you can switch from a client level to a material level.

Maintaining Batch Master Records

Working with batches involves setting up the batch masters, loading stock to batches, and determining the relevant batch during sales and distribution processing. A batch master record holds batch-specific information for a material. You can either create the batch master records manually prior to loading stock using the maintenance transactions provided by the SAP system or leave it up to the inventory load transaction to automatically create the batch master record while loading stock. You can only create a batch record for a material if the batch management is activated with the required batch level and the material is batch relevant. While activating batch management is part of the customization setting, marking material as batch relevant is a master data setting that you can set by selecting the Batch Management check box available in the Sales: General/Plant view of the material master record for the material. Remember that you cannot remove the batch relevancy indicator from a material that already contains the batch stock for the current or previous period. In such scenarios, you need to first clear the batch stock and then proceed with removing the batch relevancy indicator from the material master.

You can create a batch master record by using the transaction code MSC1N or by following the Easy Access menu path SAP Menu ➢ Logistics ➢ Central Functions ➢ Batch Management ➢ Batch.

The Batch Master Record Creation Screen

A batch is created for a material, and therefore the structure of a batch object consists of a material number, a batch number, and a plant. Whenever you create a batch master record, you enter a material number and a batch number combination as a unique key. Plant entry is optional and is required to be maintained if you have activated the batch at the material/plant level.

Figure 13.7 represents the batch master record creation screen and the Basic Data 1 tab. The screen is divided into two parts. The upper part of the screen shows the unique composite key that represents the batch master record. Here, in Figure 13.7, the batch master record is unique for each unique combination of material number and batch number (batch management at the material level). You can see a Plant entry on the screen because we maintained the optional Plant field while setting up the batch master record—just to give you a visual picture of all three fields from the batch structure.

FIGURE 13.7 Basic Data 1 screen for creating a batch master record

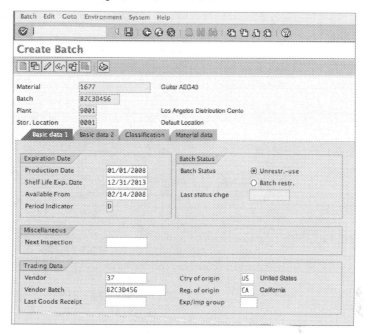

The lower part of the screen consists of various fields and tabs where you store the attributes of the batch record. Let's look at these fields in more detail:

Expiration Date   This is where you can maintain the date when the batch was produced (Production Date), when the shelf life of the batch will expire (Shelf Life Expiration Date), and when the batch will be freely available for sale (Available From). If the batch is for refurbished units, you can also use the Production Date field to represent the final date that is the last stage in the refurbishing process and marks the product good for resale. This may be the refurbished date, testing date, or last inspection date.

Miscellaneous   This is where you maintain the date on which the next inspection of the shelf stock from the batch will be due.

Batch Status   The Batch Status field allows you to maintain the status of the batch master record. You can set the status to restricted use or unrestricted use. You can also create your own user-defined statuses using the classification system to further classify the batches as damaged, blocked, require refurbishing, inspection pending, and so on. When a batch status changes from restricted to unrestricted, or vice versa, the SAP system automatically posts an internal transfer-posting document to transfer the underlying stock from restricted to unrestricted or from unrestricted to restricted stock. This material document is posted for all the storage locations where stock for this batch exists. Even for inventory movement for a batch-managed stock, the SAP system decides whether to post to restricted or unrestricted stock based on whether the batch status is restricted or unrestricted.

TIP You can use batch status as one of the search parameters to include/exclude a particular batch while carrying out the batch determination in a sales transaction.

Trading Data A batch material can be produced internally or procured from a vendor. The Trading Data part of the maintenance screen allows you to capture the vendor details when a batch was externally procured. This helps you track the source of the batch along with important information about the source, such as the vendor number, vendor batch, last goods receipt date, country of origin for the batch, region of origin, and export/import group.

The Basic Data 2 tab on the maintenance screen (Figure 13.8) allows you to capture any text or date information related to the unrestricted use of the batch. This screen also captures the administrative details about who created or changed the batch master record.

FIGURE 13.8 Basic Data 2 screen for creating a batch master record

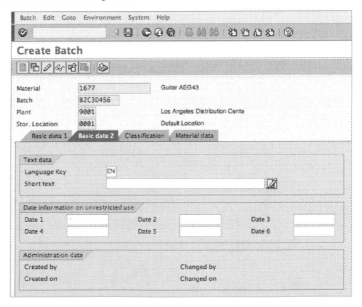

You can use batch management with and without classification. Using the Classification tab in batch management (Figure 13.9) allows you to maintain additional characteristics in the batch master records that can be used later as the search criteria for determining the relevant batch while processing deliveries and other batch-relevant business transactions. For example, if your customer only wants goods that are produced in the United States, you can maintain the country of origin (COO) as US on the Classification tab of the batch master record. You then maintain the customer requirement for COO as US in the batch determination condition records. During automatic batch determination, SAP treats the COO information maintained in the batch determination condition record as the selection parameter, and searches the relevant batch with COO set to US for delivering goods to the customer.

FIGURE 13.9 Classification screen for creating a batch master record transaction

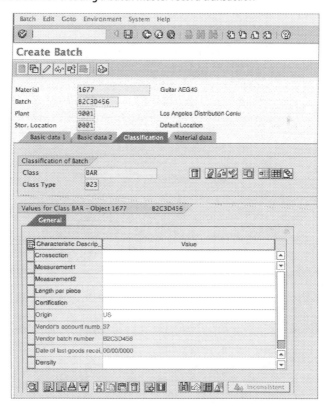

TIP   While creating a batch master using MSC1N, if you don't have the complete data to maintain the classifications, you can put the classification under incomplete status using the ✅ button and can later maintain the classification data using transaction code MSC2N (Batch Master Record Change).

Customizing Batch Management

In the following section, we will discuss the customization settings for batch management and automatic batch determination in SAP SD. We will then discuss the batch determination condition master record maintenance and will show batch determination in action using a sales order example.

Preliminary Setup and Activation

Setting up batch definition is a prerequisite for using batch management in the SAP system. By *setting up batch definition*, we mean setting up the batch level and activating batch management in the SAP system. You can customize the batch definition by using transaction code OMCT or by following menu path IMG ➢ Logistics General ➢ Batch Management ➢ Specify Batch Level And Activate Status Management.

Figure 13.10 represents the Batch Definition overview screen. The three settings of greatest interest on this screen are Batch Level, Batch Status Management, and Initial Status Of A New Batch. The setting for Plants With Batch Status Management is optional. Use it if you want to activate the batch status management at the plant level. You can also reach the customization screens for these three customization options using direct transactions—OMCE for setting up batch levels, OMCS for managing batch status, and OMAB for setting up the initial status for a new batch.

Selecting the relevant option in Figure 13.11 allows you to activate batch management at the required level. Activating batch status management as per Figure 13.12 allows you to maintain the batch status as restricted or unrestricted in the batch master record. The settings in Figure 13.13 allow you to set the default initial status for a new batch. The status is customized based on the material type. If the Initial Status check box is selected, the batch's initial status is defaulted to restricted, and when it is not selected, the batch's initial status is defaulted to unrestricted.

FIGURE 13.10   Batch definition overview screen

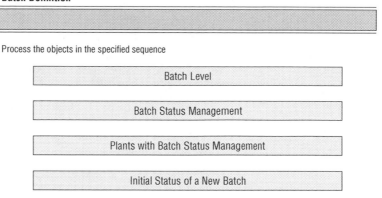

FIGURE 13.11   Defining the batch level

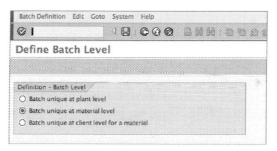

FIGURE 13.12   Defining the batch status management

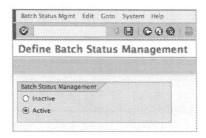

FIGURE 13.13 Setting up the initial status for a new batch

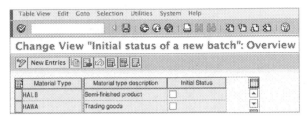

Batch Number Ranges

You can have batch numbers generated internally by the SAP system or have the user provide them externally. In the standard SAP system, number range 01 with starting number 0000000001 and ending number 9999999999 is provided to internally assign the batch numbers. The number range object is BATCH_CLT.

The customization of the internal number range involves two steps. In the first step, you need to activate the internal batch number range assignment using transaction code OMCZ, and in the second step you need to set up the actual internal numbers range using transaction code OMAD. Figure 13.14 and Figure 13.15 show the customization screen for these two steps. You can also use user exits EXIT_SAPLV01Z_001 and EXIT_SAPLV01Z_002 to assign your own batch number range parameters.

For an external number range, the SAP system does not provide any visible number range in the object BATCH_CLT, but internal number range 02 is reserved for external number assignments. You could use user exit EXIT_SAPLV01Z_003 to define your own number range parameters for external number assignment for batches.

FIGURE 13.14 Activating the internal number range

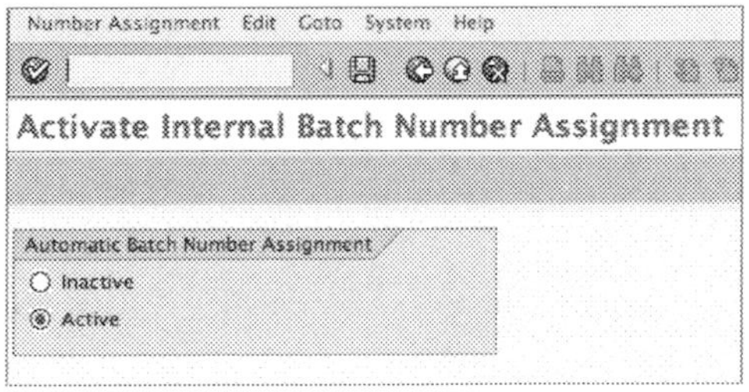

FIGURE 13.15 Setting up the internal number range

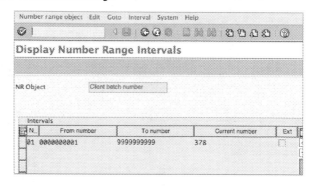

Batch Determination

Like other basic functions in the SAP SD application, batch determination uses the condition technique, and the steps for determination are very similar. Let's take a quick look at these steps:

1. Setting up a condition table

2. Setting up an access sequence

3. Defining strategy types

4. Creating a batch determination procedure

5. Setting up a batch determination rule

6. Activating automatic batch determination in SD

Setting Up a Condition Table

Here you define the condition table that will store the condition records for your batch determination. You can choose from the ones that are available in the standard SAP system, or you can create your own in the customer namespace (that is, 500 and greater). The transaction code is V/C7, and the menu path is IMG ➢ Logistics – General ➢ Batch Management ➢ Batch Determination And Batch Check ➢ Condition Tables ➢ Define Sales And Distribution Condition Tables. Figure 13.16 shows the customization screen for defining the batch condition table.

FIGURE 13.16 Setting up the batch condition table

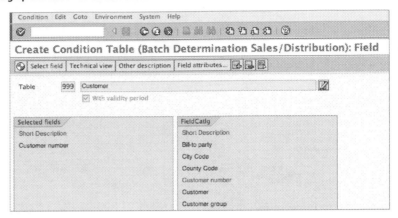

ADDING NEW FIELDS TO THE FIELD CATALOG

Adding new fields to the field catalog involves three steps: adding the fields to the header and item structures, adding the fields to the field catalog, and populating the fields. Let's look at these steps in order:

Step 1: Add new fields to the header and item structures.   Add new fields to header structure KOMKH using include KOMKDZ and to item structure KOMPH using include KOMPDZ. Once added to these structures, the fields will automatically get added to the KOMGH structure.

Step 2: Add the fields to the field catalog.   Once the new fields are added to the structure, use transaction V/C6 to add them to the field catalog. Remember that you will not be able to see the fields on the selection screen for V/C6 unless they are added to the structures as per the first step. Now you can use these newly added fields in your condition table.

Step 3: Populate the fields during order/delivery processing.   Once fields are added to the structure and field catalog and used in the condition table, the next step is to populate the values into these newly added fields. If you added fields to the header structure KOMKH, use USEREXIT_MOVE_FIELD_TO_KOMKH from include MV45AFZB for populating the values into the newly added fields. For populating the values into the newly added fields to item structure KOMPH, use USEREXIT_MOVE_FIELD_TO_KOMPH.

Setting Up an Access Sequence

Here you arrange the condition tables in the sequence in which you want them to be accessed by the SAP system when batch determination is carried out. Again, you can use the ones available in the standard SAP system or define your own. To define your own, use a four-character identification key starting with the prefix Z and add a meaningful description. Do not forget to generate your access sequence once you're done. The transaction code is V/C2, and the menu path is IMG ➤ Logistics General ➤ Batch Management ➤ Batch Determination And Batch Check ➤ Access Sequences ➤ Define Sales And Distribution Access Sequences. Figure 13.17 represents the customization screen for defining the batch access sequence.

FIGURE 13.17   Defining the batch access sequence

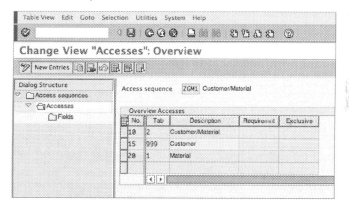

NOTE   Unlike other condition techniques based on access sequences, access sequence for batch determination does not have an Exclusive check box, and you can't define requirements at the access sequence level.

Defining Strategy Types

The next step is to define a strategy type and assign the access sequence to the relevant strategy types. *Strategy types* are the condition types that control the search criteria. The transaction code is V/C1, and the menu path is IMG ➤ Logistics – General ➤ Batch Management ➤ Batch Determination And Batch Check ➤ Strategy Types ➤ Define Sales And Distribution Strategy Types. Figure 13.18 represents the customization screen for strategy types.

CASE STUDY—GALAXY CUSTOMIZATION ANALYSIS: BATCH CONDITION TABLES AND ACCESS SEQUENCES

At Galaxy Musical Instruments, a variety of rules exist that determine the batch selection during sales and distribution processing. One of the important rules for determining batch selection in Galaxy is the country of origin. Some of Galaxy's customers only want goods that are made in United States. Sometimes, this country-of-origin requirement from customers is specific to materials, and sometimes it is a generic requirement applied to all materials sold to that customer. For all other customers, Galaxy wants to send the batch materials that were produced/procured first to be delivered first. To achieve this search logic, Galaxy chose standard condition tables 002 (Customer/ Material) for maintaining customer/material-specific batch determination rules, chose 001 (Material) for defining material-specific rules, and created the new table 999 (Customer), as shown in Figure 13.16, for defining customer-specific rules. These three tables were then put into access sequence ZGM1 with access to condition records, as shown in Figure 13.17.

FIGURE 13.18   Defining the strategy type

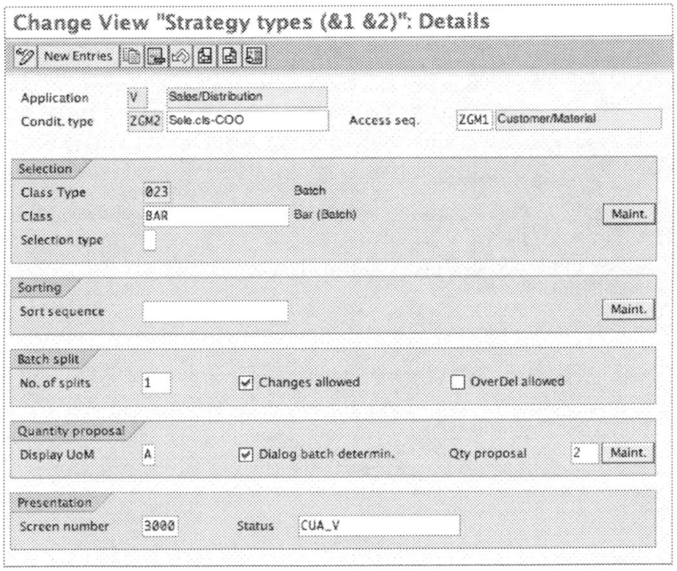

The important fields on this customization screen are as follows:

Condition Type   The Condition Type field on the screen represents the four-character strategy type identification key, ZGM2.

Access Sequence   Access sequence ZGM1 represents the access sequence assigned to strategy type ZGM2.

Class Type   The class type is always 023—the batch class provided in the standard SAP system for use with batch management, except for the material/plant level batch maintenance scenario, where the class type is 022.

Class   Using Class, you can define a default classification to your strategy type. Remember that you can search for batches using batch determination only if the batches are classified.

Selection Type   The Selection Type field defines how the selection for a batch needs to happen. When left blank, the system immediately displays the batches that meet the selection criteria when the batch search is executed in a document.

Sort Sequence   The Sort Sequence field allows you to define your own sort display for batches.

Batch Split   The Batch Split field controls the number of batch splits that are allowed during batch determination.

CASE STUDY—GALAXY CUSTOMIZATION ANALYSIS: BATCH STRATEGY TYPES

At Galaxy Musical Instruments, a variety of rules can determine a batch search. There are searches based on the country of origin and searches based on some other classes. To cover these, Galaxy created two strategy types: ZGM2 with default class BAR (for the country-of-origin information) and ZGM3 without any default class. This way, ZGM3 can have any class when the batch search condition record is finally maintained.

Creating a Batch Determination Procedure

Next you assign the strategy types to a determination procedure that will help determine the required batch during a sales transaction. The transaction code is V/C3, and the menu path is IMG ➢ Logistics – General ➢ Batch Management ➢ Batch Determination And Batch Check ➢ Batch Search Procedure Definition ➢

Define Sales And Distribution Search Procedure. Add your strategy type into the procedure as shown in Figure 13.19.

FIGURE 13.19   Creating the batch determination procedure

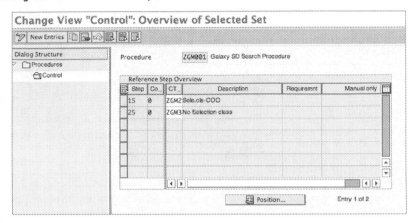

Setting Up a Batch Determination Rule

Finally, you define the determination rule. The transaction code is V/C5, and the menu path is IMG ➤ Logistics – General ➤ Batch Management ➤ Batch Determination And Batch Check ➤ Batch Search Procedure Allocation And Check Activation ➤ Allocate SD Search Procedure/Activate Check.

Here, a combination of sales area and document type helps you determine the relevant determination procedure for a sales transaction, as shown in Figure 13.20. This can be represented in equation form as follows:

Sales area + Document type = Determination procedure

FIGURE 13.20   Setting up a batch determination rule

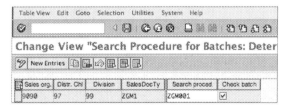

Activating Automatic Batch Determination in SD

If you want the SAP system to automatically determine the relevant batches during sales order and delivery processing, you can specify that here by selecting the automatic determination check box for each sales and delivery item category for which you would like the automatic batch determination. The transaction code is V/CA for sales and V/CL for delivery. The menu path is IMG ➢ Logistics – General ➢ Batch Management ➢ Batch Determination And Batch Check ➢ Activate Automatic Batch Determination In SD.

Maintaining Condition Master Records for Batches

Table 13.2 represents the transaction codes available in the standard SAP system for maintaining condition records for batch determination. To maintain a record, use the relevant transaction to call up the maintenance screen and maintain the record for the strategy type (condition type) you defined in customizing.

TABLE 13.2   Transaction Codes for Maintaining Batch Determination Condition Records

Transaction Code	Menu Path	Description
VCH1	SAP Easy Access Menu Path ➢ Central Functions ➢ Batch Management ➢ Batch Determination ➢ Batch Search Strategy ➢ For Sales And Distribution ➢ Create	Creates batch condition record
VCH2	SAP Easy Access Menu Path ➢ Central Functions ➢ Batch Management ➢ Batch Determination ➢ Batch Search Strategy ➢ For Sales And Distribution ➢ Change	Changes batch condition record
VCH3	SAP Easy Access Menu Path ➢ Central Functions ➢ Batch Management ➢ Batch Determination ➢ Batch Search Strategy ➢ For Sales And Distribution ➢ Display	Displays batch condition record

For batch determination strategy type ZGM2, Figure 13.21 represents the condition record maintenance screen, and Figure 13.22 represents the selection criteria for the batch determination. Here, entering the country of origin as US in the selection criteria tells SAP to look only for batches where the country of origin is set to US when it's assigning stock to the delivery document for customer 10012 and material 1677.

FIGURE 13.21   Creating the batch condition record

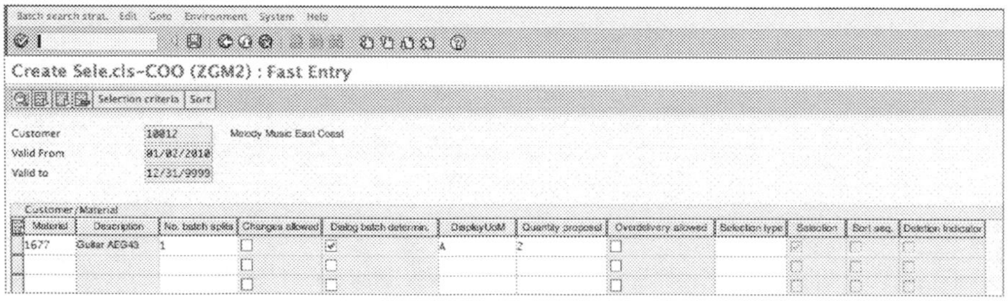

FIGURE 13.22 Creating the batch condition record, selection criteria screen

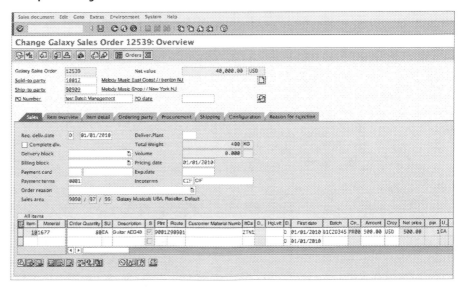

Batch Determination in Action

Figure 13.23 shows an example of batch determination in action using customer 10012 and material 1677. As you can see, the system automatically determined batch B1C2D345 using batch determination. Let's take a look at how the SAP system arrived at this batch number.

FIGURE 13.23 Example showing batch determination in a sales order

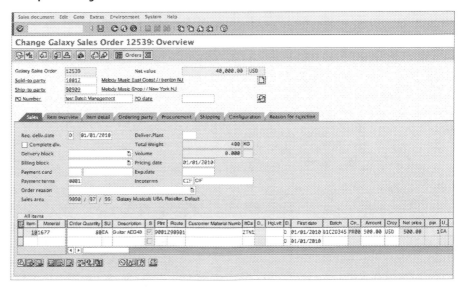

Select line item 10, and click the 🔍 button; you will be taken to the batch determination analysis screen, as shown in Figure 13.24.

FIGURE 13.24 Batch determination analysis screen

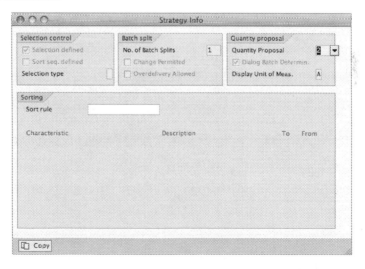

Clicking the Strategy Info button takes you to the screen in Figure 13.25 that shows all the strategy information that was used by SAP during batch determination.

FIGURE 13.25 Strategy information

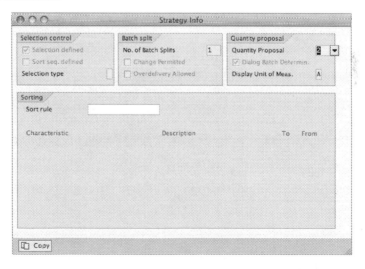

Clicking the Selection Criteria button takes you to the screen in Figure 13.26 that tells you what selection criteria SAP used to determine the batches.

FIGURE 13.26 Selection criteria

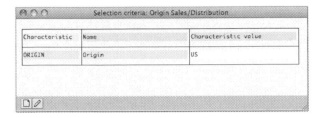

Clicking the Log button takes you to the log screen shown in Figure 13.27 that tells you how SAP determined the batch. As you can see, the two available batches for material 1677 were selected. On these two batches, SAP applied the selection criteria of the country of origin as US and found that both the batches had a country of origin set to the United States. It then checked the availability of batches in storage location 0001 and found that the batches were available.

FIGURE 13.27 Batch determination log analysis

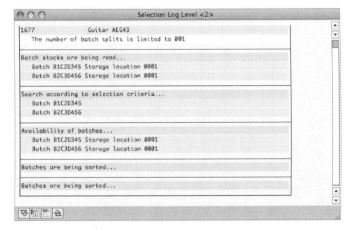

Clicking the Strategy Analysis button takes you to the batch condition record determination analysis screen (Figure 13.28), and clicking the Classification button will show the classification details of the selected batch that you maintained while setting up the batch master record (Figure 13.29).

FIGURE 13.28 Strategy analysis

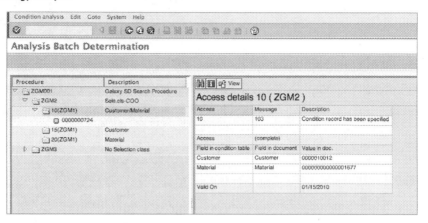

FIGURE 13.29 Batch classification

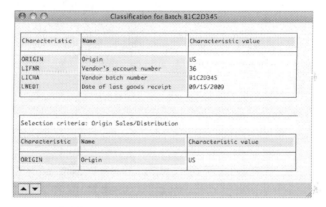

If you want to see the availability check overview for the selected batch stock, you can do so by clicking the Availability button. Figure 13.30 shows the availability check overview screen for material 1677.

FIGURE 13.30 Stock availability at the batch level

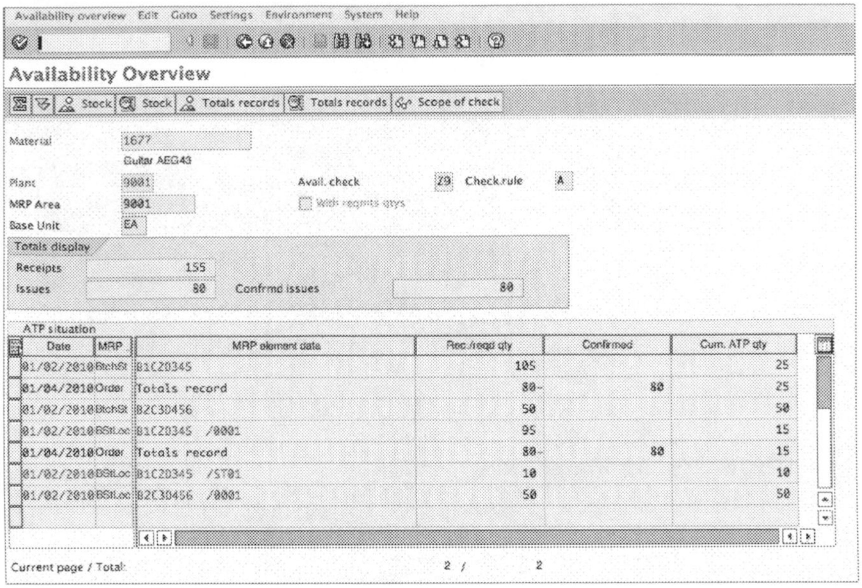

Summary

Serial numbers and batch management are important components of SAP's logistics central function because they provide great levels of tracking and traceability to organizations. In this chapter, we discussed the setup and use of serial numbers and batch management in the SAP system. In the next chapter, we will cover various advanced topics in the SAP SD application and briefly touch upon enhancement packages.

Advanced Techniques

n this chapter, we will introduce some advanced tools and techniques. We will introduce *enhancement packages*, which is the new delivery model that SAP will follow from ECC 6.0 onward. We will also discuss the new switch framework.

In the next part of this chapter, we will discuss some important tools for reporting and the mass changing of data and documents.

We will also touch upon the options available to customize SAP programs such as user exits, SAP enhancements, and business add-ins (BAdIs).

Some of these concepts are vast and beyond the scope of the regular work of an SD expert. You will require help from other technical experts, such as the Basis and ABAP teams to implement some of the tools and techniques covered here. This chapter is meant only to provide an introduction to these concepts and will not serve as an implementation guide.

Enhancement Packages

After the release of ECC 6.0, SAP changed its software delivery strategy for rolling out further innovations. In the earlier model, new enhancements were delivered only when a new version of SAP was launched. For example, version 4.6C had new features not included in 4.0B. However, it required a system upgrade before you could use the new innovations.

This process has been simplified from ECC 6.0 onward. You can easily add the new features to SAP ERP 6.0 in small bundles or packages, called *enhancement packages*. These are delivered by SAP more frequently and can be adopted with little disruption.

We'll discuss the changes that you need to know as an SD expert to implement these innovations from ECC 6.0 onward. However, our objective is not to explain each functionality and how to implement it. There are too many to do that, and they're updated frequently. Rather, we will focus on the fundamentals of enhancement packages so that you can continue to explore and adapt to these new innovations from SAP.

Introduction to Enhancement Packages

Enhancement packages are software innovations that overlay new or enhanced functionality and new processes on SAP ERP 6.0. They offer the flexibility to selectively install new software components that are relevant to you. Further, the installed components remain dormant in the system, without affecting the existing functionality until you activate them. In other words, installation and activation can be done at different points in time, as per your convenience. The differentiating feature is a new switch framework that controls the activation. Once the new functionality is "switched on," you can carry out the configuration steps to set up the new feature.

From an SD functional expert's point of view, the new switch framework is a critical step that you need to know before you can work with enhancement packages. We will discuss it later in this chapter.

The following terms are important to understand:

Business functions   The new innovations are grouped together into small bundles called *business functions*. They represent the smallest switchable unit; that is, they can be activated as a unit. Before installation, you have to study the features of the business function and its relevance to your business processes. If you decide to go ahead, you have to then install the technical usage required for the business functions.

Technical usages   The business functions require software components that must be installed together. Some of the business functions may require Java components, portal content, and so on, besides ABAP software components. These components are bundled together as *technical usages*.

On the SAP Service Marketplace website, you'll find notes for mapping business functions to the corresponding technical usages. OSS note 1083576 is one such note, explaining the software components for enhancement package 3 (EhP 3). You will have to look up OSS note for the latest version of enhancement packages in circulation.

Implementation Process

SAP delivers the enhancement packages at regular intervals. At the time of writing this book, the fourth set of enhancement packages (commonly called EhP4 or 604) has already been released. The packages are cumulative in nature. That is, EhP4 has all the features of the previous packages plus some additional new features. Also note that the enhancement packages are different from the support packages that SAP releases at regular intervals. Support packages deliver corrections and legally mandatory changes to existing programs. Enhancement packages deliver innovations and process improvement features.

The process of implementing a new business function can be broken down into four steps: identification, installation, activation, and configuration (Figure 14.1).

FIGURE 14.1 Enhancement package Implementation process

> Identify   Install   Activate   Implement

Identification   In this stage, you will study the documentation about the new features offered in the latest enhancement package and determine what is relevant and useful to your business process. You will work with experts from other functional applications and the Netweaver team to compile a list of all the business functions and the corresponding technical usages that are required for your organization.

Installation   In this stage, you will schedule the download of the required enhancement package. It is recommended that this activity is done when you periodically apply support packages, which is a regular maintenance activity. This saves additional efforts in installation. This activity is carried out by the Basis and technical teams; hence, your participation at this stage is little. The new software components remain dormant in the system. Therefore, there is no impact on the regular business processes.

Activation   Since activation is separate from installation, you can choose the right time to implement the new business functions. At this time, you will use the switch framework to activate the business functions. (We will discuss this later in the chapter.) Once activated, the changes take effect; that is, you may notice changes to screens, transactions, and nodes in the Implementation menu and Easy Access menu. Activation cannot be reversed.

T I P   Remember that the installation and activation of enhancement packages is irreversible. It is advisable to install the enhancement in a sandbox client and check the functionality before installing it in the regular SAP system.

Configuration   After activation, you may be required to configure the new business function and carry out settings in the Customizing menu (IMG), as per the instructions in the documentation. From here on, you will follow the regular change management process to configure changes, test, document, and transport to the production environment.

Switch Framework

The *switch framework* is used to control the activation of business functions that are delivered in an enhancement package. Figure 14.2 shows a conceptual model of how this works. An enhancement package delivers several business functions. You can individually activate a business function using the switch. Once activated, you will notice the changes caused by the new functionality, such as changes to screens, new transactions, or the addition of new nodes in the IMG menu.

FIGURE 14.2 Switch framework model

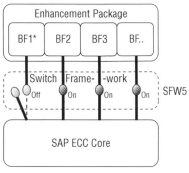

* BF = Business Function

You can access the switch framework from the menu path IMG ➤ Activate Business Functions (SFW5).

The switch framework will display a list of business functions, as shown in Figure 14.3.

FIGURE 14.3 Switch framework: Change Business Function Status screen

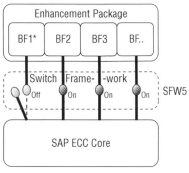

Name and Description   Each row contains name and a description of the business function.

Dependencies   This feature lists the dependencies between business functions. For example, if the business function requires the activation of any other business functions, they would be listed here. It helps guide you in the implementation process.

Documentation and Release Information   If you need more information about a business function, choose the Documentation and Release Information icons. These links lead you to all the details about each function, including the prerequisites, new features, and benefits. Make sure that you have studied them thoroughly before activation.

Release   This specifies the release number or the enhancement package number where this feature was first delivered. Note that enhancement package releases are denoted as 602 (for EhP2) , 603 (for EhP3), and so on.

SAP Test Catalog   Along with the new business function, there is a SAP Test Catalog. It is a set of predefined test scripts from SAP to help you test the impact of the activation.

Activated On   This shows the date and time on which the business function was activated.

Impact Analyzer   If you right-click the name of a business function, you will find a new menu with a feature called Impact Analyzer. This tool helps you assess the impact of the new functionality. It will list the transaction codes, the user profiles, and the user IDs that will be impacted by the change. This can help you plan change management, testing, and training that will be required before you can activate the change in your production environment.

For example, Logistics S&D Simplification (SD_01) is an important business function. The release information tells you that it was delivered with enhancement package 2 (602). The documentation about SD_01 informs you that this feature will deliver the business packages for the implementation of Internal Sales Representative roles on the portal, for enhanced material search and material view in sales order processing, for integrating the search engine (TREX), and for a new business add-in for credit cards.

To activate a business function, select the row, and click Activate Changes.

WARNING Always remember that activation is irreversible.

Important Tools and Techniques

In the following sections, we will discuss some of the important tools and techniques that are available in SAP. You can use them to meet specific requirements such as communicating with other partners and systems, reporting, mass updating, and carrying out custom enhancements to SAP.

QuickViewer

QuickViewer is a simple tool to design custom reports without the need for any programming. You can use it to design and run QuickViews (reports designed using QuickViewer) and export them to spreadsheets. Note that these reports are user-specific and cannot be shared with other users.

Before you start, identify the following:

- ▶ The fields required in your report

- ▶ The selection screen and criteria on which you will run the report

- ▶ The source of data fields, in other words, the database tables where the data is stored

- ▶ The key fields linking the tables together, in case the data is scattered over multiple tables

- ▶ The layout of the report and arrangement of fields

To access this tool, the path is SAP Menu ➢ Tools ➢ ABAP Workbench ➢ Utilities ➢ QuickViewer (SQVI).

On the initial screen (Figure 14.4), you can edit or execute a QuickView that you may have created earlier, or create a new one.

FIGURE 14.4 QuickViewer: Initial Screen

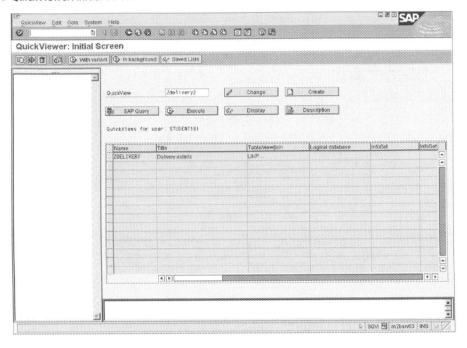

To create a new QuickView, start with a meaningful name for your report, and click the Create option. A pop-up Choose Data Source box appears, as shown in Figure 14.5. Enter a report title and comments if any.

FIGURE 14.5 Creating a QuickView

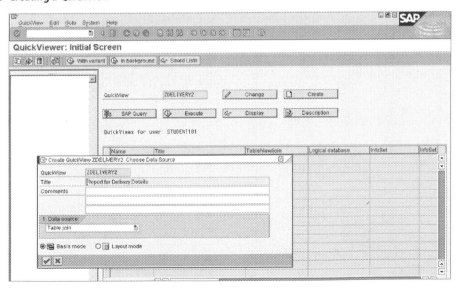

As an example, we'll show you how to set up a QuickView to display delivery-related information. The major tables that you will use in the example are LIKP and LIPS.

In the Choose Data Source box, select an option for a data source. You can choose a single table or a join of more than one table. As we said, for this example, use the join of two tables, LIKP and LIPS.

If it were a single table, you could choose the table name in the Table/View field. When you opt for a table join, you can enter the table names in a subsequent screen (we will come to that soon).

Next is the choice between Basis and Layout modes. Choose Basis mode if you want your report design in a standard format. However, if you want to design a custom layout for the report, choose Layout mode. We will explain both the modes as we go along. For now, select Basis mode.

On the next screen, you have to add the tables. As shown in Figure 14.6, select Edit ➣ Insert Table for each table that you have to add to the QuickView. The system automatically proposes the key fields linking the tables. You can check and confirm (or override) the proposed keys using the Join Condition button.

FIGURE 14.6 Inserting tables in the QuickView

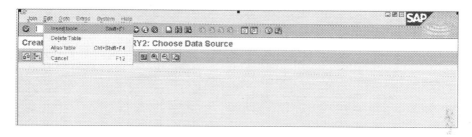

As shown in Figure 14.7, the key joining LIKP and LIPS is the delivery number (VBELN). It is denoted by a line joining the VBELN fields in both tables.

After maintaining this setting, hit the back arrow navigation key. This leads you to the screen shown in Figure 14.8. The left window contains a list of all the fields available in the joined tables. The window to the right has the same information in a different presentation format. You can use either window to select the fields that you require in the report and on the selection screen.

FIGURE 14.7 Basis mode, displaying the table join

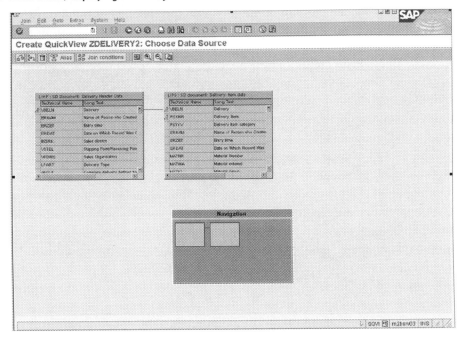

FIGURE 14.8 Field selection

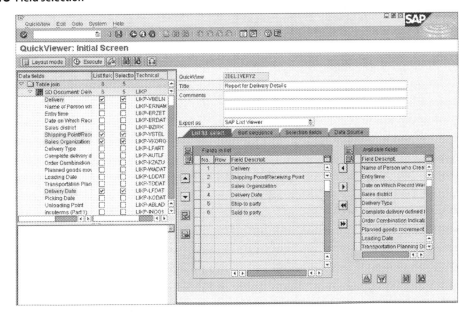

We will use the left window for this example. Here, you'll see two sets of check boxes provided next to each field, one for list display and the other for selection screen display. Select the fields based on your reporting requirements.

> **TIP** While you are selecting the fields that you'll need in your report, make sure you are choosing the correct fields by verifying the field names. It is always helpful to have another session with SE16 open. Display records from the tables you have selected, and verify the field names that you are going to use.

At this stage, if you want to customize the layout of your report and the placement of fields, you can switch to the Layout mode using the button in the top row. Customizing the layout is an optional step.

Figure 14.9 shows the layout mode. You can drag and drop fields to their required positions and customize the layout. You can also change the name of the field as it appears in the header columns and add header and footer text.

FIGURE 14.9 Layout mode

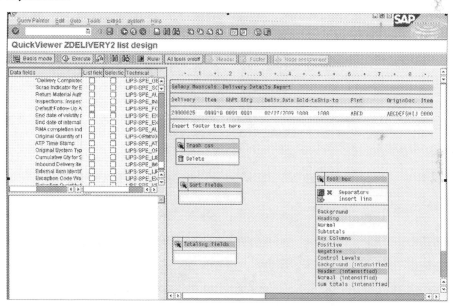

At any stage, you can execute the report. Check whether the fields appearing on the selection screen are as per your requirements. You can always go back using the Change mode and make corrections.

Figure 14.10 shows the QuickView report. It extracts information from the joined tables and displays the records as per the selection criteria. The next time you go back to SQVI, you will find this new report added to your list.

FIGURE 14.10 Result of QuickView execution

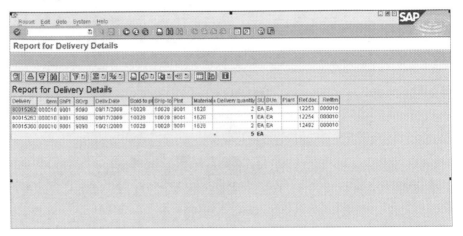

SAP Query

SAP Query is another tool to create reports without any programming. Query has more features than QuickView. The main advantage is that a query can be shared with a group of users.

Setting up SAP Query is a three-step process:

1. Create an InfoSet. This process is similar to the QuickView setup discussed earlier. Create an InfoSet by choosing the source tables.

2. Set up a groups of users who will be authorized to use the InfoSets. You assign user IDs to each group and specify the list of InfoSets that the group can use.

3. Design queries using the fields in the InfoSets.

For example, say Galaxy Musical Instruments needs a report with information about billing documents. We will show how to extract data from tables VBRK and VBRP. Specifically, you will learn how to set up a user group for the billing department so that only this group can use the InfoSet. Then you will learn how to design a query using the InfoSet.

Create an InfoSet

The first step is to create an InfoSet. Follow the path SAP Menu ≻ Tools ≻ ABAP Workbench ≻ Utilities ≻ SAP Query ≻ InfoSets (SQ02).

On the InfoSet: Initial Screen screen, shown in Figure 14.11, enter a suitable name. Choose a data source. Based on your requirement, choose either Table Join Using Basis Table, Direct Read Of Table, or Logical Database as a source.

FIGURE 14.11   InfoSet: Initial Screen

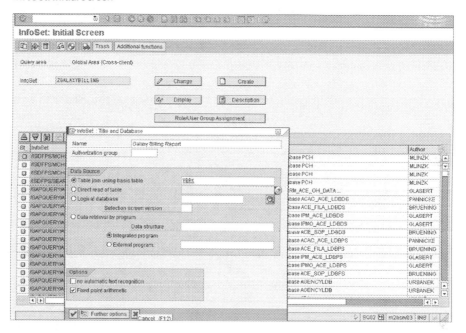

In the example, the InfoSet ZGALAXYBILLING is being created. In the Data Source fields, select the Table Join Using Basis Table option and specify the first table VBRK as the source of data. The next screen, which is identical to Figure 14.7, is where you can add the other tables.

After adding all the tables and checking the join conditions, you can save the InfoSet.

Upon saving, you will see a Field Group Defaults dialog box (Figure 14.12). Always choose the Create Empty Field Groups option.

FIGURE 14.12   Field group defaults

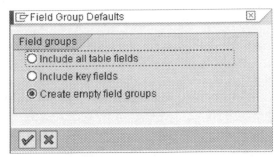

As a result, on the next screen (Figure 14.13), there are empty field groups created, as shown in the top-right window. In this case, there are two tables, and hence there are two empty groups. Now choose the fields from the tables VBRK and VBRP, and add them to the field groups. Thus, you filter only the required fields into the groups for further processing.

FIGURE 14.13   Selecting fields for the InfoSet

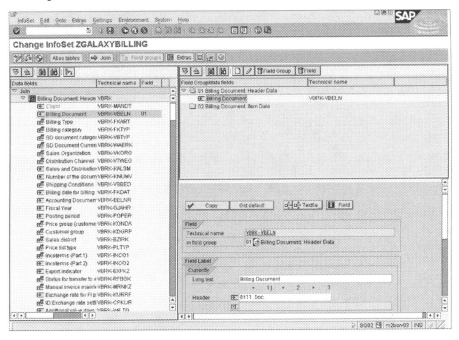

You can click the list of fields (on the left), and the attributes are displayed in the lower-right window.

You can drag and drop the field into the field groups on the right. Figure 14.13 shows that the first field (Document Number) has been added to the field group Billing Document: Header Data field. Similarly, you can proceed to add the other fields that you require in your InfoSet.

Save and generate the InfoSet once you have updated the field groups. You can choose to save it as a local object or a transport relevant object. If you plan to transport the query to other systems, you can choose the latter option.

Create a User Group

To create a user group, use the following menu path: SAP Menu ➤ Tools ➤ ABAP Workbench ➤ Utilities ➤ SAP Query ➤ User Groups (SQ03).

Select a name for the user group, and choose Create (Figure 14.14). You can save it as a local or a transport relevant object. We will set up a user group named Z_GALA_BILL for the Galaxy billing department.

FIGURE 14.14   User Group: Initial Screen

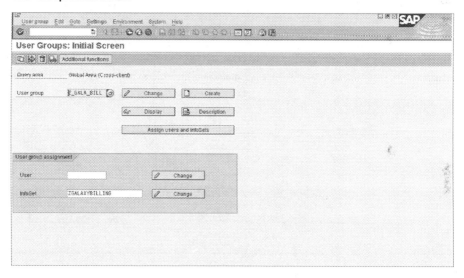

Next, on the initial screen, select the Assign Users And InfoSets option. You can assign the users to the newly created group. Figure 14.15 shows this assignment.

FIGURE 14.15 Assigning users to a user group

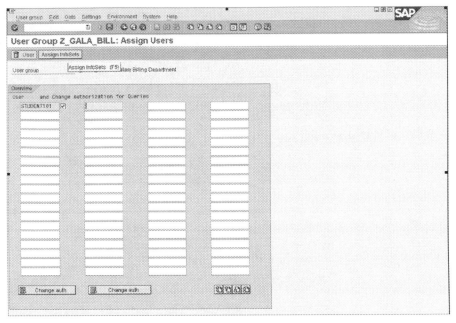

From the same screen, you can launch Assign InfoSets to add the list of InfoSets that this group is authorized to use. For this example, assign the InfoSet ZGALAXYBILLING to the user group Z_GALA_BILL.

Create a Query

For this example, you have defined InfoSet and assigned it to a user group. Now you can create a query to generate a report you require. The menu path is as follows: SAP Menu ➤ Tools ➤ ABAP Workbench ➤ Utilities ➤ SAP Query ➤ Queries (SQ01).

You can use this transaction code either to execute any existing queries or to define a new one. To start with, select the user group to which you belong by clicking the Other User Group icon  .

Based on the group you choose, the existing queries (if any) for this group will be displayed in the list. You can choose and execute these queries directly from the list.

For this example, start by creating a new query. Enter a name for the query, and click Create, as shown in Figure 14.16. A dialog box will allow you to choose the InfoSet you want to use for your query.

FIGURE 14.16   Creating a query

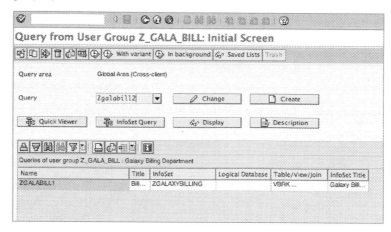

On the next screen, add a description (as shown in Figure 14.17), and specify the output display parameters.

FIGURE 14.17   Creating the query name and attributes

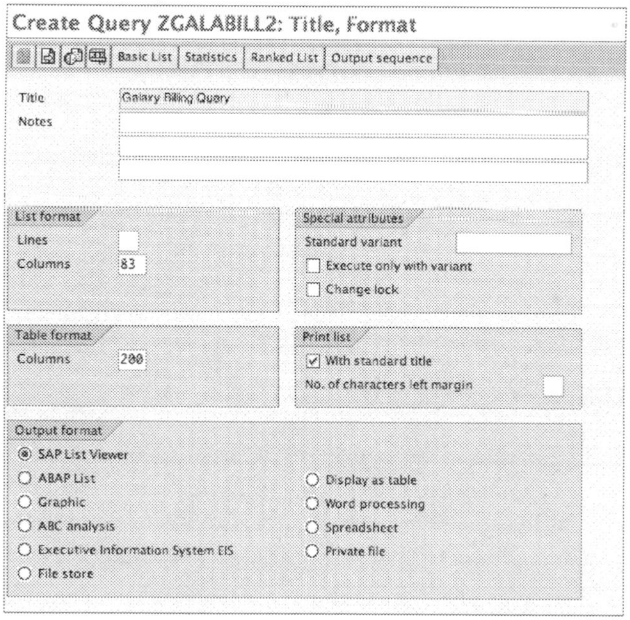

The Next icon on this screen will guide you through the other steps in query creation ![icon]. Select the field groups and the fields that you plan to use in this specific query (Figure 14.18).

FIGURE 14.18   Selecting the field groups and fields

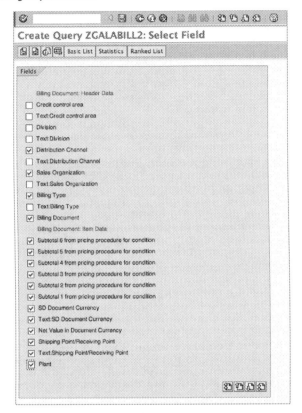

On the Selections screen (Figure 14.19), select the fields required as selection parameter for the query. You can arrange the selected fields in any order (by specifying the position number in the No column). The fields SV and 1Z allow you to further control the selection parameters. If you select the SV box next to a selection field, you cannot specify a range of values in the selection screen for that field (that is to say, the To Value box is suppressed). On the other hand, if you select the 1Z box, you cannot specify multiple values in the selection screen.

FIGURE 14.19 Choosing fields for selection screen

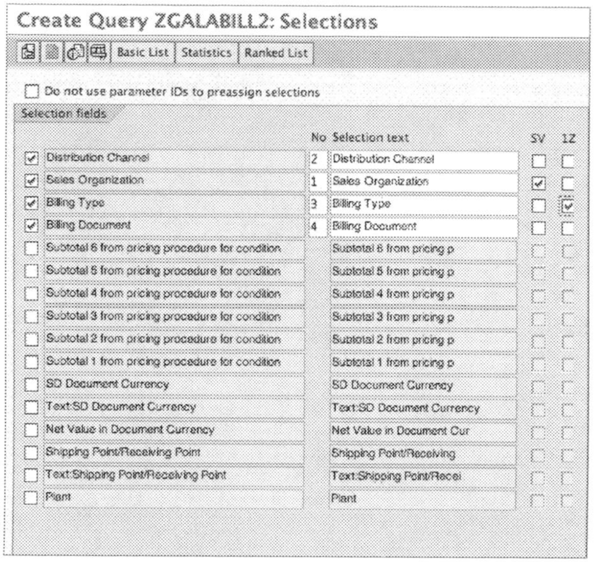

Create Query ZGALABILL2: Selections

☐ Do not use parameter IDs to preassign selections

Selection fields

		No	Selection text	SV	1Z
☑	Distribution Channel	2	Distribution Channel	☐	☐
☑	Sales Organization	1	Sales Organization	☑	☐
☑	Billing Type	3	Billing Type	☐	☑
☑	Billing Document	4	Billing Document	☐	☐
☐	Subtotal 6 from pricing procedure for condition		Subtotal 6 from pricing p	☐	☐
☐	Subtotal 5 from pricing procedure for condition		Subtotal 5 from pricing p	☐	☐
☐	Subtotal 4 from pricing procedure for condition		Subtotal 4 from pricing p	☐	☐
☐	Subtotal 3 from pricing procedure for condition		Subtotal 3 from pricing p	☐	☐
☐	Subtotal 2 from pricing procedure for condition		Subtotal 2 from pricing p	☐	☐
☐	Subtotal 1 from pricing procedure for condition		Subtotal 1 from pricing p	☐	☐
☐	SD Document Currency		SD Document Currency	☐	☐
☐	Text:SD Document Currency		Text:SD Document Currency	☐	☐
☐	Net Value in Document Currency		Net Value in Document Cur	☐	☐
☐	Shipping Point/Receiving Point		Shipping Point/Receiving	☐	☐
☐	Text:Shipping Point/Receiving Point		Text:Shipping Point/Recei	☐	☐
☐	Plant		Plant	☐	☐

On the Selections screen, click the Basic List button to configure the layout of your report. This leads you to the Layout mode that we covered when discussing QuickView. You can select the layout of the fields on the screen and save the layout.

This completes the query setup. You can test the query using the Test option 🔲.

Note the selection screen shown in Figure 14.20. Since we've used the SV box for the Sales Organization field, we cannot specify a range here. Similarly, we used the 1Z option for the field Billing Type, so we can specify a range but cannot list multiple entries.

FIGURE 14.20 Selection screen for the query

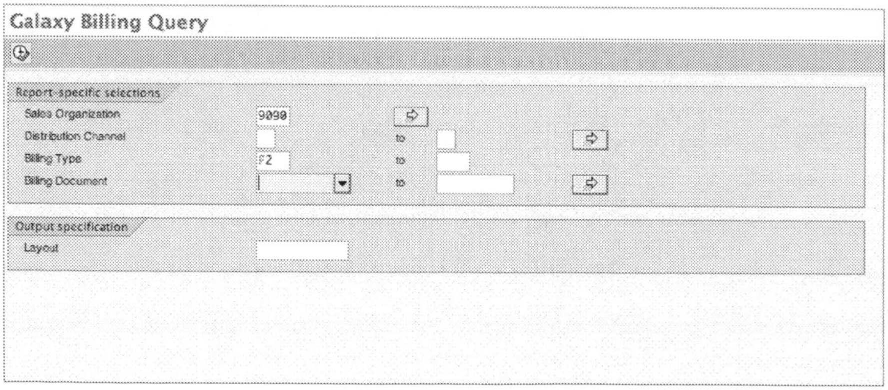

Galaxy Billing Query

Report-specific selections

Sales Organization	9090		
Distribution Channel		to	
Billing Type	F2	to	
Billing Document		to	

Output specification

Layout	

Enter the selection parameters, and execute the query. The system will search for database records that meet the criteria and display the results, as shown in Figure 14.21.

FIGURE 14.21 Query execution

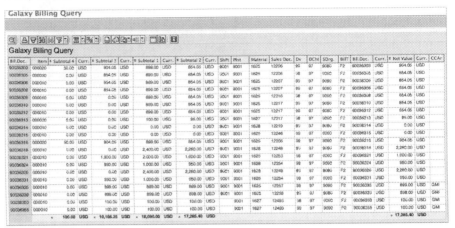

The next time you use SQ01, this new query will be added to the list of existing queries that are available to you for execution.

Mass Maintenance

Many organizations deal with a large volume of data. Mass changes to the master data (such as the customer or material master) or transaction data (such as the open sales orders) are often required. To facilitate mass changes, SAP has provided a cross-application mass maintenance tool. The user can choose the object to be changed (customer, vendor, and so on) and the fields that are to be updated. The changes are then carried out en masse, and the log is displayed to the user. This saves a lot of time and effort in carrying out mass changes.

You can access the tool by the transaction code MASS. The menu path is SAP Menu ➢ Logistics ➢ Central Functions ➢ Mass Maintenance ➢ Mass Maintenance ➢ Dialog Processing (MASS).

Use the Object Type field to specify the object that you want to change. As shown in Figure 14.22, there are numerous options such as Sales Orders (BUS2032), Customers (KNA1), and Materials (BUS1001).

FIGURE 14.22 Mass Maintenance screen, selecting the object type

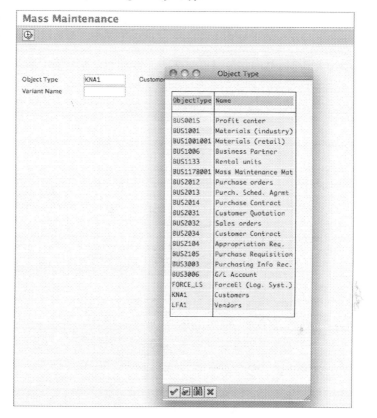

We'll now show you an example of making a mass change to the customer master. Suppose Galaxy Musical Instruments decided to reorganize the grouping of customers. As a result of this change, all the customers belonging to group G1 are to be updated to group G3. We'll show you how MASS functionality helps you make this change, and the steps to follow.

1. Launch the MASS transaction and enter **KNA1** in the Object Type field. Execute the transaction.

2. Next, select tables and fields. The screen will display the various tables and fields in which customer data is stored. As shown in Figure 14.23, there are two tabs. Go to the Tables tab. The customer group is stored in the KNVV table. Hence, select this table. Similarly, in the Fields tab, you can select all the fields that you would like to check or update. For your convenience, you can use the Find function to search for the required fields from the list. For this

example, choose the Customer group field KNVV-KDGRP. While you are visiting KNVV, you can also verify some other fields such as price group, so add KNVV-KONDA to the list of fields, and execute the transaction.

FIGURE 14.23 Selecting tables and fields

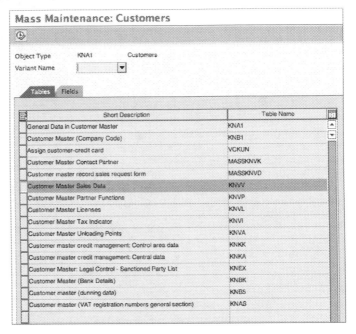

3. Next you select data records to be changed or created. Figure 14.24 shows the next screen. You can enter selection parameters to find records that are to be updated. There are two tabs here: one to change existing records and the other to create new records. We will proceed with the change option. The Choose Selection Fields option ▦ allows you to change the fields appearing on the selection screen. In this example, add the Customer group to the list.

4. Enter the selection parameters, and execute this query. Records matching the selection criteria are listed in the report.

TIP If you plan to run this report again, you can save the selection screen as a variant. This way, you can call up the variant without having to customize the selection screen again.

FIGURE 14.24 Selecting tables and fields

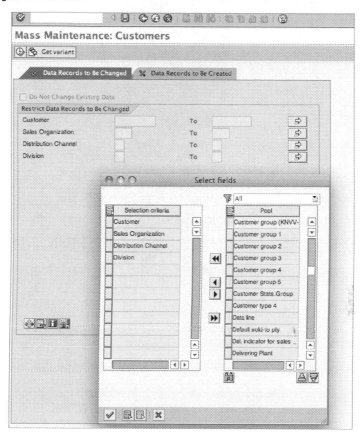

5. In the next step, you specify new values for each record. Figure 14.25 shows a list of master data records that are to be changed. The list allows you to overwrite the values to certain fields that you had chosen earlier (Customer Group and Price Group). Suppose you have to update all the customers to customer group G3. You can either overwrite G1 with G3 in each record or enter **G3** in the header record (in the upper window) and click Carry Out A Mass Change. This copies the header value to all the selected records. The effort of manually entering a value in each record is thus saved.

FIGURE 14.25 Changing values in selected records

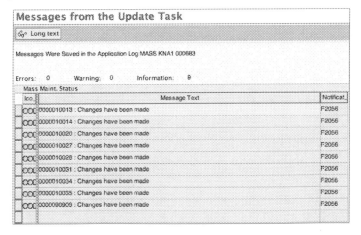

WARNING If you leave the header record blank and click Carry Out A Mass Change, the existing field value in all selected records will be wiped out (blanked).

6. When you update the changed values and click Save, a warning message reminds you that a mass change is about to be done. After the update is carried out, a log file is displayed confirming the change (Figure 14.26).

FIGURE 14.26 Change log

In SAP, you can use transaction code VA05 to perform mass change of pricing, material number, plant and currency data in sales documents. You can also use MASS for the same purpose. Just select the object as BUS2032 for Sales Orders. This offers many more fields to choose from.

In our discussion about Figure 14.24, we noted that there are two tabs. We discussed the tab for changing records. We'll now discuss the option of creating new records.

You can use MASS to generate new data records. An example is if you have created general data for a set of new customers and you want to create sales area data en masse. From the MASS transaction, choose the Data Records To Be Created tab (shown in Figure 14.27). On the lower part of this screen, there are fields to specify a reference customer record. By executing the transaction, the fields from the reference customer record will be copied into the new records being created.

FIGURE 14.27 Creating new records using MASS

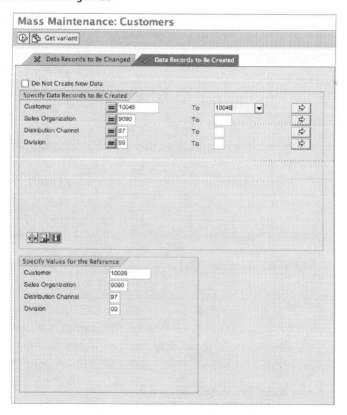

> **TIP**   MASS is a very powerful tool. Besides changing and creating records, it can also serve as a quick reporting tool. As shown in our example, you can customize the selection screen and the fields to be displayed in the report!

Logistics Information System

Logistics Information System (LIS) is a data warehouse solution provided by SAP. It consists of components for each logistics application such as sales, purchasing, inventory control, and so on. Sales Information System (SIS) is part of LIS that deals with sales-related data.

The purpose of Logistics Information System is to help generate key reports. To enable this, an information system first collects and aggregates transaction information into information structures. A typical structure consists of characteristics (that is, the basis on which data is to be aggregated, such as the sales organization, the distribution channel, the customer group), key figures (statistics such as the order quantity, the net value, and the gross value), and a period unit (a time element such as daily, weekly, or monthly). The value of the key figures are aggregated at a regular time interval specified by the period for each characteristic in the information structure. This enables you to generate analysis reports such as the total monthly (a period unit) order value (a key figure) by the sales organization (a characteristic).

The configuration of LIS is a vast topic that cannot be compressed into this chapter. The purpose of this discussion is to provide a basic understanding and to get you started with the standard information structures and standard analysis.

We'll now discuss the steps in maintaining an information structure and setting up rules to control how it is updated with data.

Managing Information Structures

The first step is to define the information structures that you want to use in your system. You can choose from the standard structures created by SAP or define a custom information structure by following the path IMG ➢ Logistics - General ➢ Logistics Information Systems (LIS) ➢ Logistics Data Warehouse ➢ Data Basis ➢ Information Structures ➢ Maintain Self-Defined Information Structures.

From this node, you can create (MC21), change (MC22), or display (MC23) information structures. SAP delivers several standard information structures, such as the following:

- ► S001: Customer
- ► S002: Sales Office

- ► S003: Sales Organization

- ► S004: Material

- ► S005: Shipping Point

- ► S006: Sales Employee

- ► S020: Credit Management

Figure 14.28 shows the details of standard information structure S001. As you can see, it has characteristics such as the sold-to party and statistics such as incoming orders and open orders as key figures.

FIGURE 14.28 Info structure details

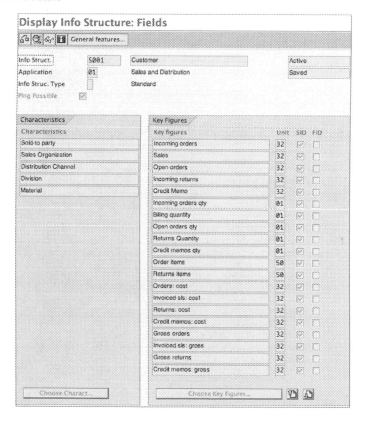

You can also define a custom information structure by choosing from a catalog of characteristics and key figures.

After selecting the information structure, you can control how the structures are updated with data flowing in from various sales transactions using statistics groups and update groups.

Statistics groups help in controlling *which* data elements (documents, item categories, materials, and customers) update the information structure. Update groups help in controlling *when* the updates should occur. Next we'll cover the steps in setting up these groups.

Defining and Assigning Statistics Groups

Statistics groups are used to filter the data that is updated in the information structure. Sometimes you have to control the customers and materials that should be updated. Similarly, you may want to segregate sales document types and item categories (such as regular orders and return orders). Statistics groups help you in controlling the updates.

There are statistics groups for materials, customers, sales documents, and item categories. The statistics groups are freely definable. You can add new groups as per your requirements. Then assign the statistics groups to sales documents and item categories. Similarly, customer master and material master data have to be updated with the appropriate value in the statistics group field.

Configuring Statistics Groups

Table 14.1 shows the steps in creating and assigning a statistics group from the configuration menu.

TABLE 14.1   Statistics Group Settings

Menu Path	Transaction Code	Action
IMG ➤ Logistics - General ➤ LIS ➤ Logistics Data Warehouse ➤ Updating ➤ Update Control ➤ Settings: Sales ➤ Statistics Group ➤ Maintain Stat Group For Customers	OVRA	Define customer statistics group.
IMG ➤ Logistics - General ➤ LIS ➤ Logistics Data Warehouse ➤ Updating ➤ Update Control ➤ Settings: Sales ➤ Statistics Group ➤ Maintain Stat Group For Materials	OVRF	Define material statistics group.

TABLE 14.1 Statistics Group Settings *(continued)*

Menu Path	Transaction Code	Action
IMG ➤ Logistics - General ➤ LIS ➤ Logistics Data Warehouse ➤ Updating ➤ Update Control ➤ Settings: Sales ➤ Statistics Group ➤ Maintain Stat Group For Sales Documents	OVRN	Define statistics group for document type and item categories.
IMG ➤ Logistics - General ➤ LIS ➤ Logistics Data Warehouse ➤ Updating ➤ Update Control ➤ Settings: Sales ➤ Statistics Group ➤ Assign Stat Group For Each Sales Document Type		Select sales documents, and assign statistics group
IMG ➤ Logistics - General ➤ LIS ➤ Logistics Data Warehouse ➤ Updating ➤ Update Control ➤ Settings: Sales ➤ Statistics Group ➤ Assign Stat Group For Each Sales Document Type Item		Select item categories, and assign statistics group.
IMG ➤ Logistics - General ➤ LIS ➤ Logistics Data Warehouse ➤ Updating ➤ Update Control ➤ Settings: Sales ➤ Statistics Group ➤ Assign Stat Group For Each Delivery Type		Select delivery document type, and assign statistics group.
IMG ➤ Logistics - General ➤ LIS ➤ Logistics Data Warehouse ➤ Updating ➤ Update Control ➤ Settings: Sales ➤ Statistics Group ➤ Assign Stat Group For Each Sales Delivery Type Item		Select delivery item category, and assign statistics group.
IMG ➤ Logistics - General ➤ LIS ➤ Logistics Data Warehouse ➤ Updating ➤ Update Control ➤ Settings: Sales ➤ Statistics Group ➤ Determine Billing Document Types Relevant To Statistics		Select billing document types, and check the ones relevant for statistics.

As a sample, Figure 14.29 shows the setup of statistics groups for customers using transaction OVRA. We will use the values defined here in the customer master data in the next step.

FIGURE 14.29 Maintaining customer statistics groups

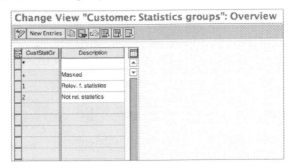

Maintaining Statistics Groups in Master Data

Besides the customization setting, the master data also needs to be updated so that data flows to the information structures. You have defined the customer and material statistics group. You have to maintain these fields in the customer master and material master records, respectively.

In the customer master, this field appears on the Sales tab in the Sales Area Data screen (Figure 14.30). Note that the values defined in Figure 14.29 are assigned here.

FIGURE 14.30 Customer statistics group field in customer master data

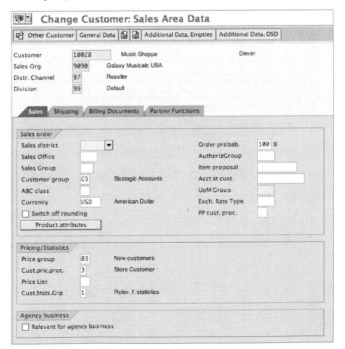

In the material master, this field appears in the Sales: Sales Org 2 view (Figure 14.31).

FIGURE 14.31 Material statistics group field in material master data

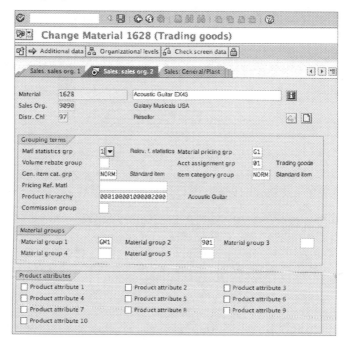

TIP   If you have already created customer and material master records in the system and you have to do a mass update for the statistics group field, try using the MASS function. Both the customer master (object KNA1) and the material master (BUS1001) are supported by the MASS transaction. The customer statistics group is the field KNVV-VERSG. The material statistics group is MVKE-VERSG.

Defining and Assigning Update Groups

You can use update groups to control the events that trigger the update of an information structure. Statistics groups are linked to update groups and control the updates. The following are the steps for maintaining update groups.

Defining Update Groups

To check the list of update groups, follow the path IMG ≻ Logistics - General ≻ Logistics Information Systems (LIS) ≻ Logistics Data Warehouse ≻ Updating ≻ Update Definition ≻ General Definition Using Update Groups ≻ Maintain Update Groups.

Update groups 1 and 2 are commonly used in SIS. Usually, you will not require more groups; however, there is a provision to set up new entries.

Maintaining Update Rules

You can use the update groups to define update rules. These rules control the events that are to be used to update the information structure. The path is IMG ≻ Logistics - General ≻ Logistics Information Systems (LIS) ≻ Logistics Data Warehouse ≻ Updating ≻ Update Definition ≻ Specific Definition Using Update Rules ≻ Maintain Update Rules (MC24).

Select the information structure and an update group. For this combination, maintain rules for updating each characteristic and key figure.

Figure 14.32 displays the rules for each key figure (using MC26, Display Transaction) in the standard information structure S001 with update group 1.

For each key figure, you can specify the event (EV), such as a sales order (VA) or a billing document (VD), that should trigger the update of the key figure. We'll present an example so you can understand the importance of events. The information structure S001 has certain statistics such as the incoming order value that would come from sales order data. Others such as the gross invoice sales would be updated only when a billing document is created. You will specify different events to control these updates.

The updating type (U) specifies how the statistic is to be updated. You can choose from A (Cumulative Updating) to add the statistics (such as values), B (Data Transfer Only) to overwrite the value, and C (Counter) to keep a count of items.

The Unit field specifies the unit of measurement for the statistic. For example, you can measure a document value in terms of document currency or statistics currency. Quantity can be measured in base units or sales units.

You can also add a formula (Form) and requirement routines (Req.) to control the update of a key figure.

This completes the setup for key figures. To set up rules for characteristics, click the Rules For Characteristics button at the bottom of the screen. As shown in Figure 14.33, you can control the source table and fields for each characteristic.

FIGURE 14.32 Update rules for key figures

Display Updating: Rules

Info structure	S001	Customer
Update group (stats)	1	SIS: Sales Document, Delivery, Billing Document
Status	Active	saved

Update Rules

Key Figures	Ev	U	Unit	Form	Req.
Incoming orders	VA	A	32		
Open orders	VA	A	32		
Sales	VD	A	32		
Gross orders	VA	A	32		
Net orders 1	VA	A	32		
Net orders 2	VA	A	32		
Orders: freight	VA	A	32		
Orders: subtotal 5	VA	A	32		
Orders: subtotal 6	VA	A	32		
Invoiced sls: gross	VD	A	32		
Net invoiced sls 1	VD	A	32		
Net invoiced sls 2	VD	A	32		
Inv. freight chrgs.	VD	A	32		
Bill. docmt: PS5	VD	A	32		
Billing docmt: PS6	VD	A	32		
Order items	VA	C	50		
Incoming orders qty	VA	A	01		
Open orders qty	VA	A	01		
Billing quantity	VD	A	01		
Orders: cost	VA	A	32		
Invoiced sls: cost	VD	A	32		

Rules for Key Fig...	Rules for Charact...

FIGURE 14.33 Update rules for characteristics

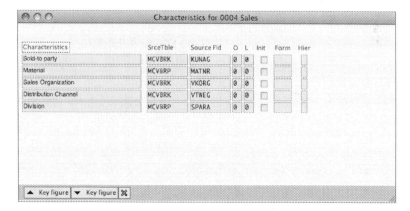

Characteristics for 0004 Sales

Characteristics	SrceTble	Source Fld	O	L	Init	Form	Hier
Sold-to party	MCVBRK	KUNAG	0	0			
Material	MCVBRP	MATNR	0	0			
Sales Organization	MCVBRK	VKORG	0	0			
Distribution Channel	MCVBRK	VTWEG	0	0			
Division	MCVBRP	SPARA	0	0			

▲ Key figure   ▼ Key figure   ✖

Assigning Update Groups

This step links together the statistics groups with the update groups. The menu path is IMG ➤ Logistics - General ➤ Logistics Information Systems (LIS) ➤ Logistics Data Warehouse ➤ Updating ➤ Update Control ➤ Settings: Sales ➤ Update Group ➤ Assign Update Group At Item Level (OVRP).

In this step, assign an update group for a combination of the following:

► Sales area

► Customer statistics group

► Material statistics group

► Sales document statistics group

► Sales document item statistics group

As shown in Figure 14.34, for the sales area (9090, 97, 99), update group 1 is assigned to sales documents. Update group 2 is attached to return documents.

FIGURE 14.34 Updating the group at the item level

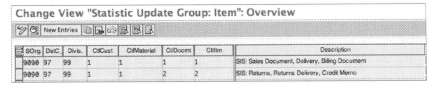

SOrg.	DstC.	Divis.	CtlCust	CtlMaterial	CtlDocmt	CtlItm	Description
9090	97	99	1	1	1	1	SIS: Sales Document, Delivery, Billing Document
9090	97	99	1	1	2	2	SIS: Returns, Returns Delivery, Credit Memo

Similarly, you have to assign the update group at a header level (Figure 14.35). The path is IMG ➤ Logistics - General ➤ Logistics Information Systems (LIS) ➤ Logistics Data Warehouse ➤ Updating ➤ Update Control ➤ Settings: Sales ➤ Update Group ➤ Assign Update Group At Header Level (OVRO).

In this step, assign an update group for a combination of header-level fields:

► Sales area

► Customer statistics group

► Sales document statistics group

With this setting, you have extended the update rules to the sales area and various statistics groups.

FIGURE 14.35 Updating the group at the header level

Change View "Statistics Update Sequence: Document Header": Overview

New Entries

SOrg.	DstC.	Divis.	CtlCust	CtlDocmt	Description
9090	97	99	1	1	SIS: Sales Document, Delivery, Billing Document
9090	97	99	1	2	SIS: Returns, Returns Delivery, Credit Memo

Activating Update

With this setting, you can control the frequency of updating the information structure and the period unit at which data is to be aggregated.

The menu path is as follows: IMG ≻ Logistics - General ≻ Logistics Information Systems (LIS) ≻ Logistics Data Warehouse ≻ Updating ≻ Update Control ≻ Activate Update.

Choose the application (such as Sales and Distribution). From the list, choose the information structure to be activated. Figure 14.36 shows the details screen for parameters.

FIGURE 14.36 Updating parameters

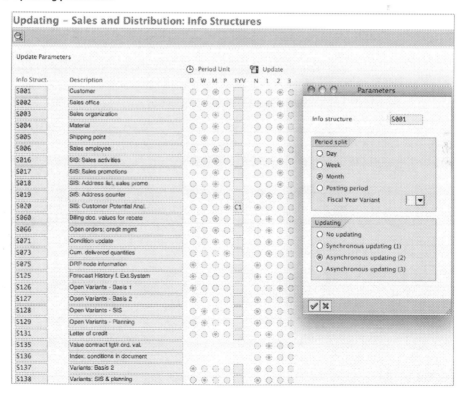

Choose the period split (such as daily, weekly, or monthly) at which the data is to be aggregated. For example, you may require monthly sales statistics or daily volumes of orders shipped.

In the options for updating, you can control when the information structure is to be updated:

No Updating   With this option, the information structure is not updated at all.

Synchronous Updating (1)   If you select Synchronous Updating (1), the structures are updated at the time of saving the transaction document. But you have to remember that if there is any problem during the update that results in process termination, then the original document is not saved.

Asynchronous Updating (2)   If you select Asynchronous Updating (2), the document update happens separately from the statistics update. Unlike synchronous updating, a termination of the statistics update does not affect the document.

Asynchronous Updating (3)   This option is similar to the previous one with one added feature: a time schedule. The update can be executed at a later time. Moreover, as opposed to the earlier options, the update is carried out for a batch of documents. Hence, it is also called *collective update*.

Accessing Reports

The data updated in the information structure can be queried and accessed based on your reporting requirements. SAP provides a set of standard reports (standard analyses) using the standard information structures.

We'll focus on the standard analyses for the Sales Information System. The menu path is SAP Menu ➢ Logistics ➢ Sales and Distribution ➢ Sales Information System ➢ Standard Analyses.

In this menu, you can get a list of available reports. Figure 14.37 shows an example of Customer Analysis (MCTA). It shows the statistics related to incoming orders for the customers of Galaxy Musical Instruments. There are several special functions in the menu bar (at the top of Figure 14.38) that help provide detailed analysis. For example, the Switch Drilldown function allows you to run the analysis at different characteristic levels. Thus, you can execute the same report at a sales organization level or a material level.

The Time Series option can split the data further into time buckets. In Figure 14.38, the statistics are reported on a monthly basis.

FIGURE 14.37 Customer Analysis screen

Customer Analysis: Basic List

Switch drilldown... Top N...

No. of Sold-to party: 4

Sold-to party	Incoming orders	Tot.order qty	Net orders 1	Orders: cost
Total	19,330.00 USD	309 EA	19,330.00 USD	308,000.00 USD
Melody Music East	1,230.00 USD	1 EA	1,230.00 USD	1,000.00 USD
Melody Music Kiosk	0.00 USD	300 EA	0.00 USD	300,000.00 USD
Music Shoppe	11,500.00 USD	5 EA	11,500.00 USD	4,000.00 USD
Style Music Store	6,600.00 USD	3 EA	6,600.00 USD	3,000.00 USD

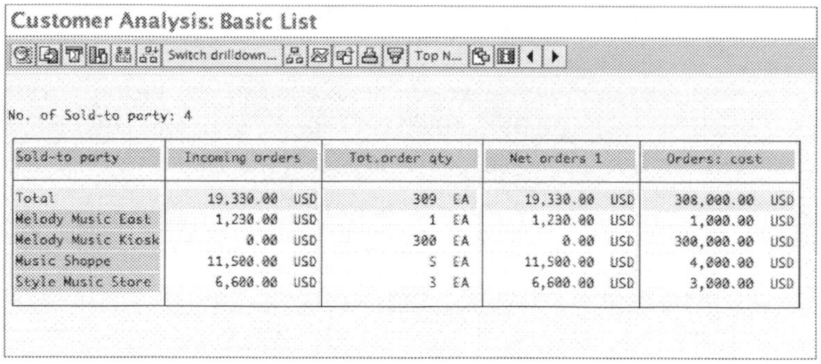

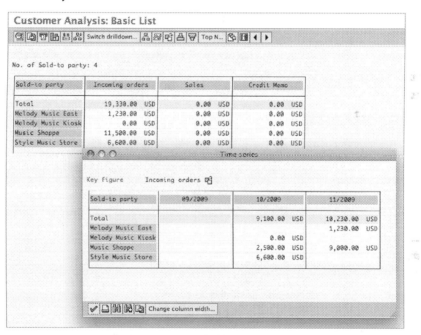

FIGURE 14.38 Time series analysis

Customer Analysis: Basic List

Switch drilldown... Top N...

No. of Sold-to party: 4

Sold-to party	Incoming orders	Sales	Credit Memo
Total	19,330.00 USD	0.00 USD	0.00 USD
Melody Music East	1,230.00 USD	0.00 USD	0.00 USD
Melody Music Kiosk	0.00 USD	0.00 USD	0.00 USD
Music Shoppe	11,500.00 USD	0.00 USD	0.00 USD
Style Music Store	6,600.00 USD	0.00 USD	0.00 USD

Time series

Key figure Incoming orders

Sold-to party	09/2009	10/2009	11/2009
Total		9,100.00 USD	10,230.00 USD
Melody Music East			1,230.00 USD
Melody Music Kiosk		0.00 USD	
Music Shoppe		2,500.00 USD	9,000.00 USD
Style Music Store		6,600.00 USD	

Change column width...

Before you exit from the report, a dialog box helps you save the analysis. This is known as a *selection version*. At any point, this version can be called up to get a "snapshot" of the report as of a particular time.

If the standard analyses do not meet your reporting requirement, you can customize your analysis using the flexible analyses option.

There is also a provision to update planned data. You can generate reports that show planned vs. actual statistics for comparison and ease of decision making.

An early warning system allows you to set up exception messages. You can set up requirements and specify a threshold value for a key figure. If the threshold is crossed, the system can perform a "follow-up" action. Such an analysis can bring the exceptional record to the attention of the decision maker. For example, you can define a warning that if the total order value is less than $1,000 for a customer, the records should be highlighted in red. Use transaction MC/Q to create an exception rule. Specify a requirement that the order value is less than $1,000. Then define follow-up processing to flag the item in red.

EDI/ALE/IDoc

Intermediate Document (IDoc) is a document-exchange format used by SAP to transmit and receive messages between two application systems. Using IDoc, you can send and receive structured messages for transactions with business partners, such as vendors and customers. The standard structure is understood by both the sending and receiving systems. Since the message has a specific structure, it can be processed automatically. In contrast, if transaction details are sent by mail or fax, the receiver has to read and enter the data manually in their system. Structured messages save you from this effort and also ensure consistency and speed.

EDI and ALE

EDI and ALE are two techniques that use IDoc for exchanging business data.

Electronic Data Interchange (EDI) is the electronic exchange of business data between two partners. From an SD point of view, a common use of EDI is to exchange transactions about sales orders, deliveries, and invoices with your customers.

Application Link Enabling (ALE) enables the linking together of different applications running on different systems. For example, if you have other SAP or non-SAP systems in the landscape, you can share customer master or material master data with all the systems using ALE.

Setting up the EDI/ALE interface and IDoc is a vast topic that is outside the scope of this book. In this chapter, we will introduce you to some of the fundamentals that you will require as an SD expert.

The IDoc Structure

An IDoc is structured into three parts:

Control record   The control record contains administrative information about the IDoc. This includes information about the IDoc being sent, the sender, and the recipient. It can be compared to a cover letter that precedes and introduces the main correspondence.

Data records   There can be several data records structured logically. They contain the transaction information such as sold-to party, material, quantity, price, and so on.

Status record   The status records contain information about the processing status of the IDoc along with a time stamp. The status records get added over time, based on the progress of the IDoc. For example, there will be a status record when the IDoc has been generated, when the IDoc is ready for dispatch, and when it has been processed successfully. In the case of any error, the message and code are displayed in the status record.

To display an IDoc, the path is as follows: SAP Menu ➤ Tools ➤ ALE ➤ ALE Administration ➤ Monitoring ➤ IDoc Display ➤ Display (WE02).

On the selection screen, you can search for a list of IDocs. For a selected IDoc, you can see the details of the control, data, and status records. Figure 14.39 shows an IDoc for a sales order.

FIGURE 14.39 Structure of an IDoc

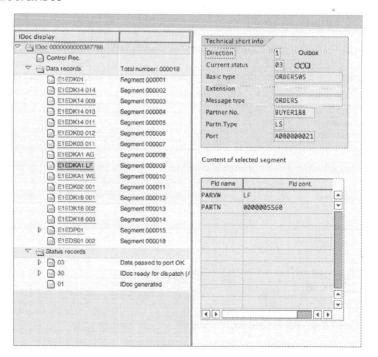

Let's look at some of the IDoc details, as shown in Figure 14.39:

Technical Short Info The Technical Short Info box contains some of the control information. Among other details it has the Message Type field. ORDERS conveys that this IDoc is about a sales order. Similarly, DESADV is used for delivery-shipping notification, and INVOIC is used for billing documents.

Data segments Within the data records, there are data segments. The data is stored within the segments. If you examine the segment E1EDKA1 LF, as shown in Figure 14.39, you can see it contains information about the ship-to party. The segment consists of field names and actual field contents (data). In the example, one of the fields in the segment is the partner number (PARTN), and the value is 5560. Similarly, other segments contain all the data required to create a sales order. The data segment E1EDP01 contains item data such as the material number, quantity, and price.

One of the important fields in E1EDP01 is the customer expected price. This feature helps avoid price-related disputes. Often there are pricing agreements between the two parties recorded in contracts or catalogs. To make sure that they agree on the same price, the customer can send an expected price along with the purchase order. During the processing of the IDoc, the customer expected price is compared with the item price in sales order creation. If the difference is beyond a tolerance limit, the order can be placed on a block, and corrective action is required. This step reduces price-related disputes at a later stage.

The customer expected price is mapped in E1EDP01. It can either be a unit price (such as $10 per unit) or a value (such as the total item value of $100). When a sales order is created by processing the IDoc, the expected price gets copied to pricing condition type EDI1 (expected price) and EDI2 (expected value) in the pricing procedure. The value is then compared with the net price of the sales order item. The pricing routines 8 and 9 are used with pricing condition types, respectively. They control the deviation that is permitted.

NOTE One of the important uses of IDoc is in the intercompany billing scenario discussed in Chapter 9, "Billing." The invoice sent by the supplying company code to the receiving company code has to be entered at the receiving end as a vendor invoice. In this case, the two company codes are set up as customers and vendors to each other. The intercompany invoice can be transmitted via IDoc and processed at the receiving end as a vendor invoice. This saves time and effort and ensures consistency of intercompany data.

IDoc Processing

IDocs are processed in the background with regular jobs. You can monitor and process an IDoc manually using transaction BD87. The menu path is SAP Menu ➢ Tools ➢ ALE ➢ ALE Administration ➢ Monitoring ➢ IDoc Display ➢ Status Monitor (BD87). Enter the IDoc number in the selection screen and process. The outcome will be displayed in the status monitor, as shown in Figure 14.40.

FIGURE 14.40   Status monitor

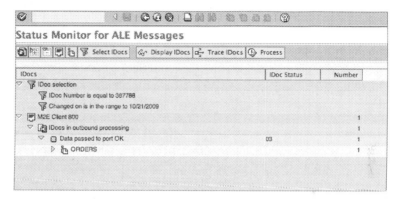

Output Processing for ALE and EDI

In our discussion on output determination in Chapter 4, "Partner, Text, and Outcome Determination," we showed you how output types are configured and how an output medium is assigned to them. In the case of transmitting the outbound message via EDI, the output medium is 6. In the settings for the processing routine, assign the form routine EDI_PROCESSING in the program RSNASTED. For ALE, the communication medium is A. Use the routine ALE_PROCESSING of the program RSNASTED. Figure 14.41 shows a typical output type setup for EDI and ALE.

FIGURE 14.41   Output processing for ALE and EDI

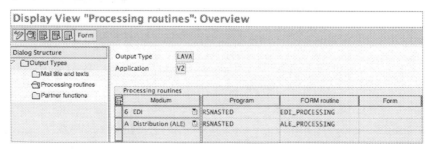

Custom Enhancements in SAP

During the course of this book, we have covered different functionalities and how they can be configured to suit the requirements of your organization. The customization menu provides these options to tailor the system response as per your requirements. However, it may not be adequate to meet certain needs specific to your organization or industry. In such cases, you can introduce changes to the program code in a controlled way. It is very important that the changes introduced do not have any side effects on the core functionality offered by SAP.

The following sections introduce the various options for carrying out enhancements to programming code. You will always require an ABAP expert to write the program code. This is just an overview and not a complete guide to implementing enhancements.

User Exits

There are specific points in standard programs where the user can attach their custom logic. These are called *user exits*. The common analogy used is that these are like hooks provided by SAP, where you can attach your custom code to the main programs. You have already seen some examples of user exits in earlier chapters such as Chapter 5 and 8.

User exits are available for different functionality, such as sales order user exits, delivery-related user exits, and so on. In the customization menu, user exits are listed under the System Modification nodes in each application area.

SAP Enhancements

SAP enhancements are customer exits provided by SAP as a controlled way to carry out changes. They consists of a function module that has an include statement where the custom code can be introduced. The input and output parameters control the data that can be brought in and sent out from the enhancement.

You can check the available enhancements using transaction SMOD. The menu path is SAP Menu ➤ Tools ➤ ABAP Workbench ➤ Utilities ➤ Enhancements.

If you have to use an enhancement, you have to first create a project using transaction CMOD and assign the SAP enhancement to the project. Then you can introduce your code below the include statement.

Figure 14.42 shows enhancement V45A00002 in SMOD. You can use this enhancement to define a default sold-to party when a sales document is being created.

FIGURE 14.42 Enhancements

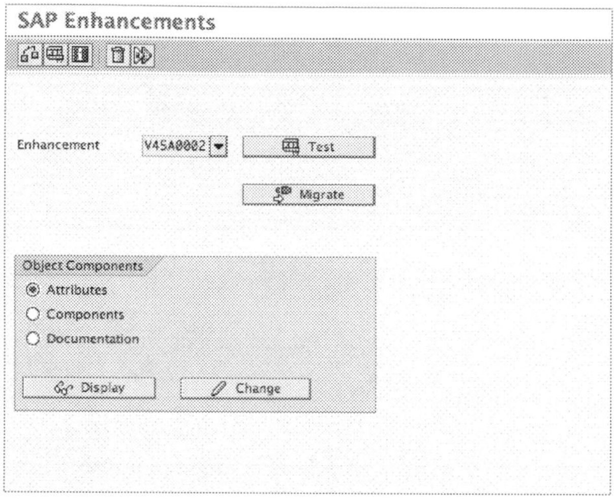

Within this enhancement is the function module EXIT_SAPMV45A_002 with an include statement (Figure 14.43). The export parameter listed for this function module includes the customer number (KUNNR). This means that you can write a custom code that will export a customer number to the main program. This number will then appear in the sales document.

FIGURE 14.43 Function module within the enhancement V45A00002

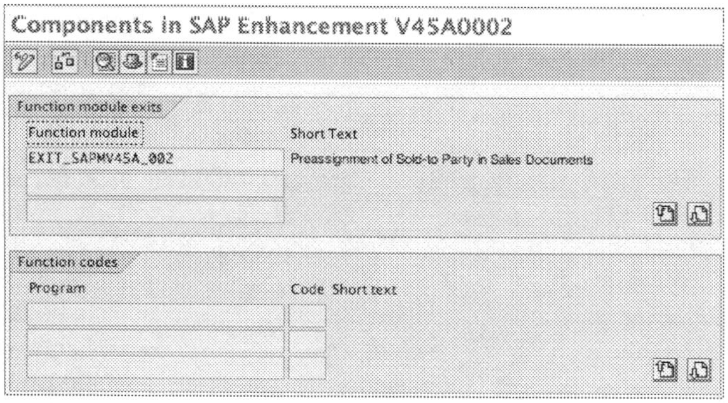

Business Add-ins (BAdI)

A *business add-in* is a new technique provided by SAP for carrying out enhancements. With the release of Netweaver 7.0, the concept of BAdI has been further enhanced.

In the customization menu, BAdIs are listed under the System Modification nodes in each application area. From the list, you can select the BAdI based on your requirement.

BAdIs are also accessible using the BAdI builder transaction SE18. The menu path is as follows: SAP Menu ➤ Tools ➤ ABAP Workbench ➤ Utilities ➤ Business Add-Ins.

Consider the example of the BAdI LE_SHP_DELIVERY_PROC in Figure 14.44. It enables you to carry out enhancements in delivery processing.

FIGURE 14.44 BAdI builder

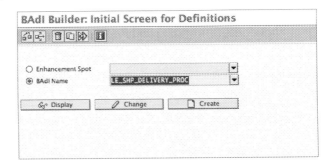

This BAdI has the interface IF_EX_LE_SHP_DELIVERY_PROC with methods such as SAVE_DOCUMENT_PREPARE, as shown in Figure 14.45. Using this method, you can perform additional checks or changes to data just before the delivery document is about to be saved.

FIGURE 14.45 Details of a BAdI

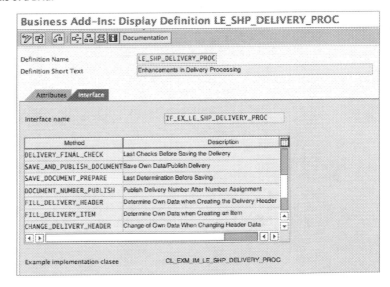

Summary

In this chapter, we discussed the concept of enhancement packages and switch frameworks that will help in implementing innovations released after ECC 6.0. We also covered the following important tools and techniques:

► QuickViewer and SAP Query, which are reporting tools

► MASS, a tool for mass update of documents

► Logistics Information System, a reporting tool

► EDI/ALE/IDoc, which are tools for communicating with other systems and partners

► User exits, enhancements, and business add-ins, which are used in making custom enhancements to SAP standard programs

This is the concluding chapter of this book. In these 14 chapters, you should have gained insights into the various steps in a sales cycle and the associated functionalities. Armed with this knowledge, you should continue to explore SAP further and leverage it to meet the changing needs of your organization.

We wish you all the best in your SAP adventures!

Transaction Codes and Database Tables

This appendix recaps the transaction codes presented in the book. We have also listed database tables and transaction codes not covered in the chapters. Although the arrangement of the transaction codes in the appendix corresponds to the chapters of the book, the database tables are grouped in logical sequence based on the nature of data that is stored in the table. For example, Table A.16 lists all the database tables that store master data information such as customer master, material master, and so on, whereas Table A.17 lists all the database tables that store SD transaction data such as sales order data, delivery document data, and so on. You use transaction code SE16 and SE16N to browse the data stored in the database tables. To make it easier to search the data from the tables, standard SAP also provides composite views on database tables. For example, rather than browsing KNA1 and KNVV separately, you can use KNA1VV to browse KNA1 and KNVV data together. Table A.19 lists the composite database views that are available in SAP SD.

For the database tables that store condition record data, SAP follows a naming convention. Pricing tables start with A, account determination tables start with C, material determination tables start with D, and so on. So if you would like to browse pricing condition table 901 where you maintained the customer-specific price (for example), use table name A901 in the data browser transaction (SE16N). Table A.20 lists the naming conventions for condition tables based on various determination techniques.

Transaction Codes

Table A.1 through Table A.14 recap the transaction codes used in this book, as well as additional ones.

TABLE A.1 Codes Related to Chapter 1, "Introduction to Sales and Distribution"

Tcode	Description
SEARCH_SAP_MENU	Transaction to Search Transactions in SAP Easy Access Menu
SPRO	Transaction to Access IMG Menu
SE10	Transport Organizer
SE01	Transport Organizer (Extended View)
SE11	ABAP Dictionary

TABLE A.1 Codes Related to Chapter 1, "Introduction to Sales and Distribution" *(continued)*

Tcode	Description
SE16	Data Browser
SE16N	Data Browser—General Table Display
SE38	ABAP Editor

TABLE A.2 Codes Related to Chapter 2, "Enterprise Structure"

Tcode	Description
OVX3	Assign Sales Organization to Company Code
OVX3N	Assign Sales Organization to Company Code
OVX4	Define Sales Group
OVX5	Define Sales Organization
OVX6	Assign Plants to Sales Org./Distr.Channel
OVX6N	Assign Plants to Sales Org./Distr.Channel
OVX7	Loading Points
OVX8	Check Report Organization Sales
OVX8N	Check Report Organization
OVXA	Assign Division to Sales Organization
OVXAN	Assign Division to Sales Organization
OVXB	Divisions
OVXC	Assign Shipping Point to Plant
OVXD	Shipping Points
OVXG	Define Sales Areas
OVXGN	Define Sales Areas
OVXI	Distribution Channels
OVXJ	Assign Sales Group to Sales Office
OVXJN	Assign Sales Group to Sales Office
OVXK	Assign Distribution Channels to Sales Organization
OVXKN	Assign Distribution Channels to Sales Organization
OVXM	Assign Sales Office to Sales Area
OVXMN	Assign Sales Office to Sales Area

TABLE A.2   Codes Related to Chapter 2, "Enterprise Structure" *(continued)*

Tcode	Description
OVXT	Transportation Planning Points
OVZ4	Maintain Factory Calendar
OX09	Customize Storage Locations
OX10	Customize Plant
OY05	Factory Calendar
SCAL	Factory Calendar with GUI
VOR1	Common Distribution Channel
VOR2	Common Division

TABLE A.3   Codes Related to Chapter 3, "Master Data in SD"

Tcode	Description
VD01	Create Customer (Sales View)
VD02	Change Customer (Sales View)
VD03	Display Customer (Sales View)
VD04	Customer Changes (SD)
VD05	Block Customer (Sales View)
VD06	Mark Customer for Deletion (Sales View)
FD01	Create Customer (Accounting View)
FD02	Change Customer (Accounting View)
FD03	Display Customer (Accounting View)
FD04	Display Customer Account Changes (Accounting View)
FD05	Block Customer (Accounting View)
FD06	Mark Customer for Deletion (Accounting View)
XD01	Create Customer (Centrally)
XD02	Change Customer (Centrally)
XD03	Display Customer (Centrally)
XD04	Customer Changes (Centrally)
XD05	Block Customer (Centrally)

TABLE A.3 Codes Related to Chapter 3, "Master Data in SD" *(continued)*

Tcode	Description
XD06	Mark Customer for Deletion (Centrally)
XD07	Change Customer Account Group
XD99	Customer Master Mass Maintenance
XDN1	Maintain Number Ranges (Customer)
OVT0	Define Account Group and Field Selection for Customer
OB20	Define Transaction-Dependent Screen Layout
VAP1	Create Contact Person
VAP2	Change Contact Person
VAP3	Display Contact Person
V-12	Create Customer Hierarchy Node
OVH1	Define Hierarchy Type
OVH2	Allowed Account Group Assignment for Customer Hierarchy
OVH3	Allowed Sales Area Assignment for Customer Hierarchy
OVH4	Hierarchy Type for Pricing
VDH1	Customer Hierarchy Maintenance (SD)
VDH1N	Display/Maintain Customer Hierarchy
VDH2	Display Customer Hierarchy
VDH2N	Display Customer Hierarchy
MM01	Create Material Master
MM02	Change Material Master
MM03	Display Material Master
MM04	Display Material Changes
MM06	Flag Material for Deletion
MM16	Schedule Material for Deletion
MMAM	Change Material Type
MMPV	Close Material Period

TABLE A.4   Codes Related to Chapter 4, "Partner, Text, and Output Determination"

Tcode	Description
VOPAN	Customizing Partners
VOTXN	Maintain Text Customizing
V/56	Create Output Condition Table (Sales Document)
V/57	Change Output Condition Table (Sales Document)
V/58	Display Output Condition Table (Sales Document)
V/48	Maintain Output Access Sequences (Sales Document)
V/30	Maintain Output Types (Sales Document)
V/32	Maintain Output Determination Procedure (Sales Document)
V/59	Create Output Condition Table (Delivery Document)
V/60	Change Output Condition Table (Delivery Document)
V/61	Display Output Condition Table (Delivery Document)
V/50	Maintain Output Access Sequences (Delivery Document)
V/34	Maintain Output Types (Delivery Document)
V/36	Maintain Output Determination Procedure (Delivery Document)
V/77	Create Output Condition Table (Shipment & Transport)
V/78	Change Output Condition Table (Shipment & Transport)
V/79	Display Output Condition Table (Shipment & Transport)
V/80	Maintain Output Access Sequences (Shipment & Transport)
V/82	Maintain Output Types (Shipment & Transport)
V/84	Maintain Output Determination Procedure (Shipment & Transport)
V/93	Create Output Condition Table (Packaging)
V/94	Change Output Condition Table (Packaging)
V/95	Display Output Condition Table (Packaging)
V/96	Maintain Output Access Sequences (Packaging)
V/97	Maintain Output Types (Packaging)
V/99	Maintain Output Determination Procedure (Packaging)
V/62	Create Output Condition Table (Billing Document)
V/63	Change Output Condition Table (Billing Document)

TABLE A.4   Codes Related to Chapter 4, "Partner, Text, and Output Determination" *(continued)*

Tcode	Description
V/64	Display Output Condition Table (Billing Document)
V/54	Maintain Output Access Sequences (Billing Document)
V/40	Maintain Output Types (Billing Document)
V/42	Maintain Output Determination Procedure (Billing Document)
VV11	Create Output Condition Records: Sales
VV12	Change Output Condition Records: Sales
VV13	Display Output Condition Records: Sales
VV21	Create Output Condition Records: Shipping
VV22	Change Output Condition Records: Shipping
VV23	Display Output Condition Records: Shipping
VV31	Create Output Condition Records: Billing
VV32	Change Output Condition Records: Billing
VV33	Display Output Condition Records: Billing
VV61	Create Output Condition Records: Handling Units
VV62	Change Output Condition Records: Handling Unit
VV63	Display Output Condition Records: Handling Unit
VV71	Create Output Condition Records: Transportation
VV72	Change Output Condition Records: Transportation
VV73	Display Output Condition Records: Transportation
VF31	Output from Billing Documents
VL70	Output from Picking Lists
VL71	Output from Outbound Deliveries
VL72	Output from Groups of Deliveries
VL74	Output from Handling Units
VL75	Shipping Notification Output
VT70	Output for Shipments
SO10	Standard Text Maintenance

TABLE A.5   Codes Related to Chapter 5, "Pricing and Tax Determination"

Tcode	Description
OV24	Field Catalog for Pricing Condition Table
V/03	Create Pricing Condition Table
V/04	Change Pricing Condition Table
V/05	Display Pricing Condition Table
V/07	Maintain Pricing Access Sequence
V/06	Maintain Pricing Condition Type
OVB2	Define Upper and Lower Limit for Pricing Conditions
V/08	Maintain Pricing Procedure
OVKI	Define Document Pricing Procedure
OVKJ	Assign Document Pricing Procedure to Sales Document
OVTP	Assign Document Pricing Procedure to Billing Documents
OVKP	Define Customer Pricing Procedure
OVKK	Define Pricing Procedure Determination
OVKO	Pricing for Item Categories
VCHECKT683	Customizing Check Pricing Procedure
VCHECKT685A	Customizing Check Condition Types
VK11	Create Pricing Condition Record
VK12	Change Pricing Condition Record
VK13	Display Pricing Condition Record
VK31	Condition Maintenance: Create
VK32	Condition Maintenance: Change
VK33	Condition Maintenance: Display
OV23	Condition Exclusion Indicator
OV30	Condition Exclusion: Procedure Assignment
OV31	Maintain Exclusion Group
OV32	Maintain Condition Types for Exclusion Group
VOK8	Maintain Condition Exclusion for Pricing Procedure
OVSI	Price List Categories
OVSJ	Material Condition Group
OVSL	Pricing Groups for Customers

TABLE A.5   Codes Related to Chapter 5, "Pricing and Tax Determination" *(continued)*

Tcode	Description
V/LA	Create Pricing Report
V/LB	Change Pricing Report
V/LC	Display Pricing Report
V/LD	Execute Pricing Report
V/LE	Generate Pricing Reports
V/N1	Maintain Accesses (Free Goods—sls)
V/N2	Create Free Goods Table
V/N3	Display Free Goods Table (SD)
V/N4	Free Goods Types—Sales
V/N5	Free Goods: Procedure for SD
V/N6	Free Goods Procedure Determ. SD
V-45	Create Price List
V-46	Create Price List w/Ref.
V-47	Change Price List
V-48	Display Price List
V_NL	Edit Net Price List
S_ALR_87100142	Price List Report
S_ALR_87100160	Price List Report
OVK1	Taxes: Tax Catg./Country
OVK2	Taxes: Regions
OVKF	US Tax—Set Up Ctry/Region/County
OVKG	US Tax—Set Up Ctry/Region/City
OVK3	Taxes: Customer Taxes
OVK4	Taxes: Material Taxes
FTXP	Maintain Tax Code
OVKB	Tax Record Conditions VK11—Selection by Country
OVKC	Tax Record Conditions VK12—Selection by Country
OVKD	Tax Record Conditions VK13—Selection by Country
OVKE	Tax Record Conditions VK14—Selection by Country

TABLE A.6 Codes Related to Chapter 6, "Availability Check, Transfer of Requirements, and Backorders"

Tcode	Description
OVZ0	Activate AC & TOR at Requirement Class Level
OVZG	Activate AC & TOR at Requirement Class Level
OVZH	Requirement Class Assignment to Requirements Types
OVZI	Rules for Determining Requirement Type Using Transactions
OVZ8	Availability Check Procedure by Schedule Line Category
OVZ2	Define Checking Group
OVZ9	Define Scope of Availability Check
OVZ3	Define Checking Group Default Value
OVZJ	Default Values for Availability Check by Sales Area
OVZ1	Define Material Block for Other Users
OVZ7	Block Quantity Confirmation in Delivery Block
OVZK	Procedure per Delivery Item Category
OMIH	Check. Rule for Updating Backorders
CO09	Availability Overview
MB53	Display Plant Stock Availability
MD04	Display Stock/Requirements Situation
MMBE	Stock Overview
V.15	Display Backorders
V_R1	List of Backorders
V_R2	Display List of Backorders
V_RA	Backorder Processing: Selection List
V_V2	Updating Sales Documents by Material

TABLE A.7 Codes Related to Chapter 7, "Sales"

Tcode	Description
VA00	Initial Sales Menu
VA01	Create Sales Order
VA02	Change Sales Order
VA03	Display Sales Order

TABLE A.7   Codes Related to Chapter 7, "Sales" *(continued)*

Tcode	Description
VA05	List of Sales Orders
VA05N	List of Sales Orders
VA11	Create Inquiry
VA12	Change Inquiry
VA13	Display Inquiry
VA14L	Sales Documents Blocked for Delivery
VA15	Inquiries List
VA15N	Inquiries List
VA21	Create Quotation
VA22	Change Quotation
VA23	Display Quotation
VA25	Quotations List
VA25N	List of Quotations
VA26	Collective Processing for Quotations
VA31	Create Scheduling Agreement
VA32	Change Scheduling Agreement
VA33	Display Scheduling Agreement
VA35	List of Scheduling Agreements
VA35N	List of Scheduling Agreements
VA41	Create Contract
VA42	Change Contract
VA43	Display Contract
VA45	List of Contracts
VA45N	List of Contracts
VA46	List of Contracts for Subsequent Processing
VOV6	Maintain Schedule Line Categories
VOV7	Maintain Item Categories
VOV8	Document Type Maintenance
VTAA	Copy Control—Sales Document to Sales Document
VTAF	Copy Control—Billing Document to Sales Document

TABLE A.7   Codes Related to Chapter 7, "Sales" *(continued)*

Tcode	Description
OVAO	Allowable Sales Document by Sales Area—Combine Sales Organization
OVAM	Allowable Sales Document by Sales Area—Combine Distribution Channels
OVAN	Allowable Sales Document by Sales Area—Combine Divisions
OVAZ	Assign Sales Order Type permitted for Sales Area
OVAU	Define Order Reasons
OVAS	Define Blocking Reasons
OVAL	Assign Blocking Reasons to Sales Document Types
OVAG	Define Rejection Reasons
OVA0	Define Status Groups for Incompletion Procedure
OVA2	Define Incompletion Procedure
V_UC	Incomplete Sales Documents
V.00	List of Incomplete Documents
V.01	List of Incomplete SD Documents
V.02	List of Incomplete Sales Orders
V.03	List of Incomplete Inquiries
V.04	List of Incomplete Quotations
V.05	List of Incomplete Scheduling Agreements
V.06	List of Incomplete Contracts
V23	Sales Documents Blocked for Billing
VCHECKTVCPF	Customizing Check Copying Control
VCU3	Display Incompletion Log
VOVL	Cancellation Rules
VOVM	Cancellation Procedures
VOVN	Assignment Rules/Cancellation Proc.
VOVO	Val. Period. Category
VOVP	Rule Table for Date Determination
VOVQ	Cancellation Reasons

TABLE A.8 Codes Related to Chapter 8, "Shipping and Transportation"

Tcode	Description
VL01N	Create Delivery Document
VL02N	Change Delivery Document
VL03N	Display Delivery Document
VL10	User-Specific Delivery Scenario
VL10A	Sales Order, Fast Display
VL10B	Purchase Order, Fast Display
VL10C	Sales Order Item Display
VL10D	Purchase Order Item Display
VL10E	Sales Orders, Schedule Lines
VL10F	Purchase Order Item Schedule Lines
VL10G	Sales and Purchase Orders Fast Display
VL10H	Sales and Purchase Order Items Fast Display
VL10I	Sales and Purchase Order Schedule Lines
VL06P	Outbound Deliveries for Picking
LT03	Create Transfer Order
LT21	Display Transfer Order
LT12	Confirm Transfer Order
LT15	Cancel Transfer Order
HUPAST	Packing Station
VT01N	Create Shipment
VT04	Collective Processing of Shipments
VT02N	Change Shipment
VT03N	Display Shipment
VT70	Output for shipment
VL06G	Outbound Deliveries for Goods Issue
VL09	Cancel Goods Issue
VTRK	Parcel Tracking
OVLK	Define Delivery Types
OVLP	Define Item Categories for Deliveries
0184	Define Item Category Determination

TABLE A.8   Codes Related to Chapter 8, "Shipping and Transportation" *(continued)*

Tcode	Description
VTLA	Define Copy Controls for Deliveries
OVLP	Maintain Delivery Item Categories for Picking
0VTC	Define Routes And Stages
MCTA	Customer Analysis Report
MCTC	Material Analysis
MCTE	Sales Organization Analysis
MCTK	Shipping Point Analysis
MCTI	Sales Employee Analysis
MCTG	Sales Office Analysis
MCYI	Exception Analysis
MCSI	User-Defined Analysis
MC/Q	Create Exception
MC/R	Change Exception
MC/S	Display Exception

TABLE A.9   Codes Related to Chapter 9, "Billing"

Tcode	Description
VF01	Create Billing Document
VF02	Change Billing Document
VF03	Display Billing Document
VF04	Maintain Billing Due List
VF05	List Billing Documents
VF05N	List of Billing Documents—New Worklist in ECC
VF06	Batch Billing
VF08	Billing for External Delivery
VFRB	Retro-Billing
VF11	Cancel Billing Document
VF21	Create Invoice List
VF22	Change Invoice list
VF23	Display Invoice List

TABLE A.9   Codes Related to Chapter 9, "Billing" *(continued)*

Tcode	Description
VF24	Edit Work List for Invoice Lists
VF25	List of Invoice Lists
VF26	Cancellation Invoice List
VFX2	Display Blocked Billing Documents
VFX3	List Blocked Billing Documents
VOEX	Incompleteness: Billing Document
VOF1	Configuration: Collective Billing
VOF2	Configuration Invoice List Info
VOF3	Edit Work List for Invoice Lists
VOFA	Billing Doc: Document Type
VOFM	Configuration for Requirements, Formulae
VOFS	Billing: Document Types
OVV7	Assign Invoice List to Billing Documents
OVV4	Billing Blocking Reasons
OVVA	Sales Organization Assignment to Intercompany Customer Number
OVV8	Sales Order Types to Intercompany Billing Document Type Assignment
OVVR	Processing Groups for Invoice List
VTFF	Copy Control from Billing Document to Billing Document
VTFL	Copy Control from Delivery to Billing Document
VTFA	Copy Control from Order Document to Billing Document
CMP_PROCESSING	Complaint Processing
SCAL	Billing Schedule
OVBI	Maintain Billing Plan Type for Periodic Billing
OVBO	Maintain Billing Plan Type for Milestone Billing
OVBM	Maintain Date Proposals for Billing Plan
OVBJ	Maintain Date Category for Billing Plan Type
OVBL	Assign Date Category Proposal for Billing Plan
OVBS	Maintain Rule for Date Determination
OVBP	Assignment of Billing Plan Type
OVBR	Assignment of Billing Plan Type to Item Category

TABLE A.9   Codes Related to Chapter 9, "Billing" *(continued)*

Tcode	Description
OVBN	Maintain Date IDs
VCHECKVOFA	Customizing Check Billing Types
VBO1	Create Rebate Agreement
VBO2	Change Rebate Agreement
VBO3	Display Rebate Agreement
OVB3	Reorganization of Billing Index for Rebates
OVB1	Rebate Activation at Sales Organization Level
VB(1	Rebate Number Ranges
VB(2	Set Up Rebate Agreement Type
VB(3	Rebate Condition Type Groups Overview
VB(4	Condition Types in Condition Type Groups
VB(5	Assignment Condition -> Condition Type Group
VB(6	Rebate Group Maintenance
VB(7	Rebate Agreement Settlement
VB(8	List Rebate Agreements
OV20	Create Condition Table for Rebates
OV21	Change Condition Table for Rebates
OV22	Display Condition Table for Rebates
OV28	Field Catalog for Rebates
VCHECKBONUS	Customizing Check for Rebate
FCRD	Payment Card User Menu
FKPC	Payment Card Processing
FPPCSL	Log Display for Payment Card
FPPCTC	Payment Card—Items to Be Invoiced
FPPCAI	PCARD: Items in Card Account
FPPCAS	PCARD: Invoiced items
FPPCBP	PCARD: Business Partner with Cards
FPPCDL	PCARD: Delete Logs
FPPCDS	PCARD: Perform Invoicing
FPPCLI	PCARD: Log (Paid Items)

TABLE A.9   Codes Related to Chapter 9, "Billing" *(continued)*

Tcode	Description
FPPCLP	PCARD: Log (Payments)
FPPCSF	PCARD: Display Invoicing File
OV80	Create Condition Table for Payment Card Account Determination
OV81	Change Condition Table for Payment Card Account Determination
OV82	Display Condition Table for Payment Card Account Determination
OV83	Field Catalog for Condition Tables for Payment Card Account Determination
OV84	Access Sequence for Payment Card Account Determination
OV85	Condition Type for Payment Card Account Determination
OV86	Condition Procedure for Payment Card Account Determination
OV87	Credit Card Accounts
OV88	Assign Billing Type to Credit Card Procedure
OV9A	Card Authorization Requirements
PACC1	Verification Rule for Card Numbers
PACC2	Maintain Payment Card Type
VCC1	Payment Cards Worklist
S_ALR_87014369	Payment Card Authorization in Background

TABLE A.10   Codes Related to Chapter 10, "Account Assignment and Revenue Recognition"

Tcode	Description
OVK5	Material Account Assignment Groups
OVK8	Customer Account Assignment Groups
OV25	Field Catalog
V/12	Create Account Determination Condition Table
V/13	Change Account Determination Condition Table
V/14	Display Account Determination Condition Table
V/10	Maintain Access Sequence for Account Determination
V/09	Maintain Condition Types for Account Determination
V/11	Maintain Account Determination Procedure
VKOA	Assign GL accounts for Account Determination
OVUR	Assign Accounts for Unbilled Receivables

TABLE A.10 Codes Related to Chapter 10, "Account Assignment and Revenue Recognition" *(continued)*

Tcode	Description
OVEP	Set Revenue Recognition for Item Categories
VF44	Revenue Recognition Worklist
VF45	Revenue Report
VF46	Revenue Recognition Cancellation
VF47	Revenue Recognition Consistency Check
VF48	Revenue Recognition Compare Report

TABLE A.11 Codes Related to Chapter 11, "Credit Management"

Tcode	Description
F.28	Customers: Reset Credit Limit
F.31	Credit Management—Overview
F.32	Credit Management—Missing Data
F.33	Credit Management—Brief Overview
F.34	Credit Management—Mass Change
F.35	Credit Master Sheet
FCV1	Create A/R Summary
FCV2	Delete A/R Summary
FCV3	Early Warning List
FD10N	Customer Balance Display
FD11	Customer Account Analysis
FD24	Credit Limit Changes
FD32	Change Customer Credit Management
FD33	Display Customer Credit Management
FD37	Credit Management Mass Change
FDK43	Credit Management—Master Data List
OB01	Define Risk Categories
OB12	Define Credit Management Groups
OB45	Define Credit Control Area
OB51	Define Credit Representative
OBY6	Assign Credit Control Area to Company Code

TABLE A.11   Codes Related to Chapter 11, "Credit Management" *(continued)*

Tcode	Description
OBZJ	Define Client Specific Setting for Credit Management—AR Summary and DSO Calculation Setup
OBZK	Permitted Credit Control Area for Company Code
OVA6	Define Credit Groups
OVA7	Credit Relevancy of Item Categories
OVA8	Automatic Credit Checks
OVAD	Assign Credit Groups to Delivery Document Type
OVAK	Assign Credit Groups to Sales Order Type
OVBD	Assign Credit Control Area
OVFL	Assign Credit Control Area to Sales Area
S_ALR_87012214	Customers with Missing Credit Data
S_ALR_87012215	Display Changes to Credit Management
S_ALR_87012216	Credit Limit Overview
S_ALR_87012217	Credit Overview
S_ALR_87012218	Credit Master Sheet
S_ALR_87012219	Credit Mgmt: Early Warning List
S_ALR_87012220	Reset Credit Limit for Customers
S_ALR_87012221	Credit Limit Data Mass Change
VKM1	Credit Management—Process Blocked SD Documents
VKM2	Credit Management—Process Released SD Documents
VKM3	Credit Management—Process Sales Documents
VKM4	Credit Management—Process SD Documents
VKM5	Credit Management—Process Delivery Documents

TABLE A.12   Codes Related to Chapter 12, "Material Determination, Listing, Exclusion, and Proposals"

Tcode	Description
OV05	Material Listing/Exclusion—Condition Table Create
OV06	Material Listing/Exclusion—Condition Table Change
OV07	Material Listing/Exclusion—Condition Table Display
OV27	Material Listing/Exclusion—Field Catalog

TABLE A.12 Codes Related to Chapter 12, "Material Determination, Listing, Exclusion, and Proposals" *(continued)*

Tcode	Description
OV01	Access Sequence Maintenance for Material Listing/Exclusion
OV02	Condition Type Maintenance for Material Listing/Exclusion
OV03	Determination Procedure for Material Listing/Exclusion
OV04	Procedure to Sales Document Type Assignment
VB01	Create Material Listing/Exclusion
VB02	Change Material Listing/Exclusion
VB03	Display Material Listing/Exclusion
VB04	Reference Material Listing/Exclusion
OV16	Create Condition Table for Material Determination
OV17	Change Condition Table for Material Determination
OV18	Display Condition Table for Material Determination
OV11	Material Determination Access Sequence
OV12	Material Determination Condition Type
OV13	Material Determination Procedure
OV14	Material Determination Procedure Assignment to Sales Document
OV26	Material Determination Field Catalog
OVRQ	Material Determination Substitution Reasons
VB11	Create Material Substitution
VB12	Change Material Substitution
VB13	Display Material Substitution
VB14	Reference Material Substitution
VA51	Create Item Proposal
VA52	Change Item Proposal
VA53	Display Item Proposal
VA55	List of Item Proposals
VD51	Create Customer-Material Info Record
VD52	Change Customer-Material Info Record
VD53	Display Customer-Material Info Record
VD54	Display Customer-Material Info Records
VD59	List of Customer-Material Info Records

TABLE A.13   Codes Related to Chapter 13, "Serial Numbers and Batch Management"

Tcode	Description
OIS2	Maintain Serial Number Profile
OIS1	Global Parameters for Serial Numbers
IQ01	Create Material Serial Number
IQ02	Change Material Serial Number
IQ03	Display Material Serial Number
IQ04	Create Material Serial Number (List Entry)
IQ08	Change Material Serial Number (Serial Number Selection)
IQ09	Display Material Serial Number (Serial Number Selection)
MSC1N	Create Batch
MSC2N	Change Batch
MSC3N	Display Batch
MSC4N	Display Change Documents for Batch
MSC5N	Mass Processing for Batch
MSC6N	Batch Worklist
OMAB	Initial Status of a New Batch (Material Type)
OMAC	Definition Initial Status Batch (Plant and Material Type)
OMAD	Number Ranges for Batch Numbers
OMCZ	Activate Batch Number Allocation
OMCE	Define Batch Level
OMCS	Activate Batch Status Management
OMCT	Batch Definition
V/C1	Maintain Strategy Types for SD Batch Determination
V/C2	Maintain Access Sequence for SD Batch Determination
V/C3	Batch Determination: Procedure for SD
V/C5	Batch Search Procedure Determination
V/C6	Field Catalog for Batch
V/C7	Create Condition Table for SD Batch
V/C8	Change Condition Table for SD Batch
V/C9	Display Condition Table for SD Batch
V/CA	Automatic Batch Determination in Sales Order

TABLE A.13   Codes Related to Chapter 13, "Serial Numbers and Batch Management" *(continued)*

Tcode	Description
V/CL	Automatic Batch Determination in Delivery
VCH1	Create Batch Search Strategy
VCH2	Change Batch Search Strategy
VCH3	Display Batch Search Strategy

TABLE A.14   Codes Related to Chapter 14, "Advanced Techniques"

Tcode	Description
BAPI	BAPI Repository
WE02	Display IDOC
WE20	Set Up EDI Partner Profile
WE19	Test Tool for IDOC Processing
WEDI	EDI/IDOC Basis
WE60	Documentation for IDOC Types
BD87	Process Failed IDOCs
SM37	Job Selection Screen
SM36	Define Background Job
SE37	Function Builder
SM35	Process BDC Session
SCAT	Computer Aided Test Tool
SECATT	Extended Computer Aided Test Tool
SHDB	Transaction Recorder
LSMW	Legacy System Migration Workbench
SQ01	Create User
SQ02	Create Infoset
SQ03	ABAP Query
SQVI	ABAP Query—Quick Viewer
SMOD	SAP Enhancements
CMOD	Project Management for SAP Enhancements
SE18	BADI Builder
SE11	ABAP Dictionary

TABLE A.14   Codes Related to Chapter 14, "Advanced Techniques" *(continued)*

Tcode	Description
SE16	Data Browser
SE16N	Data Browser—General Table Display
SE38	ABAP Editor
SE80	ABAP Development Workbench
SE93	Maintain Transactions
/h	Activate Debugging from a Transaction
SFW5	Switch Framework Customizing
MASS	Mass Update
MC21	Create Info Structure
MC22	Change Info Structure
MC23	Display Info Structure
OVRA	Maintain Statistics Group for Customer
OVRF	Maintain Statistics Group for Materials
OVRN	Maintain Statistics Group for Document and Item Categories
MC24	Maintain Update Rules
MC25	Change Update Rules
MC26	Display Update Rules
OVRO	Assign Update Group at Header Level
OVRP	Assign Update Group at Item Level

Database Tables

TABLE A.15   General Utility Tables

Table	Description
TSTC	Transaction Code with Corresponding Program Names
TSTCT	Text for TSTC Table Entries
TBTCP	Program Names with Corresponding Batch Job Names

TABLE A.16   Master Data Tables

Table	Description
MARA	Material Master—General Material Data
MAKT	Material Master—Material Descriptions
MARC	Material Master—Plant Data for Material
MARD	Material Master—Storage Location Data for Material
MARM	Material Master—Units of Measure for Material
MDTB	Material Master—MRP Table
MLAN	Material Master—Tax Classification for Material
MVKE	Material Master—Sales Data for Material
STKO	BOM Header
STOP	BOM Item
STPU	BOM Subitem
STAS	BOMs Item Selection
STPN	BOM Follow-up Control
STPF	Structure Tree of the Exploded BOM
STST	Standard BOM Link
MAST	Material to BOM Link
KNA1	Customer Master—General Data
KNB1	Customer Master—Company Code Data
KNVV	Customer Master—Sales Area Data
KNBK	Customer Master—Bank Details
KNVP	Customer Master—Partner Functions
KNVA	Customer Master—Loading Points
KNVS	Customer Master—Shipping Data
KNVT	Customer Master—Sales Text
KNVK	Customer Master—Contact Person
KNVH	Customer Master—Customer Hierarchy
KNVI	Customer Master—Tax Indicator
KNMT	Customer-Material Info Record Data
KNMTK	Customer-Material Info Record Header
KNKK	Customer Credit Master Data
KNKKF1	FI Status Data

TABLE A.16   Master Data Tables *(continued)*

Table	Description
KNKKF2	Open Items by Days in Arrears
KONP	Pricing Condition Values

TABLE A.17   Tables Storing SD-Related Transaction Data

Table	Description
VBAK	Sales Document Header
VBAP	Sales Document Item
VBEP	Sales Document Schedule Line Category
VBPA	Sales Document Partners Data
VBKD	Business Data
VBBE	Sales Requirements: Individual Records
VBBS	Sales Requirement Totals Record
KONV	Sales Document Pricing Conditions—Transaction Data
VBFA	Sales Document Flow
VBUK	Sales Document Header Status
VBUP	Sales Document Item Status
VEDA	Contract Data
KDST	Sales Order to BOM Link
CDHDR	Change Record for SD Documents—Header
CDPOS	Change Record for SD Documents—Items
LIKP	Delivery Document Header
LIPS	Delivery Document Item
MKPF	Material Document—Header
MSEG	Material Document—Item
LTAK	Transfer Order—Header
LTAP	Transfer Order—Item
VTTK	Shipment Header
VTTP	Shipment Item
VTTS	Stage in Transport
VTSP	Stage in Transport per Shipment Item

TABLE A.17 Tables Storing SD-Related Transaction Data *(continued)*

Table	Description
VTPA	Shipment Partners
VEKP	Handling Unit—Header Table
VEPO	Handling Unit—Item Table
VTFA	Shipment Document Flow
VBRK	Billing Document Header
VBRP	Billing Document Item
VBOX	Rebate Index
VBREVK	Revenue Recognition—Control Lines
VBREVE	Revenue Recognition Lines
VBRL	Invoice List
FPLTC	Payment Card Data
CCARDEC	Payment Card Encryption Data
SER00	General Header Table for Serial Number Management
SER01	Document Header for Serial Number for Deliveries
SERI	Serial Numbers
MCHA	Batches
MCH1	Batches (If Batch Management Cross Plant)
MCHB	Batch Stocks
MCHBH	Batch Stocks: History
MCHP	Batch Record for a Batch

TABLE A.18 Miscellaneous Tables

Table	Description
NAST	Output Message Control—Status
NACH	Printer Determination for Output
TNAPR	Processing Program for Outputs
STXB	SAPscript: Texts in Non-SAPscript Format
STXH	SAPscript Text File Header
STXL	SAPscript Text File Lines
EDIDC	Control Record (IDOC)

TABLE A.18   Miscellaneous Tables *(continued)*

Table	Description
EDIDD	Data Record (IDOC)
EDIDS	Status Record (IDOC)
EDPAR	Convert External < > Internal Partner Number
EDPVW	Partner Functions Allowed for EDI
EDPI1	EDI: Partner Profiles (Inbound)
EDPO1	EDI Table for Partner Profiles (Outbound), Level 1
EDPO3	EDI Table for Partner Profiles (Outbound), Level 2

TABLE A.19   Composite Views on Database Tables

Table	Description
VB_DEBI	View of KNA1, KNB1, and BSID
KNA1VV	View of KNA1 and KNVV Table
MAPOV	View of MARA, MAKT, and MVKE Table
MAWEV	Material/Plant/Sales View (MARA, MARC, MLAN Table)
VBAKUK	View of VBAK and VBUK Table
LIKPUK	View of LIKP and VBUK
LIPSUP	View of LIPS and VBUP
VIVEDA	View of VBAK and VBAP

TABLE A.20   Condition Tables

Table	Description
Axxx	Pricing Condition Tables
Bxxx	Output Condition Tables
Cxxx	Account Determination Condition Tables
Dxxx	Material Determination Condition Tables
Exxx	Rebate Condition Tables
Gxxx	Material Listing/Exclusion Condition Tables
Hxxx	Batch Determination Condition Tables
Nxxx	Free Goods Determination Condition Tables

Recommended Web Resources

The following are some additional resources:

► SAP SDN website: `http://sdn.sap.com`

► SAP Help website: `http://help.sap.com`

► SAP service marketplace website: `http://service.sap.com`

► For supplementary information, updates, and useful tips and tricks: `http://sapsdbook.wordpress.com`

INDEX

Note to the Reader: Throughout this index **boldfaced** page numbers indicate primary discussions of a topic. *Italicized* page numbers indicate illustrations.

profiles
  activity, **366–367**, *367*
  rounding, 506
  sales contracts, **313**, **319**, *319*
  serial, **524–525**, *525*
Profl. field, 525
Prompt For Workbench Request dialog box, 139
Proposal Based On Billing Plan Start Date option, 447
Proposal Based On Contract Start Date option, 447
Proposal For Pricing Date field, **263**
Proposal For Valid From Date field, **264**
Proposal Valid-From field, **410**
Proposal Valid-To field, **410**
proposals, item. *See* item proposals
Propose Delivery Date field, 263
Propose Items dialog box, 514, *514*
Propose PO Date field, 264
Proposed start date for accrual period field, 447
Provision Acc. field, 448
provisional accounts for rebate expense, 415
PT field, 353
purchase orders, 270
    numbers, **256–257**
    types, **287**, *287*
Purchase Requisition Delivery Schedule option, 276
Purchasing view for material masters, **95**

Q

quantity contracts, **319–320**, *320*
Quantity Stipulations field, **93–94**
Quantity tab, 330–331
queries, **562**
    InfoSet creation, **563–565**, *564–565*
    query creation, **566–570**, *567–570*
    user group creation, **565–566**, *565–566*
Queries (SQ01) option, 567
QuickViewer tool, **557–562**, *558–562*
Quotation Messages field, 259
quotations for sales documents, 259, **300–302**, *301*

R

Re-explode Structure/Free Goods option, 281
Reaction fields, **476**
Read Info Record option, 255–256
Reason For Complaint field, 389
Reasons For Rejection field, 290
Rebate Agreement screen, 407
Rebate Proc. Active field, 34
rebate recipients, 404
Rebate Settlement field, 378–379, 407
rebates, **403**
    account assignments for, **415–416**, *416*
    accruals, **406**, *407*
    activating, **408**, *408–409*
    agreements, **403–405**, *405–406*, **409–412**, *409*
    billing documents, 378–379
    pricing conditions, **412–415**, *413–415*
    settlements, 403, **406–407**
Receipt In Past field, **228**
receivables accounts
    payment cards, **425–426**, *425–426*
    unbilled, 440
recipients, rebate, 404
Recog. Rev. field, 441
reconciliation accounts for payment cards, **425–426**, *425–426*
records
    batch management, **532–536**, *533–535*
    data browser, 17, *18*
    item proposal, **512–513**, *513*
    material determination, **485–488**, *485–487*
Records For Access field, 166
Redetermine Freight Conditions rule, 198
Reference Application field, 168
reference billing number plan numbers, 398
Reference Condition Type field, 167
Reference/Duplication Indicator For Copying Text option, 131
Reference Mandatory field, **254**
Reference Number field, 379–381
Reference tab for customer master data, 72, *73*
RefSorg SalesDoc Type field, 34
regional codes for taxes, **200–201**, *201*
rejections for sales documents items, **290–291**, *290*
RelChkPlan field, 225